# growing up GLOBAL

## THE CHANGING TRANSITIONS TO ADULTHOOD IN DEVELOPING COUNTRIES

Panel on Transitions to Adulthood in Developing Countries

Cynthia B. Lloyd, *Editor*

Committee on Population

Board on Children, Youth, and Families

Division of Behavioral and Social Sciences and Education

NATIONAL RESEARCH COUNCIL *AND*
INSTITUTE OF MEDICINE
*OF THE NATIONAL ACADEMIES*

THE NATIONAL ACADEMIES PRESS
Washington, D.C.
**www.nap.edu**

THE NATIONAL ACADEMIES PRESS • 500 Fifth Street, N.W. • Washington, DC 20001

NOTICE: The project that is the subject of this report was approved by the Governing Board of the National Research Council, whose members are drawn from the councils of the National Academy of Sciences, the National Academy of Engineering, and the Institute of Medicine. The members of the committee responsible for the report were chosen for their special competences and with regard for appropriate balance.

This study was supported by a cooperative agreement between the National Academy of Sciences and the United States Agency for International Development (CCP-3078-A-00-5024) and from grants from the Andrew W. Mellon Foundation, the William and Flora Hewlett Foundation, the David and Lucile Packard Foundation, The John D. and Catherine T. MacArthur Foundation, and The World Bank. Any opinions, findings, conclusions, or recommendations expressed in this publication are those of the authors and do not necessarily reflect the views of the organizations or agencies that provided support for the project.

Library of Congress Cataloging-in-Publication Data

National Research Council (U.S.). Panel on Transitions to Adulthood in Developing Countries.
  Growing up global : the changing transitions to adulthood in developing countries / Panel on Transitions to Adulthood in Developing Countries ; Cynthia B. Lloyd, editor ; Committee on Population [and] Board on Children, Youth, and Families, Division of Behavioral and Social Sciences and Education.
     p. cm.
  Includes bibliographical references and index.
  ISBN 0-309-09528-X (pbk.) — ISBN 0-309-54739-3 (pdf)  1.  Young adults—Developing countries. 2.  Youth—Developing countries. 3.  Adulthood—Developing countries. 4.  School-to-work transition—Developing countries.  I. Lloyd, Cynthia B., 1943- II. National Research Council (U.S.). Committee on Population. III. National Research Council (U.S.). Board on Children, Youth, and Families. IV. Title.
  HQ799.8.D45N37 2005
  305.242′09172′4—dc22
                                    2005002187

Additional copies of this report are available from the National Academies Press, 500 Fifth Street, N.W., Lockbox 285, Washington, DC 20055; (800) 624-6242 or (202) 334-3313 (in the Washington metropolitan area); http://www.nap.edu.

Printed in the United States of America.

Suggested citation: National Research Council and Institute of Medicine (2005). *Growing Up Global: The Changing Transitions to Adulthood in Developing Countries*. Panel on Transitions to Adulthood in Developing Countries. Cynthia B. Lloyd, ed. Committee on Population and Board on Children, Youth, and Families. Division of Behavioral and Social Sciences and Education. Washington, DC: The National Academies Press.

# THE NATIONAL ACADEMIES
*Advisers to the Nation on Science, Engineering, and Medicine*

The **National Academy of Sciences** is a private, nonprofit, self-perpetuating society of distinguished scholars engaged in scientific and engineering research, dedicated to the furtherance of science and technology and to their use for the general welfare. Upon the authority of the charter granted to it by the Congress in 1863, the Academy has a mandate that requires it to advise the federal government on scientific and technical matters. Dr. Bruce M. Alberts is president of the National Academy of Sciences.

The **National Academy of Engineering** was established in 1964, under the charter of the National Academy of Sciences, as a parallel organization of outstanding engineers. It is autonomous in its administration and in the selection of its members, sharing with the National Academy of Sciences the responsibility for advising the federal government. The National Academy of Engineering also sponsors engineering programs aimed at meeting national needs, encourages education and research, and recognizes the superior achievements of engineers. Dr. Wm. A. Wulf is president of the National Academy of Engineering.

The **Institute of Medicine** was established in 1970 by the National Academy of Sciences to secure the services of eminent members of appropriate professions in the examination of policy matters pertaining to the health of the public. The Institute acts under the responsibility given to the National Academy of Sciences by its congressional charter to be an adviser to the federal government and, upon its own initiative, to identify issues of medical care, research, and education. Dr. Harvey V. Fineberg is president of the Institute of Medicine.

The **National Research Council** was organized by the National Academy of Sciences in 1916 to associate the broad community of science and technology with the Academy's purposes of furthering knowledge and advising the federal government. Functioning in accordance with general policies determined by the Academy, the Council has become the principal operating agency of both the National Academy of Sciences and the National Academy of Engineering in providing services to the government, the public, and the scientific and engineering communities. The Council is administered jointly by both Academies and the Institute of Medicine. Dr. Bruce M. Alberts and Dr. Wm. A. Wulf are chair and vice chair, respectively, of the National Research Council.

**www.national-academies.org**

# PANEL ON TRANSITIONS TO ADULTHOOD
## IN DEVELOPING COUNTRIES

# Preface

As chair of the Panel on Transitions to Adulthood in Developing Countries, I would like to say on behalf of the panel that we have been privileged and challenged by our task of examining the changing lives of young people in developing countries at the beginning of the twenty-first century. *Growing Up Global: The Changing Transitions to Adulthood in Developing Countries* is the product of a three-year effort during which time the panel reviewed many different literatures and conducted much new data analysis.

Throughout the project, the panel was committed to focusing on the links and interconnections between the productive and reproductive domains of young peoples' lives that have typically been treated in isolation from each other. It is our hope that this approach will inspire a next generation of researchers and policy makers to see the different aspects of young peoples' lives in a more interconnected way, allowing new insights for policies and programs.

This report would not have been possible without the help of numerous people and organizations. First, we wish to thank the report's sponsors: the U.S. Agency for International Development, the David and Lucille Packard Foundation, The Andrew W. Mellon Foundation, the William and Flora Hewlett Foundation, the World Bank, and the John D. and Catherine T. MacArthur Foundation.

This report reflects the intense deliberations of the panel (see Appendix C for biographical sketches) who met multiple times over the course of the project. At an early stage of the project, I formed working groups to take up certain cross-cutting topics in support of the panel's work. These met either in person or by conference call and built on the expertise of various panel members. With the formation of these groups, panel members were able to get fully engaged in the work of the panel in order to ensure their collective input at an early stage of the project. The first group, the theory group, held two meetings, one hosted by Richard Jessor at the University of Colorado. This group included Kuate Defo, Nan Astone, Nelly Stromquist, Richard Jessor, Jere Behrman, Anastasia Gage, Kaushik Basu, Cynthia Lloyd, and Valerie Durrant. A data group was formed to assess the availability of census and survey data from two recent points in time to undertake analyses of the interrelationships between various role transitions. The data group included David Lam, Jere Behrman, Susheela Singh, Cynthia Lloyd, and Valerie Durrant. A program evaluation group was formed to set standards of evidence for the evaluation of programs; this group included Robert Magnani, Robert Blum, Jere Behrman, Carlos Aramburú, Nelly Stromquist, Kuate Defo, Cynthia Lloyd, and Valerie Durrant. Finally, a reproductive health working group consisted of Barbara Mensch, Anastasia Gage, Robert Blum, Carlos Aramburú, Shireen Jejeebhoy, Susheela Singh, Valerie Durrant, and Cynthia Lloyd.

The panel also commissioned papers by panel members and other experts to provide background information on which the panel report could build. These papers helped fill some of the knowledge gaps and thus provided useful analyses, all of which are cited and some of which are incorporated into the panel report. But a number of these background studies, in addition to providing inputs for the panel report, constitute useful contributions to the knowledge of transitions to adulthood in developing countries that are richer and broader than what is incorporated into the report itself. The panel therefore established an editorial committee for these papers composed of Jere Behrman, Barney Cohen, Cynthia Lloyd, and Nelly Stromquist. They took responsibility for reviewing the papers directly and oversaw a process of external review and revision according to National Research Council (NRC) procedures. The table of contents for this edited volume titled, *The Changing Transitions to Adulthood in Developing Countries: Selected Studies* (editors, Cynthia B. Lloyd, Jere R. Behrman, Nelly P. Stromquist, and Barney Cohen) appears in Appendix B of this report.

After five meetings of the full panel, I appointed an editorial committee, with the support of the full panel, to carry forward the preparation of draft chapters on behalf of the panel, and this group of panel members spent significant time in the last year of the project attending two additional meetings and sharing the responsibility for the final preparation of the manuscript. Members of the editorial committee were: Nelly Stromquist, Nan Astone, Jere Behrman, David Lam, Barbara Mensch, Richard Jessor, and Cynthia Lloyd. I then took primary responsibility, with the support of Barney Cohen, for the final revision and editing of the manuscript in preparation for review.

Consequently, this report is truly the collective product of panel members and staff. Its content reflects the deliberations of the full panel who reviewed and revised all contributions. The purpose of the following list, therefore, is to give credit to individuals but not to assign final responsibility for the published text.

Executive Summary: This is the collective product of the deliberations of the entire panel
Chapter 1:  C. Lloyd and R. Jessor
Chapter 2:  B. Cohen, R. Jessor, H. Reed, C. Lloyd, J. Behrman, and D. Lam
Chapter 3:  C. Lloyd, D. Lam, J. Behrman, and N. Stromquist
Chapter 4:  A. Blanc, R. Magnani, S. Singh, S. Jejeebhoy, and R. Bulatao
Chapter 5:  C. Lloyd, D. Lam, and J. Behrman
Chapter 6:  M. Grant, N. Varia, V. Durrant, and N. Stromquist
Chapter 7:  B. Mensch
Chapter 8:  C. Lloyd, S. Singh, N. Astone, B. Mensch, and S. Jejeebhoy
Chapter 9:  C. Lloyd
Appendix A: C. Lloyd and V. Durrant

It should be noted that the authors listed for each chapter include those who took up major writing responsibilities at various stages of each chapter's preparation. The first author listed is the person who took the major responsibility for putting the chapter into final shape for review. These chapters occasionally contain additional paragraphs from other hands.

I want to single out for special mention the panel members who served as members of the editorial committee because of their continuing involvement in the work of the panel report from beginning to end as well as in the preparation of the accompanying volume of papers. Their involvement went well beyond what could be fully reflected in the chapter authorship list above. As chair, I want to thank each of them individually for their contributions as well as for their strong support and steady partnership throughout the volume.

Richard Jessor served as the panel's theoretician and conscience. He challenged us to develop a conceptual framework that would outlive the temporal nature of our material, provided all of us with lots of good humor along the way, and provided me most importantly with a helpful sounding board throughout the project. He also collaborated on the drafting of Chapters 1 and 2.

Jere Behrman was a constructive partner and critic at each stage of the drafting of two of the longest and most challenging chapters—3 and 5. In addition, he wrote several commissioned papers in order to strengthen the panel's treatment of policy and program evaluation throughout the volume as well as of issues of global convergence and divergence covered in Chapter 2. He also served as a coeditor of the volume of papers.

Nelly Stromquist brought a critical perspective to our work from an intellectual tradition that lay outside the tradition common to many panel members. She provided patient, persistent, and constructive input to the work of the panel throughout the life of the project. This included collaborating on the drafting of Chapters 3 and 6 and serving as coeditor of the volume of papers.

David Lam was a strong supporter of the project from its inception as a member of the NRC's Committee on Population and undertook substantial new data analysis with census and survey data to explore the interrelationships between various transitions to adulthood. He also collaborated on the drafting of Chapters 3 and 5.

Nan Astone brought her experience and expertise in the study of adolescents in the United States to our panel discussions, thus helping to shape our conceptual approach and our comparative perspective. She also played a major role in the drafting of Chapter 8 on parenthood.

Barbara Mensch, who works next door to me at the Population Council, not only became the sole author of Chapter 7 on marriage but also provided me with a steady dose of solidarity, comradeship, and advice throughout the project.

Several other individuals made key contributions that deserve special mention. Susheela Singh, Shireen Jejeebhoy, and Robert Magnani, members of the panel but not members of the editorial committee, took up drafting roles for Chapters 4 and 8. Amanda Ritchie, as a consultant to NRC, was our resident anthropologist. She wrote all of the boxes in Chapters 4, 7, and 8 and some others scattered throughout the volume, took the lead on the comparative analysis of time use data that is featured in Chapter 5, and undertook substantial background research for Chapter 4. Monica Grant, research coordinator in the Policy Research Division of the Population Council, in addition to being a lead author on Chapter 6, was responsible for most of the data analysis for Chapters 4, 7, and 8. Her speed and agility at programming 50 data sets simultaneously was truly extraordinary and was also complemented by her good understanding of the material and her many good ideas about how to handle the data. Barbara Miller, my staff assistant at the Population Council, has been my right hand throughout the project. She set up the original files to handle all the weighted regional averages for the analysis of Demographic and Health Surveys (DHS) data and undertook endless revisions and updates with good cheer. She was also responsible for handling all the references for Chapters 3, 5, 7, and 8. Paul Hewett, my collaborator on the paper on primary schooling in

Africa, took responsibility for the original data analysis for Chapter 3 and provided technical support and advice throughout the project. Holly Reed at the NRC prepared a preliminary draft of Chapter 2 as did Jonathan Zaff, a consultant, for Chapter 5. Ann Blanc and Randy Bulatao served as consultants for Chapter 3 and Nisha Varia for Chapter 6. Richard Anker provided advice on Chapter 5 at an informal meeting of interested panel members scheduled when he was on this side of the Atlantic, and Ron Kassimir of the Social Science Research Council and Martin Riesebrodt of the University of Chicago provided valuable advice and literature reviews on religion that served as background material for Chapter 2. Others who assisted in the analysis of data or who provided us with access to data include Sara Zellner, Suhaila Khan, Erin Murphy-Graham, Georgeann Higgins, Rubina Hussain, Christine Schippers, Claudia Stilman, Djavad Salehi, Matthew Sobek, Anil Deolalikar, Jed Friedman, and Lupin Rahman.

Several experts participated in a planning meeting in January 2001 to help formulate a plan for the panel's contributions. We acknowledge the collective contribution of the following members of the planning group who are not members of the panel: Richard Anker, Julie DaVanzo, Bessie Lee, Marlaine Lockheed, Anju Malhotra, Karen Mason, Susan Newcomer, Agnes Quisumbing, and Peter Xenos.

The panel was fortunate to hold one of its meetings in Mexico City, which was hosted by Consejo Nacional de Población (CONAPO) in February 2002, and would like to thank Rodolfo Turian, Elena Zuniga, and Cristina Gil Villegas for their help in making the meeting possible. During the visit, the panel received a special briefing on Programa de Educación, Salud y Alimentación (PROGRESA) from Santiago Levy and heard presentations from several researchers at the Colegio de Mexico—Claudia Stern, Rosa Maria Camareno, and Carlos Echarri—who had undertaken research on transitions to adulthood among Mexican adolescents. The panel also met with youth from Gente Joven and Balance, a young women's network in Mexico City promoting citizenship rights and political participation. Virginia Rodriquez coordinated the visit to Gente Joven. Staff from Balance included Maria Antonieta Alcalde Castro, Esteban Inzua, Belén Gutierrez, Nancy Olguin, and Mariana Pérez Ramirex.

The panel also cosponsored an expert meeting with the World Bank on Assessing the Economic Benefits of Investments in Youth in collaboration with Elizabeth Lule and Jim Rosen. Papers were presented by Jere Behrman, Jim Knowles, Wendy Cummingham, Paolo Belli, and Olivier Appaix. Others who attended the meeting and provided valuable discussion include: Robert Holzmann, Jane Ross, Maureen Lewis, Mayra Buvinic, Jacques van der Gaag, Alex Preker, Nancy Williamson, Christine Norton, Matilde Maddaleno, Laura Laski, and Aleksandra Posarac.

Many other colleagues supplied the panel with research in the form of background papers. The panel benefited greatly from these papers and thanks the following individuals for their contribution: Patrick Emerson, André Portela Souza, Shireen Jejeebhoy, Shiva Halli, Agnes Quisumbing, Kelly Hallman, Emily Hannum, Jihong Liu, Piyali Sengupta, Jere Behrman, Jim Knowles, David Lam, Leticia Marteleto, Sajeda Amin, Cynthia Lloyd, Paul Hewett, Monica Grant, Barbara Mensch, Susheela Singh, John Casterline, Peter Xenos, Sulistinah Achmad, Hui Sheng Lin, Ping Keung Luis, Chai Podhisita, Corazon Raymundo, Shyam Thapa, Nan Astone, Ken Hill, Margaret Wedon, Barthelemy Kuate Defo, Robert Blum, and Kristin Nelson-Mmari.

No project of this magnitude could be undertaken without able staff. Valerie Durrant was staff director for our panel at the NRC from the panel's inception in early 2001 until September 2003, initially as a fellow of the University of Michigan Population Fellows Program and later as a regular NRC employee. She did an excellent job of coordinating the work of the panel, arranging meetings of the panel and its various working groups, arranging for literature reviews and data analyses, working closely with our sponsors, co-organizing the expert group meeting on Assessing the Economic Benefits of Investment in Youth (October 15, 2002) in collaboration with the World Bank, and most particularly supporting me in my role as chair. She also did some major background research for Chapter 3 and did some data analysis and rewrote parts of Chapter 6. Her enthusiasm for the subject was infectious and she had a full mastery of the panel's scope. She was sorely missed after her departure, which came at the time the project had originally been scheduled for completion. Barney Cohen, director of the Committee on Population, oversaw the work and managed the final stages of the process, including the response to review. The panel owes a huge debt to both Valerie Durrant and Barney Cohen, and we are deeply grateful for their support throughout the project.

In addition, special thanks are due to Christine Covington-Chen for her superb administrative and logistic support, to Christine McShane for skillfully editing the manuscript, to Kirsten Sampson Snyder for navigating the report through review, to Anthony Mann for preparing the final manuscript, and Yvonne Wise for steering the manuscript through the production process.

This report has been reviewed in draft form by individuals chosen for their diverse perspectives and technical expertise, in accordance with procedures approved by the NRC's Report Review Committee. The purpose of this independent review is to provide candid and critical comments that will assist the institution in making its published report as sound as possible and to ensure that the report meets institutional standards for objectivity, evidence, and responsiveness to the study charge. The review comments and draft manuscript remain confidential to protect the integrity of the deliberative process. We thank the following individuals for their review of this report: Jeffrey Jensen Arnett, *Journal of Adolescent Research,* University Park, MD; Suzanne Duryea, Research Department, Inter-American Development Bank, Washington, DC; Constance A. Flanagan, Agricultural Sciences, Pennsylvania State University; Stephen F. Hamilton, Family Life Development Center, Cornell University; John Hobcraft, Department of Social Policy and Demography, University of York, United Kingdom; Reed Larson, Department of Human and Community, University of Illinois, Urbana, IL; Thomas LeGrand, Demography Department, University of Montreal, Canada; Anju Malhotra, Population and Social Transitions, International Center for Research on Women, Washington, DC.

Although the reviewers listed have provided many constructive comments and suggestions, they were not asked to endorse the conclusions and recommendations nor did they see the final draft of the report before its release. The review of this report was overseen by Marshall S. Smith, Education Program, The William and Flora Hewlett Foundation. Appointed by the NRC, he was responsible for making certain that an independent examination of this report was carried out in accordance with institutional procedures and that all review comments were carefully considered. Responsibility for the final content of this report rests entirely with the authoring committee and the institution.

Finally, I owe a special debt of gratitude to the Population Council, where I work, which has stood behind me during the three years of the project and supported my time on the project. The Population Council has made a substantial commitment to research on transitions to adulthood over the past eight years, thanks to generous funding from the U.K. Department for International Development, the Rockefeller Foundation, the Andrew W. Mellon Foundation, the William and Flora Hewlett Foundation, the U.S. Agency for International Development, and the Spencer Foundation, among others. Many colleagues of mine at the Population Council have shared in this collective effort, and I owe them all a debt of gratitude. They include, but are by no means limited to, Sajeda Amin, Martha Brady, Judith Bruce, Judy Diers, Anabel Erulkar, Nicole Haberland, Kelly Hallman, Paul Hewett, Barbara Ibrahim, Shireen Jejeebhoy, Barbara Mensch, Mark Montgomery, Zeba Sathar, and Minhaj ul Haque. John Bongaarts, vice president of the Population Council in charge of the Policy Research Division, has also been an enthusiastic supporter and a patient listener through the project, and it is his support most of all that has allowed me the time and space to embark on this major undertaking and follow it through until its very end.

For me it has been an honor and a privilege to serve as chair of this panel. I have met and become friends and colleagues with so many people I otherwise would not have known and have learned so much in the process. The product is truly a collective one, enriched and strengthened by the passions, ideas, knowledge, talents, and good humor of all my fellow panel members. To them all, I am most deeply grateful.

Cynthia B. Lloyd, *Chair*
Panel on Transitions to Adulthood in
Developing Countries

# Contents

## PART III
## TRANSITION TO ADULT ROLES

## PART IV
## CONCLUSIONS

# Executive Summary

The transition to adulthood is a critical stage of human development during which young people leave childhood behind and take on new roles and responsibilities. It is a period of social, psychological, economic, and biological transitions, and for many young people it involves demanding emotional challenges and important choices. To a large degree, the nature and quality of young people's future lives depend on how successfully they negotiate through this critical period. Yet in many developing countries, it is a stage of life that has only recently begun to receive focused attention.

The challenges for young people making the transition to adulthood are greater today than ever before. Globalization, with its power to reach across national boundaries and into the smallest communities, carries with it the transformative power of new markets and new technology. At the same time, globalization brings with it new ideas and lifestyles that can conflict with traditional norms and values. And while the economic benefits are potentially enormous, the actual course of globalization has not been without its critics who charge that, to date, the gains have been very unevenly distributed, generating a new set of problems associated with rising inequality and social polarization. Regardless of how the globalization debate is resolved, it is clear that as broad global forces transform the world in which the next generation will live and work, the choices that today's young people make or others make on their behalf will facilitate or constrain their success as adults. Traditional expectations regarding future employment prospects and life experiences are no longer valid.

Concerns about how global forces are altering the passage into adulthood are all the more urgent because of the changing demographic profile of many developing countries. The acceleration of these global changes has coincided with unprecedented growth in the size of the population of young people in developing countries. By 2005, the total number of 10-24-year-olds is estimated to have reached 1.5 billion, constituting nearly 30 percent of the population of these regions and 86 percent of all young people in the world. And each subsequent cohort of young people in the developing world is projected to continue to increase until 2035, as rapid growth in Africa and parts of Asia counteracts some slow declines in absolute numbers elsewhere in Asia and in Latin America and the Caribbean.

Recognizing the need to learn more about this crucial period of life, the National Research Council convened a panel of experts to examine how the transition to adulthood is changing in developing countries, and what the implications of these changes might be for those responsible for designing youth policies and programs, in particular, those affecting adolescent reproductive health.

According to the panel's findings, important transformations in young peoples' lives are under way. In much of the developing world, adolescence is a stage of life that is gaining in significance. In the past, young men and women tended to move directly from childhood to adult roles. But today the interval between childhood and the assumption of adult roles is lengthening. Compared to the situation 20 years ago, young people are

- entering adolescence earlier and healthier,
- more likely to spend their adolescence in school,
- more likely to postpone entry into the labor force, and
- more likely to delay marriage and childbearing.

As a result of these changes, on average, young people in the developing world now have more time and opportunities than ever before to acquire the information and skills necessary to become effective participants in decisions about their own lives and futures.

These broad statements capture only the average tendencies for young people in developing countries, which tend to be statistically dominated by trends in developing Asia, where 70 percent of young people in developing counties live, 42 percent in India and China alone. Differential rates of change have led, in some cases, to growing differences among adolescents within and across countries, as some young people experience progress while others are left behind. Over the past 20 years, economic growth rates in Latin America and the Caribbean and in sub-Saharan Africa have diverged negatively from economic growth rates in developed countries, while growth rates in East and South Asia, where the majority of young people live, have converged toward economic growth rates in developed countries.

These very different circumstances across regions mean that the experiences of today's young people, as well as the implications of globalization for them, vary enormously. And even in countries in which the rate of economic growth has been very high, for some young people, particularly those in rural areas, the outward patterns and rhythms of life may appear to be largely unaffected.

Because of rapid population growth, young people who are poor are about as numerous today as they were in the past despite declining poverty rates; current estimates imply that roughly 325 million young people in developing countries are growing up on less than $1 a day. Furthermore, the continuing growth in the absolute numbers of young people as well as the lengthening period of years spent unmarried (and in many cases sexually active) ensure a rapid and continuing growth in young peoples' need for education, as well as for reproductive and other health services. Further challenges include relatively poor learning outcomes in school among enrolled students and persistent disadvantages for young women, young people from low-income families, and young people living in the least developed countries.

Sub-Saharan Africa is a region of special concern. Not only are poverty rates rising and population growth rates proceeding at unprecedented levels, but also the risks of HIV/AIDS for young people are very high and increasing. Furthermore, recent data on school participation suggest that, in some settings during the 1990s, school attendance rates for boys fell as the prevalence of child labor rose. Growing pressures on school systems may further compromise school quality, which is already poor. While fewer African young people marry or bear children during adolescence relative to previous generations, many lack opportunities to use this lengthening adolescent phase of their lives to acquire needed education and training.

## CRITERIA FOR SUCCESS

The panel's policy and program recommendations emerge from a conceptual framework that we developed to organize and guide this report. The framework identifies criteria for successful transitions in the context of contemporary global changes. We identified the importance of adequate preparation for five key adult roles: adult worker, citizen and community participant, spouse, parent, and household manager.

The defining attributes of such a conceptualization of successful transitions to adulthood, which must be seen within the constraints of personal endowments and capabilities, include at least the following:

- Good mental and physical health, including reproductive health, and the knowledge and means to sustain health during adulthood.

- An appropriate stock of human and social capital to be a productive adult member of society.
- The acquisition of prosocial values and the ability to contribute to the collective well-being as citizen and community participant.
- Adequate preparation for the assumption of adult social roles and obligations, including the roles of spouse or partner, parent, and household and family manager.
- The capability to make choices through the acquisition of a sense of self and a sense of personal competence.
- A sense of well-being.

While success is ultimately measured at the individual level, societies and their institutions at the international, national, and local levels, including governments of developed countries, can enhance successful transitions to adulthood. In the panel's view, policies that support universal primary schooling of adequate quality, that support the expansion of good secondary schooling, and that promote good health during this phase of the life cycle are essential in their own right but also important because of their role in promoting success in these other domains. In the panel's judgment, poverty is the greatest enemy of successful transitions.

## PREPARATION FOR ADULT ROLES

### Schooling

Young people in developing countries are spending more of their adolescence in school than ever before. Recent growth rates in all indicators of school participation and grade attainment have been substantial, historically unprecedented, and greater for girls than for boys. For example, on the basis of survey data representing 60 percent of the population of the developing world, mean grades attained have risen over the past 20 years from 6.0 to 7.4 (23 percent) for young men ages 20-24 on average and from 3.8 to 6.0 (58 percent) for young women ages 20-24. Furthermore, the percentage who have never attended school has fallen from 21 to 11 percent for boys ages 10-14 and from 39 to 18 percent for girls of the same age over the same period. These positive overall trends in schooling, while typical, are not universal.

Despite these trends, there remain large differences in school attendance rates according to wealth and residential status, with poor girls suffering particular disadvantage. Recent well-designed evaluation studies have shown that conditional grants or targeted subsidies can be effective strategies for increasing school attendance and progression rates among economically disadvantaged groups.

Global trends in population, health, urbanization, and education have all contributed positively to the growth in the demand for schooling. In most parts of the developing world today, young people live within reasonable proximity of a primary school—a notable achievement given the rapid growth in the school-age population. The results of recent internationally comparable standardized tests, however, raise serious concerns about how much students are actually learning in school—and therefore about school quality. Poor school quality and poverty remain major factors limiting enrollments, encouraging dropout, and compromising learning outcomes.

## Health

The health of young people in developing countries is improving. Young people are entering the transition to adulthood healthier and with improved chances of surviving to old age. And continued reductions in mortality seem likely, with the major exception of countries strongly affected by the HIV/AIDS epidemic.

HIV/AIDS is now the leading cause of death among young people in sub-Saharan Africa. In other regions, it is among the least significant causes of death; instead, noncommunicable diseases predominate as well as injuries for men. Nevertheless, given the much higher mortality rates in sub-Saharan Africa than in the rest of the world, HIV/AIDS is now the leading cause of death for women ages 15-29 for the world as a whole and one of the leading causes of death for men in the same age group. Moreover, given the much larger population of young people in Asia, an increase in the epidemic there, which is projected by many, would mean that the numbers of young people affected would increase substantially.

Mortality and morbidity related to pregnancy and childbirth (particularly in sub-Saharan Africa and South Asia, where levels of early childbearing remain high) and as a direct consequence of unsafe abortion across all developing regions remain among the most significant risks to young women's health. Although young women appear less likely than older women to seek abortion, they are more likely to have the abortion later in the pregnancy and to choose an unsafe provider, thus putting them at greater risk.

Behaviors that young people adopt at this age have critical implications for their future health and mortality. In particular, unprotected sex is one of the riskiest behaviors that young people can undertake, particularly in settings in which HIV/AIDS is widespread. Evidence from Latin America and sub-Saharan Africa suggest that contraceptive use rates are increasing among sexually active young women, especially unmarried ones. Condom use, however, remains relatively low but is increasing rapidly in Latin America and the Caribbean as well as Eastern and Southern Africa. Poverty and economic vulnerability enhance the likelihood that young people will engage in risky sexual behaviors. Furthermore, there is growing evidence that coercive sex is not an uncommon experience for many girls and young women.

However, sex is not being initiated at an earlier age relative to the past in most countries. While there has been an increase in the percentage having premarital sex before age 18 in many countries over the past 20 years, delays in the age of marriage in most countries have meant that, on balance relative to 20 years ago, fewer young women report themselves to have been sexually active before age 18. Thus while sex is being delayed, the context of first sexual experience is changing, with a greater likelihood now than in the past that first sex will be experienced prior to marriage.

Other adolescent behaviors with compromising long-term implications for health include smoking, drinking, and using illicit drugs. Across the developing world, tobacco use is increasing, and the gender gap in smoking prevalence is closing rapidly. There is also evidence that the prevalence of illicit drug use among young people is rising slowly. Alcohol intake is highest among affluent and urban young people and thus is also expected to increase with continued urbanization.

## THE TRANSITION TO ADULT ROLES

### The Transition to Work

The rise in school enrollment and the delay in the timing of school exit have resulted in a delay in the timing of labor force entry and a concomitant decline in the percentage of young people participating in the labor force, particularly at younger ages. Household poverty is strongly associated with the likelihood that children will participate in the labor force; thus a global decline in poverty is an important explanation for declines in the prevalence of labor market work among children. Rising poverty rates in sub-Saharan Africa imply a less positive outlook for trends in children's labor force participation, however.

The rise in school enrollment and attainment and the rapidly closing gender gap in schooling is leading to a growing equalization of work burdens between young men and women during their adolescent years. This is because students spend relatively little time in the labor market, and gender differences in mean daily hours spent by students in noneconomic household work (e.g., household chores) are relatively small. This equalization in work roles is further reinforced by the rise in the proportion of young women entering the labor force, in particular the paid labor force.

The economic returns to schooling at the secondary and tertiary levels are consistently high (and differentially high for young women). The gap between the returns to higher and lower levels of schooling is widening, thus putting an increasing premium on secondary and tertiary schooling for later success in the labor market. It is not known the extent to which this shift in rates of return is due to globalization or other factors, such as declines in primary school quality resulting from rapid growth in the student population. Nevertheless, young people with secondary or tertiary schooling are increasingly advantaged in the labor market relative to their less educated peers not only in terms of earnings but also in terms of job stability and upward mobility.

In many parts of Asia, as well as in Latin America and the Caribbean, increased numbers of young people, including a rising percentage of young women, have been absorbed into the formal or informal labor market without any large increase in unemployment rates among young people. Indeed, some countries, particularly in Asia, have succeeded in maintaining strong economic growth at the same time that the labor force has been increasing rapidly, thus reaping an economic dividend as a result of these demographic shifts. However, youth unemployment is still a substantial challenge in some of the poorer countries of Asia, sub-Saharan Africa, and the Middle East, which continue to experience unprecedented growth in the size of their 10-24-year-old populations even though in many cases rates of population growth have now peaked.

## The Transition to Citizenship

Globalization, trends toward greater democratization, rising school enrollment, and greater access to media have all increased opportunities for young people to engage in civic and political life. Recent survey data show that a majority of young men in many Latin American and Asian countries express an interest in politics and a willingness to engage in political activism, whereas young women appear somewhat less inclined to express these views. At the same time that young people are expressing greater voice at the local, national, and international levels, they are becoming increasingly aware of the growth of global diversity and inequality.

Various forms of participation in the life of the community, beyond political participation, are embraced in concepts of citizenship. A variety of institutions and programs, among them schools, employers, national service programs (including military service), sports, other nonformal programs, and the media are increasingly viewed as potentially important in citizenship formation. However, comparative data are lacking on the extent and nature of community participation among young people or on the roles that various institutions play in encouraging or discouraging participation.

## The Transition to Marriage

While the transition into marriage is a key component of the transition to adulthood in most contexts, marriage, in and of itself, is not necessarily a marker of adulthood, particularly for the numerous young women who wed during the teenage years. Substantial delays in the timing of marriage among most young people, however, are contributing to an overall lengthening of the interval between childhood and the assumption of adult roles.

Compared with previous generations, a smaller proportion of young women and men are married in most regions. Men still marry at older ages than women. While only one-third of men in the developing world are married by ages 20-24, nearly two-thirds of women are married in this age group. Moreover, in certain regions, most notably the Middle East, a large fraction of men now postpone marriage until their 30s.

The minimum legal age of marriage for both men and women has risen in many countries in the past decade, and women are less likely to be married during the teenage years than in the past. However, child marriage, defined as marriage prior to age 18, is still widespread and viewed by many as a major violation of human rights. On the basis of survey data representing 60 percent of the population of the developing world, 38 percent of young women ages 20-24 married before age 18 (down from 52 percent 20 years ago), with the highest rates of child marriage currently occurring in Western and Middle Africa and South Asia. Young women who marry as minors are more likely to come from poor households and rural areas and to have relatively few, if any, years of schooling.

The age gap between spouses—often thought of as a measure of the degree of equality in marriage—appears to be narrowing, especially in sub-Saharan Africa and South Asia. There is also some evidence of growing agency on the part of young women with regard to choice of marriage partner, suggesting that the nature of marriage itself is changing.

## The Transition to Parenthood

As in the past, entry into marriage is strongly associated with entry into parenthood. Over 90 percent of first births occur within marriage, and this percentage has changed only minimally over the past 20 years. With rising ages of marriage, the age of parenthood has been rising, but the gap between age at marriage and age at first birth has narrowed, falling from 22 to 16 months on average over the past 20 years. These postponements of marriage and parenthood allow young people more time to prepare for adult roles and provide an increasing number of young women with the opportunity to participate in the labor force prior to becoming a parent.

Rates of early childbearing remain high in many parts of the developing world because of high rates of early marriage, as noted above. Based on survey data representing 60 percent of the population of the developing world, 23 percent of young people ages 20-24 gave birth before age 18 (down from 30 percent 20 years ago).

As a result of declines in early marriage, there has been a slight rise in the percentage of births to young women that are premarital. The level of premarital childbearing varies substantially across regions: from 14 percent having a premarital birth by the age of 20 in Eastern and Southern Africa to less than 1 percent in Asia and the Middle East. While Eastern and Southern Africa and Latin America and the Caribbean have seen recent small increases in the rates of premarital childbearing, the rates in other regions appear very low, but measurement is more difficult given continuing reluctance to interview unmarried women in Asia.

Although there is plentiful evidence that early childbearing is correlated with various negative outcomes, rigorous research confirming a causal role for age at birth in producing these outcomes does not exist. Major global changes, such as increasing school enrollment during late adolescence, rising rates of labor force participation among young women, and rising HIV/AIDS prevalence among young women in Africa, are likely to have important implications for the transition to parenthood, but little is known about the implications of these trends for first parenthood.

## POLICY AND PROGRAM RECOMMENDATIONS

Policies and programs designed to achieve positive and sustainable development and combat poverty confront both the opportunity and the challenge of promoting successful transitions to adulthood for a steadily growing population of young people living in developing countries. Substantial investments in the health and schooling of young people, if designed and targeted effectively, will position these young people to participate constructively in shaping their own and their countries' futures.

The panel's policy and program recommendations were derived from a careful sifting of the empirical evidence. They address areas that are potentially encompassed by the scope of the United Nations (UN) Millennium Development Goals as well as others that are not within their current scope but are nonetheless of vital importance for young people. In the panel's view, policies and programs, if they are to be effective, will need to be evidence-based, appropriate to the local context, and developed in cooperation with developing country governments and local communities.

### Poverty

The UN Millennium Development Goals, the international community's unprecedented agreement on targets toward the elimination of extreme poverty, were not originally developed with a particular focus on young people. Nevertheless, the successful achievement by 2015 or beyond of many of these goals will require that policy makers center their attention on young people. Young people currently growing up in poverty face much greater health risks in both the short and longer term and are much less likely to attend schools of adequate quality, to complete primary school, to find secure and productive employment, to have opportunities for community participation, to marry well, or to be able to provide good care and support to their children.

Policies and programs designed to enhance successful transitions for young people, whether they are reproductive health programs, programs to enhance school quality or reduce dropout rates, job training programs, livelihood or civic education programs, or programs for first-time parents—should be targeted to the poor, particularly poor young women, who are often doubly disadvantaged. Evaluation research shows that important actors in the system—parents, students, teachers, employers, and administrators—can be very responsive to well-designed incentive programs.

## Schooling

At their best, schools have the capacity to enhance success in all transitions to adulthood through the acquisition of literacy in a commonly spoken language and the transmission of knowledge and means to sustain health, prosocial values and citizenship knowledge and skills, decision-making, negotiating, and leadership skills and skills for lifelong learning. While the panel supports the UN Millennium Development Goals for education, it does not see the achievement of these goals—universal primary school completion rates and the elimination of gender disparities at all levels of schooling—as sufficient for the next generation of young people to acquire the skills necessary for successful transitions to adulthood. The rapidity of global change and changing patterns of employment require that policy makers give equal attention to investments in school quality in order to ensure adequate learning outcomes at the primary level as well as to create a stronger base for further expansions in enrollment at the secondary level. The panel also identified carefully targeted subsidies as a particularly promising way to increase enrollment and reduce the prevalence of child labor among the poor.

Declines in fertility and improvements in child health have been shown to have contributed to past increases in the demand for schooling. Policies and programs supporting further progress in these areas are likely to continue to contribute to future growth in school enrollment and attainment.

## Gender Equality and the Empowerment of Women

Throughout its report, the panel documents systematic gender differences in pathways to adulthood as well as the universal persistence of dual social norms relating to the sexual behavior of young people. The panel's recommendations on gender equality emphasize the promotion of equitable treatment in the classroom through gender training for teachers and school administrators, the development of compensatory educational and training programs for disadvantaged and out of school youth, particularly girls, and the adoption of policies and programs that support delays in marriage in places where girls still marry before age 18. Addressing gender problems in society will call for interventions that affect all social classes and that give as much attention to boys' attitudes and behaviors as to girls'.

## Health, Particularly Reproductive Health

In developing recommendations, the panel focused on policies and programs for young people in the area of sexual and reproductive health as specified in the panel's original charge. We also documented the emergence of other areas of health and health behaviors that need policy and program attention, including mental health and health compromising behaviors such as smoking. The panel identified maternal mortality as one of the major causes of death and morbidity for young women in all developing regions except Eastern Asia and HIV/AIDS as the major cause of death and morbidity for young people in sub-Saharan Africa.

The provision of information and services for young people, married and unmarried, in the area of sexual and reproductive health is generally limited to small-scale efforts that reach a fraction of the population of young people. The panel recommends that policy makers give priority to increasing the provision of general health information and sex education, including negotiating skills, in school and out of school for all young people and to increasing the availability of services for those who are sexually active. No single approach is likely to serve the needs of all young people, however, given their diversity of life circumstances.

In the view of the panel, programs designed to reduce risky and unprotected sex among young people are critical to successful transitions and will require multipronged and multisectoral approaches that are culturally appropriate, community based, and sensitive to the needs and preferences of young people, including active collaboration between the health and education sectors. Indeed, some of the most important reproductive health interventions for young people may lie outside the health sector. For example, school participation and attainment appear to have important and mostly positive associations with young people's health; both male and female students who remain enrolled during their teens are substantially less likely to have had sex than their unmarried nonenrolled peers. Thus resources spent on expanding opportunities for secondary schooling may have a direct impact on the reproductive health of both young men and women.

## Youth Employment

Policies and programs with implications for young people's successful transition to work in developing countries exist at all levels of action. However, regulations that are commonly enacted in developing countries for the purpose of improving the terms and conditions of employment put young people at a disadvantage in competing for jobs in the formal labor market and encourage the growth of an informal, unregulated sector. Young people are likely to fare better in a labor market in which employers do not face excessive regulation or in which government incentives encourage firms to invest in training.

The panel has also noted that too often policies affecting aid and trade are not coordinated. For example, trade sanctions against products produced with child labor or against countries known to violate international labor standards relating to child labor are likely to do more harm than good in contexts in which poverty is persistent and the family economy still relies on child labor. While the focus of this report has been on policies and programs directly targeted to young people, the panel notes that agricultural and trade policies aimed at reducing nonmarket imperfections in the terms of trade between developed and developing countries could potentially be a far more effective means of helping the world's poor.

## KNOWLEDGE GAPS AND DIRECTIONS
## FOR FUTURE RESEARCH

Much more is known about basic patterns and trends than about the determinants or the consequences of these trends or about the extensive variability among young people in developing countries. Gaps in knowledge that emerge from the juxtaposition of our conceptual framework and our compilation of solid evidence form the basis of research questions that are provided at the end of each chapter. From these, many additional cross-cutting questions emerge. From the very rich experience of researchers in industrialized countries, we have learned how much there is to be gained from building multidisciplinary research teams, following cohorts over prolonged periods of time, and measuring a full range of social, psychological, health, and economic outcomes while deploying a mix of research methods.

In the final chapter, we recommend specific ways that existing data collection and compilation operations can be enhanced, identify promising quantitative and qualitative research approaches (not always new but underutilized) that would significantly deepen understanding of transitions to adulthood and suggest how findings from research and program and policy evaluation can be more effectively integrated into innovative and large-scale interventions. In particular, the panel recommends that evaluation should be adopted as an integral part of policy and program innovation for all interventions designed to enhance successful transitions to adulthood.

# PART I

# Introduction and Conceptual Framework

# 1

# Introduction

In many parts of the developing world, simultaneous changes in technology, economics, culture, politics, demographics, the environment, and education have become so pervasive and globally inclusive as to create new and emergent conditions for the coming of age of recent cohorts. These changes are reaching across national boundaries and into the smallest rural communities, carrying with them both the transformative force of markets, technology, and democracy, but also the risk of marginalization. Adolescents and young adults whose lives are affected by these changes can be beneficiaries when they are prepared for them but can also bear their scars if they are not. Those who do not feel the immediate impact of these changes will nonetheless be affected indirectly as the overall pace and pervasiveness of change continue to accelerate.

While young people—a term used in this report to capture this phase of the life cycle roughly equivalent to the age range 10 to 24—have little opportunity to affect the speed and direction of change, some will soon be taking responsibility for its management as adults. Their success in making a well-timed and proficient transition from childhood to adulthood will fundamentally affect the extent to which they will be able to become active participants in and beneficiaries of global change in the future.

Concerns about how global forces are altering the passage into adulthood are all the more urgent because of the changing demographic profile of many developing countries. The acceleration of these global changes has coincided with unprecedented growth in the size of the population of young people in developing countries. In 2005, the total number of 10-24-year-olds is estimated to reach 1.5 billion, constituting nearly 30 percent of the population of these regions. The population of young people of the world is quite unevenly distributed: 86 percent of all young people live in developing countries, and 71 percent of young people in developing countries currently live in Asia (United Nations, 2003b). Furthermore, rates of growth vary widely. In terms of absolute size, each subsequent cohort of young people in the developing world is projected to continue to increase until 2035, as the rapid growth in Africa and parts of Asia counteracts some slow declines in absolute numbers in other parts of Asia and in Latin America.

Across the developing world, the life experience of many young people today is profoundly different from the experience of their parents or even of young people growing up a decade ago. While change in and of itself is not new, the rapidity and scale of recent change has profound implications for both the opportunities and the risks faced by the current generation of young people and for relationships between the generations.

Improvements in health and survival have ensured for a great many more infants and children the opportunity to enjoy life into adolescence and beyond. These improvements, moreover, have meant that these children have developed better cognitively as well as in terms of physical health. Furthermore, the fertility transition, which is in process in most of the developing world, means that many young people are growing up with fewer siblings and in smaller households. Rapid urbanization also means that a higher percentage of young people are growing up in cities or moving to cities during their formative years. School enrollment and attainment are increasing around the world at the same time that ages of labor force entry are rising. With rising levels of education, young people have more possibilities to participate in a rapidly modernizing economy—in their local village, a nearby town, the capital city, or even another country—and experience and enjoy freer and more fulfilling lives. However, that promise cannot be realized without certain legal rights and protections and supportive institutions, including good schools, a sufficient number of remunerative and satisfying jobs, the opportunity for community participation and political voice, the absence of discrimination, good nutrition and health, access to health services, and, for women, a choice about freedom from premature marriage and childbearing.

Barriers to mobility have lessened due to reduced costs of transportation and increasingly available means of transportation at the same time that greater access to information conveys news of a wider range of geographic opportunities for schooling, jobs, and marriage partners. The development of a global youth culture is facilitated by the growing accessibility of international media and the Internet but at the same time fully effective connectivity requires adequate income to afford access, language competency, and computer literacy—skills that are hard for many young people to acquire without more and better schooling opportunities. Later ages of marriage and childbearing increase opportunities for further schooling, but they also increase the time during which adolescents are exposed to pre-marital pregnancy and childbearing.

Young people in less developed regions are confronting opportunities and challenges unique to this historical time. Young people today, especially in urban areas, are the first generation to grow up with widespread access to a radio and increasingly also to television and with the growing potential for Internet connectivity at an early age. They are also the first generation to grow up in a world in which there has always been AIDS and, at least in some parts of the developing world, the first generation with nearly universal knowledge of and access to some form of contraception. This is the first generation to be covered during their childhood by the broad protections internationally recognized in the United Nations Convention on the Rights of the Child (adopted in 1991) and supported, in many diverse local contexts, by the work of many international agencies as well as international, national, and local nongovernmental organizations.

In the context of today's rapid changes, gender role socialization, which is itself undergoing change, combines conflicting messages and contradictory experiences as the global culture interacts with cultural realities on the ground. Girls have historically experienced the transition to adulthood very differently from boys. Although gender role socialization begins at birth, it has generally led to an increasingly sharp differentiation of roles, behaviors, and expectations beginning at the time boys and girls experience puberty and continuing through the assumption of adult roles. This process of socialization is reinforced through social norms, laws, and institutions that in many countries progressively restrict the mobility and public participation of adolescent girls and in some settings makes them seemingly invisible while providing expanded liberties, opportunities, and agency for adolescent boys. Boys and girls usually enter adulthood having experienced differences in the duration and content of schooling, having taken up different work roles in the home and workplace, and having been offered different opportunities for community participation. Furthermore, young women typically assume adult family roles sooner than young men because they marry younger, while young men often assume more public adult roles sooner through their participation in work and their greater opportunities for leadership in schools, communities, work, and sports.

These broad statements capture only the average tendencies for young people in developing countries. At the same time that young people everywhere are becoming part of a more integrated world, at least some people in every country are experiencing transitions to adulthood that increasingly resemble those that are typical of young people in developed countries. But differential rates of change have led, in some cases, to growing differences among adolescents within and across countries, as some young people experience progress and others are left behind. Although poverty rates have been declining for developing countries as a whole, significant fractions of young people still live in poverty. Trends in poverty rates vary across regions, with big declines in Asia but an increase in poverty in Africa. In the panel's view, the successful achievement by 2015 of many of the United Nations Millennium Development Goals will require that policy makers center their attention on adolescents (see Box 1-1).

Critics of globalization argue that it has been associated with growing income inequality and social polarization, as some local participants in global change improve their economic situation while the livelihoods of others remain largely unchanged or decline (see, for example, Milanovic, 2003; United Nations, 2004; Wade, 2004). Over time the situation of those left behind may actually deteriorate, as their skills and assets become less

---

**BOX 1-1**
**Millennium Development Goals**

The Millennium Development Goals are a set of time-bound and measurable goals and targets designed to address the world's most compelling human development problems. Adopted by world leaders at the United Nations Millennium Summit in September 2000, they are now at the heart of the global development agenda. By adopting the United Nations Millennium Declaration, the international community pledged itself to eight development targets by 2015:

- Halve extreme poverty and hunger
- Achieve universal primary education
- Empower women and promote equality between women and men
- Reduce under-five mortality by two-thirds
- Reduce maternal mortality by three-quarters
- Reverse the spread of diseases, especially HIV/AIDS and malaria
- Ensure environmental sustainability
- Create a global partnership for development, with targets for aid, trade, and debt relief

Although for the most part not explicitly addressed, implicit in many of the Millennium Development Goals is the need for greater attention to services for young people. For example, greater investments in education and health, particularly for girls, is essential for reducing poverty, lowering infant and child mortality, and achieving greater lifelong gender equality. Similarly for a variety of reasons, slashing maternal mortality by three-quarters and reversing the spread of diseases, especially HIV/AIDS, will necessarily require far greater attention be paid to reproductive health services for young people. Finally, creating a global partnership for development will go a long way toward sustaining a healthy growth in job opportunities for young people.

and less valued. Relative and absolute poverty may increase within countries as well as across them. Growing economic inequality has reverberating consequences for the next generation. Young people growing up in poverty are the most vulnerable to the negative consequences of globalization and are in the greatest need of protection and support.

The very different demographic, political, and economic circumstances of countries throughout the developing world mean that the experiences of today's young people, and the implications of globalization for them, vary enormously. From young women in garment factories in Bangladesh, to child soldiers in Sierra Leone, to university students in Mexico, to unemployed youth in refugee communities in Palestine, to young workers in the Silicon Valley of India, to family farm workers in Egypt, to young Pakistani migrant workers in the Persian Gulf, to young wives of polygamous husbands in Senegal, one can only begin to imagine the range of experience that these examples encompass. Indeed, the diversity of experiences can only be growing, as traditional roles persist, albeit experienced in qualitatively different ways than in the past, and at the same time new opportunities and experiences emerge. Young people are adaptable and continue to demonstrate resilience in handling the contradictions of today's world. However, the challenge is to ensure successful transitions to adulthood in these rapidly changing circumstances and to spread opportunities for success more equitably given the enormous gaps that persist between rich and poor and between boys and girls. Policies and programs, if they are to be effective, will need to be evidence-based, appropriate to the local context, and embraced and supported by the local community.

## THE PANEL'S CHARGE

Recognizing the critical gaps in knowledge of the transitions to adulthood in developing countries in this time of rapid change, the National Academies convened a panel of experts to review the research in this area and related implications for policies and programs. Specifically, the panel's charge was to

- document the situation and status of adolescents and young adults in developing countries, highlighting what is known about various (and multiple) transitions to adulthood, with special emphasis on gender differences;
- ascertain the changes that are occurring in the nature, timing, sequencing, and interrelationships of transitions to adulthood in developing countries;
- assess the knowledge base regarding the causes and consequences of these changes;

- identify the implications of this knowledge for policy and program interventions affecting adolescent reproductive health; and
- identify research priorities that are scientifically promising and relevant for integrating adolescent research and policy.

The charge to the panel was intentionally very broad because the National Academies recognized that the transition to adulthood is multifaceted and comprises multiple and interrelated transitions across different spheres of life. To implement the charge, the panel reviewed knowledge on the full range of transitions to adulthood—schooling, health, work, citizenship, marriage, and parenthood, as well as policies and programs affecting all of these transitions. This was necessary because transitions are interrelated and interventions directed at any single transition can affect other transitions. The panel therefore addressed both the direct and indirect effects of policies and programs on adolescent reproductive health, to the extent possible given existing research and data.

The juxtaposition of diversity in the lives of young people in less developed regions and incomplete data coverage of the full range of contemporary experiences presented special challenges to the panel. The recognition that a study, no matter how comprehensive and empirically grounded, would inevitably neglect the experience of some young people led the panel to set the study in a conceptual framework that is neither time nor context specific. This allows the reader to adapt the framework (presented in the next chapter) to an understanding of the lives of the many young people whose stories will not be told or will be told only with respect to a specific time and place that is undergoing rapid change. Furthermore, in assessing the experiences of young people, the panel developed its own set of definitions of successful transitions to adulthood against which the actual experiences of young people could be compared. These definitions build on our understanding of adolescent development and of the contemporary global context and provide an essential yardstick with which data and research findings can be interpreted.

The panel's approach was to build on the positive while not ignoring the negative. Thus, while the emphasis is on opportunity and how it can be enhanced, the panel did not ignore the risks and constraints of contemporary life. Indeed, special attention was paid to examining both success stories and failures from past policies and programs designed to reduce risks and lift constraints, particularly as they apply to the disadvantaged. The panel gives special emphasis throughout the report to the different experiences of young men and women and to the circumstances of the poor regardless of gender. The panel views the achievement and maintenance of health, in particular reproductive health during the adolescent years, as integrally connected to success in other developmental domains.

We therefore emphasize in the report the interrelationships between these developmental domains and policies and programs that may affect these interrelationships.

The panel defined adulthood as a set of culturally, historically, and gender-specific activities, rights, and responsibilities that people acquire over time by means of a process of transition. The transition to adulthood begins during adolescence, but it continues beyond adolescence, sometimes even into the late 20s or early 30s. Therefore, in several places in the subsequent descriptive analysis, we make reference to

- an early phase of the transition (between ages 10 and 14),
- a middle phase of the transition (between ages 15 and 20), and
- a later phase of the transition (21+).

It is important for a report such as this to define terms such as "children," "adolescents," "youth," and "young people" and then use them consistently since the definitions and nuances of these terms vary from country to country and no common consensus exists. Even within the international community there is no ready and straightforward agreement. For example, the United Nations Convention on the Rights of the Child covers all children, defined as anyone under the age of 18, while the International Labour Organization (ILO)'s Minimum Age Convention (No. 138) distinguishes between acceptable "child labor" that is performed by children under the age of 15 and "child work" that may contribute to a child's healthy development. Light work may be allowed for children 12 and older (National Research Council, 2004). Given the panel's broad definition of the process of transition, developed to encompass diversities both within and across countries, our definition and terminology differ slightly from those adopted by some international agencies, for example the World Health Organization (UNICEF and WHO, 1995), which has used the terms "adolescent" for those ages 10-19, "youth" for those ages 15-24, and "young people" for those ages 10-24. Although the panel has frequently used the terms in the same way, for the most part, we prefer to use the term "young people" to refer to the relevant age range, roughly corresponding to 10- to 24-year-olds, during which time the transition to adulthood generally occurs. Note again, however, that in some cases, the transition can continue into one's late 20s or even early 30s. Recent analysis of the transition to adulthood in the West shows that the transition is being prolonged well into the third decade of life and sometimes even beyond (Arnett, 2000, 2004; Furstenberg et al., 2002). It is likely that a narrow focus on the age range 10 to 24 at this time in history in the developing world would risk missing important aspects of recent change. Consequently, in some of our detailed statistical analysis, the panel thought it more informative to present data for the broader age group 10 to 29. (See also Arnett, 2002, for a discussion of how transitions to adult roles are becoming delayed, creating a distinct period of "emerging adulthood" among the [minority but growing] middle class in developing countries.)

While the panel views marriage as an important marker of adulthood, we do not think that marriage is sufficient in and of itself to confer adulthood on a young person who has not yet achieved the age of majority or completed other transitions to adulthood. This is an important caution, because much contemporary literature on adolescents focuses primarily on the unmarried, neglecting the concerns of the married, particularly young women, who are not yet fully prepared to assume adult roles and are particularly vulnerable because society provides them with few protections.

## WHAT CONSTITUTES A SUCCESSFUL TRANSITION?

The concept of a successful transition to adulthood is inherent in the panel's larger mission: to advance understanding of the impact of rapid and pervasive global change on the adolescent-to-young-adult phase of the life course and to propose interventions for enhancing that transition in developing countries. In particular, the panel is not concerned with traditional rites of passage, such as circumcision or (arranged) marriage, or solely with the acquisition of skills that will enable young people to become more productive as adults, but more fundamentally about the enhancement of capabilities that will allow them "to lead lives they have reason to value and to enhance the substantive choices they have" (Sen, 1997:1959). This represents a very different approach to the study of adolescent development than that taken in the United States over the last few decades, in which the focus has been primarily on problem behaviors rather than on normative development (Steinberg and Morris, 2001). It is also very different from the approach to the study of child outcomes in developing countries, which views parents as decision-makers and children as having no agency of their own (Levison, 2000). Defining what is meant by "a successful transition," however, remains problematic, and it engages several important considerations about adolescent development in general.

First, the transition to adulthood has to be seen as embedded in the larger developmental life course, reflecting and constrained by what has gone before as well as by what lies ahead. From this perspective, the experiences and events of earlier adolescence—and of infancy and childhood—are not only precursors of, but also preparation for, making that transition. From this perspective, too, the opportunities and barriers of future adulthood, both real and perceived, also shape the course and content of that transition. It follows, then, that efforts to safeguard or enhance a successful transition cannot be confined to that brief segment of the life trajectory between adolescence and young adulthood alone; rather, interventions must engage both earlier and later developmental periods as well.

The interrelationship between success in adolescence and opportunities at later phases of the life cycle is particularly salient in the case of gender inequalities that are socially and institutionally embedded. There is now clear evidence that countries with more equal rights for women in various domains, including politics and the law, social and economic matters, and marriage and divorce, have smaller gender gaps in such key outcome indicators as health, schooling, and political participation (King and Mason, 2001). It is rarely noted, however, that these gender gaps, which are measured for adults, take shape during adolescence. Indeed, in most societies, local definitions of success may differ profoundly for girls and boys. By contrast, the panel's definitions of success are gender neutral and embody an emerging set of international norms about gender equality that have been embodied in many international agreements and conventions.

A second consideration in defining what is meant by successful transition to adulthood is the need to make it sensitive to the enormous diversity of developing societies, appropriate to local situations, and responsive to the dynamics of historical change. It is clear that there are prevailing cultural expectations and traditions about what constitutes the attainment of maturity, and these may vary not only in different parts of the world but also across different subgroups in the same country. For example, in some contexts, the establishment of an independent household may be a marker of adulthood, whereas in others living with one's parents is entirely consistent with the assumption of all other adult roles. Furthermore, in some cultures in which strong family and community linkages are valued more than autonomy, success may be measured by the ability to mobilize social networks rather than by the ability to act autonomously (Mensch et al., 2003c).

Finally, it is also necessary to conceptualize successful transitions relative to a particular time in history (for this report, it is the present) and to the dynamics and speed of societal change that may be under way. What might have been considered a successful transition to adulthood before the globalization of production, the pervasive spread of information technology, and the greater access to a transnational and homogenizing youth culture may no longer be considered so today. In the contemporary world, success requires competence in coping with the reverberations of rapid global and societal change on daily life—a competence that cannot be entirely provided within the family but that requires extrafamilial inputs. In short, a successful transition entails being prepared for a changing future rather than one based on extrapolations of the past.

While success is ultimately measured at the individual level, nothing is clearer than that the burden of enhancing successful transitions to adulthood in developing countries is primarily on society and its institutions at the local, national, and international level, rather than on particular individuals or their families. Essential social supports for success include access to quality schooling and other educational resources outside the classroom, adequate health care, livelihood training and job opportunities, resources for civic engagement and family and community models, and supports for positive social development. The existence of norms and the availability and effectiveness of laws and institutions that can support the accomplishment of the major developmental tasks of adolescence must become a major and obligatory concern of any society seeking to enhance successful transitions to adulthood.

In light of these various considerations, the panel sought a conceptualization of successful transitions to adulthood that is both generally and locally applicable; that is predicated on preparation in prior developmental stages, especially adolescence, but also childhood; that is appropriate despite pervasive gender and socioeconomic disparities as well as different endowments and capabilities; that is open to shaping by both antecedent and subsequent life course interventions; and that recognizes the imperatives of contemporary global change. The defining attributes of such a conceptualization of successful transition to adulthood, which must be seen within the constraints of personal endowments and capabilities, include at least the following:

- Good mental and physical health, including reproductive health, and the knowledge and means to sustain health during adulthood.
- An appropriate stock of human and social capital to enable an individual to be a productive adult member of society.
- The acquisition of prosocial values and the ability to contribute to the collective well-being as citizen and community participant.
- Adequate preparation for the assumption of adult social roles and obligations, including the roles of spouse or partner, parent, and household and family manager.
- The capability to make choices through the acquisition of a sense of self and a sense of personal competence.
- A sense of general well-being.

Although no claim can be made that this is an exhaustive listing of the attributes of successful transition to adulthood, it does capture what the panel views as essential components of that process. What can be claimed is that the essential components listed can serve as a guide for the interpretation of a conceptual framework (presented in the next chapter) as well as for the design and targeting of societal interventions to maximize the attainability of those attributes.

Furthermore, the panel was concerned not only about the acquisition of certain personal values and attributes necessary for success, but also about the timing and sequencing of their acquisition. When young people take on adult work or family obligations before finishing school, success may be compromised. If young men who have assumed other adult roles are unable to marry until their 30s because of escalating financial demands, their need for sexual expression may compromise their health and the health of others and deprive them of the pleasures of and social status that accompanies a family life. The panel recognizes that all adulthood roles are not acquired at the same time, and therefore the report refers to multiple transitions rather than a single transition. Indeed, the panel expects that success in one domain will foster success in other domains of adult life, allowing transitions in various domains to occur in a steady succession. Ultimately, the benefit and enjoyment of each role is enhanced by the acquisition of the others.

## STUDY SCOPE AND APPROACH

The panel agreed early in its deliberations that our approach to the charge would be highly empirical. The panel set high standards for evidence, placing an emphasis on comparative quantitative data of high quality, supplemented by well-designed and statistically sound experimental and observational studies along with country case studies and qualitative materials.

The panel developed its own conceptual framework in order to guide our interpretation of the empirical evidence and assess claims of causal inference. This conceptual framework is presented in Chapter 2. While the panel's ambitions were as broad as the conceptual framework, the actual scope of the report was constrained by the availability of comparative and time-series data as well as by the limitations of existing empirical analyses of transitions to adulthood in developing countries, which are largely based on cross-sectional data.

The panel's approach to addressing the questions outlined in the charge flows logically from the conceptual framework presented below and includes the following six elements:

1. To use the conceptual framework as a guide to the identification of key research questions.
2. To review existing research studies on trends in the contextual factors, transitions, and outcomes laid out in the conceptual framework and to supplement these with analysis of comparative data sets.
3. To review existing literature for insights about possible factors explaining recent changes in the transition to adulthood.

4. To review existing literature for insights into the longer term consequences of alternative individual and societal outcomes.

5. To review recent evaluations of the impact of policies and programs in order to identify promising (and ideally cost-effective) approaches to the promotion of adolescent reproductive health and other important health outcomes.

6. To identify research priorities by situating the panel's findings within the conceptual framework.

To the extent that resources would permit, in Chapters 3 through 8, the panel went beyond a mere review of the existing literature and exploited available data in new ways in order to build a more complete picture of recent trends. Whenever possible, estimates of trends that are applicable to all young people or to young people from a particular region were generated by weighting data from different countries by population size, thus allowing conclusions that are more representative of the underlying population of young people.

The panel relied on the best and most up-to-date data available for each topic, while remaining mindful of data quality issues (see Appendix A for a discussion of data quality issues.) Thus the report includes data on trends in education, marriage, childbearing, and other aspects of reproductive behavior from the Demographic and Health Surveys, data on attitudes and participation from the World Value Surveys, data on marriage trends from a United Nations data bank of censuses and national surveys, data on employment and unemployment from International Labour Organization labor force statistics, data on mortality and morbidity by age from the World Health Organization, other selected census and survey data that allow comparisons over time, and data on time use from recent Population Council surveys. While readily acknowledging that the extent of high-quality studies is highly uneven across regions, for most topics, the panel decided that we were able to make statements and draw conclusions about recent change since the 1980s or 1990s. (See Appendix A for more information about the panel's approach to data analysis, the coverage of the report, and sources of data.)

One of the important roles of the conceptual framework is to guide the interpretation of empirical evidence on causal effects in the rest of the report. Simple associations in observed data, such as between schooling and age of marriage or childbearing, are useful for *describing* the reality of the transition to adulthood and how those patterns have changed. But descriptions of patterns do not lead to confident assessment of *causality* for several reasons. Different behaviors are likely to be embedded in a "web of causality," as described above. So the association between, say, schooling and age of marriage may reflect two-way or reverse causality, or that both are determined by some third factor, such as changing labor market opportunities, and not simply that schooling affects the age of marriage or that age of marriage affects schooling. The panel's goal of comprehensively addressing the factors that determine observed outcomes, and not just measured factors and their effects, required a systematic thoughtful and rigorous approach to the sifting of evidence (Bachrach and McNicoll, 2003; Smith, 2003).[1]

One scientific method for dealing with such problems of empirical inference is to use well-designed and well-implemented double-blind experiments, with random assignment to treatment and control groups and control for such factors as spillovers. There are some empirical areas for which such experiments have been undertaken and provide some of the evidence regarding what is known about transitions to adulthood in developing countries. But these are relatively limited because of costs and ethical concerns. There are no good experiments for many questions of interest, and they may not even be feasible. Furthermore, such randomized controlled trials "championed by many economists, maximize internal validity, but often at the expense of generalizability and the ability to extrapolate findings" (Moffitt, 2003:445).

In many cases, therefore, the empirical evidence must be based on observational (or sometimes called behavioral) data. These data include imperfect measures of the transitions to adulthood that are determined directly and indirectly, with feedback in many cases, by other factors. The best empirical evidence from such behavioral data makes explicit the behavioral model underlying the determination of the transitions to adulthood. It also uses estimation techniques and data that permit control for various estimation problems, such as selectivity, measurement error, and endogeneity (or the correlation of measured variables with unobservables).

For example, if there is interest in the impact of early childbearing on some other aspects of the transition to adulthood, the best empirical studies control for measurement errors in data on childbearing and for what determines childbearing—family background, ability, motivations, cultural beliefs related to gender, labor market options—in the estimation of the impact of early childbearing on other transitions to adulthood. The failure to do so is likely to lead to misunderstanding of the impact of early childbearing—confounding the effects of childbearing with other effects, such as of those determinants of childbearing noted above.

---

[1]See also Kuate-Defo (2005) for applications of multilevel models and multistate multilevel competing risks analysis as a means to disentangle the risk and protective factors of synchronized events associated with transitions to adulthood in an African context.

Undertaking such systematic empirical research is difficult. Many studies in the literature are not explicit about what conceptual framework is being used to interpret behavioral data and often implicitly make very strong assumptions. For example, many studies of the impact of early childbearing make the implicit assumption that childbearing is assigned randomly, or that there are no factors that affect both the outcome being studied as well as the timing of childbearing itself.

This report tries to make clear the quality of the empirical evidence that is being used. At times, simple descriptions are presented because they are of interest in themselves, but they should *not* be confused with assertions about causality. In a few cases, good experimental evidence is summarized. In other cases, there are good systematic studies using behavioral data with explicit models and methods, so the nature of the underlying assumptions is transparent and the assumptions themselves are plausible. To the extent possible, this report relies on evidence from these high-quality sources. But for some topics that are important, the evidence is much weaker. Too much would be lost by complete omission of these topics. Therefore in such cases the report presents what is known and tries to be clear about why that knowledge is qualified—and thus, why more and better research is warranted in certain areas.

The panel has paid special attention to policy and programs that hold promise of supporting successful transitions in resource-constrained environments. This is an area in which the empirical evidence is particularly uneven. Most interventions that have been rigorously evaluated have relatively narrowly defined intended outcomes and a limited time frame for assessing impact (Knowles and Berhman, 2005). Various policies and programs that are designed to benefit younger children may have important benefits that extend into the second decade of life, but that are generally not measured or evaluated. Furthermore, the impact of many national policies and programs with potentially profound importance to the life course and life chances of young people, such as school reforms, marriage laws, abortion laws, and child labor laws, may never have been assessed. Whether assessing policies and programs in the area of reproductive health or in other important areas, such as education, work, and marriage, the report sets the panel's review of the empirical evidence on interventions in the larger context of the policies and programs that have the potential to affect the lives of young people.

## STRUCTURE OF THE REPORT

The report has the following plan. Part I sets the stage with this introduction, and in the next chapter, we introduce our conceptual framework and use it to guide a discussion of the key elements of global change. Because of the diversity of experiences among young people, the implications of these changes for national and local environments are illustrated using examples from the empirical literature. These serve to make more tangible the many ways in which global change is affecting the daily lives of young people.

Part II looks at the two critical elements of individual resources for which we have relatively rich data and evidence: changes in education (Chapter 3) and changes in health and reproductive health (Chapter 4). Each chapter starts by describing recent data on patterns and trends, then reviews critically what is known from the empirical literature about the factors affecting these patterns and changes and finishes with a review of relevant policies and programs designed to positively affect the necessary resources and attributes for successful transitions, including evidence (when available) about their effectiveness.

Part III is organized around four adult roles: worker (Chapter 5), citizen (Chapter 6), spouse or partner (Chapter 7), and parent (Chapter 8). As there are very few data on the role of household manager, this adult role is not treated separately, although the panel recognizes its potential importance. In Part III, we are particularly interested in how changes at the global level are affecting the very nature of the transition itself, in terms of timing, sequencing, duration, and content. Each successive chapter in this part of the report considers not just that particular adult role in isolation but explores the ways in which one transition relates to another. While considerations of the timing of work in relation to schooling or the timing of marriage in relation to parenthood are more familiar in the literature, the links between work and marriage or schooling and childbearing are less familiar. The interrelationships among transitions is a key theme in each chapter whenever data permit.

It will become obvious to the reader in proceeding from the conceptual framework in Part I to the substantive chapters in Part II and Part III that the panel's knowledge falls far short of its curiosity. The gaps between the conceptual framework and the empirical evidence remain huge. Nonetheless, the panel's comparative empirical approach does allow new facts and insights to emerge, some of which have implications for the design of policies and programs. The panel's conceptual framework highlights the gap between theory and evidence with clear implications for future research priorities. Part IV's Chapter 9 summarizes the findings from Chapters 2 through 8 and identifies promising avenues for future research that can provide important insights for understanding and for policy choices.

# 2

# Conceptual Framework

## INTRODUCTION

The largest cohort of young people living in developing countries ever is currently coming of age in a rapidly changing world. Simultaneous changes in technology, economics, culture, politics, demographics, the environment, and education are creating greater connectivity among countries, communities, and individuals. These changes have lowered the importance of geographic distance between different places. Advances in technology make travel easier, faster, or even unnecessary (because of the growth of electronic communication). Changes in politics make national boundaries easier to cross, and shifts in economic structures routinize the flow of goods, services, and capital. Globalization per se is not new, but what is new is the speed, scale, scope, and complexity of this process.

Because of these changes, the ecology of daily adolescent life is no longer circumscribed by geographic boundaries. Information is disseminated and available instantaneously nearly everywhere, financial transactions and production networks are organized globally with few impediments, transportation makes high-income and lower income countries immediately accessible to one another, and migration is no longer simply from the farm to the city, but across international boundaries. All of this makes the transition to adulthood a new, transformed, and "emergent" process at the beginning of the twenty-first century. Many young people today are truly "growing up global."

While the economic benefits of globalization are potentially enormous, the course of globalization has not been without its critics, who charge that it has introduced new kinds of international conflicts and problems such as rising inequality, social polarization, and the demise of the nation-state (see, for example, Lechner and Boli, 2000; Milanovic, 2003; Wade, 2004). Some authors have even argued that young people who are "outside" the global economy and culture may be better off in some ways; they may maintain stronger family and community ties or be less likely to be exposed to risky behaviors.

Regardless of how the globalization debate is finally resolved, one thing is clear: as broad global forces transform the world in which the next generation will live and work, the choices that today's young people make or others make on their behalf will facilitate or constrain their success as adults. Old expectations regarding employment or life experiences are not valid any more. Furthermore, the transition to adulthood is no longer just a matter of familial and individual choices but is greatly shaped by global contexts, increased contact across cultures and geographical space, and the repercussions that are associated with multiple and simultaneous events across countries. And the traditional values and norms that informed and influenced these choices in the past may not lead to the best decisions in the changing global context in which adolescents find themselves. Arnett (2002) has argued that young people worldwide now develop a bicultural identity that integrates their local identity with new elements derived from their exposure to and interpretation of global culture.

The purpose of this chapter is to introduce a conceptual framework that traces the effect of broad global changes on the process of transition from childhood to young adulthood in developing countries. It describes the most important elements and discusses the diversity of adolescent experience across regions and the suitability of the framework across the developing world as a whole. A special effort is made to note the similarities and differences that young people face in different regions of the world as well as the differences between men and women and among different socioeconomic groups.

## A CONCEPTUAL FRAMEWORK

Figure 2-1 presents the conceptual framework that the panel has adopted to guide our efforts and structure the report. Although the focus of concern is on young people in developing countries and their entry into adult status in their own societies, the perspective of the framework is that much of what happens to them, and indeed what constitutes their daily experience, is shaped by the contexts of their lives. As the figure shows, context has been divided into three analytic levels. Most remote of these is *changing global context* (Box A), next is *changing national context* (Box B), and the most immediate or proximal context is *changing local community*

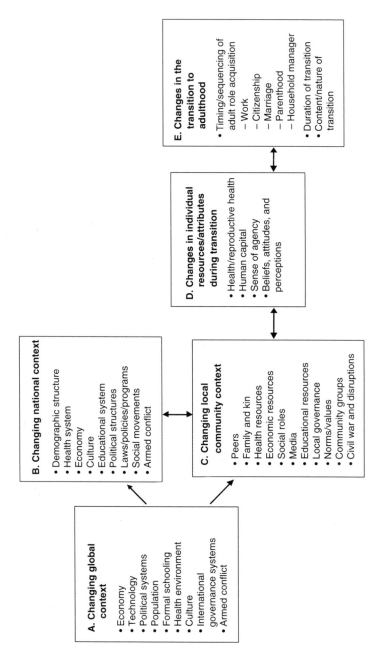

FIGURE 2-1 A conceptual framework for the study of changing transitions to adulthood in developing countries.

*context* (Box C). The embeddedness of young people's lives in these contexts entails the proposition that changes in those contexts, whether distant or immediate, will have reverberating implications for individuals.

Several aspects of the framework deserve mention. First, its emphasis throughout is on change; change is represented in the global environment, in the more immediate environments, in young people themselves, and, ultimately, in the course and contours of the transition process. Although such changes may not as yet have reached every corner of the developing world, their pervasiveness and the rapidity with which they are occurring suggest that most young people in developing countries have felt at least some impact.

Second, although the focus of concern is on young people in developing countries and on their entry into adult status in their own societies, the perspective of the framework is that much of what happens to them and, indeed, constitutes their daily experience, is shaped by the contexts in which their lives are embedded. The framework gives causal precedence to the changes under way in the global environment. As Figure 2-1 shows, the arrows originating at Box A are unidirectional, whereas all the other arrows in the figure are bidirectional. The intent in representing the change process in this way is simply to capture the panel's commitment to address the impact on individual young people of those macro forces at the global level, the dynamics of which are likely to be consequential for their development.

Third, the framework highlights the interlinkages and influences between the context and individual behavior. It is an attempt to articulate the major processes and structures that are undergoing significant change at three contextual levels and to represent their potential influence, both direct and indirect, on young people and their development. Although not exhaustive, the contents of each box in the figure can be conceptually linked to the contents of the other boxes, and, in many cases, it is possible to invoke empirical support for those linkages. Of special interest to the panel are *changes in individual resources/attributes during transition* (Box D) and *changes in the transition to adulthood* (Box E). The emphasis there is on changes in the acquisition of various kinds of attributes or capabilities and in orientation toward the changing structure of opportunity, all logically relevant to changes in the timing and nature of the transition to adulthood. The framework represents the panel's vision of a "web of causality" in which various loci of influence operate in multiple directions.

Finally, it is understood, although not made explicit in the figure, that how the forces of global change affect the national and local environments will have different implications for young men and women as well as for young people from different family backgrounds defined by such characteristics as class, caste, race, or ethnicity. To begin with, gender differences in opportunity structures and constraints pervade the institutions that shape young peoples' lives at all levels, from political structures, laws, and national education systems on one hand, to the family, the classroom, and the local youth center on the other. At the same time, some of the new opportunities that have resulted from globalization have been gender specific, such as new employment opportunities for young women in garment factories in Bangladesh and for young men in construction in the Persian Gulf. In subsequent chapters as we work through the consequences of these global changes for various domains of young peoples' lives, we give special attention to gender differences.

## KEY ELEMENTS OF THE CONCEPTUAL FRAMEWORK

Below we expand on some of the elements of the conceptual framework in Boxes A-C. Boxes D and E are the focus of the rest of the book.

### Changing Global Context (Box A)

Young people today are coming of age in a world in which the process of economic and cultural integration is accelerating. Driven by an astounding rate of technological change, particularly in transportation, computerization, and telecommunications, globalization has radically reduced the need for spatial proximity between producers and consumers and consequently reshaped the organization, management, and production of industries and firms. Globalization has also been facilitated by a more favorable international political climate, the collapse of communism and increasing democratization, and financial deregulation that has allowed capital to become more mobile than ever before (Berry, Conkling, and Ray, 1997). Yet globalization has not been without its critics, who argue that while the economic benefits are potentially enormous, in some places it has resulted in new problems related to the clash of traditional and modern cultures, rising income inequality, and social polarization (see, for example, Milanovic, 2003; United Nations, 2004; Wade, 2004).

Globalization brings both potential risks and benefits for young people. Theoretically, as the economies of the world become more interconnected, factors of production can be used more efficiently and the opportunities for wealth creation expand. At the same time, there is also a down side. Open borders and financial deregulation mean that capital can just as easily flow out of a country as it can flow in, leading to a heightened degree of instability in a local economy. Young people's employment status is often more vulnerable to the uncertainties and risks associated with globalization than any other age group, given their lack of labor market experience and the relative fragility of their tenure of employment.

Furthermore, while global change is important in the lives of many young people, its impact around the world has been highly uneven: Over the last 20 years, gross domestic product (GDP) per capita has risen spectacularly in India, China, and parts of Pacific Asia, roughly stagnated in Latin America, and fallen dramatically in the former Soviet Union, Central and Eastern Europe, and across sub-Saharan Africa (Wade, 2004).

Even in countries in which the rate of economic growth has been very high, for some young people, particularly those in rural areas, the outward patterns and rhythms of life may appear to be largely unaffected. The growing gap between those who are caught up in global change and those who are not is a particular concern. Traditional cultures may control which young people are given the opportunity to fully participate in the best that the new global economy and lifestyle has to offer, and which will maintain traditional ways of life and possibly suffer as their standards of living fall farther behind their peers in their adult years.

## Pervasiveness of Market-Led Economic Change

Although the origins of globalization can be traced back hundreds of years, there is no doubt that since the 1980s rapid technological change combined with major political reforms have accelerated the transformation of the world's economic system. Improvements in transportation and communication technology together with advances in computer power have contributed to a new international division of labor characterized by the rise of multinational companies, increased international financial flows, and the transfer of manufacturing jobs from the developed to the developing world. These technological advances have occurred at the same time that major political reforms, including the collapse of communism, have opened up markets and removed previous institutional barriers to trade and development.

Again it is important to stress that the extent of global economic change has been very uneven across the developing world. While the restructuring of global production has brought numerous benefits to many, others have been virtually unaffected and as a result increasingly marginalized. The region that has benefited the most from globalization is Pacific Asia, while large parts of Africa have been effectively bypassed. In fact, in 24 sub-Saharan African economies, GDP per capita is lower today than it was 20 years ago: and in 12 countries it is even below its 1960 level (Milanovic, 2003). In Asia, some of the populous economic giants that have gained the most overall from globalization, including China, India, and Indonesia, have experienced widening income gaps as their economies went global (Williamson, 2002). This is because the benefits of globalization have been very unevenly distributed, being concentrated in some of the larger cities and special economic zones.

For millions of adolescents throughout the developing world, this global economic restructuring has dramatically transformed possible life trajectories. Multinational companies seeking to lower production costs have greatly accelerated the processes of industrialization and global economic integration, bringing manufacturing and other types of jobs to areas in which previously they had not existed. Companies like Levi Strauss & Co. once made jeans in a single factory in San Francisco; now they manufacture and sell their products in over 100 countries around the world. As economic development progresses, adolescents with secondary schooling are more marketable in the labor force and therefore more likely to enjoy the benefits of the globalization of labor. At the same time, greater investments in human capital are usually associated with a more prolonged period of dependence, as young people stay in school longer and enter the labor market, marriage, and childbearing later.

While some young people are able to take advantage of these changes, others are not. As Basu (2003b:10) notes: "While globalization creates, on the whole, more opportunities than it destroys, it can have the negative fall-out of marginalizing some people." People pursuing traditional livelihoods without the benefits of improved technology may find they are losing out to competitors with more efficient production techniques. Furthermore, life for the illiterate and those with few years of education has become more difficult, as their skills are becoming less valued in the labor market.

## Technological Change

Technological change—new invention and innovation—is at the very heart of economic growth and development. In today's highly competitive global environment, multinational companies strive to produce goods and services as cheaply and efficiently as possible. Constant innovation and improvement in all aspects of production, distribution, and organization have become virtually essential for firms to remain competitive and survive.

Advances in computerization and in the fields of transportation and communication have been critical factors facilitating global economic integration. Advances in computer power over the last 20 years and in communication technology using satellite communication, digital systems, and fiber-optic cables have dramatically increased the speed at which information flows from one place to another, making it easier for firms to establish and manage global networks of production. At the same time, the development of superfreighters and the introduction of containerization have lowered the cost of transporting raw materials and finished products around the world, enabling multinational companies to establish new markets and to move their points of production away from their traditional consumers.

Rapid technological change presents young people with many opportunities and challenges. Globalization has resulted in a world in which change is the only constant, competitive advantage is constantly being challenged, and methods of production and distribution are constantly being reinvented. The growing interconnectedness and rapid communications seen in the spread of the Internet, the World Wide Web, and the widening availability of computers are allowing some adolescents, especially middle-class ones and elites in urban areas, to access many of the benefits of globalization, while leaving many others, who remain unconnected, farther behind.

The most obvious impact that these changes have on young people relates to the nature of the labor market that they face. A constantly changing labor market driven by rapid technological change favors those with more education. The information age demands computer skills and knowledge for the most coveted positions in the labor market. But in addition to improving their employability, access to and understanding of computers and the Internet expose young people to many of the aspects of global youth culture—including television, music, films, and fashion—that link young people around the world.

## Democratization and the Rise of Civil Society

Along with technological change, globalization of the world's economies has also been facilitated by many far-reaching political changes. Throughout the developing world, more and more authoritarian and single-party regimes are being replaced with some form of democratic government. In Eastern Europe, the collapse of communism fundamentally altered the global political landscape, which had been in place since the end of World War II. Consequently, authoritarian and single-party regimes were no longer able to rely on U.S.-Soviet tension to garner favor. The percentage of countries with some form of democratic government has risen from 57 percent in 1973 to 75 percent in 2003 (Freedom House, 2004). In China, the largest remaining communist world power, communist leaders have managed to retain control while opening up parts of the country to private investors. As a result, the percentage of China's industrial output produced in state-owned enterprises has fallen dramatically, from 78 percent in 1978 to 43 percent by 1994 (Berry et al., 1997). Throughout the developing world, greater political openness has resulted in the liberalization of global financial markets and the removal of other institutional barriers to trade and development.

The trend toward greater democratic rule has been accompanied by greater citizen participation through local social and environmental move-ments, community interest groups, and other nongovernmental organiza-tions. It has also been accompanied by a growing trend toward decentrali-zation of power and responsibility to local government authorities. These political changes have been associated with more participatory government and increasing opportunities for young people to participate in civil society, in the life of the community, and in politics.

### Changes in Population Size and Distribution

Rapid globalization has coincided with unprecedented growth in the size of the population of young people in developing countries. Large young cohorts challenge nations to achieve and sustain access to basic health and education services to all sectors of society. Although the total fertility rate is falling throughout the developing world (i.e., women are having fewer children, on average) the total number of adolescents remains very large due to high fertility in the recent past. The total population of young people ages 10-24 in the world is estimated by the United Nations to have reached 1.76 billion by 2005, approximately 27 percent of the world's total popula-tion (see Table 2-1). While young people constitute approximately 20 per-cent of the total population of more developed regions, in the developing world the population of young people ages 10 to 24 is estimated to reach approximately 1.5 billion in 2005, or 29 percent of the total population of those regions. In the least developed countries, the proportion of young people in the overall population is even greater: over 33 percent in 2005. Generally the poorer a country is, the younger its population.

In terms of absolute size, it is important to remember that the youth population in the developing world is itself quite unevenly distributed geo-graphically and that the regional distribution continues to shift as a result of differential fertility, mortality, and migration rates across regions. By 2005, it is estimated that over 70 percent of the young people in the less developed world will live in Asia, with 42 percent of all young people living in China and India alone. The population in Africa is projected to rise to 26 percent of all developing country young people by 2030 (435 million) from its level in 2005 of 19 percent (294 million). This is primarily a result of continued decline in developing Asia's share of young people, which is estimated at 75 percent in 1980 (807 million), 70 percent in 2005 (1,060 million), and 64 percent in 2030 (1,075 million). Latin America and the Caribbean's share of the total developing country young is projected to decline slightly from 10.5 percent in 2005 to 9.5 percent in 2030 (see Table 2-1).

In all developing regions, each subsequent cohort is projected to con-tinue to increase steadily as the rapid growth in Africa and parts of Asia counteracts some slow declines in absolute numbers in other parts of Asia and in Latin America. While the population of young people in Eastern Asia (largely China) peaked at 410 million in 1985 and will peak in 2030 in South Central Asia (549 million), it is not expected to peak in Western Asia (largely Pakistan) before 2050. Similarly, while the population of young people in Southern Africa reached its peak in 2005 (17 million), the most populous parts of Africa—Eastern, Western, Middle, and Central Africa—will still be growing in 2050. Thus, with the exception of Eastern Asia and Southern Africa, the absolute size of young cohorts continues to grow, peaking for Asia as a whole in 2010, in Latin America and the Caribbean by 2015, and sometime after 2050 in Africa (United Nations, 2003b).

As fertility declines, child dependency ratios decline, implying a population with relatively more working-age adults (ages 15-64) and relatively fewer nonworking-age dependents (Bongaarts, 2000). (The child dependency ratio is calculated as the ratio of children ages 0-14 to working-age adults.) But as economic development progresses, the age of dependency becomes more prolonged, stretching beyond childhood as young people stay longer in school and entry into the labor market is postponed along with marriage and childbearing. Delays in the full assumption of adult roles generally reflect greater investments in human and social capital, signaling a longer phase of economic dependency. Table 2-2 shows the percentage of the population by various broad age groups for various points in time. In Latin America and the Caribbean and Asia, the percentage of the population ages 25-64 grew substantially between 1980 and 2005. In Latin America the 25-64 age group increased from 36 to 45 percent, while in Asia it grew from 39 to 48 percent. Because Africa's fertility transition began only recently, the age structure of the African population changed relatively little over the last 25 years. But, in spite of the effects of the HIV/AIDS pandemic, between 2005 and 2030, the percentage of the population ages 25-64 is expected to grow from 34 to 41 percent in Africa. Smaller positive changes are also expected in Asia and Latin America and the Caribbean. When dependency burdens are high, transitions to adulthood are likely to be shorter; when dependency burdens are lower, transitions to adulthood are likely to be longer. The higher ratios for some parts of Africa highlight the special challenges for young people in those regions. The disadvantages they face in cohort size, particularly as they relate to the older working-age population, suggest that there will be less societal resources to invest in this stage of development, thus reducing the length of transitions and compromising chances for success.

The rapid growth in the total number of young people should also not obscure the fact that many are growing up in smaller families with fewer siblings. This is a function of the fertility transition that is well under way in

TABLE 2-1 Population of Young People by Region

| Region | Total Population (millions) | | | Population Ages 10-24 | | |
|---|---|---|---|---|---|---|
| | 1980 | 2005 | 2030 | 1980 | 2005 | 2030 |
| WORLD | 4,435 | 6,454 | 8,130 | 1,336 | 1,755 | 1,875 |
| More Developed Regions | 1,083 | 1,209 | 1,242 | 263 | 237 | 201 |
| Less Developed Regions | 3,352 | 5,245 | 6,888 | 1,072 | 1,518 | 1,673 |
| Least Developed Regions | 400 | 753 | 1,257 | 127 | 246 | 389 |
| Africa | 470 | 888 | 1,398 | 147 | 294 | 435 |
| Eastern | 144 | 282 | 462 | 45 | 96 | 152 |
| Middle | 53 | 106 | 191 | 16 | 35 | 64 |
| Northern | 111 | 190 | 267 | 35 | 60 | 68 |
| Southern | 33 | 52 | 49 | 11 | 17 | 14 |
| Western | 128 | 257 | 429 | 40 | 86 | 137 |
| Asia (excluding Japan) | 2,515 | 3,790 | 4,766 | 807 | 1,060 | 1,075 |
| Eastern[a] | 1,061 | 1,404 | 1,538 | 346 | 338 | 282 |
| South-central | 981 | 1,615 | 2,192 | 307 | 493 | 549 |
| South-eastern | 358 | 558 | 711 | 117 | 165 | 162 |
| Western | 115 | 213 | 324 | 36 | 64 | 83 |
| Latin America and the Caribbean | 361 | 558 | 711 | 117 | 161 | 159 |
| The Caribbean | 29 | 39 | 45 | 9 | 11 | 10 |
| Central America | 90 | 147 | 194 | 30 | 45 | 45 |
| South America | 242 | 372 | 472 | 77 | 105 | 104 |
| Oceania[b] | 5 | 9 | 13 | 1 | 3 | 3 |

[a]Excludes Japan.
[b]Excludes Australia and New Zealand.
NOTE: Population estimates for 2005 and projections for 2030 are for United Nations Medium Variant.
SOURCE: United Nations (2003d).

most of Asia and Latin America and parts of Africa. Using Demographic Health Survey (DHS) data from 52 developing countries, Pullum and Zellner (2000) estimated the average number of living siblings ages 0-15 for children ages 0-15 according to total fertility rates. They found a steady decline in the mean number of siblings with declining total fertility rates from 5 to 2 children per woman as well as a rise in the percentage of children with no siblings from 9 to 20 percent over the same range (see Table 2-3). Declines in sibship size reflect parental decisions to emphasize child quality over child quantity, in the context of rapid urbanization and changing economic opportunities. This change can result in increased gains in familial (and ultimately societal) investments in child health and education, with important implications for the life chances of young people, particularly girls, who may benefit from an increasing share of family income as average family size declines (Lloyd, 1994; Kelley, 1996).

| % Population Ages 10-24 | | | Annual Growth Rate | |
|------|------|------|-----------|-----------|
| 1980 | 2005 | 2030 | 1980-2005 | 2005-2030 |
| 30.1 | 27.1 | 23.0 | 1.1  | 0.3   |
| 24.2 | 19.6 | 16.1 | −0.4 | −0.6  |
| 31.9 | 28.9 | 24.3 | 1.4  | 0.4   |
| 31.8 | 32.6 | 30.9 | 2.6  | 1.8   |
| 31.3 | 33.1 | 31.1 | 2.8  | 1.6   |
| 31.2 | 34.0 | 32.9 | 3.0  | 1.8   |
| 30.2 | 33.0 | 33.5 | 3.1  | 2.4   |
| 31.5 | 31.6 | 25.5 | 2.2  | 0.5   |
| 33.3 | 32.7 | 28.6 | 1.7  | −0.8  |
| 31.2 | 33.5 | 31.9 | 3.0  | 1.9   |
| 32.0 | 27.9 | 22.6 | 1.1  | 0.6   |
| 32.6 | 24.0 | 18.3 | −0.1 | −0.7  |
| 31.3 | 30.5 | 25.0 | 1.9  | 0.4   |
| 32.7 | 29.6 | 22.8 | 1.4  | −0.1  |
| 31.3 | 30.0 | 25.6 | 2.3  | 1.0   |
| 32.4 | 28.9 | 22.4 | 1.3  | −0.1  |
| 31.0 | 28.2 | 22.2 | 0.8  | −0.4  |
| 33.3 | 30.6 | 23.2 | 1.6  | 0.0   |
| 31.8 | 28.2 | 22.0 | 1.2  | −0.04 |
| 20.0 | 33.3 | 23.0 | 4.4  | 0.0   |

Continued global integration is also being accelerated by and accelerating growth in the proportion living in urban areas. Throughout the developing world, economic growth and development are virtually synonymous with rapid urbanization and city growth. And according to recent population projections, virtually all the population increase expected over the next 30 years—approximately 2.2 billion additional people—will occur in urban areas in the developing world due either to natural growth or through migration of rural residents to urban areas (United Nations, 2002a). The speed and sheer scale of the global urban transformation, often combined with weak institutional capacity at the level of local and municipal governments present significant and complex challenges for many countries in the developing world (National Research Council, 2003). Rapid urban growth challenges local governments' ability to provide basic services, including education and health to the community. These statistics also reinforce the

TABLE 2-2  Changes in Percentage of Total Population by Broad Age
Group Over Time, by Region

| Region and Age Group | Year | | |
|---|---|---|---|
| | 1980 | 2005 | 2030 |
| WORLD | | | |
| 0-9 | 23.9 | 19.0 | 15.4 |
| 10-24 | 30.1 | 27.2 | 23.1 |
| 25-64 | 40.0 | 46.5 | 49.8 |
| 65+ | 5.9 | 7.3 | 11.8 |
| Total | 100.0 | 100.0 | 100.0 |
| Africa | | | |
| 0-9 | 32.8 | 29.3 | 23.6 |
| 10-24 | 31.4 | 33.1 | 31.1 |
| 25-64 | 32.7 | 34.2 | 40.6 |
| 65+ | 3.1 | 3.3 | 4.6 |
| Total | 100.0 | 100.0 | 100.0 |
| Asia | | | |
| 0-9 | 25.3 | 18.7 | 14.3 |
| 10-24 | 31.6 | 27.6 | 22.3 |
| 25-64 | 38.7 | 47.4 | 51.8 |
| 65+ | 4.4 | 6.4 | 11.5 |
| Total | 100.0 | 100.0 | 100.0 |
| Latin America and the Caribbean | | | |
| 0-9 | 27.5 | 20.0 | 14.3 |
| 10-24 | 32.3 | 28.7 | 22.4 |
| 25-64 | 35.8 | 45.3 | 51.7 |
| 65+ | 4.5 | 6.0 | 11.5 |
| Total | 100.0 | 100.0 | 100.0 |

SOURCE: United Nations (2003d).

fact that rural economies and lifestyles are becoming increasingly scarce
and that the structure of the labor market is changing as the proportion of
the labor force working in nonagricultural activities rises. Not only do these
forces alter the types of work that adolescents can expect to perform as
adults, but they also disrupt traditional social and cultural systems, often
leading to more nuclear families and less cohesive extended community ties.

In general, large cohorts of young people mean that many developing
countries can expect a substantial increase in the supply of labor over the
next several decades. This can have both advantages and disadvantages to
the local economy. In some Asian settings, this temporarily favorable age
structure of the population, often referred to as a country's demographic

TABLE 2-3 Estimates of Mean Number of Siblings (0-15) and Percentage of Children with No Siblings According to Total Fertility Rates (Children 0-15)

| Total Fertility Rate | Mean Number of Siblings | % with No Siblings |
| --- | --- | --- |
| 5.0 | 2.8 | 9.0 |
| 4.5 | 2.7 | 10.0 |
| 4.0 | 2.5 | 11.3 |
| 3.5 | 2.4 | 12.7 |
| 3.0 | 2.2 | 14.5 |
| 2.5 | 2.1 | 16.8 |
| 2.0 | 1.9 | 19.8 |

NOTE: Based on 52 DHS surveys.
SOURCE: Pullum and Zellner (2000).

bonus, has been credited as being a major factor in enabling sustained economic growth (Bloom and Williamson, 1998; Mason, Merrick, and Shaw, 1999). At the same time, a disproportionately high proportion of young adults in a population also comes with its own set of challenges. Too many young people (particularly men) with not enough to do can be a recipe for disaster. Historical data suggest that cycles of rebellion and military or civil conflict tend to coincide with periods when young people comprise an unusally large proportion of the population (Cincotta, Engelman, and Anastasion, 2003; Goldstone, 2002; Urdall, 2004).

*Rapid Spread of Formal Schooling*

The past 30 years have seen enormous increases in educational enrollment and attainment, particularly for girls, even in the poorest countries. The potential contribution of formal education to improving labor productivity, lowering income inequality, and promoting economic development has long been well recognized, and virtually all governments allocate a considerable share of their budgets to public expenditures on education. For capital-scarce poor countries, the effective training and utilization of their human resources are essential ingredients for initiating successful development. Not surprisingly, therefore, achieving universal primary education is one of the eight Millennium Development Goals.

There is increasing evidence that, by the late 1990s, most rural residents in developing countries lived within relatively easy reach of a primary school (either within the village or within a short walk) (Filmer, 2003; Filmer and Pritchett, 1999) with some notable exceptions in particularly remote areas, in rural West Africa and for girls in parts of South Asia (e.g.,

Pakistan, Afghanistan) where government primary schools are single-sex and girls' schools are still in relatively short supply (Sathar et al., 2003a). This reflects a substantial improvement over the last 20 years in primary school access and is a particularly remarkable achievement given the rapid growth of the school-age population in recent decades.

The growing importance of the global market has also brought to the education sector a heightened concern for efficiency and accountability in the delivery of educational services. The growth in private schooling and the tendency toward greater decentralization have also been manifestations of these trends. Some have expressed a concern that the pressures of the marketplace have led to greater emphasis in public schooling on preparing students for the labor market to the detriment of other domains of schooling, which contribute to the socialization of young people into adult roles and the formation of citizenship (Stromquist and Monkman, 2000b).

Gross primary and secondary schooling enrollments have increased substantially over the past 30 years. Low-income countries in particular have achieved strong gains in both primary and secondary enrollment, so that enrollment rates have converged substantially across the developing world (Behrman and Sengupta, 2005). There has also been a substantial change in the gender bias in enrollment: the male-female gap has been significantly reduced, and in some cases even reversed (Behrman and Sengupta, 2005).

Education is widely viewed as critical to improving many aspects of the transition to adulthood and the overall quality of life. Globalization and new technological advances favor those with more education, and researchers have documented increasing rates of return to secondary and tertiary levels of schooling over the past 20 years. Young people in developing countries with little or no formal education will be at a disadvantage in the workplace their entire lives. But apart from its productivity-enhancing effect in the labor market, education has many other benefits that support successful transitions to adulthood, some very familiar (Herz and Sperling, 2004) and some newly documented in this report (see Chapter 4).

## Changes in the Health Environment

During the second half of the 20th century, there were dramatic improvements in health in most developing countries, and life expectancy at birth rose from around 41 years to 63.4 years between 1950 and 2000 (United Nations, 2003d). Even in the poorest countries in the world, rising rates of female education, the diffusion of health care knowledge, better nutrition, the increased ability of public health departments to control vectors of infectious diseases, and the introduction of widespread immunization have combined to produce widespread reductions in infant and child mortality. Although there remain substantial inequalities in health between countries, regions, socioeconomic groups, and individuals, 85 percent of children born in the developing world now survive to age 5 (Leon and Walt, 2001). Overall, aside from some countries with very high prevalence of HIV/AIDS, young people in developing countries are entering adolescence healthier than ever and with a better chance of surviving to old age. Improvements in the health environment are important not only for the immediate survival chances of young people, but also as they affect other aspects of the transition to adulthood: healthy individuals make better students, more productive workers, more active community members, more attractive marriage partners, and better parents and caregivers than those who suffer from poor health.

In sub-Saharan Africa, the greatest immediate threat to adolescents' health relates to the HIV/AIDS pandemic. Globally, almost 12 million people ages 15-24 were estimated to be living with HIV/AIDS in 2002, and about half of all new infections are now occurring among this age group (Summers, Kates, and Murphy, 2002; UNAIDS, 2002). Until recently, antiretroviral drugs have been largely unavailable in developing countries. As a result, those with HIV/AIDS have a relatively short life expectancy. In the future, with expectations that these drugs will become increasingly available at reasonable cost, young people infected with HIV in developing countries will have a greater chance of treatment and thus living a longer and healthier life than they do now.

Adolescence is a time when many people first engage in sexual activity, potentially increasing their risk of unplanned pregnancy and unsafe abortion as well as of sexually transmitted infections (STIs), including HIV/AIDS. Delays in the age of marriage, however, have not resulted in a decline in the age at first sex; quite to the contrary, in most countries it appears that because of delays in the age of marriage there has been no change or a delay in the percent having first sex before the age of 18 (see further discussion in Chapter 4). However, even in places where there has been no decline in the age of first sex, sex may have become riskier than in the past because of the heightened risks associated with the AIDS epidemic in places where it has been growing.

HIV/AIDS is now the leading cause of death among 15-29-year-olds in the poorest and highest mortality countries. (Injuries and noncommunicable diseases remain the primary sources of deaths and are much more important than HIV/AIDS in the low- and medium-mortality developing countries.) However, in high-mortality countries and among women ages 15 to 29, maternal conditions are an equally important cause of loss of healthy years of life. In the context of risks of HIV infection, as well as other undesirable reproductive health outcomes (STIs and unwanted pregnancies), the availability of family planning and reproductive health services, in particular access to contraceptives and condoms and to testing and treatment for STIs, including HIV/AIDS, are a critical feature of the health service environment for young people.

Over two-thirds of people in developing countries now live in countries in which family planning programs are rated as relatively strong. This represents a substantial improvement in the access to and quality of family planning and reproductive health services over the last 20 years, although not necessarily for young people, particularly if they are unmarried (Ross and Stover, 2000). On average, contraceptive use, including condom use, has risen among young people in developing countries. Nevertheless, large proportions of young women do not use a method of contraception, and levels of unplanned childbearing among young women are significant (see Chapter 4 for further discussion).

For young women in the developing world, maternal mortality and the negative consequences of pregnancy, abortion, and childbearing continue to represent a considerable proportion of their health burden, despite declines in the percentage having births as children. Because adolescents who give birth early tend to be rural, less well educated, and poor, early pregnancy and childbearing can pose significant health risks. There is some evidence that in recent years, the service environment for childbirth has improved somewhat. The proportion of pregnant women who are attended by a professional at their delivery showed some small gains from 1985 to 1996 (WHO, 1997). Adolescents, who seek abortion, often because they fear disclosure and stigma or because they can stay in school, are at greater risk because they are more likely to delay the procedure and use unsafe providers. A little more then 50 percent of women in the developing world live in countries in which abortion is either entirely legal without restriction or available on very broad grounds, including physical and mental health as well as socioeconomic conditions. The overwhelming majority of these women live in two countries: India and China. (In the developed world, 86 percent of women live in countries with liberal laws.) Only a few developing countries have eased their restrictions since 1985. Regardless of legal status, abortion rates are similar in developed and developing countries. The easing of abortion laws has been associated with dramatic declines in levels of maternal death and illness due to abortion (The Alan Guttmacher Institute, 1999).

Other changes in the health environment for young people in developing countries include the aggressive marketing of tobacco to young people, the availability of illicit drugs, and the growing incidence of road traffic-related fatalities, with the increase in vehicular traffic and the growing network of roads. War and violence continue to take a toll as well, mainly on young men.

## Cultural Diffusion and Ideational Change

Young people's frames of reference are influenced on one hand by traditional cultural norms and values passed on to them from their parents, family members, teachers and other members of the community, and on the other hand by new and emergent ideas, beliefs, and ideologies that are brought about by the global age in which they live and spread transnationally. Global change, including access to Western and other international media, markets, and youth culture on one hand and the spread of transnational religious movements on the other, are potentially important new elements shaping the contemporary lives of young people in their local context.

Globalization contributes to the construction of a global culture. The proliferation of fast food outlets, chain stores, and homogeneous shopping malls in cities throughout the world means that parts of many cities come to resemble one another. Mass media are also an extremely influential agent for imparting knowledge to young people and socializing them to particular aspirations, values, and attitudes, often in contradiction to the traditions of their culture (see, for example, Condon, 1988). Western films, radio, and television have contributed to a global teen culture of music and fashion. Reading the newspaper, listening to the radio, or watching the news on television are not only important for the effects that they have on a young person's attitudes and behaviors, but also for signifying inclusion and access to knowledge in an increasingly interconnected world. The associated effects may be viewed both positively and negatively: positively for the transmission of knowledge and exposure to different ideas and cultures, and negatively for the promotion of materialistic values, for exposure to graphic sex and violence, and for time spent in front of the television rather than in more interactive activities.

Access to mass media varies substantially by geographic region as well as by social class. In Latin America, which is now a predominantly urban region, the vast majority of young people have practically universal access to information through radio or television, and e-mail is now a common means of communication, particularly among urban middle- and upper-class adolescents (Welti, 2002). At the other end of the spectrum, large numbers of young people, primarily in sub-Saharan Africa and South Asia, report that they still do not have access, either in their homes or outside them, to radio, television, or a newspaper.

It is not clear, however, whether the emergence of a global teen culture of music and fashion really has had an impact on issues related to sexuality, marriage, and reproduction. According to Stromquist and Monkman (2000a:21), "local groups often reshape their local identities when they meet challenges related to globalization processes, but they do not abandon these identities to become entirely globally oriented." Surface-level similarities in teenage culture obscure the huge regional differences in family structures, behavioral expectations, and patterns of sexuality, marriage, and reproduction. This suggests that the dominant factor in any region continues to be the traditional underlying culture (Caldwell et al., 1998). Nevertheless, at the macro level, there is evidence of a very substantial association between access to mass media and the level of fertility of a country, for example (Hornik and McAnany, 2001).

In many traditional cultures, globalization and the exposure to Western influences have been met with a mixed reception. The dramatic resurgence of religious movements over the last 30-40 years, for example, has caught many people by surprise (Riesebrodt, 2000). Forty years ago, most people simply assumed that, as the world modernized, people would become less zealous and that religion in general would become a weaker sociopolitical force. In fact, the opposite has happened. There has been a strong global revival in religion (Moghadam, 2003). Furthermore, fundamentalism has taken root and grown in many of the world's major religions, including Christianity, Islam, and Judaism. Even Buddhism, Sikhism, Hinduism, and Confucianism have developed fundamentalist factions (Marty and Appleby, 1993). From the dramatic rise of Islam in the Middle East, South-eastern Asia, and South-central Asia to the steep increase in the number of Christians in Africa and Latin America, in particular the growth of transnational Pentecostal movements (Corten and Marshall-Fratani, 2001), religion has reemerged as a major public force and a powerful shaper of world politics.

Transnational Pentecostalism is one religious movement that seeks to shape the public sphere and influence the structure of society. In Latin America, the size and reach of the Pentecostal churches serve as a powerful base for political mobilization, such as in Brazil and Argentina, although the time young people spend participating in religious activities often reduces the time available for political engagement other than voting (Corten, 2001; Oro and Semán, 2001). These emerging networks connect spiritual and material resources in ways that transcend traditional forms of ethnic, kinship, and professional identity, opening opportunities for employment and economic exchange to believers. For instance, in rural Africa, Pentecostalism offers young people the chance of upward mobility and a reconstruction of social relations and obligations (Corten and Marshall-Fratani, 2001).

Another notable example of religious resurgence is occurring among Muslim populations in developing countries, particularly, but not by any means exclusively, in the Middle East. Islam has reemerged as a major force in political and social development. This revival is frequently viewed as a backlash against the corrupting influence of Western-dominated global culture on traditional social boundaries, particularly those related to the role of women (Booth, 2002). While moderate Islamists have called for the re-Islamization of society, more radical elements have repeatedly engaged in various acts of terror in order to win dominance in multiethnic contexts or to destabilize or overthrow governments. However, the practice of Islam among a majority of the growing population of observant young people is more likely to take the form of increased personal piety manifested in dress, prayer, and avoiding "loose" Westernized behaviors.[1] For example, young people in Kenya have used Islam as an alternative to antisocial behaviors, drawn to its rejection of alcohol and drugs (Beckerleg, 1995).

Local cultures vary in the extent to which they respond to and are reshaped by these various transnational influences, and young people themselves are often important actors in this process of adaptation and response. Cross-generational changes in gender role attitudes across societies provide a good example of the relative weight of these competing international influences in shaping local attitudes. Inglehart and Norris (2003) compared the generational differences in gender role attitudes between the postindustrial societies of the West, the industrializing developing countries, and the more agrarian least developed countries. They found that while gender role attitudes among young people in the postindustrial societies of the West and the industrializing developing countries are becoming more liberal and egalitarian in comparison to the older generation, the same trends are not apparent in the least developed countries, in particular those in which the population is predominantly Muslim. As a result, gender role ideologies are diverging relative to the past, when they were more similar across societies, as some societies undergo change in response to the spread of liberal Western values and others resist change in response to the resurgence of traditional religious values.

A good example of the resilience of some aspects of local culture, even in the face of many modernizing and Western influences, comes from a recent study of emerging adulthood in urban China. Based on responses obtained from a survey of approximately 200 students from Beijing Normal University, the authors argue that young people in urban China are experiencing emerging adulthood in a different way from other cultural settings because of their unique cultural beliefs and values (Nelson, Badger, and Wu, 2004). In the United States, regardless of ethnicity, young people place prominence on criteria for adulthood that reflect independence, such as "accept responsibility for the consequences of your actions," "decide on personal beliefs and values," "financially independent from parents," and

---

[1]Personal communication with Barbara Ibrahim, regional director for Western Asia and North Africa, Population Council, November 2004.

"establish equal relationship with parents" (Arnett, 2003). Chinese young people appear to place greater emphasis on the development of attitudes and behaviors that appear to be reflective of a collectivistic culture, such as learning to always have good control of one's emotions, becoming less self-oriented, and developing greater consideration for others (Nelson et al., 2004).

### Emergence of Systems of International Governance

With greater global integration, more economically powerful countries have greater opportunities to influence the lives of people outside their own countries. Thus, while there is a tendency toward greater democratization within countries, globalization has the contrary tendency to reduce "global democracy" (Basu, 2003b).

The proliferation of international agreements and conventions under the aegis of the United Nations (UN) system, often supported by elements of civil society, including international and local nongovernmental organizations (NGOs), are a manifestation of and response to globalization and its consequences. Although not universally adopted, these agreements serve to set common goals, norms, and standards for children, young people, and adults in all domains of life that support development and protect human rights or to act as a system of checks and balances at the international, national, and local levels to the negative consequences of global change.

Important conventions, which carry the force of international law, have sought to create beneficial conditions for certain populations, including children and youth. Notable among these global conventions are the Universal Declaration on Human Rights (1948); the International Covenant on Economic, Social, and Cultural Rights (1966); the International Covenant on Civil and Political Rights (1966); the Convention on the Elimination of all Forms of Discrimination Against Women (1981); the Convention on the Rights of the Child (1989); and the Convention on the Elimination of the Worst Forms of Child Labor (1999).

In addition, international agreements (less binding upon signatory countries than conventions) in a range of social sectors were signed by participating countries at the following important international conferences over the last decade and a half: the UN Conference on the Environment and Development (Rio, 1992); the World Conference on Human Rights (Vienna, 1993); the International Conference on Population and Development (Cairo, 1994); the World Summit for Social Development (Copenhagen, 1995); the Fourth World Conference on Women (Beijing, 1995); the Second UN Conference on Human Settlements (Istanbul, 1996); the World Food Summit (1996); the Education for All Conference (Dakar, 2000); and the Millennium Summit (New York, 2000).

The Convention on the Rights of the Child marked a significant turning point for child policy for several reasons. First, for the first time ever, a dependent phase of life from 0 to 18 was separately delineated and addressed. Previous agreements had concentrated on the rights of adults, including women, but not children separately. Second, the convention defines anyone under the age of 18 as a child and thus identifies adolescents, regardless of marital, parental, or work status, as in need of protection. And third, by recognizing that children are growing and changing through this phase of life, the convention attempts to serve the best interests of the child through a combination of international, societal, and familial protections, nondiscrimination, identification of rights, and opportunity for voice. Were all governments to implement their commitments in these areas, the situation of children would be much better than it is today.

Civic participation has risen in much of the developing world with increasing democratization. In the post-World War II era, NGOs, international organizations, and civil society coalitions have proliferated throughout the world. In addition to large international actors, such as the United Nations, the World Health Organization, and the International Red Cross, there are coalitions of smaller NGOs that band together for specific causes ranging from promoting reproductive health to banning land mines. This system of transnational civil society helps to keep governments in check and serves to educate the public, promote particular policies, and advocate for change on behalf of particular interest groups. Young people are often key players in their local civic institutions (neighborhood clubs, social welfare organizations). Moreover, at many recent UN conferences, for example, delegations of young people from around the world have participated in the debate and discussions and contributed products to the process of negotiations.

## Changing National Context (Box B)

Just as the transition to adulthood has been affected by the global restructuring of the world economy and by other global forces described above, it has also been affected by a changing national context. And the same forces affecting the global context also affect the national context, including the economy (e.g., size, organization, types of technology); political structures (e.g., representative government, role for civil society); demographic structures (e.g., total population, age distribution, family size, household structure); the education system (e.g., access to schooling, attendance rules, teacher training, curriculum); the health system (e.g., availability of services for young people); culture (e.g., kinship systems, roles of women, religious ideology, media content); laws, policies, and programs (e.g., ages of majority, minimum ages for marriage, working, voting, and driving); laws mandating working conditions and benefits; rules prohibiting married or pregnant girls from attending school; protective labor legislation that affects the work opportunities of children and mothers; social movements (e.g., for human rights; women's, children's, and minority rights; and environmental protections); and armed conflict.

Because every country is unique, each aspect of the changing global environment plays out slightly differently in each country. In some parts of Asia, the results of the transformation of the global economy have been both spectacular and profound. The growth of East Asia's share of world economic output has grown from 4 percent in 1960 to 25 percent in 1995 (Yeung, 2000). Such cities as Tokyo, Seoul, Taipei, Hong Kong, Manila, Bangkok, Kuala Lumpur, Singapore, Jakarta, Shanghai, and Mumbai have flourished over the last 20 years, recording spectacular increases in gross domestic product (Lo and Yeung, 1996). Similarly, in China, as soon as the government began to open up the country in 1978, the transformation was dramatic. In Shenzhen, for example, which was chosen as one of the four initial special economic zones because of its close proximity to Hong Kong, the value of industrial output in 1987 was almost 70 times the value of industrial output in 1980, implying an annual rate of growth of 60 percent per annum (Yeung and Chu, 1998). Similarly, Xiamen, situated directly opposite the island of Taiwan, has enjoyed staggering export-led growth and industrialization over the last 20 years (Yeung and Chu, 2000). Xiamen's gross domestic product increased more than 57-fold over the period 1980-1997 (Howell, 2000). Other coastal cities, including Dalian, Guangzhou, Qingdao, Shenzhen, and Tianjin, have all undergone remarkable transformations since the Chinese government began its open policy (Yeung and Hu, 1992).

While it is impossible to describe completely the exact circumstances of every country, the final section of this chapter addresses broad questions of regional similarity and differentiation. Here we make a few general remarks about the extent to which the forces promoting globalization either promote or reduce the role of the nation-state.

Nation-states have become far weaker than previously. As foreign exchange controls have been lifted, global capital has become far more mobile, which has weakened the ability of national governments to formulate monetary policy. Foreign exchange reserves held by national governments pall in comparison to foreign exchange transactions executed on a daily basis in the world's financial markets (Berry et al., 1997). Consequently, market forces, not state policy, largely determine a country's foreign exchange rate, trade balance, and price of money.

At the same time, there has been a convergence across developing countries of laws and policies affecting young people in response to various international conventions and agreements agreed to by states through their participation in international meetings under the aegis of the United Nations (see above). The effects of some of these changes, such as laws and policies affecting equality of opportunity and treatment of women, are monitored occasionally for compliance. Many of these laws, however, remain relatively unenforced or apply only partially (e.g., employment law that affects only the formal sector).

But far from implying a world of borderless space, globalization actually strongly reinforces the importance of the subnational or local environment. The growth and development of cities in newly industrializing countries is strongly tied to the ability of cities to attract foreign companies, capital, and technology. Successful cities, particularly in Pacific Asia, that are able to attract large amounts of direct foreign investment have been able to accelerate their economic growth to spectacular heights and to break away from the fate of their national economies (Yeung, 2000). This feeds the demand by municipal authorities for increased political autonomy and fiscal authority. Cities, or in some cases extended metropolitan areas, are not only growing in size, but also gaining in economic and political influence (Yeung, 2002). Therefore, globalization has been linked to the tendency of many countries toward decentralization of responsibilities and resources to local and municipal authorities. Decentralization in the management of health and educational delivery systems are two important examples. As decentralization progresses, there is greater opportunity for regional diversity not only in access but also in terms of the content of actual services delivered.

## Changing Local Community Context (Box C)

Finally, the global and national influences affecting the transition to adulthood described above are filtered through particular local contexts. Thus the third box of our conceptual framework emphasizes the importance of peers, family and kin, health resources, economic resources, social roles, media, educational resources, and local governance; norms and values, community groups, and civil war and disruptions. The proximal context constitutes the immediate setting of social expectations, opportunities, and constraints in which young people's development proceeds.

Although adolescence is a time when young people move out of childhood to begin to take up adult roles and responsibilities of their own, parents and other family members, more than anyone else, critically influence the choices available to young people and the decisions that they make. Yet the nature of young peoples' family experience varies enormously from individual to individual: from large multigenerational families that provide young people with a plethora of relationships and interactions to small nuclear or even single-parent households in which young people may spend much less time with adults. Similarly, some young people grow up in traditional rural households, while others grow up in more progressive urban areas. In many settings, traditional family configurations are changing with fertility decline and rising divorce and remarriage rates, implying smaller average household size and more complex and multi-residence families. A recent cross-national study of living arrangements in Africa found that nuclear households—that is, households consisting only of parents and their biological children—were the predominant living arrangement in 4 of the 11 countries examined. In four other countries, extended households—consisting of parents, their biological children, and other family members or nonrelatives—were predominant. In three other countries, children were almost equally divided between nuclear and extended households (Gage, Sommerfelt, and Piani, 1996).

In many settings, including large parts of Asia, Africa, and the Arab world, many families continue to be quite authoritarian and patriarchal, despite the social pressures of the modern world. In India, for example, parental involvement and control is still very high, particularly with respect to issues related to gender socialization and marriage (Verma and Saraswathi, 2002). A survey of adolescent respondents found that even among the privileged Westernized upper middle class, a large majority of boys and girls still prefer arranged marriages (Pathak, 1994, cited in Verma and Saraswathi, 2002).

Parents and other family members are important actors in many other aspects of young peoples' lives, including influencing decisions regarding when to leave school. For example, Lloyd and Blanc (1996) examined the role of parents and other household members on schooling outcomes in seven African countries. They found that the resources of a child's residential household—in particular the education of the household head as well as the household's standard of living—are determining factors in explaining variations in children's schooling. The authors also found that children living in female-headed households have better school outcomes than children living in male-headed households, when households with similar resources are compared. More recently, Case, Paxson, and Ableidinger (2004) found that orphans in Africa are particularly disadvantaged in terms of school enrollment, and this is largely explained by their greater tendency to live with distant relatives or with unrelated caregivers.

Family members are also frequently portrayed as being influential in young people's decision making in matters of sexual and reproductive health. But too few studies have addressed this issue adequately (Gage, 1998). For example, little information is available with regard to the exact nature and frequency of discourse between young people and their parents on reproductive health matters, which can be a source of embarrassment and discomfort on both sides. Furthermore, there is very little information available on how often discussions occur, the nature of these interactions, or what other indirect (and often conflicting) signals parents give off (see, for example, Gorgen, Laier, and Diesfeld, 1993). Finally, many other family members besides parents can also play important and influential roles in young peoples' lives. In some African cultures, for example, the responsibility for transmitting sexual information to children lies not with parents but with other adult relatives, such as grandmothers or paternal aunts (Blanc et al., 1996; Cattell, 1994; Gage, 1998).

Young people also rely on peers for information and support. As young people grow and develop their own self-identity, they often begin to call into question the values and principles of their parents and other adults. The peer group can become increasingly important, and many young people can feel an intense need to belong. Consequently, just as in the developed world, peer groups in developing countries tend to play a large part in shaping many young peoples' values and beliefs during their formative years, particularly among young people from middle- and upper-class families. Peers provide young people with alternative viewpoints and sources of information as well as providing points of reference for certain norms and behaviors.

Peer influence can be positive or negative: for example, peers can support and reinforce family values, while they can also encourage certain problematic behaviors. There are many cross-national studies in developing countries that have investigated young people's source of information about contraceptives or their decision to use or to forgo using them. But without the benefit of longitudinal data, it is not possible to assign causality. Nevertheless, perceived expectations of consistent condom use among one's peers have been found to be an important predictor of young men's consistent condom use with commercial sex workers in Thailand (see VanLandingham et al., 1995). Peer pressure may also have quite negative effects on decision-making behavior. In the same study in Thailand, young men who perceived that the group norm for condom use was one of nonuse were the least likely to report using a condom when having sex with commercial sex workers (VanLandingham et al., 1995). Similarly, Gorgen and colleagues (1998) found that young unmarried urban youth in Guinea reported that both their partners and their peers pressured them to have sex. While it is impossible to quantify the relative impact of parents, family members, and peers on the behavior of young people in developing countries, we do know that adolescents are particularly susceptible to peer pressure, especially at younger ages (Gage, 1998).

In many countries, peer educators have been deployed in combination with other intervention strategies to take advantage of the fact that young people spend a large amount of time interacting with each other. These programs typically recruit and train a core group of young people to serve as role models and sources of information for their peers. In some settings, peer educators also distribute nonclinical contraceptives. Evaluations of peer promotion strategies have found varying levels of success. An 18-month study of a peer promotion program in secondary schools in six cities in Peru found a positive association between the program and age at first sex and the probability of contraceptive use at last sexual encounter (Magnani et al., 2001). Similarly, Speizer, Tambashe, and Tegang (2001) found that a community-based peer program in Cameroon was associated with both higher levels of current contraceptive use and increased probability of using condoms at last sex among those adolescents who had had an encounter with a peer educator than among adolescents who had not. Other programs appear to have had less success, and some studies suggest that the greatest program impacts are on the peer educators themselves (see Chapter 4).

The relative importance of family, peers, community, and schools on young people's decision making obviously varies from individual to individual. Generalization on this point is difficult if not impossible, because the relative importance of various factors in the local context, such as the weight of peer versus family influences, is likely to depend on an individual's age, sex, and years of education, as well as whether he or she is in or out of school, working or unemployed, living at home or elsewhere, and in a stable or a casual relationship. There are also broad regional differences in norms and values. In the final section of this chapter, we highlight some of the main similarities and differences across regions.

## IS THE WORLD CONVERGING?

Not only is the world changing rapidly, it may be becoming more homogenous. If so, young people in developing countries are making the transition to adulthood in economies and societies that are becoming ever more similar to those in developed countries. In order to investigate whether regions are becoming more or less similar, Behrman and Sengupta (2005) compiled data from six developing country regions across numerous indicators. The authors found that developing countries have tended to converge toward developed countries in a number of important respects in recent decades. But there also has been significant divergence in some other respects (Behrman and Sengupta, 2005). The tendency for convergence has been considerable for indicators of health, education, environment, transportation, communication, and gender differences but somewhat less so for other indicators. And although there has been a tendency toward convergence for many aspects of the economy, the pattern is mixed for economic growth rates and per capita product. This is also true of trends in poverty, which have fallen in some regions, not changed in others, and risen in sub-Saharan Africa (see Box 2-1).

Two of the regions in particular—Latin America and the Caribbean and sub-Saharan Africa—have diverged negatively with regard to economic growth rates and only two of the regions—East Asia and the Pacific and South Asia—have been converging in terms of per capita real product. Although the majority of young people in the developing world live in the latter two regions, there is a significant minority that lives in the other regions for which there has been a tendency for divergence in per capita real product. The region of East Asia and the Pacific generally has converged most toward developed economies and sub-Saharan Africa least. The other regions are in between, with Europe and Central Asia in several cases diverging from developed economies but converging toward the more developed of developing regions. Even where there has been a tendency toward convergence, however, there remains a gap that continues to exist with the developed world, primarily because economic growth during these years in the developed countries has also been considerable. Thus, the overall economic contexts in which most young people in the developing world have been making their transitions to adulthood have changed, and these changes have varied substantially among regions, with more positive aggregate economic experiences in Asia, where the majority of young people in developing countries live, than elsewhere.

Behrman and Sengupta's (2005) results may indicate that the dominant thrust, as suggested by many observers of globalization, has been toward convergence as an increasing percentage of young people in developing countries are growing up in an environment that is getting more similar in certain ways to that experienced by young people in developed countries. However, young people in developed countries represent only 14 percent of all young people worldwide. Thus, there is likely to be greater diversity among young people worldwide today than in the past. Some young people in developing countries are becoming more like their peers in developed countries, but others have stayed behind.

Trends in early childbearing are a good example. In some developing countries, high rates of early childbearing persist among adolescents; in most, rates are declining, some more slowly, some more rapidly, and in a few, due to a rise in the percentage of adolescents having premarital sex and delays in marriage, early childbearing is actually on the increase.

This divergence of experience among young people in developing countries is a phenomenon of particular importance. Analyses of changing transitions to adulthood in developing countries need to be sensitive both to the tendencies toward convergence and to some important tendencies toward divergence as well as to systematic differences among developing country regions and increasingly within developing countries.

Given the many global changes that form the backdrop of this report, one of the most basic questions that could be asked about the situation of

---

**BOX 2-1**
**Trends in Poverty**

Measuring poverty rates in developing countries is a complex and challenging task that has been the focus of extensive research. The absence of reliable and consistent data to estimate poverty was one of the main motivations for the World Bank's major effort to collect comparable household surveys on income and consumption in a large number of countries (Grosh and Glewwe, 2000). The issue has produced extensive debate over issues of measurement, analysis, and interpretation, much of which has played out in the context of larger and highly contentious debates about the impact of globalization, international trade, and the actions of international agencies.

The ideal way to measure trends in poverty in any country would be to have a consistent series of large, nationally representative household surveys with detailed information on income and consumption for a number of years. Very few developing countries met this ideal before the mid-1980s, and even after the launching of the World Bank's ambitious Living Standards Measurement Study (LSMS) surveys, many issues of incomplete coverage and data comparability remain.

Most estimates of poverty use a combination of household survey data and national accounts data (Deaton, 2001, 2002, 2003; Ravallion, 2003). The survey data are used to provide detailed information on the distribution of income or consumption across households, but are often available only for one or two points in time. National accounts statistics can be used to estimate changes in mean income in every year, with the combination of the survey data and national accounts being used to estimate the percentage below a given poverty line in years when complete survey data are not available. An additional key methodological issue is the comparison of incomes across countries. It is standard to use purchasing power parity (PPP) indexes based on the cost of purchasing a comparable basket of goods in each country to compare income and consumption across countries.

The most comprehensive attempts to estimate poverty in this way have been done by researchers at the World Bank. Chen and Ravallion (2001) present estimates of poverty covering the period 1987 to 1998 based on two simple benchmark poverty lines that are often used: $1 per day and $2 per day in per capita household consumption. The household surveys used for these estimates cover 88 percent of the developing country population. For the combined developing country population, Chen and Ravallion's estimates indicate a decline in the percentage of the population in poverty by the $1 per day measure from 28.3 percent

---

young people in developing countries today is whether the economic conditions of the households they are growing up in are better or worse than the conditions that were experienced by their parents. One basic question is: has the percentage of young people growing up in poverty been increasing or decreasing in recent decades? While the answer to such a question is complicated by the need for both a definition of poverty and a demanding amount of data (see Box 2-1), there is strong evidence that poverty rates

in 1987 to 23.4 percent in 1998. This decline in the percentage in poverty was just large enough to offset the substantial population growth in developing countries during this period, leading to almost no change in the total number of people in poverty.

Impressive declines in poverty rates in China play a large role in the overall trend, although the poverty rate still declines from 28.5 percent to 25.6 percent when China is excluded. The largest declines in poverty over this period took place in East Asia and the Pacific, where the $1 per day poverty rate when China is excluded fell by well over half. Smaller declines in poverty took place in Latin America, the Middle East, and South Asia. It is important to note that poverty rates in Africa increased over this period, rising from the already very high level of 46.6 percent to 48.1 percent by the $1 per day measure. Combined with rapid population growth, this implied an additional 80 million people living in poverty in Africa.

In addition to the large regional differences in both levels and trends in poverty, there are often large differences within a given country. A detailed examination of poverty in India by Deaton and Dreze (2002) shows significant declines in poverty in the 1990s, but with regional differences in poverty increasing over the period, including no reduction in poverty in some of the states that already had the highest levels of poverty. A number of studies also indicate that income inequality has increased in India and China, even though poverty has declined, with higher income growth in the highest income deciles (Chen and Wang, 2001; Deaton and Dreze, 2002). These increases in income inequality in some of the most rapidly growing economies are closely related to increases in the returns to high levels of schooling observed in many countries, an issue with important implications for the schooling investments of young people discussed in Chapter 3.

Although data on poverty rates prior to the mid-1980s is much more limited, most evidence indicates that the declines in poverty for the 1990s were a continuation of declines in poverty over several decades. Sala-i-Martin (2002) combines national accounts data from 1970 to 1998 with the available data on individual country income distributions to estimate changes in the distribution of income in each country and for the world as a whole. Applying the $1 per day poverty line to these distributions, he estimates that there have been substantial declines in poverty rates for the developing world as a whole over the entire period. His estimates of the levels of poverty are considerably lower than those estimated by Chen and Ravallion, but the estimated trends show a similar pattern. According to Sala-i-Martin's estimates, poverty fell rapidly in Asia, fell more slowly in Latin America, and increased substantially in Africa between 1970 and 1998.

have declined for the developing world as a whole over the last 30 years. Nevertheless, a significant fraction of young people in developing countries continue to live in poverty. Taking the $1 per day measure as an indicator of extreme poverty, one simple estimate of the probability that a young person in a developing country lives in poverty is about 23 percent, the average observed for the developing country population in 1998 (see Table 2-4). With the growing number of young people, however, this decline in

poverty rates has had little impact on the numbers of young people estimated to be living in extreme poverty. Using the poverty rate estimates
presented in Table 2-4 and interpolations of UN population estimates of
young people in the same years (1.2 billion in 1987 and 1.39 billion in
1998), the panel has estimated that the absolute number of young people
living in poverty would have declined from approximately 350 million in
1987 to approximately 325 million in 1998—a decline of less than half a
percent in 11 years.

TABLE 2-4  Absolute Number and Percentage of Population in Poverty in
World Regions, 1987 and 1998

| | % of Population Covered by at Least One Survey | $1 Per Day Poverty Line | | | |
| | | Number of People in Poverty (millions) | | % of Population in Poverty | |
| Region | | 1987 | 1998 | 1987 | 1998 |
|---|---|---|---|---|---|
| East Asia and the Pacific | 90.8 | 417.5 | 267.1 | 26.6 | 14.7 |
| East Asia and the Pacific (excluding China) | 71.1 | 114.1 | 53.7 | 23.9 | 9.4 |
| Eastern Europe and Central Asia | 81.7 | 1.1 | 17.6 | 0.2 | 3.7 |
| Latin America and the Caribbean | 88.0 | 63.7 | 60.7 | 15.3 | 12.1 |
| Middle East and North Africa | 52.5 | 9.3 | 6.0 | 4.3 | 2.1 |
| South Asia | 97.9 | 474.4 | 521.8 | 44.9 | 40.0 |
| Sub-Saharan Africa | 72.9 | 217.2 | 301.6 | 46.6 | 48.1 |
| TOTAL | 88.1 | 1,183.2 | 1,174.9 | 28.3 | 23.4 |
| TOTAL excluding China | 84.2 | 879.8 | 61.4 | 28.5 | 25.6 |

NOTES: The $1 per day is in 1993 purchasing power parity terms. The numbers are esti-
mated from those countries in each region for which at least one survey was available during
the period 1985-1998. The proportion of the population covered by such surveys is given in
column 1. Survey dates often do not coincide with the dates in the above table. To line up
with the above dates, the survey estimates were adjusted using the closest available survey for

The overall declines in poverty rates are based on quite different experiences in different regions, however, as poverty rates vary widely across regions, ranging from 12-15 percent for Latin America and East Asia to almost 50 percent in Africa. Impressive declines in poverty have been recorded in China and India, which together make up roughly half of the developing world. Modest declines have also been recorded in Latin America. But, at the other extreme, sub-Saharan Africa appears to have experienced increasing poverty rates (see Table 2-4).

$2 Per Day Poverty Line

| Number of People in Poverty (millions) | | % of Population in Poverty | |
|---|---|---|---|
| 1987 | 1998 | 1987 | 1998 |
| 1052.3 | 884.9 | 67.0 | 48.7 |
| 299.9 | 252.1 | 62.9 | 44.3 |
| 16.3 | 98.2 | 3.6 | 20.7 |
| 147.6 | 159.0 | 35.5 | 31.7 |
| 65.1 | 85.4 | 30.0 | 29.9 |
| 911.0 | 1,094.6 | 86.3 | 83.9 |
| 356.6 | 489.3 | 76.5 | 78.0 |
| 2,549.0 | 2,811.5 | 61.0 | 56.1 |
| 1,796.6 | 2,178.7 | 58.2 | 57.9 |

each country and applying the consumption growth rate from national accounts. Using the assumption that the sample of countries covered by surveys is representative of the region as a whole, the numbers of poor are then estimated by region.
SOURCE: Chen and Ravallion (2001).

# PART II

# Preparation for Adult Roles

# 3

# Schooling

## INTRODUCTION

Learning occurs more intensely during childhood and adolescence than during other phases of the life cycle in all domains, whether it is the development of physical or cognitive skills or the acquisition of knowledge and the shaping of values and beliefs. This is not just because of the obvious fact that growth always appears more rapid when starting from a lower base. During these same years, physical and intellectual capacities are growing rapidly, allowing for the more rapid acquisition of skills and accumulation of knowledge than at other phases of the life cycle. Interventions affecting the timing and sequencing of learning and the quality of the learning environment during these years can have important implications for the development of adult productive capacities. Investments in learning in these earlier stages of the life cycle tend to yield relatively high returns in comparison to learning later in life, because there are expected to be more decades of subsequent adulthood for returns to be obtained. Failure to invest at this stage is extremely unlikely to be compensated for in any later stage.

For all these reasons, this phase of the life cycle has typically been associated with a focus on learning. This learning can take many forms, ranging from learning by doing and imitating around the household and in family economic activities, to learning in the labor market or in military service, to formal training and schooling. Education is a central aspect of preparation for the multiple aspects of the transition to adulthood and indeed interacts with and affects each of them.

This chapter explores the process of becoming an educated adult during the second decade of life and beyond in the context of rapid global change. This process involves the acquisition of relevant capacities, including cognitive competencies, marketable skills, social capital, and complementary values and motivations, that enable individuals to function effectively in a range of adult roles, including worker, household provider, parent, spouse, family caretaker, citizen, and community participant. While education is not synonymous with going to school, the formal schooling system has become the preeminent institution worldwide dedicated to the education of young people. As a result, it is a place in which a growing percentage of young people spend significant amounts of their time. In major part, this is because the rapid changes that are discussed in Chapters 1 and 2 have substantially increased the benefits from both a more intensive as well as an extended period of learning at this stage of the life cycle. Indeed, schools are widely seen to be institutions in which young people can best develop their capacity for lifelong learning and thus are critical institutions in creating the enabling conditions for successful transitions to adulthood.

The strong link between schooling levels and subsequent earnings is well documented in the empirical literature (e.g., Knight and Sabot, 1990; Krueger and Lindahl, 2001; Psacharopoulos, 1994), as is the link between schooling levels, particularly for females, and various nonmarket or social outcomes, such as subsequent fertility and child health and educational outcomes (e.g., National Research Council, 1999; Jejeebhoy, 1995; Knowles and Behrman, 2005; Schultz, 2002; Summers, 1994; World Bank, 2001). In some parts of the developing world, however, the opportunities that education opens up for girls in the marriage market may be even more salient for parents making decisions about their girls' schooling (see Chapter 7 for further discussion of the links between schooling and various aspects of marriage). While many of these studies characterize static relations between schooling and various outcomes, a subset of studies provides evidence of a causal effect of schooling on the capacity to deal with change in markets and technologies, a capacity that is likely to be of increasing importance given the acceleration of change that motivates this report (e.g., Rosenzweig, 1995; Schultz, 1975; Welch, 1970). The quantity and quality of schooling experienced by today's young people in developing countries will have important effects on them as well as on future economic growth and development and on trends in inequality and poverty.

The chapter begins with a review of the basic facts and figures with respect to changes in schooling participation, attainment, and academic performance. We then explore some of the forces that have led to these changes, not only factors affecting demand for schooling, but also facts about some of the critical features of school systems, including recent reform efforts. Throughout these discussions, we recognize that changes in the quantity and quality of schooling provided are to an important extent a response to increased demand for schooling on the part of young people and their families. Both increases in demands for schooling and various proposals for school reform have emerged in response to the global changes, including changes in policies and programs outside the educational sphere, described in Chapters 1 and 2. The chapter also reviews the evidence about the effectiveness of existing educational policies and programs in improving the schooling environment and achieving various educational goals. The chapter ends with a summary of key findings, policy recommendations, and research questions.

## WHAT ROLES DO SCHOOLS PLAY?

In traditional and slowly changing societies, the acquisition of productive capacities or human capital was largely taken up in the family or kin group through informal on-the-job apprenticeships, which taught agricultural techniques or various traditional trades. Over the course of economic development, with the growth of the monetized economy and the shift in the occupational structure from agriculture to industry to services, the inputs required to develop productive skills have shifted. These changes have led to a growing demand in the job market for literacy and numeracy—skills more efficiently provided in a formal classroom setting with specially trained teachers—as well as for the broader knowledge base and reasoning and problem-solving skills that are acquired in school. In response to these worldwide changes, mass formal schooling has become a global institution with commonly recognized features in all countries of the world (Meyer, 1992). These include courses in reading, mathematics, language, history or social studies, and science. While formal schools occasionally include religious education and religious groups sometimes run formal schools,[1] we do not include in our definition of formal schools those schools that are solely dedicated to providing a religious education to the exclusion of other subjects.[2] The gains from extended formal schooling, as noted, are expected to

---

[1]In Egypt, there is a separate government ministry that is responsible for religious schools, but these schools are required to include all elements of the formal school curriculum in addition to religious instruction, and we would therefore include them as part of the formal schooling system. In a nationally representative survey of youth in Egypt fielded in 1997, it was found that 6 percent of all students attending formal schools attend school supervised by Al-Azhar (el-Tawila et al., 1999).

[2]In some cases these religious schools complement other forms of schooling and children attend both, but, in other cases, children attend religious schools exclusively and are therefore not exposed to the formal school curriculum.

increase with the more rapid changes that are being experienced by young people today.

The acquisition of human capital is only one of several types of capital potentially acquired in school. Social capital, defined as "the ability of actors to secure benefits by virtue of membership in social networks or other social structures" (Portes, 1998), can be acquired in school through the formation of peer networks, parents' networks, or student-teacher networks.[3] An additional domain of learning important to our subject is the acquisition of values or "cultural capital" (a termed coined by Bourdieu, 1985, as cited in Portes, 1998) that enhances an individual's effectiveness in the culture, in the community, and in the workplace. In a modernizing society, formal schooling, particularly Western-style schooling, provides a major counterpoint to the family in the socialization of the young. One important example concerns gender. While boys and girls are mostly taught the same curriculum when it comes to academic subjects, the process of socialization that occurs in the schoolyard and the classroom is often quite different for boys and girls, as are some of the traditional nonacademic subjects, such as home economics and agriculture, that are still provided in some school systems on a sex-segregated basis. In traditional societies, gender role socialization occurred primarily in the home and the community. The school, through the authority of the teacher, also has enormous potential to influence the values, expectations, and behaviors of boys and girls with respect to gender roles in the family as well as the workplace, either by reinforcing traditional roles or by sharing in the classroom changing international norms regarding human rights and gender equality.[4] Therefore, the role of schools in the socialization of the young is another factor to consider in the progress of children in school and their transition to adulthood.

A final aspect of formal schooling relates to becoming a citizen and a community participant and is treated more fully in Chapter 6. Effective citizenship at the community, national, and global levels requires a broad knowledge of the world and the acceptance of certain common values. As articulated by the Convention on the Rights of the Child, these include respect for human rights and fundamental freedoms, respect for local cul-

---

[3]School attendance, by taking children away from an exclusive reliance on family networks, may result in a decline in some types of social capital at the same time that it may provide access to other sources of social capital.

[4]Other important examples include attitudes about roles, potentialities, and interactions with other members of society who may differ in respects other than gender—race, ethnicity, class, caste, clan, or tribe—and their value as individuals independent of these differences in background.

ture and language, respect for the natural environment, and the acquisition of a spirit of understanding, peace, tolerance, and gender equality (United Nations, 1989). Most national governments and educational ministries typically include at least some aspects of citizenship training in their educational curricula.

The universal desire of governments to control the education of children and youth through the provision of public formal schooling can be largely explained by the need perceived by all governments to shape citizens' values and beliefs in ways that are consonant with prevailing culture, predominant religious beliefs, and national political ideology. A recent assessment of the centralized public school curriculum in Pakistan, for example, has concluded that "an overemphasis on Islamic interpretations in the government-prescribed syllabus has distorted historical data, nurtured intolerance for other religions and confined the scope of the physical and social sciences" (International Crisis Group, 2004).

In recent years, there has been a growing concern that nonformal religious schools, in particular Islamic schools, are capturing a growing share of school enrollment in parts of the Muslim world. The panel, however, could not find any solid evidence that this is indeed the case. Nonetheless, we did have access to recent nationally representative data from Pakistan from a survey of youth fielded in 2001-2002 that shows that 3.2 percent of young men ages 15-19 and 1.7 percent of young women of the same age had ever attended religious schools; less than 0.05 percent of young people attended religious schools exclusively.[5]

## TRENDS AND PATTERNS OF SCHOOLING PARTICIPATION AND ATTAINMENT

The panel used data from a number of recent nationally representative household surveys—particularly Demographic and Health Surveys (DHS)—to describe various important aspects of formal schooling in this chapter. For most topics, we use these data in preference to United Nations Educational, Scientific, and Cultural Organization (UNESCO) data because they permit the exploration of differentials in formal school participation and attainment by household background characteristics and because they permit the derivation of trends over the last two decades on a consistent basis across countries. A full discussion of the strengths and weaknesses of alternative sources of data on schooling and the reasons for our choice of data sources can be found in Appendix A. Appendix tables to this chapter pro-

---

[5]Tabulations from Adolescents and Youth in Pakistan, 2001-2002 Survey data.

vide country by country data to complement the tables in the text that are based on regional and country income groups.

## Current Patterns of School Participation

Table 3-1 presents aggregate country-level data on patterns of current school attendance[6] by age according to regional and income grouping (see definitions in Appendix A) based on all DHS data from the 1990s. Data for China and India are presented separately in Table 3-2. Data for these two countries, representing the education experience of two-fifths of all young people in the developing world, are not available for the full range of ages presented in Table 3-1, but are available for two recent points in time, revealing very recent changes for these two important countries.

On average, the estimates presented in Table 3-1 suggest that roughly three-quarters of 10-14-year-olds, who are in the early phase of their transitions to adulthood, are attending school. This is probably a reasonable estimate of attendance rates for all developing countries, since India and China, with roughly equal numbers of young people in these ages, would exert countervailing and roughly balancing influences on the average if included (see Table 3-2). Attendance rates in low-income countries are about 16 to 18 percentage points lower than in the upper middle-income group. The gender gap in attendance rates among younger adolescents is also slightly larger in the lower income countries (6 versus 4 percentage points). Attendance rates for the 10-14 age group fall below 75 percent for boys and girls in sub-Saharan Africa and for girls in the Middle East. Gender equality in attendance rates during the early adolescent years has essentially been achieved in China, the former Soviet Asia, and Central and South America. The distribution of this attendance between primary and secondary school for this age group varies substantially across regions. This is partly a result of differences in the age at entry and the duration of the primary school cycle, but it is also affected by variation in progression rates from primary to secondary school across countries. Over 50 percent of 10-14-year-old students are attending secondary school in Asia, but no more than 3 percent are in Eastern and Southern Africa (data not shown).

In the later teenage years, attendance rates fall off substantially, gender gaps widen, and regional differences become more pronounced. Roughly 50 percent of boys and 41 percent of girls in the 15-19 age group are attending school in the countries represented in Table 3-1. Boys have higher

---

[6]We use the term "attendance" to refer to those who are reported by their household to be currently attending school, whereas we use the term "enrollment" to refer to officially reported opening day enrollment. For further discussion see Appendix A.

TABLE 3-1 Percentage Currently Attending School, DHS Countries

| | Weighted[a] Averages | | | | | |
| | Ages 10-14 | | Ages 15-19 | | Ages 20-24 | |
| Region or Income Level | Boys | Girls | Boys | Girls | Boys | Girls |
|---|---|---|---|---|---|---|
| Region | | | | | | |
| Africa | | | | | | |
|   Eastern/Southern Africa | 74.1 | 70.6 | 52.2 | 39.4 | 16.4 | 9.1 |
|   Western/Middle Africa | 66.1 | 57.6 | 48.1 | 34.3 | 24.2 | 12.2 |
| Asia[b] | | | | | | |
|   South-central/South-eastern | | | | | | |
|     Asia[c] | 81.0 | 76.0 | 47.1 | 37.3 | 16.9 | 9.8 |
|   Former Soviet Asia[d] | 98.4 | 98.9 | 56.1 | 54.4 | 13.2 | 11.7 |
| Latin America and Caribbean | | | | | | |
|   Caribbean/Central America | 80.0 | 77.8 | 50.9 | 44.2 | 21.3 | 16.5 |
|   South America | 92.9 | 93.1 | 60.5 | 61.7 | 22.0 | 23.8 |
| Middle East | | | | | | |
|   Western Asia/Northern Africa | 81.0 | 67.6 | 47.7 | 37.4 | 17.5 | 10.3 |
| Income Level[e] | | | | | | |
|   Low | 75.3 | 69.2 | 46.4 | 34.0 | 17.5 | 8.8 |
|   Lower middle | 86.6 | 84.1 | 57.4 | 54.0 | 20.1 | 16.5 |
|   Upper middle | 91.4 | 87.2 | 59.6 | 58.1 | 22.1 | 22.1 |
| TOTAL—All DHS | 79.8 | 74.6 | 50.4 | 41.2 | 18.7 | 12.2 |

[a]Weighting is based on United Nations population estimates for year 2000 (*World Population Prospects: The 2000 Revision*).

[b]Eastern Asia not included; no DHS available.

[c]India's DHS does not include current enrollment data for 18-24-year-olds and has been removed from this table.

[d]Former Soviet Asia includes former Soviet Republics in South-central and Western Asia.

[e]World Bank income classifications, World Bank (2002b).

NOTE: See Appendix Table 3-1 for the data from each country.

attendance rates than girls in all regions except South America. While over 50 percent of 15-19-year-olds are attending school in middle-income countries, this is not the case for the low-income countries. Among those who are attending school, over 70 percent of 15-19-year-old students are currently attending secondary school (data not shown). However, in Eastern and Southern Africa, where children get a late start in school and many primary school cycles are more than six years, no more than 31 percent of male students and 38 percent of female students ages 15-19 are enrolled in secondary school (data not shown).

TABLE 3-2  Recent Trends in School Attendance in India and China

| Sex and Age | China | | | India | | |
|---|---|---|---|---|---|---|
| | 1989 | 1997 | % Growth | 1992 | 1999 | % Growth |
| Boys 12-13 | 93 | 96 | 3.2 | 76 | 81 | 6.2 |
| Girls 12-13 | 92 | 96 | 4.3 | 56 | 67 | 19.6 |
| Boys 14-15 | 77 | 85 | 10.4 | 35 | 69 | 74.3 |
| Girls 14-15 | 69 | 84 | 21.7 | 23 | 52 | 126.1 |
| Boys 16-17 | 38 | 65 | 71.1 | n.a.[a] | 54 | n.a.[a] |
| Girls 16-17 | 31 | 59 | 90.3 | n.a.[a] | 37 | n.a.[a] |

[a]Information on attendance was not asked of those over the age of 15 in 1992 survey.
NOTE: n.a. = not available
SOURCES: Hannum and Liu (2005); DHS data.

In some parts of the developing world, a substantial minority of young people ages 20-24 are still in school—over 20 percent of young men and women in South America and of young men in Western and Middle Africa and in the Caribbean and Central America. For boys at this age, the differences in attendance rates between low and upper middle-income countries are not large (18 versus 22 percent), whereas for girls the gap is much larger (9 versus 22 percent). The reasons for these patterns vary substantially. In some cases, grade attainment is high, leading to continuing school attendance at later ages; in other cases, lower grade attainment combined with late ages of entry and repetition have led to similar patterns of attendance by age despite poorer grade attainment (see further discussion of schooling beyond the secondary level below).

In Table 3-2, we compare recent changes in attendance by age in India and China. China has made impressive progress in extending school participation later into the adolescent years. The gender gap in attendance that had begun to emerge at the age of 14 in the late 1980s has almost been eliminated in the 14-15 age group and is now apparent only to a small degree among 16-17-year-olds who have showed extraordinary growth in school participation over the past 8 years. By ages 16-17, 59 percent of girls and 65 percent of boys are still attending school. India has also seen exceptional growth in school participation during the same period, particularly among the 14-15-year-olds. While the absolute gender gap in attendance rates has widened at this age, the percentage growth for girls exceeds that for boys because girls' attendance rates started from a much lower base.

## Differentials in Attendance by Wealth and Residence and Other Characteristics

Globalization is sometimes claimed to benefit most those who are relatively better off. Thus, it is interesting to look separately at current enrollment patterns among the most privileged in each country. We can do that by using the wealth index developed by Filmer and Pritchett (1999) especially for use with DHS data. It is based on a common set of indicators capturing the ownership of a set of consumer durables (e.g., radio, bike, car) as well as various indicators of quality of housing, including the availability of piped water, electricity, and finished flooring. Table 3-3 mirrors Table 3-1, but includes only those in the top 20 percent of the wealth

TABLE 3-3 Percentage Currently Attending School, Wealthiest 20 Percent of Households, DHS Countries

| Region or Income Level | Weighted[a] Averages | | | | | |
|---|---|---|---|---|---|---|
|  | Ages 10-14 | | Ages 15-19 | | Ages 20-24 | |
|  | Boys | Girls | Boys | Girls | Boys | Girls |
| Region |  |  |  |  |  |  |
| Africa |  |  |  |  |  |  |
|   Eastern/Southern Africa | 88.6 | 84.8 | 60.9 | 49.4 | 21.2 | 12.7 |
|   Western/Middle Africa | 86.7 | 80.0 | 67.4 | 53.7 | 40.2 | 26.8 |
| Asia |  |  |  |  |  |  |
|   South-central/South-eastern Asia[b] | 90.7 | 88.3 | 67.3 | 58.1 | 31.7 | 20.3 |
|   Former Soviet Asia | 98.6 | 98.9 | 64.0 | 63.6 | 24.8 | 22.1 |
| Latin America and Caribbean |  |  |  |  |  |  |
|   Caribbean/Central America | 96.3 | 92.6 | 81.0 | 74.0 | 50.0 | 43.1 |
|   South America | 98.1 | 97.0 | 73.2 | 72.8 | 31.9 | 36.9 |
| Middle East |  |  |  |  |  |  |
|   Western Asia/Northern Africa | 93.5 | 88.9 | 61.8 | 60.3 | 27.7 | 20.4 |
| Income Level |  |  |  |  |  |  |
|   Low | 88.8 | 85.0 | 64.4 | 53.8 | 31.3 | 19.9 |
|   Lower middle | 96.6 | 93.6 | 74.5 | 66.8 | 32.9 | 26.9 |
|   Upper middle | 96.6 | 95.5 | 67.8 | 70.8 | 27.4 | 30.8 |
| TOTAL—All DHS | 91.4 | 88.1 | 66.7 | 58.7 | 31.0 | 22.8 |

[a]Weighting is based on United Nations population estimates for year 2000 (*World Population Prospects: The 2000 Revision*).

[b]India's DHS does not include current enrollment data for 18-24-year-olds and has been removed from this table.

NOTES: For source of regional and income groupings and population data for weighted averages, see Table 3-1. Further detail can be found in Appendix A. See Appendix Table 3-2 for the data from each country.

distribution in each country. While the top 20 percent in Mali may not resemble the top 20 percent in South Africa, they share in common their relative position in their own countries. Looking at the average for these relatively high-income households across all DHS countries, Table 3-3 shows that about 90 percent of 10-14-year-olds are in school, with nearly two-thirds of boys and 60 percent of girls still in school in the 15-19 age range. Gender gaps are small among the 10-14-year-olds regardless of region or country income level (with the possible exception of Western and Middle Africa), but they become greater among 15-19-year-olds, particularly in Africa, where male attendance exceeds female attendance by over 10 percentage points. Adolescents from these relatively high-income households have somewhat higher attendance rates when they live in higher income countries. In the upper middle-income countries in Table 3-3, current attendance rates among 10-14 year-olds are roughly 95 percent for both boys and girls.

To further explore the question of how gender interacts with other sources of difference, such as wealth and residence, we introduce an index of relative inequality in school participation that can be used to capture relative urban and rural differences or relative differences between extremes of the wealth distribution.[7] The index ranges from 0 to 100, with 0 representing complete parity of attendance between the groups and a value of 100 representing the complete nonparticipation of the disadvantaged group. A measure of 50 implies that the one group has obtained 50 percent of the schooling participation rate of the other group.

Table 3-4 presents these measures of inequality in school attendance for males and females in the 10-14 and 15-19 age groups, using the same classification of countries. On average, young poor adolescents (ages 10-14) have attendance rates that are 25 percent lower than young rich adolescents. Relative inequality is nearly double during the later adolescent years, when transitions to secondary school are made and the differential disadvantage of poor girls widens as well.

Relative inequality varies dramatically from country to country and across regional groups. Relative inequality is highest in Western and Middle Africa and the Middle East and is also very high during the later adolescent years in South-central and South-eastern Asia and the Caribbean and Cen-

---

[7]The index is calculated as one minus the ratio of current attendance rate of the more disadvantaged group (rural residents or those in the bottom 40 percent of the wealth distribution) relative to the attendance rate of the most advantaged groups (urban residents or those in the top 20 percent wealth distribution), then multiplied by 100. It is calculated separately for boys and girls.

TABLE 3-4 Index of Inequality in School Attendance by Wealth, DHS Countries, High versus Low Wealth

| Region or Income Level | Weighted Averages[a] | | | |
| --- | --- | --- | --- | --- |
| | Ages 10-14 | | Ages 15-19 | |
| | Boys | Girls | Boys | Girls |
| Region | | | | |
| Africa | | | | |
|   Eastern/Southern Africa | 24.7 | 27.3 | 18.8 | 33.3 |
|   Western/Middle Africa | 45.1 | 54.9 | 55.8 | 70.2 |
| Asia | | | | |
|   South-central/South-eastern Asia[b] | 20.2 | 25.1 | 52.1 | 63.5 |
|   Former Soviet Asia | 0.6 | 0.5 | 19.5 | 29.2 |
| Latin America and Caribbean | | | | |
|   Caribbean/Central America | 24.6 | 24.2 | 52.3 | 61.0 |
|   South America | 10.1 | 8.5 | 33.9 | 33.3 |
| Middle East | | | | |
|   Western Asia/Northern Africa | 24.1 | 43.8 | 41.7 | 65.7 |
| Income Level | | | | |
|   Low | 27.2 | 33.7 | 46.5 | 61.8 |
|   Lower middle | 18.8 | 21.2 | 42.1 | 43.5 |
|   Upper middle | 10.5 | 15.7 | 25.9 | 34.6 |
| TOTAL—All DHS | 23.1 | 28.7 | 42.5 | 54.3 |

[a]Weighting is based on United Nations population estimates for year 2000 (*World Population Prospects: The 2000 Revision*).

[b]India's DHS does not include current enrollment data for 18-24-year-olds and has been removed from this table.

NOTES: For source of regional and income groupings and population data for weighted averages, see Table 3-1. Further detail can be found in Appendix A. See Appendix Table 3-3 for the data from each country.

tral America. By contrast, there is almost no inequality in current enrollment during early adolescence in the countries of the former Soviet Asia. During the young adolescent years, poor girls are more disadvantaged than poor boys in South-central and South-eastern Asia, Eastern and Southern Africa, Western and Middle Africa, and the Middle East and suffer the greatest relative disadvantage in the Middle East. During the later adolescent years, the relative disadvantage of poor girls grows dramatically as overall levels of inequality grow during these years. The inequality index is highest in the lowest income countries for both girls and boys, where overall attendance rates are lower to begin with. Variations in relative inequality can be even more extreme within countries. For example, in India the index of inequality, based on the current attendance of both boys and girls

TABLE 3-5 Index of Inequality in School Attendance by Rural-Urban
Residence, DHS Countries

| Region or Income Level | Weighted Averages[a] | | | |
| --- | --- | --- | --- | --- |
| | Ages 10-14 | | Ages 15-19 | |
| | Boys | Girls | Boys | Girls |
| Region | | | | |
|   Africa | | | | |
|     Eastern/Southern Africa | 14.5 | 11.4 | 38.1 | 34.6 |
|     Western/Middle Africa | 24.8 | 33.6 | 37.9 | 46.9 |
|   Asia | | | | |
|     South-central/South-eastern Asia[b] | 7.1 | 13.2 | 23.0 | 41.7 |
|     Former Soviet Asia | 0.0 | 0.8 | 4.5 | 14.6 |
|   Latin America and Caribbean | | | | |
|     Caribbean/Central America | 14.5 | 11.4 | 38.1 | 34.6 |
|     South America | 7.4 | 8.8 | 32.2 | 31.4 |
|   Middle East | | | | |
|     Western Asia/Northern Africa | 15.2 | 34.1 | 31.5 | 54.6 |
| Income Level | | | | |
|   Low | 14.1 | 20.3 | 25.1 | 40.4 |
|   Lower middle | 11.4 | 16.3 | 28.2 | 32.7 |
|   Upper middle | 7.5 | 12.9 | 26.5 | 30.6 |
| TOTAL—All DHS | 12.6 | 18.4 | 25.9 | 37.5 |

[a]Weighting is based on United Nations population estimates for year 2000 (*World Population Prospects: The 2000 Revision*).

[b]India's DHS does not include current enrollment data for 18-24-year-olds and has been removed from this table.

NOTES: For source of regional and income groupings and population data for weighted averages, see Table 3-1. Further detail can be found in Appendix A. See Appendix Table 3-4 for the data from each country.

combined (ages 6-14), ranges from 9.0 in Kerala to 59.9 in Bihar (Filmer and Pritchett, 2001).[8]

Table 3-5 presents indices of inequality in school attendance by rural-urban residence. Calculated in the same way as the wealth inequality indices these compare attendance rates for rural and urban households rather than attendance rates for rich and poor households. Looking at the indices for 10-14-year-olds for all DHS countries combined, rural boys have 12.6 percent lower attendance rates than urban boys, while rural girls have 18.4 percent lower attendance rates than urban girls. Rural-urban inequalities

---

[8]These values are derived from data presented by Filmer and Pritchett (2001) in their Appendix Table A1, p. 129.

are greatest in the low-income countries (where attendance rates are lower) and much higher among older adolescents. This is likely to be affected by the much longer distances that rural adolescents need to travel to secondary school. In most regions (although not the Caribbean and Central America for both age groups or Eastern and Southern Africa and South America for the 15-19 age range), rural-urban inequality in school attendance is higher for girls than for boys, suggesting that rural girls are differentially disadvantaged. The highest rural-urban disparities in school attendance are found in Western and Middle Africa, the Middle East, and South-central and South-eastern Asia. Comparing the rural-urban inequality indices in Table 3-5 with the wealth inequality indices in Table 3-4, there appears to be greater inequality in attendance by wealth than by rural-urban residence, with the notable exception of Eastern and Southern Africa.

The relative differences in schooling between the top and bottom wealth quintiles and between urban and rural areas are greater than relative differences in schooling by gender (not shown) regardless of region, because there is an interaction between wealth and gender and between residence and gender. Girls are differentially disadvantaged among the poor and those who live in rural areas, particularly in later adolescence.

Gender, income, and residence differentials in schooling participation lend themselves more easily to comparative analysis. Other schooling differentials by ethnicity, race, caste, or religion can be as important in particular settings but do not lend themselves easily to comparative analysis. A review of studies focusing on these more country- or region-specific differentials reveals their importance. Typically, residential and income differentials can provide only a partial explanation for observed ethnic, racial, caste, or religions differences. Results from Israel, South Africa, Nepal, India, and China all attest to the persistence of these differentials over time, even as overall schooling trends improve (Borooah and Iyer, 2002; Hannum, 2002; Munshi and Rosenzweig, 2003; Shavit and Kraus, 1990; Stash and Hannum, 2001; Treiman, McKeever, and Fodor, 1996).

## Trends in School Participation and Attainment

In the previous section, we presented a snapshot of school attendance patterns by age for the late 1990s. In this section, we present trends in school participation and attainment. Changes by decade are derived by comparing educational participation rates for cohorts that are 10 years apart in age. For each measure of participation or attainment, the youngest cohort chosen for the derivation of trends has reached a sufficient age to complete the transition in question.

The most basic measure of school participation that can be used to derive trends from a single survey is the percentage who have ever attended

TABLE 3-6 Trends in Percentage Ever Attended School, DHS Countries

| Region or Income Level | Weighted Averages | | | | | |
| --- | --- | --- | --- | --- | --- | --- |
| | Ages 10-14 | | Ages 20-24 | | Ages 30-34 | |
| | Male | Female | Male | Female | Male | Female |
| Region | | | | | | |
| Africa | | | | | | |
|   Eastern/Southern Africa | 81.1 | 77.8 | 83.4 | 74.4 | 81.5 | 68.3 |
|   Western/Middle Africa | 74.0 | 65.9 | 72.3 | 56.6 | 64.8 | 46.2 |
| Asia | | | | | | |
|   South-central/South-eastern Asia | 90.6 | 82.3 | 85.9 | 67.6 | 76.9 | 54.7 |
|   Former Soviet Asia | 99.5 | 99.8 | 99.7 | 99.5 | 99.6 | 99.7 |
| Latin America and Caribbean | | | | | | |
|   Caribbean/Central America | 92.0 | 91.7 | 89.7 | 85.7 | 84.6 | 77.6 |
|   South America | 98.2 | 98.8 | 95.6 | 97.1 | 94.1 | 93.9 |
| Middle East | | | | | | |
|   Western Asia/Northern Africa | 92.6 | 83.4 | 91.5 | 77.1 | 84.4 | 65.1 |
| Income Level | | | | | | |
|   Low | 87.0 | 79.1 | 83.5 | 66.2 | 75.3 | 54.0 |
|   Lower middle | 95.2 | 91.0 | 93.9 | 87.1 | 89.7 | 80.4 |
|   Upper middle | 97.8 | 97.4 | 95.9 | 95.4 | 93.9 | 91.0 |
| TOTAL—All DHS | 89.0 | 82.3 | 85.9 | 71.4 | 78.8 | 60.7 |

NOTES: For source of regional and income groupings and population data for weighted averages, see Table 3-1. Further detail can be found in Appendix A. See Appendix Table 3-5 for the data from each country.

school. Table 3-6 presents comparable data weighted by population size across region and country income group on trends in the percentage ever enrolled over the last two decades based on the DHS data.[9] The weighted average for all 49 DHS countries for the most recent period is 82 percent ever attended for girls and 89 percent for boys. This reflects a gain over the last 20 years of more than 10 percentage points for boys and 20 percentage

---

[9]We can reasonably assume that most children who ever enter school will have done so by the age of 10. Therefore, young adolescents (10-14) are the youngest group for which we can present data on trends in school participation. For example, in Tanzania, where age of entry is known to be late, Bommier and Lambert (2000) found that the mean age of entry for those over the age of 12 was 8.57 years despite a recommended starting age of 7, suggesting that some are still entering at ages 9 and 10. On the other hand, in Pakistan, which is known to have a relatively early age of entry, the mean age of entry is roughly 6 years and does not vary much by residence, gender, or income status (Sathar, Lloyd, and ul Haque, 2000; Sathar et al., 2003a).

| % Change | | | | | | |
|---|---|---|---|---|---|---|
| Most Recent Decade | | Earlier Decade | | Over 20 Years | | |
| Male | Female | Male | Female | Male | Female | |
| -2.7 | 4.5 | 2.3 | 9.0 | -0.5 | 14.0 | |
| 2.4 | 16.4 | 11.6 | 22.4 | 14.2 | 42.5 | |
| 5.6 | 21.7 | 11.6 | 23.5 | 17.8 | 50.3 | |
| -0.2 | 0.2 | 0.1 | -0.2 | -0.1 | 0.0 | |
| 2.6 | 7.0 | 6.2 | 10.5 | 8.9 | 18.2 | |
| 2.7 | 1.7 | 1.7 | 3.5 | 4.5 | 5.3 | |
| 1.2 | 8.1 | 8.5 | 18.5 | 9.7 | 28.1 | |
| 4.2 | 19.5 | 10.7 | 21.1 | 15.2 | 44.7 | |
| 1.4 | 4.5 | 4.8 | 8.3 | 6.2 | 13.2 | |
| 2.0 | 2.0 | 2.2 | 4.9 | 4.2 | 7.0 | |
| 3.6 | 15.1 | 8.8 | 16.8 | 12.7 | 34.4 | |

points for girls. As a result, the gender gap has narrowed considerably. It is particularly striking to see the dramatic growth in girls' attendance over the last 20 years in the low-income countries in which the gender gap has narrowed from 21 to 8 percentage points. By the late twentieth century, most children even in low-income countries have had at least some minimal contact with formal schooling. All countries in which ever attendance rates for both boys and girls ages 10-14 in the most current period fall below 70 percent are in sub-Saharan Africa (see Appendix Table 3-5).[10]

---

[10]They include Benin, Burkina Faso, Chad, Ethiopia, Guinea, Mali, Niger, and Senegal. Additional countries in which ever attendance rates fall below 70 percent for girls only include the Central African Republic, Comoros, Cote d'Ivoire, Morocco, Nepal, and Pakistan. There are still countries in which 50 percent or more of children have never been to school: these include for boys, Burkina Faso (59 percent), and for girls Benin (62 percent), Burkina Faso (73 percent), Chad (65 percent), Ethiopia (60 percent), Guinea (60 percent), Mali (64 percent), Niger (73 percent), and Senegal (60 percent).

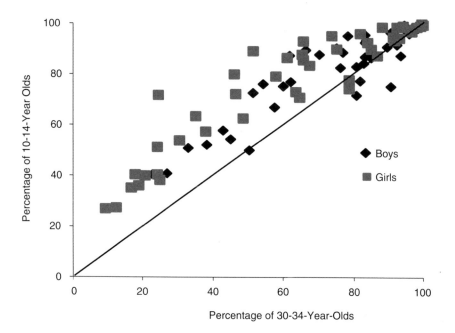

FIGURE 3-1 Percentage ever attending school, all DHS countries.
SOURCE: Appendix Table 3-2.

Figure 3-1 shows the change in the percentage ever attending school for males and females for all of the DHS countries included in our analysis. The figure plots the attendance rates of 10-14-year-olds against the attendance rates of 30-34-year-olds. Note that in all but a very few countries the percentage attending school among 10-14-year-olds is well above the 45-degree line, indicating improvements in school attendance over a 20-year period. The points for females tend to be even further above the 45-degree line than the points for males, indicating that girls have made even more progress than boys over the last two decades in most countries, consistent with the regional patterns shown in Table 3-6.

However, we should note some worrying recent declines in participation rates for boys in the last 10 years (see Table 3-6). In Eastern and Southern Africa and Latin America and the Caribbean, small gains for boys made in the previous decade have been erased in the more recent decade. A variety of conditions may have contributed to these declines, depending on the country, including worsening economic conditions, the spread of HIV/AIDS, rapid population growth, rising cost of schooling, and declines in school quality. As a result, in seven countries in Eastern and Southern Africa—Madagascar, Malawi, Namibia, Rwanda, South Africa, Zambia, and Zimbabwe—girls' attendance rates equal or exceed those of boys, a phenomenon already apparent in almost all of Latin America (Behrman, Duryea, and Szekely, 2004; Hewett and Lloyd, 2005) (see Appendix Table 3-5).

Table 3-7 presents trends in the percentage completing at least four grades of school, a marker of progress toward the Millennium Development Goal of universal primary schooling attainment by 2015 (UNESCO, 2002a).[11] In contrast to the primary school completion rate, which is tied to the duration of the primary school cycle in each country, this indicator is comparable across countries. Grade 4 attainment rates range from 68 percent in Eastern and Southern Africa to 99 percent in the former Soviet Asia for boys and from 57 percent in Western and Middle Africa to 99 percent for girls in the former Soviet Asia. On average, the 4th grade completion rate has increased 17 percent for boys and 47 percent for girls in the last 20 years. As a result, by the late 1990s, at least two-thirds (except for girls in Western and Middle Africa) of adolescents have completed at least four years of schooling. Increases for girls have been particularly dramatic in the low-income countries (59 percent). For boys, more than half of this growth, however, occurred in the previous decade; more recent growth rates have been much more modest. The average gender gap has narrowed considerably in the last 20 years as well, from 20 to 9 percentage points. Indeed, for some regions—the former Soviet Asia, Latin America and the Caribbean—4th grade attainment rates for girls now equal or exceed those for boys. For the 15-19 age group 4th grade completion rates are about 2 percentage points higher for girls than for boys in the Caribbean and Central America and 6 percentage points higher for girls in South America.

Trends in primary school completion rates tell a very similar story. Close to three-quarters of young men and 60 percent of young women have completed primary school in the most recent period (data not shown). Stagnation and decline in primary school completion rates for boys and continuing but slower increases for girls in sub-Saharan Africa suggest that the gender gap in primary school completion rates is rapidly disappearing, at levels of completion that remain unsatisfactorily low. Figure 3-2 shows estimates made by Hewett and Lloyd (2005) of trends in the percentage of males and females completing primary school in different age groups in sub-Saharan Africa from recent DHS data. While they find evidence of a

---

[11]We can reasonably assume that most young adolescents have completed grade 4 by the age of 15. For this reason, the youngest ages for which we can present data on completion of grade 4 is 15-19. Because there are still many countries in which children start school late (even up to the age of 9 or 10), grade 4 completion rates would be underestimated for the most recent period if we selected a younger group.

TABLE 3-7 Trends in Percentage Completing Four or More Years of Schooling, DHS Countries

| Region or Income Level | Weighted Averages | | | | | |
| | Ages 15-19 | | Ages 25-29 | | Ages 35-39 | |
| | Male | Female | Male | Female | Male | Female |
|---|---|---|---|---|---|---|
| Region | | | | | | |
| Africa | | | | | | |
|   Eastern/Southern Africa | 68.3 | 63.8 | 71.2 | 61.3 | 67.6 | 48.2 |
|   Western/Middle Africa | 68.4 | 56.6 | 64.6 | 48.0 | 59.4 | 37.0 |
| Asia | | | | | | |
|   South-central/South-eastern Asia | 81.4 | 69.1 | 75.2 | 53.5 | 66.3 | 43.5 |
|   Former Soviet Asia | 99.0 | 99.4 | 99.4 | 99.6 | 99.7 | 99.5 |
| Latin America and Caribbean | | | | | | |
|   Caribbean/Central America | 69.6 | 71.8 | 69.4 | 62.0 | 59.0 | 48.6 |
|   South America | 81.8 | 87.8 | 82.0 | 82.3 | 77.8 | 75.7 |
| Middle East | | | | | | |
|   Western Asia/Northern Africa | 88.8 | 76.8 | 84.0 | 65.7 | 76.9 | 52.3 |
| Income Level | | | | | | |
|   Low | 77.4 | 65.7 | 72.7 | 52.3 | 64.8 | 41.4 |
|   Lower middle | 88.5 | 84.3 | 85.0 | 76.9 | 78.9 | 68.1 |
|   Upper middle | 84.6 | 88.5 | 84.8 | 82.7 | 81.6 | 75.4 |
| TOTAL—All DHS | 79.4 | 70.1 | 75.3 | 58.1 | 68.0 | 47.8 |

NOTES: For source of regional and income groupings and population data for weighted averages, see Table 3-1. Further detail can be found in Appendix A. See Appendix Table 3-6 for the data from each country.

convergence in male and female primary school completion rates, they estimate that only 53 percent of girls ages 10-14 and 58 percent of boys ages 10-14 in the late 1990s in sub-Saharan Africa completed primary school.[12]

Table 3-8 summarizes trends in mean grades attained among 20-24-

---

[12]Because of late ages of entry, repetition, and long primary school cycles, many 15- to 19-year-old students in Africa are still attending primary school. In order to estimate primary school completion rates for those currently ages 10-14, the authors deflated the percentage of the age group that ever attended using the ratio of the percentage completing relative to the percentage ever entering based on the experience of older cohorts. As these ratios have been stable over time and 81 percent of the population of sub-Saharan Africa is covered by DHS surveys, these projections are likely to be reliable.

| % Change | | | | | | |
| Most Recent Decade | | Earlier Decade | | Over 20 Years | | |
| Male | Female | Male | Female | Male | Female | |
|------|--------|------|--------|------|--------|---|
| −4.1 | 4.1 | 5.3 | 27.0 | 1.0 | 32.2 | |
| 5.8 | 17.7 | 8.8 | 29.7 | 15.1 | 52.7 | |
| 8.2 | 29.2 | 13.4 | 23.1 | 22.7 | 59.0 | |
| −0.4 | −0.2 | −0.4 | 0.1 | −0.7 | −0.1 | |
| 0.3 | 15.7 | 17.6 | 27.5 | 18.0 | 47.6 | |
| −0.3 | 6.7 | 5.5 | 8.7 | 5.2 | 16.0 | |
| 5.7 | 16.8 | 9.2 | 25.7 | 15.5 | 46.8 | |
| 6.5 | 25.6 | 12.3 | 26.3 | 19.6 | 58.6 | |
| 4.2 | 9.6 | 7.7 | 13.0 | 12.2 | 23.8 | |
| −0.3 | 6.9 | 4.0 | 9.7 | 3.7 | 17.3 | |
| 5.4 | 20.6 | 10.7 | 21.6 | 16.7 | 46.5 | |

year-olds using DHS data.[13] It is supplemented by Table 3-9 which shows comparable data from Latin America based on 1970 and 1980 birth cohorts, including countries from the upper middle and lower middle income category. Here there is a great diversity of schooling achievement across countries. Nonentry, late ages of entry, high grade repetition rates, and early dropout rates all contribute to low average grade attainment. Mean grades attained range from 4.8 for girls in Western and Middle Africa to 10.8 in the former Soviet Asia and from 6.2 for boys in Eastern and Southern Africa to 10.6 in the former Soviet Asia. As of the mid- to late 1990s, the mean grades attained for the population represented by DHS surveys is 6.0 for girls and 7.4 for boys.

---

[13]As shown in Table 3-1, the overwhelming majority of young people have exited from school by the age of 20.

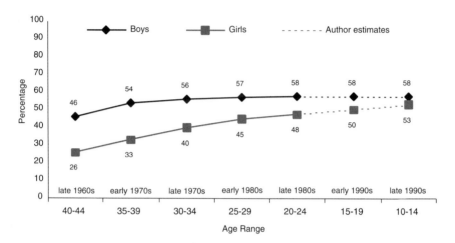

FIGURE 3-2 Trends in proportion completing primary school, 24 African countries.
SOURCE: Hewett and Lloyd (2005).

TABLE 3-8 Trends in Mean Grades Attained, DHS Countries

| | Weighted Averages | | | | | |
|---|---|---|---|---|---|---|
| | Ages 20-24 | | Ages 30-34 | | Ages 40-44 | |
| Region or Income Level | Male | Female | Male | Female | Male | Female |
| Region | | | | | | |
| Africa | | | | | | |
| Eastern/Southern Africa | 6.2 | 5.5 | 6.3 | 4.8 | 5.3 | 3.3 |
| Western/Middle Africa | 6.5 | 4.8 | 6.1 | 3.8 | 5.3 | 2.5 |
| Asia | | | | | | |
| South-central/South-eastern Asia | 7.6 | 5.7 | 6.7 | 4.2 | 5.9 | 3.5 |
| Former Soviet Asia | 10.6 | 10.8 | 11.0 | 11.0 | 11.2 | 10.9 |
| Latin America and Caribbean | | | | | | |
| Caribbean/Central America | 6.7 | 6.4 | 6.5 | 5.7 | 5.1 | 4.0 |
| South America | 7.4 | 8.0 | 7.4 | 7.4 | 6.7 | 6.4 |
| Middle East | | | | | | |
| Western Asia/Northern Africa | 8.6 | 6.8 | 7.8 | 5.5 | 6.9 | 3.9 |
| Income Level | | | | | | |
| Low | 7.2 | 5.4 | 6.5 | 4.1 | 5.7 | 3.2 |
| Lower middle | 8.9 | 8.5 | 8.4 | 7.5 | 7.6 | 6.3 |
| Upper middle | 7.5 | 7.7 | 7.4 | 6.9 | 6.6 | 5.8 |
| TOTAL—All DHS | 7.4 | 6.0 | 6.8 | 4.7 | 6.0 | 3.8 |

NOTES: For source of regional and income groupings and population data for weighted averages, see Table 3-1. Further detail can be found in Appendix A. See Appendix Table 3-7 for the data from each country.

Across the board, the rate of growth in grade attainment for girls has exceeded that for boys, with the result that the gender gap has narrowed considerably. The average growth rates for both boys and girls living in low-income countries are particularly striking. Most notably, there are dramatic improvements for girls in South Asia—a region heavily weighted by data from India that are very recent. Mean grade attainment for boys has declined slightly in the most recent decade in Eastern and Southern Africa, the former Soviet Asia, and Latin America. These declines in Latin America have not occurred only among the lower income countries, but also in some upper middle-income countries, for example Costa Rica and Panama (see Table 3-9). Indeed, it is interesting to note that the mean grade attained varies substantially even in the upper middle income group of Latin American countries, from 6.5 in Brazil to 11.3 in Chile for boys and from 7.0 in Brazil to 10.8 in Chile for girls. In many countries of Latin America, including the most populous ones (e.g., Brazil, Mexico, Colombia), grade attainment for girls has exceeded that for boys since the 1970 birth cohort.

| % Change | | | | | |
| Most Recent Decade | | Earlier Decade | | Over 20 Years | |
| Male | Female | Male | Female | Male | Female |
|---|---|---|---|---|---|
| −2.1 | 14.7 | 19.1 | 43.7 | 16.7 | 64.8 |
| 5.6 | 26.5 | 16.9 | 51.9 | 23.4 | 92.1 |
| 13.7 | 36.1 | 12.8 | 20.1 | 28.3 | 63.4 |
| −3.7 | −1.9 | −1.3 | 1.1 | −5.0 | −0.9 |
| 2.8 | 12.2 | 28.3 | 43.8 | 31.9 | 61.3 |
| −0.8 | 8.4 | 11.6 | 16.3 | 10.8 | 26.1 |
| 10.2 | 24.3 | 12.1 | 39.4 | 23.6 | 73.3 |
| 10.9 | 33.1 | 14.0 | 26.8 | 26.4 | 68.8 |
| 5.4 | 12.7 | 10.5 | 19.7 | 16.5 | 35.0 |
| 1.8 | 11.1 | 11.8 | 19.4 | 13.8 | 32.7 |
| 9.1 | 26.3 | 13.3 | 24.4 | 23.6 | 57.0 |

TABLE 3-9 Trends in Mean Grades Attained—Latin America

| Income Level and Country | 1970 Cohort | | 1960 Cohort | | % Change | |
|---|---|---|---|---|---|---|
| | Boys | Girls | Boys | Girls | Boys | Girls |
| Upper Middle Income | | | | | | |
| Brazil | 6.5 | 7.0 | 6.0 | 6.4 | 8.3 | 9.4 |
| Chile | 11.3 | 10.8 | 10.3 | 10.0 | 9.7 | 8.0 |
| Costa Rica | 8.2 | 8.7 | 9.3 | 8.3 | −11.8 | 4.8 |
| Mexico | 8.9 | 9.0 | 8.3 | 7.7 | 7.2 | 16.9 |
| Panama | 9.5 | 10.7 | 10.0 | 10.6 | −5.0 | 0.9 |
| Venezuela | 8.0 | 8.6 | 8.1 | 7.7 | −1.2 | 11.7 |
| Lower Middle Income | | | | | | |
| Bolivia | 9.5 | 7.9 | 7.9 | 6.3 | 20.3 | 25.4 |
| Colombia | 8.2 | 8.5 | 8.0 | 7.4 | 2.5 | 14.9 |
| Dominican Republic | 8.8 | 9.4 | 9.1 | 8.1 | −3.3 | 16.0 |
| Ecuador | 9.2 | 9.8 | 8.5 | 8.4 | 8.2 | 16.7 |
| El Salvador | 6.7 | 7.2 | 6.2 | 5.4 | 8.1 | 33.3 |
| Honduras | 6.2 | 6.1 | 5.8 | 5.6 | 6.9 | 8.9 |
| Jamaica | 10.4 | 10.7 | 9.7 | 9.5 | 7.2 | 12.6 |
| Paraguay | 7.4 | 7.1 | 7.2 | 7.6 | 2.8 | −6.6 |
| Peru | 10.9 | 9.3 | 9.7 | 9.1 | 12.4 | 2.2 |
| Low Income | | | | | | |
| Nicaragua | 6.4 | 6.3 | 6.4 | 4.4 | 0.0 | 43.2 |

SOURCE: Behrman, Duryea, and Szekely (1999a).

Table 3-10 summarizes recent changes in the percentage ever attending school beyond secondary school by comparing the experience of the 25-29- and 35-39-year-old cohorts. Because many are still enrolled in school in their early 20s, change cannot be assessed until most have had a chance to complete. Overall, 16 percent of the youngest men and 10 percent of the youngest women have had some postsecondary schooling. However, levels vary widely across regions, from a low of 5 percent for men and 3 percent of women in Eastern and Southern Africa to a high of 20 percent of men in South Asia and 15 percent of women in the former Soviet Asia. While trends have been impressive on average and greater for women than men, this largely reflects the experience of a few subregions, South Asia most dramatically and the Middle East and the Caribbean as well. Other regions have seen a decline in postsecondary enrollment in recent years, including all of sub-Saharan Africa, the former Soviet Asia, and South America for males and Western and Middle Africa, the former Soviet Asia, and South America for women. The most impressive increases for women have occurred in South Asia, the Middle East, and Eastern and Southern Africa, from a much lower base.

TABLE 3-10 Trends in Percentage Ever Attended School Beyond Secondary School, DHS Countries

| Region or Income Level | Weighted Averages | | | | % Change Most Recent Decade | |
| | Ages 25-29 | | Ages 35-39 | | | |
| | Men | Women | Men | Women | Men | Women |
|---|---|---|---|---|---|---|
| Region | | | | | | |
| Africa | | | | | | |
|   Eastern/Southern Africa | 4.7 | 3.3 | 5.3 | 2.6 | −13.2 | 21.6 |
|   Western/Middle Africa | 10.5 | 5.2 | 11.9 | 5.4 | −14.2 | −4.4 |
| Asia | | | | | | |
|   South-central/South-eastern Asia | 19.9 | 10.9 | 14.8 | 7.0 | 25.8 | 36.1 |
|   Former Soviet Asia | 17.1 | 14.8 | 21.0 | 17.0 | −22.6 | −14.9 |
| Latin America and Caribbean | | | | | | |
|   Caribbean/Central America | 9.3 | 8.1 | 8.4 | 7.0 | 9.0 | 13.2 |
|   South America | 12.1 | 12.2 | 12.6 | 12.6 | −4.1 | −3.2 |
| Middle East | | | | | | |
|   Western Asia/Northern Africa | 15.3 | 11.1 | 13.3 | 7.3 | 13.1 | 34.1 |
| Income Level | | | | | | |
|   Low | 16.2 | 8.2 | 12.7 | 5.3 | 21.8 | 35.3 |
|   Lower middle | 22.2 | 20.8 | 20.1 | 17.8 | 9.3 | 14.6 |
|   Upper middle | 9.1 | 8.9 | 9.6 | 8.7 | −5.6 | 2.0 |
| TOTAL—All DHS | 16.2 | 9.7 | 13.2 | 7.1 | 18.3 | 27.3 |

NOTES: For source of regional and income groupings and population data for weighted averages, see Table 3-1. Further detail can be found in Appendix A. See Appendix Table 3-8 for the data from each country.

Relative to historical experience, the speed of the schooling transition in the developing world, particularly in the poorest countries, has been very rapid (Clemens, 2004). This accelerating pace of change supports the panel's view that various elements of global change that were not present historically are contributing to this rapid pace of change. In some cases, rapid improvements in primary school enrollment have come at the expense of school quality. In spite of this rapid rate of improvement, however, it appears that the Millennium Development Goals are unlikely to be met in many of the poorer countries. The patterns shown in Figure 3-2, for example, suggest that the goal of achieving universal primary schooling by 2015 in sub-Saharan Africa is unrealistic.

## Student Performance

There are few comparable data on student performance in developing countries, whether measured by literacy rates or standardized tests. The best known data regularly published by UNESCO on literacy, which are based on self-reports, are now widely acknowledged by UNESCO and other United Nations agencies to be seriously flawed and are not presented here.[14] In the discussion below, we present some very recent but incomplete data that begin to show what schooling participation may be yielding in terms of learning outcomes as measured by literacy or by the results of standardized texts in reading, mathematics, and science in the few developing countries that have participated in these cross-national testing exercises. As yet, there are no data on trends in learning outcomes.

### Literacy

Recent DHS surveys have collected data on literacy using a minimal but "objective" measure that provides suggestive evidence of the possible link between poor school performance and attrition. In seven African countries, literacy among young adult women (15-24) has been measured directly by asking respondents to read a whole sentence out loud as part of an interview process.[15] These data, presented in Figure 3-3, measure variations in very minimal levels of literacy among women who dropped out of school prior to primary school completion according to grade attained.[16] Levels of literacy appear to vary dramatically across this set of countries by grade,

---

[14]While the ratio of literate females to males among 15-24-year-olds had been chosen as an indicator to monitor Millennium Goal 3 on gender equality, the Millennium Project's Task Force on Gender Equality chose not to use literacy rates as an indicator because of their well-known shortcomings (Millennium Project Task Force, 2004). In acknowledgment of these data limitations, UNESCO, along with the World Bank and United Nations Children's Fund (UNICEF), has launched a new program to measure literacy through direct measurement in surveys. This new program, called the Literacy Assessment and Monitoring Programme (LAMP), was just getting under way as the panel was finalizing this chapter (see UNESCO Institute of Statistics web site).

[15]The interviewer has several simple sentences printed on cards that are chosen at random for each interview (in the language spoken locally). For example, the four sentences used in the Uganda survey are as follows: (1) "Breast milk is good for babies," (2) "Most Ugandans live in villages," (3) "Immunization can prevent children from getting diseases," (4) "Family planning teaches people to be responsible for their family."

[16]The line for each country terminates the year before the last year of primary school in each country. This is because the successful completion of primary school is predicated on success in the national exam and therefore literacy rates jump to 100 percent in the last year of primary school.

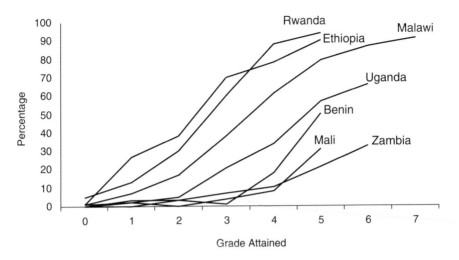

FIGURE 3-3 Percentage of young women who can read a simple sentence by grade attained.
SOURCE: Lloyd and Hewett (2004).

but typically fall well below 50 percent among those dropping out before the completion of grade 4. As success in primary school requires literacy, those who fall behind during the first few grades are more likely to get discouraged and drop out. Given that the poor have much higher attrition rates, these literacy rates disproportionately represent the poor (Lloyd and Hewett, 2004). Another factor contributing to these lower literacy rates in some settings may be differences between the language spoken locally, the official medium of instruction in primary school, and the language spoken by the primary school teacher, whose natal language may differ from the local language or the medium of instruction.

### Standardized Test Scores

A few international data sets are beginning to emerge that allow one to compare results of standardized tests typically administered in high-income countries with results from a handful of lower income countries. These results can be supplemented using data from several regional efforts in Latin America, French West Africa, and Southern Africa.

The most comprehensive and rigorous of these international efforts is Programme for International Student Assessment (PISA) of the Organisation for Economic Co-operation and Development (OECD) (Organisation for

Economic Co-operation and Development, 2001).[17] This involved the testing of 15-year-old students in reading, mathematics, and science literacy in 32 countries in 2000 (including two developing countries, Mexico and Brazil) with five more developing countries added in 2002 (Argentina, Chile, Indonesia, Peru, and Thailand) (Organisation for Economic Co-operation and Development and UNESCO Institute for Statistics, 2003).[18] The participating developing countries follow the patterns of the other OECD countries in showing better performance for girls relative to boys in reading, worse performance in mathematics, and about the same performance in science.

For each of the PISA test scores—reading, mathematics, and science—all seven participating developing countries had scores falling well below the OECD average (see Table 3-11, which provides a comparison with the results for Japan, Korea,[19] Canada, the United States, and France). Brazil, Indonesia, and Peru ranked at the bottom of the developing country group for the literacy score, with Thailand and Mexico at the top. These lower average scores reflect the fact that many tested students could not read sufficiently well to apply reading to the acquisition of knowledge and skills in other areas. For example, 54 percent of students in Peru fell below even level one, indicating the most minimal functional levels of literacy. In other Latin American countries the percentages falling below level one ranged from 16 percent in Mexico to 23 percent in Argentina and Brazil, and the percentage ranged from 10 percent in Thailand to 31 percent in Indonesia. By contrast, in the United States, 6 percent fell below level one.

Another international testing study was undertaken in 1999 by the International Study Center at Boston College—the Third International Mathematics and Science Study (TIMSS) (Martin, Gregory, and Stemler, 1999; Mullis et al., 2000). It involved the testing of students in 8th grade in 38 countries.[20] A total of 12 developing countries participated in the 1999

---

[17]PISA is based on a dynamic model of lifelong learning and seeks to assess how students can apply what they have learned to real-life situations. This approach helps ensure greater international comparability, as students' responses do not depend heavily on specific curricular material that might be highly variable from country to country.

[18]Because eligibility for testing was based on age rather than grade attained, there is the possibility that the lower scores in some developing countries were partially related to older ages of entry and higher rates of repetition, leading many 15-year-olds to have attained fewer grades by a given age than their peers in the OECD member countries. It should also be kept in mind that many fewer students in developing countries are still attending school at age 15 (see Table 3-1), so these scores are less representative of all young people in developing countries than of young people in developed countries.

[19]Korea, which is now a high-income country, has scores on all three subject areas well above the OECD average.

[20]A two-stage stratified cluster sample was used: the first stage was a sample of schools and the second stage was a randomly selected classroom in the school.

TABLE 3-11 PISA Test Scores by Country

| Region and Country | PISA 2000-2001 Test Scores | | |
| --- | --- | --- | --- |
| | Reading | Math | Science |
| Developed Countries | | | |
| Japan | 522 | 557 | 550 |
| Canada | 534 | 533 | 529 |
| United States | 504 | 493 | 499 |
| France | 505 | 517 | 500 |
| Korea | 525 | 547 | 552 |
| Developing Countries | | | |
| Argentina | 418 | 388 | 396 |
| Chile | 410 | 384 | 415 |
| Brazil | 396 | 334 | 375 |
| Peru | 327 | 292 | 333 |
| Mexico | 422 | 387 | 422 |
| Thailand | 431 | 432 | 436 |
| Indonesia | 371 | 367 | 393 |
| OECD Average (including Mexico) | 500 | 500 | 500 |

SOURCE: OECD and UNESCO Institute for Statistics (2003).

round—Chile, Cyprus, Indonesia, Iran, Jordan, Malaysia, Morocco, the Philippines, South Africa, Thailand, Tunisia, and Turkey—but only two of these (Cyprus and Iran) participated in the earlier 1995 round. With the exception of Malaysia, all the developing countries in the sample had average scores below the international median for mathematics and science (see Table 3-12 for relative scores). Furthermore, less than 50 percent of students in Chile, Morocco, the Philippines, and South Africa were able to reach the lower quarter benchmark (based on the international lower quartile) indicating that students can do basic computation with whole numbers (i.e., add and subtract).[21] Less than a third of students in Chile, Indonesia, Iran, Morocco, the Philippines, South Africa, Tunisia, and Turkey were able to achieve the international median benchmark indicating that students can apply basic mathematical knowledge.

---

[21]The lower quarter benchmark represents the 25th percentile of the distribution of scores from all the students in the combined sample of 38 countries. The few items that anchor at this level provide some evidence that students can add, subtract, and round with whole numbers. When there is the same number of decimal places, they can subtract with multiple regrouping. Students can round whole numbers to the nearest hundred. They recognize some basic notation and terminology.

TABLE 3-12 Percentage of Students Reaching TIMSS
1999 International Benchmarks

| Country | Lower Quartile[a] | Median[b] |
|---------|-------------------|-----------|
| Japan | 98 | 89 |
| Netherlands | 96 | 81 |
| Canada | 96 | 77 |
| United States | 88 | 61 |
| Malaysia | 94 | 69 |
| Thailand | 81 | 44 |
| Cyprus | 84 | 51 |
| Jordan | 62 | 32 |
| Indonesia | 52 | 22 |
| Turkey | 65 | 27 |
| Iran | 63 | 25 |
| Chile | 48 | 15 |
| Tunisia | 80 | 32 |
| Philippines | 31 | 8 |
| South Africa | 14 | 5 |
| Morocco | 27 | 5 |

[a]Median benchmark: Student can apply basic mathematical knowledge in straightforward situation.
[b]Lower quarter benchmark: Students can do basic (add, subtract) computation with whole numbers.
SOURCE: Mullis et al. (2000).

The regional office of UNESCO in Latin America undertook a study of reading and mathematics performance in grades 3 and 4 using comparable instruments in 13 countries, comprising 56,000 students in at least 100 schools per country (Casassus et al., 1998).[22] The report presents results for 11 countries—Argentina, Bolivia, Brazil, Chile, Colombia, Cuba, Dominican Republic, Honduras, Mexico, Paraguay, and Venezuela—four of which participated in PISA.[23] Mexico, which ranked near the top of the developing country group on reading in the PISA assessment, was ranked relatively low on the UNESCO reading test. Brazil, which was ranked near the bottom on the PISA mathematics test, was ranked relatively higher on math-

---

[22]The development of the test took two years and much international consultation (including participation of the Educational Testing Service) and was based on the careful study of curricular material from each of the countries in order to make the test comparable within the region.

[23]See the section on child labor in Chapter 5 for further discussion of how the academic performance of students who work compares with the performance of children who do not combine work and school.

ematics in the regional test. These differences in ranking between PISA and UNESCO, while partially explained by differences in approach, suggest caution in the interpretation of comparative test scores.

We are aware of several other regional efforts at internationally comparable student assessment in Africa: one in French-speaking West Africa (Conferences des Ministres de l'Education des Pays ayant le Francais en Partage or PASEC, 2002) and one in Southern Africa (Kulpoo, 1998, Southern African Consortium for Monitoring Education Quality). Standardized tests in mathematics and French were administered in primary schools in five countries of French-speaking Africa: Burkina Faso, Cameroon, Cote d'Ivoire, Madagascar, and Senegal. Michaelowa (2001) presents results for 5th grade students from PASEC: in many cases the percentage with the correct answer was no better than what could be achieved with guesswork.[24]

Within countries, most education systems administer standardized tests at the end of primary school in order to determine eligibility for secondary school. Only those scoring above a certain percentage are guaranteed entrance to the next level. In some countries, girls score below boys in all tests—for example, Kenya (Appleton, 1995) and Bangladesh (Arends-Kuenning and Ahmed, 2004b)—whereas in others, girls are the better performers—for example, Egypt (Lloyd et al., 2003). Such widely different gender patterns in test results, which cannot be explained by underlying differences in capabilities by gender, provide indirect evidence of the importance, not only of the curriculum, but also of the school environment and teacher attitudes in affecting student performance (see further discussion of schools as socializing agents later in the chapter).

While we are not able to make statements about trends in school performance, and even data on levels are only minimally comparable, it is nonetheless clear from these data that there are serious gaps in student achievement in many of the countries of concern to us in this report, gaps that may explain part of the reason that rapid increases in enrollment have not been translated as expected into economic growth (Easterly, 2001). While all of the countries covered have achieved substantial progress in participation and attainment, it is difficult to know what that means in terms of significant changes in the knowledge and skills of young people. The poor performance results for the developing countries are even more disconcerting because these test results apply only to students currently attending school. The older the age or grade of students tested, the greater

---

[24]A student could score 30 percent just by answering questions at random. The methodology of developing the tests is not defined in the documentation that we have been able to obtain.

the selectivity of the group. Those untested represent a much larger proportion of young people in developing than in developed countries, compromising the overall comparability of results for all young people (as opposed
to only those in school).

## FACTORS AFFECTING DEMAND FOR SCHOOLING AND
## HOW THEY ARE CHANGING

There is growing evidence that parents and young people around the
world share high aspirations for schooling attainment, usually expressing a
desire for levels of schooling that are well beyond the reach of all but a
minority. For example, in a recent rural survey fielded in Kenya in 1996, an
overwhelming majority of boys and girls attending primary school expressed a desire for a university education. Percentages expressing such a
desire ranged from 84 to 92 percent in different districts (Ajayi et al., 1997)
despite the fact that DHS data indicate that less than 1 percent of young
people in Kenya go on to university. In Egypt, around 70 percent of boys
and girls ages 10-19 aspire to continue to university, based on the results of
a recent nationally representative survey, in contrast to less than 1 percent
who actually go (El-Tawila et al., 2000). In Pakistan, where many children
never go to school and where no more than 29 percent of rural girls and 66
percent of rural boys complete primary school (Sathar et al., 2003b), many
rural parents express the desire to see their children go beyond the metric
level (class 10). Roughly a third of girls' parents and two-thirds of boys'
parents express such desires (Sathar, Lloyd, and Mete, 2000). There is also
evidence from recent qualitative research in Thailand that the gap in parental aspirations for schooling for boys and girls is narrowing (see Box 3-1).

For most, reality falls far short of young people's aspirations. To what
extent do these aspirations translate into effective demand, and what are
some of the factors that may have led to an increase in demand for schooling over the last two decades? In this section of the chapter, we discuss
various global, national, and local changes that are likely to have affected
the demand for schooling, either by changing family circumstances, or by
changing the economic returns associated with different levels of schooling.
All of these changes are the product of various aspects of global change
discussed previously as well as of policies and programs supporting fertility
decline and improvements in health and socioeconomic well-being. Our
review of the effects of these changes on the demand for schooling makes
clear that policies and programs outside the education sector can have a
significant effect on schooling trends. The influence of some of the changes
in education law and policy at the national level from Box B of the conceptual framework is discussed in the next section on policy and programs.

---

**BOX 3-1**
**Typical Quotes from Focus Groups with Parents in Thailand**
**(1991-1992)**

Knodel (1997) undertook 15 focus group discussions in 1991 and 1992 in two rural districts of Thailand to explore parental attitudes about gender and schooling. A focus of the discussions was continuing schooling past the primary school level since, at the time, this was the point at which many rural Thai children drop out of school. The quotes below are representative of the attitudes reflected in the focus group discussions. These include quotes from a group who completed primary school but did not go on to secondary school as well as a group that had continued to secondary school.

**Parents of Primary School Terminators, Northeast, Group 7**

Parent 1: In this high-tech age, they [boys and girls] are the same.
Parent 2: You have to see each person for himself, whether girl or boy. Depends on who is interested. If the boy does well, let him go on and if the girl is smart then she should get high education.

**Parents of Secondary School Continuers, Central Region, Group 8**

Moderator: Comparing a boy and a girl, if both go to school, who will get more advantages?
Parent 1: Now they have equal rights.
Parent 2: It's the same for boys and girls.
Moderator: The boys won't be more advanced later?
Parent 2: No, not nowadays.
Parent 3: Today women can be soldiers.
Parent 1: and police officers. . . . No difference, equal rights.

SOURCE: Knodel (1997:74).

---

Not all elements of the conceptual framework are discussed here. While all are conceptually relevant, systematic studies are lacking on some.

### Changing Family Circumstances and the Demand for Schooling

Young people in developing countries in the early twenty-first century live in families that are different in important ways from the families of young people 10, 20, or 30 years ago. A number of these differences may have a significant impact on schooling outcomes, and they may help explain the increases in schooling participation that are taking place in much of the developing world. In this section we review some important features of the families of young people, noting both areas of change and areas of relative stability. These include changing family size, improvements in child health, changes in family income, improvements in parents' schooling, and rapid urbanization.

*Family Size*

One of the interesting demographic paradoxes affecting many young people in the developing world today is that they have grown up during a period in which family size was falling but cohort size was increasing (Lam and Marteleto, 2005). Most developing countries (with the exception of parts of sub-Saharan Africa) have reached the stage in the demographic transition at which declining fertility has more than offset declining infant and child mortality, leading to reductions in the number of surviving children per family. From the standpoint of the children themselves, the large declines in fertility translate into declines in the number of siblings. For example, the number of preschool-age siblings, which appears to be negatively associated with school enrollment in many empirical analyses, declined by over 50 percent, from 1.2 to 0.5 for Brazilian youth ages 7-17 between 1977 and 1999 (Lam and Marteleto, 2005). The biggest change was the decline in the numbers of very large families, and these are the families for whom enrollment differentials have been shown to be largest (Kelley, 1996). Using the cross-sectional relationship between family size and schooling in 1977 to project the impact of declining family size over time, Marteleto (2001) found that, after controlling for changes in other variables, the decline in numbers of siblings accounted for about 25 percent of the 1.2 year increase in schooling attainment of 14-year-olds in Brazil between 1977 and 1997.

Most empirical studies on schooling attainment based on data from countries in which family size is declining have found that a child's schooling attainment is negatively associated with the number of siblings or the number of coresidential siblings. While statistically significant, these estimated effects are, by and large, relatively small in size when measured using cross-sectional data (see extensive reviews of the literature by Kelley, 1996; Lloyd, 1994).[25] These effects are often attributed to a dilution of resources, with a smaller share of financial and interpersonal resources available for each child in larger families.

Furthermore, there is evidence from this literature that some of the gender gap in schooling can be explained by the differential response of

---

[25]The empirical relationship between family size or number of siblings and the likelihood that a particular child in a family will go to school can occasionally be just the reverse in countries at low levels of development, at early stages of the demographic transition, or in which kin networks share the costs of schooling (Kelley, 1996; Lloyd, 1994). A more recent study in Vietnam also found relatively modest effects associated with the largest family sizes (Anh et al., 1998).

parents to resource constraints brought on by larger families (Lloyd, 1994). Thus, the reduction in number of siblings may also be related to reductions in gender inequalities in schooling. There are two possible reasons for this. First, parents with fewer children may be less likely to discriminate against girls. Second, where gender preferences are strong and fertility remains high, girls may have more siblings than boys and therefore face greater resource constraints. With reductions in family size, gender disparities in schooling are likely to fall because girls will no longer tend to come from larger families.

Jensen's (2003) investigation of gender disparities in schooling in India indicates that about half of the gender disparity in the likelihood of completing primary school can be accounted for by the fact that girls on average have more siblings than boys. Since Jensen finds that children in larger families in India tend to have less schooling, this systematic relationship between gender and number of siblings contributes to the female disadvantage in schooling outcomes.

The number of siblings of school-age children can be expected to fall further in most developing countries in the future. The speed of the decline will depend at least in part on sustained investments in access to family planning for the poor who continue to experience unwanted fertility. These trends will contribute to future growth in educational participation and attainment as well as to the closing of the gender gap.

## Child Health

Another important global trend with implications for the demand for schooling is the overall improvement that has occurred in children's nutritional status and health as a result of both economic improvements and specific health interventions (de Onis, Frongillo, and Blossner, 2000). Fogel (1994) has estimated that a third or more of the gains in labor productivity that have been made in the last 200 years in Western Europe can be linked to improvements in health and nutrition. Severe malnutrition leads to stunted growth, which delays motor maturation in infants and young children and thus reduces exploratory behavior. Stunted children evoke caretaking behaviors and social responses that are otherwise reserved for younger children (Lloyd and Montgomery, 1997). This, along with their slower motor maturation, delays the acquisition of important cognitive skills and social behaviors and lessens their adult cognitive capacities, with negative effect on adult productivity (Behrman, Haddinott et al., 2003; Pollitt et al., 1993).[26]

---

[26]There is some additional evidence that iron deficiency and parasitic infections may have similar detrimental effects (Behrman, 1996).

Furthermore, the expected returns to investments in schooling are greater with longer expected lives over which to reap those returns (Lee and Schultz, 1982). As a result, we would expect lower schooling participation and achievement among children who are nutritionally deprived in the first few years of life. Improvements in nutrition have occurred primarily in Asia and Latin America, although also in parts of Africa. These trends in health need to be recognized as a factor in the pace of schooling progress in different parts of the developing world.

As later ages of entry are associated with shorter durations in school (Bommier and Lambert, 2000), the link between nutritional status and timing of entry is an important one (The Partnership for Child Development, 1999). There is some evidence to suggest that ages of entry have been falling both because of growing enrollment in preschool and because of earlier start ages for those who enter at grade 1 (Colclough and Lewin, 1993).

Several recent well-designed studies using longitudinal data in developing country settings are beginning to substantiate the existence and importance of nutrition-schooling links and to point to the possible pathways, including the timing of age of entry, through which these effects operate. A first decision point for parents is whether or not to enroll their child in school. In Pakistan, where enrollment is not yet universal, Alderman and colleagues (2001) found that children who were nutritionally deprived at age 5 were significantly less likely to enroll in school by the age 7 than other children, and the effects are greater for boys than girls. For the Philippines, where enrollment is nearly universal, Glewwe, Jacoby, and King (2001) found that better nourished children perform significantly better in primary school not only because they enter earlier (and therefore have more time to learn), but also, more importantly, because they progress through school more smoothly, losing less time to repetition. Finally, Alderman, Hoddinott, and Kinsey (2003) found that improvement in the nutritional status of preschoolers in Zimbabwe is associated with earlier ages of school entry and higher grade attainment.

## Parental Schooling

There is almost universal empirical evidence that the schooling of parents has a positive impact on the school enrollment and schooling attainment of children (Behrman and Sengupta, 2002; Behrman et al., 1999; Lam and Duryea, 1999; Schultz, 2002; Thomas, Schoeni, and Strauss, 1996).[27]

---

[27]This literature must be qualified, however, because for the most part it does not control for such endowments as genetic-related ability and motivation that would seem to be

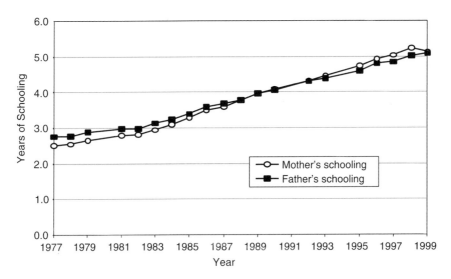

FIGURE 3-4 Means schooling of mothers and fathers of children age 7-17, Brazil 1977-1999.
SOURCE: Lam and Marteleto (2002).

Given steady improvements in schooling in most developing countries in recent decades, the parents of today's young people are on average considerably better educated than their own parents were. To illustrate this point, Figure 3-4 shows the large changes in parental schooling observed in Brazil. The schooling of mothers of children ages 7-17 more than doubled in Brazil between 1977 and 1999, from 2.5 to 5.1 years. The schooling of fathers increased from 2.7 to 5.1 years. Lam and Marteleto (2005) show that this increase in parental schooling can account for well over half of the substantial improvements in school enrollment observed for 16-year-olds in Brazil over this period.[28]

---

intergenerationally correlated and cause biases in the estimated impact of parental schooling on child schooling. Behrman and Rosenzweig (2002), for example, found that the significant positive estimate for the impact of mothers' schooling on child schooling in standard estimates for the United States became negative when data on identical twin mothers was used to control for such endowments (they speculate because more-schooled women holding ability constant spend more time in the labor market and less with their children), while those for father's schooling remained significantly positive.

[28] While conventional wisdom is that mother's schooling has a greater impact than father's schooling, an extensive review of studies from over 20 countries (mostly developing countries) reports that the estimated coefficient estimates for mothers' schooling are larger than are those for fathers' schooling in only about half of the cases (Behrman, 1997).

*Parental Income or Wealth*

Parental income or wealth can be another important determinant of schooling outcomes of children. There is a large literature documenting a positive association in the cross-section between parental income or wealth and children's schooling outcomes (e.g., Barros and Lam, 1996; Behrman and Knowles, 1999; Brown and Park, 2002; Filmer and Pritchett, 1999). Studies using time series or panel data are relatively rare, however. Using panel data for Vietnam, Glewwe and Jacoby (2004) explored the rise in secondary school enrollment from 1993 to 1998, a period of exceptional income growth in Vietnam. They found a positive and significant relationship between changes in household wealth (as approximated by a measure of consumption expenditures) and changes in schooling outcomes. These effects persist even after controlling for locally specific changes in rates of return, opportunity costs of schooling, and the supply and quality of schools.

One possible explanation of rising school participation and attainment in recent decades, therefore, would be increased parental income and other family resources. Unlike the case of parental schooling, however, in which increases are fairly universal across developing countries, the experience of income growth in developing countries is very mixed. While some regions, notably much of Asia, where the majority of young people in the developing world reside, have experienced substantial increases in family income levels, including decreases in poverty rates, much of Latin America and Africa has experienced little or no increase in per capita income in recent decades.

*Rural-Urban Residence*

Another important change that families in developing countries have experienced is increasing urbanization. Young people in developing countries today are much more likely to live in cities than they were 20 or 30 years ago (National Research Council, 2003). Urban areas are likely to differ from rural areas in both the costs and benefits of schooling. On the cost side, urban residents are more likely to live near a school or have access to public transportation, making the cost of school attendance less for urban residents. On the benefit side, urban areas may have higher returns to schooling given the concentration of manufacturing and services, including public-sector employment, in cities. It is also possible that the competition between school attendance and alternative time uses is different in rural and urban areas. Rural areas may have high opportunity cost of schooling if youth labor is important in agriculture or, as is often the case for girls, if their labor is used for water and fuel provision. In contrast, cities may offer additional economic opportunities for young people that keep the opportunity cost of schooling high. On balance, as Table 3-5 shows, attendance rates are consistently higher in urban than rural areas. We therefore expect that urbanization will be one of the factors leading to further increases in enrollment rates.

## Returns to Schooling

One of the important components of the cost-benefit calculus, driving decisions about how long to stay in school and how much effort to invest in school, is the impact of schooling on future economic opportunities.[29] In deciding whether to stay in school, young people and their parents are presumably affected by their expectations about how an additional year of schooling will affect the probability of finding a job and the wages earned in that job. The conventional method of estimating private returns to schooling is to compare the earnings of individuals with different years of schooling in a cross-sectional survey or census, usually controlling for other characteristics, such as age and labor market experience. When returns to schooling are estimated in this way, it has frequently been observed that returns to schooling in developing countries are higher than returns to schooling in high-income countries (Psacharopoulos and Patrinos, 2002), with recent estimates showing higher returns in Africa and Latin America than in Asia. One possible explanation of these high estimated rates of return is that the overall stock of human capital is low in developing countries, making the rate of return high. Returns to primary schooling are much higher for men than women; women on average have the advantage relative to men in terms of private market returns to secondary schooling.

There are many reasons why this type of estimate of returns to schooling may be misleading, however. One common argument is that there will be correlations between individuals' ability or family background and their level of schooling, generating potentially biased estimates of the impact of schooling itself on earnings. A large literature has explored these issues for several decades, and it is beyond the scope of this report to survey that literature here (see, for example, Card, 2000; Griliches, 1977). While there is some evidence that controls for family background, ability, and school quality lower the estimated returns to schooling in developing countries (Behrman and Birdsall, 1983; Case and Deaton, 1999; Lam and Schoeni, 1993), returns to schooling still appear to be quite high after controlling for these factors (Krueger and Lindahl, 2001). These conclusions are based on studies that exploited natural variations in school supply that were inde-

---

[29]The opportunity costs of school participation in terms of foregone earnings or family work time are discussed in Chapter 5.

pendent of individual schooling choices, such as Duflo's (2001) analysis of the impact of a school expansion program in Indonesia. While rates of return vary across schooling levels and across countries, the weight of evidence suggests that low schooling levels observed in many developing countries are not the result of low returns to schooling in the labor market.

Given the substantial economic changes associated with increased international trade, privatization, and market liberalization taking place in many developing countries in recent years, it is important to consider how these changes might be affecting returns to schooling for young people. It is worth considering, for example, whether the increased levels of schooling attainment described above for many countries are a response to increases in the private rate of return to schooling.

There is now widespread evidence from a range of countries representing all developing regions that rates of return to secondary and tertiary schooling are increasing relative to the past with somewhat lower returns to primary or middle schooling. For example, Behrman, Birdsall, and Székely (2003) investigated the impact of such polices as privatization, market liberalization, and free trade on the rates of return to schooling levels for urban males by combining 71 household surveys for 18 Latin American countries for the period 1977-1998 with indices of country-level policies. Their estimates control not only for all unobserved fixed country characteristics, but also for unobserved time-varying characteristics that affect basic wage levels. Their results indicate that liberalizing policy changes overall have had the effect of increasing the private returns to schooling, particularly to tertiary schooling, although this effect tends to fade over time. This effect is due to the strong impact of domestic financial market reform, capital account liberalization, and tax reform on schooling returns. Privatization, in contrast, contributed to narrowing wage differentials across schooling levels, and trade openness appeared to have had no significant effect on wage differentials across schooling levels.

Recent data from China have also allowed Heckman and Li (2003) to update estimates of rates of return to college education. They found that, after 20 or more years of economic reform with growing emphasis on markets, there has been a substantial increase in private rates of return to college. Duraisamy (2002) also estimates private rates of return to schooling in India using two national samples spread over a decade (1993-1994 and 1983-1984) and found that, in each year, returns rose up to the secondary school level and then declined. Over time, relative returns to secondary school and college have risen while returns to primary and middle school have declined.[30]

---

[30]While the estimates for each of these years may be subject to biases due to the failure to control for unobserved abilities, motivations, etc., the estimated changes in the estimates are

In Brazil, where it is possible to estimate private rates of return to schooling for large annual cross-sections from the late 1970s to the present, overall rates of return have been relatively constant at levels that are quite high in comparison to high-income countries. Average rates of return are around 15 percent, with high returns at all levels of schooling with controls for family background variables (Lam and Schoeni, 1993).[31] As in the case of India, there is some evidence that returns to schooling in Brazil are characterized by declines in the returns to schooling in the late primary and early secondary school grades at the same time that there have been increases in returns to schooling at the highest schooling levels.

A similar increase in the private returns to schooling at higher schooling levels is observed in South Africa (Lam and Leibbrandt, 2003), perhaps reflecting the same kind of increased returns to skill that has affected returns to schooling in the United States (Bound and Johnson, 1992). Schultz (2003) has also estimated recent rates of return to schooling in Ghana, Cote d'Ivoire, Kenya, South Africa, and Burkina Faso and found evidence that the returns are substantial, are likely to be growing, and are highest for those with some postsecondary education.

In addition to the strong impact of schooling on earnings, economic returns to schooling can also be affected by the impact of schooling on the probability of finding a job. As discussed in Chapter 5, evidence from most countries indicates that young people with higher levels of schooling are more likely to be employed, once they have completed schooling (O'Higgins, 2001).

In the context of recent experience in Asia, Montgomery and colleagues (2001) pose the question as to why the increase in the supply of educated young labor has not brought with it a decline in private rates of return to schooling. In the absence of other changes, such a result might be expected. There are good theoretical reasons to think that globalization and market liberalization are affecting private returns to schooling, and the recent studies cited above on Latin America, India, and China provide evidence to that effect. Furthermore, it is interesting to note that Noorbakhsh and Paloni (2001) found a correlation cross-nationally between levels of direct foreign investment and the average number of secondary years of school per working age adult, suggesting improved market opportunities for countries that have already achieved some success in secondary school completion rates.

---

still informative under the somewhat plausible assumption that theses biases are not likely to have changed much between the two years considered.

[31]Although this study controlled for standard observed family background variables, it was not able to control for such factors as genetic endowments. As a result, the estimates may be biased, perhaps considerably. For instance, most studies using data on identical twins in developed countries to control for unobserved endowments find considerable upward biases—from 12 to over 100 percent (Behrman and Rosenzweig, 1999).

While many women who go to school never enter the labor market or only work part time or for a few years, nearly all women marry. Marriage is therefore another potential pathway for young women and their parents to realize private returns on investments in schooling. These returns are likely to come in the form of a spouse who is more educated, comes from a more prosperous family, and has better earning prospects. Behrman et al. (1999) found that men in rural India who experienced significant gains from the Green Revolution married more educated women than they otherwise would have, so for women there were marriage market gains to schooling in the form of marrying into higher income households. In Cameroon, there is evidence that more educated women, if they marry men of similar schooling levels, may provide an important source of family support to family members after marriage in the form of in-fostering of relatives for school support, thus allowing families to reap a return from girls' schooling even when they do not work as adults (Eloundou-Enyegue and Calvès, 2003). Men who are more educated also have the opportunity to find a more educated wife who will be a more skilled household manager and a more effective mother. These returns, while infrequently measured, may be important factors driving the growing demand for schooling among girls in developing countries, even in settings in which female labor participation rates remain low. In countries in which the size of young cohorts continues to grow and in which women tend to marry men who are older, the competition in the marriage market is keen for women who are relatively better educated. With divorce rates still relatively low, marriage is usually for life and represents a one-time opportunity to adjust living standards and opportunities.

## SCHOOL SYSTEMS AND HOW THEY ARE CHANGING

With globalization and the diffusion of international norms regarding school accountability, governmental systems of formal schooling are coming under increasing international scrutiny both in terms of academic standards of performance and in terms of financial accountability (Carnoy, 2000; Carnoy and Rhoten, 2002). At the same time, in some parts of the developing world, particularly in Africa and the Middle East,[32] rapidly growing school-age populations are confronting greater financial stringencies, due to economic slowdown and local policy responses to debt crises and structural adjustment. Scarce resources are forcing the rethinking of

---

[32]In most of Eastern and South-eastern Asia, in contrast, the share of school-age cohorts in the population has already shrunk, and much of Latin America and South Asia is not too far behind.

priorities and processes and, in countries reliant on the assistance of international donors, leading to the imposition of conditions on multilateral and bilateral schooling grants and loans. As a result, school systems are being increasingly evaluated in terms of their contribution to labor productivity (Stromquist and Monkman, 2000a), while other aspects of schooling that contribute to the formation of cultural and social capital during adolescence, such as socialization and citizenship, are being given less attention (Libreros, 2002; Morrow and Torres, 2000).

In the discussion below, we highlight some of the most notable ways that school systems and the provision of formal schooling are changing in response to changes in demand on one hand and changes in governmental policies and programs on the other. Because there appears to be very little correlation within or across countries between education expenditures and school performance (Pritchett, 2004),[33] we focus here on evidence of actual changes in school systems rather than on trends in government expenditures on education, which UNESCO (2004) itself admits are difficult to track or compare.

## Changes in School Access

In the education literature there is often said to be a problem of lack of access to formal schools—particularly at the primary school level for the rural poor in much of sub-Saharan Africa and some parts of South Asia and particularly for girls, rural residents, and the poor at the secondary school level more broadly. The term "access" in the education literature is sometimes used interchangeably with terms that relate to school outcomes, such as enrollment, attendance, or attainment, that are the net outcome of supply and demand factors.[34] Here we use the term "access" to capture supply factors exclusively. These include the physical proximity of schools, the existence of supply-side barriers to use, and the presence of incomplete schools.[35] There is increasing evidence that, by the late 1990s, most rural

---

[33]This statement is based on a review of the literature by Pritchett (2004) that included analyses of data from OECD countries on changes in expenditures per pupil and changes in test results as well as cross-national comparisons of correlations between test scores and expenditures per pupil.

[34]"Access" also is used in apparently similar ways for other social sector services. For a critical discussion of this use for reproductive health services, see Behrman and Knowles (1998).

[35]For example, in Pakistan, where there are still many villages without a primary school, mosques are often used to house the first few grades of primary school. These schools are called mosque metabs and do not allow those enrolled to complete primary school without transferring to another school (Sathar et al., 2003b).

residents in developing countries lived within relatively easy reach of a formal primary school (either within the village or within a short walk) (Filmer, 2003; Filmer and Pritchett, 1999). Some notable exceptions are in particularly remote areas, in rural West Africa, and for girls in parts of South Asia (e.g., Pakistan, Afghanistan), where government primary schools are single-sex and girls' schools are still in relatively short supply (Sathar et al., 2003a). This reflects a substantial improvement over the last 20 years in primary school access and is a particularly remarkable achievement given the rapid growth of the school-age population in recent decades. It was not uncommon for the school-age population to have grown at rates of 2 to 3 percent per annum in many developing countries during the 1980s and 1990s.

Because there are fewer middle and secondary schools than primary schools, many more households, particularly in rural areas, face additional costs when it comes to sending their children beyond primary school. Indeed, in rural Ghana, Lavy (1996) found convincing evidence that supply constraints at the middle and secondary school level are an important factor in holding down enrollments in primary school and leading to early dropout. The shorter the primary school cycle, the younger students are when they face these constraints as well as the exams that determine eligibility for the next phase of schooling.

One response to a scarcity of school places in the public sector and the resulting excess demand for schooling has been a rise in the numbers of private formal schools, both run for profit and run by nongovernmental organizations (NGOs), including technical and vocational schools. An example is Tanzania, where from 1984 to 1990 the number of public secondary schools grew from 85 to 135 and the number of private secondary schools grew from 84 to 213 (Samoff and Sumra, 1994). As a result, no more than 40 percent of all secondary schools were public in 1990. Tanzania was a country previously noted for its restrictions on the supply of private secondary schools (Knight and Sabot, 1990). This expansion, however, appears to have had a limited impact on enhancing access for children from lower income families (Lassibille, Tan, and Sumra, 2000). In Pakistan, where access is still an issue at the primary school level, there has been a rapid rise in the availability of private formal schools at the primary level, even in rural areas in the 1990s (Sathar et al., 2000). However, at least in the case of Pakistan, it does not appear that the availability of private alternatives to formal schooling contributes strongly to higher primary school enrollment rates overall; instead it primarily affects the distribution of enrollment in formal schooling between the public and private sectors (Lloyd, Mete, and Sathar, 2005).

Supply constraints at the middle and secondary school levels have encouraged the phenomenon of "shadow schooling," which involves private and school-based tutoring and exam preparation classes that are advertised to reduce the chances of exam failure and subsequent grade repetition (Buchmann, 2002). In some contexts, shadow schooling enhances learning but in other contexts, particularly when teachers are underpaid, it may just mean that learning that would otherwise have occurred in the classroom is being shifted to other venues, as underpaid teachers use their classrooms to recruit private students to supplement their income outside the classroom.[36] There are no comparative data on trends in parental expenditures on extra classroom tutoring, but the evidence from the accumulation of many case studies suggests that a growing proportion of students are participating in shadow schooling (for a recent review, see Bray, 2003). While initially this was primarily an East Asian phenomenon, data now confirm the spread of this practice to most other parts of the world.

This rapid increase in the private provision of education services to the formal schooling sector, particularly at the secondary level, suggests the existence of an excess demand for post-primary schooling that is not being fully met by the government as well as a growing ability and willingness among parents and older students themselves to pay for schooling of adequate quality. The growth in NGO schools in some settings is also a response to the relative underenrollment of the poor in contexts in which school fees and other expenses are prohibitive and the state has inflexible pricing policies.

## Changes in School Costs

Newly formed national governments in the 1960s and 1970s made a strong financial commitment to education, including the provision of free primary schooling (Mehrotra, 1998). With the economic slowdown of the 1980s and the growing size of school-age populations, per capita schooling investments declined in many countries (Colclough and Al-Samarrai, 2000; Colclough and Lewin, 1993). As a result, many countries adopted education reform measures, often with international assistance, to improve efficiency, mobilize resources, and reallocate expenditures away from tertiary and towards more basic levels of schooling (Samoff et al., 1994). Two key elements of school reform have been policies to decentralize governance

---

[36]In Egypt the same teachers who teach students in the formal classroom moonlight for supplementary income as tutors after hours, using the classroom as a marketing tool for the recruitment of their private students. Lloyd et al. (2003) present the results of a study of preparatory schools in Egypt where members of the research field team who performed classroom observations in the schools noted that teachers gave preferential treatment in the classroom to those students who are their tutees.

structures (including devolution of responsibility for educational delivery to lower levels of government, to parent-teacher associations, and to the private sector) and to achieve greater financial accountability. There are some studies that claim that community participation in school financing increases community involvement, leading to improvements in school quality in response to community pressures for accountability (e.g., Jimenez and Paqueo, 1996).

The result of these reforms has been a fairly universal rise in the share of the total per pupil costs (typically calculated without regard to transportation costs) paid by parents—a trend that has taken different forms depending on the context (Knowles and Behrman, 2005). While we are unaware of any internationally comparable data on levels and trends in per unit school costs and changes in their distribution between various levels of government and parents, many country case studies document recent increases in school fees and complementary out-of-pocket costs, such as textbooks and uniforms.[37] The total costs of school attendance for students and their parents include both direct out-of-pocket costs and indirect opportunity costs (previously discussed). The direct costs of school enrollment include not only school fees but also the costs of uniforms, books, and other supplies, as well as the cost of travel to school and often supplementary tutoring fees.[38]

Data are lacking on trends in the total costs of public-sector schooling, whether measured from the point of view of households or from the point of view of the state. The largest component of per-pupil school costs financed by the state is the cost of teachers. Teachers' salaries are variable across countries, as are teacher-student ratios (see further discussion below on school quality). Over the last 25 years there has been a steady decline in the average teacher's salary from 6.6 to 3.7 times per capita gross domestic product, with particularly dramatic declines in French-speaking Africa, where salaries had been relatively high (Bruns, Mingat, and Rakotomalala, 2003). As there appear to be no striking trends in teacher-student ratios in

---

[37]For example, it is estimated that by 1990 in Costa Rica, the share of the total cost of public primary school paid by parents had risen to 30 percent and possibly even more in the case of public secondary school (Carnoy and Torres, 1994). Similar trends are documented in a series of case studies commissioned by a joint International Labour Office-United Nations Educational, Scientific, and Cultural Organization (ILO-UNESCO) project in Brazil, Tanzania, and Senegal (Samoff, 1994). Even in China, where the state continues to espouse a policy of equity in access to education, some school costs have been devolved onto local communities and, in the case of poorer communities, onto parents (Hannum and Liu, 2005).

[38]School fees rarely correspond to actual per pupil costs incurred by the government, however, because of government subsidies.

recent years (UNESCO, 2002b), this might suggest that per-pupil costs or investments incurred by the state are actually falling. Ideally, proper comparisons of trends in school costs would require some assumptions about school quality standards both over time and across settings.

Transportation costs, which are not typically included in the calculation of total costs, are one area in which the cost of schooling is likely to have fallen substantially in recent decades for the average young person in developing countries, given the combination of rapid urbanization, improved transportation, and expansion of schooling systems. In rural areas the total direct costs of attending secondary school may be particularly large, perhaps requiring the child to move to a town in which a school is located.

## Changes in School Quality

Pressure to expand school enrollments can have direct implications for the quality of education that young people receive. The major components of school quality identified in the literature as relevant to the development of cognitive competencies include (1) time to learn, (2) material resources, (3) curriculum, and (4) teacher knowledge and pedagogical practices (Lockheed and Verspoor, 1991). Each of these major components has many subelements too numerous to list, all of which have the potential to affect learning. Given the complexity of the schooling environment and the lack of agreement in the literature about which elements are most important for success in learning (Glewwe, 2002), it is not surprising that little is known on a comparative basis about school quality, much less about trends in school quality.

The first component of school quality—time to learn—is primarily a function of the number of contact hours per day and the length of the school year. There are internationally comparable data on time to learn for 1990 from UNESCO but no data on trends in the length of the school day over time. Reported contact hours vary from 845 in Centrally Planned Economies to 1,097 in Eastern Asia (Lee and Barro, 1997). However, in many settings the school day is very short, sometimes no more than three to four hours (see Arends-Kuenning and Amin, 2000, for Bangladesh; El-Tawila et al., 2000, for Egypt). This allows relatively little time for learning but does allow teachers the time to supplement their income with other jobs and with private tutoring and students the time to engage in various work activities.

The second element of school quality—material resources—includes class size, the supply of teachers, and the physical infrastructure and learning materials, such as textbooks. Available international data on student-teacher ratios and expenditures per student are often used as proxies for quality, despite the fact that neither of these measures is independent of enrollment trends. The latest data from UNESCO (2004) on student-teacher ratios show enormous variability across countries, with values ranging from a low of 11 to a high of 77. Data on changes in student-teacher ratios over the last 15 years since 1985 are available for 80 countries and show no consistent trend: in 44 of the 80 countries, student-teacher ratios rose, and in most others this ratio declined (UNESCO, 2002b). In some countries in which enrollments are declining, a falling ratio could be a sign of failure rather than success; alternatively where enrollments are rising, a rising ratio could be a sign of success. While some school systems have accommodated larger school-age populations through increasing class size (see Duraisamy et al., 1997, for Tamil Nadu), others have used the same school infrastructure with net additions to the teaching staff to add multiple shifts with shorter school days per session (see Lloyd et al., 2003, for Egypt). For this reason, trends in teacher-student ratios are difficult to interpret.

Curriculum—the third well-recognized component of school quality—includes the content of curriculum and the language of instruction. With the global rise in the Western approach to schooling, there has been a remarkable convergence of the core aspects of the formal curriculum, particularly in the primary school grades (Meyer, 1992). In a review of curricular material in 130 countries, including 94 low- and middle-income countries, Benavot and Kamens (1989) found that the primary school curriculum not only contained the same subjects in all countries but also gave them the same relative emphasis. Moreover, this relative emphasis has been consistent since the 1960s (Lockheed, 1993). Furthermore, at the classroom level, the experience of going to school is remarkably similar to what it was 40 years ago. "Even where parents and the local community do participate actively in school affairs, they make few attempts to change content, teaching methods or the general philosophy of education" (McGinn, 1997:48).

Language of instruction is another important aspect of the curriculum in many developing countries, particularly in sub-Saharan Africa and among the indigenous and tribal populations of South America and Asia, where a huge number of different languages are spoken.[39] Much research suggests

---

[39]For example, World Bank (1988) provides information on the number of languages spoken as well as the number of languages used for the medium of instruction for sub-Saharan Africa. Some countries, such as Cameroon, Côte d'Ivoire, Ethiopia, Ghana, Kenya, Nigeria, Sudan, Tanzania, Uganda, Zaire, and Zambia, have 30 or more spoken languages. Even if one counts only principal languages spoken by more than 10 percent of the population, most African countries have three or more (exceptions are Botswana, Lesotho, and Madagascar), and some have seven or more (Cameroon, Ghana, Kenya, Mauritius, Mozambique, Niger, Nigeria, Senegal, Sudan, Uganda, and Zambia) (World Bank, 1988).

that early learning is most effectively accomplished in a child's native tongue (UNICEF, 1999). The greater the number of languages spoken, the greater the difficulty of staffing schools with teachers who share the same languages with their students. This is in part true because certain ethnic minorities who have historically been discriminated against are less likely to have the levels of education required for the teaching profession. In countries in which many languages are spoken, however, it is very important for students to learn the national language—the language typically used in exams for promotion to the next level—and ideally an international language like Arabic, Chinese, English, French, or Spanish. There is evidence of substantially higher rates of return to French versus Arabic language schooling in Morocco (Angrist and Lavy, 1997) and English versus Marathi schooling in Bombay (Munshi and Rosenzweig, 2003). The authors of both of these studies linked these differences to the market premium associated with languages of international commerce.

There is no information available comparatively or over time on teacher qualifications and pedagogy. Even very recent information on pedagogical practices, however, suggest that rote learning and corporal punishment remain prevalent in many parts of the developing world (Fuller and Snyder, 1991; Lloyd and Mensch, 1999). Critical thinking skills are much less likely to develop in classrooms in which rote learning is the norm.

## Socialization in Schools

The formal academic curriculum reveals only part of the actual content of the school and classroom experience—an experience shaped by the principal's and teachers' attitudes and behaviors and sometimes codified in various administrative rules and practices. In this "hidden curriculum" lies a rich reality mirroring the social norms and values present in the community and beyond (if teaching staff come from outside the community). Not only can schools reinforce traditional values but they can also be the purveyors of new ideas and behaviors.

In traditional societies, elders in the community acquire power through knowledge, which is an asset to be controlled and used for personal gain (Bledsoe, 1992). In many schooling systems that are no more than a generation old, the teacher often assumes the traditional role of the village elder. Using rote learning techniques, most teachers are vocal, dominant, and often punitive in the classroom (Lloyd and Mensch, 1999). This "chalk and talk" approach to teaching takes on special meaning when seen in the context of traditional power structures that are drawn along lines of age, class, race, caste, tribe, ethnicity, religion, and gender. In many traditional contexts, the school principal and the teachers in the school hold special power and often convey very conservative values (Jeffrey and Basu, 1996).

In recent years, however, many schools have introduced new nonacademic elements to the curriculum, such as family life education or life skills, sports, and citizenship training, all of which have the potential to introduce more "modern" attitudes and behaviors. The impact of these new materials on the socialization of the young is very dependent on teacher training and motivation. Family life or life skills education taught by a teacher with no special training and traditional values can be used to purvey those values and in the process reinforce traditional behaviors. The impact of these new elements of the curriculum on the attitudes and behavior of young people have rarely been rigorously evaluated (see further discussion in Chapters 4 and 6).

Gender role socialization is a particularly important part of the hidden curriculum because it so fundamentally contributes to the very different experiences of boys and girls in their transitions to adulthood. Administrative practices, the curriculum (including the content and treatment of teaching materials), principals' and teachers' attitudes, peer subcultures, and school and classroom dynamics all contribute to the hidden curriculum on gender. For example, a common practice in many school systems is to expel girls from school when they become pregnant. Boys who make girls pregnant typically do not suffer a similar fate. Such practices convey powerful messages to boys and girls about the value associated with their schooling and the roles they are expected to play in the future.

Messages conveyed through school policies and administrative practices are heavily reinforced by centrally designed teaching materials that present cultural notions of appropriate gender roles (see Box 3-2). Independent reviews of the content of textbooks in many different parts of the developing world have found images of women appearing less frequently and, when images were depicted, women were usually shown in supporting roles and with negative character traits (Bustillo, 1993; El-Sanabary, 1993; Ibrahim and Wassef, 2000; Lloyd and Mensch, 1999; Obura, 1991; Shaheed and Mumtaz, 1993; Stromquist, 1994). Furthermore, in some parts of the world, certain aspects of the curriculum may be different for boys and girls (e.g., life skills, home science, family life, education, sports).

Probably the most important aspect of the hidden curriculum is conveyed in teachers' attitudes and behaviors. There are reports from qualitative studies in schools in different parts of sub-Saharan Africa (Guinea, Kenya, Malawi, and Togo) that both male and female teachers display negative attitudes toward girls in both their verbal comments and their behavior. Girls are viewed as lazy, less competent, and less serious about their studies (Anderson-Levitt, Bloch, and Soumare, 1998; Biraimah, 1980; Davidson and Kanyuka, 1992; Hyde, 1997; Lloyd and Mensch, 1999). Appleton (1995) asked teachers in Kenya why they thought girls did less well than boys in exams. Their response was that girls' poor exam results

## BOX 3-2
## The Treatment of Gender in Textbooks: The Case of Peru

Changes in school textbooks are by no means uniform and, since they are based on country-level studies, are difficult to generalize. Nonetheless, Peru constitutes a good case to discuss because data are available that allow comparisons over time of textbook content in primary school. Through content analysis, Mansilla (1981) found that textbooks presented women primarily in their roles as mothers and wives, thus fostering a social understanding of women as associated with emotions, whereas the portrayal of men emphasized traits such as aggression, competitiveness, and heroism. A subsequent analysis of primary school materials (Anderson and Herencia, 1983) found that men were depicted in many more instances than women and consistently as possessing more valuable intellectual and attitudinal attributes than women. The study also found that the presence of women as historical or political figures decreased in textbooks for higher grades.

Further studies analyzed social sciences textbooks for the 5th and 6th grades of elementary school in the subjects of history, geography, and civic education (Fernandez Davila et al., 1986). Military and presidential figures were found to prevail in all the textbooks on civic education that referred to the principle of equality among all citizens. The presentation of women was limited to wives and mothers who promote unity, respect, and understanding among family members, while fathers were described as the head of the family and breadwinner. Families were presented in an ideal version, denying the variety of families that exist in the country today.

Content analysis of primary school teacher guides produced since 1997 and in use now reveal the maintenance of traditional stereotypes regarding masculinity and femininity (Muñoz, 2003). For example, a guide for the 2nd grade presents 321 masculine illustrations and only 160 feminine illustrations, while the guide for the 6th grade offers 329 masculine and 269 feminine illustrations. Although the materials now make explicit reference to gender and to equity, the drawings continue to present traditional portrayals, with men occupying public spaces, working, and occupying professional roles and women at home and in private settings and portrayed mostly as teachers when in professional roles.

Since 1998, students in public schools have had access to supplementary materials on sex education that can be used in classes dealing with civics and social studies. Guides have been produced for both primary and secondary school teachers. These materials have been developed around three themes: the family, sexuality, and responsible fatherhood and motherhood. They highlight the importance of the family but consider only complete nuclear families. The materials offer very clear depictions and explanations of the reproductive system for men and women; they also address democratic and civil rights. Such issues as domestic violence, adolescent pregnancy, and the use of contraceptives are presented; there is weak discussion of other issues such as homosexuality, abortion, and incest. From 1996 to 2002, training in sex education has reached 47,000 primary and secondary school teachers, or about 11 percent of the teaching force. To our knowledge, the effects of these curricular materials on student knowledge and behavior have not been evaluated (Montoya, 2003).

were related to the effects of adolescence on them; they become disturbed by their bodily changes, lose interest in school, become more interested in boys and their appearance, and suffer from mood swings.

Attitudes are reflected in behavior when teachers actually treat boys and girls differently. Mensch and Lloyd (1998) report that girls in 8th grade classrooms in Kenya—the last year of the primary school cycle—were more likely than boys to feel that gender treatment in the school was unequal. Furthermore, in their classroom observations, they found some small but systematic differences between male and female students in the number of positively toned interactions they were observed to have with their teachers (see Box 3-3). Gender treatment varies by cultural context; in Egypt, teachers prefer teaching girls to boys and find them more hard-working and intelligent. Boys experience more physical beating in the classroom, a practice that has been made illegal but that is still relatively common. Data from a survey of students in school reveal that 22 percent of boys but only 5 percent of girls reported that they had been hit by the teacher on the previous school day (Lloyd et al., 2003).

In a more in-depth exploration of gender role attitudes among unmarried Egyptian adolescents (ages 16-19), Mensch et al. (2003) did not find that progressively higher levels of schooling in Egypt were associated with the expression of more egalitarian attitudes among either sex. Their study was based on data drawn from a national representative survey in which young people were asked about desirable qualities in a spouse as well as more direct indicators of gender role attitudes, such as opinions about whether wives should defer to their husbands, share in household decision-making, and have responsibility for performing domestic tasks. They concluded that Egyptian schools are not currently a particularly progressive force for attitudinal change.

The role of socialization in schools regarding gender has been explored much more than the role of socialization in schools regarding other differences in school, such as race, ethnicity, religion, caste, class, and tribe. This probably is the case because gender is pervasive across school systems, whereas these other groupings differ greatly across school systems. Another reason is an articulate and influential lobby on gender issues centered in the developed world and in international organizations. But causal observations in particular contexts suggest that socialization in schools about roles with regard to race, religion, ethnicity, tribe, and class may be very important in determining options for individuals and how societies function. Furthermore, it would appear that such socialization, as often is the case for socialization about gender, is dominated by conservative tendencies to maintain traditional hierarchies and power structures rather than to expand individual opportunities of those from disadvantaged groups.

**BOX 3-3**
**Gender Differences in the Schooling Experiences of**
**Adolescents in Rural Primary Schools in Kenya**

In a study designed to measure differential gender treatment in the school and classroom, Mensch and Lloyd (1998) combined school and classroom observations with interviews with students and teachers in a sample of 36 rural primary schools. In particular, they focused on the experiences of boys and girls in grades 7 and 8, the last two grades of primary school. In Kenya, the majority of school-going adolescents attend primary school. A higher percentage of girls than boys drop out of school before the end of primary school, and girls score on average lower than boys on the nationally competitive school-leaving exam at the end of primary school that determines eligibility for secondary school.

Their research had both quantitative and qualitative components. Girls were found to suffer from negative attitudes and discriminatory behavior in both low- and high-performing schools (measured using average scores on the primary school-leaving exam). Teachers' attitudes and behaviors revealed lower expectations for adolescent girls, traditional assumptions about gender roles, and a double standard concerning sex in both types of schools.

Each team of observers stayed in each school for 2-3 days. Before conducting observations of mathematics and English classes, the observers were given a short gender training course and shown videos of typical Kenyan classrooms. Some of their comments are particularly revealing of what they saw. To provide a context for each comment, the authors identified the source of each comment by whether or not the parents of children in that school were more or less well educated and by whether the school did relatively well or poorly in the primary school-leaving exam. The following quotes are examples of such comments:

"As usual, like in most Nakuru rural schools, the school is run by the cane. Students are caned severely for minor offenses and for getting low marks. The girls are caned on the thighs and hands. The students are so tense that when they see teachers passing, you can just see fear in their eyes" *(high parental education, high-performing school)*.

"The teacher told girls that they can never be household heads. This was prompted by the one girl who could not read the comprehension loudly and clearly" *(high parental education, high-performing school)*.

"Most questions were directed to boys and not girls. The teacher told the girls that if they do not improve, he could foresee them joining the local Mathenge technical institute instead of good boarding schools or institutions. . . . The teacher constantly told the class that the girls do not use common sense and that is why they might not make good sales persons. 'Lazy salesmen like some of you girls get very little commission,' the teacher told the class" *(high parental education, low-performing school)*.

"When the girls gave wrong answers, the teacher was very unhappy and pointed out that 'girls do not understand because they do not use their heads.' When marking the exercise, the teacher concentrated [on] showing girls examples he had already written on the board. When I inquired about the extra attention, the teacher said that girls in 8A are weak and lazy" *(high parental education, low-performing school)*.

## THE IMPACT OF SCHOOL POLICIES AND PROGRAMS ON SCHOOLING OUTCOMES

The provision of formal schooling for the young has traditionally been the business of the state in most societies, although in a number of cases there are also strong traditions of private, religious, or other types of formal schools.[40] With the establishment of international norms relating to the goals of universal primary school completion and gender equity in access to all levels of schooling, schooling in developing countries has also become the business of the United Nations system, multilateral and bilateral donor agencies, and a host of international and local NGOs. Along with a succession of donor-led initiatives and local school reform efforts has been a growing body of research on policy and program factors contributing to positive educational outcomes for the young including school effectiveness studies as well as evaluations of specific supply- or demand-side interventions designed to promote attendance, retention, or improved academic performance in general or among particular disadvantaged groups.

Schools have the potential to impact positively or negatively on many aspects of the transition to adulthood. As in other policy arenas, however, few of these policies or programs have been scientifically evaluated, including separately by gender. Studies of cost-effectiveness are particularly rare, and rarer yet, are estimates of rates of return to alternative interventions that would permit comparisons of uses of resources across interventions in different domains of action, such as health or labor markets. Furthermore, few of these evaluations permit identification of differences between private and social rates of return that would establish the basis for public subsidies on efficiency grounds. This paucity of adequate evaluation research may not be surprising given the complexity of the issues. Policies designed to serve one or some combination of the many goals of the formal schooling system may reinforce or jeopardize others. It is difficult to weigh competing objectives when assessing effectiveness. Schooling policies or programs have the potential to affect boys and girls and members of different ethnic, religious, caste, class, and tribal groups differently as well as to affect other aspects of the transition to adulthood indirectly, such as work and marriage. These benefits or costs of schooling policies also need to be assessed for a complete evaluation. Nonetheless, in the absence of such research, policies and programs are designed on the basis of anecdotes, nonrandom observations, and the views of those with strong vested interests or on experiences from developed countries without a sensitivity to differences in context—and the consequent result is the loss or misuse of scarce resources.

---

[40]This is not surprising given that schools shape beliefs at the same time that they promote learning, giving the government a direct interest in being the primary provider of schooling.

The good news is that the current research climate in the education field is changing fairly rapidly, and evaluations of school performance are one of the most fertile and innovative areas of research among those reviewed by the panel. Many of the studies cited below have been completed in the past few years, and we expect the field to continue to evolve rapidly. To date, the evidence of effects from well-designed studies is very eclectic, both with respect to types of interventions and countries (examples from Asia and Latin America are more frequent than examples from Africa and the Middle East). These studies often depend on the happenstance of particular types of data, the determined behavior of a few key individuals, or the particular circumstances of the intervention ex post in terms of placement.

Evaluations tend to fall in one of four categories: (1) prospective randomized experimental studies of specific interventions; (2) retrospective longitudinal studies of specific policies and programs, in some cases using so-called natural experiments;[41] (3) cross-sectional reduced-form studies of specific policies and programs on demands and supplies that approximate responses with the experience represented in the sample; and (4) studies that estimate structural models of behavior based on direct estimation of the underlying structural preferences and production function relations, allowing the simulation of alternative policy scenarios.

The first three of these alternative approaches are efforts to evaluate the effects of actual programs or policies. These approaches have the limitation that they cannot be generalized with any confidence outside the range of the experiment or the sample. The fourth, by contrast, can evaluate policies that have not been implemented. This is an approach that has some considerable advantages (at the cost of being specific about the structural relations underlying behaviors) because it usually is not possible to undertake many experiments on many different variants of a program.[42] Typically, evalua-

---

[41]Natural experiments are occurrences perhaps due to policies or perhaps to other factors, such as individual behaviors that are claimed to change some determinants of the outcome of interest, but do not directly affect the outcome. Table 3-13 gives some examples. For a critical evaluation of many so-called natural experiments, see Rosenzweig and Wolpin (2000).

[42]Todd and Wolpin (2003), for example, estimated a structural model based on the baseline data from Programa de Educación, Salud y Alimentación: The Education, Health, and Nutrition Program of Mexico (PROGRESA) and found that the model predicts well the experimental outcomes of the program. They use the structural model to estimate counterfactual policies pertaining to what would happen—not only to schooling but also to other household decisions, such as fertility—if the program were in operation for cohorts throughout their school ages and what would happen if the conditional transfers in the program had been substantially smaller or substantially larger.

tions tend to focus on schooling outcomes, including enrollment, grade attainment, and academic performance, whose improvement is associated with successful transitions in one of three domains: (1) policies affecting demand, (2) policies affecting school access, and (3) policies affecting school quality.

In the review that follows, each of these three policy domains is discussed in turn, and both direct evidence, based on scientifically sound evaluation research, and indirect evidence, based on more descriptive and qualitative material, is brought to bear on the question of school effectiveness in enhancing successful transitions to adulthood. The absence of research in particular policy domains is also noted. As success in later grades is very much linked to early success in school, our review focuses in particular on policies and programs relating to primary or basic schooling and on factors affecting progression to secondary school.

There is a large family of school-based education production function (or school effectiveness) studies that have been conducted in developing countries over the years that are not covered in this review. This is because they suffer from selectivity biases (in that they are restricted to enrolled students) that are not corrected in settings in which enrollment is less than universal (Glewwe, 2002). In addition to problems of selectivity, all studies assessing policy impact face other estimation problems.[43] Before including a study in our review, we have carefully assessed the plausibility of each study's conclusions in light of the particular research question, the context, the study design, and research techniques. Table 3-13 summarizes the major evaluation studies cited according to type of study and policy domain. This table can be referenced throughout the following discussion.

---

[43]These include measurement error, omitted variables, and endogeneity bias (Knowles and Behrman, 2005). A recent study in Kenya compared the effects of flip charts on test scores in Kenyan primary schools using prospective and retrospective techniques (Glewwe et al., 2004). In the first approach, the introduction of flip charts was randomized across schools. In the second study, conclusions were derived about the effectiveness of flip charts from a cross-sectional school survey of a different set of schools in the same Kenyan district, using data from each school on the presence and use of flip charts, unlinked with any explicit flip chart program. The prospective study found no statistically significant effect of flip charts on test scores, while the retrospective study found a statistically significant effect. The authors argued that the difference in results was caused by omitted variable bias in the retrospective study because schools with flip charts were presumably associated with other factors contributing to student performance that were not measured. The authors conclude that flip charts do not contribute to test scores and use this illustration to support the importance of random assignment and prospective approaches to intervention research. This is an important lesson because it has implications for the general approach to evaluating any intervention.

## TABLE 3-13 List of Studies of Program and Policy Impact by Type in Developing Country Settings

1. Prospective randomized experimental studies of specific interventions
   - *Demand*: PROGRESA, Mexico (Behrman et al., 2002; Schultz, 2004)
   - *Access*: Quetta girls' fellowship, Pakistan (Kim et al., 1999)
     PACES, Colombia (Angrist et al., 2002; King et al., 1999)
   - *Quality*: DIP, Philippines (Tan et al., 1999)
     Flip charts, Kenya (Glewwe et al., 2004)
     Textbooks/uniforms, Kenya (Glewwe et al., 2001)
     De-worming, Kenya (Miguel and Kremer, 2004)
     Second teacher, India (Banerjee et al., 2002)
     Teacher incentives, Kenya (Glewwe et al., 2003)
     Remedial education, India (Banerjee et al., 2003)
     School meals (Banerjee et al., 2000)

2. Retrospective longitudinal studies of specific policies and programs, including "natural experiments"
   - *Demand*: FSSAP, Bangladesh (Khandker et al., 2003)
   - *Access*: INPRES, Indonesia (Duflo, 2001)[a]
   - *Quality*: ASP, Nicaragua (King and Ozler, 1998)
     FONCODES, Peru, (Paxson and Schady, 2000)
     French language, Morocco (Angrist and Lavy, 1997)
     Class size, South Africa (Case and Deaton, 1999)[a]
     Class size, Israel (Angrist and Lavy, 1999)[a]
     Vouchers, Chile (Hsieh and Urquiola, 2003)

3. Cross-sectional studies of specific policies and programs
   - *Demand*: FFE, Bangladesh (Ravallion and Wodon, 2000; Ahmed and del Ninno, 2002; Arends-Kuenning and Ahmed, 2004a; Arends-Kuenning and Ahmed, 2004b)
   - *Access*: CSP, Pakistan (Kim et al., 1998)
     EDUCO, El Salvador (Jimenez and Sawada, 1999)
     Secondary school access, Kenya and Tanzania (Knight and Sabot, 1990)
     Tiered system, Tunisia (Mete, 2004)
     Double shift, Egypt (Lloyd et al., 2003)
   - *Quality*: Escuela Nueva, Colombia (Psacharopoulos et al., 1993)
     Class size, India (Duraisamy et al., 1997)
     Class size, Bolivia (Urquiola, 2000)
     Classroom infrastructure, Ghana (Glewwe and Jacoby, 1994)
     Pedagogical processes, Jamaica (Glewwe et al., 1995)
     Gender treatment, Kenya (Lloyd et al., 2000; Appleton, 1995)
     Local teacher, Pakistan (Lloyd et al., 2005)
     Vouchers, Chile (Contreras, 2003)
   - *All elements*: DPEP-Phase I, India (Jalan and Glinskaya, 2003)

4. Structural models of behavior
   - *Demand*: Bolsa Escola, Brazil (Bourguignon et al., 2002)
     PROGRESA, Mexico (Todd and Wolpin, 2003)

---

[a]Characterized by the authors as a natural experiment.

## Policies and Programs Affecting Demand

Governments can affect the demand for education by changing the costs or the benefits of attending school. Furthermore, regulations that restrict access to governmental schools because of such factors as age, parental status, ethnicity, race, religion, tribe, or marital status can raise the cost of education to particular subgroups in the population.

### *Laws and Rules Governing Attendance and Eligibility*

Many countries have included guarantees of compulsory schooling in their constitutions (Tomasevski, 2001), although compulsory schooling laws are rarely enforced. A total of 43 developing countries do not have such guarantees, and most of these are in sub-Saharan Africa. Among the countries that do, the legally mandated length of compulsory education varies from 4 to 11 years (Tomasevski, 2001). Effective enforcement requires that there be an adequate supply of school places for the eligible population, as well as mechanisms to ensure that students who are required to be in school actually are. In many developing countries, universal access at the primary level has been achieved; in others, this will require substantial additional investment.

We are not aware of any studies examining the impact of compulsory schooling laws on retention and on lifetime earnings in developing countries.[44] An important administrative rule governing eligibility relates to the appropriate or required age of entry. On one hand, in contexts in which parents are not yet ready to commit their children to school at a set age or doubtful about their child's prospects of continuing beyond primary school, an inflexible age of entry rule may work against universal schooling goals by limiting the window of time during which children are eligible to enter. Some experts feel that the enforcement of a rigid age of entry in the highly bureaucratized Egyptian system led to the permanent exclusion of many girls who never entered school (Lloyd et al., 2003). On the other hand, flexible age of entry rules, while more inclusive, have led to other problems.

---

[44]Angrist and Krueger (1991), using state variations in compulsory schooling laws in the United States, found that these laws can be effective in compelling a small proportion of students who would otherwise drop out to remain in school until they attain the legal drop-out age. Oreopoulos (2003), analyzing changes in minimum school leaving ages over time in three countries, found that students compelled to stay in school longer than they otherwise would have experienced substantial gains in lifetime wealth and health. While these studies suggest that enforcement of compulsory schooling laws might bring some benefits in developing country contexts, the economic constraints on many households and the limited reach of the central government in many poor countries make such an approach difficult to envision.

In Kenya, where the rules governing the timing of entry are very flexible, children continue to enter the system until age 11 (Montgomery and Lloyd, 1999). The resulting age heterogeneity in the classroom presents a challenge to teachers who are dealing with young people at very different stages of development.[45] To our knowledge, there is no proper evaluation that compares the quality of the learning environment under these very different conditions. The enforcement of age-appropriate entry requirements has been identified by some as a promising area for intervention (e.g., Pritchett, 2004) because there is clear evidence that late age of entry is associated with fewer years in school.

Certain administrative rules governing eligibility discriminate specifically against young women by prohibiting school attendance if one is pregnant, married, or a parent. These administrative rules are based on assumptions about the incompatibility of roles and concerns about contagion effects. In our review of these policies, we were able to determine that, in recent years, many of these policies and practices are being liberalized, but many still remain (see Chapter 8 for further discussion of pregnancy and school progress).

## School Fees

As previously discussed, school fees are only one component of total school costs but the one that is most easily changeable in response to market conditions or specific policy intervention. Jacoby (1994), using data from Peru, found that the school progress of children from credit-constrained households was much more responsive to changes in household economic circumstances than the school progress of children from households without credit constraints. For the many countries that have implemented structural adjustment policies in response to economic crisis in the last 15 to 20 years, the privatization of school costs through increasing user fees is thought to have had negative effects on enrollment. However, until very recently there has been no direct evidence of how changes in school fees might affect demand.

The high price elasticity of demand for basic schooling among poor parents has been dramatically demonstrated in the aftermath of the decision in 1997 by the government of Uganda to eliminate school fees for primary school, using new resources made available through debt relief (Deininger, 2003). As a direct result, by 1999, the wealth gap in enrollment had been substantially narrowed, the gender gap has been eliminated, and

---

[45]In Egypt, 88 percent of students enrolled in grade 8 range in age from 13 to 15. In Kenya no more than 50 percent of students in 8th grade classes are in this age range, while 40 percent are 16 or older (tabulations from DHS).

many fewer students were giving cost as a reason for dropping out. Success has come at a price, however, as class sizes have shot up and failure rates have increased. The experience in Malawi after the elimination of school fees in 1994 was similar (Moulton et al., 2001). More recently, fees for primary school were eliminated in Tanzania and Kenya in 2002 (Lacey, 2003; Millennium Project Task Force, 2004).

Even when rates of return to basic schooling are high, liquidity constraints may prevent parents from sending their children to school, not only because of school fees, but also because of the opportunity costs in terms of lost earnings or lost domestic product (Jacoby and Skoufias, 1997). Girls can be disadvantaged further despite relatively high rates of return (Schultz, 2002; Summers, 1994) in contexts in which parents are unable to recoup their investment through labor market returns, remittances after marriage, or reduced dowries or increased bride-prices. These research findings have led many educational policy makers to identify school grants or subsidies targeted to disadvantaged groups as potentially cost-effective interventions for boosting enrollment rates.

## Conditional Grants or Targeted Subsidies

A growing number of programs have been designed to address the enrollment gap between rural and urban areas, particularly as it relates to the poor. One of the first of the conditional grant programs was the food for education program in Bangladesh, where poor households with primary school-age children are eligible for monthly rice or wheat allotments according to their number of children, conditional on the children's maintaining an adequate attendance record at school. The program was begun on a large-scale pilot basis in 1993 and has grown to cover 27 percent of all primary schools and to benefit about 13 percent of all primary school students. Despite the large scale of the project, its design and implementation did not include a built-in evaluation component. Since its implementation, however, there have been two ex post evaluations, one using a 1995-1996 household expenditure survey (Ravallion and Wodon, 2000) and one using a survey specially designed for the evaluation (Ahmed and del Ninno, 2002). Both studies found large statistically significant effects of the program on enrollment, with the largest effects emerging in the immediate aftermath of its introduction. Furthermore, improvements in girls' enrollment have exceeded those of boys.

In 1994, the government of Bangladesh also began a female secondary school stipend program in rural areas to increase the enrollment of secondary school-age girls, to improve their secondary school completion rates and to delay their age of marriage. This stipend program, which combines both tuition coverage and a cash grant that increases with age, is complemented by other program components designed to enhance school quality. A girl is eligible to receive the stipend if she maintains a minimum level of performance, has a 75 percent attendance record, and remains unmarried. Using household and school data from two points in time, Khandker, Pitt, and Fuwa (2003) were able to conduct an ex post evaluation of the program, taking advantage of differences across villages in the timing of introduction. They found, using village fixed effects, that the duration of the program had strong statistically significant effects on the enrollment of girls but no impact on the enrollment of boys. They also found that the school enrollment benefits of the program accrue disproportionately to girls from families with larger amounts of owned land. As of 1997, the stipend budget alone was estimated to represent over 13 percent of the education sector budget. Given the large expense of the program, these conclusions may suggest that the program needs to be better targeted or abandoned; at the moment, girls are eligible regardless of family income or land ownership.

A newer version of the conditioned transfers for education has emerged more recently in Latin America, with cash grants to poor households conditioned on children's school attendance as part of an antipoverty strategy. These programs include PROGRESA in Mexico, which began in 1997, the Red de Protección Social (RPS—The Social Safety Net Program in Nicaragua), begun in 2000, and most recently Bolsa Escola in Brazil, which was expanded to a national scale in 2001 (Bourguignon, Ferreira, and Leite, 2002). The best documented in this family of programs is the PROGRESA program in Mexico. This is because the introduction of the program included a pilot evaluation phase, in which intervention and control communities were randomly selected from a group of eligible communities and their experiences were compared over a two-year period (see Box 3-4). The conditional cash grants are given to mothers for all children maintaining an adequate attendance record in grades 3-9—the higher the grade, the higher the grant, with girls in secondary school receiving a slight premium over boys.[46] A very thorough assessment after two years of the program showed strong positive effects on schooling outcomes, including earlier ages of school entry, less grade repetition, better promotion rates to secondary school, lower dropout rates, and higher school reentry rates among drop-

---

[46]The grants were larger for girls than for boys because teenage enrollment rates prior to the program were higher for boys than for girls. But in fact this gender discrepancy in enrollment rates did not mean that girls had less schooling than boys. To the contrary, boys failed and repeated grades more than girls, so they had to be enrolled more years to attain the same level of schooling—and on average girls had more schooling than boys before the program (Behrman, Sengupta, and Todd, 2002). Thus a policy designed to address a gender discrepancy that was perceived to disadvantage girls in terms of enrollments actually accentuated a gender discrepancy that disadvantaged boys in terms of school attainment.

## BOX 3-4
## PROGRESA:
## The Effect of School Subsidies for the Poor on Enrollment

At its inception in 1997, Mexico's Programa Nacional de Educación, Salud y Alimentacíon (PROGRESA) was among the most comprehensive rural antipoverty and human resource investment programs ever implemented in the developing world. Its purpose was to improve the education, health, and nutrition of poor families. Benefits consist of education grants to mothers contingent on their children's regular attendance in school and food consumption grants contingent on regular visits to health clinics, in which nutritional supplementation and basic care are provided. Oportunidades, the new name for PROGRESA, also covers urban areas and now reaches over 20 million poor individuals.

Research has played a critical role in each phase of the project's design and implementation at the instigation of the Mexican government. The decision to provide cash grants to mothers was based on research findings on intrahousehold resource allocation in developing countries showing that income received by mothers had a stronger association with positive child outcomes than the same amount of income transferred to fathers. The selection of eligible communities and households was based on careful statistical analysis based on the census. The decision to give mothers slightly larger education grants for their daughters than their sons for secondary school attendance was based on the observation that girls had lower enrollment rates than boys (although, as noted, girls had higher schooling attainment because boys repeated grades much more often than girls). Finally, the startup phase of the project was designed to allow for a scientific evaluation of the program's impact using random assignment of communities to treatment and control areas. PROGRESA, in collaboration with the International Food Policy Institute (IFPRI), undertook an extensive evaluation, using both qualitative and quantitative research methodologies, encompassing the first two years of the intervention prior to the introduction of the program in the control areas. The research team collected household-level data from 24,000 households in 506 localities, 320 of which were designated as treatment and 186 as control communities.

In the first two years of the program, some of the most dramatic positive impacts of the program related to the school attendance and work of adolescents. Behrman, Sengupta, and Todd (2002) found beneficial effects of the program at all stages of school progression, including earlier ages of entry, reduced grade repetition and better grade progression, lower dropout rates, higher school reentry rates, and, most importantly, higher transition rates from primary to secondary schools. Behrman, Sengupta, and Todd (2002) have simulated longer term effects, using the assumption that each child is a member of a PROGRESA household for eight years from ages 6 to 14, and found an average impact per child of 0.6 additional years of schooling, with a slightly greater effect for girls than boys. Such an increase in attainment was estimated to imply an increase of about 7 percent in adult earnings.

While this is a key finding, it should not overshadow the fact that PROGRE-SA had no measurable impact on regular school attendance or test scores of students in the short time frame allowed for impact evaluation (Behrman, Sengupta, and Todd, 2000; Schultz, 2000). Furthermore, no studies have been conducted on PROGRESA's impact on class size or other measures of education quality, although the available estimates find no negative spillover effects on children who were ineligible for PROGRESA but who were attending the same schools as many children supported by PROGRESA. The results of the evaluation do suggest, however, that investments in improved access to secondary schools by building additional schools so as to bring all children within four kilometers of a secondary school would have less than a tenth of the effect on enrollment than the enrollment impact attributed to PROGRESA (Skoufias and McClafferty, 2001).

Skoufias and Parker (2001) studied interrelationships between schooling and all aspects of working, including time spent in market, domestic, and farm activities. Their findings give important insight into the roles of work in the lives of adolescent boys and girls. For boys, the increases in school participation were approximately equivalent to decreases in market work, suggesting that market work and schooling are competing activities. For girls, increases in school participation were more likely to be associated with reductions in domestic work. While domestic work for girls declined with increased school participation, it did not do so to the same extent as market work for boys, suggesting that some domestic work is flexible enough to be combined with schooling or, conversely, that the domestic division of labor is not easily altered.

Despite the fact that quantitative studies find that PROGRESA effectively targets poor households in communities, qualitative interviews with beneficiaries, doctors, school directors, and nonbeneficiaries revealed that PROGRESA's system of household targeting may be problematic. All groups participating in focus groups or in-depth interviews believe that there are many families in PROGRESA communities who are poor and do not receive benefits and, to a lesser extent, people receiving benefits who do not need them (Adato, 2000). These social costs in the form of divisions in the community between beneficiaries and nonbeneficiaries merit further research. However, limiting PROGRESA to families identified as poor in the recipient communities permitted much more extensive coverage of poor communities for given program resources—about a third more communities—than would have been possible if coverage had included all households in poor communities instead of just those below the poverty line (Skoufias, 2001).

NOTE: In March 2002, Mexico's government, headed by President Vicente Fox, changed PROGRESA's name to Oportunidades, but the program retains the key elements of the PROGRESA program. Oportunidades will expand upon PROGRESA's coverage, both in urban and rural areas, with the help of a $1 billion loan from the Inter-American Development Bank (IDB), its largest ever (Krueger, 2002).

outs. Indeed, the program is encouraging even to the younger children who are not yet eligible for the subsidies (Behrman, Sengupta, and Todd, 2002). Based on projections by Schultz (2004), the benefits of PROGRESA could be as much as a 10 percent increase in grade attainment.

The two-year pilot phase of a similarly designed program in Nicaragua (Red de Protección Social, or RPS) incorporated an evaluation component as well using randomization of treatment and control areas and a panel survey design. In this pilot phase, RPS induced a net 17.7 percentage point increase in enrollment among 7-13-year-olds as well as improvements in retention (Maluccio and Flores, 2004). Bourguignon et al. (2002) used national data from Brazil to simulate some of the potential long-term effects of Bolsa Escola, a similar antipoverty program being implemented in Brazil, although one without the baseline, longitudinal, and experimental assignment features. They found that the most critical factor in the program's likely success is the fact that the grant is conditional on the attendance of school-age children. Unconditional grants to the poor that do not change the cost of education are predicted to have little effect on enrollment; increasing the size of the grant with age is not projected to have a major incremental effect. Similar results also have been reported for PROGRESA (Todd and Wolpin, 2003). This suggests that, in the absence of constraints, the poor see more pressing uses for the extra resources than supporting the attendance of their children in school. Therefore, constraining the use of these resources for the children's education is effectively an intergenerational transfer.

An alternative approach to increasing demand for schooling is the use of targeted subsidies, vouchers, or scholarships that alter the cost of private schooling directly for low-income groups. Programa de Amplicación de Cobertura de la Educación Secundaria or the PACES voucher program in Colombia is among the best known because of its careful evaluations (Angrist et al., 2002; King, Orezem, and Wohlgemuth, 1999). Between 1992 and 1997, Colombia awarded over 125,000 vouchers to secondary school pupils from poor urban neighborhoods to pay for private schooling (Angrist et al., 2002). These vouchers typically covered the tuition charged by lower cost private schools, but not the cost of more elite schools. Municipalities could choose to direct their resources to the building and maintenance of public schools or to the subsidization of existing private schools by joining the voucher program. During the five years of program operation, only 25 percent of municipalities joined the voucher program, and adoption was most likely in municipalities in which existing private schools had excess capacity, a large percentage of students were enrolled in private school, and there was a limited number of underserved students. The program was disbanded because its monitoring and administrative requirements proved too costly (King et al., 1999).

In municipalities in which the number of applicants exceeded the funds available, scholarship recipients were randomly selected through a lottery. Taking advantage of the lottery feature as a natural experiment, Angrist et al. (2002) collected data on voucher applicants in Bogota and Cali in 1998. The authors estimated that the additional 0.12-0.16 years of schooling completed by lottery winners would raise their annual incomes by about $36-48 per year.[47] In addition, the estimated increase of 0.2 standard deviations in test scores among lottery winners was estimated to be the equivalent of about one full year of schooling, which would translate into an additional gain of about $300 in annual earnings. With a favorable benefit-cost ratio,[48] this program would appear to have a high return compared with alternative marginal investments, but its ultimate demise suggests that some of the up-front costs proved daunting while the potential returns were not yet clearly visible.

There is no doubt that grants conditioned on school attendance or subsidies that are targeted to the poor can be effective in increasing enrollment, reducing dropout, and increasing grade attainment. The estimates for the Colombian voucher program (Angrist et al., 2002) indicate high benefit-cost ratios and internal rates of return. Whether conditional cash transfer schemes are cost-effective depends on whether or not all of the transfer is attributed to the educational objective or whether it is partially or fully attributed to its primary antipoverty objective (Pritchett, 2004).

Some critical questions remain: (1) How will these programs affect school quality and what implications will these changes have for the academic performance of recipients and nonrecipients who typically attend the same schools? (2) How can they be designed to achieve maximum cost-effectiveness? Few of these evaluations have given any attention to school quality. However, in the case of the food for education program in Bangladesh, schools were required to maintain certain standards to be eligible to enroll recipient children. While participating schools experienced an increase in enrollment relative to nonparticipating schools and the academic performance of participating schools declined overall, it is interesting to note that the academic achievement of nonparticipating students in participating schools did not change (Ahmed and del Ninno, 2002). Similar results are reported for PROGRESA (Behrman et al., 2002).

---

[47]These estimates are based on an estimated rate of return to schooling of 10 percent in Colombia and predicted average annual earnings of $3,000.

[48]Knowles and Behrman (2005) estimated that gain in earnings (even if heavily discounted) would exceed the program's cost. They estimated the benefit-cost ratio of this program, using broad definitions of costs and benefits. With a 5 percent discount rate they estimated that the benefits discounted to age 13 are $3,152, while the costs (also discounted to age 13) are $953. The benefit-cost ratio is 3.31, while the internal rate of return is 25.6 percent.

### Policies and Programs Affecting School Access

In many developing countries, major public works programs, such as school building, occurred at an early stage of economic development during the 1960s and 1970s. Today, primary school access exists for the majority in most countries, although often in crowded conditions, but difficult pockets remain in more remote rural areas or urban slums or squatter settlements. Secondary school access is available on a much more selective basis, and, in many systems, only a minority of primary school leavers can find a place in public secondary schools due to a shortage of places. Over the years, school access policies have included a range of approaches, including: (1) the building of new schools, (2) the development of alternative schools with lower unit costs, (3) the decentralization of school authority to the community, (4) double shifting in order to use the same school facility for several school sessions per day, and (5) the imposition of national exams at the end of primary school to restrict access to secondary schools according to a student's performance on competitive exams.

*School Construction*

Duflo (2001) was able to take advantage of rich national survey data in Indonesia to assess the impact of a major national school building program that occurred in Indonesia from 1973 to 1979. She assessed its effects on grades attained and the future wages of men by exploiting differences in the number of schools constructed by region and differences in outcomes across birth cohorts. By comparing cohorts entering school before the intervention to cohorts entering school after the intervention, she found positive and significant effects of the building program on average grades attained, the percentage completing primary school, and adult wages. She concluded that the program paid for itself many times over due to increased earnings in later life.

*Development of Alternative Schools*

Another approach to increasing school access has been to encourage the development of alternative schools that provide more flexibility and ease of access than the standard public primary school. In Egypt, the introduction of community schools in disadvantaged areas for girls who missed the entry age has been credited with a substantial increase in girls' enrollment, but this well-publicized intervention has not been subject to a proper evaluation. The even better known nonformal primary education program in Bangladesh, started by the Bangladesh Rural Advancement Committee (BRAC) on a pilot basis in 1985 to reach poor rural girls who had missed out on school, has not been properly evaluated (Ahmed, Chabbott, and Pande, 1994). BRAC schools currently enroll over a million girls, some of whom missed school altogether and others of whom may still have the opportunity to be mainstreamed back into the formal schooling system (accessible at: www.brac.net/education). The Colombian PACES voucher program for private schools discussed above is another example.

We are aware of only one intervention to develop alternative community schools that included an evaluation as part of the pilot phase of the program's introduction. This is the Quetta Girls' Fellowship program in Balochistan, Pakistan, in the city of Quetta, which began in 1994. The purpose of the study was to determine whether the establishment of private primary schools in poor neighborhoods that lack a public primary school was a cost-effective way of expanding primary schooling (Kim, Alderman, and Orazem, 1999). Subsidies were provided to private schools to establish new facilities in urban slums; the size of the subsidy was a function of the number of girls enrolled. In the start-up phase of the project (1994-1996), the program was introduced in 10 slum areas but its placement was randomized in 1 of 3 sites in each area; the other sites became the controls. In the first two years of the program, enrollment for boys increased by 24 percent and enrollment of girls increased by 28 percent. The authors concluded that this was more cost-effective than several alternative approaches, including income transfers to poor households and the construction of new public schools. The program has continued to expand since the pilot phase from 11 to 40 schools and from 2,000 to 10,000 students.

*Decentralization and Community Control*

It is probably too soon to expect solid evaluation results from the recent widespread school reform efforts aimed at decentralization of management authority and development of more participatory community governance structures for local schools. A common goal of these reforms has been to enhance efficiency, cost-effectiveness, and accountability through organizational change. Depending on the context, the reforms may be directed toward the more specific longer term goals of expanding the supply of schools in underserved areas or improving pedagogy and boosting student achievement. We are aware of only three country reform programs for which partial evaluations have been made, two of which were specifically designed to increase school access in underserved areas; the third in Nicaragua is discussed in the section on teacher knowledge and pedagogical practices because its primary purpose was to improve teaching practices and improve learning outcomes.

After the civil war in El Salvador, a community managed school program (EDUCO) was introduced in 1991 to expand school access to remote rural areas. Communities targeted for the new schools had high rates of malnutrition and grade repetition rates. The program provided for a community education association comprised of elected parents to manage the school, in particular to be responsible for administration, management, the hiring and firing of teachers, equipment and school maintenance, and teacher supervision. An ex post analysis based on a panel of EDUCO and traditional schools from 1996 to 1998 showed that access had indeed been effectively expanded and more active community involvement, a better classroom environment, and more careful teacher management have led to improved retention rates (Jimenez and Sawada, 1999).

A smaller scale intervention to develop government community partnerships to support the expansion of school access in rural Pakistan (Balochistan) was also evaluated on an ex post basis using a survey conducted in participating and control villages with similar characteristics (Kim, Alderman, and Orazem, 1998). The purpose of the program was to provide government funding and short-term teacher training to communities that could provide a temporary school facility and a local female teacher, even if she did not have the necessary credentials. Three years after the program began, the authors found a significant increase in girls' enrollment as well as an increase in boys' enrollment.

## Double Shifting

Double shifting is widely practiced in many developing countries as a way of reducing the unit costs of schooling. The same building is used twice in a day, but the school day is shorter and only the core subjects are taught. A particular school infrastructure will often have a completely different staff in the morning than the afternoon. Lloyd et al. (2003) provide evidence, based on a cross-sectional study linking a community-based sample of adolescents with the schools they attended in Egypt, that girls' retention suffers when they live in communities with double-shifting schools.[49] This effect was not observed for boys—a result that also brings out the possibility that policies and programs may have differential impacts on boys and girls.

---

[49]Few Egyptian children have a choice of school but are assigned according to their residence, so the authors suggest that this study can be seen as a sort of natural experiment. However, if there are unobserved neighborhood characteristics that affect learning and are correlated with double shifting these results are likely to be biased because the cross-sectional data do not permit control for such neighborhood effects.

*Restrictions on Secondary School Access*

In most public school systems, many fewer students can be accommodated in secondary than in primary school given a relative scarcity of school places at the secondary level. Knight and Sabot (1990) explored the implications of alternative policies on secondary school access in Kenya and Tanzania on school progression, subsequent earnings, and intergenerational mobility based on data collected from male urban wage employees in 1980 in both countries. While both countries limited entry to government secondary schools through meritocratic exams and provided extensive subsidies, Tanzania strongly discouraged the establishment of private secondary schools, while Kenya allowed the growth of private secondary schooling and even provided some subsidies. The result was a much more rapid expansion of secondary school enrollment in Kenya relative to Tanzania, resulting in a widening gap between the two countries in productivity. In a context of excess demand and constraints on the private sector, highly selective promotion practices lead to overcrowded classrooms in government schools, which become filled with grade-repeating students who are either not ready to sit for the exam or have sat for the exam multiple times. In the case of Tunisia, Mete (2004) shows how these practices impact negatively on student success rates and create a vicious cycle of inefficiency and failure.

## Policies and Programs Affecting School Quality

In contrast to evaluations of policies or programs affecting demand or school access, most evaluations of explicit interventions to improve school quality have been entirely school based and therefore restricted to currently enrolled students. Some studies of school quality, however, based on household surveys that include all children of school age, can be linked to data on schools attended by children in the community as well as to other relevant community characteristics. This permits researchers to exploit variations in measured school quality to derive implications about their effects on various educational outcomes using multilevel analysis. This second group of studies has the disadvantage of being retrospective and therefore suffers from some of the potential biases discussed earlier, including omitted variable bias and the potential endogeneity of school choice or placement. However, this approach has the advantage of being able to look at effects of school quality on the initial enrollment decision and the decision to exit from school; school studies can explore only outcomes specific to the particular school, including test scores and dropout, and are limited to selected samples of school attendees, which may make interpretation difficult.[50] The discussion of results is organized according to the major categories of school quality introduced previously but includes as well a few system-wide interventions designed to improve quality more holistically, either through promoting competition on one hand or providing an intensive infusion of resources on the other.

Time to learn, usually translated into the length of the school day, is less variable across schools in a system but is highly variable across countries. It is an assumption, but not a fact established through research, that a longer school day permits more learning because children are removed from home demands. Obviously the context is fundamentally important to how time is used, and that is why the other elements of school quality have been given more attention in evaluation research. Time to learn can also be affected by factors affecting student or teacher absenteeism. Thus, health interventions in the schools could be seen as contributing to time to learn. When teachers do not come from the villages in which they teach, have to cash or collect their wages elsewhere, or do not receive wages conditional on performance, teacher absenteeism can be a problem.

School feeding programs have been a popular approach to improving nutrition and school attendance simultaneously. Because of the possibility of substituting a meal in school for a meal at home, these programs have not been seen to be highly effective approaches to improved childhood nutrition, which has been their primary purpose (Banerjee et al., 2000). A three-cell school feeding experiment in the Philippines using random assignment compared no intervention to school feeding alone and school feeding combined with parent-teacher partnerships and did not find any statistically significant improvement in dropout rates after two years (Tan, Lane, and Lassibille, 1999).

Schools can also be used as a venue for vaccinations or the treatment of infectious diseases. A recent prospective study of deworming treatment in Kenyan schools using random assignment of schools provides a strong case for the cost-effectiveness of health interventions in schools in which certain infectious diseases are endemic (Miguel and Kremer, 2004). Two years after the intervention began, the school-based deworming program had led to at least a seven percentage point average gain in primary school participation in treatment schools, representing a 25 percent decline in absenteeism due to the improved health of both treated and untreated children.[51]

---

[50]There is no way of knowing in a school-based study whether a student who drops out is finished with his or her schooling or just transferring to a different school.

[51]The externality of untreated children benefiting from the treatment of other children means that the private incentives to obtain treatment are likely to be inadequate if families

In Pakistan, where girls' primary schools are staffed by female teachers, teacher absenteeism can be a particular problem in rural areas in which many teachers are not local residents. In a recent study in rural Punjab and the North West Frontier Province, Lloyd et al., (2005) developed a structural model of the enrollment decision and found that the presence of a local female teacher, rather than a teacher from out of town, in a village with a girls' primary school was predicted to have a greater positive effect on girls' enrollment than introducing a girls' school in a village that previously had none.

## Material Resources

Many elements of school quality are related to material resources including class size, the supply of teachers, the physical infrastructure, and learning materials often requiring parental contributions. Of these, class size—or the teacher-student ratio—has been the element to receive the most research attention. Recent studies provide persuasive evidence that increases in class size beyond some reasonable threshold have a negative impact on grade retention and average test scores.[52] Furthermore, it appears that the question of the impact of class size on learning is more complex than originally understood and the answer is likely to vary depending on the composition of students in the classroom. The study in South Africa is based on a representative household sample linked with district data on schools (Case and Deaton, 1999). The large variability in teacher-student ratios across black schools was assumed to be outside the control of students and their families because they had little voice in school budgets and

---

must pay the marginal resource costs of the treatment—everyone is tempted to ride free on the treatment of others. So there is a strong efficiency case for public subsidies of such treatment. While there are many claims of important externalities that justify public subsidies for health and education investments, this study is an exception in that it measures the extent of such externalities carefully rather than just claiming that they are important.

[52]Based on a review of 30 school-based production function studies in developing countries, Harbison and Hanushek (1992) concluded that there is no compelling evidence to support policies to reduce class size. The authors based this conclusion on estimated statistical effects from cross-sectional regressions using student samples to model the determinants of school performance or test results, with teacher-student ratios or class sizes as one of several independent variables. However, it is highly possible that variations across schools in class size are endogenous (consequences of variations across schools in other elements of school quality). More recently, Hanushek and Kim (1995) have estimated a positive but statistically insignificant relationship between teacher-student ratios and international tests in mathematics and science, but similar reservations apply to this study.

no freedom to move out of the community in search of better schools.[53] Case and Deaton found that decreasing the student-teacher ratio from 40 to 20 (the approximate means in black and white schools, respectively) would result in an increase in grade attainment by 1.5 to 2.5 years and a significant increase in students' reading test scores as well (conditional on years of school attendance). A second study, by Angrist and Lavy (1999), was able to take advantage of an unusual rule about class size in Israel, which sets a maximum for each class: class size is immediately cut in half and another teacher is hired when total enrollment exceeds 40. This nonlinearity in class size reduces the chance that class size will be correlated with unobserved determinants of learning. They found a significant negative effect of class size on reading and mathematics scores. Urquiola (2000) also found a significant negative effect of class size on test scores in Bolivia using similar techniques.

Several studies from India provide further support for these conclusions. First, a longitudinal study in Tamil Nadu showed that a decline in the pass rate for the statewide 10th grade exam (Duraisamy et al., 1997) was associated with an increase in teacher-student ratios arising from a sharp rise in enrollment triggered by numerous measures adopted by the state to encourage enrollment.[54] Banerjee and colleagues (2003) evaluated a large-scale remedial education program conducted in Mumbai and Vadodara, which included substantial reductions in teacher-student ratios for those students receiving remediation. They interpreted the measured success of the program in terms of improved learning outcomes as being at least partially attributable to smaller class sizes.

Additional insights about the effects of class size on performance come from interventions designed to increase the enrollment of disadvantaged students. In the food for education program in Bangladesh, the lower income beneficiary students performed better when attending schools with smaller class sizes than when attending schools with larger class sizes (Ahmed and del Ninno, 2002; Arends-Kuenning and Ahmed, 2004a). By contrast, in neither the Bangladesh food for education program nor the PROGRESA program in Mexico did nonbeneficiary students suffer ill effects in terms of performance when class sizes grew in response to the

---

[53]Of course, there also is the further implicit assumption that teacher-student ratios were assigned randomly across communities and were not endogenous choices in response to political pressures or perceived needs that would be likely to cause biases (e.g., Pitt, Rosenzweig, and Gibbons, 1993; Rosenzweig and Wolpin, 1986).

[54]These included free meals, uniforms, and books as well as special cash grants to schools that retain girls.

intervention (Behrman, Sengupta, and Todd, 2002). This may suggest that the performance of students from lower income families is more sensitive to class size than the average student, possibly because their families are able to provide less material and intellectual support to their schooling than the families of their better off peers. Nonbeneficiary students were, however, negatively affected in terms of their performance by the presence in the classroom of poorer performing beneficiary students, suggesting that it is not just the size of the class that is important but also its composition.

Infrastructural improvements can be an important domain of school quality in settings with difficult weather conditions and poor building materials. For example, in a study linking household and school data in Ghana, Glewwe and Jacoby (1994) found that the existence of unusable or leaky classrooms was a statistically important factor in explaining variations in test scores and student retention. A recent longitudinal study of the impact of an education program in Peru primarily devoted to funding community-based school renovation projects (a part of the larger Peruvian Social Fund known as FONCODES) found a sizeable impact of the program on the school attendance of younger children (Paxson and Schady, 2000).

Several other well-designed randomized experiments in Kenya have explored the effects of the provision of uniforms and textbooks (Kremer et al., 1997), textbooks only (Glewwe, Kremer, and Moulin, 2001), and flip charts (Glewwe et al., 2004) on various school outcomes. These studies have been small in scale and short in duration. None of these interventions found positive effects on test scores. However, the interventions themselves appear to have been poorly designed and chosen by the collaborating NGOs, although the evaluation methodology was sound. It was found, for example, that the textbooks were too advanced for the students and that the teachers were not properly trained in their use. The authors claim nevertheless that each of the interventions they consider are ones for which there are strong advocates. Thus the publication and dissemination of negative results are helpful to the policy dialogue.

## Curriculum

Language of instruction is a key aspect of curriculum that is rarely evaluated in terms of its impact. Angrist and Lavy (1997) took advantage of a natural experiment in Morocco to evaluate the impact of a change in the language of instruction in grade 6 and higher in Morocco from French to Arabic in 1983. By comparing the hourly wages of successive cohorts going through the school system, Angrist and Lavy were able to determine that the premium to postprimary education of younger cohorts was reduced by as much as one-half as a result of the language change. They were able to attribute this largely to a decline in French writing skills. Morocco is not the only country that has shifted the language of instruction away from the language of former colonial powers (e.g., Swahili in Tanzania and Urdu in Pakistan), but the consequences of these changes are not known.

## Teacher Knowledge and Pedagogical Practices

Several intervention studies have given attention to the special pedagogical needs of children in disadvantaged settings. These include greater teacher autonomy (Autonomous School Program in Nicaragua [King and Ozler, 1998]); multigrade schools and teacher training and instructional materials adapted to slow learners and local needs (Escuela Nueva in Colombia); and multilevel learning materials and parent-teacher partnerships (dropout intervention in the Philippines). King and Ozler (1998) used a matched comparison design in Nicaragua to follow a sample of treatment and no-treatment schools and found no evidence that students in schools participating in the program had better test scores. However, they did find that when schools, regardless of participation in the program showed higher levels of teacher autonomy student test scores were significantly higher.

Psacharopoulos, Rojas, and Velez (1993) have evaluated, using a cross-sectional study with a quasi-experimental design, the effects of the introduction of Escuela Nueva in villages in rural Colombia that formerly had no primary school. These multigrade schools were designed with flexible promotion, teacher training and instructional materials adapted to slow learners and local needs, intensive supervision, community involvement, and student governance, and they were introduced into rural villages. The authors found improved test scores and less dropout among students attending Escuela Nueva relative to those attending traditional schools in similar villages. In the three-cell randomized experiment in the Philippines, the introduction of multilevel learning materials combined with parent-teacher partnership did result in a reduction in dropout rates and better language learning (Tan et al., 1999).

Glewwe and colleagues (1995) simulated alternative policy scenarios for the improvement of cognitive competencies in Jamaican primary schools using data linking school and household data. They took a very comprehensive approach to the measurement of school inputs, including the traditional factors used in educational production function studies as well as measures of pedagogical processes and school management and organization. They found that material inputs were less important than the pedagogical processes in explaining variations in achievements. Among the most important factors were increasing the intensity of textbook use and decreasing the amount of time spent on written assignments in class.

An evaluation of a randomized trial of a teacher incentive scheme in Kenya documents that teachers can be extremely responsive to financial incentives if linked to improvements in students' test scores (Glewwe, Llias, and Kremer, 2003). In intervention schools, test scores increased significantly. However, teachers devoted increased class time to test preparation without improving their attendance record, their approach to homework, or their pedagogy. An implication of this study is that improvements in pedagogy are unlikely to result when incentives are tied solely to test performance.

## Gender Treatment

Boys and girls may have different experiences in the same school because of differences in curricular opportunities, differences in treatment by individual teachers, and differences in rules, regulations, and administrative practices. While some differences in gender treatment are legislated by policy (e.g., home economics for girls, required withdrawal if pregnant) and therefore uniform across schools, differences in gender treatment in the classroom, in the absence of gender training for teachers, are likely to vary both within and across schools. Few studies have attempted to quantify differences in gender treatment across schools in a way that would allow the measurement of their impact on school outcomes. Appleton (1995), exploring the determinants of gender differences in the scores of primary school-leaving exams in Kenya with his own sample of schools in Nairobi, identified teacher attitudes toward the teachability of boys and girls as a statistically significant factor associated with differences in exam scores. Specifically, girls underperform boys in schools when the staff think they are naturally less able, while boys are not significantly affected in their school performance by such attitudes. Lloyd, Mensch, and Clark (2000), using data from their own specially designed school and household survey in rural Kenya, found various measures of gender treatment, controlling for family and other more traditional school quality factors, to be statistically significant factors associated with the probability of dropout for girls but not for boys. From these results, they concluded that school environments are discouraging to girls when boys are favored in class and provided with a more supportive environment in terms of advice, teachers take the importance of more difficult subjects like mathematics less seriously for girls, boys are left free to harass girls, and girls' experience of less equality treatment is not fully recognized by boys.

## Treatment of Others Disadvantaged by Class, Race, Ethnicity, Tribe, Caste, or Religion

Although there has been relatively greater attention to gender differences in education, there are some suggestions that different treatments by other categorizations may be important and in some cases probably more important than gender differences. As noted above, for example, schooling differentials by income or wealth class tend to be larger than those for gender holding income or wealth constant both across countries and within countries. A number of programs directed toward the poor (reviewed above) show significant and possibly high rate-of-return impacts for transfers conditional on school attendance and vouchers that expand choices to private schools. We are not aware, however, of systematic evaluations of programs that are designed to change the treatment of poor students in schools.

While categorizations beyond gender and economic class may be very important in any particular context, the nature of these categorizations varies across countries. In some contexts the important distinctions involve race, in others religion, tribe, caste, language, or immigrant status. For instance, as noted above, the differential in treatment by race in apartheid South Africa was enormous. Black students typically studied in more crowded classrooms than white students with important consequences for schooling attainment. In postconflict Southeastern Europe, schools and other public institutions have been blamed for exacerbating ethnic tensions rather than healing them because there are separate sessions in some schools for children from different ethnic groups (World Bank, 2002b). As far as we are aware, however, there is no systematic documentation of the many ways schools treat students differently according to these other categorizations.

### Promotion of Competition Through School Vouchers

While voucher programs have been much discussed and experimented with in school reform initiatives in the United States, experience with vouchers is rare in developing countries. To our knowledge, among developing countries, Chile has the most extensive experience with vouchers. Chile introduced a nationwide voucher system in 1981 in order to promote competition between the public and private sectors, improve efficiency in all schools, and produce better learning outcomes. This system has now been in place for over 20 years but did receive substantial enhancements in the early 1990s in response to some disappointments relating to the unequal social distribution of learning outcomes (Cox and Lemaitre, 1999).

There are three types of schools in Chile: (1) municipal schools financed by a per-student subsidy granted by the state and run by the municipality, (2) private subsidized schools (voucher schools) financed by the same per-student subsidy but run by the private sector, and (3) private fee-paying schools financed by fees paid by parents and managed by the private sector. Both types of private schools use selection procedures and are therefore able to screen out some of the weaker or more difficult students (Cox and Lemaitre, 1999; Mizala and Romaguera, 2000).

There have been several recent rigorous evaluations of the program. Hsieh and Urquiola (2003) used data from the 1980s to assess whether the promise of the system to improve overall educational outcomes was realized. They found no evidence that choice improved overall education outcomes. Contreras (2003), using data from the 1998 college test exam and controlling for school choice, found that those who attended voucher schools have substantially higher standardized scores than those attending public schools. However, the author did not address the selectivity of private school admission. Furthermore, these results do not address the fundamental question addressed by Hsieh and Urquiola (2003) as to whether or not choice improved overall educational performance.

### Intensive Infusion of External Donor Resources

The district primary education program is the most intensive primary school education intervention ever undertaken by the government of India. Launched in 1994, it is entirely funded with donor dollars and covers 271 districts in 18 states, targeted to districts in which female literacy rates were low. The range of investments includes the building of new schools, the enhancement of existing facilities, the training of teachers, and the institution of village and school management committees. Using data from the 1991 census as well as two national surveys (1993-1994 and 1999-2000), Jalan and Glinskaya (2003) assessed the net impact of the program using propensity score matching in the absence of randomization. Despite the huge investment, they found evidence of only a very small net impact on primary school attendance and completion rates and progression to higher grades. Furthermore, most of the benefit accrued to boys and was largely concentrated in the state of Madhya Pradesh, where several other state-level interventions had been initiated. This was a very disappointing result given the amount of resources invested.

The field of evaluation of school policies and programs is in a very rich and fertile stage of development. Many lessons from the most recent and best studies reflective of this new line of inquiry have already emerged that have both methodological and substantive implications. These studies largely group in two areas: (1) large-scale studies of the enrollment effects of targeted antipoverty programs with an education component and (2) smaller scale, often local, studies of the effects of school input enhancements on enrollment, retention, and achievement. Recent research comparing the policy implications than can be derived from prospective randomized studies with research results based on retrospective designs that do not allow for the control of all unobserved community characteristics raise many questions. Natural experiments, such as the change of language of instruction in Morocco and the school building program in Indonesia, also provide a promising route for policy insight but results are less timely as sufficient time has to elapse after the change in policy to allow for an assessment of impact. The conclusions and implications of this research for policy and programs designed to enhance successful transitions are summarized below.

## CONCLUSIONS AND RECOMMENDATIONS

### Key Findings

*Young people in developing countries are spending more of their adolescence in school than previously.* The rate of growth in school attendance has been very rapid, in some cases far exceeding the pace of change that occurred in the historical transition to universal schooling in the West. Nonetheless, aspirations for schooling attainment expressed by both parents and young people far exceed actual attainment levels. This rapid pace of change is expected to continue.

*These trends, while typical, are not universal.* In sub-Saharan Africa, rates of growth in school attendance and attainment slowed in the 1990s, and in some countries boys' attendance rates have begun to decline. These trends are worrying because they are occurring in countries with rapidly growing school-age cohorts and poor economic prospects. Furthermore, in sub-Saharan Africa, the former Soviet Asia, and South America, enrollments in postsecondary school appear to have declined, in some cases dramatically, while returns to secondary and tertiary schooling are rising rapidly.

*Growth rates in all indicators of school participation and grade attainment have been greater for girls than for boys. As a result, gender gaps are narrowing rapidly and have been eliminated or reversed in some countries.* Girls now have a small educational advantage in South America in terms of grade attainment and primary school completion rates and may soon reach parity with boys in much of Africa. The gender gap in attainment remains largest in South Asia, the Middle East, and in some of the smaller countries of Western and Central Africa.

*There remain large differences, however, in school attendance rates according to wealth and residential status.* Indeed, the relative differences in schooling between the top and bottom wealth quintiles or between urban and rural areas are greater than relative differences by gender. However, there is an interaction between wealth and gender and urban-rural residence and gender such that girls are differentially disadvantaged among the poor and among rural residents, particularly in later adolescence.

*Trends in grade attainment tell only part of the story; limited data from standardized test scores provide cause for serious concern.* Limited comparative data on literacy and standardized test scores show a very loose connection between grades attained and the acquisition of basic literacy and learning skills. Standardized test results in reading, mathematics, and science administered to 15-year-old students in some of the more advantaged developing countries as well as most of the developed countries in 2000-2001 show students from all participating developing countries falling well below average scores reported by OECD countries. As of yet, there are no data on trends in test scores.

*Global trends in fertility, mortality, health, urbanization, and education, undoubtedly enhanced by policies and programs supporting these trends, have all contributed positively to current schooling trends in developing countries.* Furthermore, attendance rates have been rising not only in countries experiencing strong economic growth, but also in countries with disappointing economic performance. It is likely that rising aspirations for schooling are also driven by changing global norms about rights to and the value of schooling, as these norms have been expressed in recent United Nations agreements and conventions.

*Private rates of return to schooling at the secondary and tertiary level are consistently high and the gap between the returns at higher versus lower levels of schooling is widening.* These trends are expected to continue in countries in which liberalizing domestic policy changes are under way and in which economies are becoming more open to global economic opportunities. As a result, one expects a rapid rise of the proportion progressing on to secondary school and beyond.

*In most parts of the developing world, young people live within reasonable proximity of a primary school.* Given the rapid growth in school-age cohorts, this represents a huge achievement. However, access to secondary schooling and university and other tertiary institutions is much more limited, creating intense competition for scarce places.

*The most visible changes in the provision of education in those countries in which such data are available are the rise in private formal schooling and the increasing share of school costs (including the costs of the growing practice of supplementary tutoring) paid by parents.* The implications of these trends for the quality and quantity of educational opportunities are unclear. The rise in private schooling and the increasing share of costs borne by parents could be a response to an inadequate supply of school places relative to demand or to deteriorating quality in the public sector; it could also be a reflection of rising expectations in relation to existing school quality. Trends in other aspects of the school experience that have the potential to affect attitudes and behaviors are even more difficult to track.

*Recent studies have shown that conditional grants or targeted subsidies can be highly effective strategies for increasing school attendance and progression rates among disadvantaged groups.* Given the scarcity of resources, the challenge of these programs is twofold: (1) proper targeting, so that only those at the margin will benefit and not those who would have gone to school or stayed in school in any case and (2) proper monitoring so as to ensure that beneficiaries are indeed fulfilling the enrollment conditions of participation.

*Poor school quality is a major factor limiting enrollments and encouraging dropout.* There is growing evidence to suggest that the integration of disadvantaged groups into the school system will create additional challenges to teachers in more diverse classrooms, particularly if class sizes are allowed to rise. Successful transitions to adulthood depend on dramatic improvements in school quality. A recent experiment testing a low-cost approach to remedial education in the early grades in India shows promising results.

*A growing chorus of development experts are now calling for systemic school reform based on the knowledge and experience gained from a decade of active research and experimentation with a range of school innovations.* Most evaluation studies have measured the impact of one or no more than several discrete policy or program changes among a much wider array of factors affecting either the demand or supply of schooling. Both positive and negative results have been documented, but effects are often small in size and context specific. Systematic reforms are rarely evaluated, although they are increasingly being implemented.

## Policy Recommendations

*While the panel supports the UN Millennium Development Goals for education, it does not see the achievement of these goals—universal primary school completion rates and the elimination of gender disparities at all levels of schooling—as sufficient for the next generation of young people to acquire the skills necessary for successful transitions to adulthood.* The rapidity of global change and changing patterns of employment require that policy makers give equal attention to investments in school quality in order to ensure adequate learning outcomes at the primary level as well as to create a stronger base for further expansions in enrollment at the secondary level.

*The panel sees successful transitions to adulthood as requiring, at a minimum, that young people receive respectful and equitable treatment in the classroom regardless of gender, class, race, ethnicity, or religion and leave school literate in a commonly spoken language and endowed with skills for lifelong learning.* Success cannot be measured solely in terms of participation rates but must be evaluated also according to the nature of the educational process and the quality of educational outcomes.

*A first education policy priority is to address the needs of the poor.* School fees are not the only barrier to sustained school attendance; many poor families cannot afford to send their children to school even when schools are free and available. Antipoverty programs that provide incentives to parents to send their children to school through grants to low-income families that are conditional on children attending school have proved to be successful in increasing enrollment and reducing dropout in some settings. However, unless very carefully targeted, such programs can be prohibitively expensive.

*A second education policy priority is to achieve universal on-time enrollment.* Delayed age of entry is an area that has been underresearched, but it is increasingly recognized as a significant factor in low grade attainment and dropout prior to primary school completion.

*A third education policy priority is to enhance primary and secondary school quality so as to ensure better learning outcomes.* Poor school quality contributes to discouragement and dropout as well as poor learning outcomes. Basic school enhancements must be accompanied by better training and accountability for teachers. Few schools are currently well equipped to meet the educational needs of the disadvantaged who lack parental supports for learning.

*A fourth education policy priority is gender equality in the delivery of education services.* This includes the equal treatment of students in the classroom and the presentation of materials that do not portray stereotypical beliefs and attitudes about gender roles. While the gender gap in schooling participation and grade attainment is closing rapidly, traditional attitudes and beliefs persist and are reflected in differential treatment in the classroom and gender differences in standardized tests. Gender equality in the delivery of education services is essential if girls are to reach their full potential as adults.

*Policies outside the education sector are also critical to the achievement of education goals.* Population and health policies that reduce unwanted childbearing and improve children's health have proved to be important factors in past educational success. Furthermore, most strategies to alleviate poverty in the short run lie outside the education sector and often even outside the country. Poor countries will find it difficult to meet these challenges without assistance in the form of debt relief, human and financial resources, and fairer markets for exports from developing countries.

*While additional resources for schools will be needed, their marginal impact will be limited in many settings without systemwide reform that includes performance incentives and mechanisms for accountability.* Strategies to increase local autonomy and provide more choice have yielded disappointments in contexts in which standards are lacking, providers are poorly trained and unmotivated, and parents are ill informed.

*Evaluation research shows that important actors in the system, whether they are parents, students, teachers, or administrators, can be very responsive to well-designed incentives.* However, the results of most educational evaluation studies are very context dependent because of the complexity of school systems. It is hard to generalize, even from the very best studies.

*Policy evaluation should be adopted as an integral part of policy innovation.* A new generation of educational policy reforms is likely to emerge from current priority setting in the international debates around the Millennium Development Goals. These reforms will be multifaceted and context specific. If rigorous evaluation becomes a routine part of a phased implementation, lessons can be learned and adjustments made before implementation goes to scale that will increase the chances of success.

## Research Recommendations

Despite a rich tradition of research in the education field, many important questions remain unanswered, some of which merit particular priority given the panel's conclusions and policy recommendations. To be effective, research requires not only accurate data and skilled practitioners but also good dissemination. The current generation of research questions will challenge the most highly trained researchers but at the same time risk being lost to the policy formulation and design process if not well communicated once executed.

Important research questions remain unanswered:

• What explains the rapid rise in girls' schooling? Why are rates of girls' schooling rising more rapidly than those of boys?

• What role do various forms of nonformal education play in learning and how effective can they be as alternatives to formal schooling in the education of the young? How do they need to be adjusted to meet the needs of older adolescents?

• What is the relationship between formal schooling and self-efficacy and agency (especially for young women)?

• How important is language of instruction to the acquisition of literacy, progress to secondary school, and future productivity?

• What is the potential of formal schooling as a site for attitudinal change?

• How can teacher effectiveness in imparting basic literacy and numeracy be enhanced? In imparting learning for life skills?

• What are the implications of sensitivity training for teachers with respect to gender, race, ethnicity, class, and religious differences on student outcomes?

• What school investments will yield the greatest returns in terms of performance on internationally comparable tests, such as the Program for International Student Assessment (PISA)?

• How can adequate accountability be achieved in settings in which parents themselves are illiterate or barely literate or in which citizens have little voice?

• How have civil war, natural disasters, and other major disruptions affected educational progress in different settings?


**APPENDIX TABLES 3-1 THROUGH 3-8 FOLLOW.**

APPENDIX TABLE 3-1 Percentage Currently Attending School, DHS Countries

| Country | Survey Date | Male (age) | | | Female (age) | | |
|---|---|---|---|---|---|---|---|
| | | 10-14 | 15-19 | 20-24 | 10-14 | 15-19 | 20-24 |
| Armenia | 2000 | 97.5 | 60.5 | 12.8 | 99.1 | 65.7 | 14.0 |
| Bangladesh | 1999-2000 | 72.7 | 45.9 | 27.4 | 76.5 | 34.2 | 12.7 |
| Benin | 1996 | 59.0 | 35.3 | 12.9 | 31.6 | 16.1 | 3.5 |
| Bolivia | 1998 | 93.8 | 72.8 | 37.4 | 90.3 | 64.4 | 28.1 |
| Brazil | 1996 | 93.8 | 61.5 | 20.6 | 94.1 | 64.4 | 23.7 |
| Burkina Faso | 1998-1999 | 30.3 | 15.0 | 8.9 | 21.7 | 8.2 | 3.1 |
| Cameroon | 1998 | 81.7 | 52.9 | 21.6 | 76.5 | 35.7 | 12.4 |
| Central African Republic | 1994-1995 | 72.4 | 46.2 | 18.3 | 50.1 | 19.9 | 6.0 |
| Chad | 1996-1997 | 49.9 | 44.4 | 25.2 | 29.5 | 12.3 | 3.6 |
| Colombia | 2000 | 87.8 | 52.1 | 22.8 | 90.3 | 51.7 | 22.6 |
| Comoros | 1996 | 71.9 | 61.2 | 35.1 | 59.3 | 47.3 | 21.8 |
| Côte d'Ivoire | 1998-1999 | 65.8 | 31.7 | 14.8 | 46.3 | 16.9 | 7.7 |
| Dominican Republic | 1996 | 93.6 | 67.5 | 23.9 | 95.1 | 63.4 | 26.6 |
| Egypt | 2000 | 88.5 | 61.7 | 19.3 | 81.9 | 50.8 | 12.4 |
| Ethiopia | 1999 | 46.1 | 42.4 | 18.8 | 36.1 | 26.2 | 6.8 |
| Ghana | 1998-1999 | 82.0 | 49.6 | 15.1 | 79.8 | 37.6 | 4.0 |
| Guatemala | 1998-1999 | 82.9 | 38.5 | 17.6 | 74.2 | 34.5 | 12.4 |
| Guinea | 1999 | 38.2 | 33.7 | 17.8 | 25.8 | 13.5 | 5.4 |
| Haiti | 2000 | 65.7 | 55.1 | 24.2 | 64.5 | 37.6 | 11.0 |
| Indonesia | 1997 | 88.5 | 46.1 | 14.6 | 88.1 | 42.8 | 11.5 |
| Jordan | 1997 | 96.7 | 66.7 | 20.9 | 96.6 | 70.8 | 14.8 |
| Kazakhstan | 1999 | 98.8 | 78.5 | 17.3 | 99.1 | 76.8 | 18.9 |

| | | | | | | | |
|---|---|---|---|---|---|---|---|
| Kenya | 1998 | 93.2 | 61.6 | 11.8 | 90.7 | 50.1 | 5.7 |
| Kyrgyz Republic | 1997 | 97.3 | 51.1 | 9.3 | 97.6 | 53.7 | 11.2 |
| Madagascar | 1997 | 59.5 | 22.0 | 6.3 | 57.2 | 16.2 | 2.6 |
| Malawi | 2000 | 83.6 | 64.5 | 22.2 | 84.6 | 44.6 | 5.4 |
| Mali | 2001 | 46.5 | 30.2 | 15.8 | 32.4 | 16.8 | 6.2 |
| Morocco | 1992 | 60.1 | 34.4 | 14.1 | 41.4 | 23.5 | 7.5 |
| Mozambique | 1997 | 71.4 | 46.1 | 10.9 | 58.7 | 17.3 | 3.0 |
| Namibia | 1992 | 91.6 | 76.7 | 35.1 | 93.4 | 69.1 | 25.7 |
| Nepal | 2000-2001 | 83.5 | 51.0 | 13.6 | 65.1 | 30.6 | 5.5 |
| Nicaragua | 1997 | 77.2 | 46.0 | 20.9 | 81.7 | 47.7 | 19.6 |
| Niger | 1998 | 32.1 | 12.6 | 5.9 | 22.1 | 6.4 | 2.3 |
| Nigeria | 1999 | 74.5 | 61.5 | 33.4 | 70.1 | 49.3 | 19.0 |
| Pakistan | 1990-1991 | 69.3 | 44.5 | 15.1 | 45.0 | 21.2 | 4.6 |
| Peru | 2000 | 95.4 | 62.6 | 24.7 | 92.2 | 58.9 | 24.7 |
| Philippines | 1998 | 87.7 | 58.8 | 18.7 | 92.7 | 63.5 | 15.6 |
| Rwanda | 2000 | 41.7 | 12.4 | 4.0 | 42.4 | 8.9 | 0.9 |
| Senegal | 1992-1993 | 42.6 | 25.2 | 14.0 | 31.6 | 11.4 | 6.8 |
| South Africa | 1998-2000 | 96.6 | 84.8 | 35.2 | 97.5 | 79.4 | 34.4 |
| Togo | 1998 | 84.6 | 65.8 | 31.7 | 65.8 | 37.3 | 8.7 |
| Turkey | 1998 | 81.4 | 36.8 | 16.8 | 61.9 | 26.4 | 9.0 |
| Uganda | 2000-2001 | 91.3 | 66.1 | 19.8 | 90.1 | 45.6 | 4.9 |
| United Republic of Tanzania | 1999 | 69.3 | 30.1 | 3.6 | 69.0 | 26.3 | 0.7 |
| Uzbekistan | 1996 | 98.4 | 43.7 | 11.7 | 99.0 | 40.3 | 7.4 |
| Vietnam | 1997 | 90.4 | 43.8 | 6.7 | 85.6 | 33.7 | 5.1 |
| Zambia | 1996-1997 | 76.2 | 52.4 | 12.7 | 74.7 | 33.6 | 4.0 |
| Zimbabwe | 1999 | 93.1 | 58.1 | 8.9 | 91.8 | 42.7 | 4.1 |

APPENDIX TABLE 3-2 Percentage Currently Attending School, Wealthiest 20 of Households, DHS Countries

| Country | Survey Date | Male (age) | | | Female (age) | | |
| --- | --- | --- | --- | --- | --- | --- | --- |
| | | 10-14 | 15-19 | 20-24 | 10-14 | 15-19 | 20-24 |
| Armenia | 2000 | 99.5 | 80.6 | 20.9 | 98.7 | 78.5 | 27.7 |
| Bangladesh | 1999-2000 | 80.4 | 64.2 | 47.6 | 73.1 | 52.0 | 25.7 |
| Benin | 1996 | 85.6 | 58.2 | 28.0 | 53.5 | 29.9 | 12.7 |
| Bolivia | 1998 | 99.3 | 91.0 | 65.3 | 94.4 | 79.0 | 52.0 |
| Brazil | 1996 | 98.4 | 74.6 | 28.8 | 97.5 | 76.0 | 36.3 |
| Burkina Faso | 1998-1999 | 60.1 | 41.0 | 22.3 | 53.8 | 27.7 | 13.1 |
| Cameroon | 1998 | 95.0 | 69.0 | 39.8 | 92.2 | 59.8 | 34.6 |
| Central African Republic | 1994-1995 | 86.6 | 70.0 | 38.9 | 81.2 | 46.7 | 20.8 |
| Chad | 1996-1997 | 73.3 | 62.5 | 47.6 | 58.7 | 33.2 | 13.8 |
| Colombia | 2000 | 96.5 | 63.8 | 30.3 | 94.7 | 60.9 | 31.1 |
| Comoros | 1996 | 87.5 | 72.2 | 43.7 | 76.7 | 72.2 | 40.4 |
| Côte d'Ivoire | 1998-1999 | 88.7 | 62.3 | 41.2 | 62.5 | 37.8 | 21.3 |
| Dominican Republic | 1996 | 98.1 | 79.0 | 42.3 | 97.2 | 75.3 | 43.5 |
| Egypt | 2000 | 96.1 | 75.1 | 28.2 | 94.0 | 67.6 | 20.7 |
| Ethiopia | 1999 | 81.8 | 67.8 | 29.2 | 69.2 | 52.3 | 16.8 |
| Ghana | 1998-1999 | 95.7 | 60.9 | 28.3 | 89.6 | 43.9 | 12.0 |
| Guatemala | 1998-1999 | 98.3 | 77.0 | 45.3 | 92.8 | 67.7 | 34.0 |
| Guinea | 1999 | 61.3 | 54.9 | 31.8 | 51.0 | 30.3 | 16.8 |
| Haiti | 1994-1995 | 94.5 | 90.8 | 64.2 | 86.1 | 81.8 | 54.3 |
| Indonesia | 1997 | 96.5 | 67.6 | 31.6 | 95.8 | 62.2 | 24.3 |

| Country | Year | | | | | | |
|---|---|---|---|---|---|---|---|
| Jordan | 1997 | 98.3 | 82.3 | 37.7 | 99.1 | 84.4 | 30.5 |
| Kazakhstan | 1999 | 99.8 | 85.7 | 40.2 | 99.6 | 89.6 | 36.3 |
| Kenya | 1998 | 95.2 | 58.9 | 11.4 | 88.6 | 38.6 | 8.1 |
| Kyrgyz Republic | 1997 | 98.3 | 71.3 | 22.3 | 98.4 | 73.4 | 27.9 |
| Madagascar | 1997 | 89.6 | 52.6 | 22.2 | 86.1 | 45.7 | 10.3 |
| Malawi | 2000 | 90.4 | 75.4 | 28.9 | 88.4 | 61.0 | 10.7 |
| Mali | 2001 | 73.3 | 59.2 | 36.6 | 57.1 | 34.1 | 21.2 |
| Morocco | 1992 | 92.8 | 65.2 | 28.2 | 77.9 | 56.0 | 19.3 |
| Mozambique | 1997 | 80.5 | 59.9 | 22.8 | 78.5 | 34.9 | 11.5 |
| Namibia | 1992 | 98.4 | 80.3 | 23.3 | 94.5 | 65.5 | 22.4 |
| Nepal | 2001 | 91.3 | 64.4 | 22.5 | 85.7 | 53.0 | 15.1 |
| Nicaragua | 1997 | 91.9 | 76.5 | 48.4 | 96.2 | 72.7 | 44.0 |
| Niger | 1998 | 66.9 | 35.2 | 15.3 | 55.9 | 23.7 | 9.8 |
| Nigeria | 1999 | 93.0 | 77.9 | 48.6 | 92.9 | 71.1 | 36.2 |
| Pakistan | 1990-1991 | 85.8 | 65.2 | 27.2 | 84.9 | 51.0 | 13.6 |
| Peru | 2000 | 98.6 | 73.3 | 43.1 | 98.6 | 69.1 | 44.4 |
| Philippines | 1998 | 96.5 | 78.2 | 29.1 | 95.3 | 64.9 | 20.1 |
| Rwanda | 2000 | 40.7 | 15.1 | 11.2 | 42.2 | 15.0 | 3.0 |
| Senegal | 1992-1993 | 75.9 | 54.5 | 27.7 | 65.3 | 29.5 | 20.6 |
| South Africa | 1998-2000 | 98.5 | 77.5 | 23.8 | 99.2 | 77.6 | 26.0 |
| Togo | 1998 | 95.6 | 77.9 | 41.8 | 74.2 | 50.6 | 19.3 |
| Turkey | 1998 | 90.6 | 43.2 | 26.1 | 87.6 | 52.1 | 19.9 |
| Uganda | 2000-2001 | 94.3 | 68.8 | 30.9 | 90.5 | 54.4 | 11.1 |
| United Republic of Tanzania | 1999 | 85.7 | 29.8 | 5.9 | 91.6 | 30.1 | 1.7 |
| Uzbekistan | 1996 | 97.8 | 48.0 | 17.1 | 98.5 | 45.1 | 12.2 |
| Vietnam | 1997 | 97.4 | 65.9 | 16.5 | 96.4 | 66.0 | 14.0 |
| Zambia | 1996-1997 | 96.2 | 73.2 | 27.0 | 91.9 | 55.5 | 10.5 |
| Zimbabwe | 1999 | 99.2 | 65.9 | 16.6 | 95.9 | 46.6 | 8.0 |

APPENDIX TABLE 3-3 Index of Inequality in School Attendance by
Wealth, DHS Countries, High Versus Low Wealth

| Country | Survey Date | Boys | | | | | |
|---|---|---|---|---|---|---|---|
| | | Ages 10-14 | | | Ages 15-19 | | |
| | | SES High | SES Low | Inequality Index | SES High | SES Low | Inequality Index |
| Armenia | 2000 | 99.5 | 96.2 | 3.3 | 80.6 | 50.4 | 37.5 |
| Bangladesh | 1999-2000 | 80.4 | 64.6 | 19.6 | 64.2 | 27.8 | 56.8 |
| Benin | 1996 | 85.6 | 40.1 | 53.2 | 58.2 | 17.3 | 70.3 |
| Bolivia | 1998 | 99.3 | 89.3 | 10.0 | 91.0 | 47.7 | 47.5 |
| Brazil | 1996 | 98.4 | 89.5 | 9.0 | 74.6 | 50.0 | 33.0 |
| Burkina Faso | 1998-1999 | 60.1 | 19.6 | 67.4 | 41.0 | 3.8 | 90.8 |
| Cameroon | 1998 | 95.0 | 70.4 | 25.9 | 69.0 | 37.4 | 45.9 |
| Central African Republic | 1994-1995 | 86.6 | 56.4 | 34.9 | 70.0 | 29.1 | 58.5 |
| Chad | 1996-1997 | 73.3 | 36.6 | 50.1 | 62.5 | 31.6 | 49.4 |
| Colombia | 2000 | 96.5 | 79.5 | 17.6 | 63.8 | 38.1 | 40.3 |
| Comoros | 1996 | 87.5 | 60.3 | 31.1 | 72.2 | 50.4 | 30.1 |
| Côte d'Ivoire | 1998-1999 | 88.7 | 55.1 | 37.9 | 62.3 | 17.9 | 71.3 |
| Dominican Republic | 1996 | 98.1 | 89.4 | 8.9 | 79.0 | 58.0 | 26.6 |
| Egypt | 2000 | 96.1 | 83.6 | 13.0 | 75.1 | 51.0 | 32.1 |
| Ethiopia | 1999 | 81.8 | 34.1 | 58.3 | 67.8 | 30.7 | 54.7 |
| Ghana | 1998-1999 | 95.7 | 73.5 | 23.1 | 60.9 | 43.8 | 28.1 |
| Guatemala | 1998-1999 | 98.3 | 72.3 | 26.4 | 77.0 | 20.2 | 73.7 |
| Guinea | 1999 | 61.3 | 23.9 | 61.0 | 54.9 | 13.0 | 76.4 |
| Haiti | 1994-1995 | 94.5 | 63.9 | 32.4 | 90.8 | 59.3 | 34.7 |
| Indonesia | 1997 | 96.5 | 82.2 | 14.8 | 67.6 | 32.9 | 51.3 |
| Jordan | 1997 | 98.3 | 95.6 | 2.7 | 82.3 | 58.2 | 29.3 |
| Kazakhistan | 1999 | 99.8 | 97.8 | 2.0 | 85.7 | 74.4 | 13.2 |
| Kenya | 1998 | 95.2 | 92.4 | 2.9 | 58.9 | 61.8 | −4.9 |

| Girls | | | | | |
|---|---|---|---|---|---|
| Ages 10-14 | | | Ages 15-19 | | |
| SES High | SES Low | Inequality Index | SES High | SES Low | Inequality Index |
| 98.7 | 98.4 | 0.4 | 78.5 | 55.4 | 29.4 |
| 73.1 | 70.9 | 3.0 | 52.0 | 20.7 | 60.2 |
| 53.5 | 13.0 | 75.7 | 29.9 | 2.8 | 90.8 |
| 94.4 | 82.6 | 12.5 | 79.0 | 32.9 | 58.3 |
| 97.5 | 90.4 | 7.3 | 76.0 | 53.0 | 30.3 |
| 53.8 | 9.3 | 82.6 | 27.7 | 0.8 | 97.2 |
| 92.2 | 60.2 | 34.6 | 59.8 | 16.2 | 72.9 |
| | | | | | |
| 81.2 | 26.6 | 67.2 | 46.7 | 5.9 | 87.3 |
| 58.7 | 16.4 | 72.0 | 33.2 | 4.8 | 85.5 |
| 94.7 | 85.1 | 10.2 | 60.9 | 38.2 | 37.2 |
| 76.7 | 41.1 | 46.5 | 72.2 | 26.7 | 63.0 |
| 62.5 | 32.7 | 47.7 | 37.8 | 3.9 | 89.7 |
| | | | | | |
| 97.2 | 92.2 | 5.1 | 75.3 | 47.9 | 36.4 |
| 94.0 | 69.7 | 25.8 | 67.6 | 34.4 | 49.1 |
| 69.2 | 22.1 | 68.0 | 52.3 | 13.6 | 73.9 |
| 89.6 | 69.2 | 22.7 | 43.9 | 31.1 | 29.0 |
| 92.8 | 61.6 | 33.6 | 67.7 | 10.4 | 84.6 |
| 51.0 | 10.2 | 80.0 | 30.3 | 1.6 | 94.8 |
| 86.1 | 63.7 | 26.0 | 81.8 | 43.1 | 47.3 |
| 95.8 | 82.6 | 13.8 | 62.2 | 27.0 | 56.7 |
| 99.1 | 94.6 | 4.6 | 84.4 | 56.1 | 33.6 |
| 99.6 | 98.3 | 1.3 | 89.6 | 69.8 | 22.1 |
| 88.6 | 92.0 | −3.9 | 38.6 | 57.3 | −48.6 |

*Continued*

## APPENDIX TABLE 3-3 Continued

| | | Boys | | | | | |
|---|---|---|---|---|---|---|---|
| | | Ages 10-14 | | | Ages 15-19 | | |
| Country | Survey Date | SES High | SES Low | Inequality Index | SES High | SES Low | Inequality Index |
| Kyrgyz Republic | 1997 | 98.3 | 95.8 | 2.5 | 71.3 | 44.6 | 37.5 |
| Madagascar | 1997 | 89.6 | 48.6 | 45.8 | 52.6 | 9.7 | 81.5 |
| Malawi | 2000 | 90.4 | 80.0 | 11.4 | 75.4 | 60.0 | 20.5 |
| Mali | 2001 | 73.3 | 39.0 | 46.8 | 59.2 | 17.1 | 71.1 |
| Morocco | 1992 | 92.8 | 34.1 | 63.3 | 65.2 | 11.1 | 83.0 |
| Mozambique | 1997 | 80.5 | 64.4 | 20.0 | 59.9 | 40.6 | 32.3 |
| Namibia | 1992 | 98.4 | 89.9 | 8.7 | 80.3 | 81.2 | −1.2 |
| Nepal | 2001 | 91.3 | 76.5 | 16.3 | 64.4 | 40.4 | 37.3 |
| Nicaragua | 1997 | 91.9 | 63.3 | 31.1 | 76.5 | 20.9 | 72.6 |
| Niger | 1998 | 66.9 | 18.5 | 72.4 | 35.2 | 3.0 | 91.4 |
| Nigeria | 1999 | 93.0 | 51.4 | 44.7 | 77.9 | 40.2 | 48.4 |
| Pakistan | 1990-1991 | 85.8 | 55.7 | 35.1 | 65.2 | 29.3 | 55.1 |
| Peru | 2000 | 98.6 | 93.1 | 5.5 | 73.3 | 54.7 | 25.3 |
| Philippines | 1998 | 96.5 | 80.2 | 16.9 | 78.2 | 42.8 | 45.3 |
| Rwanda | 2000 | 40.7 | 45.4 | −11.7 | 15.1 | 11.2 | 26.2 |
| Senegal | 1992-1993 | 75.9 | 20.9 | 72.5 | 54.5 | 10.8 | 80.2 |
| South Africa | 1998-2000 | 98.5 | 94.6 | 4.0 | 77.5 | 86.1 | −11.0 |
| Togo | 1998 | 95.6 | 76.6 | 19.9 | 77.9 | 55.9 | 28.2 |
| Turkey | 1998 | 90.6 | 73.3 | 19.1 | 43.2 | 28.8 | 33.4 |
| Uganda | 2000-2001 | 94.3 | 89.2 | 5.3 | 68.8 | 63.6 | 7.6 |
| United Republic of Tanzania | 1999 | 85.7 | 54.8 | 36.0 | 29.8 | 34.7 | −16.3 |
| Uzbekistan | 1996 | 97.8 | 98.6 | −0.8 | 48.0 | 39.7 | 17.4 |
| Vietnam | 1997 | 97.4 | 85.3 | 12.5 | 65.9 | 31.9 | 51.6 |
| Zambia | 1996-1997 | 96.2 | 65.6 | 31.8 | 73.2 | 44.0 | 39.8 |
| Zimbabwe | 1999 | 99.2 | 92.0 | 7.3 | 65.9 | 57.5 | 12.8 |

| Girls | | | | | |
| --- | --- | --- | --- | --- | --- |
| Ages 10-14 | | | Ages 15-19 | | |
| SES High | SES Low | Inequality Index | SES High | SES Low | Inequality Index |
| 98.4 | 97.4 | 1.0 | 73.4 | 40.3 | 45.0 |
| 86.1 | 43.4 | 49.6 | 45.7 | 3.5 | 92.4 |
| 88.4 | 81.2 | 8.1 | 61.0 | 37.3 | 38.8 |
| 57.1 | 23.0 | 59.6 | 34.1 | 5.6 | 83.7 |
| 77.9 | 10.7 | 86.3 | 56.0 | 1.7 | 97.0 |
| 78.5 | 45.3 | 42.3 | 34.9 | 8.2 | 76.6 |
| 94.5 | 94.5 | 0.0 | 65.5 | 73.4 | −12.0 |
| 85.7 | 50.0 | 41.6 | 53.0 | 17.2 | 67.5 |
| 96.2 | 68.2 | 29.1 | 72.7 | 22.5 | 69.0 |
| 55.9 | 9.8 | 82.4 | 23.7 | 0.7 | 97.1 |
| 92.9 | 43.8 | 52.8 | 71.1 | 27.1 | 62.0 |
| 84.9 | 21.3 | 74.8 | 51.0 | 2.9 | 94.4 |
| 98.6 | 86.9 | 11.9 | 69.1 | 42.5 | 38.4 |
| 95.3 | 89.1 | 6.5 | 64.9 | 51.1 | 21.2 |
| 42.2 | 43.3 | −2.6 | 15.0 | 6.5 | 56.8 |
| 65.3 | 11.7 | 82.1 | 29.5 | 2.0 | 93.3 |
| 99.2 | 96.3 | 3.0 | 77.6 | 78.9 | −1.7 |
| 74.2 | 55.0 | 25.9 | 50.6 | 25.0 | 50.7 |
| 87.6 | 46.6 | 46.8 | 52.1 | 14.6 | 71.9 |
| 90.5 | 86.6 | 4.3 | 54.4 | 37.1 | 31.7 |
| | | | | | |
| 91.6 | 59.3 | 35.2 | 30.1 | 19.7 | 34.4 |
| 98.5 | 98.5 | 0.0 | 45.1 | 31.5 | 30.2 |
| 96.4 | 78.1 | 18.9 | 66.0 | 18.5 | 71.9 |
| 91.9 | 62.9 | 31.6 | 55.5 | 21.3 | 61.7 |
| 95.9 | 90.8 | 5.3 | 46.6 | 43.9 | 5.7 |

APPENDIX TABLE 3-4 Index of Inequality in School Attendance by Urban-Rural Residence, DHS Countries

| | | Boys | | | | | |
| | | Ages 10-14 | | | Ages 15-19 | | |
| Country | Survey Date | Urban | Rural | Inequality Index | Urban | Rural | Inequality Index |
|---|---|---|---|---|---|---|---|
| Armenia | 2000 | 98.4 | 96.4 | 2.0 | 65.9 | 53.5 | 18.9 |
| Bangladesh | 1999-2000 | 70.4 | 73.3 | −4.1 | 50.7 | 44.7 | 11.9 |
| Benin | 1996 | 74.2 | 50.4 | 32.1 | 44.2 | 28.9 | 34.7 |
| Bolivia | 1998 | 96.3 | 90.0 | 6.5 | 82.5 | 50.0 | 39.4 |
| Brazil | 1996 | 95.2 | 89.6 | 5.9 | 66.5 | 44.8 | 32.5 |
| Burkina Faso | 1998-1999 | 73.7 | 23.8 | 67.7 | 50.2 | 6.1 | 87.8 |
| Cameroon | 1998 | 89.5 | 78.2 | 12.6 | 63.2 | 45.1 | 28.7 |
| Central African Republic | 1994-1995 | 83.6 | 63.9 | 23.6 | 60.1 | 30.5 | 49.3 |
| Chad | 1996-1997 | 67.8 | 44.5 | 34.3 | 62.1 | 37.0 | 40.3 |
| Colombia | 2000 | 92.9 | 77.8 | 16.2 | 59.1 | 35.9 | 39.3 |
| Comoros | 1996 | 78.9 | 69.5 | 12.0 | 70.0 | 56.5 | 19.3 |
| Côte d'Ivoire | 1998-1999 | 75.0 | 61.9 | 17.5 | 48.4 | 20.0 | 58.7 |
| Dominican Republic | 1996 | 94.8 | 92.1 | 2.8 | 72.7 | 60.1 | 17.4 |
| Egypt | 2000 | 89.3 | 87.9 | 1.5 | 68.0 | 57.2 | 16.0 |
| Ethiopia | 1999 | 85.0 | 40.0 | 52.9 | 75.8 | 35.1 | 53.7 |
| Ghana | 1998-1999 | 91.1 | 78.1 | 14.2 | 55.1 | 46.8 | 15.0 |
| Guatemala | 1998-1999 | 91.7 | 78.0 | 15.0 | 58.1 | 25.4 | 56.3 |
| Guinea | 1999 | 61.4 | 28.6 | 53.5 | 57.1 | 18.5 | 67.6 |
| Haiti | 1994-1995 | 91.6 | 73.7 | 19.6 | 85.9 | 68.0 | 20.8 |
| Indonesia | 1997 | 93.9 | 86.6 | 7.8 | 62.2 | 38.5 | 38.0 |
| Jordan | 1997 | 96.4 | 98.1 | −1.8 | 66.8 | 66.0 | 1.2 |
| Kazakhstan | 1999 | 99.8 | 98.1 | 1.7 | 85.7 | 73.7 | 13.9 |
| Kenya | 1998 | 92.6 | 93.3 | −0.7 | 55.7 | 62.7 | −12.6 |

| Girls | | | | | |
| --- | --- | --- | --- | --- | --- |
| Ages 10-14 | | | Ages 15-19 | | |
| Urban | Rural | Inequality Index | Urban | Rural | Inequality Index |
| 99.5 | 98.6 | 1.0 | 73.4 | 54.9 | 25.2 |
| 70.4 | 77.9 | −10.6 | 39.4 | 32.9 | 16.7 |
| 45.3 | 21.5 | 52.5 | 24.8 | 8.2 | 67.0 |
| 95.6 | 81.7 | 14.6 | 75.0 | 32.4 | 56.9 |
| 95.7 | 88.5 | 7.5 | 68.0 | 49.0 | 27.9 |
| 62.5 | 14.0 | 77.6 | 34.1 | 1.4 | 95.8 |
| 87.4 | 70.7 | 19.0 | 53.3 | 25.1 | 52.9 |
| 69.8 | 33.0 | 52.7 | 33.3 | 7.6 | 77.2 |
| 52.3 | 22.9 | 56.3 | 31.8 | 6.4 | 79.9 |
| 93.9 | 81.9 | 12.8 | 57.0 | 35.0 | 38.5 |
| 67.3 | 56.3 | 16.3 | 63.4 | 40.5 | 36.2 |
| 53.7 | 41.8 | 22.1 | 28.3 | 7.3 | 74.4 |
| 96.2 | 93.6 | 2.7 | 69.2 | 52.6 | 24.0 |
| 92.0 | 75.2 | 18.3 | 65.1 | 40.1 | 38.5 |
| 78.4 | 28.4 | 63.8 | 58.8 | 17.1 | 70.9 |
| 86.2 | 76.9 | 10.8 | 41.1 | 35.6 | 13.5 |
| 81.0 | 70.0 | 13.6 | 46.4 | 25.9 | 44.1 |
| 48.3 | 14.2 | 70.6 | 26.9 | 4.6 | 83.0 |
| 83.4 | 75.2 | 9.9 | 71.9 | 58.6 | 18.5 |
| 93.1 | 86.3 | 7.3 | 60.1 | 33.5 | 44.2 |
| 96.9 | 95.1 | 1.8 | 72.1 | 65.1 | 9.7 |
| 99.6 | 98.7 | 0.9 | 80.3 | 73.9 | 8.0 |
| 86.5 | 91.4 | −5.6 | 29.6 | 55.6 | −88.3 |

*Continued*

## APPENDIX TABLE 3-4 Continued

| | | Boys | | | | | |
| | | Ages 10-14 | | | Ages 15-19 | | |
| Country | Survey Date | Urban | Rural | Inequality Index | Urban | Rural | Inequality Index |
|---|---|---|---|---|---|---|---|
| Kyrgyz Republic | 1997 | 98.5 | 96.9 | 1.6 | 60.7 | 47.8 | 21.3 |
| Madagascar | 1997 | 78.1 | 53.3 | 31.8 | 45.6 | 12.8 | 71.9 |
| Malawi | 2000 | 94.8 | 82.1 | 13.4 | 72.7 | 62.8 | 13.7 |
| Mali | 2001 | 71.8 | 37.6 | 47.6 | 58.2 | 16.5 | 71.7 |
| Morocco | 1992 | 84.6 | 42.9 | 49.3 | 53.6 | 16.3 | 69.6 |
| Mozambique | 1997 | 84.5 | 67.7 | 19.9 | 55.7 | 40.8 | 26.8 |
| Namibia | 1992 | 96.4 | 90.1 | 6.5 | 78.2 | 76.2 | 2.6 |
| Nepal | 2001 | 90.4 | 82.7 | 8.5 | 61.4 | 49.7 | 19.1 |
| Nicaragua | 1997 | 86.0 | 66.4 | 22.8 | 59.3 | 25.0 | 57.8 |
| Niger | 1998 | 65.7 | 23.0 | 64.9 | 37.3 | 3.9 | 89.5 |
| Nigeria | 1999 | 82.2 | 71.2 | 13.3 | 72.6 | 56.2 | 22.6 |
| Pakistan | 1990-1991 | 79.2 | 64.9 | 18.0 | 48.9 | 42.0 | 14.0 |
| Peru | 2000 | 97.0 | 93.3 | 3.8 | 66.7 | 55.4 | 16.9 |
| Philippines | 1998 | 92.4 | 83.9 | 9.2 | 65.6 | 51.4 | 21.6 |
| Rwanda | 2000 | 46.7 | 41.0 | 12.2 | 17.6 | 11.3 | 35.4 |
| Senegal | 1992-1993 | 69.5 | 27.0 | 61.2 | 41.3 | 13.7 | 66.9 |
| South Africa | 1998-2000 | 97.9 | 95.5 | 2.5 | 82.8 | 86.8 | −4.9 |
| Togo | 1998 | 94.2 | 80.9 | 14.1 | 75.3 | 61.0 | 19.0 |
| Turkey | 1998 | 86.7 | 73.4 | 15.4 | 41.5 | 27.9 | 32.9 |
| Uganda | 2000-2001 | 89.7 | 91.5 | −1.9 | 65.6 | 66.2 | −0.9 |
| United Republic of Tanzania | 1999 | 81.2 | 66.5 | 18.1 | 26.8 | 31.2 | −16.7 |
| Uzbekistan | 1996 | 97.5 | 98.9 | −1.5 | 42.1 | 44.5 | −5.9 |
| Vietnam | 1997 | 93.0 | 90.0 | 3.3 | 54.1 | 41.5 | 23.2 |
| Zambia | 1996-1997 | 87.0 | 69.7 | 19.9 | 60.8 | 46.1 | 24.2 |
| Zimbabwe | 1999 | 97.4 | 91.9 | 5.6 | 59.3 | 57.6 | 2.8 |

| Girls | | | | | |
|---|---|---|---|---|---|
| Ages 10-14 | | | Ages 15-19 | | |
| Urban | Rural | Inequality Index | Urban | Rural | Inequality Index |
| 99.0 | 97.1 | 1.8 | 67.7 | 47.7 | 29.5 |
| 76.5 | 51.1 | 33.2 | 37.5 | 8.0 | 78.7 |
| 86.5 | 84.3 | 2.5 | 57.5 | 42.0 | 27.0 |
| 54.0 | 24.0 | 55.6 | 33.2 | 5.4 | 83.8 |
| 73.4 | 19.1 | 74.0 | 46.6 | 4.8 | 89.7 |
| 75.6 | 53.3 | 29.5 | 33.3 | 11.1 | 66.6 |
| 95.8 | 92.6 | 3.4 | 61.8 | 72.2 | −16.9 |
| 81.4 | 63.2 | 22.4 | 54.8 | 27.7 | 49.5 |
| 89.9 | 69.9 | 22.2 | 60.3 | 26.2 | 56.6 |
| 55.9 | 11.5 | 79.4 | 25.3 | 0.8 | 96.9 |
| 82.6 | 64.3 | 22.2 | 59.9 | 45.0 | 24.8 |
| 68.4 | 33.1 | 51.7 | 41.1 | 10.0 | 75.7 |
| 95.8 | 87.3 | 8.9 | 65.9 | 43.3 | 34.3 |
| 93.9 | 91.6 | 2.4 | 65.0 | 61.4 | 5.5 |
| 46.6 | 41.8 | 10.3 | 16.7 | 6.8 | 59.1 |
| 54.8 | 16.9 | 69.2 | 22.5 | 2.3 | 89.7 |
| 98.4 | 96.8 | 1.6 | 79.4 | 79.4 | 0.0 |
| 74.5 | 61.5 | 17.5 | 45.0 | 31.2 | 30.6 |
| 72.6 | 47.1 | 35.1 | 34.4 | 13.9 | 59.5 |
| 87.5 | 90.5 | −3.4 | 48.7 | 44.9 | 7.8 |
| | | | | | |
| 76.6 | 67.1 | 12.4 | 27.6 | 25.9 | 6.0 |
| 99.4 | 98.8 | 0.6 | 44.3 | 38.1 | 14.2 |
| 94.0 | 84.3 | 10.3 | 59.8 | 28.4 | 52.5 |
| 86.2 | 67.1 | 22.2 | 43.5 | 24.6 | 43.6 |
| 92.3 | 91.6 | 0.8 | 41.7 | 43.3 | −3.9 |

APPENDIX TABLE 3-5 Percentage Ever Attended School, DHS Countries

| Country | Survey Date | Male (age) | | | Female (age) | | |
|---|---|---|---|---|---|---|---|
| | | 10-14 | 15-19 | 20-24 | 10-14 | 15-19 | 20-24 |
| Armenia | 2000 | 99.2 | 99.8 | 99.5 | 99.6 | 99.8 | 99.6 |
| Bangladesh | 1999-2000 | 87.5 | 79.4 | 61.8 | 89.1 | 68.4 | 51.3 |
| Benin | 1996 | 66.9 | 66.3 | 57.4 | 38.4 | 32.2 | 24.7 |
| Bolivia | 1998 | 99.3 | 99.0 | 98.7 | 98.8 | 96.7 | 92.6 |
| Brazil | 1996 | 97.9 | 94.4 | 92.6 | 98.7 | 96.9 | 93.3 |
| Burkina Faso | 1998-1999 | 40.6 | 36.0 | 22.7 | 27.2 | 16.8 | 9.3 |
| Cameroon | 1998 | 88.6 | 90.5 | 85.3 | 83.6 | 77.6 | 67.3 |
| Central African Republic | 1994-1995 | 82.9 | 86.1 | 80.7 | 62.8 | 56.1 | 48.7 |
| Chad | 1996-1997 | 54.5 | 61.0 | 45.1 | 35.1 | 27.2 | 16.7 |
| Colombia | 2000 | 98.0 | 97.5 | 96.1 | 99.2 | 98.0 | 96.3 |
| Comoros | 1996 | 77.1 | 78.1 | 61.9 | 63.6 | 63.8 | 35.0 |
| Cote d'Ivoire | 1998-1999 | 72.8 | 62.7 | 51.5 | 57.3 | 53.4 | 37.9 |
| Dominican Republic | 1996 | 96.2 | 91.9 | 89.8 | 97.6 | 93.8 | 91.7 |
| Egypt | 2000 | 95.6 | 92.4 | 83.4 | 86.7 | 78.1 | 61.2 |
| Ethiopia | 1999 | 49.9 | 53.5 | 50.2 | 40.0 | 30.3 | 20.6 |
| Ghana | 1998-1999 | 86.8 | 86.9 | 83.3 | 85.8 | 75.0 | 65.5 |
| Guatemala | 1998-1999 | 93.8 | 89.6 | 83.6 | 90.2 | 80.6 | 75.0 |
| Guinea | 1999 | 57.6 | 48.5 | 43.0 | 40.3 | 24.2 | 17.8 |
| Haiti | 2000 | 87.5 | 90.1 | 80.8 | 88.4 | 83.8 | 63.5 |
| India | 1998-2000 | 90.4 | 85.5 | 75.3 | 80.0 | 61.6 | 46.2 |
| Indonesia | 1997 | 98.7 | 97.9 | 95.4 | 98.8 | 97.1 | 88.3 |

| | | | | | | | |
|---|---|---|---|---|---|---|---|
| Jordan | 1997 | 99.4 | 97.6 | 94.7 | 99.2 | 98.5 | 94.2 |
| Kazakhstan | 1999 | 99.6 | 99.5 | 99.6 | 99.6 | 99.6 | 99.9 |
| Kenya | 1998 | 96.5 | 97.3 | 95.8 | 95.0 | 94.7 | 91.4 |
| Kyrgyz Republic | 1997 | 99.4 | 99.2 | 99.5 | 99.3 | 99.8 | 99.4 |
| Madagascar | 1997 | 77.6 | 81.6 | 82.0 | 77.7 | 81.4 | 78.7 |
| Malawi | 2000 | 92.6 | 90.6 | 83.4 | 93.2 | 81.2 | 65.5 |
| Mali | 2001 | 50.7 | 34.2 | 33.0 | 36.3 | 20.0 | 18.8 |
| Morocco | 1992 | 75.4 | 74.3 | 60.0 | 54.1 | 45.5 | 30.6 |
| Mozambique | 1997 | 84.5 | 81.6 | 83.0 | 70.8 | 58.7 | 64.6 |
| Namibia | 1992 | 95.1 | 88.4 | 78.4 | 96.2 | 92.7 | 82.0 |
| Nepal | 2001 | 89.6 | 83.8 | 66.4 | 71.8 | 44.4 | 24.6 |
| Nicaragua | 1997 | 88.8 | 85.2 | 85.0 | 91.3 | 87.8 | 85.2 |
| Niger | 1998 | 40.9 | 39.0 | 27.0 | 27.4 | 19.9 | 12.3 |
| Nigeria | 1999 | 82.7 | 83.0 | 76.3 | 79.2 | 69.6 | 57.9 |
| Pakistan | 1990-1991 | 76.2 | 65.9 | 54.3 | 51.3 | 36.1 | 24.1 |
| Peru | 2000 | 99.7 | 99.1 | 98.6 | 99.1 | 97.5 | 94.3 |
| Philippines | 1998 | 98.4 | 98.7 | 98.7 | 98.9 | 98.7 | 98.4 |
| Rwanda | 2000 | 87.7 | 83.2 | 70.1 | 87.9 | 81.9 | 65.1 |
| Senegal | 1992-1993 | 52.0 | 50.4 | 38.2 | 40.2 | 32.8 | 24.2 |
| South Africa | 1998-2000 | 97.9 | 97.6 | 95.3 | 98.8 | 98.0 | 92.4 |
| Togo | 1998 | 88.9 | 85.1 | 76.9 | 72.3 | 58.8 | 46.6 |
| Turkey | 1998 | 97.0 | 98.5 | 96.5 | 92.7 | 89.8 | 84.1 |
| Uganda | 2000-2001 | 96.4 | 92.5 | 90.7 | 95.4 | 84.0 | 73.9 |
| United Republic of Tanzania | 1999 | 75.3 | 88.7 | 90.7 | 74.3 | 82.9 | 78.5 |
| Uzbekistan | 1996 | 99.5 | 99.9 | 99.7 | 100.0 | 99.3 | 99.7 |
| Vietnam | 1997 | 97.2 | 94.5 | 97.2 | 96.9 | 94.4 | 96.7 |
| Zambia | 1996-1997 | 87.5 | 92.8 | 93.8 | 87.5 | 89.0 | 86.9 |
| Zimbabwe | 1999 | 98.5 | 98.5 | 97.3 | 98.6 | 98.1 | 94.0 |

APPENDIX TABLE 3-6 Percentage Completing Four or More Years of Schooling, DHS Countries

| Country | Survey Date | Male (age) | | | Female (age) | | |
|---|---|---|---|---|---|---|---|
| | | 15-19 | 25-29 | 35-39 | 15-19 | 25-29 | 35-39 |
| Armenia | 2000 | 99.2 | 99.4 | 99.3 | 100.0 | 99.8 | 99.4 |
| Bangladesh | 1999-2000 | 70.8 | 58.5 | 48.6 | 69.5 | 44.2 | 32.7 |
| Benin | 1996 | 45.9 | 44.9 | 36.8 | 25.5 | 21.6 | 10.5 |
| Bolivia | 1998 | 96.4 | 93.3 | 84.8 | 92.5 | 79.2 | 65.0 |
| Brazil | 1996 | 76.7 | 78.1 | 74.6 | 85.3 | 79.8 | 74.0 |
| Burkina Faso | 1998-1999 | 29.7 | 21.0 | 12.9 | 18.4 | 10.0 | 7.6 |
| Cameroon | 1998 | 77.9 | 82.2 | 72.6 | 72.2 | 65.4 | 54.1 |
| Central African Republic | 1994-1995 | 55.6 | 57.7 | 52.1 | 34.9 | 32.3 | 17.7 |
| Chad | 1996-1997 | 36.1 | 33.6 | 28.9 | 14.2 | 7.7 | 7.1 |
| Colombia | 2000 | 90.2 | 87.1 | 79.1 | 92.9 | 88.4 | 80.4 |
| Comoros | 1996 | 64.1 | 62.6 | 34.9 | 48.9 | 43.6 | 15.1 |
| Côte d'Ivoire | 1998-1999 | 57.1 | 59.0 | 50.5 | 40.9 | 43.5 | 27.3 |
| Dominican Republic | 1996 | 77.7 | 81.5 | 74.4 | 87.0 | 84.9 | 73.4 |
| Egypt | 2000 | 89.3 | 83.7 | 71.7 | 77.2 | 61.8 | 44.8 |
| Ethiopia | 1999 | 30.7 | 36.6 | 29.3 | 20.8 | 19.5 | 7.9 |
| Ghana | 1998-1999 | 85.0 | 83.7 | 77.0 | 79.1 | 62.4 | 60.1 |
| Guatemala | 1998-1999 | 67.3 | 62.9 | 53.0 | 62.9 | 49.5 | 41.9 |
| Guinea | 1999 | 48.9 | 35.3 | 31.1 | 25.1 | 15.1 | 12.1 |
| Haiti | 2000 | 62.2 | 66.8 | 49.2 | 65.1 | 50.2 | 28.6 |
| India | 1998-2000 | 81.5 | 75.1 | 65.4 | 64.9 | 47.0 | 38.4 |
| Indonesia | 1997 | 92.6 | 91.8 | 76.8 | 93.2 | 83.6 | 61.3 |

| | | | | | | | |
|---|---|---|---|---|---|---|---|
| Jordan | 1997 | 98.0 | 94.8 | 92.3 | 97.5 | 95.0 | 86.4 |
| Kazakhstan | 1999 | 98.9 | 99.1 | 99.8 | 99.5 | 99.8 | 99.7 |
| Kenya | 1998 | 90.6 | 93.0 | 90.9 | 90.6 | 88.5 | 72.3 |
| Kyrgyz Republic | 1997 | 99.0 | 99.4 | 99.8 | 99.3 | 99.4 | 98.8 |
| Madagascar | 1997 | 41.3 | 57.5 | 55.1 | 43.1 | 55.5 | 42.0 |
| Malawi | 2000 | 71.8 | 69.6 | 66.4 | 71.5 | 48.0 | 38.2 |
| Mali | 2001 | 35.3 | 25.0 | 25.3 | 23.0 | 14.0 | 14.9 |
| Morocco | 1992 | 69.0 | 56.5 | 50.3 | 44.5 | 32.3 | 22.2 |
| Mozambique | 1997 | 56.2 | 49.8 | 52.4 | 34.1 | 30.0 | 17.9 |
| Namibia | 1992 | 70.1 | 74.2 | 69.6 | 82.1 | 78.9 | 65.0 |
| Nepal | 2001 | 74.2 | 64.2 | 47.1 | 51.2 | 25.0 | 8.8 |
| Nicaragua | 1997 | 74.9 | 70.0 | 65.3 | 79.6 | 75.1 | 59.6 |
| Niger | 1998 | 35.7 | 26.8 | 15.8 | 18.1 | 15.0 | 7.2 |
| Nigeria | 1999 | 83.2 | 79.4 | 75.6 | 73.4 | 64.1 | 48.0 |
| Pakistan | 1990-1991 | 66.0 | 54.6 | 51.1 | 40.5 | 25.6 | 18.8 |
| Peru | 2000 | 96.1 | 95.8 | 93.2 | 95.0 | 90.3 | 82.7 |
| Philippines | 1998 | 93.5 | 92.5 | 91.0 | 97.0 | 95.5 | 92.8 |
| Rwanda | 2000 | 57.0 | 64.9 | 51.8 | 56.8 | 61.8 | 36.6 |
| Senegal | 1992-1993 | 45.6 | 38.4 | 35.0 | 34.0 | 20.7 | 18.4 |
| South Africa | 1998-2000 | 96.2 | 93.1 | 88.9 | 97.6 | 91.5 | 84.1 |
| Togo | 1998 | 68.8 | 63.9 | 61.0 | 47.5 | 32.9 | 26.8 |
| Turkey | 1998 | 97.1 | 96.8 | 94.6 | 90.6 | 84.3 | 72.9 |
| Uganda | 2000-2001 | 82.8 | 78.0 | 71.1 | 74.1 | 58.3 | 46.4 |
| United Republic of Tanzania | 1999 | 73.5 | 82.5 | 84.8 | 70.5 | 77.6 | 54.1 |
| Uzbekistan | 1996 | 99.1 | 99.6 | 99.8 | 99.2 | 99.5 | 99.4 |
| Vietnam | 1997 | 88.2 | 88.4 | 91.4 | 86.6 | 87.7 | 83.7 |
| Zambia | 1996-1997 | 80.6 | 87.4 | 90.1 | 78.4 | 74.8 | 71.1 |
| Zimbabwe | 1999 | 95.0 | 97.0 | 90.9 | 95.2 | 94.2 | 72.1 |

APPENDIX TABLE 3-7 Mean Grades Attained, DHS Countries

| Country | Age at Start | Number of Years in Primary | Survey Date | Male (age) | | | Female (age) | | |
|---|---|---|---|---|---|---|---|---|---|
| | | | | 20-24 | 30-34 | 40-44 | 20-24 | 30-34 | 40-44 |
| Armenia | 7 | 4 | 2000 | 10.7 | 11.8 | 11.7 | 11.6 | 12.0 | 11.6 |
| Bangladesh | 6 | 5 | 1999-2000 | 6.1 | 4.8 | 4.5 | 4.7 | 3.1 | 2.3 |
| Benin | 6 | 6 | 1996 | 3.8 | 4.2 | 2.8 | 1.6 | 1.6 | 0.9 |
| Bolivia | 6 | 8 | 1998 | 9.9 | 9.2 | 8.2 | 8.8 | 7.7 | 6.2 |
| Brazil | 7 | 8 | 1996 | 6.5 | 6.8 | 6.0 | 7.4 | 6.9 | 5.9 |
| Burkina Faso | 7 | 6 | 1998-1999 | 2.6 | 1.6 | 1.3 | 1.2 | 0.6 | 0.4 |
| Cameroon | 6 | 6 | 1998 | 7.5 | 7.7 | 6.1 | 6.3 | 4.8 | 3.5 |
| Central African Republic | 6 | 6 | 1994-1995 | 5.0 | 5.1 | 3.7 | 2.8 | 2.4 | 1.0 |
| Chad | 6 | 6 | 1996-1997 | 3.6 | 2.7 | 2.3 | 1.1 | 0.7 | 0.4 |
| Colombia | 6 | 5 | 2000 | 8.6 | 7.7 | 7.2 | 9.2 | 8.0 | 7.0 |
| Comoros | 7 | 6 | 1996 | 5.3 | 5.4 | 2.3 | 4.3 | 2.8 | 0.7 |
| Cote d'Ivoire | 6 | 6 | 1998-1999 | 5.0 | 4.5 | 3.9 | 3.7 | 2.6 | 2.4 |
| Dominican Republic | 6 | 8 | 1996 | 7.5 | 8.2 | 7.4 | 8.7 | 8.6 | 6.6 |
| Egypt | 6 | 5 | 2000 | 9.6 | 9.1 | 7.7 | 8.0 | 6.4 | 4.4 |
| Ethiopia | 7 | 6 | 1999 | 2.8 | 3.1 | 2.1 | 1.7 | 1.1 | 0.4 |
| Ghana | 6 | 6 | 1998-1999 | 8.6 | 8.5 | 8.6 | 6.5 | 5.7 | 5.3 |
| Guatemala | 7 | 6 | 1998-1999 | 6.3 | 5.4 | 4.4 | 5.4 | 4.5 | 3.1 |
| Guinea | 7 | 6 | 1999 | 3.8 | 3.7 | 3.9 | 1.7 | 1.4 | 1.2 |
| Haiti | 6 | 6 | 2000 | 6.8 | 6.4 | 3.6 | 5.5 | 4.1 | 2.2 |
| India | 6 | 5 | 1998-2000 | 7.9 | 6.8 | 6.1 | 5.3 | 3.6 | 3.1 |
| Indonesia | 7 | 6 | 1997 | 8.7 | 7.9 | 6.3 | 8.1 | 6.3 | 4.9 |
| Jordan | 6 | 10 | 1997 | 11.0 | 10.1 | 9.9 | 11.4 | 9.6 | 7.1 |
| Kazakhstan | 7 | 4 | 1999 | 10.7 | 10.9 | 11.0 | 11.1 | 11.3 | 11.0 |
| Kenya | 6 | 8 | 1998 | 8.5 | 8.6 | 7.8 | 8.1 | 7.3 | 4.8 |

| Kyrgyz Republic/ | | | | | | | | | |
|---|---|---|---|---|---|---|---|---|---|
| Kyrgyzstan | 7 | 4 | 1997 | 10.4 | 10.9 | 11.1 | 10.7 | 10.9 | 10.9 |
| Madagascar | 6 | 5 | 1997 | 3.8 | 5.0 | 4.2 | 3.8 | 4.3 | 3.3 |
| Malawi | 6 | 8 | 2000 | 6.4 | 5.7 | 5.4 | 4.8 | 3.4 | 2.5 |
| Mali | 7 | 6 | 2001 | 2.4 | 2.2 | 2.4 | 1.2 | 1.1 | 0.9 |
| Morocco | 7 | 6 | 1992 | 5.5 | 4.5 | 3.5 | 3.4 | 2.3 | 1.3 |
| Mozambique | 7 | 5 | 1997 | 3.9 | 4.1 | 3.2 | 2.3 | 2.2 | 0.9 |
| Namibia | 7 | 7 | 1992 | 6.1 | 6.1 | 5.1 | 6.9 | 5.9 | 4.0 |
| Nepal | 6 | 5 | 2001 | 6.2 | 4.8 | 3.3 | 3.1 | 1.4 | 0.6 |
| Nicaragua | 7 | 6 | 1997 | 6.3 | 6.5 | 5.6 | 6.7 | 6.6 | 4.8 |
| Niger | 7 | 6 | 1998 | 2.8 | 2.1 | 1.2 | 1.3 | 0.8 | 0.4 |
| Nigeria | 6 | 6 | 1999 | 8.2 | 7.8 | 6.5 | 6.6 | 5.2 | 3.0 |
| Pakistan | 5 | 5 | 1990-1991 | 5.4 | 4.5 | 3.8 | 2.8 | 1.8 | 1.2 |
| Peru | 6 | 6 | 2000 | 10.2 | 10.2 | 9.6 | 9.8 | 9.1 | 8.0 |
| Philippines | 7 | 6 | 1998 | 9.3 | 9.0 | 8.4 | 9.9 | 9.3 | 8.6 |
| Rwanda | 7 | 7 | 2000 | 4.8 | 4.9 | 3.6 | 4.6 | 4.0 | 2.4 |
| Senegal | 7 | 6 | 1992-1993 | 3.9 | 3.0 | 2.7 | 2.2 | 1.7 | 0.9 |
| South Africa | 6 | 7 | 1998-2000 | 9.8 | 9.2 | 7.9 | 10.1 | 8.5 | 7.2 |
| Togo | 6 | 6 | 1998 | 5.1 | 5.5 | 4.6 | 2.9 | 2.4 | 1.7 |
| Turkey | 6 | 5 | 1998 | 8.7 | 7.6 | 7.4 | 6.7 | 5.7 | 4.4 |
| Uganda | 6 | 7 | 2000-2001 | 6.5 | 6.4 | 6.1 | 5.1 | 4.0 | 3.5 |
| United Republic of | | | | | | | | | |
| Tanzania | 7 | 7 | 1999 | 6.0 | 6.3 | 5.0 | 5.6 | 5.3 | 2.8 |
| Uzbekistan | 6 | 4 | 1996 | 10.6 | 11.1 | 11.2 | 10.5 | 10.7 | 10.6 |
| Vietnam | 6 | 5 | 1997 | 7.4 | 8.0 | 8.1 | 7.4 | 7.5 | 6.9 |
| Zambia | 7 | 7 | 1996-1997 | 7.0 | 8.0 | 8.3 | 6.0 | 6.0 | 5.6 |
| Zimbabwe | 6 | 7 | 1999 | 9.5 | 10.0 | 7.3 | 9.0 | 8.2 | 5.0 |

SOURCE: UNESCO Statistical Yearbook (1999).

APPENDIX TABLE 3-8  Percentage Ever Attended School Beyond
Secondary School, DHS Countries

| Country | Survey Date | Male (age) | | Female (age) | |
|---|---|---|---|---|---|
| | | 25-29 | 35-39 | 25-29 | 35-39 |
| Armenia | 2000 | 23.0 | 20.8 | 21.2 | 16.4 |
| Bangladesh | 1999-2000 | 18.2 | 13.8 | 7.4 | 2.9 |
| Benin | 1996 | 3.3 | 4.9 | 0.2 | 0.7 |
| Bolivia | 1998 | 27.0 | 24.4 | 21.7 | 16.5 |
| Brazil | 1996 | 7.0 | 9.0 | 7.6 | 10.1 |
| Burkina Faso | 1998-1999 | 2.4 | 1.2 | 0.5 | 0.5 |
| Cameroon | 1998 | 7.7 | 7.1 | 2.9 | 1.2 |
| Central African Republic | 1994-1995 | 4.4 | 5.3 | 1.7 | 1.0 |
| Chad | 1996-1997 | 2.1 | 2.3 | 0.1 | 0.3 |
| Colombia | 2000 | 18.3 | 15.1 | 17.8 | 15.3 |
| Comoros | 1996 | 4.2 | 5.6 | 1.4 | 0.5 |
| Côte d'Ivoire | 1998-1999 | 7.6 | 5.7 | 3.8 | 1.2 |
| Dominican Republic | 1996 | 14.5 | 16.4 | 18.6 | 16.6 |
| Egypt | 2000 | 17.9 | 17.4 | 13.0 | 10.3 |
| Ethiopia | 1999 | 3.0 | 2.9 | 1.2 | 0.8 |
| Ghana | 1998-1999 | 6.7 | 8.2 | 2.2 | 3.1 |
| Guatemala | 1998-1999 | 8.8 | 5.2 | 4.1 | 4.4 |
| Guinea | 1999 | 5.9 | 6.6 | 2.3 | 3.0 |
| Haiti | 2000 | 5.9 | 2.7 | 3.2 | 1.0 |
| India | 1998-2000 | 25.2 | 18.3 | 12.5 | 7.7 |
| Indonesia | 1997 | 8.9 | 5.5 | 7.1 | 3.1 |
| Jordan | 1997 | 34.1 | 37.3 | 34.1 | 24.2 |
| Kazakhstan | 1999 | 14.1 | 17.8 | 18.5 | 22.7 |
| Kenya | 1998 | 6.6 | 6.2 | 3.4 | 1.7 |

## APPENDIX TABLE 3-8 Continued

| Country | Survey Date | Male (age) | | Female (age) | |
|---|---|---|---|---|---|
| | | 25-29 | 35-39 | 25-29 | 35-39 |
| Kyrgyz Republic | 1997 | 11.5 | 20.7 | 17.0 | 18.2 |
| Madagascar | 1997 | 2.6 | 6.2 | 1.8 | 2.1 |
| Malawi | 2000 | 0.7 | 1.1 | 0.3 | 0.1 |
| Mali | 2001 | 4.3 | 2.7 | 1.2 | 0.8 |
| Morocco | 1992 | 10.2 | 5.2 | 3.9 | 1.7 |
| Mozambique | 1997 | 0.2 | 0.3 | 0.0 | 0.1 |
| Namibia | 1992 | 4.3 | 6.7 | 3.2 | 2.9 |
| Nepal | 2001 | 12.4 | 7.9 | 2.6 | 0.8 |
| Nicaragua | 1997 | 8.1 | 13.1 | 9.5 | 8.6 |
| Niger | 1998 | 2.0 | 2.3 | 0.3 | 0.5 |
| Nigeria | 1999 | 16.4 | 19.3 | 8.9 | 9.9 |
| Pakistan | 1990-1991 | 6.4 | 5.2 | 2.2 | 1.6 |
| Peru | 2000 | 30.5 | 27.9 | 29.2 | 22.8 |
| Philippines | 1998 | 33.5 | 30.3 | 36.1 | 31.8 |
| Rwanda | 2000 | 1.3 | 2.1 | 0.7 | 0.2 |
| Senegal | 1992-1993 | 3.4 | 7.6 | 1.2 | 0.7 |
| South Africa | 1998-2000 | 11.1 | 10.5 | 11.2 | 8.5 |
| Togo | 1998 | 4.3 | 5.2 | 1.2 | 0.7 |
| Turkey | 1998 | 13.3 | 10.7 | 10.6 | 5.3 |
| Uganda | 2000-2001 | 8.3 | 9.5 | 5.0 | 4.6 |
| United Republic of Tanzania | 1999 | 0.1 | 0.5 | 0.0 | 0.1 |
| Uzbekistan | 1996 | 19.1 | 22.8 | 11.5 | 13.6 |
| Vietnam | 1997 | 1.3 | 2.2 | 1.3 | 3.1 |
| Zambia | 1996-1997 | 5.5 | 10.7 | 4.0 | 5.1 |
| Zimbabwe | 1999 | 7.1 | 10.4 | 4.5 | 3.9 |

# 4

# Health

## INTRODUCTION

The physical changes that signal the transition from childhood to adulthood are accompanied by changes in opportunities and risks that can profoundly affect health and well-being during adolescence and beyond. Habits acquired during these years can enhance or compromise future health, and choices made about health-related behavior have implications for the entire life course. The importance of health status for the transition to adulthood is clear; it is intimately linked with the probability of making successful transitions in other areas. Healthy individuals make better students, more productive workers, more attractive marriage partners, more active community members, and better parents and caregivers than those who experience poor health. At the societal level, a healthy population is a prerequisite for social and economic development.

After infancy, childhood is a period of relatively slow growth. Suddenly, in adolescence, growth accelerates, perhaps to twice the earlier rate for a year or two, then slows, and finally comes to a stop. Along with the growth spurt of adolescence comes the development of secondary sexual characteristics (Ellison, 2001). In the developing world these changes are occurring earlier in life; consistent evidence from various parts of the developing world shows that the average age at puberty has declined over the last several decades.

The physical growth and sexual maturation during adolescence are accompanied by social, psychological, and intellectual maturation during which individuals develop more abstract reasoning skills, consolidate their identity, become more independent and emotionally mature. The "cascade of hormonal, physical, psychological, and behavioral changes" (Cameron, 2003) that marks this stage of life inevitably has implications for health. Research over the last few decades has shown that these implications depend, to a great extent, on the social environment (Boyden, Ling, and Myers, 1998; Bronfenbrenner and Morris, 1998). In other words, the transition to healthy adulthood is dependent on the contexts in which it occurs—parents, other family members, peers, teachers, and other significant adults all play an important role, as do the communities in which young people live (Steinberg and Morris, 2001). The significance of context has become clearer in recent research that points to the many ways in which normative views of healthy childhood and adolescence vary across societies and over time (Boyden, Ling, and Myers, 1998; Caldwell et al., 1998).

Across all societies, however, physical and social gender differentiation are key features of this phase of the life cycle. Boys and girls are treated differently from birth onward, but puberty marks the beginning of a widening divide (Mensch, Bruce, and Greene, 1998). After puberty, young men and women's opportunities and experiences increasingly diverge in ways that are reflective of societal gender norms and expectations, and these differences can have direct implications for young men's and women's health as well as for health-related behaviors. While less true than in the past, young women often live more physically circumscribed lives than young men after puberty. Thus they may be relatively more "protected" than young men from some risks, such as dangerous work conditions, violence and military conflict, and road-related accidents, but they face other risks, such as early pregnancy and childbearing and gender-based violence, that are sex-specific. Furthermore, because of their greater "protection," young women may have fewer opportunities to develop the negotiating skills and the knowledge they need to protect and preserve their health and remain healthy as adults.

This chapter examines the transition to a safe and healthy adulthood in developing countries in the context of a range of rapid global transitions in health patterns and health services. For most individuals, adolescence has always been and remains a relatively healthy period of life. At any phase of the epidemiological transition in which societies experience a decline in the importance of infectious diseases and a rise in the importance of chronic conditions, death rates are at their lowest point from ages 10 to 14 and are often relatively low from ages 15 through 24 as well, particularly in countries in which obstetric care is adequate. The panel's view of a successful transition to adulthood, however, encompasses a view of health that is broader than survival and in which success includes the best possible mental and physical health and the knowledge and means to sustain health during adulthood.

The health environment in which young people are making the transition to adulthood has been dramatically altered by global epidemiological shifts as well as many other important changes, such as the rising percentage of young people attending school, changes in poverty rates, rapid urban growth, the growing presence of multinational corporations, the spread of global youth culture, technological change and medical advances, greater access to basic health care and family planning services, and growing acceptance of international norms relating to reproductive rights. Many of these changes have brought improvements in the health environment for young people; others have brought new challenges, and some have created greater risks for young people. The distribution of these changes and their implications for young people's health varies by context. For example, in many settings, schools provide an institutional setting through which various health interventions for young people can be delivered including health education, nutritional supplements, and some basic health care; thus an increase in the percentage of young people attending school has the potential to bring improved health benefits to a greater population of young people. On the other hand, in parts of sub-Saharan Africa where the HIV/AIDS pandemic is widespread, the risks to young people's health, most particularly young women, have increased substantially. By contrast, in other regions, such as the Middle East and parts of Asia and Latin America, the risks of HIV/AIDS remain relatively low. The aggressive marketing of tobacco products to young people and the increased global availability of illicit drugs present growing risks to young people, particularly in urban settings. Changing levels of violence due to war and civil disturbances are more context-specific but affect young men differentially. At the same time, some health hazards, such as those related to pregnancy and unsafe abortion, continue to disproportionately affect young women in developing countries.

While much of the literature on young people's health focuses on the problems and risks they face, there is a great deal of evidence that most young people get through the transition to adulthood without developing significant behavioral, social, or emotional difficulties (Barker, 2002; Steinberg and Morris, 2001). Furthermore, while young people may experiment with certain behaviors, such as substance abuse, this does not mean that they will continue to do so as adults. Indeed, during this period many develop positive habits that promote good health and well-being later in life (Call et al., 2002).

Puberty is a key health marker for young people, not just a period of "normative disturbance" as it is sometimes described (Steinberg and Morris, 2001). Puberty changes the way in which a young person is treated by others, increases the salience of sexuality, and introduces various reproductive health risks. It also marks the point at which individuals start to become significant actors in determining their own health. Choices about behaviors that affect health and about the use of health services and technologies are increasingly made by individual young people during this phase of life rather than by parents or other adults.[1] The design and implementation of health programs and services for young people can thus have a considerable effect on their health.

This chapter begins with a health profile of young people, which emphasizes the major health issues of this stage of life as well as evidence of recent change. The predominant causes of mortality and morbidity among developing country young people—maternal conditions, HIV/AIDS, and injuries—are given special attention. Because sexual and reproductive health constitute a key component of a healthy transition to adulthood and because they are so strongly linked with other transitions, a substantial section of the chapter is devoted to an examination of trends in various aspects of sexual and reproductive behavior. Data on each topic were carefully evaluated and were not presented unless the panel felt confident that they were the best available and provided a relatively broad comparative perspective.[2] The literature on the factors that influence such behavior is also critically reviewed. Levels and trends in risky behaviors with consequences for health, in particular smoking and illicit drug use, are also addressed. Evidence on the effectiveness of programs and policies that seek to improve health and support healthy development among young people is assessed. Finally, a series of policy and research recommendations are offered.

## HEALTH PROFILE OF YOUNG PEOPLE

Enormous changes are under way in the health context in which young people in developing countries make the transition to adulthood. While there have been some substantial negative trends—perhaps most strikingly the HIV/AIDS pandemic—positive changes in overall health have clearly outweighed the negative changes. Between 1970-1975 and 1995-2000, life expectancy at birth in the developing world increased 8.6 years, compared with an average of 5.8 years for the same period in high-income countries (United Nations Development Programme, 2001). Although there are considerable differences among regions in the developing world in the magnitude of these improvements, all regions have seen some positive change. Increases in life expectancy at birth have been strongly affected by substantial declines in infant and child mortality rates. However, life expectancy at

---

[1]It is worth noting, however, that young women in many settings have less control over decisions affecting their health than young men.

[2]A full discussion of the data is provided in Appendix A.

age 10 (i.e., among those who survive to age 10) in developing countries also rose by about one year during the 1990s and is projected to continue increasing (United Nations, 2003a).

Improvements in the health environment are important not only for survival chances, but also for overall well-being and productivity. For example, substantial decreases in malnutrition and related nutritional deficiencies have contributed to increasing survival rates in infancy and childhood as well as to improved cognitive and physical development of those entering adolescence (Smith and Haddad, 2000).[3] Advances in immunization coverage have reduced the incidence of a range of serious childhood illnesses. Many of the diseases that have contributed substantially to morbidity in developing countries, such as malaria, diarrheal diseases, and respiratory infections, have also been reduced. Furthermore, positive changes in the overall health environment affect productivity both directly and through decisions made in adolescence about investments in human capital. For example, the expected returns to investments in higher education are greater when the number of years of healthy working life increases.

Overall, aside from some countries with very high prevalence of HIV/AIDS, young people in developing countries are entering adolescence healthier than ever and with a better chance of surviving to old age. Moreover, the improving health context will enable young people to live better and more productive lives.

## Mortality and Morbidity

Having survived the relatively higher risk of death during childhood and not yet subject to the chronic and degenerative diseases of older adults, individuals are less likely to die between ages 10 and 25 than any other age range (Figure 4-1). In developing countries, the risk of dying between ages 10 and 25 is about 2.5 percent compared with roughly 9 percent between birth and age 10 (United Nations, 2003a). Although mortality rates among young people are low in developing countries, they are still above rates in developed countries by a factor of more than two between ages 10 and 25.

While data for the estimation of trends in mortality in developing countries are scarce and often of dubious quality and comparability (Hill, 2003), United Nations estimates indicate that death rates in the 2000-2005 period were slightly lower than in 1990-1995 for ages 10-25 (Figure 4-1). However, at ages 25 to 35 mortality has increased, a change that is particu-

---

[3]However, increasing consumption of foods containing fat, cholesterol, and sugar and declines in physical activity are starting to contribute to increasing levels of overweight and obesity in some countries (see the section on other risk behaviors later in the chapter).

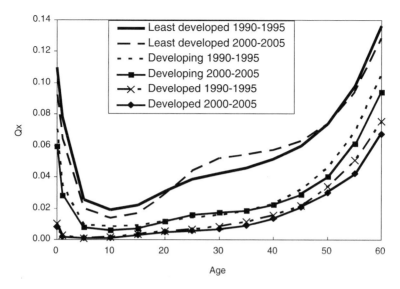

FIGURE 4-1 Probability of dying by age, according to type of country, 1990-1995 and 2000-2005.
SOURCE: United Nations (2001).

larly evident when the 48 least developed countries are examined separately; this is due primarily to the effect of the HIV/AIDS pandemic. The United Nations projects that the improvements over the 1990s among 10-25-year-olds will continue over the coming decade with mortality rates in developing countries moving downward at about the same pace although staying above the rates for developed regions. The AIDS pandemic, however, increases the usual level of uncertainty of these projections.

For developing countries as a whole, the risk of death between ages 10 and 25 is similar for both sexes, with a slightly lower risk for females (Table 4-1). This contrasts with the more developed countries where, while overall mortality risk is much lower, females have a strong survival advantage. In these regions, the female probability of dying between ages 10 and 25 is less than half that for males. This difference in the male-female ratio is due to relatively high levels of maternal and HIV-related mortality among young women in developing countries.

Reliable data on causes of death are rare for developing countries and, internationally comparable data are virtually unavailable for the specific age group of primary interest here (10-24). Nevertheless, the World Health Organization's (WHO) Global Burden of Disease project provides estimates based on existing data and various modeling techniques that illus-

TABLE 4-1 Probability of Dying Between Age 10 and Age 25 by Country Group, Years, and Sex

| Region | 1990-1995 | | 2000-2005 | |
|---|---|---|---|---|
| | Males | Females | Males | Females |
| WORLD | 0.028 | 0.024 | 0.025 | 0.021 |
| Developed regions | 0.014 | 0.005 | 0.012 | 0.005 |
| Developing regions | 0.031 | 0.028 | 0.027 | 0.024 |
| Least developed countries | 0.074 | 0.070 | 0.064 | 0.059 |
| Sub-Saharan Africa | 0.079 | 0.070 | 0.075 | 0.068 |

SOURCE: Estimated from United Nations (2003a).

trate broadly the major causes of mortality in early adulthood (ages 15-29).[4] The World Health Organization divides countries by region and level of mortality into groupings that are not exactly comparable to those used above, but countries classified as "low mortality" are roughly equivalent to the developed world, while the "medium" and "high" categories divide the developing countries by level of overall mortality (Figure 4-2).

Table 4-2 demonstrates the extent to which HIV/AIDS has come to dominate the mortality profile of young people in sub-Saharan Africa. By extension, because of the heavy weight of deaths in Africa at these ages, it also dominates the distribution of deaths in this age group for high-mortality countries as a group[5] as well as for the world as a whole (bottom panel of Figure 4-2). As many as 58 percent of deaths among 15-29-year-olds in sub-Saharan Africa can be attributed to HIV for young women and 43 percent for young men. By contrast, slightly over 10 percent of deaths among young people are due to HIV in Southeast and Southwest Asia. In North Africa, the Middle East, Latin America, and East Asia, HIV is among the least important or the least important cause of death.

Among females ages 15-29 in high-mortality countries, almost 40 per-

---

[4]WHO estimates of mortality by cause cover 191 countries, using vital registration data whenever possible. For 63 developing countries with no such data, estimates are derived from projected trends in child mortality using Brass techniques. For an additional 54 countries, vital registration data are incomplete or based on sample systems, so estimates must be adjusted. These limitations apply to data for all African countries, most countries in Asia and the Middle East, and several countries in Latin America (Murray et al., 2001). Given these procedures, as well as such additional problems as age misreporting, the data must be treated with considerable caution. They may be particularly questionable for Africa, where WHO relies perforce on old data and models devised for other regions (INDEPTH Network, 2002; United Nations, 1999a).

[5]A group of countries that include India, but not China.

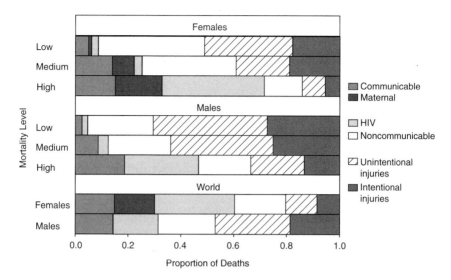

FIGURE 4-2 Percentage distribution of deaths at ages 15-29 by cause for the world as a whole, according to sex and mortality.
NOTES: Low = all developed countries (exclusively); medium = mixture of developed and developing countries; high = all developing countries.
SOURCE: World Health Organization (2001c).

cent of deaths are the result of HIV/AIDS (Figure 4-2). Close to 20 percent are due to maternal conditions, a category that includes pregnancy and delivery complications and the complications of abortion. In medium- and low-mortality countries, where the mortality rate is much lower, deaths due to these causes comprise a much smaller percentage of overall female mortality, while noncommunicable diseases (mostly cardiovascular disease and cancer) and unintentional injuries (mostly road traffic accidents) are much more important.

For young adult males in high-mortality countries, almost half of the deaths are the result of communicable diseases, the most important of which is HIV/AIDS. About one-third of deaths are attributable to either unintentional or intentional injuries. The deaths due to unintentional injuries are most commonly road traffic accidents. The intentional injury category includes violence, war, and suicide. The two injury categories predominate among male deaths in the medium- and low-mortality countries.

Estimates are also available of a measure that summarizes the loss of healthy life due to both death and ill health. This measure is called disability-adjusted life years (DALYs), and estimates are available for the

TABLE 4-2 Percentage Distribution of Deaths at Ages 15-29 by Cause, According to Sex and Region

| Region | Sex | Cause of Death | |
| --- | --- | --- | --- |
| | | Communicable Diseases | Maternal Mortality |
| WORLD | Females | 14.6 | 15.4 |
| | Males | 14.1 | 0.0 |
| Sub-Saharan Africa | Females | 12.0 | 16.6 |
| | Males | 19.8 | 0.0 |
| Southeast/Southwest Asia | Females | 20.3 | 16.7 |
| | Males | 15.6 | 0.0 |
| North Africa and Middle East | Females | 16.2 | 25.4 |
| | Males | 20.2 | 0.0 |
| Latin America | Females | 14.0 | 16.4 |
| | Males | 8.7 | 0.0 |
| East Asia | Females | 11.3 | 6.1 |
| | Males | 7.5 | 0.0 |

SOURCE: World Health Organization (2001a).

age group 15-29, for two categories of developing countries, and for each of the major categories of diseases and conditions. These data support the findings presented above based on mortality alone and in addition reveal an additional important cause of ill health among young people: neuropsychiatric or mental health illnesses and conditions, which account for about 20 percent of all DALYs lost in high-mortality developing countries and almost 40 percent of all DALYs in low-mortality developing countries (World Health Organization, 2002, 2003). In high-mortality developing countries, HIV/AIDS represents 17 percent of DALYs lost and in low-mortality developing countries 2 percent of DALYs lost. While HIV/AIDS is of considerable concern in the higher mortality developing countries, other causes of death and disability surpass it for all young people in developing countries as a whole.

Depression, anxiety disorders, and other mood disorders are among the most common mental health problems among young people with diagnoses typically peaking during the 20s (Schulenberg and Zarrett, forthcoming; World Health Organization, 2003). A number of researchers would suggest that in fact young women are more likely to suffer from depression than

| HIV | Noncommunicable Diseases | Unintentional Injuries | Intentional Injuries |
|---|---|---|---|
| 30.3 | 19.4 | 11.6 | 8.8 |
| 17.3 | 21.7 | 28.2 | 18.6 |
| 57.8 | 6.9 | 2.6 | 4.1 |
| 43.1 | 12.7 | 10.7 | 13.8 |
| 11.8 | 25.4 | 18.3 | 7.5 |
| 13.2 | 25.9 | 32.6 | 12.7 |
| 7.2 | 29.5 | 12.0 | 9.7 |
| 5.0 | 28.7 | 30.8 | 15.3 |
| 7.1 | 35.2 | 14.7 | 12.6 |
| 6.0 | 16.8 | 27.0 | 41.5 |
| 1.8 | 33.7 | 22.4 | 24.6 |
| 3.0 | 31.0 | 41.6 | 16.8 |

young men (Gureje, 1991; Lewinsohn et al., 1993; Sorenson, Rutter, and Aneshensel, 1991). Mental health problems are important not only because of the suffering they cause, but also because they are known to be linked to other health outcomes and behaviors. For example, a study in New Zealand has documented links among 21-year-olds between neuropsychiatric disorders and risky sexual behavior, as well as sexually transmitted disease (Ramrakha et al., 2000). How such findings apply to young people in developing countries is not yet known due to lack of research. The impact of war on the mental health of young people in affected countries and the effect of HIV/AIDS stigma have both received increased attention in recent years (e.g., Booth, 2002; Joint United Nations Programme on HIV/AIDS [UNAIDS], 2002; UNICEF, 2005).

Nevertheless, when young people in developing countries are asked about their lives, they appear generally content. Two questions on this subject were part of the World Values Survey (2003), which covered 21 developing countries between 1990 and 1996 (including such major countries as Brazil, China, India, and Nigeria). Males and females ages 18-24 rated their level of unhappiness at 1.9 on a scale from 1 to 4, for which a score of 4 represents "quite unhappy" and a score of 2 represents "quite happy." This was not as positive a rating as that of their counterparts in 21 countries covering Australia, Canada, Japan, the United States, and Western Europe, but clearly more positive than ratings in 24 Eastern European countries. In a recent study of nine Caribbean countries, 83 percent of in-school young people attending school reported being generally happy and 88 percent were satisfied with their appearance (Halcón et al., 2003).

Young people also tend to assess the status of their own health positively. In the World Values Survey, young people ages 18-24 rated their own health as "good" (a mean score of 2.0 on a scale that goes up to 5 for very poor health). This rating is more positive than that of any older age group (Figure 4-3). It is not as high as ratings by young people in major industrial countries, but somewhat better than ratings by young people in Eastern Europe.

A series of opinion polls conducted in 2000-2001 corroborate this generally positive outlook. On average across 17 countries in East Asia and the Pacific, 83 percent of 14-17-year-olds thought that their lives would be

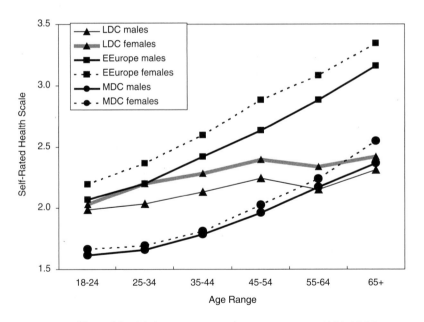

FIGURE 4-3 Self-rated health by age, sex, and country group, 1990-1996.
NOTES: 1 = very good health, 5 = very poor health. LDC = developing countries and MDC = developed countries, which in this figure exclude Eastern Europe.
SOURCE: World Values Survey (2003).

better or much better than their parents' lives (UNICEF, 2001a). Similarly, approximately three-quarters of 14-18-year-olds in 20 countries of Latin America and the Caribbean believed that they would have better lives than their parents (UNICEF, 2000).

With HIV/AIDS now the dominant cause of death among young people in sub-Saharan Africa and with other newly emerging infectious diseases, the concept of one common epidemiological transition, in which all societies evolve toward declining importance of infectious diseases and increasing importance of chronic conditions, may reflect too simple a view of long-term trends. Extensions of transition stages to accommodate further mortality declines, as well as critical exceptions to transition, notably in Africa, but also in Eastern Europe, have increasingly been noted (Caselli, Meslé, and Vallin, 2002). The health of young people in developing countries still contrasts strongly with the health of young people in developed countries, and even among developed countries, enough contrasts exist, for example, between Western and Eastern Europe, to illustrate that homogenization is far from being achieved.

## HIV/AIDS and Other Sexually Transmitted Infections

Globally, almost 12 million people ages 15-24 were estimated to be living with HIV/AIDS in 2002. About three-quarters of these live in sub-Saharan Africa. The young age structure of countries hardest hit by the pandemic means that about half of all new infections are now occurring among this age group (Summers, Kates, and Murphy, 2002; Joint United Nations Programme on HIV/AIDS [UNAIDS], 2002). Since the vast majority of HIV infections are sexually transmitted, the vulnerability of young people is strongly influenced by their sexual behavior. Thus, early age at sexual initiation, early marriage, risky sexual practices, and commercial sex work are all contributing factors. In places where HIV is linked primarily to injecting drug use, young people, who tend to be the main users, are most affected. The injection of drugs among young people has apparently increased in some countries in recent years, most dramatically among young men in Eastern Europe and Central Asia (UNICEF, 2002; United Nations, 2000b).

Table 4-3 shows estimates by the Joint United Nations Programme on HIV/AIDS (UNAIDS) of the proportions of young people infected at the end of 2001. On average, prevalence is extremely high in countries of Eastern and Southern Africa. HIV prevalence in 2001 averaged 14 percent among females ages 15-24, 6 percent among males, and 12 percent among all adults ages 15-49. Prevalence is also very high in Western and Middle Africa. In a few countries in this region, such as the Central African Republic and Cameroon, levels resemble those in Eastern and Southern Africa.

TABLE 4-3 HIV Prevalence at Ages 15-24 and 15-49, by World Region

| Region | Males 15-24 2001 | Females 15-24 2001 | Adults 15-49 1997 | 1999 | 2001 |
|---|---|---|---|---|---|
| WORLD | 0.8 | 1.4 | 1.0 | 1.1 | 1.2 |
| Eastern and Southern Africa | 5.9 | 13.7 | 11.1 | 13.0 | 12.3 |
| Western/Middle Africa | 2.9 | 6.0 | 4.2 | 4.9 | 5.4 |
| North Africa/Middle East | 0.1 | 0.3 | 0.1 | 0.1 | 0.3 |
| Caribbean | 1.9 | 2.5 | 1.8 | 2.1 | 2.3 |
| Latin America | 0.5 | 0.4 | 0.5 | 0.5 | 0.5 |
| South/Southeast Asia | 0.3 | 0.5 | 0.6 | 0.5 | 0.6 |
| East Asia/Pacific | 0.2 | 0.1 | 0.1 | 0.1 | 0.1 |
| Australia/New Zealand | <0.1 | <0.1 | 0.1 | 0.1 | 0.1 |
| Eastern Europe/Central | 1.0 | 0.3 | 0.1 | 0.2 | 0.5 |
| Asia | n.a. | n.a. | n.a. | n.a. | n.a. |
| Western Europe | 0.2 | 0.1 | 0.2 | 0.2 | 0.3 |
| North America | 0.5 | 0.2 | 0.6 | 0.6 | 0.6 |

NOTES: n.a. = not available. Midpoints are taken where only low and high estimates are provided. Estimates are for the end of the respective years. Country-level data are weighted by the population ages 15-24.
SOURCE: Joint United Nations Programme on HIV/AIDS [UNAIDS] (1998, 2000b, 2002).

Prevalence drops sharply as one moves farther north on the African continent; prevalence in North Africa and the Middle East is a fraction of that in sub-Saharan Africa. However, data are particularly sparse for countries in this region.

The Caribbean is notable for its very high prevalence of HIV. Rates in Haiti, for example, average 5 percent for females ages 15-24 and 4 percent for males. The regional average is 2.5 percent for females and 1.9 percent for males. Rates in the remaining developing regions are lower and in line with or slightly higher than prevalence rates in developed countries, but the absolute numbers of young people infected are large. Excluding sub-Saharan Africa, two-thirds of all remaining infected females ages 15-24 and one-third of all remaining infected males of that age reside in South and South-eastern Asia (Kiragu, 2001).

Most developing regions show considerably higher HIV prevalence among females ages 15-24 than among males. This is especially true in Africa, where prevalence rates among females are more than double those of males. Community studies confirm this pattern for sub-Saharan Africa (e.g., Glynn et al., 2001). Higher infection rates among females also hold, though to a lesser extent, for South and South-eastern Asia. In Latin America and the East Asia and Pacific region, higher prevalence rates appear among males, as they also do in developed regions. The ratio of female to male prevalence generally rose in 2000-2001 worldwide (the major exception being Eastern Europe and Central Asia).

Women, particularly girls and young women, face a higher risk of infection with HIV for physiological, social, and cultural reasons. The risk of infection during unprotected sex is two to four times higher for women than for men (UNFPA, 2003). There are several reasons for this disparity; the viral load is generally higher in semen than in vaginal secretions; in vaginal intercourse a larger surface area is exposed to sexual secretions for a woman than for a man; and the vagina and cervix of adolescent women are less mature, with a thinner cell structure that allows the virus to pass more easily (Berman and Hein, 1999; Watstein and Laurich, 1991).

Variation in the female-male ratio across countries among those infected is also related to differences in patterns of heterosexual relations, such as differences in the number of partners, age differences between partners, and the use of commercial sex workers, as well as to variations in the importance of other modes of HIV transmission. In sub-Saharan Africa, for example, where most infections are transmitted by heterosexual relations, young women generally face higher risks because they tend to have sex with and marry older men, who are more likely to be infected than younger men. Some of these relationships are based on economic gain, that is, they involve the exchange of gifts or money for sex. There is now a great deal of research showing that the power differentials inherent in such relationships make it difficult for young women to negotiate the use of condoms (Blanc, 2001; Luke, 2003; Weiss, Whelan, and Gupta, 1996). Furthermore, in high HIV areas, early marriage does not protect young women from risk. While marriage reduces the number of sexual partners, it increases frequency of sex, decreases condom use, and virtually eliminates a girl's ability to abstain from sex, except possibly during the postpartum period (Clark, 2004).

Sex between men accounts for at least 5-10 percent of HIV cases at all ages worldwide, and it is a predominant risk factor in some developing countries, including Brazil, Costa Rica, and Mexico (Summers, Kates, and Murphy, 2002). Young people comprise a large proportion of this population (Joint United Nations Programme on HIV/AIDS [UNAIDS], 1998, 2000a). Injecting drugs, again a particular problem among young men, accounted for over half of new cases in 1998-1999 in China, Malaysia, Russia, and Vietnam (Joint United Nations Programme on HIV/AIDS [UNAIDS], 2000b). This is a doubly disturbing trend because, in addition to the risks of transmission through injections, the use of drugs is also associated with an increased likelihood of engaging in risky sexual behavior (Summers, Kates, and Murphy, 2002).

The presence of certain other sexually transmitted infections greatly enhances the probability that HIV infection will be passed between sexual partners (Cohen, 1998). Data on the prevalence of other STIs among young people are scarce, and trends are virtually impossible to discern. Existing studies, however, give the impression that a substantial minority of young people may contract STIs. For example, studies in eight countries of various populations ranging in age from 12 to 24 show that between 3 and 12 percent of males and 1 to 14 percent of females had ever experienced an STI (Brown et al., 2001). Furthermore, WHO estimates that, globally, one in three new infections occur in people under the age of 25 (World Health Organization, 1999a).

Trends in the proportion of young people with HIV/AIDS are not available for most countries.[6] For some countries in sub-Saharan Africa (plus Haiti), however, there are now sufficient surveillance data gathered from young women attending antenatal care to begin to see some positive changes taking place. Of the 18 countries for which there are adequate data, there is evidence of stability in HIV prevalence in seven countries and of falling prevalence in eight countries (Joint United Nations Programme on HIV/AIDS [UNAIDS], 2004; personal communication, 2004). The current estimates of HIV prevalence among pregnant women ages 15-24 in these countries ranges from around 3 percent in Haiti to 33 percent in Botswana. In three countries—Lesotho, Mozambique, and Swaziland—the available evidence suggests that prevalence continues to rise.

Future trends in HIV/AIDS among young people depend on a range of factors, but basic knowledge about the disease and ways to prevent it are among the most crucial (see Box 4-1 for further discussion of the future impact of HIV/AIDS on today's young people). The proportion of females ages 15-24 who are unaware that a healthy-looking person can be infected with HIV/AIDS averages 46 percent in 73 developing countries with appropriate surveys, mostly surveys taken as recently as 2000. The level of misinformation is higher than average in sub-Saharan Africa (51 percent across 39 separate surveys), and still higher in Central Asia and the Caucasus (60 percent across 7 surveys). Only in the Caribbean does the lack of awareness fall below 10 percent (Joint United Nations Programme on HIV/AIDS [UNAIDS], 2002). In virtually every country in which comparable data on young men are available, the percentages who are unaware are lower for males than females (UNICEF, 2002). While young people may be unaware of certain dangers, they also see dangers where they do not exist. In surveys

---

[6]Although UNAIDS published prevalence estimates among 15-24-year-olds for 1999 and for 2001, it warns that these should not be interpreted as depicting trends; the uncertainty surrounding the estimates is too great at present to support age-specific trend estimates for most countries.

in 55 countries, only 40 percent on average are aware that mosquitoes cannot transmit HIV (UNICEF, 2002).

Knowledge of ways to prevent the transmission of infection is also low among young people in many countries. In 17 national surveys conducted between 1994 and 1999, 40 percent of females ages 15-19 on average could not identify any preventive measure—abstaining from sex, being faithful to one partner, avoiding multiple partners, or condom use. Males of the same age were somewhat more knowledgeable, with 27 percent not knowing how to protect themselves. Across countries, however, the level of knowledge is quite variable but nonetheless consistent with the prevailing level of risk. For example, the percentage not knowing any preventive measures was 96 percent for females and 88 percent for males in Bangladesh, where HIV represents a relatively modest risk for young people, compared with 11 and 16 percent, respectively, in Uganda, where the risks are very high (Kiragu, 2001). It is also worth noting that only a small percentage of young people who are infected report in surveys being aware that they are HIV positive (UNICEF, 2002).

The extent to which young people are able to judge accurately the risks associated with health behavior is still poorly understood overall (Blum, McNeely, and Nonnemaker, 2002), but there is some evidence that they underestimate their own risk of becoming infected with HIV/AIDS. In part this underestimation is due to a lack of accurate information, such as misconceptions about modes of transmission as well as a sense that "this cannot happen to me." But (as is true among adults generally) it is also related to a desire to be accepted, to trust one's partner, and to believe that he or she is "clean" (Brown et al., 2001). Moreover, since infection with HIV does not have immediately apparent effects, young people may find it difficult to make choices with consequences that seem very removed from their immediate situation (Weiss, Whelan, and Gupta, 1996).

Nevertheless, trends in the use of condoms by young people suggest that behavior is changing in sub-Saharan Africa and Latin America, where data on condom use have been collected for young people (see also the section below on sexual initiation). Condom use among sexually active young women is still relatively low, but increases are evident when Demographic and Health Surveys (DHS) from the late 1980s are compared with surveys about 10 years later (Table 4-4). Among young women who presumably are most likely to have high-risk sex—never married, sexually active females—the (unweighted) average increases among 15-19-year-olds from 0.3 to 8.0 percent and among 20-24-year-olds from 0.2 to 5.5 percent. The often-cited case of Uganda and its success in promoting behavior change is evident here; virtually no women ages 15-24 were recorded as using condoms in 1988-1989, whereas about 10 years later the proportions among never married, sexually active women exceed one in three and are

## BOX 4-1
## Young People Facing a Different World:
## The Future Impact of HIV/AIDS

The HIV/AIDS pandemic has profoundly affected the world for over two decades and its continued and rapid progress will have far-reaching impacts on the kind of world young people inherit. The United Nations (2003b) estimates that between 2000 and 2050, there will be 178 million fewer births due to AIDS-related deaths of women of childbearing age. While sub-Saharan Africa currently has the highest prevalence rates, epidemics are already growing rapidly in parts of Asia, Eastern Europe, and North Africa (Joint United Nations Programme on HIV/AIDS [UNAIDS] and World Health Organization, 2003). How will this deficit in human life impact the lives of young people who survive to adulthood?

The economic impacts of HIV/AIDS are difficult to predict and may not be apparent until the pandemic peaks, but they will probably include falling gross domestic product, decreased productivity and profits for businesses, and increased poverty and wealth disparities. A review of 14 studies of the economic impact of HIV/AIDS (mostly in African countries) reports the estimated effects on gross domestic product could range from "small" to 2-3 percent lower than in the absence of AIDS (United Nations, 2003c). Bell and colleagues (2003:95) conclude that unless certain measures are taken, "economic collapse is in the cards" for Southern Africa. Future generations will surely be faced with economies severely debilitated by HIV/AIDS.

The AIDS pandemic is likely to widen the gap between the rich and poor and increase poverty, especially among those households directly affected by HIV/AIDS. Early epidemiological studies showed a link between higher socioeconomic status and HIV infection; however, researchers believe that HIV infection is higher among poorer individuals as the pandemic progresses (Barnett and Whiteside, 2002; Over and Piot, 1993). Socioeconomic disparities exacerbated by HIV/AIDS could heighten political and social conflict among those who survive. Military and national police forces also expected to be affected by the pandemic, being less prepared to maintain the peace. By the mid-1990s, 21 percent of soldiers in one province in Cambodia tested HIV positive, and HIV prevalence rates among South African soldiers were estimated at double or more than civilian rates (United Nations Population Fund, 2003).

Future generations will face increased demand for health care and diminished quality of care. Studies from Southern Africa estimate that approximately 60 percent of hospital beds are occupied by HIV/AIDS patients, crowding out other patients. In Zambia, hospital bed occupancy by AIDS patients is projected to rise from 6 to 43 percent between 1990 and 2005 (Cornia, Patel, and Zagonari, 2002:7). The World Bank estimates that a country with a stable 30 percent prevalence rate could lose 3 to 7 percent of its health care workers each year due to AIDS (Cornia, Patel, and Zagonari, 2002:9). Rising health expenditures on HIV/AIDS and mounting strains on the public health systems may lead to future shortages that force people into private health services, which cost more.

In the agricultural sector, fewer people with less farming knowledge will be tasked with sustaining people's food needs. The U.S. Department of Agriculture predicts a substantial gap between agricultural production and food needs by 2010 in Eastern and Southern Africa (United Nations, 2003c:5-4). Grain production in

Kenya is expected to be 12.1 percent less than required to meet food needs in 2010. Food shortages, more malnutrition, and increased dependence on food imports are expected.

HIV/AIDS is already having significant impacts on education, which will compromise human development for generations. An estimated 860,000 African children have lost their teachers to AIDS (United Nations Development Programme, 2001). More than 100 schools have already closed in the Central African Republic because of AIDS-related teacher shortages (Kiragu, 2001). Teacher shortages are expected in Kenya, Uganda, Zambia, and Zimbabwe at least through 2010, especially in rural areas (Kiragu, 2001). More and more families will take children out of school because they cannot afford to pay their education costs and need their children's labor and because of HIV/AIDS-related stigma. In Thailand, 15 percent of rural families affected by AIDS took a child out of school (Kiragu, 2001). In the Central African Republic and Swaziland, AIDS and orphanhood is responsible for a 20-30 percent fall in school enrollment rates (United Nations Development Programme, 2001).

Household composition and structure are affected by the AIDS pandemic in numerous ways. A longitudinal study of AIDS-affected families in Haiti found that the number of household dependents decreased and unemployment, borrowing, and the sale of possessions increased as the disease progressed over time (United Nations, 2003c:3-3). In Sri Lanka, one study found that medical costs ranged from US$5,454 to 18,680 per HIV/AIDS-related case (Bloom et al., 1997, cited in United Nations, 2003c:3-5).

It is estimated that, as of 2001, approximately 14 million children under age 15 had been orphaned because of AIDS, 11 million of whom lived in sub-Saharan Africa (United Nations, 2003c). By 2010, the number of AIDS orphans is projected to rise to 20 million in sub-Saharan Africa (United Nations Population Fund, 2003). Studies have found that orphans are more likely than other children to live in poor and female-headed households, to be malnourished, to be educationally disadvantaged, and are at an increased risk of getting involved in crime, drugs, and being recruited into military activities (Bicego, Rutstein, and Johnson, 2003; United Nations, 2003c; United Nations Population Fund, 2003). In taking the lives of millions of parents, AIDS also deprives children of their parents' loving care, knowledge, and emotional support, the effects of which are impossible to know. The consequences of living in a state of nearly constant mourning for extended periods of time, as deaths to family and friends accumulate, are also impossible to predict.

It is difficult to predict what the world will be like for future generations because of HIV/AIDS. What can be surmised from the estimates and projections discussed above is grim. AIDS may, however, create unexpected opportunities in the future. In Uganda, national-level programs have galvanized people and communities around HIV/AIDS (United Nations Development Programme, 2001). The pandemic could foster increased social cohesion, especially in communities affected by AIDS. As the illness becomes more prevalent, stigma could decline significantly, leading to better treatment and prevention of further infections. While those who survive will certainly face greater burdens, they will also encounter more opportunities to lead their communities and pave the way for future development. It is critical that now, while the pandemic rages in many parts of the globe, the current generation of young people consider and prepare for the future of a world affected by AIDS.

TABLE 4-4 Percentage of Young Women Currently Using Condoms in Successive Demographic and Health Surveys About Ten Years Apart

| Age Group and Country | Year of Survey | | All Sexually Active | | Never Married and Sexually Active | |
|---|---|---|---|---|---|---|
| | 1st | 2nd | 1st | 2nd | 1st | 2nd |
| 15-19-Year-Olds | | | | | | |
| Ghana | 1988 | 1998-1999 | 0.4 | 12.1 | 0.4 | 8.6 |
| Kenya | 1989 | 1998 | 0.3 | 5.5 | 0.3 | 4.3 |
| Senegal | 1986 | 1997 | 0.0 | 3.2 | 0.0 | 2.5 |
| Togo | 1988 | 1998 | 1.8 | 14.4 | 1.8 | 13.6 |
| Uganda | 1998-1999 | 2000-2001 | 0.0 | 11.8 | 0.0 | 36.7 |
| Zimbabwe | 1988 | 1999 | 0.8 | 6.5 | 0.8 | 4.4 |
| Bolivia | 1989 | 1998 | 0.1 | 4.3 | 0.0 | 2.9 |
| Brazil | 1986 | 1996 | 1.1 | 12.0 | 0.0 | 7.9 |
| Colombia | 1990 | 2000 | 1.5 | 12.7 | 0.6 | 10.0 |
| Dominican Republic | 1986 | 1996 | 0.0 | 2.2 | 0.0 | 1.2 |
| Guatemala | 1987 | 1998 | 0.9 | 3.6 | 0.0 | 0.2 |
| Peru | 1986 | 1996 | 0.0 | 6.6 | 0.0 | 3.3 |
| 20-24-Year-Olds | | | | | | |
| Ghana | 1988 | 1998-1999 | 1.2 | 7.1 | 0.2 | 3.6 |
| Kenya | 1989 | 1998 | 1.2 | 2.2 | 0.1 | 0.8 |
| Senegal | 1986 | 1997 | 0.0 | 2.7 | 0.0 | 2.1 |
| Togo | 1988 | 1998 | 1.5 | 9.6 | 0.9 | 7.2 |
| Uganda | 1998-1999 | 2000-2001 | 0.0 | 4.5 | 0.0 | 34.9 |
| Zimbabwe | 1988 | 1999 | 1.8 | 3.8 | 0.4 | 1.7 |
| Bolivia | 1989 | 1998 | 0.4 | 5.1 | 0.0 | 1.4 |
| Brazil | 1986 | 1996 | 0.8 | 8.2 | 0.3 | 4.1 |
| Colombia | 1990 | 2000 | 2.0 | 14.2 | 0.5 | 7.7 |
| Dominican Republic | 1986 | 1996 | 0.0 | 2.0 | 0.0 | 0.3 |
| Guatemala | 1987 | 1998 | 1.5 | 1.8 | 0.0 | 0.1 |
| Peru | 1986 | 1996 | 0.0 | 6.1 | 0.0 | 2.0 |

SOURCE: DHS data.

far higher than in any other country in the table. Although the magnitude of the change varies, increases over time appear in all countries surveyed. In many countries, condom use is higher among teenagers than among women in their early 20s. This pattern has been interpreted by some as reflecting a greater willingness among those just starting their sexual lives to accept the use of condoms (Joint United Nations Programme on HIV/AIDS [UNAIDS], 2000b). It may also be partially explained by the fact that condom use tends to decline with the duration of relationships (Bankole, Darroch, and Singh, 1999; Norris and Ford, 1999), and young people in their early 20s may be more likely to be involved in long-term relationships.

In contrast to earlier studies, which tended to show higher HIV prevalence among educated individuals, recent studies based on cross-sectional data suggest that this relationship is beginning to disappear or even be reversed (Glynn et al., 2004; Hargreaves and Glynn, 2002). This is probably due to the greater ability of educated people to both access information on HIV prevention and to act on it. There is some recent evidence that more educated people are less likely to engage in various types of risky sexual behavior and more likely to use condoms when they do (Lagarde et al., 2001).[7] One study using 12 years of longitudinal data from Uganda demonstrates convincingly the evolving relationship between HIV and education (de Walque, 2002). The study found no relationship between education and HIV prevalence among young people (ages 18-29) in the early 1990s. However, 10 years later, HIV prevalence had decreased substantially more among those with secondary school education than among those with no or primary education (Figure 4-4). Based on the available evidence, trends toward improvements in education thus imply progress in the reduction of HIV, but the results of these studies also suggest that HIV/AIDS prevention campaigns may need to be targeted more effectively at those with no or low levels of education.

## Injuries

For young people, particularly for young men, injuries—mostly due to road traffic accidents, violence, war, and suicide—contribute substantially to mortality and morbidity. According to WHO data (World Health Organization, 2001a), injuries (unintentional and intentional combined) in sub-Saharan Africa make up a larger share of all deaths among males ages 15-

---

[7]Special case studies of the impact of HIV/AIDS on schooling in Botswana, Malawi, and Uganda have documented lower AIDS-related mortality among teachers (Bennell, Hyde, and Swainson, 2002).

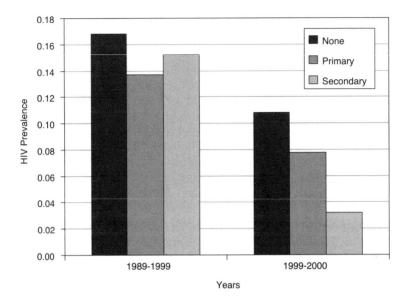

FIGURE 4-4 HIV prevalence among individuals ages 18-29 by level of education, rural Uganda (MRC General Population Cohort).
SOURCE: de Walque (2002).

29 (25 percent) than maternal deaths make up a share of all deaths among females of the same age (see Table 4-2). In other developing regions, deaths to young males attributable to injury are a relatively more important cause of death ranging from 45 to 68 percent of all deaths for young men. Injury, including injury due to domestic violence and/or gender-based violence, is also a major cause of death among females, explaining the largest share of deaths in East Asia.

The most common fatal injuries involve road traffic accidents. Road deaths per registered vehicle tend to be more numerous in the poorest countries. However, death rates from road accidents among young people tend to be highest in upper middle-income countries (Ahmed and Andersson, 2002). Regionally, some parts of South-eastern Asia, including Indonesia, Sri Lanka, and Thailand, and the Eastern Mediterranean, which includes the Gulf states, Iran, Libya, and Saudi Arabia, have higher than average death rates from road accidents among young people, a pattern that may be linked to rising affluence in these countries (World Health Organization, 2001a). In the developed countries that make up the Organisation for Economic Co-operation and Development (OECD), 48 percent of traffic fatalities in 2000 involved drivers or occupants in passenger cars or station wagons (International Road Traffic and Accident Database, 2002). In developing countries, by contrast, a much higher proportion of fatalities involve pedestrians, bicyclists, motorcyclists, and moped riders or passengers on buses and trucks (Nantulya and Reich, 2002).

As motorized transport has grown, death rates due to traffic accidents also appear to have risen over the last 20 years in developing countries as a whole, although available reports are not entirely consistent (Nantulya and Reich, 2002; Nordberg, 2000). For example, road deaths among young people are reported in one study to have risen substantially over two decades in Chile, Mexico, and Venezuela (Maddaleno and Silber, 1993), but another study asserts that death rates have fallen in the majority of countries in the Americas (Yunes and Rajs, 1994). A rise in fatalities as motor vehicle use increases in developing countries is not inevitable; the development of preventive and safety measures—safety belt and helmet use, air bags, cameras at intersections, speed reductions, enforcement of drunk driving laws[8]—have led to improvements in high-income countries and in some developing countries in which they have been introduced (Mohan, 2003; World Health Organization, 1995). For example, in Thailand, introduction of a motorcycle helmet law reduced fatalities by 56 percent (World Health Organization, 2002:72).

Violence and war account for about a fourth of male deaths due to injury at ages 15-29 (World Health Organization, 2001a). United Nations Children's Fund (UNICEF) estimates that there are approximately 300,000 soldiers under the age of 18 involved in armed conflicts globally. Some of them become soldiers voluntarily, while others are forcibly recruited. Not only may young people be involved in war as combatants, but they may also be affected as civilians. Noncombatant male young people tend to be at higher risk than females for war-related deaths. Civilian young males are often targeted by soldiers who suspect they may become future war combatants. In addition, during times of civil unrest, young males are often sent out of the security of the home environment to get food and supplies, to tend to animal herds, or to earn money. Of course, in addition to deaths caused directly by armed conflict, young people are subject to other consequences of armed conflict that affect health both in the short and the long term, including nonfatal injuries, the loss of parents and other family members, displacement, abuse in various forms, and the disruption of school and other routines.

Young males are also disproportionately affected by homicide, with male death rates (among 10-29-year-olds) exceeding those among females

---

[8]According to at least one researcher, driver education programs aimed at young people may be useful for teaching the mechanics of driving, but they have never been shown to reduce traffic accidents (Mohan, 2003).

in virtually every country with reasonable data (Krug et al., 2002). Regional differences in mortality—due to homicide among young people—show Latin America, the Caribbean, the Russian Federation, and some countries of Southeastern Europe having the highest rates. In a recent study of 24 developing countries in the mid-1990s, several in Latin America were distinguished by exceptionally high rates of mortality due to homicide for males ages 10-29: Brazil, Colombia, El Salvador, and Venezuela. The rates for these countries ranged from 1.56 per thousand (Colombia) to 0.46 per thousand (Venezuela) compared with no higher than 0.3 in the remaining 20 countries (Krug et al., 2002). At least some of these deaths are the result of violence associated with youth gangs (Rodgers, 1999), and the vast majority involve the use of guns. High and rising rates of homicide among young people in Latin America are thought to be linked to increasing income inequality, although the evidence for this assertion appears to be based mainly on associations in aggregate cross-sectional statistics (Butchart and Engstrom, 2002; Szwarcwald et al., 1999).

The share of deaths due to injury that are intentional varies by region. In some regions, including sub-Saharan Africa, young men in Latin America, and young women in East Asia, the majority of deaths due to injury are intentional. Suicide rates among young males have been increasing since the 1950s in most developed countries, but the trend in most developing countries is far less certain because reliable trend data are generally unavailable (Cantor and Neulinger, 2000; Eckersley and Dear, 2002). Although suicide rates among young males are far higher than among young females (in part because females who attempt suicide are less likely to succeed), death rates among younger males tend to be consistently lower than among older males. Among females in developing regions, however, ages 15-29 appear to be times of particular peril, with death rates 24 percent higher than at ages 30-44 (World Health Organization, 2001a).

China is notable for comparatively high rates of suicide, especially in rural areas and especially among young women (see data on East Asia in Table 4-2). Estimates for 1992 are 0.28 suicides per thousand males and 0.46 per thousand females ages 20-24, the peak age for suicide (Ji, 1999). Suicides may have declined since then, but statistics are contradictory (Hannum and Liu, 2005). The primary reasons for suicide in rural China are not entirely clear but seem to be associated with marital and family pressures and education and employment problems (Hannum and Liu, 2005; Ji, Kleinman, and Becker, 2001).

In general, little is known about the reasons that young people commit suicide in developing countries, but some research suggests that they are not substantially different from those in the developed world. Reasons linked to rapid social and economic transitions, such as loss of tradition, social cohesion, and spontaneous social support, and associated risk factors, such as alcohol and drug abuse and mental illness, have been cited as important factors (Brown, 2001). While such issues affect older adults as well, they are particularly relevant among the young because the individual developmental transitions experienced during this phase of life can be full of stress and uncertainty. Increased access to the means to commit suicide may also be a factor in rising rates in some countries (Brown, 2001; Eckersley and Dear, 2002). For example, the ingestion of powerful and readily available pesticides is the most common method used by rural Chinese women (Hannum and Liu, 2005).

## Maternal Mortality and Morbidity

Maternal mortality and morbidity are among the most significant threats to the health of young women in developing countries. Maternal mortality comprises a substantial proportion of deaths to young women in all developing country regions except East Asia (see Table 4-2). The proportion of deaths attributable to maternal causes ranges from 25 percent in Northern Africa and the Middle East to 16 percent in Africa, Latin America, and South Asia, to 6 percent in East Asia. In addition, nonfatal complications associated with pregnancy and childbirth are common and not only affect health in the short term, but they can cause or make worse some long-term morbidities, such as obstetric fistula, uterine prolapse, anemia, reproductive tract infections, and infertility (National Research Council, 1997a).

The most recent global estimates put the maternal mortality ratio (i.e., maternal deaths per 100,000 live births) in developing countries at 440. Another measure, the lifetime risk of maternal death, shows that the chance that a woman in a developing country will die of maternal causes is 1 in 61 in developing regions compared with 1 in 2,800 in developed regions. There is also enormous variation across the developing regions, with the lifetime risk reaching 1 in 16 in sub-Saharan Africa and 1 in 840 in East Asia (World Health Organization, 2003). Maternal deaths are those that occur during pregnancy and up to 42 days after birth. About 80 percent of these deaths are due directly to maternity; the most common cause is hemorrhage, followed by sepsis and complications of unsafe abortion, hypertensive disorders, and obstructed labor. The remaining 20 percent of deaths are due to conditions that are aggravated by pregnancy but may be present prior to pregnancy, such as diabetes, anemia, malaria, and increasingly HIV/AIDS.

As in the case of other cause-specific mortality data, estimates of maternal mortality are often based on partial information of variable quality, so trends can be inferred only cautiously and at the most general level. Trends related specifically to young women are not available, but a United Nations report released in 2003 states that "it does appear that globally, levels of maternal mortality remained stable between 1995 and 2000" (World Health Organization/UNICEF/United Nations Population Fund, 2003:15).

The evidence on the age pattern of maternal mortality is conflicting. Most studies suggest that the per-pregnancy risk of dying of maternal causes is higher below age 20 than among women in their 20s and 30s; there seems to be universal consensus that risks rise dramatically above age 40. A study published by WHO in 1989 (cited in Senderowitiz, 1995) asserted that the risk of dying during pregnancy or delivery is 20 to 200 percent greater for women ages 15-19 than for older women. In a later study, WHO (1995) provided data from subnational community studies or official statistics for seven developing countries. In six of seven cases, the maternal mortality ratio was higher at ages 15-19 than at ages 20-24, sometimes slightly higher, but sometimes substantially so. The results for the only national survey in this study (Egypt, 1992-1993) showed a ratio at ages 20-24 that was about a third of the ratio at ages 15-19. A surveillance study conducted over four years in one department in Guatemala showed almost identical ratios for women ages 15-19 and 20-24 (Kestler and Ramirez, 2000). Similarly, a six-year population-based study in rural Guineau-Bissau found no difference in maternal mortality by age once other factors were controlled (Hoj et al., 2002).

Two recent national surveys, however, show a different pattern. A 2001 national survey in Bangladesh examined household deaths that occurred in the three preceding years during pregnancy, delivery, or two months postpartum and related these to numbers of pregnancies (rather than live births). The resulting mortality ratios were 221 at ages 15-19 and 253 at ages 20-24 (National Institute of Population Research and Training and ORC Macro, 2002). Similarly, a reproductive age mortality survey for Egypt in 2000 gave maternal mortality ratios of 31 at ages 15-19 and 41 at ages 20-24 (Egypt Ministry of Health and Population, 2001).

The inconsistencies in these studies may reflect the fact that the number of births among young mothers (those under age 20) is relatively small, so age-specific maternal mortality ratios have high standard errors and consistent patterns are difficult to detect. Nevertheless, the dangers of childbearing among very young women, whose bodies are not yet fully grown, are well known. Preeclamptic toxemia and cephalopelvic disproportion, pregnancy-induced hypertension, vesicovaginal fistulae, and anemia pose serious problems for young mothers (Institute of Medicine, 1996; Senderowitz, 1995). Indeed, one study of Chilean data showed that young people under age 15 had a significantly higher rate of maternal mortality than those ages 15-19 (Siña, Valdivieso, and del Pinto, 2003). In addition, it is difficult to separate the effects of age from the effects of parity and other factors on maternal mortality. Young mothers are also less likely to be well nourished than older mothers. In spite of a widespread assumption that young mothers are less likely to get adequate prenatal and obstetric care, recent evidence suggests that this is not the case (Abou-Zahr and Wardlaw, 2003). However, evidence from some sub-Saharan African countries suggests that young mothers may be less likely to deliver with a skilled attendant (Magadi, Agwanda, Obare, and Raffa, 2004). Regardless of whether there is an intrinsically higher risk of death associated with young age, the physical toll of early parenthood can have significant consequences later in life, including infertility and complications in later pregnancies.

Female genital cutting is one factor that contributes to the level of maternal morbidity and mortality in a number of countries. Female genital cutting—an operation that involves the partial or total removal of female external genitalia—is a rite of passage that is traditionally carried out during childhood in some societies and during adolescence in others. In either case, the consequences continue during adolescence and adulthood. Female genital cutting is not a worldwide practice, but is confined largely to a band of countries stretching across the upper half of Africa also including some countries of the Middle East. Prevalence of the practice is as high as 97 percent in Egypt and 98 percent in Somalia and Djibouti, and it falls to 5 percent in Uganda and the Democratic Republic of Congo (Carr, 1997; Creel, 2001; Toubia and Izett, 1998). (We are not aware of regional or global estimates of female genital cutting.) The practice can have immediate health consequences (such as infection and hemorrhage) and, particularly for those who have the more extreme forms, can lead to later obstetrical complications and eventual reduced fertility as well as psychological difficulties and reduced sexual pleasure (Shell-Duncan and Hernlund, 2001).

A gradual recognition of the magnitude and consequences of this practice, a redefinition of it as a human rights issue, and a strong policy push for elimination followed the 1994 International Conference on Population and Development and the 1995 Fourth World Conference on Women. Declines in the practice are now apparent in a few countries, and there are some indications that its harmful effects are increasingly being recognized by affected populations and that disapproval of the practice is increasing. In a study based on DHS data from eight countries, women ages 20-24 in six of the countries were more likely to oppose female genital cutting than women ages 45-49 (Creel, 2001). Another study in Egypt suggests a 10 percentage point decline in prevalence from one generation to the next, around the time of the International Conference on Population and Development (El-Gibaly et al., 2002).

Despite an emerging international consensus on the issue, few sustained national-level policy initiatives have been implemented to date. However, nongovernmental organizations and community-led efforts appear to have made some progress, by breaking the silence around the issue and mobilizing local support for ending the practice (Masterson and Swanson, 2000). Mostly anecdotal evidence from some of the small-scale efforts that have been undertaken to date suggest that providing alternative rites of passage in the form of ceremonies to mark this traditional moment of transition for young females may be crucial in efforts to end female genital cutting.

## SEXUAL AND REPRODUCTIVE HEALTH BEHAVIOR

After puberty and during the teenage or early adult years, most young people normally have their first sexual experience and begin to form sexual relationship(s); in terms of development, these early sexual experiences signal an important dimension of the transition from childhood to adulthood, either because they occur at the time of marriage or because they bring with them opportunities for further emotional and relational development as well as the possibilities of marriage and/or parenthood. The negative health consequences of sexual behavior among young people—unwanted pregnancies, sexually transmitted diseases and premature parenthood—have been emphasized in the literature, yet sexual initiation can also indicate a process of increasing awareness and appreciation of one's body, consolidation of personal and sexual identity, the establishment of mature intimate relationships with others, and the development of negotiation skills (Schutt-Aine and Maddaleno, 2003).

A growing body of evidence from various parts of the developing world indicates that the age at puberty has been falling slowly over decades for both boys and girls due primarily to improvements in nutrition (e.g., Du Toit, 1987; Kac, de Santa Cruz Coel, and Velasquez-Melendez, 2000; Onat and Erten, 1995; Wong et al., 1996; Wright, 1990). For example, the decline in the mean age at menarche for girls in urban Cameroon has been estimated at roughly 2.5 to 3.2 months per decade (Pasquet et al., 1999), a decline of roughly the same pace as the long-term decline in the mean age of puberty for girls in Western industrial countries from 1850 to 1950 (Parent et al., 2003). A nationally representative survey of girls in the United States ages 8-20 (Chumlea et al., 2003) estimated a median age of puberty of 12.4 years in 1994 while a nationally representative survey of relatively well-nourished Egyptian girls ages 10-19 in 1997 estimated a median age of puberty of 13.7 years (El-Tawila et al., 1999). A compilation of recent estimates of ages of menarche for girls from around the world shows substantial differentials as wide as 2 years between the age of puberty among the better off and poorer segments of a population. Estimates vary from as low as 12.1 among the well off in India to 16.1 among the underprivileged in Senegal (Parent et al., 2003). Ages of puberty remain higher in developing countries, particularly in the poorest countries, than in the West but gaps are likely to be narrowing. Differences in patterns and trends in puberty provide an important context in which to assess changes in sexual and reproductive behavior.

The literature on young people's sexual and reproductive behavior in developing countries is vast. The HIV/AIDS pandemic has added a sense of urgency to understanding its various dimensions and determinants, and the volume of research has expanded rapidly over the last several years. What we know about sexual behavior among young people, however, is derived primarily from self-reports on interviewer-administered surveys. In settings in which privacy is rare, the responses to such sensitive and intimate questions are likely to be strongly affected by prevailing social norms and values leading in some cases to underreporting and in some cases to overreporting of sex behaviors. These limitations should be kept in mind when assessing the findings reported below. Current efforts to improve the reporting of sexual behavior among young people are described in Box 4-2.

Given the magnitude of the literature on this topic and its comprehensive treatment in a number of recent publications, the discussion here is confined to a set of key sexual and reproductive health behaviors that are likely to have the most decisive effects on a successful transition to adulthood: age at sexual initiation, risky sexual behavior, sexual violence and coercion, the use of contraception, and abortion. Information on marriage is covered in Chapter 7 and on childbearing in Chapter 8.

## Sexual Initiation

Dual social norms surrounding the sexual initiation of boys and girls persist almost everywhere in the developing world. While young women are expected to marry at a younger age than young men, they are typically discouraged from premarital sex, particularly if under a socially recognized age of maturity or with a partner that is not seen as a likely spouse or partner. These norms influence the context in which the first sexual experience takes place, which for many young women still occurs at the time of marriage and for the majority of men occurs prior to marriage. Among young people reporting premarital sex regardless of setting, it appears that females are more likely to report sexual debut with a steady partner, while males are far less likely to report this and much more likely to report that their first sexual experience was with a friend, casual contact, or sex worker (Brown et al., 2001; Choe and Lin, 2001; Rani, Figueroa, and Ainsle, 2003; Xenos, 1997). Boys are also much more likely to report satisfaction or pleasure after their first premarital sexual experience, while girls whose first sexual experience is premarital are more likely to experience shame, guilt, or pain (Rani et al., 2003). These gender differences in sexual initiation are important to keep in mind when interpreting demographic data on the timing of sexual initiation.

**BOX 4-2**
**Improving Reporting of Sexual Behavior Among Young People**
**Using Alternative Interviewing Methods**

Obtaining accurate information on sexual activity and risk behaviors among young people, particularly teens, is crucial for monitoring exposure to sexually transmitted infections and effectively addressing the reproductive health needs of young people. Reliable estimates of sexual behavior among teens are particularly important given rising rates of HIV infection and STIs in many developing countries. However, obtaining accurate reports from young people on surveys containing sensitive topics, such as alcohol and drug use, premarital sexual activity, coerced sex, and pregnancies is challenging, particularly for girls, since such behaviors are often contrary to social norms and stigmatizing (Dare and Cleland, 1994). Moreover, young people are likely to be embarrassed and uncomfortable when questioned directly by adults on sexual issues.

Studies from Africa indicate that when conventional survey methods are used to obtain information, such as face-to-face interviewing, young unmarried women tend to underreport their sexual activity. The most striking evidence that reporting of sexual activity is problematic comes from a study in Kenya that collected both survey data and blood and urine samples. This study found that among women ages 15-24 who claimed never to have had sex, STI/HIV rates ranged from 6 to 18 percent (Buvé et al., 2001). These so-called virgin infections are clear evidence of the underreporting of sexual activity by young women. The reporting for young men is no less problematic, with indications that young men overreport some sexual behaviors—because sex is considered a badge of honor and rite of passage to adulthood in many places (Erulkar and Mensch, 1997b)—while underreporting other potentially stigmatizing sexual behaviors (Mensch, Hewett, and Erulkar, 2003).

Alternative interview techniques, such as audio computer-assisted self-interviewing, potentially provide a more effective method for eliciting accurate reporting, since they offer respondents a greater degree of privacy and confidentiality when divulging sensitive information. Computerized interviewing allows the respondent to hear recorded questions through audio headphones, while entering responses directly into the computer keyboard or numeric keypad. These methodologies have also been adapted for household-based surveys and populations for which literacy is not universal (Hewett, Mensch, and Erulkar, 2003, 2004).

In a study conducted in two districts in Kenya, Mensch, Hewett, and Erulkar (2003) experimentally tested different interview modes to assess whether audio computer-assisted self-interviewing improves reporting of sexual behaviors by young people. The authors found that for both sexes, the reporting of certain activities, such as having multiple sexual partners, having sex with a stranger, and having coerced sex, was higher using computerized administration, significantly so for all three behaviors for girls and for two of the three behaviors for boys. However, contrary to expectations, reporting of ever having had premarital sex and alcohol use was higher among girls in the face-to-face interviews.

There is a general consensus that researchers and program evaluators should be circumspect regarding estimates of sexual behavior generated from survey data. Given that young people in developing countries are likely to be influenced by the context in which interviews are administered and given that truthful answers to questions regarding sexual and illegal and stigmatized behaviors may put the young person in an uncomfortable position, additional research and evaluation of the response effects in surveys is warranted.

The age at which the sexual initiation of young women and men is reported to occur varies widely across regions in which recent survey data are available (Table 4-5). Early sexual initiation is particularly variable; among females ages 20-24, the percentage who report having had sex by age 15 varies from around 1 percent in the former Soviet Asia to more than 20 percent in Western and Middle Africa. These variations in early sexual debut are due largely to differences in age at marriage. Among young men, the highest percentages reporting having sex by age 15 are found in Latin America and the Caribbean. In contrast to women, few young men are married by age 15; differences among regions are mostly a result of differences in premarital sexual activity. By age 18, more than 40 percent of young women report having had sex in Latin America and the Caribbean, close to 60 percent in sub-Saharan Africa, and about 20 percent in the former Soviet Asia. More young men than women report having had sex by age 18 in Latin America and the Caribbean, while the opposite is true in sub-Saharan Africa.

Relatively little comparable information is available from Asian countries, mainly because there are few DHS surveys conducted in the region and those that are conducted tend to exclude never married women. Nevertheless, recent data for both women and men have been collected in four countries under the Asian Young Adult Reproductive Risk project. These data show that the proportion of females reporting sex by age 20 is 54-66 percent in Indonesia and Nepal compared with 28-39 percent in the Philippines and Thailand. These differences are due primarily to earlier marriage in the former countries. In Indonesia and Nepal, lower proportions of young men than women report having initiated sexual activity by age 20, while the proportions reporting sexual initiation are higher for men in the Philippines and Thailand. This pattern is related to the differential pattern of premarital sexual activity among young men and the timing of marriage among young women in the two sets of countries (Xenos et al., 2001).

Various factors suggest that sexual initiation may be occurring at a progressively younger age. Not only is the age of puberty falling, but also various global changes discussed above, such as the penetration of Western mass media and entertainment, as well as increasingly common ideas about individualism and the erosion of traditional social controls, might be seen to favor earlier sexual experimentation outside marriage (Caldwell et al., 1998). Indeed, the median age at reported first intercourse has generally fallen in Latin America and the Caribbean while increasing somewhat in sub-Saharan Africa, but not as much as the increases in age at marriage (Zlidar et al., 2003). The increasing age at marriage observed in many developing countries also signifies a lengthening of the amount of time that women are exposed to the possibility of premarital sex.

An analysis based on data from 41 DHS surveys (see Table 4-6), including 27 in sub-Saharan Africa, 9 in Latin America and 5 in Asia, primarily

TABLE 4-5 Percentage of Females and Males Ages 20-24 Who First Had Sex by Specific Ages, Demographic and Health Surveys 1996-2001 and Young Adult Reproductive Health Surveys (YARHS)

| Region (Number of Countries for Females/Males) | Females First Had Sex by Age | | | Males First Had Sex by Age | | |
|---|---|---|---|---|---|---|
| | 15 | 18 | 20 | 15 | 18 | 20 |
| DHS Surveys | | | | | | |
| Eastern and Southern Africa (13/9) | 16.6 | 57.1 | 76.9 | 14.1 | 45.2 | 65.2 |
| Western and Middle Africa (12/11) | 21.4 | 59.3 | 76.5 | 11.5 | 40.3 | 60.6 |
| Former Soviet Asia (4) | 0.9 | 19.5 | 53.1 | n.a.[a] | n.a.[a] | n.a.[a] |
| Caribbean/Central America (4/3) | 12.7 | 44.1 | 62.4 | 31.0 | 69.6 | 84.0 |
| South America (5/3) | 9.1 | 41.4 | 61.3 | 30.9 | 72.7 | 86.6 |
| YARH Surveys | | | | | | |
| Indonesia 1999 | n.a. | n.a. | 54.0 | n.a. | n.a. | 7.0 |
| Philippines 1994 | n.a. | n.a. | 28.0 | n.a. | n.a. | 33.0 |
| Thailand 1994 | n.a. | n.a. | 39.0 | n.a. | n.a. | 57.0 |
| Nepal 2000 | n.a. | n.a. | 66.0 | n.a. | n.a. | 43.0 |

[a]Too few countries with sufficient cases to calculate regional average.
NOTE: n.a. = not available.
SOURCES: DHS data, 1996-2001; Xenos et al. (2001:Tables 1 and 2).

former Soviet Asia (Armenia, Kazakhstan, Kyrgyzstan, the Philippines, and Uzbekistan) reveals that in only 9 of 41 countries (roughly one-fifth of the sample countries) has there been an increase in the reported probability of having had sex before the age of 18 over the past 20 years (Mensch et al., 2005).[9] This is based on a comparison of the experiences reported by older women (40-44) and by younger women (20-24) before they reached age 18. In 19 countries (a little less than one-half of sample countries) there has been no change in the probability of sexual initiation before the age of 18, and in 13 countries (roughly a third of sample countries), there has actually been a decrease in the probability of reported sex by the age of 18. This can be explained by the fact that, in three-quarters of the countries included in this analysis (31 of the sample of 41 countries), there are fewer young

---

[9]The analysis uses multiple decrement life tables to model premarital sex and marriage (without prior premarital sex) among young women as competing risks. Thus, the analysis looks at the likelihood that a woman who has neither had premarital sex nor been married (i.e., not yet sexually active) will do one of the two (or neither) by a given age. The surveys included took place between 1990 and 2003 and trends are calculated by comparing the experience of 20-24-year-olds to 40-44-year-olds. Differences between cohorts of less than 5 percent are recorded as no change. This is because it is expected that there is a certain amount of "noise" in these data, given that women are being asked to report about very sensitive behaviors.

TABLE 4-6 Direction of Change in the Probability of Females Marrying, Having Premarital Sex, and Having Sex by Age 18: A Comparison of 20-24-Year-Olds and 40-44-Year-Olds, Demographic and Health Surveys (1990-2003)

|  | Number of Countries | Increase | No Change | Decrease |
|---|---|---|---|---|
| Percent Marrying by Age 18 |  |  |  |  |
| Africa | 27 | 0 | 3 | 24 |
| Asia | 5 | 1 | 3 | 1 |
| Latin America/Caribbean | 9 | 0 | 3 | 6 |
| TOTAL | 41 | 1 | 9 | 31 |
| Percent Having Premarital Sex by Age 18 |  |  |  |  |
| Africa | 27 | 20 | 7 | 0 |
| Asia | 5 | 1 | 4 | 0 |
| Latin America/Caribbean | 9 | 3 | 5 | 1 |
| TOTAL | 41 | 24 | 16 | 1 |
| Percent Having Sex by Age 18 |  |  |  |  |
| Africa | 27 | 5 | 14 | 8 |
| Asia | 5 | 2 | 2 | 1 |
| Latin America/Caribbean | 9 | 2 | 3 | 4 |
| TOTAL | 41 | 9 | 19 | 13 |

NOTE: Differences between the cohorts of less than five percentage points are recorded as "no change."

women married before the age of 18 (see further discussion in Chapter 7), counteracting the effect of a rise in the percentage reporting premarital sex by the age of 18. Indeed, 24 of the 41 countries (roughly three-fifths) report a rise in the probability of having premarital sex before the age of 18.

Thus, contrary to widespread belief, sex is not being initiated at an earlier age relative to the past in most countries. While there has been an increase in premarital sex before age 18 in many countries over the past 20 years, delays in the age of marriage in most countries have meant that, relative to 20 years ago, fewer young women report themselves to have been sexually active before the age of 18. Thus while sex is being delayed, the context of first sexual experience is changing, with a greater likelihood relative to the past that first sex will be experienced prior to marriage. Zaba and colleagues (2002) note that in countries in which HIV-related mortality has started to deplete cohorts before they reach their mid-20s, the median age at first sex would increase as cohorts age because those who initiated sex early would be those most likely to develop AIDS. It is also worth noting that results from a study of Colombia and Peru using the same data sets but different methodology show the same patterns as this analysis (Ali, Cleland, and Shah, 2003).

A review of the recent literature on the determinants of age at sexual initiation yielded a multitude of studies that have attempted to explore the potential role of risk and protective factors. Many of the studies that seek to explain variations in the reported age at first sex at the individual level using data on peer, family, and community influences, however, suffer from various methodological flaws, the most common of which is the failure to consider the endogeneity of independent variables. This is unfortunately because the richness of analysis that is possible with longitudinal data available in the United States and other developed countries, where the importance of family, peer, and community influences have been ably explored, is not possible with single point-in-time cross-sectional data (Baumer and South, 2001; Costa et al., 1995). For example, virtually all of the studies examined are based on cross-sectional data, and many incorporate variables related to the individual's perception of the sexual experience of his or her friends. While it is certainly plausible that friends influence each other's sexual behavior, it is also possible that young people choose friends whom they perceive to be similar to themselves in terms of sexual and other behavior and attitudes; it is impossible to sort out this relationship using cross-sectional data. Another example is the inclusion of contraceptive knowledge as a predictor variable. As a result, many potentially important family and peer influences remain poorly documented because of the limitations imposed on data analysis by the types of data currently available. A number of more methodologically rigorous studies, however, have produced some statistically significant findings on the determinants of sexual initiation, many of which are referenced below.

For example, earlier reported age at sexual debut is significantly associated with urban residence in the northeast region of Brazil (Gupta, 2000), in KwaZulu-Natal, South Africa (Kaufman et al., 2002), and in five of eight countries in sub-Saharan Africa (Mahy and Gupta, 2002). A study of 11 mostly sub-Saharan African countries found a positive relationship in some and a negative relationship in others between urban residence and the probability of reporting having had sex among 15-19-year-olds (Filmer, 1998). While Mahy and Gupta (2002) found that the effect of urban residence had not changed over time, a study in Cameroon found that the influence of urban residence had increased (Kuate-Defo, 1998). Oddly, a study by Zaba and colleagues (2002) found that urban residence was associated with later age at first sex in six countries in sub-Saharan Africa. Some studies have also shown significant religious differences in sexual initiation. For example, Zulu, Dodoo, and Chicka-Ezeh (2002) found that in the slums of Nairobi, Christian women started sexual activity significantly earlier than Muslim women or those who practice traditional religions. Gupta (2000) found that young women who regularly attend religious services, regardless of the religion they practice, are significantly less likely to engage in sexual activity, premarital or otherwise.

Educational attainment is shown to have an inverse relationship with the probability of initiating sex in the vast majority of studies reviewed and mentioned above that were considered to be more methodologically rigorous. Again, however, problems of endogeneity plague such studies. Since pregnancy and parenthood are often a reason for discontinuing schooling, what appears to be the preventive effect of educational attainment on sexual initiation may instead be the effect of sexual activity on the likelihood of continuing schooling. There may also be some unknown factors that affect both the likelihood of reporting sexual initiation and the propensity to continue schooling. Nevertheless, the statistical association between the two is so strong and pervasive that it is worth looking at more closely.

Figure 4-5, based on DHS data drawn from Latin America and sub-Saharan Africa, demonstrates that reported sexual initiation is later among young unmarried women enrolled in school than among those not enrolled in school at all levels of enrollment. In this figure, the proportion who ever had sex among unmarried 15-17-year-olds in each country is standardized by the mean age distribution by single years of age of unmarried women in this age group across all countries. The standardization effectively controls for differences in the age distributions of those enrolled and not enrolled as well as differences in age at marriage across countries. The ratio of the proportions who have ever had sex among those not enrolled to those enrolled averages 1.7,[10] exceeding 1.0 in 24 of 28 countries with sufficient samples sizes to make the calculations. Thus, in the vast majority of countries, young women who are currently enrolled in school are less likely to report having had sex than their unmarried age peers who are no longer currently enrolled. There is a slight tendency for the ratio to increase as overall enrollment of young women increases. A few countries—Bolivia, Guatemala, and Zimbabwe—are clear outliers. In Bolivia and Zimbabwe, the ratio is unusually high because very few of those in school reported that they had initiated sex.[11] In Guatemala, few of those in either group reported ever having sex.[12] The fact that the strong association of delayed sexual

---

[10]This average excludes the ratios for Bolivia, Guatemala, and Zimbabwe, which were exceptionally high.

[11]For Bolivia, the standardized values for nonenrolled and enrolled women, respectively, are 13.9 and 2.7 percent; for Zimbabwe, the values are 20.8 and 2.7.

[12]For Guatemala, the standardized value for nonenrolled women is 2.6 percent and for enrolled women is 0.3 percent.

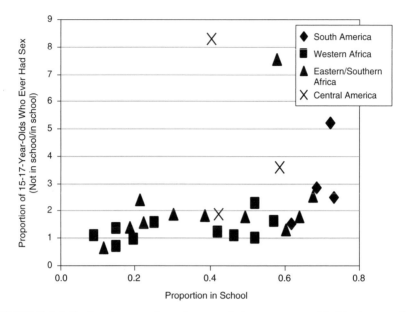

FIGURE 4-5 Ratio of proportion of unmarried women ages 15-17 who ever had sex among those not currently enrolled vs. enrolled, by overall proportion in school. SOURCE: DHS data, 1995-2001.

initiation with current enrollment persists across levels of enrollment suggests that the relationship is not the result of selectivity among either the enrolled population (at low levels of enrollment) or the nonenrolled population (at high levels of enrollment). Rather, it suggests that whether unmarried women are attending school in an environment in which most are in school or few are, being enrolled is associated with a lower likelihood of reporting ever having had sex. The reasons underlying this association, however, will need to be the focus of future research as DHS data are not sufficiently rich to provide causal explanations.

There are fewer DHS data available for unmarried men, and the sample sizes are generally too small to permit standardization by single years of age. Nevertheless, the (unstandardized) ratio of nonenrolled to enrolled is greater than 1.0 for 20 of the 28 countries. In the 24 countries for which there are data for both unmarried young men and women, the ratio is higher for women in 19 of them. Thus, enrollment in school is less strongly associated with reported sexual initiation among young men than among young women.

These descriptive findings raise further questions about the possible factors in the environment that might be protective for young people in terms of the timing of sexual initiation—factors that may be present to a greater or lesser extent in different families, different schools, and different communities. This is a relatively underresearched area, one that holds future promise given the descriptive findings highlighted above. In particular, an exploratory study in Kenya has identified some potentially important elements of school quality that merit further investigation (Mensch, Clark, Lloyd, and Erulkar, 2001). In this study, a community-based survey of young people ages 12 to 19 in three districts of rural Kenya was linked in a multivariate analysis with data collected from the schools these young people attended. The school data included interview data from students, teachers, and head teachers as well as systematic observations in classrooms and schoolyards to identify important factors affecting the likelihood of reported premarital sex and, for those who were sexually active, reported contraceptive use. Controlling for other factors, girls were found to be significantly less likely to report having engaged in premarital sex if they had attended schools in which female students reported that they were being treated equitably, and these findings were robust to many alternative specifications. This effect was not found for boys.

The rapid rise in the percentage of young people who remain in school during the later teenage years suggests that schools are becoming an increasingly important institutional environment for young people at a phase of the transition when sexual activity becomes more prevalent. Indeed, it is a possibility that increasing school enrollment may have played a role in limiting the consequences of delayed marriage for the timing and incidence of premarital sex.

## Risky Sex

Unsafe sex involves having many sexual partners, changing partners often, selecting riskier partners (such as commercial sex workers), and engaging in riskier sex acts, especially not using condoms. Despite the importance of such aspects of sexual behavior, collecting information on them is so socially sensitive that representative data are seldom available.

An analysis by Singh and Bankole (2001) provides some information on the number of reported sexual partners in the past year for men in 17 countries and for women in 12 countries (based on DHS surveys). Among unmarried men who were sexually active in the past year, a substantial proportion of those ages 15-19 reported having had two or more sexual partners during the past year: 20 to 39 percent in 5 of the 17 countries with this information, and 40 to 61 percent in the remaining 12 countries. The proportion reporting three or more partners in the past year is also substantial: 20 to 42 percent in all but 2 of these 17 countries. Unmarried young men in their 20s report similar levels of multiple sexual partnering. In all of the limited number of countries with data on sexual partners for women, the proportion reporting multiple partners is much lower among women than among men. However, in these 12 countries, 10-30 percent of unmarried women ages 15-19, who have been sexually active in the past year, report having two or more sexual partners over the recent one-year period.

Girls in sub-Saharan Africa are of particular concern because an increasing number of studies from this region document the widespread practice of sexual partnerships of girls with much older men who provide them with money, school fees, and gifts. The young girls who participate in such relationships are strongly motivated by immediate economic considerations as well as by a desire to increase their future life chances by staying in school or establishing a career. In addition, older men prefer younger sexual partners because they are believed to be less likely to be infected with HIV (Luke, 2003). While the evidence that these relationships lead to higher rates of HIV infection or lower rates of condom use is mixed, it is clear that girls have relatively little power to negotiate safe sex or condom use or to control violence in them (Blanc, 2001; Luke, 2003). In addition to the consequences for physical health, such relationships presumably promote a view of sexual relationships that emphasizes their functional rather than emotional aspects, although there is little, if any, research on this topic.

In some cultures, it is normal and acceptable for boys to experience sex for the first time with a sex worker. For example, a study of young men in Gujarat, India, found that almost 80 percent reported having had their first sexual experience with a prostitute (Sharma and Sharma, 1995). Similarly, visits to sex workers were reported to be a normal activity for peer group socializing among Cambodian young men (Tarr and Aggleton, 1999). However, there is now some evidence that the changing sexual environment and fear of HIV/AIDS may be inhibiting this practice in countries in which HIV is prevalent (e.g., VanLandingham and Trujillo, 2002).

Risky sexual behaviors are more likely to occur among young people who are in a position of economic disadvantage. In a recent study based on survey data on young people ages 14 to 24 in KwaZulu-Natal Province, South Africa, a high HIV prevalence area, Hallman (2004) found that relative economic disadvantage was positively associated with an increased likelihood of a variety of unsafe sexual behaviors, particularly for young women. These risky behaviors include multiple sexual partners, coerced sex, exchanging sex, and lower age of sexual debut, among others. Low socioeconomic status has more consistent negative effects on female than on male sexual behaviors.

## Sexual Violence and Coercion

While there is a substantial body of evidence suggesting that considerable proportions of young people report engaging in unsafe sexual relations, evidence on the wantedness of sexual activity among them is sparse. There is some evidence, however, based on findings from a few small-scale studies and from anecdotal evidence, that coercion plays a considerable role in the sexual relations of young people—not only young women but also young men. A recent review by Jeejebhoy and Bott (2003) is the most comprehensive examination to date of what is known about the reporting of sexual coercion among young people in developing countries, including the magnitude, correlates, and consequences of sexual coercion, and this section relies largely on that review. So little research had been done on this topic—until recently—that trends are virtually impossible to determine.

Sexual coercion has been defined as the "act of forcing (or attempting to force) another individual through violence, threats, verbal insistence, deception, cultural expectations, or economic circumstances to engage in sexual behavior against her/his will. As such, it includes a wide range of behaviors from violent forcible rape to more contested areas that require young women to marry and sexually service men not of their choosing" (Heise, Moore, and Toubia, 1995). In practice, sexual coercion exists along a continuum. The important point is that the victim lacks choice and may face severe physical or social consequences if she or he resists.

Jeejebhoy and Bott (2003) caution readers about the heterogeneity of definitions used in different studies, warning that cross-cultural comparisons must be interpreted cautiously. At the same time, caution must be exercised in interpreting findings. There is concern on one hand that reluctance to reveal consensual sexual relations may lead young women to report the encounter as undesired. On the other hand, sexual abuse may go unreported because of fear of stigmatization and shame among females, but also among males. The strength of each of these influences on reported experience of sexual coercion may vary from culture to culture, and between females and males, making comparisons difficult.

The magnitude of sexual coercion appears to vary widely across countries. Rates appear to be somewhat lower in studies conducted in Asia compared with those in sub-Saharan Africa and Latin America. Disturbingly high rates come from studies in South Africa that report a consistent picture of high rates of sexual coercion in adolescence. For example, results of a study in Cape Town showed that 72 percent of young women who were pregnant and 60 percent of those who had never been pregnant had reported experiencing coerced sex (Jewkes et al., 2001). In another study, 28 percent of young women reported forced sex at debut, and 20 percent reported that debut occurred as a result of peer pressure (Wood, Maforah, and Jewkes, 1998). In the South Africa DHS, 1.6 percent of women ages 15-49 reported retrospectively the experience of rape by the age of 15 (Jewkes, Levin, and Mbananga, 2002); results may well be underestimates, subject to possible recall problems among older women and to questions concerning reliability of responses. Studies from other settings in Africa report considerable variation in the prevalence of reported coerced sexual relations of young women.

Table 4-7 shows results from a range of studies in different regions on the experience of forced sexual initiation among young people. A high proportion of young women report forced initiation: 15 to 40 percent in 10 sub-Saharan Africa surveys, 20-40 percent in Peru, and 48 percent across nine Caribbean countries. Males are also affected, the rates being roughly a quarter to three-quarters as high as for females.

Perpetrators of sexual coercion and force are infrequently complete strangers. Studies in every region confirm that coercion of young people is perpetrated largely by those with whom the young person is acquainted. For example, a review of several studies reports that perpetrators were often reported to be familiar adults, often those in authority—workplace supervisors (Republic of Korea), "sugar daddies," and older male teachers, policemen, priests, and relatives (Botswana, United Republic of Tanzania) (Brown et al., 2001). A study of young people seeking counseling in clinics in Colombia and Peru suggests, likewise, that reported perpetrators were usually relatives and friends, and the coercive incident was most likely to occur in the home (Stewart et al., 1996). A study in Goa, India, reported that the most common perpetrators of forced sex reported by both young men and women were other students or friends (Patel and Gracy, 2001), and a study in Tanzania of primary school girls found that 75 percent reported being sexually harassed by a school boy, 46 percent by adult men, and 9 percent by teachers (Mgalla, Schapink, and Boerma, 1998). In Kenya, a study using trained observers noted through direct observation the sexual harassment of girls in 14-17 percent of schools (Mensch and Lloyd, 1998). While such reported sexual activity in the school environment is reported widely, it is nonetheless true that those who remain enrolled are much less likely to report ever having had sex, even coerced sex, than those of the same age who are no longer enrolled (see the discussion above under sexual initiation).

The adverse consequences of sexual coercion are multifaceted and extend from sexual and reproductive health to emotional damage to adverse school outcomes (see Heise, Ellsberg, and Gottemoeller, 1999, for a review). Several studies have suggested that young people who report experiencing coercive sex are subsequently more likely than other young people to engage in high-risk consensual sexual behavior, including early debut, multiple partners, nonuse of condoms, and even prostitution (Boyer and Fine, 1992; Handwerker, 1993; Heise, Moore, and Toubia, 1995; Stewart et al., 1996). Young people who have experienced coercion also suffer emotional and behavioral consequences. Depression, low self-esteem, posttraumatic stress, and serious consideration of suicide are more likely to characterize

TABLE 4-7 Percentage of Young People Reporting Forced Sexual Initiation in Selected Developing Countries

| Country | Study Site | Year[a] | Age Group | Sample Size | Females | Males |
|---|---|---|---|---|---|---|
| Studies Reported in Krug et al. (2002) | | | | | | |
| Cameroon | Bamenda | 1995 | 12-25 | 646 | 37 | 30 |
| Ghana | Three urban towns | 1996 | 12-24 | 750 | 21 | 5 |
| Mozambique | Maputo | 1999 | 13-18 | 1,659 | 19 | 7 |
| South Africa | Transkei | 1994-1995 | 15-18 | 1,975 | 28 | 6 |
| Tanzania | Mwanza | 1996 | 12-19 | 892 | 29 | 7 |
| Caribbean | Nine countries | 1997-1998 | 10-18 | 15,695 | 48 | 32 |
| Peru | Lima | 1995 | 16-17 | 611 | 40 | 11 |
| Studies Reported in Jejeebhoy and Bott (2003) | | | | | | |
| Ghana | Six districts | 1999 | 15+ | n.a. | 15 | n.a. |
| South Africa | Transkei | 1996 | 13-17 | n.a. | 28 | n.a. |
| South Africa | Cape Town | 2001 | < 19 | n.a. | 18-32 | n.a. |
| Central African Rep. | National | 1999 | 15-19 | n.a. | 24 | n.a. |
| Kenya | National | 1994 | 12-24 | n.a. | 40 | n.a. |
| Philippines | Duaguete city | 1998 | 15-24 | n.a. | 5 | n.a. |
| Argentina | Buenos Aires | 1991 | 13-19 | n.a. | 5 | n.a. |
| Peru | Three cities | 1996 | 13-19 | n.a. | 2-20 | n.a. |

[a]In bottom panel, "year" corresponds to the year the study was published.
NOTES: n.a. = not available. Sample populations and questions asked in surveys varied so results are illustrative, not directly comparable.
SOURCES: Top panel—Krug et al. (2002:151-153); bottom panel—Jejeebhoy and Bott (2003:40).

them than other young people (Heise, Moore, and Toubia, 1995; Luster and Small, 1997; Stewart et al., 1996; Stock et al., 1997).

A widely held norm in many settings argues that young men's sexual needs are beyond their control and demand immediate satisfaction. Sexual conquest and potency appear as related themes in many cultural definitions of masculinity, placing women at increased risk of coerced sex (Heise, Ellsberg, and Gottemoeller, 1999). Young men are perceived to have uncontrollable sexual urges, and forced sex becomes an acceptable option (see Varga, 1997, 2001). As studies of young people in Africa (Ajuwon, Akin-Jimoh, Olley, and Akintola, 2001), and India (Sodhi and Verma, 2003) show, boys are socialized in some settings into a sense of entitlement to sex—for example, as fair exchange for gifts or attention given to the girl. Case studies undertaken in Ghana, Malawi, and Zimbabwe document the predatory behavior of male students and teachers in schools in which sexual aggression goes largely unpunished and there are strong social supports for conforming to traditional gender roles (Leach et al., 2003). As a result, as several studies suggest, female victims are perceived to have invited the coercive incident. These gender double standards condone premarital and extramarital sexual relations for men but ostracize and stigmatize sexual activity among unmarried young women.

Studies of sexual coercion among young people suggest that they often fail to perceive the environments in which they live as supportive and nonjudgmental with regard to their sexual health needs in general. As a study in Kenya revealed, young females reporting coercion were reluctant to confide in parents for fear that they would blame the girl for inciting the incident or violate her privacy by discussing it in the community. Teachers and health providers are similarly perceived to be no more supportive. In one study in Goa, India, for example, only 15 percent of female victims and not a single male victim shared the experience with friends or parents (Patel and Gracy, 2001). In a similar vein, young people in Uganda report that telling family about rape leads to misunderstanding or being sent away from home (Bohmer and Kirumira, 1997). In Bohmer and Kirumira's (1997) study in Kenya, girls feel there is no avenue for recourse: parents accused them of collusion, police of prostitution. Narratives in Nigeria suggest that victims are afraid to draw attention to themselves for fear of being blamed by family and society for the incident (Ajuwon et al., 2001). Similarly, a study of young people seeking counseling in clinics in Colombia and Peru reports that as many as two-thirds of those seeking counseling had never told anyone about the coercive experience, for reasons of shame, fear, and threats from the perpetrator (Stewart et al., 1996).

## Contraceptive Knowledge and Use

The current generation of young people in the developing world is the first to grow up with nearly universal knowledge of modern contraceptive methods, at least partly as a result of the efforts of organized family planning programs. DHS data show that, in the vast majority of surveys conducted in the last five years or so, more than 9 in 10 women ages 15-24 know about at least one contraceptive method and most know more than one (ORC Macro, 2004).

The use of contraception among young people has also been increasing. In the last 20 years, there has been a substantial improvement in overall access to family planning services of reasonable quality; it is not known the extent to which young people, particularly those who are unmarried, have experienced the same increase in access. Figures 4-6a through 4-6d show how the use of contraceptive methods among women ages 15-19 changed over roughly the last decade in developing countries in which comparable DHS surveys were conducted. Some increase in contraceptive use is evident in most countries, whatever the initial level of contraceptive prevalence. Increases tend to be smaller in surveys in sub-Saharan Africa, whereas some countries in Latin America, for example, Colombia and Bolivia, have seen a very rapid rise in contraception in this age group. Among North African and Middle Eastern and Asian countries, survey data are available only for married women. With the exception of India and the Philippines, these countries also demonstrate substantial increases in contraceptive use during the 1990s.

Levels of contraceptive use are still quite low among younger females; regional averages range from 4 to 10 percent of 15-19-year-olds (Table 4-8). This is partly because of lower levels of sexual activity among the unmarried women. Indeed, when one considers only sexually active females, the proportion using contraception at ages 15-19 doubles or triples in the regions with data. Among the never married sexually active women, prevalence rates are still higher, reaching 38 percent in South America. The use of contraception is much higher among women in their early 20s than among young people. The regional averages for Eastern and Southern Africa and Latin America and the Caribbean are around 24 percent, with higher levels of use in the former Soviet Asia and lower levels in Western and Middle Africa. In broad terms, contraceptive use increases as income level increases, although there are only two countries in the upper middle-income category, so it is not possible to draw firm conclusions.

Within regions, there are large differentials in contraceptive use by level of education (Table 4-9). These differentials are largest in sub-Saharan Africa, where contraceptive use among sexually active 20-24-year-olds with secondary or higher education is 4-5 times that among those with no educa-

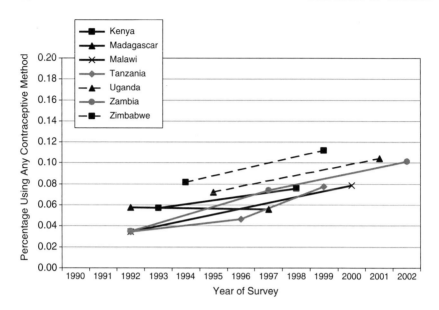

FIGURE 4-6a Percentage of females ages 15-19 using any contraceptive method, Eastern and Southern Africa.
SOURCE: DHS data, 1986-2000.

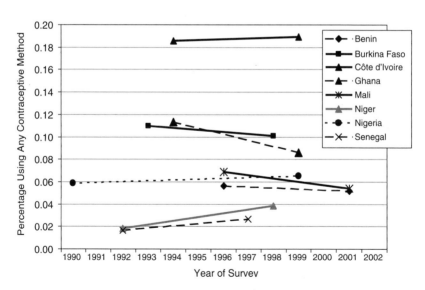

FIGURE 4-6b Percentage of females ages 15-19 using any contraceptive method, Western Africa.
SOURCE: DHS data, 1986-2000.

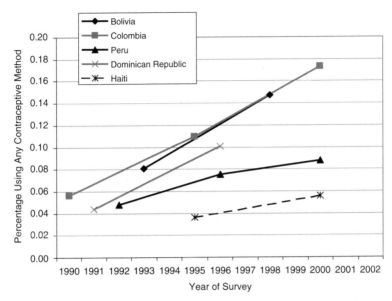

FIGURE 4-6c Percentage of females ages 15-19 using any contraceptive method, Latin America and Carribean.
SOURCE: DHS data, 1986-2000.

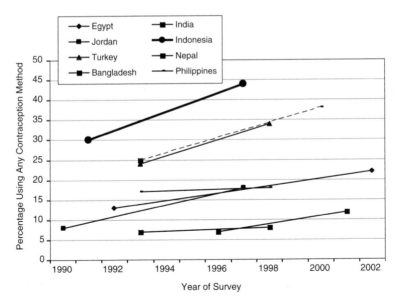

FIGURE 4-6d Percentage of married females ages 15-19 using any contraceptive method, Middle East and Asia.
SOURCE: Zlidar et al. (2003).

TABLE 4-8 Percentage of Women Ages 15-19 and 20-24 Currently Using Contraception by Region (Weighted Averages), Demographic and Health Surveys

| Region or Income Level (Number of countries) | Ages 15-19 | | | |
|---|---|---|---|---|
| | All | Sexually Active | Never Married | Sexually Active, Never Married |
| Region | | | | |
| Eastern and Southern Africa (13) | 9.4 | 21.1 | 7.7 | 27.7[a] |
| Western and Middle Africa (13) | 8.7 | 20.4 | 9.2 | 25.8[b] |
| Former Soviet Asia (4) | 3.6 | 24.5 | 1.0 | n.a.[c] |
| Caribbean/Central America (4) | 7.0 | 23.5 | 1.3 | n.a.[c] |
| South America (5) | 9.7 | 27.8 | 7.7 | 38.3 |
| Income Level | | | | |
| Low (29) | 7.0 | 17.7 | 6.1 | 29.2 |
| Lower middle (8) | 10.1 | 39.8 | 4.6 | 35.7 |
| Upper middle (2) | 12.4 | 27.8 | 12.3 | 43.2 |

[a]Due to insufficient sample size, average for sexually active never married includes 12 countries.

[b]Due to insufficient sample size, average for sexually active never married includes 11 countries.

tion. Similarly large differences in use are evident among 15-19-year-olds. Education differentials are smaller but still substantial in Latin America and the Caribbean.

Most studies of the determinants of contraceptive use do not focus specifically on young people. Those that do show that age, education (or school attendance or literacy), and urban residence are consistently positively associated with use (Ali et al., 2003; Gueye, Castle, and Konate, 2001; Gupta, 2000; Kuate-Defo, 1998). Some studies also identify various influences of religion. For example, in Cameroon, being Christian increases the likelihood of contraceptive use among women ages 15-27 (Kuate-Defo, 1998). In northeast Brazil, women ages 15-24 who regularly attended religious services (regardless of religion) were more likely to use contraception (Gupta, 2000).

Few young people, male or female, report using contraception at the time of their first sexual intercourse, although there are some exceptions; in a 1993 survey in Jamaica, for example, 43 percent of females reported using contraception the first time they had sex. The likelihood of using a method the first time increases with age at first sex (Blanc and Way, 1998). Young people often report failing to use contraception because they were

| Ages 20-24 | | | |
|---|---|---|---|
| All | Sexually Active | Never Married | Sexually Active, Never Married |
| 24.7 | 29.9 | 22.7 | 42.2[a] |
| 17.3 | 23.3 | 28.4 | 35.4[b] |
| 30.2 | 43.0 | 3.8 | n.a.[c] |
| 24.0 | 35.8 | 4.1 | n.a.[c] |
| 23.7 | 33.3 | 31.1 | 58.6 |
| 18.9 | 24.8 | 20.6 | 43.6 |
| 35.5 | 55.0 | 15.1 | 49.3 |
| 24.1 | 29.6 | 40.4 | 64.1 |

[c]Too few countries with sufficient cases to calculate regional average.
NOTE: n.a. = not available.

not expecting to have sex. Once they start to use contraception, girls are more likely to discontinue contraceptive use than older women and more likely to experience a contraceptive failure (Blanc and Way, 1998).

The proportion of young women who are not using contraception in spite of being exposed to the risk of pregnancy and not wanting to have a child ranged from 17 to 47 percent of married women ages 15-19 and 16 to 40 percent of women ages 20-24 in 26 developing countries in the early to mid-1990s (Westoff and Bankole, 1995). Young married women are about as likely as older women to have an unmet need for contraception. This is because younger women tend to want to space their births rather than stop childbearing, while older women increasingly prefer to stop childbearing; the net effect of the two tendencies is a roughly equal level of unmet need (Westoff and Bankole, 1995). Unmet need among never married women is much more difficult to assess and can vary widely depending on how it is calculated, because their exposure to the risk of pregnancy is complicated to measure accurately (Westoff, 2001).

Why young people do not use contraception, even when they are sexually active but do not intend a pregnancy, is a complex question. Lack of proper information is one possibility. While most young women have some

TABLE 4-9 Percentage of Women Ages 15-19 and 20-24 Currently Using Contraception by Region and Years of Education (Weighted Averages), Demographic and Health Surveys

| Region/Years of Education (# of Countries) | Ages 15-19 | | Ages 20-24 | |
|---|---|---|---|---|
| | All | Sexually Active | All | Sexually Active |
| Eastern and Southern Africa (13)[a] | | | | |
| 0-3 years | 8.2 | 7.2 | 16.1 | 11.5 |
| 4-7 years | 9.5 | 17.5 | 26.9 | 28.6 |
| 8+ years | 13.6 | 29.2 | 36.3 | 48.9 |
| Western and Middle Africa (13)[b] | | | | |
| 0-3 years | 3.8 | 7.4 | 7.1 | 8.6 |
| 4-7 years | 9.3 | 27.1 | 18.4 | 24.7 |
| 8+ years | 16.3 | 45.1 | 31.5 | 46.3 |
| Caribbean/Central America (4)[c] | | | | |
| 0-3 years | 6.5 | 19.5 | 19.5 | 30.1 |
| 4-7 years | 9.9 | 27.0 | 30.7 | 43.3 |
| 8+ years | 5.8 | 35.4 | 25.9 | 44.6 |
| South America (5) | | | | |
| 0-3 years | 9.5 | 23.3 | 21.7 | 26.3 |
| 4-7 years | 13.1 | 39.3 | 31.1 | 42.7 |
| 8+ years | 20.1 | 57.6 | 47.9 | 68.6 |

[a]Due to insufficient sample size, average for sexually active includes 9 countries.

[b]Due to insufficient sample size, average for sexually active includes 10 countries.

[c]Due to insufficient sample size, average for sexually active includes 3 countries.

NOTE: Former Soviet Asia is excluded because virtually all women have 8+ years of education.

level of knowledge about one or more methods of contraception, knowledge of basic sexual and reproductive information is inadequate in many settings. Moreover, their knowledge of contraceptive methods may include inaccurate or exaggerated information about the risks involved. When it is considered inappropriate for children to learn about sex from their parents—as shown for example in studies in Uganda, South Africa, and India (Jejeebhoy, 1998; Nyanzi, Pool, and Kinsman, 2001; Wood, Maforah, and Jewkes, 1998)—and when schools do not provide forthright sex education (e.g., Balmer et al., 1997; Jejeebhoy, 1998), young people can be expected to enter marriage or their initial sexual relationship with various misconceptions. In contrast, when they have good initial knowledge about such issues as HIV/AIDS, research in Zambia shows their subsequent sexual behavior is more responsible, involving fewer lifetime sexual partners and more use, including more consistent use, of condoms (Magnani et al., 2004).

## Abortion

Performed in safe conditions with modern methods, induced abortion carries little risk to women's health or mortality. In representative developed countries, the risk of dying is no more than 1 in 100,000 procedures, lower than the relatively low risks associated with pregnancy and childbirth in these countries (The Alan Guttmacher Institute, 1999). Conditions are not necessarily safe, however, for women in developing countries (for further discussion, see the section under changes in the health service environment in Chapter 2) and are particularly hazardous for young women because of the circumstances under which abortions among them are likely to occur. Research suggests that while young women are not disproportionately likely to have abortions, they are more likely to delay seeking them and more likely to use an unskilled abortion provider.

National vital statistics on abortion are incomplete for all but a handful of developing countries. Even when data are available, they are often not broken down by age. Official statistics, even when they are reasonably complete, exclude abortions that take place outside the health care system. Survey data, in which women are interviewed concerning their experience of abortion, are available for some countries. However, collecting data on induced abortion through surveys is notoriously difficult, often because abortion is legally restricted, but also because, regardless of its legal status, abortion is an extremely sensitive issue (Barreto et al., 1992; Malhotra et al., 2003; Singh, Henshaw, and Berentsen, 2003). As a result, data on the incidence of abortion among young women in developing countries are largely unavailable, and the data that are available probably underreport its incidence. The available body of research on other aspects of abortion in general, and among young women in particular, is also relatively limited. Many studies are based on samples drawn from hospitals, reflecting the population of women who obtain unsafe abortions but not those who succeed in obtaining a safe procedure; many of the available studies are small scale, and many are qualitative, with few providing quantitative information on numbers, prevalence, or rates of abortion.

There were only five developing countries with national data on abortion prevalence among young women in the mid- to late 1990s: Cuba, Kazakhstan, Kyrgyzstan, Turkey, and Uzbekistan. Among these, the abortion rate (per 1,000 women) among women under age 20 ranged from virtually zero in Uzbekistan to 91 in Cuba. For women ages 20-24, the range was from 18 to 88. Cuba is noteworthy for its extremely high abortion rate among women younger than age 20; at 91 per 1,000, it exceeds that of the 19 other developed and developing countries in this study (Bankole, Singh, and Haas, 1999). Information based on other types of data is also available from a few countries. A large-scale survey of young people in Uganda reported that 17 percent of 15-19-year-olds previously had an abortion and 53 percent of 20-24-year-olds had done so (Agyei and Epema, 1992). A study among 20-29-year-olds in Yaoundé, Cameroon, found that 21 percent of women reported ever having an abortion and 29 percent of young men reported ever having a girlfriend who terminated a pregnancy for which they were responsible (Calvès, 2002). Indirect estimates of the abortion rate in the early 1990s for young people in six Latin American countries showed that this rate (the number of abortions per 1,000 15-19-year-olds per year) ranged from 13 in Mexico to 36 in the Dominican Republic (The Alan Guttmacher Institute, 1999).

For the five countries included in the Bankole, Singh, and Haas (1999) study, the number of abortions per pregnancy rises consistently with age in all countries except one (Cuba). In contrast, population-based estimates in India for married women suggest higher abortion ratios for teenagers—1.7 percent of all pregnancies at ages 15-19 versus 1.3 percent for older women (Jejeebhoy, 1998), but these ratios are quite low in comparison to other countries, most likely because of underreporting of abortions. Based on the extremely limited data, it would appear that younger women obtain abortions less often than older women, but they nevertheless may be at greater risk when they do.

Among young pregnant women observed at a public hospital in Mexico City, 72 percent of young women who had an unwanted pregnancy that was ultimately carried to full term reported an average of 2.3 unsuccessful attempts at abortion (Ehrenfeld, 1999). For the members of the group who did abort the pregnancy, one to four abortion attempts were made before success. Many of these attempts were self-induced: typically "strong injections" of unknown drugs, the consumption of infusions of various types, and even deliberately falling down stairs. This is a common pattern followed by women of all ages seeking abortion; several attempts are usually made before succeeding in obtaining an abortion, safe or unsafe.

Furthermore, although the evidence is scattered, it suggests that young women—and particularly those who are unmarried—are considerably more likely than married adult women to delay seeking abortion and hence to undergo second trimester abortions. In India, where abortion is not restricted, a study reports that while three in five unmarried young women who had a medical termination of pregnancy at a municipal general hospital from 1978 to 1983 sought second trimester abortions, only a quarter of all married young women did so (Aras, Pai, and Jain, 1987). A more recent study in rural Maharashtra observes that, while married women regardless of age sought abortion at an average of 10.9 and 10.8 weeks of gestation, respectively, unmarried young women sought it at 12.7 weeks (Ganatra and Hirve, 2002). In Tanzania, where abortion is legally restricted, a study of young women seeking postabortion care reports that, while about half

(52 percent) sought abortion in the first 10 weeks, 37 percent sought it between 10 and 16 weeks of pregnancy and 11 percent sought it between 16 and 20 weeks (Mpangile, Leshabari, and Kihwele, 1999).

Unmarried young women, are, moreover, considerably more likely to resort to clandestine abortions and unskilled providers (Ehrenfeld, 1999; FOCUS on Young Adults, 2001; Ganatra and Hirve, 2002; Mpangile, Leshabari, and Kihwele, 1999; The Alan Guttmacher Institute, 1998; Varga, 1997). The need for confidentiality is a leading reason underlying this preference. For example, studies in India report that confidentiality was the leading criterion in the selection of a provider—outranking safety and convenience criteria. One such study observed that young women, whether married or not, were more likely to seek abortion from untrained providers, traditional birth attendants, paramedical workers, as well as medical practitioners unlicensed in providing abortion: while 22 percent of older women underwent abortion from an untrained provider, this proportion reaches almost one-third among young women who were married, and almost one-half among young women who were unmarried (Ganatra, forthcoming; Ganatra and Hirve, 2002). A study in Dar es Salaam, Tanzania, reports similarly that, of the abortion providers reported by young women who had undergone abortion, only 22 percent were identified as doctors; 65 percent were described as "other health workers" and 13 percent as "quacks" (Mpangile, Leshabari, and Kihwele, 1999). In urban Cameroon, abortions obtained before age 20 were more likely to be reported as self-induced or performed by an untrained person than were abortions performed after age 20 (Calvès, 2002).

In the study in India, while cost was cited as the leading motive for this choice among young married women, confidentiality was the leading reason reported by the unmarried; in general, young women were more likely to report, moreover, that the provider had not explained the abortion procedure (Ganatra and Hirve, 2002). The case study in Dar es Salaam also reports that cost considerations prompted provider selection, and that providers neither counseled nor gave them information or contraceptive supplies (Mpangile, Leshabari, and Kihwele, 1999).

An ethnographic study in Lombok, Indonesia, reported similarly that even though providers were willing to provide abortions to unmarried women, they remained highly critical of unmarried pregnant women and as a result the quality of services provided to them was compromised: no attempt was made to explain the abortion procedure or postabortion contraception, provider attitudes were judgmental, and no counseling was provided. Doctors themselves corroborated these attitudes, labeling unmarried young abortion seekers as immoral and bad (Bennett, 2001).

And in China, where abortion is legally available in the first trimester, a large number of migrant young women in urban areas sought abortion from private facilities because they felt their privacy would be better protected there (Zheng et al., 2001). Likewise, in Cuba, where abortion services are widely available, in order to ensure anonymity young people frequently seek services outside their local clinic (Peláez Mendoz et al., 1999). However, a study of induced abortion among single women in Sichuan province suggested that providers were well trained and abortions were performed under generally safe conditions (Luo et al., 1995). In the Republic of Korea too, single women cited privacy as an important criterion in the selection of an abortion facility (Tai-Hwan, Kwang Hee, and Sung-nam, 1999).

Reasons frequently cited by young women for obtaining abortion are to continue to attend school, a lack of commitment by their partner, and being unmarried. In a review by Bankole, Darroch, and Singh (1999), between 30 and 55 percent of women who had an abortion in four studies in sub-Saharan Africa reported that their main reason for having the abortion was concern that childbearing and rearing would disrupt their education or their employment. In urban Cameroon, being in school increased the odds that a pregnancy would result in abortion sevenfold, after controlling for other factors (Calvès, 2002). This reason was less common but still significant in studies in three Latin American countries included in the Bankole, Darroch, and Singh (1999) review, with 15 percent of women reporting it. In addition to this category of reasons, a substantial proportion (14 to 37 percent of women) in all but one of the sub-Saharan and Latin American countries reported that their main reason for seeking the abortion was that they were too young or that their parents or someone else objected to the pregnancy.

Recent studies have documented the impact of rising rates of contraceptive use on abortion rates among women in a few developing countries (Marston and Cleland, 2003; Senlet et al., 2001; Singh and Sedgh, 1997; Westoff et al., 1998). The relationship between the two is complex and a number of factors come into play, but these studies generally demonstrate that a trade-off eventually occurs between contraception and abortion, as more women use contraception and as they use it more effectively. Where the use of contraception has grown among young women, particularly among sexually active unmarried women, the last decade may have seen reduced reliance on abortion or may signal an impending decrease in the demand for abortion. In many countries, however, it will most likely be several years before abortion rates decline; increases in exposure to the risk of premarital pregnancy, reductions in the number of children desired, and the increasing competition of educational and work aspirations with motherhood suggest that, unless young women adopt family planning in rising proportions, they will increasingly resort to abortion.

## OTHER RISK BEHAVIORS AND THEIR HEALTH CONSEQUENCES

Some health behaviors that typically are initiated during the transition to adulthood can compromise current health and reduce life expectancy and well-being. WHO estimates that 70 percent of premature deaths among adults are largely due to behavior initiated during adolescence (World Health Organization, 1995). Cigarette smoking, the consumption of alcohol, and the use of illicit drugs are among behaviors that can have the most damaging effects on long-term health. These behaviors often occur together and appear to have some common underlying causes. The development of a global youth subculture that underestimates the dangers of smoking and drug use is thought to be an important factor in the growth of smoking and substance abuse in developing countries. Trends toward easier access to drugs and increasing urbanization, the influence of Western media, the relaxation of traditional social controls on young people (Mugisha et al., 2003), and the resulting "ambivalences and contradictions of a confusing cultural braid" (Nsamenang, 2002:65) are also implicated. While not further discussed due to lack of comparative data, increasing obesity and overweight among young people is another concern that is emerging in the context of rapid global change (see Box 4-3).

### Smoking

According to one estimate, between 68,000 and 84,000 people under the age of 20 in low- and middle-income countries take up smoking every day (Gajalakshmi et al., 2000). Smoking usually starts early in life. In developed countries, the majority of smokers start in their teens. In developing countries, the starting age may be slightly later, on average, perhaps in the early 20s, but the trend is toward younger ages (Jha and Chaloupka, 1999; Yang et al., 1999, cited in Hannum and Liu, 2005). Once a smoker starts, symptoms of dependence develop quickly, particularly for those who start young. A study of 12-13-year-olds indicates that two cigarettes once a week for six months are on average enough to develop 11 specifically defined symptoms of dependence in boys. In girls, it takes on average only three weeks. The development of any symptom of dependence strongly predicts continued smoking and, as is the case with other health-related behavior, there is some evidence that young people tend to underestimate the risk of becoming addicted to nicotine and the probability that they will continue to smoke into adulthood (DiFranza et al., 2002; Gruber and Zinman, 2000; Jha and Chaloupka, 1999).

More than 100 surveys on smoking among young people have been conducted since 1999 by the Global Youth Tobacco Survey (GYTS) program (World Health Organization and Centers for Disease Control and

## BOX 4-3
## The Nutrition Transition:
## Increasing Obesity and Overweight Among Young People

The nutrition transition is defined as the shift in dietary and physical activity patterns from high activity levels and diets relatively low in fat and sugar and relatively high in carbohydrates and fiber that are typical of poor rural populations to low activity levels and diets relatively high in saturated fat, sugar, and refined foods and low in fiber that are typical of wealthier, urban populations (Popkin, 2002). This transition results in increased proportions of the population who are overweight and obese and higher prevalence of chronic and degenerative diseases.

Evidence from developing countries points to increases in the prevalence of overweight and obesity among many adult populations and, in a few countries with data specific to young people, that this trend extends to young people (Popkin, 2002; Wang, Monteiro, and Popkin, 2002). For example, in Brazil, the proportion of persons ages 6-18 who were overweight increased from 4 to 14 percent between 1975 and 1997. In China, the increase was from 6 to 8 percent between 1991 and 1997. Other evidence from China shows an upward shift in the body mass index and a large increase in those in the overweight category (body mass index > 25) among adults (Popkin, 2002) (see figure below). This shift has been accompanied by a marked decline in physical activity.

These changes in the overweight and obesity profile of populations are associated with higher prevalence of nutrition-related chronic diseases, such as diabetes, hypertension, and cardiovascular disease. The treatment of such diseases entails high health care costs and can have negative effects on socioeconomic development as a result of premature death and disability. The nutritional status of young people is particularly important because overweight and obese children are at elevated risk of becoming obese adults (Wang, Keyou, and Popkin, 2000). Some developing countries have started to address these issues with both school-based and general nutrition education programs, promotion of physical activity, and food pricing and labeling policies intended to discourage the consumption of unhealthy foods (Popkin, 2002).

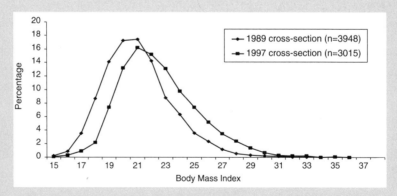

Shift in the distribution of BMI among Chinese adults: Ages 20-45 in 1989 and 1997.
SOURCE: Popkin (2002).

Prevention, 2002). The surveys use self-administered questionnaires and are nationally or subnationally representative samples of in-school students who are primarily ages 13-15 (GYTS Collaborating Group, 2002).[13] The data are limited to in-school young people attending school. Thus samples are highly selective of those populations most likely to be exposed to global youth culture and Western media and unrepresentative of the populations of these ages in settings in which the majority of young people or of girls are not attending school at this age.

The percentages currently smoking by region based on 126 GYTS surveys are shown in Table 4-10 (individual survey results are in Appendix Table 4-1). Across the developing country surveys, 15 percent of male students on average and 7 percent of females students are currently smoking cigarettes. There is substantial variation among regions, with current smoking among male students varying from 41 percent in the Russian Federation and the former Soviet Asia to less than 10 percent in Southern and Eastern Asia. Among the 23 state-level surveys conducted in India, smoking prevalence among boys ranged from 1 to 33 percent and among girls from 1 to 13 percent. The regional medians are lower for girls than boys in every developing region. Substantial proportions of young people attending school in some countries use forms of tobacco other than cigarettes (GYTS Collaborating Group, 2002).

Survey data on smoking among young people ages 15-19 have been collected recently for five Asian countries—Indonesia (1998), Nepal (2000), the Philippines (1994), Taiwan (1994), and Thailand (1994)—under the Asian Young Adult Reproductive Risk (AYARR) project and a handful of other countries under the DHS program. Among these countries, gender differences are even greater with no more than 5 percent of females reporting current smoking in any of these surveys (Choe, Westley, and Retherford, 2002; ORC Macro, 2004). It is not surprising that gender differences in smoking are reported to be smaller in student populations than in the general population, because it is by being a student that boys' and girls' exposure and experiences during these years become more similar. Nonetheless, smoking rates remain lower among girls in most places where data are limited to student populations, and this could be due to the fact that smoking is not considered ladylike or attractive for girls by young people in

---

[13]The survey respondents are all students in the grades that normally correspond to ages 13-15 in each site, but all students in those grades on the day of the survey are eligible, so some are less than age 13 or older than age 15 (GYTS Collaborating Group, 2002). In each of the Asian Young Adult Reproductive Risk surveys shown in Appendix Table 4-2, smoking prevalence was lower among in-school than out-of-school youth ages 15-19, the median gap being 15 percentage points.

TABLE 4-10 Percentage of Young People Currently Smoking by Sex

| Age Group and Region or Country | % Currently Smoking | |
| --- | --- | --- |
| | Males | Females |
| In-School Ages 13-15 (GYTS), 1999-2003 | | |
| Eastern and Southern Africa (16) | 12 | 5 |
| Western/Central Africa (10) | 24 | 6 |
| South-eastern/South-central Asia (31) | 8 | 3 |
| East Asia (5) | 9 | 2 |
| Russia/Former Soviet Asia (3) | 41 | 29 |
| West Asia/Northern Africa (19) | 14 | 4 |
| Caribbean/Central America (24) | 14 | 11 |
| South America (34) | 20 | 15 |
| Europe (14) | 24 | 20 |
| Oceania (3) | 23 | 20 |
| USA (1) | 18 | 18 |
| All, Excluding Europe and USA | 15 | 7 |
| All Ages 15-19 (DHS), 1999-2002 | | |
| Benin 2001 | n.a. | 1 |
| Malawi 2000 | n.a. | <1 |
| Rwanda 2000 | n.a. | 1 |
| Uganda 2000-2001 | n.a. | 1 |
| Zambia 2001-2002 | 2 | <1 |
| Zimbabwe 1999 | n.a. | <1 |
| Egypt 2000 | n.a. | <1 |
| Cambodia 2000 | n.a. | 1 |
| Haiti 2000 | 1 | 1 |
| All Ages 15-19 (YARHS), 1994-2000 | | |
| Indonesia 1998[a] | 38 | 1 |
| Nepal 2000[b] | 12 | 4 |
| Philippines 1994 | 28 | 3 |
| Taiwan 1994 | 30 | 5 |
| Thailand 1994 | 33 | 2 |

[a]Includes nonmetropolitan provinces in Java.
[b]Excludes the mountain ecological region. Includes cigarettes/*bidis*.
NOTES: n.a. = not available. Global Youth Tobacco Survey (GYTS) regional percentages are unweighted medians of all sites (both national and subnational).
SOURCES: Demographic and Health Survey tabulations from 1999-2002; Choe, Westley, and Retherford (2002); and GYTS (2003).

some places (e.g., Morrow et al., 2002). For example, in almost every GYTS survey in a developing country, a larger percentage of respondents said that smoking makes boys look more attractive than said it makes girls look more attractive (GYTS Collaborating Group, 2002). In comparison to the volume of research on the determinants of such risk behaviors as smoking among young people in Western countries, little is known about developing countries. We found only a few examples of multivariate studies of the determinants of smoking and even fewer that were methodologically sound. These studies and other descriptive information tend to confirm that both individual factors as well as factors present in young people's social environment "protect" them from smoking (see Box 4-4). For example, one study on the initiation of smoking among Filipino youth ages 15-19 shows that being strongly religious reduced the odds of initiating smoking, while living away from parents increased the odds (Choe and Raymundo, 2001). Among Chinese young people, problem behavior (including smoking) was reduced in the presence of support from teachers, disapproval of such behavior by adults in the neighborhood, and control of the family as well as individual intolerance of deviant behavior (Jessor et al., 2003). As in the case of studies of sexual behavior among young people, many studies of smoking and other health-related behaviors have found a strong association between the likelihood of smoking and the perceived behavior of peers (e.g., whether or not friends smoke). In cross-sectional statistical studies, these variables are most likely to be endogenous, and their introduction in the analysis may bias the results of the study.

Young smokers are not necessarily content with their habit. Across countries participating in the GYTS, approximately 70 percent want to stop smoking, and two-thirds have actually tried to stop. The desire to stop is particularly strong in low-income countries, where 80-90 percent often want to stop (Figure 4-7). Young people obtain cigarettes more often by purchasing them in a store than from any other source (Warren et al., 2000), so their cost may be a factor if incomes are particularly low. Indeed, some studies of European young people have shown that the likelihood of smoking is positively associated with increased personal income (Griesbach, Amos, and Currie, 2003; Pavis et al., 1998; also see discussion below on taxation policies under policy recommendations).

Smoking has declined in the general population in various developed countries (Cutler, 2004; Gruber and Zinman, 2000; Johnston, O'Malley, and Bachman, 2003). The trend among the adult population in developing countries, in contrast, has been upward since the 1970s, although possibly more moderate in the 1990s. Data on trends in smoking among teens and young adults are not available as yet for most developing countries, but the consensus based on the limited information available is that smoking among this group increased during the 1990s in many countries, and that the increases were particularly steep among young women (Jha and Chaloupka, 1999; Shafey, Dolwick, and Guindon, 2003). Even if this trend turns downward, however, rising numbers of deaths attributable to tobacco are expected for decades to come. In the 40 years subsequent to the peak of the tobacco epidemic in the United States in the 1950s, for example, deaths in middle age attributable to tobacco rose from 1 in 8 to 1 in 3 (Jha and

## BOX 4-4
## A Syndrome of Problem Behavior?

Experimenting with tobacco, alcohol, and illicit drugs would seem to involve interdependent decisions. A syndrome of risk may exist, with young people who are inclined to try one hazardous substance also likely to try another. Such a syndrome need not involve a psychological predisposition to addiction. It may instead be related to social context: circumstances in which one substance is available and considered acceptable may also provide opportunities to sample another. Arguably, such a syndrome could extend to other behaviors that pose immediate or delayed health risks, including early sexual activity.

Research in developed countries appears to provide confirmation of such a syndrome. Among young people living in the United States, alcohol abuse, smoking, and use of illicit drugs tend to go together, and these behaviors have been shown in some studies to correlate with precocious sexual activity. Studies in Finland and Israel show parallel interdependencies. Importantly, these problem behaviors also appear to have similar psychosocial and environmental correlates (Jessor, 1984, 1991).

It is not clear at this time, however, whether a syndrome of problem behavior extends to young people in developing countries. One indication is a recent study that assesses problem behavior (delinquency, smoking, and problem drinking) among young people ages 13-15 in Beijing schools and compares them with young people in urban U.S. schools in the Rocky Mountain area (Jessor et al., 2003). In spite of marked differences in the social context of young people at the two sites, the researchers found similar factors at work in both settings, notably the influence of peers or schoolmates on such behavior and the protective effect of personal intolerance for deviance. In the Beijing sample but not in the U.S. sample, problem behavior was also lower among those who reported stronger family controls and neighborhood disapproval of such behavior. These factors—peer influence and the protective influence of personal and social disapproval—had roughly equal, though opposite, effects. With somewhat similar dynamics across cultures, despite the variation in the effect of family controls, the existence of a similar syndrome seems plausible, but considerably more research confirmation is needed.

Could a syndrome cover such other health risk behaviors as poor diet and limited exercise? These factors appear somewhat less strongly linked to cigarette smoking and alcohol abuse, forming a separate though related class of behaviors among U.S. teens (Turbin, Jessor, and Costa, 2000). Extending the idea of a syndrome further to cover other problem behaviors, such as those mainly involving legal or normative transgressions, may be problematic. The research consensus for developed countries appears to be that, when problem behaviors are defined broadly, separate factors are identifiable for externalizing problems, such as physical aggression, and internalizing problems, such as shyness or depressed mood (Loeber et al., 1998)—suggesting two syndromes rather than one. Perhaps more critical, what is considered a normative transgression may vary across developing countries, and what is normative in a given culture is not necessarily healthy. Where social or even legal norms restrict various forms of sexual behavior, such as contraceptive use among young people, nonnormative behavior may in fact be the healthier choice.

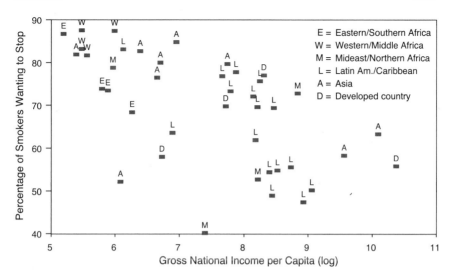

FIGURE 4-7 Percentage of student smokers ages 13-15 wanting to stop, by per capita national income and region.
SOURCES: Global Youth Tobacco Survey Collaborating Group (2002) and World Bank (2001).

Chaloupka, 1999). The health effects of a continued rise in smoking among young people in developing countries could be felt for even longer (Gajalakshmi et al., 2000).

## Drug and Alcohol Use

Not surprisingly, comparable data on illicit drug use among young people in developing countries are scarce and often of dubious quality. Nevertheless, international comparisons that provide a general picture of levels and trends are periodically compiled by the United Nations (e.g., United Nations, 1999b, 2000b). There is an enormous research literature on the correlates of alcohol and drug use among young people, although a great deal more is known about young people in developed than developing countries. A comprehensive review of this literature is beyond the scope of this chapter, but a summary of significant trends and issues is given below.

The data compiled by the United Nations show that the prevalence of drug use tends to be lower on average in developing countries than in developed countries although the gap may have decreased since the early to mid-1990s due to both stable or declining prevalence in developed regions combined with increases in developing regions. For most drugs except marijuana, however, the prevalence of drug use in the developing regions is still mostly well below Europe, North America, Australia, and New Zealand.

Research suggests that, unlike smoking, many young people who experiment with illicit drugs do not become addicted and do not continue to use when they become adults (United Nations, 1999b). This pattern is manifested in higher reported prevalence rates among young people than among the general population. It is worth noting, however, that the younger the age at first experimentation, the more likely that a serious addiction will develop; there are indications that the initiation into drug use has become earlier, especially in places where amphetamine-type stimulants (such as Ecstasy) are popular. In the developing world, these places include some countries in South-eastern Asia and Africa (United Nations, 1999b). At the same time, even short-term experimental drug and alcohol use can have detrimental effects on progress in school, and the impaired judgment that results can increase the likelihood of engaging in other risky behavior, such as unprotected sex, drunk driving, and violence (Call et al., 2002).

In 1990, alcohol use was responsible for 5 percent of all deaths of young people ages 5 to 29 worldwide (Jernigan, 2001). The link between alcohol use among young people and adult alcohol dependence has also been documented in at least one developing country—Costa Rica—where a 1995 study showed that 55 percent of those identified as alcoholic and 40 percent of those drinking "excessively" began drinking before age 15 compared with 31 percent of those drinking at lower levels (Jernigan, 2001). Compared with developed countries, studies on alcohol consumption among young people in developing countries are scarce and rarely comparable in terms of age groups or categories of use (lifetime, current, or heavy use). Overall, rates of alcohol use among young people tend to be lower in developing countries than developed countries. However, as corporations intensify marketing campaigns and increase the sale of new types of alcohol products in developing countries, alcohol consumption patterns are predicted to rise. In Mexico, new types of sweeter alcoholic beverages, combining cola and liquor, are appearing on the market and are consumed more among young people in urban areas who are under the age of 18 (World Health Organization, 2001b). Data from Brazil, Chile, and Mexico already indicate an increase in drinking among all young people, especially girls.

Generally speaking, boys are more likely to drink and drink heavily than girls, and alcohol consumption tends to become more prevalent with age. Surveys conducted in Africa, Latin America, and China consistently show higher rate of alcohol use among boys than girls (Jernigan, 2001).

At-risk young people may initiate drinking earlier and drink more than other young people. For example, a study of Brazilian street youth found that 33 percent of young people ages 9-11 and 77 percent of those ages 15-

18 reported heavy use of alcohol (Jernigan, 2001). Young people in developing countries are increasingly engaging in binge drinking, which until now has been a type of drinking associated only with developed countries.

It is difficult to link trends in alcohol use among young people in developing countries with other global trends, given data limitations. For example, since most data on drinking among young people comes from surveys of students, little is known about nonstudent alcohol consumption and what the impact will be of worldwide rising school enrollment rates. However, it is clear that as developing countries become more urban and as the marketing and proliferation of alcohol products intensifies, patterns of drinking among young people in developing countries will become more similar to those of developed countries.

## POLICIES AND PROGRAMS AIMED AT YOUNG PEOPLE'S HEALTH

Young people become increasingly important actors in shaping their own health during adolescence. As described above, adolescence entails making choices concerning lifestyles and actions that have significant short-term and long-term health implications—for example, choosing health-promoting activities such as regular school attendance, participation in sports, participation in community-based youth groups or activities, and abstinence or contraceptive use or choosing health-compromising activities such as smoking, alcohol and drug use, joining gangs, or unprotected sex. Other challenges entail contending with adverse circumstances not of their own making—for example, exposure to infectious disease (especially tuberculosis and malaria) and parasites, exposure to environmental contaminants, and malnutrition related to poverty.

At the same time, young people increasingly become "clients" for policies and programs aimed at protecting their health, gradually eliminating the fiduciary role that parents and guardians play. It should be noted, however, that although many relevant policies and programs aim to directly influence young people as primary decision-makers on matters related to health, others recognize the important role that the context or environment in which young people are raised play in influencing their behaviors; these programs thus seek positive health outcomes indirectly by influencing environmental factors.

Numerous health-related policies and programs directed toward protecting the health of young people have been implemented in developing country settings over the years. To what extent have these policies and programs increased the likelihood of a healthy transition to adulthood? Despite the emergence of a global consensus that young people are a population subgroup having special needs and warranting special attention, the empirical evidence on the impact of relevant health policy and program initiatives remains thin. Careful studies of the impact of health-related policies are particularly lacking, and cost-effectiveness studies are virtually nonexistent. The existing body of evidence supports only the most tentative conclusions as to the effectiveness of health policy and program efforts undertaken to date, and it is insufficient to make meaningful comparisons as to the relative effectiveness of many promising policy and program approaches. One tentative conclusion that can be reached, however, is that a more recent generation of programs with multiple components appears to be more effective in changing behavior than single-strategy interventions, particularly if drawn on local institutions and are designed to be culturally appropriate to the local context.

In this section we review the available evidence on the impact of policies and programs in two areas: reproductive and sexual health and smoking. These were chosen because they are areas in which the choices made by young people can have an enormous impact on both their current and future health. Moreover, they are areas in which global trends, such as increasing education, the rise of market economies, and the diffusion of a global youth culture, are likely to play a major role. In addition, in both areas, one or more comprehensive reviews of the evidence on the effectiveness of interventions has recently been carried out. The discussion of reproductive and sexual health interventions is based largely on a review prepared as part of the final project activities of the U.S. Agency for International Development (USAID)-funded FOCUS on Young Adults project (Speizer, Heller, and Brieger, 2000) as well as on a summary of 10 subsequent studies conducted primarily under the FRONTIERS and Horizons projects (YouthNet/Family Health International, 2003).[14] The discussion of smoking interventions draws heavily on the World Bank's 1999-2000 work on the economics of tobacco control.

### Policies and Programs Directed Toward Improving Sexual and Reproductive Health Outcomes

The number of small-scale programs and interventions addressed to adolescent reproductive health needs that have been implemented has greatly increased since the U.N. International Conference on Population and Development in 1994, when member states agreed that young people have special reproductive health needs and recommended that special pro-

---

[14]While these reviews are comprehensive in the sense that they report on the evidence available from relatively rigorous evaluations, it is not known how well they represent the entire universe of sexual and reproductive health interventions for developing country youth.

grams be developed to address those needs (United Nations, 1994). As experience with programming has evolved, it appears that multicomponent programming is becoming more common. At the same time, the level of attention to assessing the impact of reproductive health programs for young people has also increased in the 1990s, although the proportion of programs that are subjected to rigorous evaluation remains small.

Many reproductive and sexual health programs have been evaluated using designs that are methodologically flawed and preclude drawing strong conclusions about the impact of the program being evaluated. This situation has improved over the last several years, however; much of the available evidence as to the impact of reproductive health interventions for young people in developing country settings now comes from matched quasi-experimental evaluations of small- to modest-scale programs and, in a few cases noted below, from randomized trials.[15] Unfortunately, however, it is not known how well the distribution of intervention studies in terms of type of program evaluated mirrors the underlying distribution of programs that have been developed over the last 10 years.

While these studies represent a substantial improvement in rigor, they are nevertheless subject to a number of important limitations. Generally, the available studies have measured only short-term effects, within 6 to 18 months after the intervention, and many of the interventions themselves have had very short durations. This is a potentially important limitation because some studies have suggested that the impact of such programs, school-based sexual and reproductive health education for example, may be transitory in nature (Eggleston et al., 2000; Jackson et al., 1998; Kirby, 1997). In addition, many of the matched quasi-experimental studies undertaken to date have failed to adequately account for possible endogeneity with regard to selectivity of program exposure. Also, the outcomes of most existing studies have been (self-reported) knowledge, attitudes, or behaviors that put young people at risk for adverse reproductive health outcomes (early sexual debut, unprotected sex, multiple sexual partners) rather than ultimate outcomes (pregnancy, HIV infection). The most common outcomes measured are knowledge or attitudes, intended behavior, condom use, any type of contraceptive use, initiation of sex, and frequency of sex.

All of the evidence discussed below comes from studies with random-

---

[15]In quasi-experimental designs, randomization is not used to assign subjects or groups of subjects to experimental groups. Instead, one or more control groups are identified that are as similar as possible to the treatment group on as many factors as possible. Alternatively, geographic areas that are similar to the treatment area population may be chosen (Bertrand, Magnani, and Rutenberg, 1996).

ized or matched control designs, some with pretest and posttest measurements and some with posttest-only measurements. Studies with less rigorous designs are not included in the discussion. The first part of the review focuses on the more traditional single-component programs, whereas the second part of the review focuses on the newer multicomponent programs.[16]

## Sexual and Reproductive Health Education in Schools

Undertaking sexual and reproductive health education programs in schools has the potential to reach a large number of young people in countries in which school enrollment rates are high. Although the reach of school-based programs is not universal, enrollment rates among adolescents are now relatively high in many developing country settings, and recent data indicate that they are rising more or less throughout the developing world, particularly among females. The curricula, content, duration, and format of these interventions varies. Overall, the programs attempt to impart information on one or more of the following areas: sexuality, HIV/AIDS transmission and prevention, family planning, condoms, sexually transmitted diseases, and decision-making and refusal skills.

Findings from studies in developing country settings suggest somewhat higher levels of intervention success in comparison to school-based programs in the United States and Canada, where a recent review has found minimal impact (DiCenso et al., 2002). A review of 22 evaluation studies by Speizer, Heller, and Brieger (2000) found that a large majority of the programs reviewed (17 of 21) were able to demonstrate impact on knowledge and attitudes. However, only 4 of 11 programs that sought to delay age at first sex and 3 of 6 seeking to reduce numbers of sexual partners were able to demonstrate impact. As with U.S. and Canadian programs, programs in developing countries in the aggregate appear to have been somewhat more successful in increasing contraceptive or condom use (impact was observed in 6 of 10 programs seeking this outcome). However, among the programs that were able to demonstrate behavioral impact, the magni-

---

[16]An increasingly popular approach to HIV/AIDS prevention among young people is the multicomponent "ABC" approach (i.e., Abstain, Be faithful, use Condoms). The implementation and evaluation of these programs have become issues of contention in HIV/AIDS prevention circles, so we have avoided characterizing programs as "ABC" or not and have simply described the specific activities undertaken in each intervention reviewed. The relative emphasis given to each component of an intervention is often impossible to determine from published sources.

tude of impact has generally been modest and limited to a subset of the behavioral outcomes targeted.

Examples of the results achieved by some of these school-based interventions include:

- A randomized control trial of an after-school intervention (14 sessions) undertaken in Namibia found that young women who had never had sex (at baseline) in the intervention group were more likely to have remained celibate at the 12-month follow-up (Fitzgerald et al., 1999; Stanton et al., 1998).
- A randomized control trial of a "drama-in-education" program in KwaZulu-Natal Province, South Africa, found that at the 6-month follow-up sexually active participants from project schools reported an increase in condom use compared with sexually active participants from control schools (Harvey, Stuart, and Swan, 2000).
- A randomized control trial of a skills-based, 90-minute intervention in Zimbabwe found that at 4-months' follow-up, students in the intervention group reported fewer sexual partners and fewer episodes of unprotected sex in the last month than control students (Wilson, Mparadzi, and Lavelle, 1991).
- A randomized control trial of a program for young people (ages 18-25) who worked full time and attended junior high or high school in the evening in Sao Paulo, Brazil, found that at 1-year follow-up female participants reported improved communication with partners and a decrease in unprotected sex (Antunes et al., 1997). No impact was observed, however, among the male participants.

Two linked school- and health facility-based programs are also among those that reported behavioral impact. For example, an intervention in Benin City, Nigeria, was implemented in 1998 to teach young people attending school about STIs and encourage them to receive treatment from trained private medical doctors (Coplan et al., forthcoming). At the 12-month follow-up, students in the intervention schools reported significant increases in the use of condoms and knowledge of the correct treatment-seeking behavior for STIs compared with students in the control schools. Moreover, prevalence of self-reported symptoms of STIs in the prior 6 months was lower in intervention than control schools, the use of private physicians increased, and the use of patent medicine dealers or pharmacists decreased. The Integrated Adolescent Development Program in Chile, an integrated school- and health facility-based reproductive health intervention implemented over three school years for urban teenagers in Santiago, reported an increase in age at sexual debut among intervention males compared with no change among control males (Murray et al., 2000). The intervention resulted in a greater increase in contraceptive use among girls from program schools than among those from nonprogram schools. Overall, however, use of contraceptives at last sex remained low in both groups, and no significant increase in the volume of young clients at health facilities over the 2-year follow-up period was observed.

Three studies published after the Speizer, Heller, and Brieger (2000) review reported findings consistent with the above summary. A randomized trial of a 1.75-hour in-class peer education program implemented in secondary schools in Zambia indicated significant effects on knowledge, attitudes, and beliefs toward abstinence and condom use and higher levels of perceived risk, but it did not measure impact on behaviors (Agha, 2002). An assessment of the South African national Life Skills Program undertaken in KwaZulu-Natal Province indicated statistically significant but modest program effects on some areas of knowledge and perceived condom self-efficacy and larger effects on condom use, but no consistent effects on age at sexual debut, secondary abstinence, or numbers of sexual partners (Magnani et al., 2003). Finally, a randomized trial of an extracurricular school-based program in Masaka, Uganda, failed to detect any significant program effects (Kinsman, Nakiyingi, and Kamali, 2001).

Although behavioral impact was not always achieved in school-based sexual and reproductive health programs, no developing country study to date has found evidence that providing young people with sexual or reproductive health information results in increased sexual risk-taking.

## Mass Media and Social Marketing Programs

The use of mass media is an appealing strategy for reproductive health programs for young people because of its potential to reach large numbers of young people and the opportunity to introduce new ideas and topics. Although less research has been undertaken on mass media-based sexual and reproductive health interventions directed specifically to young audiences, communications research indicates that the media can be an effective strategy for influencing adult behaviors (Rogers, 1995).

Six quasi-experimental studies of mass media-based interventions aimed at influencing knowledge, attitudes, and behaviors among young people are reported in the research literature. All but one was successful in improving knowledge or attitudes in the intervention community, and all five of the evaluations that measured behavioral impacts found impact on at least one behavioral outcome.

One project, the Arte y Parte project in Paraguay, which had as explicit goals to increase sexual and reproductive health knowledge and communication skills among young people, used various mass media products and activities to disseminate information to young people on adolescent health issues, as well as workshops conducted in schools (Magnani et al., 2000). The program trained peer educators, who assisted in the development of media products and interacted regularly with their peers. After 30 months, nearly 44 percent of young people were exposed to at least one project activity, with radio programming having the greatest reach. Exposure to the program was found to be associated with changes in relevant knowledge and attitudes, but not with sexual or contraceptive behaviors, although the program probably contributed to an observed increase in the proportion of young people reporting condom use at first sex.

Four mass media projects with social marketing were undertaken in Africa by Population Services International (PSI) in Botswana (Meekers, Stallworthy, and Harris, 1997), Cameroon (Van Rossem and Meekers, 1999a), Guinea (Van Rossem and Meekers, 1999b), and South Africa (Meekers, 1998). All had similar intervention and evaluation designs (see Agha, 2000). The projects included a mass media component (radio and print media in Botswana and Cameroon; print media in Guinea; radio, television, and print media in South Africa), as well as social marketing of condoms and peer educators who sold condoms. In addition, the Botswana Tsa Banana Program referred young people to the Tsa clinics and included education sessions in schools, the program in Cameroon worked with clubs in schools to increase their reach, and the program in Guinea had a small "youth-friendly services" component that involved providing special hours for young people at selected clinics linked to the program.

The evaluation findings indicate that these mass media strategies achieved high coverage, especially of radio messages. The media campaigns also increased recognition of the brand of condoms being promoted in Guinea (Van Rossem and Meekers, 1999b) and Cameroon (Van Rossem and Meekers, 1999a). The primary behavioral impact of these programs was on condom use (ever use and recent use). In Guinea, women and men in the intervention group reported greater use of condoms at last sex than young people in the comparison group (Van Rossem and Meekers, 1999b). In Cameroon and South Africa, women in the intervention group reported greater experience with condoms at follow-up; however, this did not translate into greater recent condom use (Meekers, 1998; Van Rossem and Meekers, 1999a). Finally, the project in Cameroon found that women in the intervention group reported delayed sexual initiation, and significantly fewer men in the intervention group reported having multiple partners in the last 12 months (Van Rossem and Meekers, 1999a).

The sixth mass media project, the Promotion of Youth Responsibility Project in Zimbabwe, had both individual and community-level objectives (Kim et al., 1998, 2001). The project employed two strategies: a 6-month multimedia campaign directed toward young people and training of providers in interpersonal communication and counseling skills. Evaluation findings indicated broad reach of the radio program, especially in rural areas. Young people exposed to the intervention also reported being more likely to abstain from sex and have fewer recent sexual partners, and use of contraceptives and clinic services increased significantly in campaign sites between the surveys. Comparable increases were not found in comparison sites. The campaign had the greatest impact on clinic attendance among some of the groups least likely to seek services: males, single young people who are unmarried, and sexually inexperienced young people (Kim et al., 2001).

### Youth-Friendly Health Services

Youth-friendly service initiatives are geared toward making the use of existing reproductive health services more acceptable and less traumatizing to young people. Youth-friendly services placed in existing facilities can also provide a wide range of services for young people in a single setting.

To date, only a small number of youth-friendly service programs in developing country settings have been rigorously evaluated. Among the three with reported evaluation results, one found solid evidence of positive impact on service utilization by young people, one nominal impact, and one no impact. The strongest impact was observed in connection with the Zimbabwe mass-media-based program discussed above that also included training of health service providers in youth counseling skills (Kim et al., 2001).

The second study, which yielded mixed results, was undertaken in Ecuador. This intervention combined education, counseling, and clinical services provided by trained clinic personnel in service delivery and reproductive health issues for young people (i.e., a "reproductive health awareness" approach) (Institute for Reproductive Health, 2001). The evaluation findings indicate that the program did not increase the number of new clients visiting the project clinics, but it did increase the number of young people who returned, thus improving continuity of care at intervention facilities.

The third program involved the testing of three separate youth-friendly service pilot projects in Lusaka, Zambia, in the late 1990s (Mmari and Magnani, 2003). No statistical relationship between the degree of clinic youth-friendliness and trends in service utilization was found. Instead, rank-order correlation tests indicated that service utilization by young people was more closely related to community attitudes toward the provision of reproductive health services to young people.

Although the available evidence is thin, it suggests that some form of community outreach might be necessary in conjunction with health facility-based programs in order to attract young people to health facilities. For example, an evaluation of a community-based program implemented by family planning workers, village doctors, and women's leaders in 20 townships in Jiangsu Province, China, observed significant increases at the 12-month follow-up in condom use at last sex among villages participating in the project versus no change in condom use in control villages (Xiaoming et al., 2000).

*Peer Promotion Programs*

Peer programs take advantage of the fact that young people spend a large amount of time interacting with other young people similar to themselves in school, at work, or in the community. These programs recruit and train a core group of young people to serve as role models and sources of information for their peers. In some settings, peers have been able to distribute or sell certain types of contraceptives, thus increasing access to nonclinical contraceptives in a nonthreatening environment. Peer educators (or promoters) have been deployed in combination with other intervention strategies (e.g., some school-based programs), and many mass media programs use peer educators.

Peer promotion strategies have been associated with positive behavioral outcomes in several studies. Evaluation findings from a matched quasi-experimental study of a peer-promotion program in secondary schools in six cities in Peru demonstrated a positive association with age at sexual initiation and use of a contraceptive method at last sexual encounter over an 18-month observation period (Magnani et al., 2001). A peer-based program worked with youth-serving organizations in Nigeria and Ghana in three types of sites: secondary schools, postsecondary schools, and out-of-school sites (Brieger et al., 2001; Speizer, Tambashe, and Tegang, 2001). The only behavioral change associated with the program was that young people attending intervention schools reported greater recent use of protective methods against STIs than comparable young people from nonintervention schools. The program was not associated with any behavioral change for out-of-school young people who do not attend school. A third peer program used a community-based peer education strategy in one city of Cameroon to promote contraceptive use and reduce the prevalence of STIs/HIV and unintended pregnancies among young people (Speizer, Tambashe, and Tegang, 2001). At the 16-month follow-up, having had an encounter with a peer educator was associated with current contraceptive use and use of condoms at last sex.

It should be noted that the recurring costs of peer programs are high, and several studies in the United States suggest that the largest program impacts are on the peer educators themselves (Barnett, 2000; Flanagan, Williams, and Mahler, 1996; Philliber, 1999; Randolph, 1996).

*STI/HIV Counseling and Testing*

Evidence from the United States indicates that HIV counseling and testing can be effective in changing high-risk sexual behaviors and reducing new STIs among both adults and young people (Bolu et al., 2002; Kamb et al., 1998). The evidence from developing country settings is sparse. However, the findings from a randomized control trial of a program for unmarried young adults in northern Thailand indicated a significant effect on the proportion of young people seeking HIV testing. The magnitude of the effect (8 percent) was modest, and no increases in other risk-reduction behaviors (e.g., condom use) were observed (Jiraphongsa et al., 2002).

*Youth Centers*

In recent years the use of youth centers to reduce barriers to reproductive health information and services for young people has been largely limited to Africa. Youth centers generally have recreational and educational components, as well as reproductive health counseling and clinical components. Most youth centers also include peer educators who refer young people to the center for both recreational and health service visits.

The evidence on the impact of youth centers on service utilization is limited. The only rigorous study currently available is an evaluation of the Association Togolaise pour le Bien-Etre Familiale youth center in Lomé, Togo (Speizer et al., forthcoming). The study found that, while awareness of the youth center increased from 6 percent in 1998 to 42 percent in 2000 among young people in Lomé, actual use only rose moderately, from 3 percent in 1998 to 8 percent in 2000 and 10 percent in 2001. Multivariate analyses demonstrated an association between youth center use and both reproductive health knowledge and contraceptive use. However, the study was unable to rule out selection effects, that is, the possibility that young people who were predisposed to use contraception were also more likely to visit a youth center.

Situation analysis studies in other African youth centers have also demonstrated that the majority of youth center use is for recreation rather than for health services (Erulkar and Mensch, 1997a; Glover, Erulkar, and Nerquaye-Tettah, 1998; Kouwonou and Mukahirwa, 2000; Phiri and Erulkar, 1997). Several studies have observed that young people coming for clinical services tend to be older than the target age range for programs focused on teenagers (Erulkar and Mensch, 1997b; Glover, Erulkar, and Nerquaye-Tetteh, 1998; Phiri and Erulkar, 1997).

## Programs Targeting Parents

Recognizing that parents play a key role in shaping young people's behaviors and that parents in many settings are uncomfortable counseling their children on matters related to sex and contraception, a number of sexual and reproductive health and HIV/AIDS education programs for parents have been designed both as stand-alone efforts and as components of larger programs directed to young people. The impact of such programs in developing country settings has yet to be rigorously measured. In the United States, the available evidence suggests that parents are often unwilling to participate in such programs (Kirby, 2001). When they do, however, it appears that parent-child communication about sexuality increases. However, in the only two rigorous studies available, neither of the programs evaluated were able to demonstrate an effect on the likelihood of initiating sex during the teen years, the primary objective of both programs (Miller et al., 1998; Nicholson and Postrado, 1991).

## Workplace-Based Programs

Reaching young people with sexual and reproductive health information in out-of-school sites is essential in places in which large numbers of young people do not attend school. Placing reproductive health activities in workplaces that attract large numbers of young people is a logical strategy in such places.

Four evaluations of workplace-based reproductive health programs for young people appear in the research literature, only two of which measured impact on behaviors, and both reported significant impact.[17] The first program was the government of Thailand's national 100 percent condom promotion program to increase condom use among visitors to brothels (Celentano et al., 1998, 2000). One aspect of the project emphasized conscripts into the Thai army (ages 19-23). The activities aimed at conscripts included a communications strategy, free condom distribution in brothels, and promotion of condom use at brothels, especially among men previously treated for STIs. Over the follow-up period, there was a tenfold decline in STI incidence observed among conscripts between 1991-1993 and 1993-1995. Moreover, HIV incidence declined in successive cohorts of recruits over the same period, from 2.48 per 100 person-years to 0.55 per 100 person-years. Note, however, that it is difficult to separate

---

[17]The two that did not measure behavioral impact were an intervention for garment factory workers in Cambodia (Focus on Young Adults, Care International, 2000) and an AIDS prevention education intervention among northern Thai migratory factory workers (Cash, Anasuchatkul, and Busayawong, 1995). Both reported impacts on knowledge and attitudes.

the impact of the Thai army program from other activities under way in Thailand given the intensity of efforts to reduce STI/HIV at the national level in Thailand in the early 1990s.

The second was an STI/HIV intervention undertaken among commercial sex workers and madams in the red light district of Bombay (Bhave et al., 1995). The intervention involved group sessions in which the sex workers watched motivational and educational videos about HIV, participated in small group discussions about HIV, and were exposed to visual materials about HIV. Of the sex workers included in this study, more than 80 percent were between the ages of 15 and 25. Evaluation findings indicated that, although higher HIV prevalence was observed among both intervention and control groups at follow-up, the increase was significantly smaller in the intervention group. Moreover, the intervention group had significantly higher levels of knowledge regarding HIV and was more likely to say that they would insist on condom use postintervention.

## Multicomponent Community-Based Programs

In response to the limited success of narrowly focused programs, typically relying on one programmatic modality and in recognition of the multiple risk and protective factors present in the environment, multiple-component community-based reproductive health programs for young people are increasingly being tried. The integrated school- and health-based facility programs in Chile, Nigeria, and Zimbabwe described earlier are steps in the direction of integrated efforts. There are four recent studies of multicomponent interventions conducted in the late 1990s in Bangladesh, Kenya, Mexico, and Senegal. These studies included three types of interventions: a community sensitization program for community leaders, parents, and out-of-school youth; youth-friendly clinic services; and a school-based reproductive health information program (YouthNet/Family Health International, 2003). In all four countries, the study design included one or more sites that received only the community and clinic interventions and one or more sites that also included the school-based intervention as well as control sites. The results were mixed. In some sites, positive changes were observed in behavior, but these changes tended to be small and mostly statistically insignificant. Knowledge and attitudes did change in many of the sites. Increases were observed in knowledge of several aspects of reproductive health, such as family planning methods, women's fertile period, and transmission modes for HIV. There was no consistent evidence that the three-component intervention achieved better results than the two-component intervention (YouthNet/Family Health International, 2003).

Another multicomponent community-based intervention in the

Mwanza region of Tanzania is unique because the evaluation incorporated the measurement of biological markers as outcome measures: HIV incidence, genital herpes, other STIs, and pregnancy rates (YouthNet/Family Health International, 2003). This randomized trial intervention had four components: community activities, sexual and reproductive health education in schools, youth-friendly reproductive health services, and community-based condom promotion and social marketing by young people. Comparing intervention with control sites showed significantly greater changes in knowledge and attitudes, greater delays in sexual initiation and reduced numbers of sexual partners among males but not females, and more condom use among both males and females. The intervention did not have any effect, however, on any of the biological outcomes.

A careful evaluation of behavioral change over three years in response to the Nyeri Youth Health project in Kenya provides a promising example of a multicomponent community-based model of youth services designed with input from the local community (Erulka et al., 2004). The project had at its core trained community-based counselors who drew on existing community structures to meet with young people and provide educational and motivational activities at the same time that they worked with parents, schools, teachers, and service providers. The design of the project emerged from a year-long research and planning phase in the community. It drew on several principles of youth programming: "begin with what young people want and what they are already doing to obtain sexual and reproductive health information and services; include skills building; engage adults to create a safe and supportive environment; use a variety of settings and providers and make the most of existing infrastructure" (Erulkar et al., 2004:59). Using a quasi-experimental design with one control and one intervention municipality and a 3-year follow-up period, baseline and endline surveys were based on random samples of young people in each community, selected regardless of program participation. Controlling for differences between the intervention and control sites, the researchers found that females at the project site were significantly more likely than those at the control site to adopt secondary abstinence and less likely to have had three or more sex partners. Males at the project site were more likely to use condoms than those at the control site. Thus, the program achieved significant behavioral change but that change differed by gender. Furthermore, there was no evidence that the project resulted in increased experimentation with sex or promiscuity, as many had feared.

## Comprehensive Youth Development Programs

Another type of comprehensive program, youth development programs or livelihood programs (discussed further in Chapter 6) consist of the provision of a range of development activities in one program that address a wide range of needs of young people during the transition from adolescence to adulthood. These projects go beyond simply providing sexual and reproductive health education to also focusing on life options, educational aspirations, employment considerations, and psychosocial development needs. They also promote a safe environment in which young people can develop and are often focused on vulnerable populations, those who have missed the opportunity to go to school or dropped out prematurely (Kirby and Coyle, 1997). The only youth development program in a developing country for which evaluation data are currently available is the Better Life Options Project designed by the Centre for Development and Population Activities and initially implemented in India in 1987 (Levitt-Dayal and Motihar, 2000).[18] This program included nonformal education (literacy, postliteracy, and linkages with formal education), family life education, vocational skills training, health education and services, public awareness creation, and advocacy. The evaluation study found that females (ages 15-26) who had participated in the program had a higher age at marriage and fewer children; were more likely to have participated in formal schooling; were more likely to be employed and earning cash; had greater confidence and self-efficacy; and had higher rates of contraceptive use, antenatal care, hospital deliveries, and use of oral rehydration solutions compared with girls with no program exposure. While these results are promising, it should be noted that the extent to which the program evaluation effectively controlled for participation (i.e., selection) bias is questionable.

### Policies and Programs to Reduce Smoking Among Young People

As cigarette consumption in Europe and the United States declines, the tobacco industry is increasingly directing its attention to untapped markets in developing countries, especially the female youth market (Global Youth Tobacco Survey Collaborating Group, 2003). According to the Global Youth Tobacco Survey Collaborating Group (2003), "selling tobacco products to women and girls currently represents the single largest product marketing opportunity in the world (p. 215)." Documents released from

---

[18]A program for out-of-school female orphans ages 16-19 in Zimbabwe will be the subject of an evaluation with a rigorous randomized control design (Dunbar, 2004). The intervention combines an integrated micro-credit program with a life-skills education curriculum. The control group will receive the life-skills education curriculum without the economic components. Outcome measures include the incidence of herpes simplex virus type 2 and unintended pregnancy as well as risk behaviors including unprotected sex, number of partners, transactional sex, and early sexual debut.

the tobacco litigation trials in the United States show that the tobacco industry is intensely interested in trends in the attitudes and smoking habits of young people (World Health Organization, 1999b).

The literature that addresses the effect of programs and policies on smoking among young people tends to focus on a few antismoking strategies: the provision of information, media campaigns, price increases, and restrictions on access and smoking in public places. Few rigorous evaluations of the impact of these strategies have been carried out for developing countries, and this lack of evidence has hampered efforts to develop appropriate interventions (Baris et al., 2000).

The strategy that has been shown to be most effective in deterring young people from initiating smoking and cutting down on consumption in developed countries is increasing the price of cigarettes through taxes. Young people in developed countries have been shown to be more price-responsive than older people, presumably because they have less disposable income and are likely to be less heavily addicted (Jha and Chaloupka, 1999; Gruber and Zinman, 2000).

According to the World Bank, most measures intended to reduce tobacco supply are ineffective as well as difficult and costly to enforce, including banning tobacco sales to young people (World Bank, 2004). Whether advertising has an effect on the initiation of smoking among young people is a hotly debated question. The tobacco industry consistently claims that it does not market its products to children and young people and that the purpose of advertising is to encourage current smokers to switch brands (World Health Organization, 1999b). A recent comprehensive review of both econometric and noneconomic studies of the effects of tobacco advertising concluded that a complete ban on smoking advertising reduces tobacco use more quickly and to lower levels than a partial ban and that counteradvertising is generally associated with a decline in smoking prevalence among the general population (Saffer, 2000). Antismoking messages that emphasize identity and empowerment may be most effective among young people who tend to misunderstand and underestimate the health effects of tobacco use (World Health Organization, 1999b).

## CONCLUSIONS AND RECOMMENDATIONS

### Key Findings

*The health of young people in developing countries is improving overall.* Young people are entering the transition to adulthood healthier and with improved chances of surviving to old age. While slight declines in mortality rates among young people are evident in the aggregate for developing countries in recent years, increases in mortality among 25-35-year-olds are evident in the least developed countries, raising cause for some concern.

*Continued reductions in mortality seem likely, with the major exception of countries strongly affected by the HIV/AIDS pandemic.* The HIV/AIDS pandemic has already taken a huge toll on the population of young people in sub-Saharan Africa and a few other places. It poses a serious and imminent threat in many other places, including countries with the largest populations of young people, China and India.

*Most developing regions show considerably higher HIV prevalence among females ages 15-24 than among males.* This is especially true in Africa, where prevalence rates among females are more than double those of males. Globally, almost 12 million people ages 15-24 were estimated to be living with HIV/AIDS in 2002. About three-quarters of these live in sub-Saharan Africa. The young age structure of countries hardest hit by the pandemic means that about half of all new infections are now occurring among this age group.

*Mortality and morbidity related to pregnancy and childbirth, a substantial proportion of which is a direct consequence of unsafe abortion, are one of the most significant risks to the health of girls and young women.* The lifetime risk of dying from maternal causes is more than 40 times greater among women in developing than developed countries. This disparity in risk indicates that the vast majority of these deaths are preventable.[19]

*Compared with young women, young men in developing countries are disproportionately likely to be affected by road traffic accidents, violence, war, and suicide.* There are some striking geographic patterns in these health risks that appear to be linked to other regional trends. For example, comparatively high and rising rates of homicide among young people in Latin America have been linked to rising income inequality, and high rates of road traffic fatalities in South-eastern Asia to increasing affluence. In some countries, for example, Liberia, Sierra Leone, and Sudan, violence caused by civil war has characterized the experience of an entire generation of young men.

---

[19]A number of major ongoing research programs are investigating the effectiveness of interventions to reduce maternal mortality in developing countries. These include the IMPAACT project at the University of Aberdeen, the Averting Maternal Death and Disability project at Columbia University, and the Safe Motherhood Initiative at Family Care International.

*Mental health problems account for a substantial and possibly increasing share of illness among young people.* This finding is significant not only because it directs increasing attention to the problems of young people who suffer from mental health problems but also because mental health problems are associated with various other behaviors, including alcohol and drug use and risky sexual behavior.

*Substantial proportions of young people are sexually active at a young age in some parts of the world, most notably sub-Saharan Africa.* The HIV/ AIDS pandemic has made it inescapably clear that young people are sexually active. While most young women first have sex in a marital relationship, substantial proportions do not. Moreover, in areas with high HIV prevalence, marriage does not protect young women from risk. While marriage reduces the number of sexual partners, it increases the frequency of sex, decreases condom use, and virtually eliminates a girl's ability to abstain from sex.

*There has been an increase in the percentage of women having premarital sex before age 18 in many countries over the past 20 years.* However, delays in the age of marriage in most countries have meant that, relative to 20 years ago, fewer young women report themselves to have been sexually active before age 18. Thus, while sex is being delayed, the context of first sexual experience is changing, with a greater likelihood relative to the past that first sex will be experienced prior to marriage.

*There is increasing evidence that coercive sexual initiation is not uncommon among young people.* The individuals responsible for this coercion are likely to be known to the young person and are sometimes people in authority, such as teachers. Studies suggest that those who experience coercive sex are subsequently more likely than others to engage in higher risk consensual sexual behavior.

*Contraceptive use is increasing among sexually active young women, especially those who are unmarried.* Rising contraceptive prevalence is most evident in Latin America and the Caribbean and in Eastern and Southern Africa. In Western and Middle Africa, the trends are variable. In other regions—the Middle East and Asia—data on contraceptive use are available only for married women in a limited number of countries. When data are available, they also indicate increases in contraception among married young people in most countries.

*Condom use among sexually active young women is still relatively low but increasing rapidly in some places.* Although the magnitude of the increases in condom use varies, increasing trends are evidenced in all countries with data.

*Although young women are generally less likely than older women to obtain an abortion, they are more likely to have the abortion later in pregnancy and to choose an unsafe provider, thus putting themselves at greater risk.* Reliable data on induced abortion are severely lacking. It appears, however, that young people are more likely to delay seeking an abortion even in settings in which abortion is not restricted. The need for confidentiality and privacy is the main reason that young women choose unskilled providers.

*The use of tobacco among young people in developing countries is high, and the gap in smoking prevalence between young men and women small.* Although few data exist on trends in smoking among young people in developing countries, indications are that smoking is increasing generally and perhaps more rapidly among young women. The marketing of tobacco to young people in developing countries, rising affluence in some countries, and the relaxation of traditional social controls, particularly on girls' behavior are all factors implicated in these trends. The negative consequences of increasing prevalence of smoking for the future health of the current generation are considerable.

*Trends in the use of illicit drugs are difficult to characterize, but it appears that incidence in much of the developing world is rising slowly.* In contrast to the rest of the developing world, trends in Eastern Europe and Central Asia show rapid increases. The increase in injecting drug use among young males in Eastern and South-eastern Asia and the Russian Federation does not bode well for the health of these populations, particularly because of the double risk of the drug use itself and the transmission of HIV/AIDS.

*The consumption of alcohol is greater among young males than young females, among the affluent, and among those living in urban areas.* Some evidence suggests that young people in developing countries are initiating drinking earlier and are increasingly engaging in binge drinking. Marketing campaigns aimed at young people and the promotion of new types of sweeter alcoholic beverages directed at the under age 18 market, suggest the continuation of these trends.

*School participation and attainment have important and mostly positive connections to young people's health. It is expected that rising school enrollment rates should contribute to further improvements in reproductive health among young people.* Grades attained as well as current enrollment status are associated with delayed sexual initiation among young women and men and a greater likelihood of contraceptive use. Recent evidence shows that, in contrast to earlier patterns, progressively higher levels of schooling completed are linked with higher rates of condom use and lower rates of HIV infection. However, the effect of schooling on health can vary with school quality. For example, young women and men in some settings experience sexual coercion and harassment at the hands of teachers and classmates, which may lead to earlier sexual initiation. Others may attend schools in which teachers show girls respect and provide equitable treatment in the classroom, which may lead to delayed sexual initiation and the avoidance of risky behaviors.

*Young people whose families are poor suffer from higher rates of mortality and morbidity wherever they live.* This is because they are less able to pursue a healthy lifestyle, are more likely to be exposed to health risks, to have families with fewer resources to pay for preventative and curative health services, and to have less access to health, family planning, and safe delivery services. Economic vulnerability and risky sexual behavior interact in many and complex ways, including, for example, the exchange of sex for money, housing, food, or education, as well as exposure to a greater number of sexual partners.

*Most sexual and reproductive health interventions have not been rigorously evaluated, but the quality of evaluation is beginning to improve.* Recently published and ongoing evaluations are using more rigorous evaluation designs and more appropriate statistical methods. To date, insufficient data exist to evaluate the relative effectiveness of different approaches. Furthermore, the cost-effectiveness of various approaches has not been assessed.

*To date, sexual and reproductive health interventions have generally been more successful at influencing knowledge and attitudes than at changing behavior. There is no evidence that these interventions contribute to greater sexual experimentation among young people.* Among those programs that were able to demonstrate behavioral impact, the magnitude of the effect has generally been modest. Multiple-component community-based strategies appear more promising than single-component strategies, particularly when designed to be culturally sensitive and to make use of the traditional strengths of local institutions.

### Policy Recommendations

*The rising proportions of young people attending school provide opportunities to reach more people with school-based sex education classes and health interventions.* The years between roughly ages 10 and 14 are a window of opportunity to reach young people before they become sexually active (or start injecting drugs or become involved in sex work). Antismoking and drug use programs can also form part of school-based health education.

*Sexual activity among young people is unlikely to decline, so programs should focus on improving negotiating skills and making sex, among those who do engage in it, wanted and safe.* Coercion appears to play a substantial role in the sexual experience of young people. Among the factors that need to be addressed are gender double standards, the perception that the victim is responsible, lack of negotiation skills, and unsupportive family and institutional environments.

*Special attention needs to be paid to the provision of appropriate family planning services for young women and men, including both the married and unmarried populations.* The overall success of family planning programs in developing countries, the demands made by the HIV/AIDS pandemic on health services and donor funding, and the absence of specific reproductive and sexual health goals in the Millennium Development Goals have reduced the international attention paid to family planning programs in the last several years. Yet there are still large proportions of young women in some countries who are not using contraception in spite of a preference to delay or avoid pregnancy. Moreover, due to the very large cohorts of young people in developing countries, the absolute numbers of contraceptive users needed to simply maintain current rates of contraceptive use will rise. Where appropriate, family planning services for young people should be integrated in HIV/AIDS programs.

*No program strategy can work for all young people.* Some young people attend school while others do not; some live with parents while others do not; some work outside the home while others do not; some are married while others are not; some are HIV positive while others are not; some are parents while others are not. Programming for young people must recognize this diversity.

*Multiple component community-based reproductive health programs for young people appear to be a promising approach to addressing reproductive health needs, particularly if they are designed to be culturally appropriate in the local context, sensitive to the expressed needs of young people, and built on the strength of local institutions.* Now that the magnitude and scope of the interventions that will be needed to both prevent and treat

HIV/AIDS are becoming apparent, many national governments and inter-national organizations have turned their attention to young people as key to defeating the pandemic. Because the issues surrounding HIV/AIDS deal with sensitive issues about what is appropriate for young people to know and to do, interventions are often highly controversial. Yet the effectiveness of various prevention strategies is not a political or moral question, but an empirical one. The evidence suggests that a combination of strategies—increasing knowledge of mechanisms of transmission and of the three prin-cipal means of preventing infection (abstinence, monogamy, and the use of condoms), providing youth-friendly services, promoting voluntary counsel-ing and testing, providing diagnosis and treatment of sexually transmitted infections, implementing public education campaigns to reduce stigma, and creating safe and supportive environments—is more effective than any single strategy for reducing risky sexual behavior, the most important transmis-sion mechanism in developing countries. Clearly, national policy strategies to reduce HIV/AIDS must have as an essential component a sustained infor-mation and prevention program that begins before puberty and continues through the transition to adulthood.

*Some of the most important interventions to improve the reproductive health of young people may lie outside the health sector.* For example, improvements in school quality, particularly those elements relating to the treatment of girls by their teachers, can have important reproductive health benefits.

*The prevention of tobacco use among young people must be a priority for developing countries.* This is an area in which much research in developed countries has been done and in which lessons learned could usefully be applied in developing countries. For example, increasing the price of ciga-rettes through taxes has been shown to be the most effective strategy for deterring young people from smoking.

*The disparity in maternal risk between developing and developed countries can be reduced with appropriate interventions.* The use of skilled atten-dants at delivery and access to emergency obstetric care for the treatment of pregnancy, delivery, and postpartum complications are key actions to re-duce maternal health risks. Safe abortion in countries where it is legal and postabortion care everywhere are also essential components of maternal health programs. The provision of contraceptive services in the context of postpartum and postabortion care is an important means of increasing young women's ability to space births and to avoid unwanted pregnancies.

## Research Recommendations

Throughout this chapter, the lack of data on some topics has hampered our ability to describe the current health situation of young people and, more often, trends in health indicators. A key recommendation is therefore that improvements need to be made in both the coverage and quality of data collection on health among young people. Many of the areas in which data on young people are deficient apply to all age groups. For example, data on causes of death are inadequate, as are reliable data on induced abortion, mental illness, and illicit drug use. While the available information on sexual behavior among young people has greatly improved and expanded over the last decade or so, many questions remain about the quality of the data and their comparability across settings and over time. Methodological research that would help to improve data collection methods in this area is urgently needed. Data from Northern Africa, the Middle East, and Asia are particularly lacking. Aside from the data needed simply for monitoring the health of young people, the deficiencies of the available data for answering research questions on the factors affecting health outcomes are clear. Suitable data collection strategies, which probably require longitudinal data and more data from carefully constructed experiments with random assignment of treatment, are necessary to sort out these questions.

Unanswered research questions span all of the topics covered in this chapter. Some of the most urgent are:

- What are the factors that predict a healthy transition to adulthood among young people? Do these differ between developing and developed countries and among regions in the developing world?
- Are dual social norms relating to the sexual behavior of boys and girls changing? What implication do such changes have, if occurring, for gender differences in healthy development during this phase of the life cycle?
- What are the factors that inhibit or facilitate safe sexual behavior among young females and males? And how do these differ by sex and marital status?
- What are the implications of rising school enrollment during the later teen years for young people's reproductive health? In particular, what are the factors in the school environment that are protective of young people's reproductive health?
- What are the consequences of the HIV/AIDS pandemic for the future life course of the current generation of young people?
- What are the risk factors associated with road traffic accidents among young people? Under what circumstances do most accidents happen?

- What is the abortion rate among young women, and what factors determine their decision to terminate a pregnancy and their choice of provider? What are the consequences of unsafe abortion?
- What factors increase or decrease the probability that a young person will commit suicide?
- What are the most common mental health problems among young people in developing countries? What is the status of diagnosis and treatment of mental illnesses? What is the relationship between mental illness and risky behaviors?
- What has been the effect on young people in countries in which prolonged wars have occurred? What are the physical, psychological, and emotional consequences of making the transition to adulthood in such an environment?
- What are the factors that prevent young people from using contraceptive methods even when they do not want to become pregnant?
- Are younger women more or less likely to die of maternal causes than older women? How do the risk factors for maternal mortality and morbidity differ between younger and older women?
- What explains the rise in drug use among young people in developing countries? What specific factors explain the recent rapid increases in injecting drug use in some countries?

Further study is also needed of health among young people in the context of the life course. Some early life events, possibly even in the womb (Barker, 1998, 2003), have consequences for young people, and events during the transition to adulthood have consequences for health later in life. In general, the contribution of events during this phase of the life cycle—intermediate between infancy and old age—to later health needs clarification. As countries progress through a nutritional transition toward a better fed, sometimes overfed, populace, the contribution of youthful diet and exercise patterns to late life chronic conditions will become of increasing concern.

The systematic evaluation of interventions has been limited mostly to sexual and reproductive health, and many studies are largely inconclusive. These inconclusive results are sometimes due to flawed evaluation designs. There is a clear need to improve the level of methodological rigor in the evaluation of reproductive health interventions. Interventions in other areas, such as smoking and drug use, are largely untested and require basic research. Some of the most significant questions about interventions include:

- What is the most effective way to transform knowledge about sexually transmitted infections into behavior change among young people?

- Which combination of interventions is most cost-effective and sustainable for delaying the age at sexual initiation?
- What aspects of school quality are most salient for young people's reproductive health?
- Which combination of interventions is most cost-effective and sustainable for promoting the use of condoms, as well as other contraceptive methods, among young people? How can the use of condoms be sustained at high levels among young people, and how can the effectiveness and consistency of use be increased?
- How can girls and young women best be protected from sexual violence and coercion? How can boys and young men best be brought up and taught to reject sexual violence and coercion?
- What is the best way to introduce and sustain reproductive and sexual health services for young people? How should providers be trained to deal with young clients? How can both married and unmarried young people be served?
- What are the most effective interventions for reducing maternal mortality and morbidity, and do these differ depending on the age of the mother?
- Which interventions are most likely to prevent the adoption of smoking among young people? Do interventions need to be gender-specific? How can cessation of smoking among young smokers be promoted?

**APPENDIX TABLE 4-1 FOLLOWS**

APPENDIX TABLE 4-1 Smoking Among Students Ages 13-15, Global
Youth Tobacco Survey, 1999-2003 (Percentage)

| Region and Country | | Ever Smoked Cigarettes | | Currently Smoke Cigarettes | |
|---|---|---|---|---|---|
| | | Male | Female | Male | Female |
| Eastern and Southern Africa | | | | | |
| Botswana | 2001 | 24.1 | 10.0 | 8.7 | 2.6 |
| Kenya | 2001 | 21.0 | 8.5 | 10.1 | 4.2 |
| Lesotho | 2002 | 40.0 | 15.1 | 23.0 | 6.0 |
| Seychelles | 2002 | 56.4 | 42.9 | 31.3 | 21.7 |
| Swaziland | 2001 | 27.5 | 10.6 | 14.6 | 4.6 |
| Malawi: Blantyre | 2001 | 22.3 | 7.8 | 4.1 | 1.6 |
| Malawi: Lilongwe | 2001 | 28.6 | 10.1 | 9.1 | 2.8 |
| Mozambique: Gaza Inhambe | 2002 | 12.7 | 7.2 | 4.3 | 3.3 |
| Mozambique: Maputo City | 2002 | 23.9 | 10.7 | 5.9 | 2.6 |
| Uganda: Arua | 2002 | 38.2 | 21.7 | 24.3 | 15.7 |
| Uganda: Kampala | 2002 | 22.8 | 11.5 | 6.7 | 3.3 |
| Uganda: Mpigi | 2002 | 23.7 | 14.2 | 11.5 | 3.3 |
| Zambia: Chongwe / Luangwa | 2002 | 30.5 | 28.1 | 14.9 | 12.4 |
| Zambia: Kafue | 2002 | 23.4 | 15.3 | 12.2 | 8.2 |
| Zambia: Lusaka | 2002 | 36.0 | 22.3 | 10.8 | 8.3 |
| Zimbabwe: Harare | 1999 | 30.1 | 21.5 | 11.4 | 10.1 |
| Zimbabwe: Manicaland | 1999 | 29.0 | 16.3 | 12.6 | 9.7 |
| Central and Western Africa | | | | | |
| Ghana | 2000 | 14.7 | 13.0 | 5.3 | 3.8 |
| Mauritania | 2001 | 38.9 | 22.9 | 24.1 | 10.6 |
| Niger | 2002 | 43.2 | 11.9 | 24.8 | 6.5 |
| Togo | 2002 | 31.8 | 10.0 | 14.9 | 4.0 |
| Burkina Faso: B. Dioulasso | 2001 | 58.4 | 23.5 | 31.2 | 8.3 |
| Burkina Faso: Ouagadougou | 2001 | 61.9 | 27.4 | 30.9 | 9.1 |
| Mali: Bamako | 2001 | 59.0 | 14.7 | 43.7 | 7.6 |
| Nigeria: Cross River State | 2001 | 20.4 | 13.7 | 9.7 | 5.7 |
| Senegal: Dakar | 2002 | 36.0 | 6.8 | 20.8 | 5.6 |
| Senegal: Diourbal | 2002 | 35.8 | 3.7 | 23.0 | 1.8 |
| South-eastern/Southern-central Asia | | | | | |
| Cambodia | 2002 | 11.3 | 1.2 | 7.9 | 1.0 |
| Iran | 2003 | 19.1 | 9.4 | 4.2 | 0.4 |
| Myanmar | 2001 | n.a. | n.a. | 29.1 | 3.1 |
| Nepal | 2001 | 12.0 | 3.8 | 6.3 | 0.6 |
| Philippines | 2000 | 57.0 | 32.0 | 32.6 | 12.9 |
| Singapore | 2000 | 29.5 | 21.9 | 13.4 | 8.8 |
| Sri Lanka | 1999 | 17.5 | 6.8 | 6.8 | 1.7 |
| India: Andara Pradesh | 2002 | 14.9 | 9.6 | 3.5 | 1.4 |
| India: Arunachal Pradesh | 2001 | 29.8 | 8.4 | 21.9 | 3.0 |
| India: Assam | 2001 | 23.5 | 9.3 | 14.6 | 4.4 |

| Currently Use Any Tobacco Products | | Never Smokers Likely to Initiate Smoking Next Year | Smokers Wanting to Stop | Smokers Who Have Tried to Stop |
|---|---|---|---|---|
| Male | Female | | | |
| 17.0 | 11.6 | 8.1 | 63.5 | 68.3 |
| 15.8 | 10.0 | 19.7 | 73.5 | 70.2 |
| 31.6 | 19.7 | 35.1 | 80.1 | 73.5 |
| 36.0 | 24.5 | 16.4 | 76.1 | 76.4 |
| 20.7 | 10.0 | 17.4 | 76.3 | 75.3 |
| 17.9 | 15.3 | 15.3 | 91.4 | 61.0 |
| 21.1 | 14.7 | 17.1 | 82.0 | 92.1 |
| 10.0 | 10.5 | 28.6 | n.a. | n.a. |
| 12.8 | 9.7 | 28.6 | n.a. | n.a. |
| 35.0 | 27.7 | 11.0 | 80.7 | 71.8 |
| 15.2 | 12.2 | 5.8 | 77.9 | 76.9 |
| 23.0 | 12.1 | 9.1 | 68.7 | 70.7 |
| 27.1 | 27.9 | 36.0 | 75.7 | 67.8 |
| 22.7 | 21.6 | 34.0 | 77.5 | 67.9 |
| 25.7 | 23.7 | 34.9 | 70.2 | 61.7 |
| 21.5 | 17.2 | 29.8 | 66.2 | 49.1 |
| 23.0 | 20.0 | 36.6 | 70.6 | 60.3 |
| | | | | |
| 19.5 | 18.8 | 16.5 | 87.4 | 78.4 |
| 33.7 | 22.7 | 17.6 | 78.8 | 73.7 |
| 27.3 | 14.2 | 12.5 | 71.8 | 75.9 |
| 19.5 | 9.7 | 6.7 | 91.7 | 82.8 |
| 31.5 | 11.3 | 14.6 | 87.3 | 86.9 |
| 32.1 | 12.1 | 16.8 | 87.8 | 82.1 |
| 44.9 | 12.6 | 8.6 | 83.2 | 78.2 |
| 23.9 | 17.0 | 20.4 | 81.7 | 66.4 |
| 25.1 | 7.7 | n.a. | 86.6 | 84.8 |
| 25.6 | 3.5 | n.a. | 86.1 | 79.2 |
| | | | | |
| 11.4 | 3.2 | 12.0 | n.a. | 87.0 |
| 14.0 | 4.5 | 13.6 | n.a. | n.a. |
| 37.3 | 4.7 | n.a. | 86.5 | 83.2 |
| 15.3 | 6.4 | 10.6 | 81.9 | 69.7 |
| 37.3 | 18.4 | 26.5 | 84.8 | 84.0 |
| n.a. | n.a. | 9.0 | 63.3 | 79.6 |
| 14.5 | 6.1 | 4.9 | 80.0 | 40.5 |
| 11.3 | 6.3 | 8.0 | 82.2 | 57.8 |
| 54.2 | 43.9 | 23.1 | 60.3 | 34.7 |
| 45.2 | 25.0 | 22.5 | 67.3 | 21.0 |

*Continued*

APPENDIX TABLE 4-1 Continued

| Region and Country | | Ever Smoked Cigarettes | | Currently Smoke Cigarettes | |
|---|---|---|---|---|---|
| | | Male | Female | Male | Female |
| India: Bihar | 2000 | 23.3 | 8.1 | 16.5 | 4.6 |
| India: Calcutta | 2000 | 15.4 | 9.5 | 8.8 | 2.6 |
| India: Central Bihar | 2001 | 9.6 | 3.1 | 4.6 | 1.1 |
| India: Delhi | 2001 | 5.7 | 2.2 | 1.5 | 0.7 |
| India: Goa | 2000 | 5.0 | 2.5 | 1.0 | 0.6 |
| India: Hyderabad | 2001 | 6.2 | 5.8 | 2.4 | 0.2 |
| India: Maharashtra | 2000 | 10.2 | 9.6 | 3.0 | 4.2 |
| India: Manipur | 2001 | 31.8 | 9.8 | 24.9 | 5.6 |
| India: Meghalay | 2001 | 22.8 | 14.2 | 16.5 | 6.5 |
| India: Mizoram | 2001 | 38.9 | 21.5 | 32.8 | 13.4 |
| India: Mumbai | 2000 | 5.9 | 1.7 | 2.4 | 0.2 |
| India: Nagaland | 2001 | 37.0 | 20.3 | 25.7 | 12.9 |
| India: Navoday | 2001 | 8.2 | 2.0 | 1.0 | 0.2 |
| India: Orissa | 2002 | 8.4 | 3.5 | 2.8 | 0.6 |
| India: Rajasthan | 2002 | 18.1 | 7.7 | 3.9 | 1.8 |
| India: Sikkim | 2001 | 31.9 | 15.5 | 24.1 | 10.5 |
| India: Tamil Nadu | 2000 | 6.3 | 4.1 | 2.3 | 1.0 |
| India: Tripura | 2001 | 16.0 | 8.0 | 13.4 | 6.6 |
| India: Uttar Pradesh | 2002 | 14.8 | 10.2 | 8.3 | 6.4 |
| India: West Bengal | 2000 | 14.1 | 6.3 | 6.1 | 1.4 |
| Indonesia: Jakarta | 2000 | 69.3 | 18.8 | 37.1 | 4.4 |
| Eastern Asia | | | | | |
| China: Chongqing | 1999 | 42.4 | 18.5 | 11.5 | 1.8 |
| China: Guangdong | 1999 | 27.1 | 17.4 | 7.3 | 2.3 |
| China: Shandong | 1999 | 26.5 | 7.6 | 4.9 | 0.2 |
| China: Tianjin | 1999 | 36.5 | 11.0 | 12.0 | 1.5 |
| Macau | 2001 | 33.0 | 23.4 | 8.5 | 6.0 |
| Russia/Former Soviet Asia | | | | | |
| Russian Fed.: Moscow | 1999 | 71.4 | 61.7 | 38.3 | 28.7 |
| Russian Fed.: Sarov | 2002 | 70.1 | 51.7 | 40.8 | 25.0 |
| Ukraine: Kiev City | 1999 | 84.0 | 69.1 | 46.8 | 33.8 |
| Western Asia/Northern Africa | | | | | |
| Bahrain | 2001 | 41.5 | 14.1 | 23.1 | 4.6 |
| Gaza Strip | 2001 | 56.2 | 24.4 | 18.5 | 3.8 |
| Georgia | 2002 | 55.5 | 32.7 | 32.6 | 12.1 |
| Jordan | 1999 | 44.1 | 25.8 | 22.6 | 11.4 |
| Kuwait | 2002 | 37.6 | 17.6 | 21.1 | 6.7 |
| Lebanon | 2001 | 39.9 | 27.1 | 16.1 | 7.4 |
| Libya | 2003 | 22.0 | 6.7 | 9.4 | 1.7 |
| Morocco | 2001 | 19.4 | 5.9 | 6.3 | 1.5 |
| Oman | 2003 | 31.4 | 6.8 | 16.2 | 1.8 |

| Currently Use Any Tobacco Products | | Never Smokers Likely to Initiate Smoking Next Year | Smokers Wanting to Stop | Smokers Who Have Tried to Stop |
|---|---|---|---|---|
| Male | Female | | | |
| 61.4 | 51.2 | 22.7 | 66.7 | 56.7 |
| 18.6 | 14.6 | 29.3 | 48.0 | 51.8 |
| 12.2 | 9.4 | 9.1 | 67.2 | 60.4 |
| 5.5 | 3.1 | 8.3 | n.a. | n.a. |
| 5.5 | 3.2 | 9.4 | n.a. | n.a. |
| 9.4 | 3.3 | 8.5 | n.a. | n.a. |
| 13.2 | 11.1 | 13.7 | n.a. | n.a. |
| 74.4 | 47.2 | 38.4 | 21.6 | 12.0 |
| 54.7 | 32.0 | 22.2 | 59.3 | 45.1 |
| 58.4 | 48.7 | 45.9 | 85.3 | 79.3 |
| 5.9 | 1.6 | 6.3 | 80.9 | 72.8 |
| 69.1 | 56.4 | 26.7 | 81.3 | 55.3 |
| 13.0 | 7.5 | 9.5 | 92.1 | 92.2 |
| 16.8 | 10.3 | 23.4 | n.a. | n.a. |
| 21.7 | 10.3 | 13.3 | 70.9 | 64.7 |
| 68.1 | 38.3 | 46.1 | 27.2 | 8.3 |
| 8.0 | 5.3 | 5.6 | 72.9 | 76.5 |
| 50.4 | 36.9 | 20.1 | 32.9 | 10.7 |
| 23.2 | 16.1 | 12.0 | n.a | 97.8 |
| 16.5 | 8.1 | 26.9 | 76.1 | 65.8 |
| 36.7 | 5.0 | 13.6 | 82.7 | 91.2 |
| | | | | |
| 19.8 | 9.8 | 5.4 | 73.2 | 64.5 |
| 13.9 | 7.6 | 4.7 | 64.5 | 62.8 |
| 11.1 | 6.4 | 4.3 | 86.2 | 81.6 |
| 16.0 | 5.5 | 4.9 | 82.1 | 70.3 |
| 9.4 | 6.2 | 11.4 | 58.3 | 64.1 |
| | | | | |
| 40.6 | 29.8 | 31.1 | 69.8 | 74.8 |
| 42.5 | 25.5 | 34.5 | 69.5 | 73.1 |
| 46.1 | 34.6 | 26.3 | 58.0 | 62.3 |
| | | | | |
| 33.5 | 11.9 | n.a. | 65.3 | 62.8 |
| 24.3 | 6.6 | 8.1 | 60.5 | 64.8 |
| 33.8 | 13.0 | 22.7 | 41.2 | 49.0 |
| 27.5 | 15.2 | 13.9 | 40.2 | 79.3 |
| 33.3 | 18.4 | 20.0 | 63.9 | 27.6 |
| 45.5 | 39.6 | 16.9 | 52.7 | 49.6 |
| 18.7 | 9.4 | 19.8 | 80.0 | 85.3 |
| 17.4 | 9.3 | 12.5 | 76.3 | 62.8 |
| 27.3 | 8.9 | 14.3 | 77.7 | 67.3 |

*Continued*

## APPENDIX TABLE 4-1 Continued

| Region and Country | | Ever Smoked Cigarettes | | Currently Smoke Cigarettes | |
|---|---|---|---|---|---|
| | | Male | Female | Male | Female |
| Sudan | 2001 | 30.0 | 10.0 | 14.1 | 2.1 |
| Syrian Arab Republic | 2002 | 15.4 | 6.1 | 8.4 | 3.8 |
| Tunisia | 2001 | 39.0 | 11.8 | 23.1 | 4.2 |
| United Arab Emirates | 2002 | 29.5 | 10.9 | 14.3 | 2.9 |
| West Bank | 2001 | 70.4 | 41.4 | 29.4 | 5.9 |
| Saudi Arabia: Riyadh | 2001 | 34.5 | n.a. | 10.8 | n.a. |
| Yemen: Aden | 2002 | 16.4 | 6.3 | 6.4 | 0.9 |
| Yemen: Hadhramout | 2002 | 16.1 | 4.6 | 7.5 | 1.6 |
| Yemen: Sanaa | 2002 | 21.3 | 13.9 | 7.5 | 4.5 |
| Egypt | 2001 | 16.2 | 10.7 | 4.4 | 3.4 |
| | | | | | |
| Caribbean/Central America | | | | | |
| Antigua/Barbuda | 2000 | 29.2 | 18.2 | 5.9 | 4.2 |
| Bahamas | 2000 | 33.6 | 27.5 | 9.0 | 6.0 |
| Barbados | 2002 | 35.0 | 30.0 | 7.0 | 7.0 |
| Belize | 2003 | 48.1 | 28.9 | 20.2 | 11.1 |
| British Virgin Islands | 2001 | 28.6 | 19.0 | 4.9 | 2.6 |
| Costa Rica | 2002 | 44.7 | 41.9 | 16.6 | 17.4 |
| Cuba | 2001 | 27.7 | 32.3 | 13.0 | 11.9 |
| Dominica | 2000 | 42.7 | 30.9 | 13.7 | 11.4 |
| El Salvador | 2003 | 45.1 | 27.4 | 18.8 | 11.3 |
| Grenada | 2000 | 34.0 | 20.9 | 9.7 | 6.8 |
| Haiti | 2001 | 22.6 | 24.6 | 11.0 | 12.1 |
| Jamaica | 2001 | 39.3 | 28.9 | 19.3 | 11.7 |
| Montserrat | 2000 | 21.1 | 23.1 | 4.0 | 5.3 |
| Panama | 2002 | 35.1 | 26.5 | 13.2 | 10.7 |
| St. Kitts/Nevis | 2002 | 25.4 | 12.1 | 8.0 | 2.5 |
| St. Lucia | 2001 | 45.3 | 27.7 | 13.5 | 6.5 |
| St. Vincent/Grenadines | 2001 | 43.0 | 27.7 | 17.6 | 11.5 |
| Trinidad/Tobago | 2000 | 46.5 | 32.6 | 17.6 | 9.5 |
| Guatemala: Chimaltenango | 2002 | 38.6 | 26.8 | 9.5 | 7.6 |
| Guatemala: Guatemala City | 2002 | 52.7 | 44.5 | 18.1 | 11.3 |
| Honduras: San Pedru Sula La Ceiba | 2003 | 48.5 | 37.6 | 17.9 | 9.2 |
| Honduras: Tegucigalpa | 2003 | 51.3 | 46.7 | 17.4 | 15.0 |
| Mexico: Guadalajara | 2003 | 52.2 | 51.4 | 17.9 | 20.3 |
| Mexico: Monterrey | 2000 | 57.3 | 43.7 | 22.3 | 14.6 |
| | | | | | |
| South America | | | | | |
| Guyana | 2000 | 36.7 | 22.2 | 11.1 | 5.5 |
| Suriname | 2000 | 62.8 | 46.0 | 23.4 | 10.0 |
| Venezuela | 1999 | 22.6 | 18.0 | 6.1 | 7.0 |
| Argentina: Buenos Aires | 2000 | 57.3 | 62.6 | 27.8 | 31.8 |

| Currently Use Any Tobacco Products | | Never Smokers Likely to Initiate Smoking Next Year | Smokers Wanting to Stop | Smokers Who Have Tried to Stop |
|---|---|---|---|---|
| Male | Female | | | |
| 20.3 | 12.9 | 24.6 | 73.9 | 79.2 |
| 23.7 | 15.2 | 9.6 | 71.6 | 67.2 |
| 28.7 | 7.2 | 20.6 | 80.6 | 69.7 |
| 29.7 | 12.6 | 11.1 | 66.8 | 64.2 |
| 31.8 | 8.3 | 10.9 | 59.8 | 66.8 |
| 20.2 | n.a. | n.a. | 72.8 | 54.8 |
| 19.4 | 11.7 | 31.3 | 91.8 | 77.0 |
| 21.8 | 11.2 | 29.4 | 83.4 | 66.8 |
| 22.4 | 17.7 | 39.6 | 79.7 | 65.9 |
| 22.8 | 15.8 | n.a. | 61.9 | 63.5 |
| 15.5 | 11.3 | 8.6 | n.a. | n.a. |
| 22.5 | 14.3 | 15.8 | 75.2 | 77.3 |
| 16.0 | 13.0 | 15.0 | 45.0 | 53.0 |
| 23.9 | 13.9 | 19.9 | 75.3 | 67.8 |
| 18.0 | 10.1 | 8.5 | 47.5 | 40.6 |
| 19.5 | 19.3 | 18.7 | 52.2 | 59.4 |
| 16.8 | 18.3 | 11.9 | 58.8 | 65.6 |
| 23.8 | 16.0 | n.a | 54.8 | 52.4 |
| 25.1 | 15.3 | 11.5 | 97.1 | 74.0 |
| 17.9 | 13.8 | 11.3 | 72.1 | 69.8 |
| 18.1 | 18.4 | 22.3 | 83.1 | 81.4 |
| 24.1 | 14.7 | 14.8 | 73.3 | 68.1 |
| 14.3 | 13.9 | 12.8 | n.a. | n.a. |
| 19.4 | 15.5 | 13.2 | 57.5 | 68.6 |
| 20.4 | 15.7 | 15.2 | 64.7 | n.a. |
| 18.5 | 10.1 | 13.0 | 75.7 | n.a. |
| 27.3 | 19.9 | 12.8 | 77.8 | 83.9 |
| 19.5 | 11.7 | 12.4 | 69.4 | 76.5 |
| 12.6 | 12.3 | 9.9 | 77.0 | 74.0 |
| 20.8 | 12.6 | 15.2 | 60.9 | 66.5 |
| 28.7 | 17.4 | 24.9 | 60.0 | 63.3 |
| 26.0 | 19.4 | 25.4 | 60.4 | 67.5 |
| 21.4 | 22.8 | 28.1 | 52.7 | 62.0 |
| 26.7 | 16.2 | 25.0 | 54.4 | 58.5 |
| 21.1 | 10.8 | 14.2 | n.a. | n.a. |
| 28.3 | 13.5 | 18.8 | 75.0 | 68.3 |
| 15.4 | 12.3 | 11.6 | 69.6 | 69.4 |
| 30.9 | 33.8 | 25.1 | 47.4 | 51.6 |

*Continued*

## APPENDIX TABLE 4-1 Continued

| Region and Country | | Ever Smoked Cigarettes | | Currently Smoke Cigarettes | |
|---|---|---|---|---|---|
| | | Male | Female | Male | Female |
| Bolivia: Cochabamba | 2000 | 61.2 | 45.7 | 29.7 | 17.7 |
| Bolivia: La Paz | 2000 | 63.5 | 47.5 | 32.2 | 22.4 |
| Bolivia: Santa Cruz | 2000 | 60.7 | 49.7 | 29.5 | 20.8 |
| Brazil: Goiania | 2002 | 48.2 | 46.5 | 16.0 | 23.5 |
| Brazil: Matto Grosso do Sul | 2002 | 48.9 | 48.1 | 20.6 | 18.3 |
| Brazil: Paraiba | 2002 | 45.3 | 42.2 | 14.4 | 12.4 |
| Brazil: Rio Grande do Norte | 2002 | 40.1 | 38.7 | 14.5 | 13.1 |
| Chile: Coquimbo | 2000 | 65.1 | 69.7 | 35.4 | 40.8 |
| Chile: Santiago | 2000 | 67.4 | 74.7 | 30.9 | 43.8 |
| Chile: Valparaiso V. del Mar | 2000 | 61.7 | 71.6 | 31.3 | 40.6 |
| Colombia: Bogota | 2001 | 63.4 | 58.7 | 28.4 | 27.2 |
| Ecuador: Guayaquil | 2001 | 31.1 | 26.9 | 9.2 | 7.5 |
| Ecuador: Quito | 2001 | 62.1 | 40.4 | 23.8 | 11.1 |
| Ecuador: Zamora | 2002 | 64.0 | 46.8 | 26.6 | 17.4 |
| Paraguay: Altoparana Ituapua | 2003 | 36.8 | 30.1 | 15.4 | 12.3 |
| Paraguay: Amambay Caaguazu | 2003 | 30.0 | 27.1 | 14.1 | 13.3 |
| Paraguay: Asuncion | 2003 | 36.0 | 37.0 | 18.4 | 17.0 |
| Paraguay: Central | 2003 | 26.0 | 25.1 | 11.7 | 12.2 |
| Peru: Huancayo | 2000 | 60.0 | 37.9 | 22.7 | 10.8 |
| Peru: Ica City | 2002 | 48.6 | 37.5 | 19.6 | 11.8 |
| Peru: Lima | 2000 | 63.1 | 48.9 | 23.6 | 17.4 |
| Peru: Tarapoto | 2000 | 56.2 | 32.2 | 21.7 | 10.1 |
| Peru: Trujillo | 2000 | 59.9 | 38.2 | 27.1 | 10.5 |
| Uruguay: Colonia | 2001 | 32.4 | 41.2 | 15.1 | 17.1 |
| Uruguay: Maldonado | 2001 | 49.4 | 51.8 | 15.7 | 24.6 |
| Uruguay: Montevideo | 2001 | 52.2 | 52.3 | 20.5 | 26.5 |
| Uruguay: Rivera | 2001 | 42.7 | 48.7 | 18.1 | 21.0 |
| Venezuela: Tachira State | 2001 | 23.8 | 21.2 | 7.8 | 6.5 |
| Venezuela: Yaracuy State | 2001 | 14.5 | 10.0 | 4.4 | 3.5 |
| Venezuela: Zulia State | 2001 | 24.2 | 17.2 | 11.3 | 5.9 |
| Oceania | | | | | |
| Fiji | 1999 | 47.4 | 27.2 | 18.8 | 9.6 |
| Northern Marianas | 2000 | 78.2 | 81.3 | 37.5 | 40.7 |
| Palau | 2000 | 63.0 | 60.1 | 23.3 | 20.0 |
| Europe | | | | | |
| Bosnia and Herzegovina | 2003 | 45.5 | 38.5 | 16.8 | 10.0 |
| Bulgaria | 2002 | 64.4 | 73.4 | 31.3 | 42.7 |
| Croatia | 2002 | 62.5 | 56.3 | 18.5 | 14.3 |
| Czech Republic | 2002 | 75.0 | 71.2 | 34.4 | 34.9 |
| Estonia | 2002 | 82.4 | 73.8 | 33.9 | 29.8 |
| FYR Macedonia | 2002 | 25.8 | 19.5 | 9.3 | 6.7 |

| Currently Use Any Tobacco Products | | Never Smokers Likely to Initiate Smoking Next Year | Smokers Wanting to Stop | Smokers Who Have Tried to Stop |
|---|---|---|---|---|
| Male | Female | | | |
| 33.2 | 21.7 | 25.8 | 56.3 | 59.8 |
| 36.8 | 25.9 | 28.0 | 64.7 | 66.9 |
| 34.3 | 25.3 | 24.1 | 69.8 | 63.7 |
| 21.8 | 17.5 | 12.5 | 69.9 | 64.1 |
| 26.2 | 21.0 | 15.9 | 67.4 | 75.9 |
| 18.1 | 16.6 | 14.1 | 83.2 | 82.0 |
| 18.4 | 16.3 | 13.6 | 72.0 | 70.0 |
| 36.3 | 41.3 | 27.5 | 51.7 | 61.2 |
| 32.6 | 43.0 | 28.4 | 44.3 | 59.7 |
| 31.8 | 39.9 | 21.9 | 50.8 | 61.3 |
| 30.2 | 28.7 | 22.9 | 69.5 | 69.8 |
| 14.4 | 13.7 | 14.0 | 67.2 | 65.6 |
| 23.1 | 15.5 | 16.7 | 72.5 | 65.6 |
| 32.5 | 28.6 | 21.0 | 79.0 | 66.1 |
| 24.3 | 22.5 | 18.3 | 61.8 | 69.3 |
| 24.8 | 24.0 | 17.8 | 74.1 | 73.2 |
| 27.2 | 24.5 | 22.7 | 49.8 | 62.2 |
| 21.6 | 19.5 | 15.0 | 59.5 | 67.5 |
| 27.7 | 13.7 | 31.4 | 75.1 | 68.0 |
| 21.6 | 13.8 | 24.5 | 82.9 | 76.7 |
| 26.9 | 20.1 | 24.4 | 67.7 | 63.4 |
| 23.4 | 13.2 | 20.1 | 86.3 | 80.3 |
| 28.0 | 14.1 | 25.9 | 78.3 | 76.5 |
| 17.1 | 19.8 | 19.4 | 46.0 | 50.4 |
| 19.9 | 26.9 | 18.9 | 52.1 | 58.2 |
| 26.2 | 28.8 | 23.0 | 58.7 | 63.6 |
| 22.1 | 22.8 | 16.8 | 65.5 | 60.6 |
| 14.1 | 11.5 | 14.1 | 53.1 | 58.4 |
| 14.6 | 7.8 | 11.0 | 74.2 | 69.9 |
| 19.0 | 25.4 | 16.6 | 67.7 | 64.3 |
| | | | | |
| 24.1 | 13.4 | 21.4 | 79.7 | 82.3 |
| 68.4 | 57.1 | 35.9 | 80.7 | 76.8 |
| 54.8 | 62.3 | 16.8 | 76.8 | n.a. |
| | | | | |
| 18.8 | 12.2 | 24.6 | 58.4 | 69.9 |
| 33.0 | 42.4 | 30.5 | 63.6 | 71.0 |
| 19.3 | 14.8 | 17.0 | 49.9 | 73.5 |
| 35.8 | 33.4 | n.a. | 48.8 | 69.1 |
| 34.9 | 29.8 | 35.5 | 60.9 | 69.0 |
| 11.7 | 7.9 | 15.9 | 59.9 | 77.3 |

*Continued*

## APPENDIX TABLE 4-1 Continued

| Region and Country | | Ever Smoked Cigarettes | | Currently Smoke Cigarettes | |
| --- | --- | --- | --- | --- | --- |
| | | Male | Female | Male | Female |
| Latvia | 2002 | 86.6 | 72.7 | 38.2 | 29.7 |
| Montenegro | 2003 | 34.8 | 26.5 | 3.7 | 3.4 |
| Republika Srpska | 2003 | 49.6 | 45.2 | 14.0 | 12.2 |
| Serbia | 2003 | 54.4 | 55.2 | 15.5 | 16.8 |
| Slovakia | 2002 | 69.9 | 58.0 | 25.5 | 22.5 |
| Slovenia | 2003 | 66.5 | 65.7 | 25.4 | 29.9 |
| Poland: Rural | 1999 | 68.2 | 49.8 | 21.7 | 11.6 |
| Poland: Urban | 1999 | 71.8 | 67.0 | 30.0 | 27.3 |
| United States | 2000 | 50.5 | 48.6 | 17.8 | 17.7 |

NOTE: n.a. = not available.
SOURCES: World Health Organization and Centers for Disease Control (2002).

| Currently Use Any Tobacco Products | | Never Smokers Likely to Initiate Smoking Next Year | Smokers Wanting to Stop | Smokers Who Have Tried to Stop |
|---|---|---|---|---|
| Male | Female | | | |
| 41.4 | 33.0 | n.a. | 75.0 | 71.6 |
| 4.9 | 5.0 | 15.2 | n.a. | 83.0 |
| 14.5 | 12.2 | 23.0 | 53.9 | 73.2 |
| 16.2 | 17.2 | 19.1 | 54.4 | 77.8 |
| 26.6 | 23.3 | 22.9 | 64.0 | 80.8 |
| 27.1 | 29.3 | 27.3 | 41.6 | 68.5 |
| 25.2 | 14.5 | 21.6 | 79.5 | 79.1 |
| 37.2 | 30.3 | 23.7 | 74.6 | 73.5 |
| 26.0 | 20.1 | n.a. | 55.8 | 58.2 |

# PART III

# Transition to Adult Roles

# 5

# The Transition to Work

## INTRODUCTION

One of the most important transitions young people make as they grow older is the transition from being dependent on the economic support of their parents or other adults to being economically productive in their own right with the ability to support themselves and others. This productivity can take many forms, for example, working on the family farm, caring for children at home, working for wages in a factory, or running an independent business. Whatever form this work takes, the transition to becoming a productive member of society depends for its success, at least in part, on the achievement and maintenance of good health and the acquisition of marketable skills as well as capabilities for lifelong learning (topics covered in the previous two chapters). This transition differs significantly across regions of the world, and it has been affected in important ways by global demographic, social, and economic changes.

In response to global economic change, the reward structures of many labor markets are changing to favor those with secondary education or beyond. Perhaps in part as a result, there has been an enormous shift in the use of children's time from work (mostly in family enterprises and in noneconomic household work[1]) to schooling. Nevertheless, in many develop-

---

[1]The term "noneconomic household work" was developed by statisticians specializing in gender issues to capture domestic chores that are noneconomic in nature. As some economic activity occurs in the household, it is important to distinguish between economic household work and noneconomic household work (United Nations, 2000c:134-135).

ing countries experiencing economic growth, low-cost child labor still can give producers a competitive edge. The heightened concern about child labor in developing countries reflects these two contradictory realities. When children take up full-time work responsibilities in the home or labor market too soon, their future productive potential can be comprised.

Throughout history, much learning has been acquired in the context of work through formal or informal apprenticeships. However, certain important skills that are increasingly required in today's job market are rarely acquired on the job, but are more typically acquired in school. These include proficiency in reading, writing, mathematics, abstract reasoning, critical thinking, and computer literacy as well as skills in lifelong learning. Given the early and rapid development of the brain, children benefit most when these skills are acquired at a young age. For these reasons, successful transitions to adult work roles in today's workplace are likely to be completed later, involve more formal schooling, and possibly play out more gradually than in the past.

The pathways of young men and women typically diverge as they prepare for adult work roles. The socialization of young people for adulthood starts in the family and is usually modeled on the norms and values of adult family members, as colored by their own life experiences. The traditional division of labor between the sexes—which has been reinforced over the generations through this socialization process—stems from a universal concern with the protection, feeding, and rearing of the young and a recognition of the importance of maintaining physical proximity between mother and child. Women's productive activities have traditionally remained close to home and have been less likely than men's to yield direct personal remuneration in the form of cash income. As a result, young women have been trained for and aspired to adult work roles and livelihoods that are compatible with mothering, whereas young men have pursued a wider set of potentially more remunerative options.

The growing importance of a cash economy brings with it both opportunities and pitfalls for a current generation of young women who are anticipating and planning for adult lives that are likely to be quite different from their mothers'. On one hand, the growth in remunerative market job opportunities, particularly for those with secondary schooling, has the potential to attract young women into the labor force, put cash in their hands, and give them opportunities for greater agency in their lives, whether it is a better choice of spouse, an opportunity to save, a greater say in the family, or more money for personal consumption. On the other hand, the growing importance of a cash economy can also ultimately reinforce existing intrahousehold inequalities, if young women revert to traditional roles after marriage and childbearing while young men gain increasing control of the disposition of their family's financial resources as they age.[2] Furthermore, rising rates of female household headship around the world suggest that women who have the ability to generate income through their work will be better prepared to face future uncertainties.[3] Thus, our definition of a successful work transition for young women today has to include, as it does for young men, the opportunity or potential to earn cash.

Probably the most dramatic social transformations that have occurred in developed countries over the last 30 years have been the growing labor force participation of women, accompanied by a rising percentage of women working outside their homes or farms for cash—first young unmarried women, then older married women, and most recently young mothers in the labor force—and the narrowing gap between men's and women's pay.[4] These changes permit young women greater agency in all aspects of their lives both over the course of the transition to adulthood and beyond (Blau, 1997; Goldin, 1990). These changes have been very much supported and reinforced by women's ability, for the first time in history, to limit their fertility and control the timing of their children's births so as to enhance their career building over the life cycle—a possibility that now potentially exists for all women thanks to dramatic improvements in birth control technology (Birdsall and Chester, 1987). The experience of women in the

---

[2]These intrahousehold inequalities emerge due to the strong link between access to cash and bargaining power over the allocation of resources in the home or family, as presented in the seminal papers by Manser and Brown (1979, 1980) and McElroy and Horney (1981). These led to a large subsequent literature, some important examples of which include Browning et al. (1994), Dwyer and Bruce (1988), Haddad, Hoddinott, and Alderman (1997), Lundberg and Pollak (1993), Lundberg, Pollak, and Wales (1997), and Rubalcava, Teruel, and Thomas (2002). Most of the literature interprets the associations between intrahousehold allocations and cash income of women as reflecting causal effects, although most studies do not distinguish persuasively between the effect of increased cash income of women and the possibility that women with greater unobserved motivations and abilities for those reasons have both greater cash income and more impact on intrahousehold allocations (see Behrman, 1997). The Lundberg, Pollak, and Wales study noted above is an exception: it uses a change in the recipients of English child support payments from fathers to mothers to identify such effects. Another exception is Rubalcava, Teruel, and Thomas (2002), which used the random assignment of transfers to women in some poor rural Mexican household to identify these effects.

[3]It is estimated that women in developing countries can expect to spend roughly a quarter to a third of their adult years outside marriage due to nonmarriage, widowhood, and divorce (Bruce, Lloyd, and Leonard, 1995).

[4]However, the available data on manufacturing wages by gender as of the mid-1990s did not show a narrowing of the gender gaps in most fast-growing East Asian economies, some of which are currently included in the developed country group (Behrman and Zhang, 1995).

world of work in the developed world over the last 30 years suggests a further prerequisite for successful work transitions—the opportunity to earn cash in the labor force before marriage—a possibility that has always been available to men.

Due to changing family circumstances, rising educational attainment, greater mobility, and rapid economic changes, one can confidently predict that the transition to work in developing countries today will be different from that in the past and is increasingly likely to be multistaged. The type of part-time work that is appropriate while one is still a student during the teen years will be different from the type of full-time work that may be desired if one is planning for and saving for marriage. Furthermore, the type of work undertaken if one is still living at home with one's parents may be different from the type of work desired if one is managing one's own home. Increasingly, a successful transition to adult work roles will be one that accommodates these stages and allows greater flexibility and mobility over time for both young men and young women.

Given all these considerations, a successful transition depends not only on appropriate preparation, but also, equally importantly, on a healthy and growing economy that generates a diversity of adequate jobs or other forms of livelihood for each new cohort as it approaches adulthood as well as equal opportunities, regardless of gender, race, or class. Young people and their parents respond to the incentives that surround them and cannot be expected to carry the responsibilities of success on their shoulders alone. Thus, in this chapter, as we review trends in work participation among young people in developing countries, we are interested not only in explaining current trends, but also in drawing lessons from current policies and programs that may hold promise for the future.

As in other chapters, we begin with a discussion of current patterns and recent changes in the transition to work, including some of the links between this transition and other transitions previously discussed, while drawing on available data from household surveys and censuses. The determinants of these changes are discussed next, using as a guide the conceptual framework laid out in Chapter 2. We conclude with a discussion of policies and programs operating at the international, national, and local levels that directly or indirectly have implications for preparation for and acquisition of adult work roles.

The panel was unable to explore some potentially important aspects of the transition to adult work roles due to lack of data. These include the links between work experience during the transition to adulthood and the development of a sense of identity, agency, competence, and decision-making skills and the implications of these potential benefits of labor market work during the transition for successful transitions in other domains. We address this gap in our research recommendations.

The chapter focuses primarily on formal or informal work in the labor market, the kind of work that is typically measured in labor market surveys.[5] This is in part because the data are more complete for labor market work than they are for noneconomic household work. But more importantly, it is because of the particular importance we have attached to paid work, which represents a growing share of labor market work everywhere, in our definition of successful work transitions. Special topical themes covered in the chapter include child labor, the changing roles of young women in the labor market, youth unemployment, and migration for work. Because comparable data on many of these topics are lacking, we often rely on case studies to illustrate key points that, in our view, have the potential for wider applicability. The chapter begins with an introductory discussion of work defined in its broadest sense to include noneconomic household work, drawing on time use data among adolescents in order to provide a context for the subsequent discussion of recent trends and determinants of labor force participation.

## PATTERNS AND TRENDS IN WORK PARTICIPATION AMONG YOUNG PEOPLE

This section presents empirical evidence on patterns of work by age and sex as derived from recently collected time use data as well as on trends in the labor force participation of young people as measured in conventional survey and census data. The distinction between the terms "work" and "labor force participation" is an important one for our purposes. Standard labor force statistics typically divide the population into three groups based on responses given in censuses or household surveys to questions about economic activity in the week, month, or year prior to the survey. Those who report that they did any work for pay, or a certain number of hours of self-employed work or unpaid work in a family farm or business working during the reporting period, are considered employed. This group includes both formal and informal employment. The second group—the unemployed—are generally defined as those who report that they were not doing any of the specified types of work during the reporting period, but were looking for a job. The employed and unemployed groups are both considered to be economically active and together make up the labor force. The

---

[5]Informal employment is comprised of both self-employment in informal enterprises (i.e., small and/or unregistered) and wage employment in informal jobs (i.e., without secure contracts, worker benefits, or social protection [International Labour Office, 2002a]). In developing regions, a majority of those who are employed informally are self-employed. By contrast, formal employment involves secure contracts, worker benefits, and/or social protection.

third group is those who are neither employed nor unemployed. This group is considered out of the labor force or "not economically active." However, many young people who are defined as out of the labor force or not economically active are actually working in areas not well covered by labor force surveys and censuses. The types of work rarely measured include noneconomic household work or domestic work (which falls outside the definition of economic activity) as well as various forms of remunerative but informal, episodic, or casual work, as well as illegal or socially sanctioned work (which fall within the definition of economic activity).

Time use data, when available, can provide an alternative and more comprehensive perspective on patterns of work over the transition to adulthood as well as on gender differences in work burdens by age. This is because typically these include not only time doing labor market work but also time spent in noneconomic household work. Because most reported labor force participation data do not distinguish part-time from full-time employment and do not include participation in noneconomic household work, it is difficult to get a complete sense of the number of hours worked overall or the extent to which young people combine school with various types of work. However, data on trends in time use are not available. Thus, time use data are mainly useful in setting the context in which to interpret the more available data on labor force participation, because they include various categories of work time, including unpaid work and noneconomic household work, that are not captured in labor force surveys.

### Patterns of Time Use

From an overall review of the literature on the time use of adolescents and youth, three fairly universal patterns emerge: (1) There are significant differences in the way boys and girls spend their work time, regardless of age, with boys more likely to work for pay or family economic gain and girls more likely to do noneconomic household work (i.e., domestic chores); (2) The total amount of time devoted to all work activities (labor market activities and noneconomic household activities combined) rises with age for both boys and girls; (3) Girls tend to work longer hours in total than boys, leaving boys more time for leisure activities (Ritchie, Lloyd, and Grant, 2004). Levison, Moe, and Knaul's (2001) analysis of time use data for 12-17-year-olds in urban Mexico illustrates these points well (Figure 5-1).[6]

Rising rates of school attendance during the adolescent years have

---

[6]Neither of these studies, however, explored differences in work patterns by family income or wealth, which are likely to be important as well.

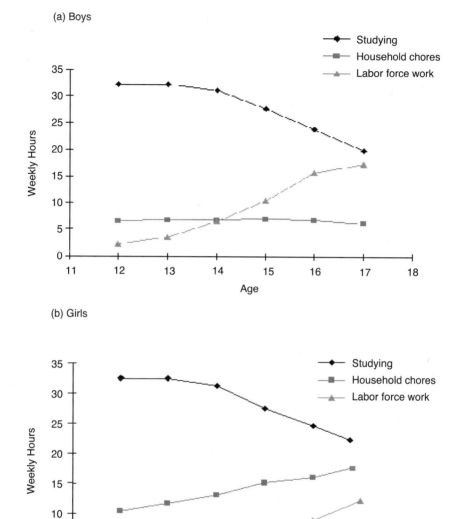

FIGURE 5-1 Weekly hours by type of work, urban Mexico, 1996 (ages 12-17).
SOURCE: Levison, Moe, and Knaul (2001:171).

implications for time use among young people. A recent comparative analysis of time use data for young people ages 15-19 from an eclectic group of developing countries, including Kenya, India, Nicaragua, Pakistan, and South Africa, allows comparisons of time use between students and nonstudents (Ritchie, Lloyd, and Grant, 2004). Figure 5-2 shows gender differences in mean hours per day spent in school as well as gender differences in mean hours per day spent in all types of work (labor market work and noneconomic household work combined). The patterns shown in the figure describe associations that are similar across countries representing a wide range of school attendance patterns among 15-19-year-olds.

Figure 5-2 shows that there are large variations across countries in the average time currently enrolled students spend attending school and doing schoolwork, variations that largely reflect variations in the length of the school day. For example, the average time devoted to school is almost twice as high in rural Kenya as it is in rural South Africa. The longer the school day, the shorter the time students have available for any type of work. One of the major concerns about child labor is that it interferes with the ability of young people to attend and learn effectively in school (Anker, 2000). These data suggest that the extent to which this may be true varies across countries in accordance with school schedules.

As far as the overall distribution of total work burdens (combining time spent in paid work, unpaid work, and domestic work) is concerned, Figure 5-2 shows that in every case, those who are not enrolled in school report substantially more total work hours than enrolled students, regardless of the reference period. This is not surprising given that school takes up a significant portion of the day. It is also true that, in every case but rural Nicaragua, girls report more total work hours than boys, whether or not they are students. Among students, gender disparities in total work time are greatest for urban India, with girls reporting on average 2 more hours of work on days when school is in session than boys. Gender differences in students' total work time on a school day are typically about an hour. Among nonenrolled adolescents as well, gender differences in total work time are typically about an hour. Thus, while those who attend school have less total work demands, female students still work longer total hours than male students.

Figure 5-3 provides a further breakdown of daily time use into noneconomic household work and labor market work. Here we can see that the gender division of labor in this phase of the life cycle is most sharply etched among those who are not attending school. While boys who are students share noneconomic household work roles with girls, boys who are not in school spend the majority of their work day in economic activity, while girls who are not in school are largely limited to noneconomic household work. Indeed, boys contribute more to the household in terms of noneconomic household work than economic activities when they are enrolled. Female students, however, still do more noneconomic household work than male adolescents who are not enrolled in school.

These data provide suggestive evidence that the sharp increases in school participation and attainment that have occurred around the world in the last 20 years are likely to be associated with simultaneous declines in overall work burdens as well as declines in labor force participation rates among adolescents (Ritchie, Lloyd, and Grant, 2004). As these data are very recent and gender gaps in enrollment are closing rapidly, these findings also imply that the time use of male and female adolescents, at least during the early and middle phases of the transition to adulthood, is becoming more similar despite the fact that the work burdens that accompany school attendance are still greater for girls.

## Trends in Labor Force Participation

This section presents empirical evidence on recent trends in the labor force participation of young people ages 15-24 as measured in conventional surveys and censuses. [7] As defined above, the labor force participation rate is the proportion of the population that is economically active and includes both the employed and the unemployed. The International Labour Organization (ILO) plays an important role in developing standards for the collection of labor force statistics at the national level, compiling these national statistics in a variety of publications and data bases. We restrict our analysis to those data provided by the ILO that are the direct result of dedicated data collection exercises and choose not to present estimated participation rates, whether prepared by the ILO or by national statistical offices. [8] While it is important to keep in mind that the data are not necessarily perfectly comparable across countries because of differences in the wording of questions, the length of the reference periods, definitions of work or unemployment, and the design of household surveys, these compilations provide the best available international source of information on labor force statistics and, therefore, the best place to begin. Under the assumption that individual countries typically apply internally consistent definitions of labor force participation over time, these data are particularly appropriate for the comparison of trends across countries.

---

[7]Because of the sensitivity of issues associated with work among children ages 10-14, data on this age group are less often collected and, when collected, harder to interpret. Recent data collection efforts by the United Nations Children's Fund and the International Labour Organization are discussed later in the chapter in the section on child labor.

[8]Such estimates are difficult to evaluate because the assumptions that underlie them are not known.

274

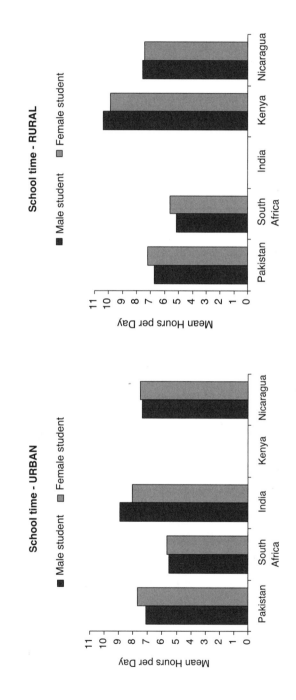

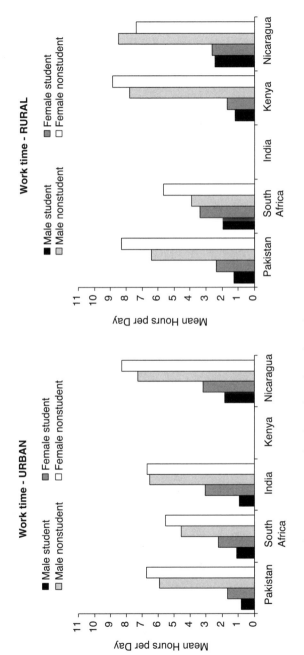

FIGURE 5-2 Mean hours spent on school work and total work (ages 15-19).
NOTE: Reported on a school day.
SOURCE: Ritchie, Lloyd, and Grant (2004).

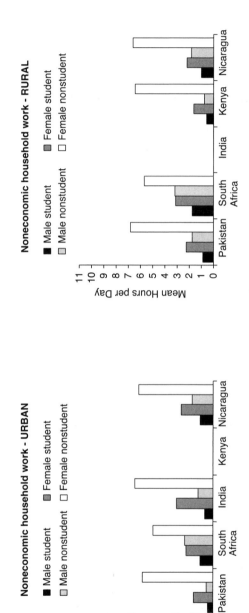

277

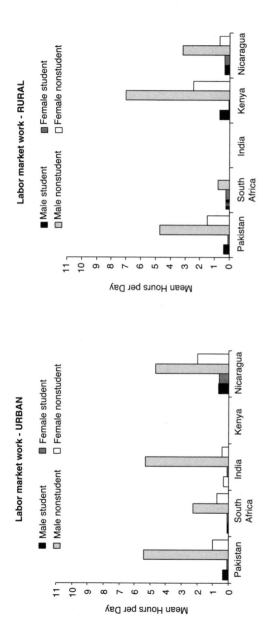

FIGURE 5-3 Total time spent in noneconomic household work and labor market work (ages 15-19).
NOTE: Reported on a school day.
SOURCE: Ritchie, Lloyd, and Grant (2004).

Tables 5-1 and 5-2 summarize trends in labor force participation rates for 15-19-year-olds and 20-24-year-olds, respectively, by five-year age groups over the last 20 years for all countries for which we could compile, at a minimum, data for the most recent time period (1995-present) and at least one five-year period in the recent past (1980-1984 or 1985-1989). Because of the heavy influence of the business cycle on year-to-year trends, we did not want business cycle fluctuations to obscure longer term trends. For this reason, we chose to present data for longer time intervals: 1980-1984, 1985-1989, 1990-1994, and 1995+. The rates presented for each five-year time period represent an average of available data for that time period.[9] Some countries from all regions but Africa are represented in these data (25 countries in all) but not a sufficient number to present regional averages.

Among boys in the later teens (ages 15-19), participation rates are highly variable, from 18 percent in Suriname to 65 percent in Bangladesh and Brazil in the most recent period (Table 5-1), reflecting a huge variation in timing across countries in the acquisition of adult work roles among young men.[10] The overall tendency is one of decline in participation rates for young men over the last two decades, mirroring the rising percentage of this age group that is enrolled in school. Some countries have experienced a much sharper drop than others, however, and some have not shown any decline despite rising enrollment rates in this age group (Bangladesh and Mexico, among others). Among 15-19-year-old women, rates tend to be much lower than those of men, but trends are less consistent. In 10 of the 26 countries, participation rates for women have risen despite rising enrollments. However, given much lower levels of participation, there is less likely to be a direct trade-off between school enrollment and labor force participation. In several countries, including Bangladesh, Ecuador, and Egypt, female participation rates went up at the same time that participation rates for men went down.

Typically by the age of 20-24, participation rates for young men come close to or exceed 80 percent (Table 5-2). This is universally true in Asia and Central America. Exceptions include Chile, Egypt, Peru, Suriname, and Tunisia.[11] In most cases, trends over the last two decades are less dramatic,

---

[9]Data for at least two of the five years covered in each time period were required for an average to be presented for that period for a particular country.

[10]While Standing (1999) notes a long-term decline in the labor force participation rates of adult men in most developing countries since 1975, we would still expect labor force participation rates to peak by the late 20s at well over 80 percent.

[11]In some cases, military service during these ages can be a factor explaining unusually low recorded labor force participation. Egypt is a prime example (for further discussion of military service, see Chapter 6).

with some ups and downs. Female participation rates, which were at considerably lower levels than those of men in this age group in the early 1980s, have tended to increase over time. Most countries have shown a rise in participation rates among young women over the last two decades, suggesting that transitions to adulthood in the domain of labor force participation are undergoing significant transformation.

Table 5-3 presents trends in the female-male ratio in participation rates for the same age groups. A pattern of steadily rising ratios is readily apparent. Except in a few countries, in which the female-male ratio was already quite high in the early 1980s (e.g., Malaysia, the Philippines, and Turkey), one can see a consistent rise in the ratio over time, both among the 15-19-year-olds and the 20-24-year-olds, signaling an important change in work roles among younger cohorts of women. Nonetheless, the persistence of substantial diversity across countries is apparent in the range of recent ratios (from 0.2 for Pakistan to over 0.8 in Colombia, Peru, and Thailand).

China and India together represent 42 percent of the population of young people in the developing world. While data on trends in labor force participation rates for these two important countries were not available from the ILO database, data from alternative sources show similar patterns (see Table 5-4 for China and Figure 5-4 for India). For China there are data on employment by single years of age for 1989 and 1997 (Hannum and Liu, 2005). Substantial declines in employment rates are evident through age 20 for both sexes and through age 22 for boys. Gender differences in employment rates are relatively small. In India, there is a slight decline in labor force participation rates for men ages 15-19 and 20-24 from 1987-1988 to 1993-1994, as well as a slight rise in labor force participation rates for women of the same ages. While the gender gap in labor force participation in India remains huge, it is narrowing.

## Youth Employment: Measurement Issues

In many developing country settings, the terms "labor," "employment," and "paid work" are used interchangeably. The status of being unemployed or looking for work is a refinement of measurement that emerges with development, as the formal sector of the labor force grows. Most poor people are engaged in subsistence economic activities that do not require an application or an interview. Thus, in the poorest and most underdeveloped economies, unemployment is a luxury that few young people can afford.[12]

Nonetheless, it is important to know what is included in the definition

---

[12]Indeed, many fewer developing countries report unemployment data separately to the ILO for that very reason.

TABLE 5-1 Trends in Labor Force Participation Rates (Ages 15-19), Selected Developing Countries

| Region and Country | Male | | | | Female | | | |
|---|---|---|---|---|---|---|---|---|
| | 1980-1984 | 1985-1989 | 1990-1994 | 1995+ | 1980-1984 | 1985-1989 | 1990-1994 | 1995+ |
| Middle East | | | | | | | | |
| Egypt | 44.5 | 38.0 | 33.2 | 33.3 | 9.8 | 11.5 | 12.2 | 12.1 |
| Syria | 50.8 | n.a. | n.a. | 54.3 | 9.7 | n.a. | n.a. | 18.5 |
| Tunisia | 56.8 | 45.3 | 44.5 | 37.1 | 24.4 | 22.6 | 24.9 | 21.1 |
| Turkey | 69.4 | 64.8 | 56.6 | 48.5 | 51.8 | 45.5 | 38.3 | 29.2 |
| South America | | | | | | | | |
| Argentina | 51.6 | n.a. | n.a. | 36.9 | 27.8 | n.a. | n.a. | 24.2 |
| Brazil | 64.8 | 73.3 | 72.4 | 64.9 | 31.2 | 41.3 | 44.4 | 42.2 |
| Chile | 28.2 | 30.2 | 28.7 | 20.5 | 12.0 | 12.1 | 12.5 | 10.1 |
| Colombia | 38.2 | 39.7 | 38.5 | 38.2 | 19.0 | 29.6 | 29.4 | 30.7 |
| Ecuador | 47.8 | n.a. | 52.4 | 44.2 | 14.6 | n.a. | 19.0 | 29.4 |
| Peru | 34.0 | 36.7 | 32.9 | 41.9 | 22.0 | 32.7 | 25.3 | 34.5 |
| Suriname | 13.3 | n.a. | 22.5 | 18.3 | 3.8 | n.a. | 10.3 | 5.7 |

| | | | | | | | | |
|---|---|---|---|---|---|---|---|---|
| Caribbean/Central America | | | | | | | | |
| Costa Rica | 61.1 | 61.8 | 56.6 | 53.9 | 23.7 | 26.0 | 26.3 | 24.5 |
| El Salvador | 60.9 | n.a. | 54.6 | 53.4 | 29.4 | n.a. | 27.0 | 21.7 |
| Mexico | 55.9 | 56.9 | 57.7 | 58.4 | 26.8 | 30.0 | 26.1 | 29.6 |
| Panama | 41.3 | 44.5 | 45.8 | 45.0 | 17.9 | 19.6 | 21.7 | 21.9 |
| Trinidad and Tobago | 52.2 | 46.5 | 41.9 | 39.3 | 20.1 | 20.6 | 23.1 | 21.7 |
| Asia | | | | | | | | |
| Bangladesh | 67.7 | 69.5 | 72.8 | 65.2 | 5.6 | 23.5 | 59.5 | 47.3 |
| Indonesia | 48.0 | 45.1 | 46.3 | 44.8 | 32.3 | 34.5 | 34.5 | 33.3 |
| Malaysia | 47.8 | 38.2 | 36.7 | 32.4 | 33.9 | 24.5 | 25.6 | 21.1 |
| Pakistan | 66.2 | 65.5 | 52.3 | 53.7 | 10.3 | 8.5 | 12.1 | 10.9 |
| Philippines | 50.1 | 49.4 | 46.4 | 45.8 | 34.9 | 31.2 | 28.6 | 27.2 |
| Sri Lanka | 42.1 | 44.2 | 33.9 | 33.5 | 19.0 | 23.4 | 22.7 | 19.9 |
| Thailand | 70.6 | 70.0 | 59.3 | 40.4 | 71.4 | 71.3 | 58.7 | 34.1 |

NOTES: n.a. = not available. Each data entry is an average of two or more data points within each time interval.
SOURCE: International Labour Office, Labor Statistics Division (2003).

TABLE 5-2 Trends in Labor Force Participation Rates (Ages 20-24), Selected Developing Countries

| Region and Country | Male | | | | Female | | | |
|---|---|---|---|---|---|---|---|---|
| | 1980-1984 | 1985-1989 | 1990-1994 | 1995+ | 1980-1984 | 1985-1989 | 1990-1994 | 1995+ |
| Middle East | | | | | | | | |
| Egypt | 67.5 | 65.4 | 53.2 | 60.7 | 19.9 | 28.7 | 32.9 | 28.2 |
| Syria | 72.3 | n.a. | n.a. | 81.5 | 15.3 | n.a. | n.a. | 25.7 |
| Tunisia | 82.6 | 69.7 | 65.0 | 64.8 | 31.8 | 30.1 | 34.5 | 34.2 |
| Turkey | 90.6 | 88.2 | 85.5 | 78.2 | 49.5 | 44.3 | 41.7 | 36.2 |
| South America | | | | | | | | |
| Argentina | 85.5 | n.a. | 82.9 | 78.9 | 42.2 | n.a. | 52.4 | 53.4 |
| Brazil | 90.0 | 92.6 | 91.6 | 89.5 | 39.1 | 51.9 | 57.5 | 61.4 |
| Chile | 77.0 | 79.2 | 77.9 | 71.8 | 40.2 | 39.3 | 41.2 | 41.3 |
| Colombia | | | | | | | | |
| Ecuador | 75.3 | n.a. | 79.3 | 81.2 | 22.7 | n.a. | 29.3 | 56.1 |
| Peru | 69.2 | 72.8 | 73.8 | 73.5 | 39.9 | 55.1 | 54.2 | 56.1 |
| Suriname | 57.7 | 74.4 | 67.8 | 62.6 | 25.3 | 44.8 | 38.9 | 28.1 |
| Uruguay | 91.2 | 88.0 | 88.0 | 88.8 | 65.6 | 48.1 | 65.5 | 70.7 |

Caribbean/Central America

| | | | | | | | | |
|---|---|---|---|---|---|---|---|---|
| Costa Rica | 82.3 | 87.7 | 88.0 | 86.0 | 27.7 | 41.1 | 43.8 | 47.9 |
| El Salvador | 86.7 | n.a. | 83.2 | 84.0 | 45.7 | n.a. | 47.3 | 44.6 |
| Mexico | 83.4 | 83.0 | 82.1 | 84.9 | 37.3 | 40.9 | 37.5 | 43.0 |
| Panama | 81.3 | 85.2 | 84.7 | 87.2 | 40.1 | 44.1 | 44.2 | 51.1 |
| Trinidad and Tobago | 90.6 | 86.6 | 83.0 | 88.4 | 48.3 | 49.8 | 53.9 | 64.6 |
| Asia | | | | | | | | |
| Bangladesh | 83.2 | 85.3 | 85.5 | 81.5 | 6.6 | 27.4 | 59.8 | 58.2 |
| Indonesia | 81.5 | 77.7 | 75.4 | 80.2 | 37.8 | 48.9 | 47.0 | 50.9 |
| Malaysia | 89.0 | 79.4 | 80.0 | 85.4 | 52.6 | 51.4 | 53.7 | 60.0 |
| Pakistan | 88.5 | 89.1 | 84.9 | 85.1 | 11.1 | 8.6 | 14.0 | 14.0 |
| Philippines | 71.8 | 80.2 | 79.6 | 81.1 | 51.1 | 48.9 | 51.8 | 52.4 |
| Sri Lanka | 78.7 | 87.6 | 84.5 | 82.0 | 36.8 | 47.7 | 59.2 | 51.4 |
| Thailand | 89.5 | 91.1 | 89.1 | 81.4 | 81.0 | 82.7 | 75.9 | 70.1 |

NOTES: n.a. = not available. Each data entry is an average of two or more data points within each time interval.
SOURCE: International Labour Office, Labor Statistics Division (2003).

TABLE 5-3 Trends in Female/Male Ratio in Participation Rates, Selected Developing Countries

| Region and Country | Ages 15-19 | | | | Ages 20-24 | | | |
|---|---|---|---|---|---|---|---|---|
| | 1980-1984 | 1985-1989 | 1990-1994 | 1995+ | 1980-1984 | 1985-1989 | 1990-1994 | 1995+ |
| Middle East | | | | | | | | |
| Egypt | 0.22 | 0.30 | 0.37 | 0.36 | 0.29 | 0.44 | 0.62 | 0.46 |
| Syria | 0.19 | n.a. | n.a. | 0.34 | 0.21 | n.a. | n.a. | 0.31 |
| Tunisia | 0.43 | 0.50 | 0.56 | 0.57 | 0.38 | 0.43 | 0.53 | 0.53 |
| Turkey | 0.75 | 0.70 | 0.68 | 0.60 | 0.55 | 0.50 | 0.49 | 0.46 |
| South America | | | | | | | | |
| Argentina | 0.54 | n.a. | n.a. | 0.65 | 0.49 | n.a. | 0.63 | 0.68 |
| Brazil | 0.48 | 0.56 | 0.61 | 0.65 | 0.43 | 0.56 | 0.63 | 0.69 |
| Chile | 0.43 | 0.40 | 0.44 | 0.50 | 0.52 | 0.50 | 0.53 | 0.58 |
| Colombia | 0.50 | 0.75 | 0.76 | 0.80 | n.a. | n.a. | n.a. | n.a. |
| Ecuador | 0.31 | n.a. | 0.36 | 0.66 | 0.30 | n.a. | 0.37 | 0.69 |
| Peru | 0.65 | 0.89 | 0.77 | 0.82 | 0.58 | 0.76 | 0.73 | 0.76 |
| Suriname | 0.29 | n.a. | 0.46 | 0.31 | 0.44 | 0.60 | 0.57 | 0.45 |
| Uruguay | n.a. | n.a. | n.a. | n.a. | 0.72 | 0.55 | 0.74 | 0.80 |

| | | | | | | | | |
|---|---|---|---|---|---|---|---|---|
| **Caribbean/Central America** | | | | | | | | |
| Costa Rica | 0.39 | 0.42 | 0.46 | 0.45 | 0.34 | 0.47 | 0.50 | 0.56 |
| El Salvador | 0.48 | n.a. | 0.49 | 0.41 | 0.53 | n.a. | 0.57 | 0.53 |
| Mexico | 0.48 | 0.53 | 0.45 | 0.51 | 0.45 | 0.49 | 0.46 | 0.51 |
| Panama | 0.43 | 0.44 | 0.47 | 0.49 | 0.49 | 0.52 | 0.52 | 0.59 |
| Trinidad and Tobago | 0.38 | 0.44 | 0.55 | 0.55 | 0.53 | 0.58 | 0.65 | 0.73 |
| **Asia** | | | | | | | | |
| Bangladesh | 0.08 | 0.34 | 0.82 | 0.73 | 0.08 | 0.32 | 0.70 | 0.71 |
| Indonesia | 0.67 | 0.76 | 0.75 | 0.74 | 0.46 | 0.63 | 0.62 | 0.63 |
| Malaysia | 0.71 | 0.64 | 0.70 | 0.65 | 0.59 | 0.65 | 0.67 | 0.70 |
| Pakistan | 0.16 | 0.13 | 0.23 | 0.20 | 0.13 | 0.10 | 0.16 | 0.16 |
| Philippines | 0.70 | 0.63 | 0.62 | 0.59 | 0.71 | 0.61 | 0.65 | 0.65 |
| Sri Lanka | 0.45 | 0.53 | 0.67 | 0.59 | 0.47 | 0.54 | 0.70 | 0.63 |
| Thailand | 1.01 | 1.02 | 0.99 | 0.84 | 0.91 | 0.91 | 0.85 | 0.86 |

NOTES: n.a. = not available. Each data entry is an average of two or more data points within each time interval.
SOURCE: International Labour Office, Labor Statistics Division (2003).

TABLE 5-4 Trends in Employment Rates Among Youth in China

| | Men | | Women | |
|---|---|---|---|---|
| Age | 1989 | 1997 | 1989 | 1997 |
| 16 | 43.5 | 20.4 | 55.2 | 24.1 |
| 17 | 63.6 | 31.3 | 61.1 | 55.6 |
| 18 | 75.2 | 59.7 | 76.3 | 52.7 |
| 19 | 79.6 | 70.1 | 80.9 | 66.3 |
| 20 | 90.4 | 72.3 | 86.4 | 79.2 |
| 21 | 87.5 | 79.2 | 86.2 | 85.4 |
| 22 | 94.1 | 80.0 | 87.5 | 83.3 |
| 23 | 93.5 | 89.6 | 87.5 | 86.6 |
| 24 | 94.4 | 86.8 | 93.6 | 89.0 |
| 25 | 92.4 | 91.5 | 93.9 | 89.1 |

SOURCE: Hannum and Liu (2005).

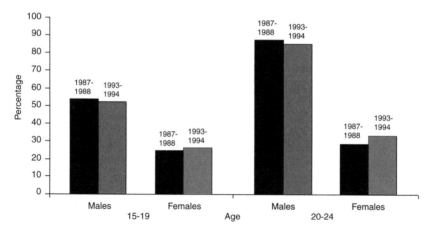

FIGURE 5-4 Trends in labor force participation rates among youth in India (ages 15-24).
NOTE: Based on weekly status.
SOURCE: Visaria (1998).

of work in order to understand the employment patterns of young people. Because they are among the least likely to be employed at a steady formal job, their work patterns are particularly challenging to measure. Using comparisons from a special survey conducted in South Africa on work among children, Box 5-1 illustrates what a difference definitions can make. Several conclusions from this illustration have potential generalizability.

**BOX 5-1**
**Alternative Estimates of Employment Patterns**
**Among Young Africans Ages 15-17 in South Africa, 1999**

As part of the ILO's International Programme on the Elimination of Child Labour, member countries have undertaken, with ILO assistance, dedicated surveys on child labor called the Statistical and Information Monitoring Programme on Children (SIMPOC). Using the South African SIMPOC survey that was fielded in 1999 as an illustration, one can compare estimated employment rates for 15-17-year-old black South Africans using three alternative definitions of work that are based on activity in the seven days before the survey and are successively more inclusive: (1) any work for wage or payment, (2) work 1 plus self-employment, unpaid work for family business, and/or catch fish or other animals for sale or family food, (3) work 2 plus help on family plot, garden, or cattle post. In this age group, 90 percent of boys and 88 percent of girls were currently enrolled in school.

|  | Work 1 | | Work 2 | | Work 3 | |
|---|---|---|---|---|---|---|
|  | Male | Female | Male | Female | Male | Female |
| Work only | 4.4 | 3.6 | 6.5 | 6.2 | 9.0 | 9.5 |
| Work and school | 3.8 | 4.1 | 20.1 | 34.0 | 64.2 | 63.3 |
| Total work | 8.2 | 7.7 | 26.6 | 40.2 | 73.2 | 72.8 |

Percentage of workers attending school

|  | 46 | 53 | 76 | 85 | 88 | 87 |
|---|---|---|---|---|---|---|

SOURCE: Tabulations courtesy of David Lam, 1999 Survey of Activities of Young People in South Africa, Statistics South Africa.

First, work for cash is relatively rare even among older children. Second, most children engage in some form of economic activity while enrolled in school.

## Changes in the Timing and Sequencing of Transitions to Labor Market Work

In order to study how the timing and sequencing of labor market work have been changing over the last decade in relationship to school departure, one would ideally like to compare the experiences of successive birth cohorts over the transition by using either a panel design and successive samples of children at the eve of adolescence or successive cross-sectional surveys of young adults who are taken through a life event history to trace their adolescent experience retrospectively. Neither type of data is currently available. However, a partial picture of the transition to labor market work can be obtained from microdata using several large surveys or census samples to look at recent changes in economic activity in relationship to changes in school enrollment by single years of age. In this section we present results from seven countries that have large surveys and census extracts available for two points roughly 10 years apart.[13] These include Brazil, China, Iran, Kenya, Mexico, South Africa, and Vietnam. Such data must be interpreted with caution, however, given the rapidity with which enrollment rates and employment rates are changing in some settings. These data combine different cohorts, each of which is at a different phase of its own transition to adulthood.

Figure 5-5 first compares transitions out of school and into labor market work from ages 10-29 for boys and girls separately for the most recent date available—typically around the year 2000. To facilitate comparisons across countries, we divide each transition into three phases: early (10-14), middle (15-19), and late (20 and older). During the early phase of the transition, the proportion working in the labor market never exceeds the proportion out of school at any age except in Brazil. The percentage currently reported to be working in the labor market at age 15 is quite low in some countries (less than 10 percent in Kenya and South Africa, less than 20 percent in Iran), but much higher in others (between 20 and 35 percent in Brazil, Mexico, and Vietnam). In Vietnam, a higher percentage of girls are reported to be working in the labor market than boys at age 15. Over the course of the middle phase of the transition, labor market work transitions become highly variable across countries. At age 20, 65 to 70 percent of young men are reported to be working in the labor market in Brazil, China, Mexico, and Vietnam and a similar number of young women in China and Vietnam. At the other extreme, no more than about 35 percent of men are working in the labor market in Kenya and South Africa, with 45 percent reported working in Iran. While school enrollment is still high at this age in South Africa, the same cannot be said for Iran or Kenya. By age 20, not more than 10 percent of young women in Iran and Kenya are working in the labor market. In contrast, rates are 30 to 45 percent in Mexico and Brazil and as high as 70 percent in China and Vietnam.

---

[13]Large public use samples from the two most recent censuses for Mexico (1990 and 2000), Kenya (1989 and 1999), and Vietnam (1989 and 1999) are available from the Integrated Public Use Microdata Series (IPUMS) International web site at the University of Minnesota (www.ipums.umn.edu). We also use the 1992 and 1999 surveys of Brazil's Pesquisa Nacional por Amostra de Domicilios (PNAD); the 1993 South Africa Integrated Household Survey, SALDRU/World Bank, and September 2000 South Africa Labour Force Survey, Statistics South Africa, courtesy of David Lam (University of Michigan); the Child Health and Nutrition Survey in China from 1989 and 1997, courtesy of Emily Hannum (University of Pennsylvania); the 1987 Social and Economic Survey of Households, Statistical Center of Iran, and 1998 Household Expenditure and Income Survey, Statistical Center of Iran, courtesy of Djavad Salehi-Isfahani (Virginia Polytechnic University).

As a crude indicator of the lag between school leaving and employment, we look at the gap in years between the age at which 50 percent are out of school and 50 percent are working in the labor market. In every case but Brazil, the gap for boys is positive, meaning that the age at which half the youth are out of school is generally lower than the age at which half the youth are employed. In some countries the gap is relatively short—about a year in China, Mexico, and Vietnam—but in others it is much longer. In Iran it is about three years, in South Africa about five years, and in Kenya, the gap is too long to be measured because less than 50 percent of young men are estimated to be employed in the labor market by the age of 29.

The transition to labor market work for girls is highly variable. While all young women take up adult work roles, the degree to which this involves entry into the labor market differs enormously across countries. In China and Vietnam, the transitions to labor market work for men and women look very similar at least up to the age of 20, with the overwhelming majority of women working in the labor market by that age in both societies. The only other country, among those considered here, in which labor market work rates for young women exceed 50 percent in the latter phase of the transition is Brazil. South Africa also comes close to 50 percent by age 29. It is interesting to note that in no country does the percentage working among women under 30 decline in contrast to typical labor force participation profiles of young women in the West 30 years ago.

Figure 5-6 shows changes in these transitions from school to work in the same seven countries over the decade of the 1990s. In most cases, transition profiles for enrollment and labor market work have been shifting to the right. This means that the percentage not enrolled at each age has been falling, as has the percentage currently working in the labor market. The one exception to this is Kenya, where the percentage not currently enrolled rose from 1989 to 1999 for both men and women, while the lag between school exit and labor force entry increased.[14] In Mexico and Vietnam the shift in enrollment transitions for men has been more significant than the shift in work transitions, a fact that may be particularly surprising in Vietnam, where dramatic economic growth occurred in the 1990s. In China, the shifts for men have been of about the same magnitude, whereas in Iran and South Africa, the wait for employment for men seems to be growing if measured by the changing gap between the profiles. In Iran and Mexico, women's employment rates are rising at each age, but in Brazil and South Africa they have remained about the same, and in Kenya employment rates for women seem to be falling slightly.

While the operational definition of labor market work varies across

---

[14]This is consistent with trends in school attendance by age presented in Chapter 3.

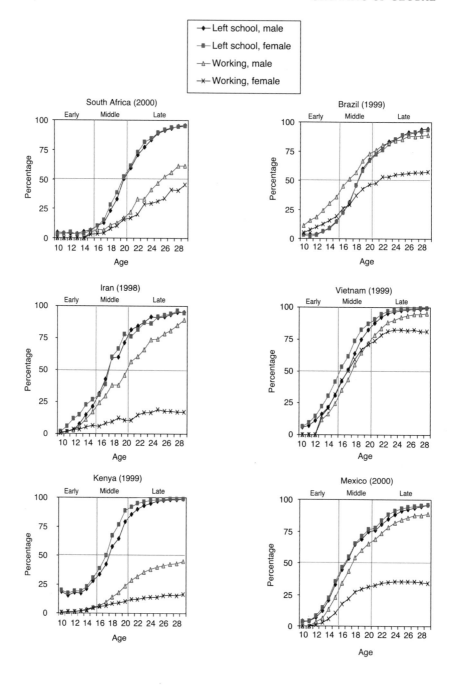

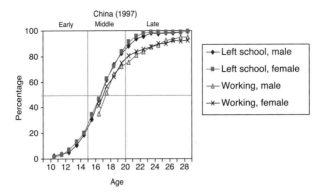

FIGURE 5-5 School and employment status by single years of age, most recent year (ages 10-29).
SOURCE: See text, footnote 13.

countries, the direction and pace of trends within countries can be compared. These examples depict the highly variable transitions to labor market work currently being experienced by young people across societies. Not only does the timing vary, but so does the sequencing of work and schooling (e.g., Brazil) as well as the length of the lag between school exit and labor market employment.

Without comparing transitions over a longer period of time, it is difficult to see the kind of shift that is taking place in women's work roles. One of the common patterns of change for young women is a decline in the proportion of time spent working in the labor market in adolescence and an increase in the proportion of time spent working in the labor market during their 20s. This pattern can be illustrated in the case of Brazil by taking advantage of the large annual household surveys called Pesquisa Nacional por Amostra de Domicilios (PNAD) (Figure 5-7). The figure shows the clear rotation in the age profile of labor force participation for young women between 1977 and 2001. The teenage years are characterized by a decline in the proportion of time spent in the labor force working, corresponding to an associated increase in the proportion of time spent enrolled in school. Employment rates above age 20 have increased, indicative of the increased labor force participation of Brazilian women in recent decades. The proportion of women employed at age 20 remained roughly constant over this period, with rates falling at all ages below 20 and rising at ages above 20. The transition to adulthood for young women in Brazil has clearly shifted, so that the teenage years are now primarily a period for acquiring human capital, with the returns on this human capital being realized in the early 20s in the form of increased labor force participation.

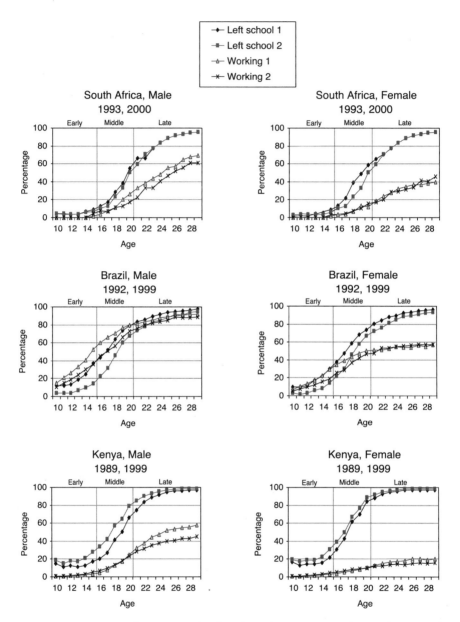

FIGURE 5-6 Recent changes in school and employment status by single years of age (ages 10-29); South Africa, Brazil, Kenya, Iran, Vietnam, Mexico, and China. SOURCE: See text, footnote 13.

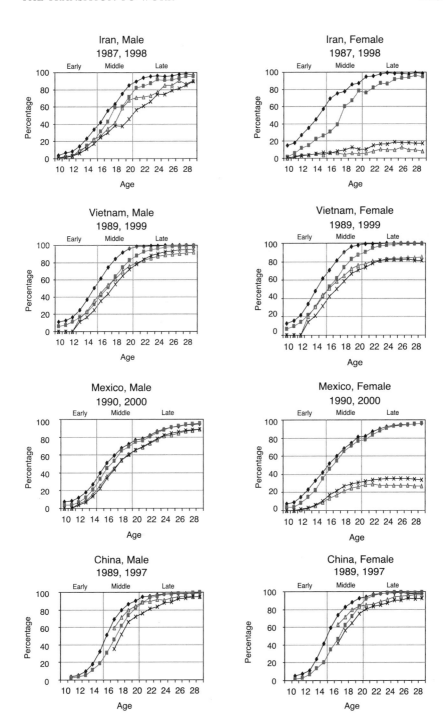

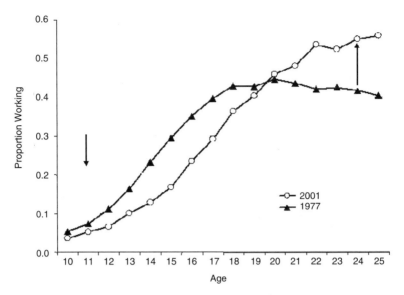

FIGURE 5-7 Female employment rate by age, Brazil, 1977 and 2001 (ages 10-25).
SOURCES: Brazil Pesquisa Nacional por Amostra de Domicilios, 1977 and 2001.
Tabulations courtesy of David Lam.

## SPECIAL ISSUES OF RELEVANCE TO YOUTH EMPLOYMENT

There are several employment-related topics that merit some discussion here because they have been the subject of much debate and media attention and have important implications for the ways in which young people first experience gainful employment as well as for their likelihood of a successful transition to adult work roles. These are child labor, the growing presence of young women in the workplace, youth unemployment, and migration for work.

### Child Labor

Despite the enormous international attention and concern about child labor issues, it is amazing to discover that there are actually no data collected on a fully comparable basis that can be used to measure recent trends in child labor in developing countries. Instead there are recent counts produced by the ILO of the number of child laborers in different categories. This lack of trend data can be explained by recent changes in the definition of child labor. Difficulties of measurement also play an important role.

The changing definitions of child labor reflect an evolution of international norms and standards, beginning with the ILO Minimum Age Convention of 1973 (No. 138) and continuing with the U.N. Convention on the Rights of the Child (1989) and the ILO Convention on the Worst Forms of Child Labour (No. 182) adopted in 1999 (Myers, 2001). The ILO Minimum Age Convention of 1973 (No. 138) established a general minimum age for work of 15 but did allow some exceptions for "light work," defined as safe part-time work starting at age 13 that did not interfere with schooling.[15] The U.N. Convention on the Rights of the Child (1989) does not prohibit all types of work below a certain age, but it does seek to protect children from harmful types of work (United Nations, 1989). The ILO Worst Forms of Child Labour Convention No. 182, which was adopted in 1999, enumerated various categories of the worst forms of work that should be prohibited and eliminated, including hazardous work,[16] and unconditional worst forms of child labor, including trafficking, forced or bonded labor, armed conflict, prostitution and pornography, and illicit work (Myers, 2001).

Formerly, estimates of children's economic activity rates were used as a proxy for the prevalence of child labor (Ritualo, Castro, and Gormly, 2003). As of 2000, the ILO estimated that economic activity rates among children ages 10-14 ranged from 35 percent in sub-Saharan Africa to 20 percent in the Middle East and North Africa. Estimated rates for Asia are 27 percent and for Latin America and the Caribbean, 22 percent (International Labour Office, 2002a).

Currently, however, the ILO's definition of a child laborer varies according to the age of the child and the type of work. All children, regardless of age, who are involved in the worst forms of work are counted as child laborers. In addition, all economically active children under age 11 are counted as child laborers, as are children ages 12-14 who spend more than 14 hours a week in economic activity. Thus, the percentage of children ages 12-17 who are defined as child laborers according to this definition form a subset of all children who are economically active because of the additional qualifications required to be defined as child laborers. The ILO estimates

---

[15]Convention No. 138 depicts children largely as victims who need adult protection rather than as individual actors with potential rights. Despite the fact that this convention is now seen to be ethnocentric and insensitive to cultural perceptions of child development in other parts of the world (Boyden, 1997, as cited in Myers, 2001), many developing countries have recently signed Convention No. 138 in order to receive financial and technical assistance from the ILO's International Programme for the Elimination of Child Labor.

[16]The term "hazardous work" is defined as work in specified hazardous industries and occupations or work in other industries or occupations that exceeds 43 hours per week, (International Labour Office, 2002b).

that in 2000 there were 211 million children ages 5-14 engaged in economic activity of which 186 million were child laborers.[17] If one includes all children ages 5-17, the estimates are 351 million children engaged in economic activity of whom 245 million were child laborers (International Labour Office, 2002a)

### Trends in the Economic Activity of Children

While the ILO's international data base provides estimates and projections of economic activity rates for 10-14-year-olds, these estimates are known to be biased substantially downward, particularly for girls, at least for the most recent period (Basu and Tzannatos, 2003; Ritualo, Castro, and Gormly, 2003). This is because earlier labor force surveys and censuses on which these data rely did not use probing techniques to elicit information on economic activity. Furthermore, if reference periods are too short, much of children's work may be missed because of its intermittent nature (Duryea et al., in press). When comparisons are possible between more recent surveys sponsored under SIMPOC and other data sources for the same country, the differences can be substantial.[18] Data on economic activity rates among children have become more inclusive, with growing sensitization to measurement issues in many country statistical offices.

Even though changes in estimation techniques compromise the assessment of trends, it is nonetheless striking that the ILO estimated that there were 206 million economically active children ages 5-14 in developing countries in 2000, down from its 1995 estimate of 250 million. Given that current estimates are based on a much more inclusive approach to measurement and that the overall population of children ages 5-14 in developing countries is estimated to have risen by almost 50 million from 1995 to 2000,[19] it is undoubtedly true that the overall percentage of children who are economically active has indeed declined, and it is therefore likely to be true that the percentage of children counted as child laborers has also declined. This conclusion appears consistent with trends in economic activ-

---

[17]To derive these estimates, the ILO has relied on the results of the SIMPOC series of recent surveys (see Box 5-1) as well as other recent suitable national household surveys.

[18]Another potential source of bias seems to be less important. In most labor force surveys and censuses, a responsible adult or household responds to all questions on behalf of the household, whereas in the SIMPOC surveys, both parents and children are asked separately about children's participation to see whether or not levels of reporting differ. A recent study comparing these responses for nine recent surveys finds a reasonable consistency between these two sources of information (Ray and Lancaster, 2003).

[19]The more precise estimate is 48.7 million (United Nations, 2003b).

ity rates among 15-19-year-olds, considering the rapid rise in school participation during this same period.[20]

While some insights are available into trends in economic activity rates, there is almost no knowledge about trends in mean hours of work among working children or trends in the intermittent nature of work and therefore about whether or not there has been a change in the context of work with implications for the compatibility of child labor and schooling.[21]

## Consequences for Health

Given the enormous international concern about this issue, it may be surprising that evidence on the link between child labor and health and mortality is lacking. This is because health and mortality data are never linked with young people's work status or work history, so there is no way of investigating the context or the cause. In reviewing the scant evidence on the subject, Boyden, Ling, and Myers (1998) based their conclusions about the health-compromising nature of child labor on three key observations: (1) children are more susceptible to environmental hazards than adults, (2) excessive work compromises the healthy physical development of children because they expend more energy than adults for the same level of activity, and (3) children are more susceptible than adults to accidents and injury. Unstated assumptions underlie these observations: that working children are more exposed to environmental hazards than nonworking children, that working children expend more energy per hour than nonworking children, and that working children are more likely to face the risk of accidents and injury than nonworking children. However, relatively little is known about the risks poor children face in their home or school environment or the risks that all children face regardless of work or enrollment status. This is clearly an area in which more research is needed.

## Consequences for Learning

A principal social concern with child labor is that it competes with schooling either directly or indirectly (Anker, 2000; Basu, 1999; Emerson

---

[20]This is also consistent with the declines implied by the ILO database; although the estimates in this database are now recognized to be biased downward (Dehejia and Gatti, 2002), it is unlikely that such biases have changed so much over time that the implied direction of trends would be reversed if not for these biases.

[21]Duryea et al. (in press) are able to illustrate the intermittent nature of children's work using 20 years of panel data from metropolitan Brazil.

TABLE 5-5 Percentage Combining Work and Schooling by Single Years of Age, Weighted Average for All Sub-Saharan Africa Countries Participating in UNICEF Surveys, 1995

| Age | All in School | School Only | % School Only | % Work Combined with School |
|-----|---------------|-------------|---------------|------------------------------|
| 5   | 7.5           | 6.5         | 86.7          | 13.3                         |
| 6   | 23.4          | 19.8        | 84.6          | 15.4                         |
| 7   | 42.3          | 33.8        | 79.9          | 20.1                         |
| 8   | 54.3          | 40.3        | 74.2          | 25.8                         |
| 9   | 60.4          | 41.7        | 69.0          | 31.0                         |
| 10  | 64.1          | 36.5        | 57.0          | 43.0                         |
| 11  | 68.5          | 37.1        | 54.2          | 45.8                         |
| 12  | 68.0          | 32.6        | 47.9          | 52.1                         |
| 13  | 66.9          | 31.1        | 46.5          | 53.5                         |
| 14  | 65.1          | 31.0        | 47.6          | 52.4                         |

SOURCE: Huebler and Loaiza (2002).

and Souza, 2003). It competes directly if work takes place during school hours and precludes school attendance. It competes indirectly if it is combined with school attendance, but affects academic performance and school progress either because of poor attendance or inadequate time or energy for school work. As the school day is short in many countries, it is not difficult to combine work with school attendance, and school holidays and weekends allow additional opportunities for work. Indeed, estimates based on 15 UNICEF household surveys fielded in Africa in 1995 suggest that the percentage of enrolled students combining work with schooling rises with age (see Table 5-5), reaching a majority by age 12 (Huebler and Loaiza, 2002). This may suggest that, with later ages of school exit, there is an increasing tendency for children to combine work with schooling. Furthermore, for some students, taking up cash work may provide the money for school fees that support continuing enrollment. Box 5-2 describes the kind of trade-offs that children face in managing work and schooling, drawing on an anthropological study from Northeastern Tanzania.

Child laborers are not the only children who spend significant hours working. As mentioned in the discussion of children's time use, girls spend a significant amount of time doing domestic chores. Indeed, if all types of work are counted, they work more total hours than boys. This nonmarket work time also has opportunity costs in terms of schooling. Long hours of domestic work are often required in settings in which basic amenities such as clean water, electricity, and fuel are lacking. Girls' ability to attend

---

**BOX 5-2**
**Managing Work and Schooling in the Mountains of**
**Northeastern Tanzania**

Anthropologist Karen Porter (1996) explores the agency of children, work, and social change in the South Pare Mountains of Tanzania. She challenges various assumptions in the literature, including that children's involvement in the cash economy is always exploitative and that households act as homogenous decision-making units.

Porter provides a case study of 14-year-old Stefano to illustrate the importance of work for school attendance and the degree of agency children can have, particularly boys, in juggling work-school trade-offs:

> Stefano is a fourteen-year-old boy born out-of-wedlock. He and his younger brothers and sisters have few clothes and a relatively poor diet; their mother has great difficulty paying school fees. With no social father, Stefan stands little if any chance of inheriting land or being assisted with bride-wealth payments when he is old enough to marry. To offset his vulnerable position, Stefano willingly works for his grandmother's patri-lineal kinsmen, distant relatives, but close neighbors. He runs errands, works on their farms, and generally does their bidding. Though he received no cash payment for such work, his strategy for securing attention and support succeeds; his school fees are paid and the household receives intermittent gifts of food.

Porter's observations lead her to conclude that, with the rise in the market economy, children's agency increases along with conflicts in the household.

---

school and women's ability to participate in the labor force can be compromised when basic infrastructure is lacking (e.g., Desai and Jain, 1994). Data from Mexico and Peru document the strong negative association between hours spent in household chores and school attendance and participation (Levison and Moe, 1998; Levison, Moe, and Knaul, 2001).

Because decisions about children's work and schooling are joint decisions, it is difficult to assess, without a randomized experiment or longitudinal data with specified instrumental variables, whether the elimination of child labor would increase school attendance and improve learning outcomes. The parents of children who work are a selective group; they might be less likely to send their children to school even if no work were available. Furthermore, the children themselves may also be selective, with parents more likely to send those children to work who have greater earning capabilities or lesser academic promise. While all empirical studies of the association between children's work and schooling attendance or learning outcomes show a negative relationship, in most cases, the reported empirical associations cannot be interpreted as causal.[22]

Recent empirical analyses by Rosati and Rossi (2003) and Canals-Cerda and Ridao-Cano (2003) illustrate this estimation problem clearly. Rosati and Rossi (2003) present maximum likelihood estimates of the determinants of hours spent in child labor and enrollment for Nicaragua and Pakistan that allow correlations between the unobserved characteristics that determine these two forms of time use. Their estimates suggest that these unobserved characteristics are significantly negatively correlated across these two forms of time use, that failure to control for the simultaneous determination of the two types of time use results in biases, and that the estimated impact of marginal effects of household background variables on these two forms of child time use differs depending on a child's latent propensity to enroll. Similarly, Canals-Cerda and Ridao-Cano (2003), using retrospective schooling and work histories in Bangladesh, found that the measured effect of work on schooling differs among those with a propensity to work from those who do not have such a propensity.

A recent study, using panel data in Vietnam and a set of plausible instrumental variables, provides the most persuasive evidence to date of the negative effects of child labor on school participation and attainment (Beegle, Dehejia, and Gatti, 2004). Focusing on children ages 8-13 who were enrolled in school during the first wave of the data collection (1992-1993), they found that having worked during the first period of observation, controlling for the selectivity of children who worked, had a negative and significant impact on enrollment and attainment during the second period of observation (1997-1998).[23] Furthermore, the negative effects are much greater for girls than boys.

Further evidence of these trade-offs comes from the experience of the Food for Education program in Bangladesh. Ravallion and Wodon (2000) used a 1995-1996 rural sample of the Household Economic Survey to test whether a discount on the price of primary school, created by the food subsidy, might lead children who were previously working to attend school. Given that school subsidies are targeted to the poor, however, program placement had to be controlled for in the model. They found that school subsidies led to higher enrollment rates and lower work participation rates among program participants, but the decline in recorded work was only a

---

[22]See for example, Patrinos and Psacharopoulos (1995, 1997), Akabayashi and Psacharopoulos (1999), Ray and Lancaster (2003), Binder and Scrogin (1999), Heady (2003), Post and Pong (2000, as cited in Post [2001]).

[23]The instruments used are measured at the community level during wave 1 rice prices and crop shocks and were chosen only after they were thoroughly tested and determined to be transitory and at least conditionally exogenous.

quarter of the increase in enrollment. This finding suggests that much of the increase in school enrollment was drawn from the pool of children who were not previously reporting work (including household work) as their "normal" activity.[24] These findings led the authors to conclude that work does not necessarily compromise school attendance.

For currently enrolled students who combine work with schooling, an added question of interest is whether or not time spent working affects learning outcomes. This is a difficult question to answer not only because it requires data on standardized tests, but also because of the difficulties of teasing out causality when one has a selective sample of students. Taking advantage of the unusual opportunity provided by the first comparative study of language and mathematics achievement for 3rd and 4th graders in Latin America (see discussion in Chapter 3), Gunnarsson, Orazem, and Sanchez (2003) were able to use information on the policy environment in each country[25] to create instruments for predicting the likelihood of child labor and thus to at least partially correct for the problem of mutual causation, using a sample of students ages 8-15. By pooling data from 11 countries and controlling for individual, family, teacher, and school characteristics, the authors estimate that working outside the home has a strong negative and significant effect on performance on standardized mathematics and language tests—in fact a stronger effect than would have been estimated without using proper statistical techniques to control for mutual causation. Furthermore, the greater the time spent working, the larger the negative effects. The students in this sample ranged in age from 8 to 15.

The long-term consequences of child labor for later success in the labor market in adulthood are difficult to assess for the reasons discussed above as well as because data demands become even greater when data are needed over a substantial period of time.[26] Taking a shorter term time horizon over five years, Beegle, Dehejia, and Gatti (2004) found that children in

---

[24]Work status was determined in response to a question about normal activity last week and includes those children ages 5-16 who reported that their normal activity was employment, household work, or seeking work. Furthermore, it is highly likely that many enrolled children are also engaged in some part-time work that goes unreported when work participation is recorded only if work is seen to be the normal activity.

[25]Policy variables include the beginning and ending ages for compulsory schooling, whether or not preprimary schooling is available, and measures developed by Kaufmann, Kraay, and Zoida-Lobatón (2002) of the country's level of political stability, market-friendly regulatory policies, and ability to enforce laws.

[26]Two studies based on retrospective data from Brazil about adults' experience with work as children explore the longer term relationship between the experience of child work and later outcomes. Ilahi, Orazem, and Sedlacek (forthcoming) found a negative relationship between working before age 12 and adult hourly wages. Emerson and Souza (2002) also found that early exposure to child labor had a negative association with adult earnings.

Vietnam who had worked when they were ages 8-13 in 1992-1993 were twice as likely to be working five years later as those who had not previously worked and were earning significantly higher wages, despite their lower levels of education, than children who started work for the first time in the intervening period. Again, the effects are larger for girls than boys. The authors use these results to underscore the policy challenge of eliminating child labor given its economic benefits to families at least in the short to medium term.

### The Growing Presence of Young Women in the Workplace

The data presented above document the growing presence of young women in the labor force. However, these data are silent with respect to the motivations for and the implications of these trends for young women's transitions to adulthood. For men, the transition into the labor force that occurs during these years is presumably a permanent role shift that will last until retirement, disability, or death. For women, however, it is not clear whether the recent changes observed during the young adult years presage a more fundamental shift in adult work roles for women, or whether these changes represent the increasing prevalence of a temporary phase in the work lives of young women, preceding marriage or childbearing.

The experience of the developed countries over the last 30 years may suggest that the rise in young women's participation in wage work is likely to be part of a more fundamental shift in work and family roles. In the United States, for example, there has been a substantial rise in the participation of young women in the formal labor market in the last 25 years (Blau, 1997). This can be partially attributed to a decline in fertility and a rise in the divorce rate, because divorced women and those with fewer children have higher participation rates, but it is also due to the fact that young mothers are much more inclined than they were in the past to work for pay outside the home. Thus it would appear that women's participation in the United States, as in most of the rest of the developed world, is increasingly determined by their own opportunities and less by their family circumstances (Blau, 1997).[27]

In developing countries, the long-term rise in young women's labor force participation rates, which is linked to a shift from agriculture to industry and services, implies a change in adult work roles as well. Indeed,

---

[27]Jacob Mincer's (1962) seminal work on the determinants of a married woman's labor force participation emphasized the contrary effects of a rise in her wage (substitution effect) and the effects of a rise in her husband's wage (income effect) on her decision to participate in the labor market. While this model worked well to explain changes in labor force participation in the early post-war period, it predicts very little of the recent change.

Standing (1999) suggests that the labor force is actually becoming more "feminine" in its characteristics, partly as a result of the rise in women's labor force participation, but more importantly because of the changing nature of work. Due to growth in international trade and stiffening international competition, markets for wage work have been increasingly deregulated and thus become more informal. At the same time, the female share of nonagricultural employment has been rising, despite a decline in the share of employment represented by the public sector—a sector in which women typically had a higher share of employment than in other sectors. These trends have also been accompanied by a small decline in the extent of sex-based occupational segregation in many parts of the world in which such data are available to document trends. Occupational segregation nonetheless continues to be extensive and persistent, particularly in China, the Middle East, and North Africa (Anker, 1998).

In many settings better educated women are more likely to report economic activity in the middle to later phases of the transition to adulthood than their less educated peers (Celli and Obuchi, 2003). And in some settings, they are also more likely to report work before marriage despite later ages of school leaving (Malhotra and deGraff, 1997). The rise in labor force participation of young women can transcend their changing educational distribution. An in-depth exploration of recent changes in the Egyptian labor market concludes that the small rise in women's overall labor force participation rates during the 1990s can be explained largely by a rise among the least educated women; labor force participation rates among women with intermediate levels of education actually fell (Assaad, 2002). In Pakistan, a rise in the percentage of young women entering the paid labor force has been coincident with a rise in girls' primary school completion rates. One might conclude that these two trends are associated. However, Lloyd and Grant (2005) use life history data from a recent national survey of youth (2001-2002) to show that the recent rise in labor force participation among young women during the middle phase of the transition (ages 15-19) has occurred among those who have ever been to school as well as those who have not (see Figure 5-8). In both cases, these changes are statistically significant. During the same period, there was no change in the pace of labor force entry for young men. These data cannot indicate, however, whether these changes will persist as these young women age or whether this is a temporary phenomenon that may be linked to changes in the timing and context of marriage (for further discussion see Chapter 7).

The very rapid rise in the factory employment of young women in Bangladesh provides an interesting case study of the implications of improved opportunities for private-sector wage employment on the transition to adulthood in a very traditional setting. Bangladesh has experienced a significant increase in employment in the garment industry; by 1995 the

(a) Never attended school

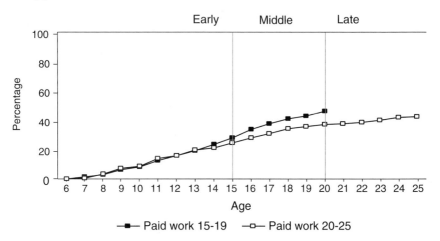

(b) Ever attended school

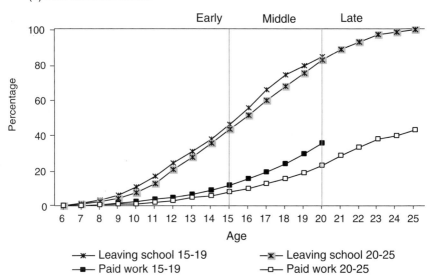

FIGURE 5-8 Changes in school and work transitions, females.
SOURCE: Lloyd and Grant (2005).

sector employed about 1.2 million, of whom 90 percent were women. Bangladesh is a society in which girls are typically confined to the home after puberty and marriage for girls typically occurs before the age of 18. The rapid rise in factory employment occurred during the 1990s as Bangladeshi factory owners were able to gain a global competitive edge in the mass production of clothing for export.

In 1996, Amin and her colleagues (1998) conducted a survey of garment workers with both qualitative and quantitative elements. By listening to their life stories the researchers were able to learn more about how and why they sought factory employment, how their work lives have changed as they have aged, and how their perceptions and aspirations differ from their nonworking peers. While most young women report that their decision to work was part of a household strategy, there were some exceptional cases of young women who made the decision on their own. Most factory workers in Dhaka come from rural areas; in some cases the migration to work represented a move on the part of the whole family; in other cases young women moved to the city where they live with or have connections with local family members. Most workers experienced rapid wage growth in the first year of work, which is typically the result of job mobility between factories, and reported this mobility as a positive feature of their work experience. Despite the stigma and physical stress associated with garment work, most young women reported that they value the work and the independence associated with it and feel that it is less of a hardship than agricultural work. Indeed, Amin and her colleagues (1998) conclude that this new opportunity for work has created a period of adolescence for young girls that did not previously exist as a life cycle phase. Nonetheless, almost all of these unmarried workers pool some or all of their income with their households, whether they live with their family or not and do not express any particular desire to retain control over the dispensation of their income. It is not known what percentage of these women leave factory work when they marry or give birth.

In contrast to Bangladesh, there has been a decline in the labor force participation of young unmarried women in Egypt in the last 10 years, which corresponds to a significant rise in school leaving ages (Assaad, 2002). This has occurred despite the implementation of structural economic reforms that were expected to create new wage work opportunities for young women. In a qualitative study of young female wage workers and their mothers, Amin and Al-Bassusi (2003) found that, among the minority of young women who work, the primary reason reported for working is to save for marriage. Being a wage worker is seen by young women themselves as a temporary role and not as an appropriate role for married women or mothers (see Box 5-3). In order to allow a couple to realize their aspiration to start married life in their own home and to

**BOX 5-3**
**The Role of Work in Preparing for**
**Marriage and Motherhood in Egypt**

As a result of increasing consumerism and rising material expectations in Egypt, young couples are now less likely to join an extended household upon marrying and instead must accumulate considerable resources before they marry to establish their own household. In a study of young women's perceptions of marriage and work in Egypt, Amin and Al-Bassusi (2003) analyzed national labor survey data and conducted in-depth interviews with young women working for pay in industrial, periurban, and rural areas. The women interviewed consistently reported that their primary reason for working was to save money and prepare for marriage. Their desire to earn money reflects not only the rising expectations regarding the possessions and assets that one brings to marriage, but also economic realities of raising a family. As the mother of a young, working woman explained:

> Men like to marry girls who are rich or at least prepared well. I will tell you why: after one year of a marriage, they will get a child. The new child needs a budget for him only (clothes, diapers, doctors, milk, medicine, and so on). Also a couple needs a budget for food, clothes, doctors, medicine, rent, compliments [gifts], and so forth. In the second year, they may receive their second child who needs another budget. Some years later the children will go to school and need a new budget. The wife has to stay home in order to take care of the children. Do you think the salary of whatever type of earnings that the husband makes will enable him to do all that and more? This means the couple will not have a chance to prepare themselves after they are married. They have to start as perfect as possible, because there is no other chance to improve their living standard later.

Women are also motivated to work to provide a greater *gehaz* (trousseau) to enhance their status and improve their bargaining position in their new marital family. They often set aside earnings that are put into traditional savings pools until they are married.

Aisha of Helwan pays 45 pounds a month from her salary for transportation and saves the rest for her marriage trousseau. She explained that the gehaz is an expensive undertaking for her parents, so she works to save in order that her marriage will not be a burden to them. Another respondent, Abeer, a factory worker in the investment zone who was recently married, reported that she contributed 3,000 out of the 8,000 pounds required for her marriage. One of the items she acquired and was proud to show was an ornate sideboard for the dining room.

In general, working for pay does not interfere with being a wife and mother, because women are expected to stop working once they are married. The interviews with young women indicated that none was postponing marriage due to work. Several working women did, however, describe making a trade-off between working and pursuing an education in preparation for marriage. These women considered education a potential barrier to saving money for their marriages and thus opted to work instead.

preserve traditional gender roles in the family after marriage, work before marriage is seen as a means to an end rather than as preparation for an adult work role in the labor force.

Earlier studies of the motivations for young women's work in export-oriented industries in Taiwan (Greenhalgh, 1988) and Hong Kong (Salaff, 1981) also depict this as a temporary phase of life during which parents were able to exploit the earnings of their more educated daughters for their own ends by sending them to work before marriage. The question remains as to whether this experience of earning money in one's own right early in life is transformative for young women in terms of self-esteem and agency or predictive of labor force participation later in adult life. A very preliminary answer can be found in the case of Argentina from the results of a small study of the views of young people in their mid 20s on the criteria for defining adulthood (Facio and Micocci, 2003). The study found that young women were more likely than young men (90 versus 65 percent) to view women's capability of supporting a family financially as a marker of adulthood.

Indeed, the process of social change is complex. In a period of rapid change, it is difficult for young people to make decisions about educational investments and labor force participation by modeling their behavior on the experiences of the older generation. They are expecting to have more education, marry later, and have fewer children than the older generation. As Goldin said in reviewing the historical experience in the United States (1990:154): "Each generation passes its norms and expectations to the next in a manner than often impedes social progress." Taking the example of the Egyptian mother's view of work and marriage above, we might expect that her daughter will stay home after marriage and not return to the labor force. However, recent trends in women's labor force participation in Egypt may suggest otherwise. For every age group beyond the early 20s, women's labor force participation rates have been rising in both rural and urban areas, suggesting that the persistence of labor force participation after marriage is rising as well, although slowly (Assaad, 2002).

An additional important factor to consider is that young women in developing countries can model their behavior not only on their peers and their parents in their own country, but also potentially on the behavior of younger women in other parts of the world. Relative to the historical experience of the West, this creates the possibility of more rapid social change.[28] Indeed, the very rapid decline in marital fertility that has oc-

---

[28]In the case of fertility decline, the later in historical time the decline began, the more rapid the fertility decline has progressed. This has been partially explained by the rapid diffusion of ideas from developed to developing countries, allowing a speedier transition (Bongaarts and Watkins, 1996).

curred in many parts of the developing world may bring with it the seeds of change in gender work roles in the family, as family size diminishes and women's childrearing responsibilities occupy fewer years of their productive lifetime (Amin and Lloyd, 2002). The very recent and rapid rise in the number of young women working in the export sector in Bangladesh is an example of this possibility in a poor country that has experienced a very rapid fall in family size over the last 30 years.

## Youth Unemployment

Unemployment rates among youth are typically higher than unemployment rates among adults. This is a common pattern in both developed and developing countries. This is not surprising given that the process of entering the labor force requires some time without a job before the first job is obtained, and there may be employment lapses between jobs as youth and their employers each search for mutually good matches. It is also well established that trends in youth unemployment tend to follow trends in adult unemployment. In countries in which overall unemployment rates are high, youth unemployment rates also tend to be relatively high (O'Higgins, 2001). A growing concern with youth unemployment in developing countries can be explained in part by the growth in the size of the youth population, by the growth of the share of that population searching for wage employment instead of working in family enterprises, and in part by recent declines in economic growth in many countries.

It can be a challenge to measure unemployment in many developing countries. Much work takes place in the agricultural sector, which is subject to day-to-day and seasonal volatility in activity rates, and poverty, even in urban areas, often precludes waiting for a formal job. Instead in very poor settings, people have to make do with whatever casual or part-time work they can find. Thus, for measurement purposes, they are counted as employed, despite the fact that they are actually underemployed, or as out of the labor force when they are actually willing to work but discouraged from looking for work. As a result, measured unemployment in developing countries is typically higher in urban than rural areas (O'Higgins, 2001).

These points are well illustrated in Table 5-6 with data from India on youth employment measured according to three different reference periods: (1) the last day, (2) the last week, or (3) a "usual" week (Visaria, 1998). First, the longer the reference period, the lower the estimated rates of unemployment, suggesting that many of those included among the employed (if usual status is used as the reference period) are not employed on a steady basis and that many of those usually classified as unemployed are not unemployed on a steady basis. Second, we can see that estimates of urban unemployment can be as much as three times rural unemployment

TABLE 5-6 Recent Patterns and Trends in Youth Unemployment in India

| Location, Type of Work, and Time Period | Ages 15-19 | | | Ages 20-24 | | |
|---|---|---|---|---|---|---|
| | Male | Female | Female/Male | Male | Female | Female/Male |
| Rural | | | | | | |
| Usual | | | | | | |
| 1987-1988 | 4.6 | 3.6 | 0.8 | 5.0 | 3.9 | 0.8 |
| 1993-1994 | 3.3 | 1.9 | 0.6 | 4.9 | 2.8 | 0.6 |
| Weekly | | | | | | |
| 1987-1988 | 8.7 | 7.6 | 0.9 | 8.8 | 6.5 | 0.7 |
| 1993-1994 | 5.7 | 5.1 | 0.9 | 7.2 | 5.9 | 0.8 |
| Daily | | | | | | |
| 1987-1988 | 9.0 | 9.2 | 1.0 | 9.2 | 9.8 | 1.1 |
| 1993-1994 | 9.0 | 8.3 | 0.9 | 10.3 | 8.2 | 0.8 |
| Urban | | | | | | |
| Usual | | | | | | |
| 1987-1988 | 17.2 | 13.6 | 0.8 | 14.9 | 17.8 | 1.2 |
| 1993-1994 | 11.9 | 12.8 | 1.1 | 12.6 | 21.7 | 1.7 |
| Weekly | | | | | | |
| 1987-1988 | 20.4 | 19.3 | 0.9 | 17.7 | 24.4 | 1.4 |
| 1993-1994 | 13.4 | 15.7 | 1.2 | 14.7 | 25.8 | 1.7 |
| Daily | | | | | | |
| 1987-1988 | 23.3 | 24.0 | 1.0 | 20.3 | 27.2 | 1.3 |
| 1993-1994 | 16.2 | 18.6 | 1.1 | 17.0 | 28.5 | 1.7 |

SOURCE: Visaria (1998).

estimates, with even higher multiples in the case of female "usual" unemployment.

Given the recent rise in labor force participation rates among young women, it is interesting to see how gender differences in unemployment rates may be changing. Again, using India as an example (Table 5-6), we can see that from 1987-1988 to 1993-1994, urban unemployment rates have been rising for young women (20-24) at the same time that unemployment rates for young men have been falling, regardless of which reference period is used. Such relative shifts in the distribution of unemployment can be expected if the growth in new female labor force entrants exceeds the growth of young male entrants. While urban unemployment rates among those ages 15-19 have been falling for both young men and women, the decline for men has been greater than for women, with the result that unemployment rates for young women in this age group now exceed those of young men. In rural areas, in contrast, gender differences in unemployment rates according to most measures are to the advantage of women.

It is often claimed that youth unemployment rates are highest among the most educated (O'Higgins, 2001). However, a strict comparison between the unemployment rates of more and less educated people may overstate the significance of the problem. First, the more educated have spent less time in the labor market at a comparable age than the less educated, given later ages of school leaving, and therefore have had less time to find work. Second, the labor force participation rates of the less educated tend to be lower than the labor force participation rates of the more educated, suggesting the possibility that there may be a problem of discouraged workers among the uneducated who are not recorded as in the labor force (O'Higgins, 2001). Third, the more schooled generally come from more advantaged families and generally have better support networks for financing longer job searches for better job matches. Thus, higher unemployment rates for those with more schooling may not reflect a problem for them but rather a problem for those with less schooling who have much more limited support networks.

In South Africa, where the black population has suffered a historic disadvantage due to apartheid, the discouragement factor has a substantial effect on estimates of unemployment. Using data from the 2000 South African Labour Force survey, we compared the official unemployment rates for blacks and whites with an expanded definition of unemployment that includes those out of the labor force who would accept work if a suitable job were offered (Table 5-7). The first two columns contrast the official unemployment rates for blacks and whites. These unemployment rates are very high for young black South Africans (47 percent for men and 55 percent for women ages 20-24). The second two columns present unemployment rates using the broader definition that is often used in labor

TABLE 5-7 Unemployment Rates According to Alternative Definitions, South Africa, 2000

| Sex and Age Group | Unemployment Official | | Unemployment Expanded | |
|---|---|---|---|---|
| | African | White | African | White |
| Male | | | | |
| 15-19 | 49.4 | 33.8 | 64.5 | 43.5 |
| 20-24 | 47.1 | 10.1 | 61.1 | 14.5 |
| 25-29 | 30.8 | 1.6 | 41.5 | 3.7 |
| 30-34 | 23.8 | 0.8 | 32.8 | 1.0 |
| N | 8,309 | 854 | 9,409 | 861 |
| Female | | | | |
| 15-19 | 58.0 | 38.5 | 74.4 | 43.3 |
| 20-24 | 55.5 | 6.0 | 71.1 | 10.6 |
| 25-29 | 42.3 | 4.9 | 55.7 | 10.8 |
| 30-34 | 31.2 | 3.0 | 45.0 | 6.9 |
| N | 7,459 | 694 | 9,100 | 722 |

SOURCES: September 2000, South African Labour Force Survey (Statistics South Africa). Tabulations courtesy of David Lam.

market debates. Unemployment rates by this measure rise substantially, to over 60 percent for 20-24-year-old black men and over 70 percent for 20-24-year-old black women. It is worth noting that even at ages 30-34, an age at which male unemployment rates are usually low in most countries, unemployment by the narrower definition is 24 percent, and unemployment by the broader definition is 33 percent, with only 62 percent of men reporting labor force participation.

The best data on recent unemployment trends come from Latin America. In a review of recent trends in Latin American labor markets during the 1990s, Duryea, Jaramillo, and Pagés (2003) conclude that, in the context of an overall rise in unemployment rates from 5.3 to 7.5 percent in the region as a whole, youth unemployment rates rose but at a slower rate. As a result, the ratio of youth to adult unemployment rates declined (see Figure 5-9). The youngest workers have the highest unemployment rates. Ratios have declined in the 1990s in all countries shown except Panama.

## Migration for Work

One of the important transitions that many young people make in all parts of the world is leaving their place of birth to migrate to a different village, city, or country. This migration is frequently motivated by search

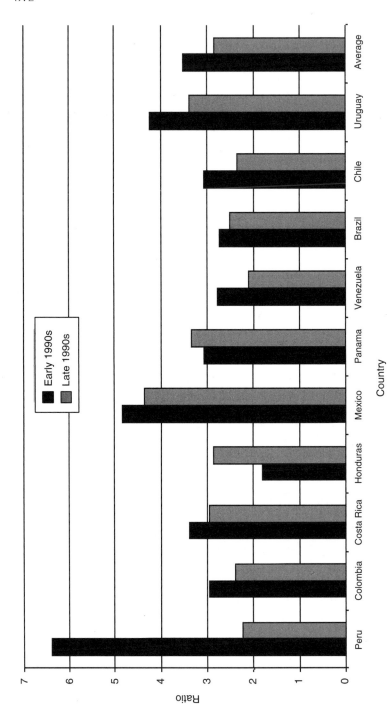

FIGURE 5-9 Relative unemployment rate, Latin America (ratio youth unemployment and adult unemployment).
SOURCE: Duryea, Jaramillo, and Pagés (2003).

for employment, although other considerations, especially education and marriage, can also play a role. Researchers who study migration have long recognized the almost universal pattern that probabilities of migration are much higher for individuals in the 15-30 age range than for those in other age groups. Dorothy Thomas concluded from her broad study of migration in 1938 that "the one generalization about migration differentials which can be considered definitively established" is that "there is an excess of adolescents and young adults among migrants, particularly migrants from rural areas to towns, compared with the . . . general population" (Thomas, 1938:11). The age pattern of migration observed by Thomas for the United States and Europe in the early twentieth century has also been widely documented in developing countries.[29] These age patterns of migration continue to be evident in developing countries today.

Like formal schooling and vocational training programs, migration can be viewed as an investment that individuals make with the expectation that the discounted lifetime benefits will exceed the discounted lifetime costs.[30] The costs and benefits of migration include both direct economic considerations, such as wages and employment prospects, and nonpecuniary considerations, such as social amenities, the psychic costs of leaving family, and potential marriage opportunities. Economists have used this human capital approach to migration to consider why migration probabilities are so much higher in the 15-29 age group than they are in older age groups. One potential explanation is that young people have more years in which to reap the benefits from investing in a new location. As noted by such economists as Sjaastad (1962), however, a more important factor is probably that young people face lower opportunity costs of migration, having not yet become firmly established in jobs that compete with migration and having not yet married or had children.

One common source of basic information on migration is census data. Figure 5-10 shows the age profile of migration for Brazil and Kenya using the two most recent censuses for each country.[31] The top panel of the figure

---

[29]A vast literature has documented the fact that young people have dominated migration flows in developing countries for decades, such as Caldwell's analysis of rural-urban migration in Ghana in the 1960s (Caldwell, 1969) and Schultz's analysis of rural-urban migration in Colombia (Schultz, 1971).

[30]For a survey of economic literature on internal migration in developing countries, see Lucas (1997).

[31]Similar patterns for Mexico are not shown. The census data from Kenya and Mexico used for results in this section were taken from the IPUMS-International web site at the University of Minnesota (Sobek et al., 2002). The Brazilian census results are based on public use samples obtained from the Instituto Brasileiro de Geografia e Estatística, the Brazilian statistical agency.

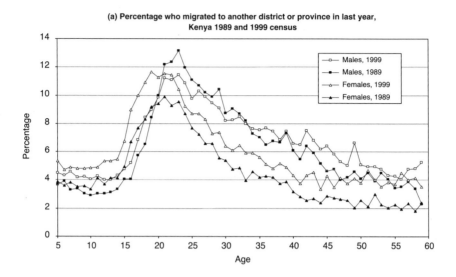

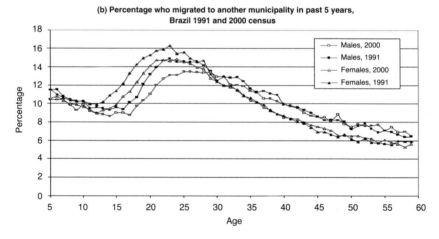

FIGURE 5-10 Migration rates by age for Kenya and Brazil, males and females (ages 5-59).
SOURCES: Kenya 1989, 1999 Census and Brazil 1991, 2000 Census. Tabulations courtesy of David Lam.

shows the proportion of Kenyan men and women at each age who had migrated during the previous year. The probability of migrating rises sharply beginning around age 15 for both young men and women, with young women migrating at higher rates than men during the period from age 15 to age 20. The fact that over 10 percent of Kenyan men and women in their late teens and early 20s moved across district boundaries in a single year is an impressive indicator of the mobility of young Kenyans. Migration rates fall rapidly as individuals age into their late 20s and early 30s. For women, the probability of migrating at age 20 is more than double the probability at age 10 and almost double the probability at age 30. While migration is observed at all ages, migration is clearly a phenomenon that is especially important during the transition to adulthood.

The bottom panel of Figure 5-10 shows migration rates by age for men and women in Brazil, measured according to whether individuals changed their municipality of residence during the five years preceding the census. While the Brazilian data are not strictly comparable to the Kenyan data, the overall age patterns of migration are very similar. The highest migration rates are observed in the 15-29 age range, with female migration rates rising at a faster rate than those of young men beginning around age 15. Women peak at higher migration rates than men in both 1991 and 2000. As in Kenya, the continuity in the age profile of migration in Brazil over the 1990s is probably more noteworthy than any recent changes.

Relatively few surveys or censuses collect data on the reasons for migration. The Mexican census is one example that does (Table 5-8). Combining the first two labor market related categories (looking for work and changing place of work), about 53 percent of men and 34 percent of women ages 20-24 gave work-related reasons for migration. About 23 percent of women ages 20-24 said they migrated to get married or form a union, compared with only 5 percent of men. Similar proportions—about 9 percent of women and 11 percent of men in the 20-24 age group—migrated to study. While these results indicate that in Mexico women are much more likely than men to migrate because of marriage, it is important to note that, even among women, work-related migration is more common than migration to marry. In a very different context—rural Burkina Faso—where child labor is likely to be more prevalent, households with a child migrant ages 6-17 were asked the reasons for migration. A surprisingly high 41 percent of boys were reported as having migrated for work (Kielland and Sanogo, 2002). Only 16 percent of girls the same age had migrated for work. Thus, even at a younger age, work can be an important reason for migration for younger boys.

Migration from rural to urban areas continues to be one of the most important components of migration in developing countries. Due to data limitations, the results reported above show migration only as defined by moving across municipality or state boundaries, without indicating whether migration is from rural to urban areas. In the case of the 2000 Brazilian census, however, it is possible to identify the rural-urban location of both the previous and current residence of individuals who migrated across municipal boundaries during the five years before the census. Table 5-9 shows

TABLE 5-8 Reasons for Migration by Age and Sex, Mexico 2000

| Reason | Ages 10-14 | | Ages 15-19 | | Ages 20-24 | | Ages 25-29 | |
|---|---|---|---|---|---|---|---|---|
| | Male | Female | Male | Female | Male | Female | Male | Female |
| Look for work | 6.8 | 6.9 | 31.0 | 29.1 | 42.6 | 27.2 | 37.3 | 21.3 |
| Change workplace | 4.2 | 4.5 | 5.9 | 4.4 | 10.9 | 6.4 | 18.7 | 10.4 |
| Study | 6.4 | 6.4 | 12.6 | 10.6 | 10.8 | 8.9 | 4.1 | 2.9 |
| Reunite with family | 46.8 | 47.1 | 28.6 | 27.5 | 18.2 | 21.8 | 17.4 | 25.1 |
| Get married | 0.1 | 0.4 | 1.0 | 11.4 | 5.3 | 22.8 | 8.1 | 20.7 |
| Health reasons | 2.4 | 2.0 | 1.3 | 1.1 | 0.9 | 1.1 | 1.3 | 1.6 |
| Violence or safety | 4.0 | 3.7 | 2.7 | 1.7 | 1.3 | 1.2 | 1.3 | 1.9 |
| Other reason | 29.4 | 29.0 | 17.0 | 14.3 | 10.2 | 10.6 | 11.9 | 16.0 |

SOURCES: 2000 Mexico Census. Tabulations courtesy of David Lam.

TABLE 5-9 Percentage of Migrants Migrating to an Urban
Area by Previous Residence, Brazil 2000

|  | Previous Residence (1995) | |
| --- | --- | --- |
| Age Group | Urban | Rural |
| 5-9 | 89.2 | 61.3 |
| 10-14 | 90.4 | 63.7 |
| 15-19 | 91.4 | 72.6 |
| 20-24 | 91.7 | 73.8 |
| 25-29 | 90.9 | 68.2 |
| 30-34 | 91.0 | 65.0 |
| 35-39 | 91.8 | 64.6 |
| 40-44 | 91.1 | 62.8 |
| 45-49 | 90.6 | 64.9 |
| 50-54 | 88.9 | 62.0 |
| 55-59 | 89.3 | 63.9 |

SOURCES: 2000 Brazil Census. Tabulations courtesy of David Lam.

the percentage of Brazilian migrants who migrated to an urban area. Migrants from both rural and urban areas tend predominantly to migrate to
urban areas. Among 10-14-year-olds, 90 percent of migrants who were
previously in an urban area migrated to another urban area, while 64
percent of migrants who were previously in a rural area migrated to an
urban area. While over 60 percent of migrants from rural areas move to
urban areas at all ages, the probability that migrants from rural areas move
to urban areas is highest in the 15-19 and 20-24 age groups. Almost 75
percent of migrants from rural areas in these age groups migrate to an
urban area. Since these are also the age groups with the highest migration
rates, the migration of young adults is clearly a major driving force for
rural-urban migration.

Finally, young people are more likely to cross international borders in
search of work than older adults. Data on the age composition of U.S.
immigrants shows the predominance of youth in immigrations flows. Immigrants entering the United States between 1992 and 1994, for example,
were much younger in age than the U.S. population, with significantly
higher percentages among 15-34-year-olds (National Research Council,
1997b). The age distribution of immigrants peaks in the early to mid-20s.
The age distribution of an earlier wave of immigration in 1907-1910 was
even more strongly skewed.[32]

---

[32]Family reunification is playing an increasing role in recent migration flows. Thus, the age
pattern in more recent flows is becoming more diffuse.

## DETERMINANTS OF CHANGING WORK TRANSITIONS AMONG YOUNG PEOPLE

In Chapter 3, we discussed some of the factors affecting changes in the demand for schooling as well as some of the most notable features in the changing landscape of educational service provision. In many ways, a discussion of the determinants of changing work transitions should mirror our previous discussion. Clearly many of the same determinants feature in an explanation of the rising age of school exit as feature in an explanation of the rising age of labor force entry. Furthermore, rising levels of educational attainment are usually explained by increases in the rates of return to secondary and higher levels of schooling; increases that are manifest in rising wage rates among young people as well as shifts in the occupational distribution of younger workers toward employment sectors with higher entry-level skill requirements.

However, there are other features of changing work transitions whose determinants have not been fully discussed and, as a result, questions remain. For example, what are the implications of rising cohort size for successful labor market absorption, particularly given evidence of rising labor force participation rates for young women? Behrman and Birdsall (1983), for example, reported inverse associations between earnings and cohort size in Brazil. Is the economics of the family changing in ways that may have implications for the supply and distribution of entry-level workers as well as for the distribution of skills that they bring with them? What are the major factors affecting the demand for entry-level workers, and how are they changing? These may include shifts in the composition of production, technological change, the pace and stability of economic growth, and changes in patterns of employment discrimination.

Some of these changes are occurring in the household, some in the community, and others at a national level. They include changes in family size, shifts in the size and age composition of the labor force, urbanization, trends in poverty, the growth in the share of employment in the private sector, a decline in trade barriers, and growth in the relative economic importance of the export sector. They also include changes in the availability, cost, and quality of schooling—all factors discussed in Chapter 3. Finally globalization means a tighter link between the economies of developed and developing countries through trade and international financial flows, creating both opportunities and vulnerabilities. While human capital investments are made with long-term returns in mind, the success of young people's labor market transitions are not only a function of the training and skills that they bring to the market but also of the labor market conditions at the time they seek to make those transitions.

In the discussion that follows we explore successively some of the factors on the supply and demand sides of the labor market that may play a role in explaining the patterns and trends observed. On the supply side, we explore first the changing demography of the labor force and then look at some of the factors at the household level that may be affecting changes in the composition of new labor market entrants, including family size and the incidence of poverty. On the demand side, we explore the size of the economy and the composition of production, opportunities for decent and productive work, employment discrimination, and technological change. We save, for the next section on policies and programs, a discussion of existing evidence on the effectiveness of a range of policy interventions on smoothing transitions to work and enhancing their success.

### Factors Affecting the Supply of Entry-Level Workers

*Changes in the Demography of the Labor Force*

Many developing countries, especially those in Latin America and Asia, are moving into a period in which the age structure will be characterized by high proportions of the population in the working ages. This so-called demographic dividend (Bloom, Canning, and Sevilla, 2002), characterized by several decades in which both children and the elderly will be relatively small proportions of the population, will be a dividend for the growth of the economy only to the extent that the working-age population succeeds in finding productive employment. This demographic "dividend" comes bundled with a demographic and economic challenge: the provision of jobs for the largest labor force in history. Evidence from a comparative analysis of labor force trends in 15 advanced economies over the last 25 years (Korenman and Neumark, 1997) provides evidence that relative cohort size is positively correlated with youth unemployment rates, suggesting that relative cohort size will also be a factor in developing country labor markets.

Following the themes set out in Chapter 2, it is important to begin a discussion of youth labor markets with a look at the sheer numbers involved. The increase in the absolute numbers of young workers in developing countries can seem staggering, even overwhelming. In order to put these numbers in perspective and to consider how the growth of the youth labor force will differ across regions, it is instructive to look at estimates of the actual and projected numbers of young people ages 15-24, looking back 50 years and looking forward 50 years. Figure 5-11 shows the changes in the absolute number of 15-24-year-olds based on an index of 1950 = 100 using five countries as examples: Brazil, Kenya, Mexico, Pakistan, and Thailand, representing different regions and phases of the demographic transition (United Nations, 2003d). One type of pattern is demonstrated by Brazil,

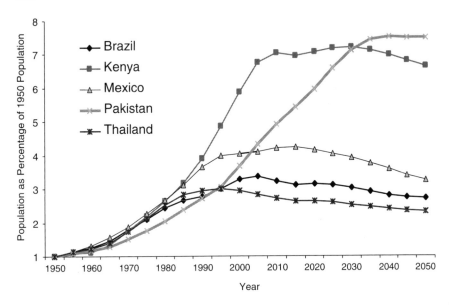

FIGURE 5-11 Size of population 1950-2050, ages 15-24.
SOURCE: United Nations (2003d).

Mexico, and Thailand, where rapid fertility decline has occurred in recent decades. In these three countries, the potential numbers of new labor force entrants peaked around 1990-1995 and have now stabilized. Growth patterns in Kenya and Pakistan are strikingly different. While the growth of the 15-24 age group, between 1950 and 2000 in Kenya, was roughly similar to the growth observed in three other countries until 1985, it has diverged sharply since. In Kenya, where fertility was historically high and has come down rapidly in the last 15 years, the size of the youth population will level off in 2010 at about seven times its level in 1950. In the meantime, the size of the youth population in Pakistan will continue to grow steadily until 2040, reaching nearly eight times its size in 1950. In Pakistan, fertility decline has begun much more recently and taken off much more slowly than in Kenya.

To put the absolute numbers in further perspective, Figure 5-12 plots the annual growth rates for five-year periods for the same set of countries, beginning with the 1950-1955 period. The growth rate of this age group peaked at rates of 4 percent and above around 1970 for all countries except Pakistan. In Kenya, growth rates peaked at over 6 percent, nearly double the growth rates in Pakistan in the same year. Growth rates in Pakistan peaked in 2000 at around 4 percent, roughly the same growth rate as that of Kenya in 2000. In almost all developing countries, the growth rate of the

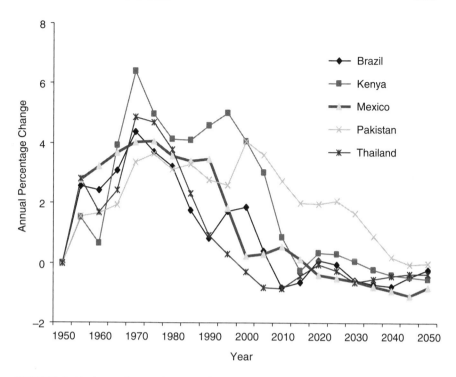

FIGURE 5-12 Annual growth rates of population, ages 15-24.
SOURCE: United Nations (2003d).

youth labor force has been higher in recent decades than it will be in the coming decades. So while the challenge for youth employment will be substantial in countries, like Kenya and Pakistan, that have experienced unprecedented growth in the size of their youth population, the problem in proportional terms will be somewhat smaller in the future than it has been in the past, particularly for Brazil, Mexico, and Thailand, where growth rates are now near zero or negative.

While it is tempting to attribute recent increases in youth unemployment rates to the increasing size of the youth cohorts, it is important to recognize that in many of these countries the absolute numbers of young people were increasing much more rapidly in the 1970s and 1980s than they were in the 1990s. In Brazil, for example, the 15-24 age group grew at over 3 percent per year in the early 1980s, an increase of almost 1 million new young people every year, but the youth unemployment rate stayed at the relatively low levels of 6-7 percent. In the 1990s, the 15-24 age group grew only half as fast as it did in the 1980s, but the youth unemployment rate rose to over 20 percent (Inter-American Development Bank, 2003a).

While the entry into the labor market of the large youth cohorts will create a need for millions of new jobs in developing countries, it is important to recognize that many Asian and Latin American countries successfully absorbed increases in the numbers of young workers in the 1970s and 1980s of similar proportions.

Sustained economic growth, much of it concentrated in the urban economy, clearly played an important role in the historically unprecedented job creation that took place in many developing countries in the 1970s and 1980s. Whether economic growth of a similar magnitude will enable the countries of Southern Asia and sub-Saharan Africa to create jobs for the large cohorts of young people that will enter the labor market in the coming decades is clearly an open question. Later we discuss some issues in international economic policy that may have an important impact on this question.

### Poverty

In the very extensive literature that has analyzed the determinants of child labor, poverty, often associated with capital market failure and liquidity constraints, features as the most prominent explanation. Basu and Van (1998) hypothesize that in many poor settings, parents may actually be caught in a low-level equilibrium trap in which they have no choice but to send the children to work because their own low wages are not sufficient to provide subsistence consumption.[33] This implies a backward-bending supply curve for child labor, with more child labor provided at lower wages. As a result, there *may* be multiple equilibria, with a "good" equilibrium at high wages (with no child labor) and a "bad" equilibrium at low wages (with considerable child labor).[34] If there are multiple equilibria, legal prohibitions on child labor may move the economy from the bad to the good equilibrium. However, in very poor countries there may not be a good

---

[33]In contrast to many economic models of the household that see children as assets for their parents to manipulate for their own economic self-interest, Basu and Van (1998) assume that parents are fundamentally unselfish and only send their children to work when household income falls below a critical threshold or when liquidity constraints prevent them from weathering temporary economic shocks.

[34]Subsequent papers have developed more nuanced models of child labor and other kinds of multiple equilibria. Basu and Tzannatos (2003) review and give references to this literature in a symposium on child labor and development. Work by Horowitz and Wang (2004) is an even more recent contribution that shows that, with heterogeneous children, bans on child labor may either increase (e.g., if the practice is stopped of altruistic parents making more talented children work to increase intrahousehold equity) or reduce (e.g., if the practice is stopped of having less talented children working while their more talented siblings attend school) efficiency. The papers by Bourguignon et al. (2003) and Rosati and Rossi (2003) in the same symposium provide related estimates of decisions about children's labor-school time use.

equilibrium, and in such cases, a ban, if effective, may leave poor families and their children impoverished.

A recent empirical test of this hypothesis in Vietnam provides strong empirical support (Edmonds, 2003). Using data from a panel survey of households, Edmonds (2003) is able to observe changes in economic circumstances and children's labor force participation in the same households over time. He found that households whose per capita expenditure rose sufficiently to push them above the poverty threshold between 1993 and 1998 experienced an 80 percent decline in child labor. While he found per capita household expenditures to be negatively associated with child labor throughout the income range, improvements in household economic status had more power in explaining declines in child labor over the five-year period of observation among low-income families than did improvements in household economic status in other groups.

Another way to explore the relationship between poverty and the incidence of child labor is to look at the impact of economic shocks, such as job loss, family disruption, and bad agricultural harvests on the work activity of young people. Poor families, because they lack access to credit or risk insurance, are much less likely than other families to be able to weather an economic shock without calling on other family members to increase their work effort to compensate for the loss. Concern about the impact of economic shocks (including the consequences of structural adjustment) on young people has been an important focus of attention in the international community (see, for example, Jolly, 1991).

While some studies have found positive statistical associations between work rates among children and adolescents in response to adverse shocks (e.g., Rucci, 2003, for Argentina from 1998-2002 in response to currency fluctuations; Beegle, Dehejia, and Gatti, 2003, for Tanzania in the early 1990s due to crop loss; Cunningham and Maloney, 2000, for Mexico from 1987 to 1997 due to parental job loss), others have found little relationship (e.g., Skoufias and Parker, 2002, for Mexico from 1995-1997 due to parental job loss, divorce, and marriage or Duryea, Lam, and Levison, 2003, for Brazil due to male job loss) or a negative association (e.g., Behrman et al., 2000, for Thailand after the 1997 financial crisis; Duryea and Arends-Kuenning, 2003, for Brazil from 1977 to 1998 due to labor market fluctuations). When shocks affect the supply of jobs in the market, the increased need for family income is counterbalanced by a decline in labor market opportunities. In comparisons of the effects of shocks on the poor and nonpoor, children in poor families appear more likely than others to increase their work rates in response to adverse shocks (e.g., Beegle, Dehejia, and Gatti, 2003, for Tanzania; and Neri et al., forthcoming, for Brazil). These results provide further support for the notion of a backward bending supply of labor in very poor settings or among poor families.

In most parts of the world, the percentage of the population living on less than $1 per day has declined over the last decade (Chen and Ravallion, 2001). However in sub-Saharan Africa it is rising. Given long-term trends in the incidence of poverty, one would expect to see declines in the incidence of child labor in countries in which the percentage living in poverty has declined, but increases in countries in which that percentage has increased. At the same time, changes in the structure and function of labor markets (see discussion below) as well as changes in the accessibility of credit and risk insurance can affect families' ability to absorb temporary economic shocks due to a bad harvest, a business failure, or a job loss, with attendant implications for the timing of young people's transitions to work.

### Family Size

Throughout the developing world, except possibly in some parts of sub-Saharan Africa, family size is declining rapidly and the educational levels of parents are substantially higher than they were in previous generations. At the same time, the burdens of domestic work that depend to a large extent on the availability of electricity, cooking fuel, and water are likely to be declining as countries become more fully electrified, as public services become more widely accessible, and as a growing proportion of the population lives in cities in which services are much more accessible (National Research Council, 2003). These trends that are associated with positive demographic and economic changes might be expected to free young people up from domestic responsibilities as well as from the need to contribute to family income at a young age or while still a student, thus allowing time for longer and more effective learning in school.

At the same time, female household headship is rising throughout the developing world, and mothers are more likely to work outside the home than in the past (Bruce, Lloyd, and Leonard, 1995). Rising female headship means fewer adult earners in the household, possibly increasing the need for young people to contribute to household income. Lloyd and Blanc (1996) found in sub-Saharan Africa that children living in female-headed households actually had an educational advantage over children in male-headed households once income was controlled, because of the tendency of these households to be more child-oriented in the allocation of family resources. However, female-headed households are more likely to be poor; the net effect of rising female headship on the incidence of child labor should depend on trends in the relative incidence of poverty in these households. Increasing rates of female labor force participation also lead to a reduction in the number of adults in the household available to take up domestic responsibilities, with possible implications for children's domestic work responsibilities. Unless the family is poor, the increased family income resulting from women's labor force participation should reduce children's work requirements, if that increased income can be applied to the purchase of child care and domestic help, thus freeing children to go to school and to stay in school longer.

A rich literature on the relationship between family size and children's school has shown how key elements of context (e.g., level of economic development, government expenditure on education, family systems and gender role ideology, and phase of the demographic transition) mediate that relationship and explain its direction and strength across countries. The same is true of estimated relationships between family size and patterns of child labor (e.g., DeGraff, Bilsborrow, and Herrin, 1993; Jejeebhoy, 1993). Because of differences in gender roles in the family, the consequences of having fewer siblings may play out differently for the work roles of boys and girls. In the case of girls, the greater likelihood that their mothers are working for pay may increase the need for help at home (e.g., Basu, 1995, for the case of poor urban slums in India; Ray, 2002, for Pakistan) but fewer siblings at home may reduce the need for child care. For boys, fewer siblings at home may reduce the need to supplement family income in some settings but may increase it in rural areas in which families have large land holdings or in settings in which family enterprises are important. Edmonds (2003), using panel data from Vietnam, found that per capita expenditure improvements predicted declines in child labor better for boys than for girls; they also predicted changes in large households better than changes in smaller households.

## Factors Affecting the Demand for Entry-Level Workers

### Size of the Economy and Composition of Production

Over the last few decades, the economies of Eastern and Southern Asia, where the majority of young people in developing countries live, have been growing more rapidly than the economies of the developed countries. As a result, the very large gap between these economies has narrowed slightly (Behrman and Sengupta, 2005). In other parts of the developing world, per capita income levels, which were previously much higher than levels in Eastern and Southern Asia have been diverging from per capita income levels in the developed world, most dramatically in the Middle East and the transition economies of Europe and Central Asia, but to some extent in Latin America as well. Per capita income levels in sub-Saharan Africa, which were always among the lowest in the world, have been diverging further from developed country levels. Thus, the overall economic contexts in which most young people in the developing world have been making their transitions to adulthood have changed, and these changes have varied substantially among regions, with much more positive aggregate economic experiences in Asia, where the majority of young people in developing countries live, than elsewhere.

The composition of production across economic sectors substantially shapes the employment options for young people. Conventional wisdom is that production shares of agriculture decline steadily in the process of development from about half or more to levels of about 5 percent, industrial shares increase initially and then peak and decline somewhat, after which service shares tend to increase. As noted in Chapter 2, recent patterns for most developing regions are mostly consistent with these characterizations. However the relatively large movements toward developed country service shares for Latin American and the Caribbean, Southern Asia, and sub-Saharan Africa—given their respective levels of development—raise some concerns that the service sector in these regions may be absorbing labor at too rapid a rate given more limited job expansion in goods-producing sectors, leading to lower average levels of productivity. These rapid changes in the growth of different sectors have implications for returns to different forms of human capital (e.g., increased returns to formal schooling in comparison to informal learning in family enterprises) and have involved some dislocation (including physical migration) to adjust to the changes.

Another factor that shapes economic growth and employment options for young people is the extent of engagement in international markets. Four of the six developing country regions have converged toward the developed countries in a standard measure of openness—the share of exports plus imports in national product (Behrman and Sengupta, 2005). The exceptions are Eastern Asia and the Pacific and, to a much lesser extent, Southern Asia. For Eastern Asia and the Pacific (but not for Southern Asia), the divergence has been more rapid increases in openness than in developed countries—a trend that has often been interpreted as being an important causal factor in the relatively successful recent economic progress of this region.

The 1980s and 1990s have been a period of structural reforms implemented in concert with international development-oriented agencies in many developing countries, particularly in sub-Saharan Africa and Latin America and the Caribbean.[35] The stated objective of adjustment lending programs,

---

[35]Many countries in Asia also have changed their economic policies in ways that are consistent with—and indeed have been the inspiration for—structural reform associated with international development agencies. But, with the exception of the post-1997 Asian financial crisis period, for the most part these policy changes in Asia have not been formally related to international development agencies and are not considered in usual discussions of structural reform.

initiated in the late 1970s and early 1980s by the International Monetary Fund and the World Bank, was the promotion of long-term economic growth (Haddad et al., 1995). These structural reforms include the lifting of restrictions on international trade, privatization, and tax reform, which were expected to improve economic efficiency and promote economic growth. In Latin America these adjustments often included various labor market reforms as well, such as the loosening of various regulations designed to make the labor market more flexible.

While poverty provides a persuasive explanation for child labor in rural areas, job opportunities for children could be a factor pulling them into the labor market in urban areas. This is the conclusion of a comparative study of the determinants of child labor and schooling using cross-sectional survey data from Nepal, Peru, and Zimbabwe that estimated the effects of wages on child labor separately in urban and rural areas (Ersado, 2002). Other studies of the determinants of child labor that are confined to urban populations also have found evidence of a significant demand effect on child labor. For example, using an urban sample in Mexico, Levison, Moe, and Knaul (2001) found that a rise in the urban wage for girls did increase their likelihood of combining work and school; the same was not true for boys. Using a sample of urban schoolchildren in Mexico, Binder and Scrogin (1999) found that the likelihood of combining work with school was significantly and positively related to children's wage opportunities. Finally, Duryea and Arends-Kuenning (2003), using a series of household surveys from 1977 to 1998 representing urban populations in Brazil, found employment rates for 14-16-year-old boys and girls increase as local labor market conditions improve (see further discussion in the section on factors affecting the supply of entry-level workers).

With population growth primarily concentrated in urban areas in developing countries, it is important to understand the implications of these trends for work transitions. Family farms and enterprises have traditionally been an important source of employment for children. With the shift of employment from agricultural to industry with development, one would expect that family farms would be less of a source of demand than in the past for child workers, but not much is known about trends in the prevalence of other types of family enterprises and wage employment opportunities that may be prevalent in urban areas. Thus, little is known about how the demand for child labor may be changing with development and urbanization.

## Opportunities for Decent and Productive Work

One of the targets agreed to as part of the Millennium Development Goals is "to develop and implement strategies for decent and productive work for youth" (United Nations General Assembly, 2003). While the term "decent" is not defined, we assume that it relates to various job characteristics, such as pay, hours, benefits, and security. We understand the term "productive" to mean that jobs are well matched with workers' skills in addition to possibly providing on-the-job training. These targets, however, need to be understood in the context of rapidly changing labor market structures in many developing countries.

Around the world as labor markets are being deregulated, the public sector as a share of total employment is declining and the share of nonagricultural employment in the informal sector is growing. A key feature of informal markets is wage flexibility. Furthermore, most working children are employed in the informal sector. Data from case studies suggest that children who work are typically paid less than adults even when they do the same task (Grootaert and Kanbur, 1995). It is unknown whether the growth in the informal sector has led to an increased demand for child labor. A careful study of children working in the carpet industry in India found that adult workers are entirely substitutable for child workers and have similar productivity, yet for many smaller weaving establishments there can be a cost advantage to hiring child labor because of their lower pay (Levison et al., 1996).

As part of this tendency toward deregulation and privatization, the informal sector is becoming increasingly diverse and contains a growing number of high-wage job opportunities that lack job protection and often benefits. The high-wage part of the informal sector represents the most dynamic sector of the economy. At the same time, even conditions of employment in the formal sector are becoming "informalized," and thus the distinctions between the formal and informal sectors are becoming increasingly blurred (Roberts, 1991; Vandemoortele, 1991).

For example, in Egypt, an increasing number of government employees are being hired on a temporary basis (El Mahdi, 2002). In Latin America, there appears to be a high degree of mobility between sectors, with 32 percent of workers in Mexico and 22 percent of workers in Argentina estimated to move either in or out of an informal job in a 6-month period (Inter-American Development Bank, 2003b). What implications does this growing informalization of the labor market have for new labor market entrants?

China is a dramatic example of these changes and their implications. A series of reforms was adopted in the late 1980s that have abolished the former system of work units organized by the public sector, which provided housing as well as cradle-to-grave job security. This allowed a labor market to emerge in which worker skills can be better matched with jobs (Hanuum and Liu, 2005). The results have been a rapid rise in the private sector as well as a rise in rates of return to higher levels of schooling. Both public-sector and private-sector jobs have less stability and fewer benefits than past jobs, but compared with earlier cohorts, young people in China today enjoy substantially higher incomes.

Egypt is another interesting case. In Egypt all graduates of secondary or postsecondary institutions are guaranteed, at least in principle, employment in the public sector. Over time, real wages have eroded, but the queue for government jobs has lengthened as the growth in secondary and university graduates has outpaced the growth in government jobs, in the absence of sufficient growth in the private sector (Assaad, 1997a, 2002). Thus, graduates today have a choice of queuing for public-sector jobs that still provide pay and benefits that compare favorably to the private sector or entering the private sector, where they have a greater likelihood of finding a job as a result of recent growth in that sector. Furthermore, with the increasing informalization of both the public and private sectors, the informal sector has become the most important source of labor absorption in the last decade (Assaad, 1997b, as cited in Ahlburg and Amer, 2004; El Mahdi, 2002). In exploring the labor market mobility of young Egyptians, Ahlburg and Amer (2004) found that students who left school in the 1990s were more likely to be employed than students in the 1980s, but at the same time, among those employed, they were more likely to work in the private (and often informal) sector. Indeed, rates of employment in the informal sector have risen more rapidly for young men and women in Egypt than for any other age group (Moktar and Wahba, 2002).

Most importantly, Ahlburg and Amer (2004) also found that the more educated had greater upward mobility in the labor market over time. For the purposes of their study, they created a hierarchy of types of mobility starting with a move from out of the labor force into it, from unemployment to employment, from nonwage to wage employment, from irregular to regular employment, from unprotected to protected employment, and from protected private- to protected public-sector employment, with the assumption that these options are successively more desirable from the point of view of a potential employee. Using this hierarchy, they found that education is important to long-term job mobility, with the more educated the most likely to upgrade their employment status over time. They also concluded that labor market mobility for young graduates has increased in the last 10 years.

A potentially important aspect of "decent and productive" work is on-the-job training. A recent comparison of job stability for men of prime working age in private-sector wage employment in urban Colombia and the United States confirms anecdotal and case study evidence that jobs may be less stable in developing than in developed countries. Schaffner (2001) found, after controlling for differences in employment growth rates between Colombia and United States, that four-year job retention probabilities are substantially higher in the United States than in Colombia, particularly in the first few years of a job, when on-the-job training should be most cost-effective. Even after further controlling for the fact that the occupational and industrial distribution of the workforce in the two settings differs in ways that would predict such differences, jobs in Colombia remain on average shorter in duration. These results suggest that young workers entering the private wage sector in Colombia will have substantially less opportunity for on-the-job training than their U.S. peers, with long-term consequences for productivity and wage growth over time.[36] Various hypotheses to explain these differences between the United States and Colombia, including lower levels of development, greater volatility in the lives of workers and firms, financial constraints faced by employers and workers, and the inferior quality of formal schooling, remain untested.

### Employment Discrimination

We are unaware of any studies specifically focusing on the role of employment discrimination according to gender, race, ethnicity, caste, or religion in transitions to work among young people. There is an entire literature on occupational stratification that the panel did not explore, but a cursory glance at materials focusing on labor market issues specific to young people in developing countries revealed little on this topic that would address our concerns with the occupational barriers that might affect new labor force entrants in the context of recent change.

While rising private rates of return to secondary schooling for girls in the labor market as well as growing opportunities for young women in factories around the world may be factors contributing in some countries to the breaking down of traditional employment barriers to women, patterns of occupational segregation by gender are pervasive. Indeed, according to Anker (1998), approximately half of all workers in the world are in occupations in which at least 80 percent of workers are of the same sex, with the least educated being the most segregated by occupation (Deutsch et al., 2002). Furthermore, in the cases of Costa Rica, Ecuador, and Uruguay, there appears to be no evidence that occupational segregation has decreased during the decade of the 1990s (Deutsch et al., 2002). Indeed, the degree of occupational segregation in these three countries is similar despite very different economic conditions.

One question that remains is what implications the trend toward privatization and informalization of the labor market may have for patterns

---

[36] Indeed, there is evidence from the United States that early job stability is associated with higher wages as an adult (Neumark, 1998).

of employment discrimination for new labor force entrants. In Egypt, for example, the private sector appears to be virtually closed to women outside manufacturing and finance. Assaad (2002) found that, in the last decade, women's share of employment in nonagricultural wage employment has actually declined. If it had not been for growth of jobs in the public sector for women, female unemployment rates might have risen sharply.

## Technological Change

An additional factor that may affect changes in the demand for labor is technology. The introduction of labor-saving technology can cut down on the demand for low-cost child labor. There are many examples of this in the literature. In Egypt, the mechanization of agriculture, in particular the expanded use of tractors and irrigation pumps, reduced the demand for child labor, such as picking cotton or driving animals to power waterwheels or haul freight (Levy, 1985). In Ethiopia, the availability of labor-saving agricultural machinery was found to reduce child labor (Admassie and Singh Bedi, 2003). In the Philippines, having electricity in the community reduced both market and domestic work by children (deGraff, Bilsborrow, and Herrin, 1993). However, not all technological change is labor saving. Take for example the case of higher yield seeds that increase the productivity of the land. In Ethiopia, Admassie and Singh Bedi (2003) found that the introduction of higher yield seeds, in the absence of other labor-saving technology, actually led to an increase in the prevalence of child labor, at least in the short run.

Technological change can also contribute to changing rates of return to different levels of schooling, benefiting some young people and disadvantaging others in the search for remunerative work. Much evidence from developing countries suggests that technology can contribute to rising rates of return to higher levels of schooling (Montgomery et al., 2001). However, directions of causation can be difficult to establish, because a labor force with higher levels of education is more likely to generate innovations than one with lower levels of education. In many developing countries, in which technologies have been imported and are not the result of indigenous invention, this is less of a problem. The case of the green revolution, which initially relied on research and technology developed in international agricultural research stations, is a good example. Foster and Rosenzweig (1996) found evidence for such an effect in India in connection with the importation of high-yielding variety seeds. Their results indicate a rise in the returns to schooling during the period of rapid technological change, particularly in the states experiencing the most rapid growth rate. They conclude that the more educated are better able to manage the new technologies or to access information about them sooner. They further conjectured that the relationship between technological change and schooling is synergistic, with technological change having the biggest payoff in settings in which the labor force is more educated.

In the context of recent experience in Asia, Montgomery et al. (2001) pose the question as to why the increase in the supply of educated young labor has not brought with it a decline in rates of return to schooling. In the absence of other changes, such a result would be expected. Evidence of rising rates of return to secondary and tertiary education might appear counterintuitive. The authors raise the possibility of technological change as an explanation. In their cross-country regression analysis of factors associated with rates of return to schooling at the primary, secondary, and tertiary levels, the variable measuring trade openness was found to be significant. The authors speculate about the possibility that trade may serve as a conduit for technological transfer. Estimates by Wood and Calandrino (2000) project that greater trade openness in India will raise the demand for education in India, partly by shifting employment toward more skill-intensive sectors, but mainly by increasing the need for more educated workers in each sector, because of more technologically sophisticated methods of production. However, Behrman, Birdsall, and Szekely (2003b) did not find that trade openness was an important factor in Latin America in explaining the widening of wage differentials between the more and less educated; instead they identified other factors, such as tax and financial market reform, as being important.

## POLICIES AND PROGRAMS

One challenge in designing effective policies to support successful transitions to adult work roles is to make sure that these transitions do not take place too early or too late. Another is that those making the transition have the skills and the information necessary to find decent and productive work in a very diverse and rapidly changing marketplace. Yet another is ensuring equal opportunities. While much is written about the prevention of child labor and the promotion of jobs for young people, there has been almost no sound scientific evaluation of policies and programs designed to support these goals. This is in sharp contrast to the field of education, in which policy evaluation is increasingly recognized as an essential element of proper policy formulation. Indeed, the one area in which there is some evidence of program effects is child labor, and this evidence is derived largely from evaluations of various antipoverty schemes that promote school attendance.

In the overview of relevant policies and programs that follows, we explore several domains of action, some with intended consequences for youth employment and some with objectives not specific to youth employment but with consequences for youth. First, there are policy actions at the international or national level that take place outside the country in question but are intended to discourage child labor or to limit competition and thereby protect workers in developed countries. These include international labor standards and trade sanctions against countries with labor practices that are seen to be deleterious to children as well as certain features of macroeconomic policy.

Second, there are actions taken by developing country governments, which fall into three major categories: (1) laws and regulations governing employment practices, including the employment of children and youth, (2) programs designed and directed to the promotion of youth employment, and (3) poverty reduction programs targeted to poor families with school-age children. This list, however, neglects policies and programs that may have beneficial effects for young people, particularly girls and young women, whose work is hidden but who labor for long hours on unnecessarily time-consuming domestic chores, because many poor households still lack access to certain shared amenities of development, such as electricity, water, fuel, and transportation. Public works projects designed to free poor families from these burdens would lead to greater possibilities for schooling as well as remunerative work, particularly for girls and young women. However, such projects are rarely discussed alongside youth employment promotion schemes, despite their obvious benefits for young women.

### International Policies

The International Labour Organization, in the early years after its founding in 1919, was focused primarily on labor policies in the industrialized north, in particular the needs and concerns of organized labor. In more recent years, the ILO has shifted its emphasis to improving working conditions in developing countries through the adoption of various international agreements and conventions that, at least in theory, bind their signatories to the enforcement of national labor standards. Among those of particular salience to our discussion are (1) the elimination of all forms of forced or compulsory labor, (2) the effective abolition of child labor, and (3) the elimination of discrimination in employment (Engerman, 2003). The ILO has no powers of enforcement, but it plays a useful role in developing consensus around an internationally shared set of norms and in educating the international community about basic human rights in the areas of labor and employment.

In recent years, trade policy has become a new tool being used in the international arena to "enforce" labor standards through product-labeling or trade sanctions against trading partners who are known to violate international labor standards relating to child labor. There has been much recent debate about the motives as well as the effects of unilateral actions by developed countries to ban imports of products produced by child labor. First, while there is some evidence that the use of child labor in unskilled-labor-intensive export industries can have some modest positive effect on a country's comparative advantage, these effects are far outweighed by the importance of a country's labor endowment and the overall educational level of the working-age population in determining comparative advantage in a particular industry (Busse, 2002). Second, while many assume that the motivation for trade sanctions is primarily protectionist, Krueger (1997) has done some interesting analysis of voting patterns in the United States that may suggest that humanitarian concerns play an important role in the adoption of these policies as well. Third, as stated by Brown, Deardorff, and Stern (2003:240) "trade sanctions do little to address the underlying market failure that gives rise to offending child labor practices."

As discussed earlier, poverty is the primary cause of child labor. A loss of jobs in the export sector in a country that has many families living in poverty with little access to credit and where labor standards are weak or poorly enforced will lead poor children to seek work in other informal, less remunerative, and potentially more hazardous conditions. Indeed, there is evidence that this actually happened in Bangladesh after children were dismissed from factories in 1993 (Boyden, Ling, and Myers, 1998). Furthermore, sudden loss of jobs for children may also further exacerbate the incidence of poverty among families if such actions lead to a decline in the overall demand for labor (Basu, 1999; Basu and Van, 1998; Jafarey and Lahiri, 2002). Indeed, a country's openness to trade (as measured by the sum of imports over gross national product) has been shown empirically to be negatively associated with the incidence of child labor (Edmonds and Pavcnik, 2002; Shelburne, 2001). Furthermore, the majority of working children in developing countries remain outside the reach of labor regulations because they work in the informal economy or at home. Thus, policy makers motivated by humanitarian concerns for children will be more likely to succeed if they shift their energies to policies designed to attack the root causes of poverty.

Many other aspects of macro policy in developed countries influence the job prospects of young people in developing countries. While talking about increasing aid to the Third World, industrialized nations often follow trade policies and fiscal subsidy strategies in their own nations that may far outdo the good of the increased aid. Yet too often decisions made by foreign aid agencies in industrialized countries are not coordinated with trade policy.

Consider farm subsidies in developed nations as an example. By using taxpayer money to subsidize their farmers, rich countries tend to outcompete poor farmers in poor nations and also their export prospects.

This policy alone can have huge consequences for poverty in rural regions of developing nations, causing agricultural wages to be low, contributing to underemployment, and diminishing young people's opportunity for work in rural areas.[37]

## National Labor Policies and Programs

### Laws and Regulations

Some labor laws and regulations, such as minimum ages of employment and youth-specific minimum wages, are specifically adopted with young people in mind. Others, such as rules governing employment contracts, conditions of employment including hours and wages, and job security or antidiscrimination legislation, are more general but may have particular consequences for new labor market entrants. Typically, these laws or regulations, while commonly adopted in developing countries, apply only in the formal sector, which, in many settings, appears to be declining in relative importance even as economies are growing.

There have been few studies of the effects of minimum wage legislation on youth employment in developing countries. This is probably because so few youth work in the formal sector and because, even in the formal sector, enforcement of minimum wage laws, where they exist, tends to be weak. Furthermore, minimum wages are typically set very low and, even if set at a relevant rate, are often quickly eroded by inflation. A recent review of the literature (Ghellab, 1998) found only one study of the specific effects of the minimum wage on youth employment in urban Indonesia, where its effects were found to be statistically insignificant (Rama, 1996, as cited in Ghellab, 1998).

The story of the enforcement of stricter child labor standards in Nepal (see Box 5-4) is a particularly poignant example of the complexity of applying labor standards in a poor country in which many children work outside the reach of the government's potential enforcement capacities (Baker and

---

[37]The International Food Policy Research Institute (2003) estimates that total support to agriculture in Organisation for Economic Co-operation and Development member countries in 2001 was over $US300 billion and that this support costs agriculture and related industries in developing countries at least $US24 billion annually (not counting some possibly important spillover and dynamic effects) and displaces over $US40 billion annually in developing country agricultural exports. Thus OECD agricultural policies not only have major negative effects on income and employment to produce that income in developing countries, but also on the most productive allocation of labor and other resources in developing countries (International Food Policy Research Institute, 2003).

---

**BOX 5-4**
**Child Workers in the Carpet Industry in Nepal**

Through the enforcement of child labor laws, children working in large and highly visible carpet factories in Nepal, which were deemed to have hazardous work conditions, were expelled from their workplaces and disallowed from income-generating activities (Baker and Hinton, 2001). In the mid-1990s, these expelled child workers were then enrolled in a rehabilitation program funded by the Nepal Rugmark Foundation, which was funded by contributions from factory owners and set up to enable them to attach "child labor free" labels to their carpets. Children were placed in residential hostels; provided with health care, nonformal education, and counseling; and, ultimately reunited, if possible, with their families in rural areas. However, many children worked alongside other family members and being reunited with their family meant being allowed to remain near them in their factory environments. Thus, there has been increasing attention to the need to provide day nurseries, nonformal education, and health facilities in the factory environment. The authors of the study point to the need for protective policies that will allow children to combine work with schooling.

---

Hinton, 2001). While children under the age of 16 no longer work in the largest carpet factories, which have been subject to government inspections and extensive media attention, employers in the smaller and medium-sized factories remain ignorant of the law or able to circumvent it.

In a recent comparative study of the employment effects of labor regulations in 85 countries that included over 50 developing countries, Botero and colleagues (2003) found no evidence that the regulation of labor, while more extensively practiced in poorer than richer countries, is beneficial. Indeed, they found that young people suffer differentially from labor regulations. For this analysis, they developed an index of employment laws related to conditions of employment, job security, and alternative employment contracts that ranges in value from 0.87 to 2.40, with higher values reflecting a greater degree of regulation. Developing countries, which have tended to adopt legal traditions from former colonial powers, are distributed through the range. An increase of the employment laws index by 1 point raises the average unemployment rate for young men by 6 percent and of young women by nearly 10 percentage points. More extensive labor regulations are also associated with a relatively greater share of the economy being situated in the informal sector.

*Policies and Programs Promoting Youth Employment*

Policies and programs designed to promote youth employment or livelihoods can be grouped in four categories: (1) vocational education and training, (2) information sharing, (3) direct job creation, and (4) support for self-employment and enterprise creation, including various livelihood schemes promoted by nongovernmental organizations (NGOs). We also include military or national service here. While military service is rarely discussed in this context, it should be recognized that it often provides employment and training for young people, mainly young men. For those who do not make a long-term career in the military, it also provides a transition back into the regular labor market with marketable skills (see further discussion of military service and its role in citizenship formation in Chapter 6).

A recent report of the secretary general of the ILO stated that "training is in crisis everywhere in the developing world" (International Labour Office, 2003:38). In many developing countries, a large part of vocational training has traditionally taken place in the schooling system in the form of a specialized track at the secondary level, with per-student costs that can be as much as twice those of general secondary schooling (Gill and Fluitman, 1997). Employers, unions, and other government agencies often play a role as well. Typically the types of skills provided are geared to jobs in the formal sector. However, bureaucratic rigidities and outdated curricula have combined to raise questions about the cost-effectiveness of an approach that is slow to respond to rapidly changing skill requirements in the marketplace. Nonetheless, many countries continue to focus employment policies for young people around vocational education.

For example, in the 1992 revision of the National Policy on Education in India, high priority was assigned to the "vocationalisation" of secondary education, but subsequent follow-up suggests that progress was sluggish and the links between the schools and industry were weak (Visaria, 1998). In Mexico, the National College of Vocation Studies—a decentralized federal institution that provides mid-level technical training at the postsecondary level—has been criticized for its inflexibility and its inability to build an adequate relationship with the private sector (Lugo, 1999). This is made all the more challenging by the fact that most firms in the formal sector have relatively few employees and a growing number of young people work in the informal sector.

Egypt is well known for its large system of technical secondary schooling. Two-thirds of graduates from basic schools go to technical secondary schools rather than academic secondary schools. However, many of the concerns raised above have stimulated thinking about alternative approaches. The Mubarak-Kohl initiative conceived in 1991 and piloted in some of Egypt's new cities in 1995 hoped to create a cooperative system of internship training using public-private partnerships (van Eekelen, de Luca, and Ismail, 2001). So far this initiative has not taken off and is unlikely to spread beyond the internationally competitive sector of the economy because of its costs (Gill and Fluitman, 1997). Furthermore, concerns have been expressed that vocational training that was previously open to young men and women equally would begin to favor young men, because students in the program would be selected by private companies and the private sector is largely closed to women in Egypt (Assaad, 2002).

Vocational training is distinguished from vocational education by being outside the formal school system, but also outside the workplace, while in-service training occurs in firms. The Chile Joven program represents a model combining both approaches, which has now been replicated in three other Latin American countries (Gallart, 2001). Aedo and Núñez (2001) evaluate the effectiveness of Programa Joven in Argentina, a program targeted to young people from poor households with low levels of school and no work experience. The training combines a classroom and an internship phase lasting from 14 to 20 weeks. The program showed statistically significant positive wage effects for young men and adult women as well as statistically significant positive employment effects for adult women only, controlling for selection into the program.[38]

The authors interpret these results as reflecting the different market conditions faced by different groups rather than differences in their training experiences. Using data on program costs and estimated benefits, the authors conclude that it would take 9-12 years for the net present value of the program to become positive. Given evidence of the relatively modest returns associated with job training, the Inter-American Development Bank in its latest report on the Latin American labor market recommends that governments "should move away from the direct provision of training and improve the incentives of firms, workers and training providers to fund, seek and provide high quality training" (Inter-American Development Bank, 2003a).

Job counseling and job registries do not create jobs or provide training, but they can improve the effectiveness of the search process through information sharing and better matching of jobs with potential applicants. In India, the national employment service operates over 900 employment exchanges, primarily in large towns and cities, and the overwhelming majority of registrants are young people ages 15-29 in search of their first jobs (Visaria, 1998). However, employers do not find that they meet their needs and, as a result during 1995, there were 5.9 million job seekers registered but only 386,000 vacancies listed. Evidence from evaluations in member

---

[38]The authors estimate a model of program participation and, based on the estimated propensity scores, they use the nearest neighbor matching estimator to estimate the impact of the program separately.

countries of the Organisation for Economic Co-operation and Development suggests that job registries can be cost-effective if properly managed, however (Inter-American Development Bank, 2003a).

Labor-intensive public works projects have been a long-standing approach to job creation. For example, the Public Works Programme (PWP) in Egypt was set up in 1991 to apply and institutionalize, at the national level, labor-intensive techniques in infrastructure projects to create employment in rural areas. While young people have not been specifically targeted, young men have been the principal beneficiaries (van Eekelen, de Luca, and Ismail, 2001). The long-term success of such programs is significantly enhanced if there are spillover effects in the local economy that encourage sustained employment and growth. Furthermore, since these projects are likely to lighten domestic work burdens, they may free many young women for participation in the nonagricultural wage sector—a sector that has traditionally been closed to them.

A final approach to youth employment is the promotion of self-employment and entrepreneurship through various livelihood schemes. Livelihood schemes have as their objective the promotion of self-employment and entrepreneurship among traditionally disadvantaged groups and have recently been promoted as a promising approach to the integration of girls and young women into an increasingly informal labor market. Livelihood schemes can encompass the development of capabilities, resources, and opportunities (Population Council and International Center for Research on Women, 2000). This has been a fertile arena for NGOs in many settings and goes beyond training to encompass access to financial services, access to markets, the creation of safe spaces, the empowerment of young women, and the protection and promotion of rights, among other goals (see further discussion of the role of livelihood interventions in the acquisition of citizenship in Chapter 6). While there is strong evidence that young women's labor force participation rates are on the rise, there is no comparable evidence about trends in domestic work burdens or patterns of labor market discrimination. By adopting an integrated approach to addressing the needs of young women, these programs are trying to address simultaneously many of the traditional disadvantages that these women have faced in making the transition to adult work roles and responsibilities. Evaluations of some of these programs are currently under way.

### Antipoverty Programs Promoting Children's Schooling

In Chapter 3, grants to poor families conditional on their children's school attendance were featured as a promising new approach to increasing school participation and attainment among the poor. In most cases these same evaluations, which have been heavily concentrated in Latin America, have documented program effects on children's work participation as well. Variations in key features of program design, as well as in the contexts in which these programs have been applied (e.g., prevalence and depth of poverty, previous school participation, school quality, opportunities for children to work for pay), will clearly lead to differences in outcomes.

The most comprehensive assessment of time-use impacts on children of conditional grants for school has been done in connection with the evaluation of PROGRESA: poor families were eligible to receive monthly grants on a per-child basis as long as the child maintains an 85 percent attendance record in school (Skoufias and Parker, forthcoming). The percentage decline in labor force participation rates for boys was roughly in balance with the rise in school enrollment, except among boys ages 16-17 who showed no significant reduction in the probability of working. For girls, however, the decline in their labor force participation was much lower than the recorded rise in their enrollment rates, because they had much lower levels of labor force participation to begin with. However, by looking more comprehensively at all aspects of time use, the researchers were able to document that PROGRESA also lowered the time girls spend on domestic chores, which can also be an important barrier to school attendance. Thus it appears that PROGRESA has the promise of contributing to a more successful transition to adult work roles for many poor Mexican youth.

A pilot project in Nicaragua with a similar design but with a slightly younger group of children targeted for education support (ages 7-13) also found that the percentage of children working after the program had been in operation for a year was lower in every age group, but only significantly so in the case of children ages 12-13 (Maluccio, forthcoming). Because of the younger ages of the children, their participation rates were lower than in Mexico, where children enrolled in secondary school were also included. This is likely to explain the less significant effects.

The experience of the Program to Eradicate Child Labor (PETI) in rural Brazil is of particular interest because its primary goal was to eliminate child labor. This program provides a per-child stipend to poor households conditional on the school attendance of those children that households designate as participants; it is also conditional on the attendance of participating children in an after-school program (Jornada Ampliada), which effectively doubles the length of the school day. In addition, it includes a contract signed by the parents agreeing that their participating children will not work. The evaluation was based on a cross-sectional survey conducted in participating and nonparticipating communities (matched on socioeconomic status) three years after the initiation of the program (Yap, Sedlacek, and Orazem, forthcoming). In the statistical analysis, PETI was found to be more successful in removing children who were working part time from the labor force than removing children working full time. This result was seen to be due to the availability of the after-school program, particular in Bahia—an region with high rates of child labor—where nonprogram children were also allowed to participate in the after-school program. PETI participants were also more likely than nonparticipants to progress to the next grade and less likely to engage in various types of hazardous work. It is not known whether the after-school program had a direct effect on better grade progression rates through the provision of more educational inputs or an indirect effect through the reduction of work hours.

## CONCLUSIONS AND RECOMMENDATIONS

### Key Findings

*The rise in school enrollment and the delay in the timing of school exit have resulted in a delay in the timing of labor force entry and a concomitant decline in the prevalence of child labor.* Not only is the average educational attainment of new labor force entrants rising, but so are the earnings of secondary and university graduates compared with those who lack an education or have only completed primary school. As a result, working children in developing countries are experiencing a growing disadvantage relative to their more educated peers.

*The rapidly closing gender gap in school attendance and participation implies a growing equalization of work burdens between young men and women as their daily lives become more similar to each other.* These changes in gender roles during a critical phase of the transition to adulthood are creating opportunities for greater gender equity in adulthood. Nonetheless, young women's work burdens still exceed those of young men even when they are students, because they spend relatively more time than young men on noneconomic household work.

*The longer young people stay in school, the more likely they are to combine schooling and work.* Indeed, part-time or intermittent work can provide the means to make continued enrollment possible in many poor settings. Unambiguous evidence of the negative effects of child labor on learning outcomes is limited but is most persuasive in the case of children of primary school age who combine work and schooling.

*In many parts of Asia and Latin America, increased numbers of young people have been absorbed into the labor market without any large increase in unemployment rates among youth, despite a rapid rise in the size of cohorts entering the labor force. However, the challenge for youth employment remains substantial in some of the poorer countries of Asia, sub-*

*Saharan Africa, and the Middle East, which are currently experiencing unprecedented growth in the size of their youth populations.* Rates of growth in the size of the potential youth labor force (ages 15-24) have now peaked in most countries even though the absolute numbers continue to grow. Because youth opportunities for employment depend on broader economic trends that can vary greatly over time and across countries, significant fluctuations are likely to occur in how well youth are integrated into the labor market in the future.

*Household poverty is strongly associated with child labor; trends in poverty are an important explanation for trends in child labor.* While most young people live in parts of the world in which poverty rates are falling, a rising proportion of young people in sub-Saharan Africa are growing up in poor households. And it is in sub-Saharan Africa where there is evidence that rates of child labor are growing. These trends in sub-Saharan Africa widen the gulf between young Africans and their peers in other parts of the developing world, raising further concerns about Africa's future prospects.

*A rising proportion of young women are entering the labor market, particularly in paid employment, but rates of participation among young women still vary widely across the developing world.* Thus, for more and more women, adult work roles will include paid employment in the labor market. For an increasing number of young women who have the opportunity to earn money in the labor market before marriage, paid work is likely to mean that they can have greater control in meeting their own needs as well as contributing to family income and, through these changes, they may have greater say in decision-making in the family.

*More educated young workers have higher earnings, greater job stability, and greater upward mobility over time compared with their less educated peers.* These patterns, however, coexist with strong labor market trends toward deregulation and privatization that may have made labor markets more unstable relative to the past.

## Policy Recommendations

Policies and programs with implications for young people's successful transitions to work in developing countries exist at all levels of action: international, national (both developed and developing country policies), and local. Policies that enhance successful transitions to work include those that attack the root causes of poverty, enhance economic growth, improve learning outcomes in school and on the job, ensure equity of opportunity and pay regardless of race, gender, or class, and prevent harmful and unfair practices. Relatively few of these have been evaluated for their effectiveness. However, basic labor force trends direct attention to various fruitful avenues for intervention.

*The panel supports the United Nations (UN) Millennium Development Goals relating to the reduction of extreme poverty and the fostering of a global partnership for development.* The achievement of these goals will foster a climate in which a higher percentage of youth will be able to attend school into late adolescence, thus avoiding premature work responsibilities and ensuring a more successful transition to adult work roles.

*Antipoverty programs providing financial assistance to poor families that keep their children in school have been successful in reducing child labor by increasing enrollment.* Their cost-effectiveness depends primarily on careful targeting of benefits. The success of these programs in the longer run will need to be judged by whether improvements in education stimulated by these programs lead to declines in poverty in the next generation so that the conditions that fostered child labor are alleviated.

*Tax, trade, and aid policies in developed countries need to be coordinated so that tax and trade policies do not take away with one hand what is given with the other hand in the form of development assistance.* Otherwise, rather than providing value added in addressing issues of poverty and productivity, development assistance can do no more than mitigate the harmful effects of agricultural subsidies and restrictive trade policies on developing country economies and, by extension, on decent and productive job opportunities for youth.

*Labor market regulations that are commonly enacted in developing countries for the purpose of improving the terms and conditions of employment put youth at a disadvantage in competing for jobs in the formal labor market and encourage the growth of the informal sector.* Youth are likely to fare better in a labor market in which employers do not face excessive constraints governing employment contracts.

*Trade sanctions against products produced with child labor or against countries known to violate international labor standards relating to child labor are likely to do more harm than good in contexts in which poverty is persistent and the family economy still relies on child labor.* In the presence of such sanctions, children who need to work have often been forced to find more hazardous work in the unprotected sectors of the economy, with risks to their health and safety.

*Government incentives for firms to invest in training, for training providers to provide high quality and relevant training, and for workers to invest in training have been identified as promising alternatives to the direct government provision of training.* Evidence suggests that government-sponsored vocational education and training are often relatively expensive and inefficient at matching training curricula and training opportunities with job demands.

## Research Recommendations

Important research questions remain unanswered:

- Is globalization changing the types of jobs that child laborers do and the extent of such work?
- How prevalent are the "unconditionally worst forms of child labor," including trafficking, forced or bonded labor, armed conflict, prostitution, pornography, and illegal activities? How is their prevalence changing?
- What are the long-run consequences of child labor for children's health, education, and well-being?
- How does combining school attendance with work affect learning outcomes among adolescents attending secondary school?
- What are the trends in time spent working by age, including domestic work and economic activity? Is the distribution of work by gender being spread more evenly than in the past?
- How will opportunities for young women to work before marriage affect their timing of marriage, their marital relationship, their agency in marriage, and their probability of working after marriage?
- With the delay in labor force entry, young people are more mature and more educated when they start to work. As labor force choices become more their own and less those of their parents, what implications will this have for the types of choices they make?
- Why do better educated women in different settings make such different choices with respect to labor market participation? How are these choices changing?
- Has the growing tendency toward deregulation and privatization in many labor markets contributed in a positive or negative way to the effective absorption of growing cohorts of young people into the labor force?
- Do young women, the poor, ethnic minorities, and other disadvantaged groups face more or less discrimination in the labor market than in the past?

- How can labor market policies encourage employers to invest in on-the-job training for young workers?
- How do national educational and labor market policies in developed countries affect international labor migration among youth?
- How do labor market regulations affect the migration of youth to urban areas?
- How are rates of unemployment and underemployment changing among youth? Do these trends differ by educational attainment?

# 6

# The Transition to Citizenship

## INTRODUCTION

The transition to adulthood includes the acquisition of civic rights and responsibilities by young people and the possibility for heightened social, civic, and political participation. Opportunities for participation are important for both an individual's development and socialization as well as for larger social and political goals such as maintaining social contracts, nation building, fostering political and economic stability, and ensuring the sustainability and strength of democracy (Erikson, 1968; Putnam, 2000; Youniss et al., 2002).

During this phase of the life cycle, young people assume legal rights and responsibilities in relation to the state and forge identities and relationships with society and groups outside their immediate families. As young people explore and assume active roles in their societies, they develop a sense of belonging and hone decision-making skills that are important for psychosocial development (Erikson, 1968). These relationships and experiences facilitate the growth of social capital, as young people build social networks and gain access to the resources and opportunities that these connections regulate (Portes, 1998). Many of the behaviors and attitudes that individuals adopt as young people predict lifelong civic affiliations and perspectives (Flanagan et al., 1999; Youniss, McLellan, and Yates, 1997).

Many of the attributes of successful transitions as defined by the panel— including the acquisition of an appropriate stock of social capital, the acquisition of prosocial values and the ability to contribute to the collective well-being, and the capability to make choices through the acquisition of a

346

sense of self and a sense of personal competence—are all part of effective citizenship in its best sense. Furthermore, the rights and opportunities that young people are granted and the agency they develop as part of the transition to adult citizenship are often closely linked to the outcomes of other important transitions to adulthood, including health, schooling, work, and the acquisition of adult roles in the family, as well as the range of social spaces they are ultimately able to inhabit.

In this chapter, we examine the practice of citizenship among young people as well as the institutions, policies, and programs that can foster effective citizenship in the developing world. We define citizenship broadly to encompass not only legal rights and obligations in formal political processes but also engagement with diverse social, cultural, and economic institutions and integration and full participation in families and communities. The nature of citizenship can range widely: at the most constructive end of the spectrum, it is characterized by the guarantee of voice, the development of agency, and the ability to exercise leadership in governing social and political structures; at the other end, it may be characterized by exclusion and repression. Individuals who experience successful transitions to adult citizenship feel invested and engaged; those who don't often feel isolated and powerless. Individuals excluded from full citizenship may express apathy toward civic involvement, while others may turn to violence in a struggle, either to disrupt the system that denies them full rights and status or to create alternative social orders in which they find belonging and opportunities for participation.

Given the enormous political changes that have occurred in many countries in the developing world over the past few decades, we pay particular attention to the ways in which citizenship and community participation may be changing, especially as the "communities" with which young people can engage expand and evolve. Globalization provides them with new opportunities to participate as world citizens. Citizenship is not defined solely by national boundaries or relationships to state governments, but increasingly by interaction with global and local institutions. Young people growing up throughout the world, and especially in developing countries, must be able to negotiate a world with immense political and economic inequities and with societies torn by ethnic or religious conflict. International conventions and agreements have enshrined a set of human rights, state responsibilities, and principles for democratic governance. The young people of today and the leaders of tomorrow will be responsible for promoting, realizing, and enforcing these ideals. As the world is interconnected in ways never before, adults in the twenty-first century need to be prepared to act as global and local citizens who can effectively communicate and cooperate on such issues as the economy, the environment, and security.

Although there is a growing body of literature on young people and citizenship in the United States and other developed countries (Flanagan et al., 1999; Putnam, 2000; Torney-Purta et al., 2001; Yates and Youniss, 1999), research dedicated to this subject in most developing countries is only just emerging. The dramatically different histories, sociopolitical arrangements, and cultural conceptions of citizenship and participation of nations in Africa, Latin America, Asia, and the Middle East preclude easy comparisons with the United States and Europe and, similarly, with each other. However, when adequate data from developing countries are not available, we use data from the United States and Europe to illustrate important themes related to the transition to adult citizenship and to highlight potential areas for future research.

This dearth of data from developing countries—including ethnographic studies and large-scale statistical analyses—poses a considerable challenge. The entrance of young people into civic and political participation and the factors that affect their attitudes and behavior have not been a subject of much analysis in the development literature until very recently, despite the belief that young people are often the leaders of change and those most willing to critique their government or challenge existing norms (Braungart and Braungart, 1993; Erikson, 1968). Correspondingly, literature on young people has emphasized traditional development imperatives, such as education and health, with only peripheral treatment of the emerging roles of young people as community participants and decision-makers. For example, none of the indicators in the United Nations Children's Fund's (UNICEF's) State of the World's Children Report, the United Nations Development Programme's Human Development Indicators, or the World Bank's World Development Indicators looks at youth civic engagement.[1] While many nongovernmental organizations (NGOs) and programs have been addressing citizenship themes for some time, there is little rigorous documentation or evaluation of these efforts.

In this chapter, we bring together the limited knowledge that is available to examine when and how individuals become citizens at the global, national, and local levels. We begin by reviewing changing notions of citizenship in the globalizing world. We then examine when and how individuals receive formal recognition and rights at these multiple levels. The next section examines the practice of citizenship by young people—primarily in Latin America and Asia, where cross-national data on young people are available—including political and civic participation and the modes of so-

---

[1]However, the 2003 UNICEF State of the World's Children report focuses on child participation. Although no measures of child participation have been permanently incorporated into this report, this edition highlights the important role of civic engagement in the successful development of young people around the globe.

cial connectedness. We then address the formation of citizenship by young people, with specific attention to how the transition to adult citizenship relates to other important transitions. Finally, we summarize key findings and make recommendations for policy and research.

## CITIZENSHIP: AN EVOLVING CONCEPT?

Historically, concepts of citizenship have been rooted in Western liberal thought regarding the relationship between individuals and the nation-state. Thus, in its narrowest historical meaning, citizenship refers to membership in the nation-state and the formal rights and obligations this membership entails (Shapiro, 2000). Civic participation has been associated with practices that support democratic governance, such as voting, staying engaged with or taking leadership positions in political parties or the government, and staying informed about political affairs. Correspondingly, civic education has generally referred to developing citizens who are well informed, patriotic, and moral and who have an understanding of political processes, systems of government, and citizens' rights and responsibilities (Morris and Cogan, 2001; Torney-Purta et al., 2001).

The pivotal work of T. H. Marshall extended the concern with civil and political rights to social and economic rights (1950). His approach recognizes that the social relationships between individuals and the state and those between individual citizens shape access to the resources and opportunities necessary for people to fully participate as citizens (Ellison, 1997; Lister, 1997; Turner, 1999). Another strand of citizenship theory expands the discussion further by focusing on the attitudes and shared values that form the cultural underpinnings of citizenship (Almond and Verba, 1963). However, the formalized rights and responsibilities outlined by the nation-state are never perfectly achieved by all eligible citizens; it is the set of social practices that connect the individual to the state that give citizenship meaning. The balance and tension between institutionalized rights and responsibilities and the strength of civic culture highlight the ambiguity and dynamism of citizenship in modern society (Mische, 1996).

Definitions of citizenship developed in liberal Western democracies cannot simply be transferred to other parts of the world. In particular, the meaning of citizenship and ideas of belonging and identity are often more complex, but no less meaningful, in postcolonial societies. At independence, many new nations have found themselves struggling to create a cohesive identity out of the diverse ethnic, language, and religious groupings that had been brought together by colonialism (Abah and Okwori, 2002; Anderson, 1983; Gaventa, 2002). Rather than coming together under a single nationalism, these alternate sites of identity serve as the foundation for political and economic power in many countries in sub-Saharan

Africa. These relationships of ethnic, religious, and language identities mediate both access to rights and resources and the way that individuals relate to the nation-state (Mamdani, 1996). In these constructed nation-states that encompass populations with multiple identities and loyalties, young people from minority communities face particular challenges as they seek access to opportunities that are regulated by a dominant group, such as enrollment at public universities and employment in the civil service (Adebanwi, 2002; Fokwang, 2003).

In many developing countries, an individual's roles and privileges in society may be influenced by their status in kinship, ethnic, and age hierarchies. Typically, these relationships have deeper roots and greater weight than connections to the modern state (Joseph, 1997). The lack of political institutions that link the citizen to the state as well as cultural considerations are important factors to consider when evaluating levels and types of participation (Bratton, 1999). Furthermore, postindependence nation-building has closely linked citizenship with economic growth and opportunities (Khilnani, 1997). As many of the economies and governments in developing countries find themselves unable to deliver on their promises, poverty may contribute to a sense of disenfranchisement or political unrest.

A resurgence of interest in citizenship occurred in the late 1980s and 1990s, following the end of the Cold War, the rise of market-led economic policies, and the democratization of many countries in Asia, Africa, Latin America, and the former Soviet Union (Acharya, 1999; Youniss et al., 2002). In many places, these effects of globalization have changed the sociocultural landscape of the nation-state (Appadurai, 1996; Featherstone, Lash, and Robertson, 1995). These changes have meant that civic learning could not simply be passed down from generation to generation, but that all citizens were novices (Flanagan et al., 1999; Marr and Rosen, 1998).

Several forces, such as the pervasiveness of market-led economic change, the revolution in information and communication technology, and transnational flows of people, have made a rethinking of citizenship imperative. The types of skills needed to become effective participants in a global society are changing rapidly, and people's movements across borders result in transnational identities and obligations. The idea of citizenship itself is in great flux as the ingredients for meaningful participation in society evolve. For example, access to media and information technology has become an essential way for staying engaged in society. Furthermore, greater mobility and better communication technology allow religious, ethnic, or ideological groups to organize across national borders in order to fight for rights and hold states accountable for their actions (Castells, 2000; Keck and Sikkink, 1998).

The acceleration of the *pace* of change, another contemporary feature of globalization, has created additional challenges for the formation of citizens. For example, urbanization and industrialization can often be disruptive to existing social and cultural systems, making it more difficult for young people to integrate into cohesive community networks, and making it more likely that they resort to violence in order to establish their membership and status (Heitmeyer, 2002). Furthermore, the rapidly growing populations of young people present challenges to governments to provide adequate education, employment, and health services (Brockerhoff, 2000). The challenges of participating in a highly competitive market economy have also made traditional livelihoods less sustainable, with many communities and young people getting left behind (Richards, 1996). All of these changes can contribute to the alienation of young people and the potential for harmful activities.

Globalization has been associated with rising awareness of deep economic and political inequalities. The disparity between universalistic concepts of citizenship, which guarantee rights for all, and the actual reality, in which poverty, gender, race, and ethnicity inhibit individuals from full participation, has spurred renewed theorization about this subject. "Inclusive" citizenship refers to a situation in which no one is disenfranchised or unable to participate fully in civic or political affairs. Kabeer (2002) outlines what she thinks are the most critical barriers to inclusive citizenship: ethnic and religious divides in postcolonial societies, such social inequities as gender and poverty, and issues of culture and identity. Inclusive citizenship encompasses a broad set of meanings, central to which are ideas of participation and agency (Lister, 1997). These definitions are not confined solely to interactions with the state but extend to individuals' engagement with all of civil society.

Feminist critiques of citizenship theory bring attention not only to the degree to which women may not be able to participate in formal political life but also to the domestic sphere of life as a crucial terrain in which citizenship is exercised on a daily basis (Dietz, 1998; Pateman, 1988; Phillips, 1998). Even in societies in which the domain of women is separate from that of men, women may still exercise power and influence when they are able to create a public world of their own (Rosaldo, 1974). For young women making the transition to adulthood, the existence of safe social spaces in which girls can interact with their female peers serves as a critical site for the development of self-esteem and identity, building the foundations for future community engagement.

The recognition of citizenship as an expression of agency expands the understanding of the subtleties that influence participation. In this context, agency is more than the capacity to make choices and act on those decisions; it involves a conscious capacity to act (Lister, 1997). This conscious sense of agency operates at both the personal and the political levels and is crucial for the full realization of one's capabilities. Self-esteem and a sense that one is worthy of participation in political life mediate decision-making and one's ability to utilize the resources of human and social capital. Together these build a sense of political competence that is a necessary condition of active citizenship (Kabeer, 2000; Lister, 1997).

Modern conceptions of citizenship are interconnected with development and human rights approaches. These approaches insist that individuals be active participants in development projects, and that they be engaged in the decisions and processes that affect their lives (Holland, Blackburn, and Chambers, 1998). The participation-in-development approach arose from efforts to foster decision-making by the poor, promote a good governance agenda for governments, and advocate a rights-based approach to development (Gaventa, 2002). Combating the formal and informal forces of social exclusion, particularly as it extends to forms of economic inequality, has become a key theme in recent development policy (United Nations Development Programme, 2002). Active citizenship is also an integral component of human rights discourse, which has become increasingly influential as a framework for pursuing development goals in a sustainable and just manner (Sen, 1999). Despite this new thinking, however, most indicators of citizenship—reflected in the literature cited in this chapter—continue to be oriented toward the measurement of conventional forms of political party participation and voting for candidates to public office.

In the current global era, citizenship must be understood to encompass multiple meanings, from membership and participation in the nation-state to various other social and political interests, activities, and memberships, ranging from the household to the local community to the global arena. Furthermore, citizenship must be understood to encompass not only the rights and responsibilities of membership but also the acquisition of the capabilities to exercise those rights and responsibilities. In the discussion we give special attention to the transition to full citizenship and civic participation, a process that, if it occurs at all, typically occurs during adolescence. Given the panel's criteria for successful transitions, the definition of a successful transition to adult citizenship must include the capability to make choices through the acquisition of a sense of self and a sense of personal competence, as well as the acquisition of prosocial values and the ability to contribute to the collective well-being as citizen and community participant.

## FORMAL AND LEGAL RIGHTS OF CITIZENSHIP

The ages at which individuals are granted rights by the state or held accountable for their actions indicates social recognition of accountability and the responsibilities often associated with the onset of adulthood. Most of the formal norms granting rights and recognizing individuals occur at the national level. However, global platforms and local communities have become critical sites in promoting young peoples' rights, social spaces, and status.

## Youth Citizenship Rights at the Global Level

Since the inception of the United Nations (UN), important conventions (which carry the force of international law among signatory countries) and agreements (derived from international meetings and conferences and thus less binding upon signatory countries) have sought to establish rights and create beneficial conditions for people, including children and young people. Notable among these global commitments are:

- the Universal Declaration of Human Rights (San Francisco, 1948),
- the International Covenant on Economic, Social, and Cultural Rights (New York, 1966),
- the International Covenant on Civil and Political Rights (New York, 1966),
- the World Summit for Children (New York, 1990),
- the United Nations Conference on the Environment and Development (Rio, 1992),
- the World Conference on Human Rights (Vienna, 1993),
- the International Conference on Population and Development (Cairo, 1994),
- the World Summit for Social Development (Copenhagen, 1995),
- the Fourth World Conference on Women (Beijing, 1995),
- the Second United Nations Conference on Human Settlements (Istanbul, 1996), and
- the World Food Summit (Rome, 1996).

International agreements and conventions have broadened interpretations of citizenship and rights, spawned social action and political activity, and provided a political forum beyond the nation. The approaches promoted in these documents have been adopted by such implementing agencies as UNICEF and the United Nations Development Programme as well as many international and national NGOs.

Few agreements and conventions specify an age at which individuals are guaranteed rights. The Convention on the Rights of the Child defines children as those under age 18, but it includes limited language that differentiates adolescents from younger children. Ratified by all countries except Somalia and the United States, it outlines such child rights as freedom to express views in all matters affecting the child, freedom of thought and religion, freedom of association, access to national and international media, and entitlements to education, health care, a safe living environment, and nationality (United Nations, 1989). Articles and conventions providing protections for young workers (discussed in Chapter 5) and juvenile offenders also specify minimum ages.

Nevertheless, attention by international agencies and national governments to young people as a population with particular attributes and needs emerged with great force in the mid-1980s, with the enactment of the International Youth Year in 1985, followed by special sessions of the UN General Assembly in 1985 and 1995. These discussions culminated in the adoption of the UN World Program of Action for Youth in the Year 2000 and Beyond (PAY)—a document that builds on the various references to young people expressed in previous global forums, including the 1992 UN Convergence on Environment and Development, 1993 World Conference on Human Rights, 1994 International Conference on Population and Development (ICPD), 1995 World Summit for Social Development, and 1995 UN Fourth World Conference on Women. PAY commits governments to adopt a series of actions, beginning with the formulation of a national youth policy, progressing toward the translation of this policy into a youth program of action, and then implementing these activities. As in previous instances of other global agreements, the declarations of intent exceed by far actions taken by governments at the national level. Commitments made at the Children's World Summit in 1996 have been poorly followed. At present, 13 years after the ratification of the Convention on the Rights of the Child and almost 10 years after the Children's World Summit, very few countries in the world have developed action plans for children.

Girls and young women have received specific mention in several conventions, complementing the rights established for adult women in the Convention on the Elimination of All Forms of Discrimination Against Women, first adopted in 1979 and ratified by 177 countries as of March 2004.[2] Most attention in these conventions has been given to civil rights and the legal status of women as well as to their reproductive rights. The Program of Action of the World Social Summit for Social Development devotes particular attention to younger women because of the recognition that gender equality and equity and the full participation of women in all economic, social, and political activities are essential to attain social development (United Nations, 1989:Point 15.g). Similar objectives were further reiterated at the Fourth World Conference on Women in Beijing in 1995

---

[2]A list of countries that have ratified the convention is regularly updated and available at: http://www.un.org/womenwatch/daw/cedaw/states.htm.

(United Nations, 1996). Likewise, the International Conference on Population and Development (ICPD) Program of Action dedicates substantial attention to adolescents in Chapter VII, on "Reproductive Rights and Reproductive Health."[3] Global commitments by states are not always implemented, but some of them do have significant impacts. According to the UN Economic Commission for Latin America and the Caribbean (Durston, 1995), the 1990 World Summit for Children and the 27 specific goals it identified have served as a powerful stimulus for improvements in the health, nutrition, and education of children in Latin America.

In addition to establishing the rights of young people, international governmental and nongovernmental organizations have granted young people some opportunities to participate in international conventions, conferences, and dialogues. Each member country of the UN is invited to include a youth representative in their delegation to the General Assembly; however, as of 2003 only six countries had appointed such representatives.[4] Youth delegates have played a more active role at recent UN conferences, such as the World Summit for Social Development in 2002, at which the youth caucus led debates on energy and labor, and the five-year review meeting of the UN International Conference on Population and Development (ICPD+5), at which young participants formed the Youth Coalition, an international group of 15-29-year-olds committed to promoting adolescent and youth sexual and reproductive health rights and knowledge.

Other nongovernmental organizations have supported international organizations of young people, such as the Global Youth Action Network,[5] which mobilizes youth organizations for participation and collaboration on international issues, and Oxfam International, which organizes the International Youth Parliament.[6] However, many global youth activism groups acknowledge that announcements of forthcoming conferences and meetings are primarily posted on web sites and listservs, thereby restricting participation to those with access to the Internet (Lombardo, Zakus, and

---

[3]Only once does it refer explicitly to male adolescents, when they appear mentioned together with adolescent females concerning the need of governments to provide them with "information, education, and counseling to help them delay early family formation, premature sexual activity, and first pregnancy" (United Nations, 1994:Paragraph 8.24).

[4]At the 2003 session of the United Nations General Assembly, youth representatives were part of the delegations from Australia, Denmark, Finland, the Netherlands, Norway, and Sweden. The session in 2000 also included youth representatives from Bangladesh and India. A complete list is available at: http://www.un.org/esa/socdev/unyin/youthrep.htm.

[5]Information about the Global Youth Action Network can be found at: http://www.globalyouthactionnetwork.org.

[6]Information about the International Youth Parliament can be found at: http://www.iyp.oxfam.org.

Skinner, 2002). Furthermore, for almost all of these organizations, young people are chosen to participate after completing lengthy applications that describe their past commitments to youth activism and social justice; of the few young people who do participate in discussions at the international level, the voices heard are often those with the most resources and the best education.

### National Citizenship Rights: Young People and the State

An essential component of citizenship and political participation is an individual's relationship with the state. This relationship can include formal citizenship privileges, such as the right to vote and the ability to run for office; entail the laws governing military service or access to health care, education, and employment opportunities; involve the treatment of individuals in the criminal justice system; and define the treatment of foreign visitors, immigrants, and refugees. It is during the period of adolescence that individuals assume adult status in the eyes of the state. In this section we look at how different governments legally define the transition to adult citizenship by reviewing the age at which young people gain full rights and responsibilities.

Table 6-1 presents the legal ages at which young people are able to vote, leave school, begin work, join or be conscripted into the army, and be held responsible for their actions in the criminal justice system. (The legal age at marriage, a particularly important indicator of adulthood in the eyes of the state, is discussed in Chapter 7.) The table documents the variability in the minimum ages at which individuals are granted rights by the state within and across countries. In countries that have a minimum age for leaving school or starting work, the ages tend to fall in the mid-teens. The majority of countries listed in the table allows young people to exercise the right to vote at 18, although a small number of countries give citizens this right at slightly older or younger ages. In many countries there is no minimum age for school leaving, employment, or military recruitment, if there is parental consent. Although minimum age laws set national standards for the timing of various status transitions, these laws often differ vastly from actual practice.[7] When information is available, the table also notes when military service is open to females in addition to males.

Policies pertaining to education, work, and marriage are covered in other chapters, but policies on juvenile crime deserve closer attention here.

---

[7]Although not listed in Table 6-1, representation in government offices is another way to formally recognize social groups. However, comparative data on the minimum age at which individuals can hold public office and on whether there are government positions set aside for young people are not available.

As with other policy arenas, the legal frameworks concerning the treatment of young people in the criminal justice system vary widely by country; multiple systems may operate simultaneously, and practice may diverge from the actual law. Information on the age at which young people are tried as adults is listed in Table 6-1. Data on the actual incidence of juvenile crime would be useful to monitor patterns and trends; however, due to differences in legal categories, data collection, and reporting in each country, it is difficult to find comparable statistics.

Human rights organizations such as Amnesty International and Human Rights Watch have documented the abuse and age-insensitivity of many criminal justice systems. In many instances, children have little or no understanding of why they were arrested or what the charges against them mean. They are often held in adult jails and given limited access to lawyers. The incarceration of young people in adult facilities not only leaves them vulnerable to abuse, but also inhibits any potential rehabilitation or positive socialization. When these young people are released, they are often less equipped with the human and social capital necessary to succeed than when they were first arrested (Amnesty International, 2000, 2002, 2003; Human Rights Watch, 1994a, 1994b, 1996, 1997a, 1999a, 1999b). The Convention on the Rights of the Child, other international agreements,[8] and many child and youth advocacy agencies promote the use of separate court systems and detention facilities for young people.

Police brutality is especially rampant against poor young people, whose survival strategies are often criminalized (e.g., street children, sex workers). In Kenya, the three most common reasons for the detention of children were "destitution and vagrancy," being "beyond parental control," and "begging" (Human Rights Watch, 1997b). Although there is reason to believe that the vast majority of "infractions" are related to economically motivated, nonviolent crimes, in many countries there is a popular imagery that associates lower class children and adolescents with violent and organized crime (Adorno, 2002; UNICEF, 1998).

Many international organizations have also fought to raise the minimum age for military recruitment or participation in armed conflict to age

---

[8]Several international norms exist for the treatment of juveniles in the criminal justice system. These include the 1955 Standard Minimum Rules for the Treatment of Prisoners, the 1966 International Covenant on Civil and Political Rights, the Beijing Rules (United Nations Standard Minimum Rules for the Administration of Juvenile Justice, 1985), United Nations Rules for the Protection of Juveniles Deprived of their Liberty 1990, and the Riyadh guidelines (United Nations Guidelines for the Prevention of Juvenile Delinquency 1990) (UNICEF, 1998). The minimum guidelines set out in these provisions include separating young prisoners from adults in custodial facilities and prohibiting the death penalty for crimes committed when younger than age 18 (UNICEF, 1998). However these international norms have not been fully integrated into national legislation and enforcement.

## TABLE 6-1 Age of Majority for Various Activities

| Region and Country | Voting | Leaving School | Employment |
|---|---|---|---|
| South-central/South-eastern Asia | | | |
| Bangladesh | 18 | | 12 |
| Bhutan | varies | no min. | |
| Cambodia | 18 | no min. | 16 |
| East Timor | | | |
| Fiji | | no min. | 12 |
| India | 18 | 14 | 14 |
| Indonesia | 17 | | |
| Iran | 15 | 11 | 15 |
| Laos | 18 | 11 | 15 |
| Malaysia | 21 | | |
| Myanmar | | no min. | no min. |
| Nepal | 18 | | |
| Pakistan | | | |
| Philippines | 18 | | |
| Singapore | | | |
| Sri Lanka | 18 | | |
| Thailand | 18 | | 13 |
| Vietnam | 18 | | |
| | | | |
| Eastern Asia | | | |
| China | 18 | | |
| Korea, Democratic Peoples | 17 | 16 | |
| Korea, Republic | 20 | | |
| Mongolia | 18 | | |
| | | | |
| Middle East | | | |
| Algeria | 18 | 16 | 16 |
| Bahrain | | no min. | 14 |
| Egypt | 18 | 14 | 14 |
| Iraq | 18 | | |
| Jordan | 19 | 16 | 16 |
| Lebanon | 21 | 11 | 13 |
| Libya | 18 | 15 | 15 |
| Morocco | 20 | | |
| Oman | | no min. | 13 |
| Palestine | | | |
| Qatar | | no min. | |
| Saudi Arabia | | | 13 |
| Sudan | 17 | no min. | 16 |
| Syria | 18 | 12 | 12 |
| Tunisia | 20 | 16 | 16 |
| Turkey | 18 | 14 | no min. |
| United Arab Emirates | | 11 | 15 |
| Yemen | 18 | no min. | 16 |

| Voluntary Military Recruitment | Compulsory Military Recruitment Age | Criminal Responsibility | Women Allowed in Military[a] |
|---|---|---|---|
| 16 | b | 7 | Noncombat |
| 18 | b | | |
| 18 | b | no min. | |
| 18 | b | | |
| | | 10 | |
| 16 | b | 7 | Noncombat |
| 18 | 18 | 16 | |
| 16 | 18 | | |
| | | 15 | |
| 18 | b | | Noncombat |
| | 18 | 7 | Nurse corps |
| 18 | b | 10 | Medical corps |
| 18 | b | 7 | |
| 18 | 18 | 9 | Yes |
| 16.5 | 18 | | |
| 18 | b | 8 | Yes |
| 18 | 18 | 7 | Yes |
| | 18 | 14 | |
| | | | |
| no min. | 18 | 14 | |
| 16 | 17/18 | 14 | |
| 17/18 | 18/20 | 12 | |
| | 18 | 16 | |
| | | 13 | |
| 18 | b | no min. | |
| | 18 | 7 | Noncombat |
| 15 | 18 (<18 in war) | 9 | |
| 17 | b | 7 | Yes |
| 18 | 18 | 7 | No |
| 14/16 | 17-19 | 7 | |
| 18 | 18 | 12 | |
| | | 9 | Yes |
| 18 | | | |
| 18 | b | 7 | |
| | b | 10 | No |
| | 17 | 7 | |
| | 19 | 7 | Noncombat |
| 18 | 20 | 13 | Noncombat |
| 19 | 19 | 11 | Yes |
| | b | 7 | Yes |
| | 18 | 15 | No |

*Continued*

## TABLE 6-1 Continued

| Region and Country | Voting | Leaving School | Employment |
|---|---|---|---|
| Western/Middle Africa | | | |
| Angola | 18 | | |
| Benin | 18 | | 14 |
| Burkina Faso | 18 | no min. | no min. |
| Cameroon | 20 | no min. | 14 |
| Cape Verde | 18 | 16 | 14 |
| CAR | 18 | | 14 |
| Chad | 18 | 15 | no min. |
| Congo | | | |
| Côte d'Ivoire | 21 | no min. | no min. |
| DRC | | no min. | no min. |
| Gabon | 21 | 16 | 16 |
| Gambia | 18 | no min. | |
| Ghana | 18 | 15 | no min. |
| Guinea | 18 | 16 | |
| Guinea-Bissau | 18 | no min. | no min. |
| Liberia | 18 | | |
| Mali | 18 | | no min. |
| Mauritania | 18 | no min. | 14 |
| Niger | 18 | 16 | 14 |
| Nigeria | 18 | | |
| Senegal | 18 | | |
| Sierra Leone | 21 | 15 | no min. |
| Togo | 18 | 15 | 14 |
| South America | | | |
| Argentina | 18 | 15 | 14 |
| Bolivia | 18/21[e] | | |
| Brazil | 18 | | |
| Chile | 18 | 14 | 14 |
| Colombia | 18 | 15 | 14 |
| Ecuador | 18 | | 14 |
| Guyana | 18 | | |
| Paraguay | 18 | 12 | no min. |
| Peru | 18 | 18 | 12 |
| Suriname | 18 | no min. | 14 |
| Uruguay | 18 | | |
| Venezuela | 18 | 14 | 14 |

| Voluntary Military Recruitment | Compulsory Military Recruitment Age | Criminal Responsibility | Women Allowed in Military[a] |
|---|---|---|---|
| | 17 | | |
| 21 | 21 | 13 | |
| 20 | 18 | 13 | Yes |
| 18 | b | 10 | Yes |
| | | 16 | |
| 18 | 18 | 13 | |
| 18/any age[c] | 20/any age[c] | 13 | Yes |
| 18 | b | | |
| 18 | 18 | 10 | Yes |
| | | 16 | |
| 18 | b | 13 | |
| 18 | b | 7 | |
| 18 | 18 | 7 | Yes |
| | 18 | 18 | |
| | 18 | 16 | |
| 18 | b | | Yes |
| 18 | 18 | 13 | Noncombat |
| 18/16[c] | 17 | no min. | Yes |
| | 18 | 13 | |
| 18 | b | 7 | |
| 18 | 18 | 13 | No |
| consent or 18 | 18 | 10 | |
| 18 | 18 | no min. | |
| 18 | b | 16 | Yes |
| 14 | 18 | 16 | Yes |
| 17 | 19 | | Yes |
| 18/16? | 18 | 16 | Yes |
| 18 | 18 | 18 | Noncombat |
| | 18 | 18 | Yes |
| | b | | Yes |
| 18 | 18 | 14 | No |
| | b | 12 | Yes |
| | b | 10 | |
| 18 | 18 | 18 | Yes |
| 18 | 18 | 18 | Noncombat |

## TABLE 6-1 Continued

| Region and Country | Voting | Leaving School | Employment |
|---|---|---|---|
| Former Soviet Asia | | | |
| Azerbaijan | 18 | | |
| Belarus | 18 | | |
| Kazakhstan | 18 | | |
| Kyrgyzstan | | | 15 |
| Tajikistan | | | 14 |
| Turkmenistan | | | |
| Uzbekistan | | | 16 |
| Caribbean/Central America | | | |
| Bahamas | 18 | | |
| Barbados | | 16 | no min. |
| Belize | 18 | 14 | 12 |
| Costa Rica | 18 | no min. | 15 |
| Cuba | 16 | | 17 |
| Dominican Republic | 18 | 14 | 14 |
| El Salvador | 18 | | |
| Guatemala | 18 | | no min. |
| Haiti | 18 | | |
| Honduras | 18 | 13 | 14 |
| Jamaica | 18 | | |
| Mexico | 18 | 15 | no min. |
| Nicaragua | 16 | | 14 |
| Panama | 18 | | 14 |
| Trinidad & Tobago | | 12 | 12 |
| Eastern and Southern Africa | | | |
| Botswana | 18 | | |
| Burundi | 18 | 12 | 12 |
| Comoros | | 14 | no min. |
| Djibouti | 18 | | 13 |
| Eritrea | | | |
| Ethiopia | 18 | no min. | 14 |
| Kenya | 18 | no min. | no min. |
| Lesotho | 18 | | no min. |
| Madagascar | 18 | | |
| Malawi | 18 | no min. | no min. |
| Mauritius | 18 | | |
| Mozambique | 18 | no min. | |
| Namibia | 18 | | |
| Rwanda | | | |

| Voluntary Military Recruitment | Compulsory Military Recruitment Age | Criminal Responsibility | Women Allowed in Military[a] |
|---|---|---|---|
| 18 | 18 | 14 | |
| | 18 | 16 | |
| | 18 | | |
| | 18 | 14 | |
| | 18 | | |
| 18 | 18 | | |
| | 18 | 13 | Yes |
| | b | | |
| 18[c] | b | 7 | |
| 18 | b | 7 | |
| 18 | 18 | 18 | |
| | 16/17 | 16 | |
| 18 | b | 12 | |
| 16 | 18 | 16 | Noncombat |
| 18 | 18 | 12 | Yes |
| 18 | b | | |
| 18 | b | 12 | Yes |
| 18 | b | 12 | |
| 16[c] | 18 | no min. | |
| 17 | b | 13 | Yes |
| 18 | b | 18 | |
| 18 | b | 7 | Yes |
| 18 | b | | Admin. only |
| 16 | 16 | 13 | |
| | | 13 | |
| | b | 13 | |
| 18 | 18 | | |
| 18 | 18 | 9 | Noncombat |
| 18 | b | 8 | Yes |
| | b | 7 | |
| | | 13 | |
| 18 | b | 7 | Noncombat |
| 18 | b | 14 | |
| | 18 | 16 | Yes |
| 18 | | 7 | |
| 16 | b | 14 | |

*Continued*

TABLE 6-1 Continued

| Region and Country | Voting | Leaving School | Employment |
|---|---|---|---|
| South Africa | 18 | 15 | no min. |
| Swaziland | 18 | | |
| Tanzania | 18 | 13 | no min. |
| Uganda | 18 | | no min. |
| Zambia | 18 | | |
| Zimbabwe | 18 | | |

*a*This category is based upon the best available information. These countries that allow women in the military may restrict their participation to certain divisions.
*b*No compulsory conscription.
*c*With consent of parents.
*d*Graduates of secondary school.
*e*18 for married, 21 for single.

18. In 2002, the UN Optional Protocol to the Convention on the Rights of the Child on the involvement of children in armed conflict, entered into force.[9] This agreement raised, from 15 to 18, the minimum age for direct participation in hostilities, compulsory military recruitment, and any recruitment by nongovernmental armed groups.[10] Table 6-1 shows that while most countries with compulsory military recruitment limit conscription to those ages 18 and older, many countries do not place the same restrictions on those who enlist voluntarily. However, most compulsory recruitment laws apply only to men; most countries prohibit women from enlisting in the military or else restrict them to noncombat units (Table 6-1).

Significant gender differences also remain in social protections and legal access to resources in many countries.[11] Table 6-2 shows whether

---

[9]The status of ratifications of the Optional Protocol to the Convention on the Rights of the Child on the involvement of children in armed conflict is regularly updated at: http://www.unhchr.ch/pdf/report.pdf.

[10]The Africa Charter on the Rights and Welfare of the Child, ratified in November 1999, also prohibits the recruitment or direct participation of young people under the age of 18 in armed conflicts. Furthermore, the International Labour Organization's Convention 182 includes "forced or compulsory recruitment of children for use in armed conflict" among the worst forms of child labor (Article 3).

[11]The Center for Reproductive Law and Policy analyzes national legislation around the world to investigate the legal norms and protections regarding women's rights in different countries (1997a,b, 1999, 2001). Their Women of the World series provides one of the comprehensive sources of information about gender equity in national legislation not only in terms of reproductive and sexual rights, but also in property and inheritance laws.

| Voluntary Military Recruitment | Compulsory Military Recruitment Age | Criminal Responsibility | Women Allowed in Military[a] |
|---|---|---|---|
| 18 | b | 7 | |
| 18 | b | | |
| 15 | 18[d] | | |
| 18 | b | 7 | Yes |
| 18, <18[c] | | | Yes |
| 18 | b | 7 | Yes |

NOTES: No min. = no minimum. Most of the above sources relied on country reports submitted to the United Nations in compliance with the Convention on the Rights of the Child to monitor changes in national legislation regarding minimum age restrictions. Different sources and often the legislation itself contain contradictions regarding minimum age laws, and every attempt has been made to include the most recent and reliable information. SOURCES: Coalition to Stop the Use of Child Soldiers (2001); Melchiorre (2002); UNICEF International Child Development Centre (1998); Marshall (2000).

men and women have equal inheritance, property, and divorce rights. Although these rights typically apply to adults, they shape young people's expectations with respect to opportunities for livelihoods and marriage prospects, affect rates of return to schooling and other forms of training, and perpetuate a traditional division of labor by gender.

Independent country case studies corroborate that there are significant and pervasive gender differences in the ability to inherit, own, or acquire property, an important asset that is critical not only for economic prosperity and security but also for social status, agency, and equal domestic power relations (Agarwal, 1994). Women's access to land and other natural resources, such as water and forests, is limited not only by formal laws, but also by cultural norms (Meinzen-Dick et al., 1997). This is an important area for research and intervention as women's ability to own property is linked to their empowerment, the health and wealth of the household, efficiency of resource use, and equity of resource allocation (Agarwal, 1994; Meinzen-Dick et al., 1997; Quisumbing and Otsuka, 2001). While deep gender inequities in property rights continue to exist in many societies, other countries have begun to reform their laws, especially at the national level. However, these regulations may vary within countries according to customary or religious law, or by national and regional dictates, creating multiple legal frameworks (Meinzen-Dick and Pradhan, 2001).

TABLE 6-2 Access of Women to Equal Inheritance, Property, and
Divorce Rights

| Region and Country | Equal Inheritance Rights | Equal Property Rights | Equal Divorce Rights |
|---|---|---|---|
| **South-central/South-eastern Asia** | | | |
| Bangladesh | no | no | n.a. |
| Bhutan | yes | n.a. | yes |
| Cambodia | n.a. | yes | yes |
| Fiji | yes | yes | n.a. |
| India | no | no | no |
| Indonesia | no | yes | no |
| Laos | n.a. | yes | n.a. |
| Malaysia | no | no | no |
| Myanmar | yes | yes | yes |
| Nepal | no | no | no |
| Pakistan | n.a. | n.a. | no |
| Philippines | no | no | no |
| Singapore | n.a. | n.a. | no |
| Sri Lanka | yes | yes | no |
| Thailand | no | n.a. | no |
| Vietnam | yes | n.a. | yes |
| **Eastern Asia** | | | |
| China | yes | yes | yes |
| Korea, Republic | yes | yes | no |
| Mongolia | n.a. | yes | yes |
| **Middle East** | | | |
| Algeria | no | n.a. | n.a. |
| Egypt | no | n.a. | no |
| Iraq | no | yes | no |
| Jordan | no | no | no |
| Lebanon | no | no | no |
| Libya | no | n.a. | no |
| Morocco | no | n.a. | no |
| Tunisia | no | no | no |
| Turkey | no | no | no |
| Yemen | n.a. | n.a. | no |
| **Western/Middle Africa** | | | |
| Angola | yes | yes | yes |
| Benin | no[a] | no[a] | n.a. |
| Burkina Faso | no | yes | no |
| Cameroon | no | no | no |
| Cape Verde | yes | n.a. | yes |
| CAR | yes | yes | yes |
| Chad | yes | yes | n.a. |

## TABLE 6-2 Continued

| Region and Country | Equal Inheritance Rights | Equal Property Rights | Equal Divorce Rights |
|---|---|---|---|
| Congo | no | no | no |
| DRC | no | no | no |
| Gabon | no | no | no |
| Gambia | no | n.a. | no |
| Ghana | no | no | no |
| Guinea | no | no | no |
| Guinea-Bissau | no | no | no |
| Mali | no | no | no |
| Niger | no | no | no |
| Nigeria | no | no | no |
| Senegal | no | no | yes |
| Sierra Leone | no | no | n.a. |
| Togo | no | no | no |
| **South America** | | | |
| Argentina | yes | yes | yes |
| Bolivia | no*a* | no*a* | yes |
| Brazil | yes | yes | yes |
| Chile | yes | no | n.a. |
| Colombia | yes | yes | yes |
| Ecuador | n.a. | yes | yes |
| Guyana | no | n.a. | no |
| Paraguay | yes | n.a. | yes |
| Peru | yes | yes | yes |
| Uruguay | yes | n.a. | yes |
| Venezuela | n.a. | n.a. | no |
| **Former Soviet Asia** | | | |
| Azerbaijan | n.a. | yes | n.a. |
| Belarus | yes | yes | no |
| Kazakhstan | yes | yes | n.a. |
| Kyrgyzstan | yes | yes | yes |
| Tajikistan | yes | n.a. | yes |
| Turkmenistan | yes | yes | n.a. |
| **Caribbean/Central America** | | | |
| Barbados | n.a. | n.a. | yes |
| Costa Rica | n.a. | yes | yes |
| Cuba | yes | yes | yes |
| Dominican Republic | yes | yes | no |
| El Salvador | yes | n.a. | no |
| Guatemala | yes | yes | yes |
| Haiti | n.a. | n.a. | no |
| Honduras | n.a. | yes | yes |
| Jamaica | no | yes | no |

*Continued*

TABLE 6-2 Continued

| Region and Country | Equal Inheritance Rights | Equal Property Rights | Equal Divorce Rights |
|---|---|---|---|
| Mexico | n.a. | yes | yes |
| Nicaragua | n.a. | n.a. | yes |
| Panama | yes | yes | yes |
| Trinidad & Tobago | n.a. | n.a. | no |
| Southern/Eastern Africa | | | |
| Botswana | n.a. | no | no |
| Burundi | no | no | n.a. |
| Comoros | n.a. | yes | no |
| Eritrea | n.a. | no | n.a. |
| Ethiopia | yes | yes | no |
| Kenya | no | no | no |
| Lesotho | no | no | no |
| Madagascar | no | no | n.a. |
| Malawi | n.a. | yes | yes |
| Mauritius | n.a. | yes | no |
| Mozambique | no | no | n.a. |
| Namibia | yes | yes | yes |
| Rwanda | n.a. | n.a. | yes |
| South Africa | no | no | no |
| Tanzania | no | no | no |
| Uganda | no | no | no |
| Zambia | no | no | no |
| Zimbabwe | no | no | yes |

aProperty and inheritance rights are equal in the civil code, but according to customary law and in practice, women are restricted from inheriting or holding property.
NOTE: n.a. = not available.
SOURCES: International Planned Parenthood Federation and International Women's Rights Action Watch (IWRAW) (2000); Center for Reproductive Rights (1997a, 1997b); and Center for Reproductive Rights (1999).

## THE PRACTICE OF CITIZENSHIP

We now move from the formal legal relationship between young people and the state to examine the ways in which they participate in social and political arenas. Specifically, we look at youth participation in and attitudes toward formal politics and activism. The data on youth civic participation, attitudes, and perceptions are scant. Large-scale surveys that either address young people specifically or disaggregate by age tend to focus on health and economic indicators, with little or no attention to political or civic participation. The panel was unable to identify any cross-national set of public opinion polls or surveys of civic and political participation that spanned the entire transition to adulthood. Commonly cited data sets, such as the World Values Survey (WVS)[12] and the Barometer surveys in Latin America and Africa, include only respondents ages 18 and older, while surveys that target young people—such as the UNICEF Young Voices Surveys in Latin America, the Western Pacific, Europe, and Central Asia and the civic education and knowledge surveys conducted by the International Association for the Evaluation of Educational Achievement (IEA)—are restricted to those ages 17 and younger. In particular, it is important to note the scarcity of cross-national quantitative data on the practice of citizenship among young people in sub-Saharan Africa and the Middle East. Whenever possible, these shortcomings are supplemented by ethnographic data that highlights the diversity of the practice of citizenship in these regions. For further discussion of the data, see Appendix A.

Not only are there few cross-national, representative surveys of public opinion and political behavior conducted among young people in developing countries, but the content of these surveys also has several limitations. First, these surveys are grounded in the measurements of citizenship and political participation derived from traditional Western understandings of the subject, in particular the relationship of the individual to the nation-state and of the individual to the community. However, as mentioned earlier, this is not an accurate representation of all forms of social organization. Joseph (1996) points out that many Middle Eastern nations recognize citizens as members of family units, religious sects, and ethnic, tribal or other subnational groups; citizenship, its rights, and its responsibilities are not constructed entirely in terms of the individual. It is important to collect data that are grounded in local social and political realities. Although this makes cross-national comparisons, such as the ones in this chapter, more difficult, the recognition of the diversity of political experiences and modes of expression enriches the understanding of youth citizenship formation.

Second, the surveys that we will rely on for our discussion have not fully encompassed in their questionnaire designs the diverse realizations of democracy that exist globally. Although democratic principles are broadly compatible with diverse religious and cultural traditions, there is growing divergence in the quality or depth of democracy in recently democratized nation-states (Diamond and Plattner, 2001). The levels of participation discussed here provide some insight into diverse patterns of engagement

---

[12]As this report was being prepared, data from the 2000 World Values Survey were not publicly available. Unless otherwise noted, the tables included in the text use data from the 1995-1996 WVS.

with the community and the nation-state, but they do not provide any information about what meanings young people themselves attach to these structures and relationships. At this stage, more in-depth qualitative studies are needed, in order to document the range of local possibilities for young people to engage with their communities.

Although data are scarce, it is important to consider the processes by which young people acquire political and civic values and begin to participate and assume adult responsibilities in the public sphere. When possible, the established literature and the above-mentioned data sets are used to illustrate current patterns of political and civic activism across the transition to adulthood. Furthermore, we draw on the qualitative research of political scientists, sociologists, and anthropologists in order to understand the heterogeneous ways in which young people engage with their communities.

## Participation in Formal Politics

*Knowledge and Interest in Politics*

Interest in politics is a well-tested variable included in most public opinion surveys to assess levels of engagement and concern about politics and current events. Dalton (1996) calls political interest "cognitive political mobilization" and found that it is one of the strongest predictors of voting in Western countries. The IEA studies showed that, in Australia, several European countries, Russia, and Hong Kong, men tended to express more interest in politics than women (Amadeo et al., 2002; Torney-Purta, Schwille, and Amadeo, 1999). This gender gap is closing in some countries, including Chile and Colombia, where the gender difference was not statistically significant.

In the World Values Surveys, more than half of all respondents ages 18-34 discuss politics with friends[13] (Table 6-3). Young men are more likely than young women to discuss politics in every country surveyed, although the size of the gender difference varies widely, from almost 24 percentage points in India to 3 in Georgia and 2 in the Dominican Republic. Young people in Asian countries are collectively the most likely to discuss politics, while young people in South America are least likely to do so. In almost all developing regions except Southeastern and Southwestern Asia, the younger cohort of 18-34-year-old men is less likely to discuss politics than the

---

[13]The sample size of young adults ages 18-24 in the World Values Surveys is too small to produce valid statistical results at the country level. Following the example of Tilley (2002), all our tables that use WVS data are based on 18-34-year-olds.

TABLE 6-3 Percentage Discussed Politics with Friends ("frequently" or "occasionally")

| Region and Country | Male (Ages) | | Female (Ages) | |
|---|---|---|---|---|
| | 18-34 | 35+ | 18-34 | 35+ |
| Caribbean/Central America | | | | |
| Mexico | 68.3 | 68.6 | 53.6 | 51.1 |
| Dominican Republic | 80.0 | 86.7 | 78.0 | 77.8 |
| Eastern/Southern Africa | | | | |
| Nigeria[a] | 76.8 | 76.6 | 56.5 | 56.0 |
| South America | | | | |
| Argentina | 65.5 | 76.0 | 53.9 | 55.7 |
| Brazil | 58.6 | 68.2 | 52.6 | 52.8 |
| Chile | 52.5 | 51.4 | 43.6 | 38.6 |
| Peru | 70.1 | 67.5 | 56.9 | 51.1 |
| Uruguay | 57.7 | 60.6 | 51.3 | 43.7 |
| Venezuela | 55.8 | 59.5 | 48.9 | 45.5 |
| SE/SW Asia | | | | |
| Bangladesh | 86.4 | 79.7 | 69.2 | 54.8 |
| China | 79.8 | 72.2 | 64.9 | 59.9 |
| India[b] | 77.2 | 71.2 | 52.8 | 37.6 |
| Pakistan | 72.4 | 66.9 | 46.0 | 41.5 |
| Philippines | 75.5 | 78.0 | 74.6 | 71.9 |
| Middle East | | | | |
| Turkey | 75.4 | 77.5 | 58.5 | 56.4 |
| Former Soviet Asia | | | | |
| Armenia | 78.8 | 84.0 | 68.5 | 72.2 |
| Azerbaijan | 60.1 | 60.7 | 45.1 | 41.6 |
| Georgia | 66.6 | 82.0 | 63.9 | 78.3 |
| Developed Countries | | | | |
| Germany | 94.4 | 93.2 | 85.0 | 85.7 |
| Japan | 47.6 | 69.7 | 32.2 | 56.3 |
| South Korea | 89.5 | 89.3 | 83.5 | 70.6 |
| Spain | 66.2 | 57.8 | 63.8 | 37.0 |
| USA | 71.6 | 79.9 | 62.1 | 68.8 |
| TOTAL | 70.7 | 71.8 | 61.0 | 57.4 |

[a]The sample in Nigeria is restricted to urban areas.
[b]The sample in India is restricted to those who are literate.
NOTE: All figures are percentages.
SOURCE: 1995-1998 World Values Surveys.

cohort of men older than 35, while more young women appear to discuss politics than older women among the developing countries participating in the survey. Inglehart and Norris (2003) suggest that, as the education and labor force participation of women increase, the gender gap in political interest should decrease. Using data from the 2000-2001 World Values Surveys[14] to analyze this hypothesis, they found that the gender gap in political interest and political discussion was smallest in postindustrial countries and largest in agrarian countries.

Using Barometer surveys that cover 41 countries from Western Europe, Eastern Europe, and Latin America, Lagos and Rose (1999) found that age was not an important variable when looking at interest in politics, having a positive attitude toward democracy, or rejecting undemocratic alternatives. Instead, they found that economic status and education were positively associated with these democratic values. The only category in which age was significant was voting, which the authors felt could be attributed to life-cycle differences. However, these overall conclusions hide some of the heterogeneity found in the results from South America and Central America. Respondents in Latin America showed a lower degree of interest in politics than respondents from the established democracies in Europe (34 compared with 46 percent). In this sample of countries, age had a more significant impact: the younger the respondent, the less likely he or she was to vote, express interest in politics, express satisfaction with democracy, or be proud of his or her country.

As Lagos and Rose (1999) concluded, these results highlight the complexity of political behavior and the difficulty inherent in reducing political participation to social differences in age, education, and economic conditions. In post-Communist Europe and Latin America, the explanatory variables (age, gender, education, material prosperity, and church attendance) did not capture much significant variance in political involvement. For the

---

[14]Inglehart and Norris (2003) used the values of the 1998 United Nations Development Programme Human Development Index to group the 2000-2001 World Values Surveys into the following categories:

• *Postindustrial*—Australia, Austria, Belgium, Canada, Denmark, Finland, France, Germany, Iceland, Ireland, Italy, Japan, Luxembourg, The Netherlands, New Zealand, Norway, Spain, Sweden, Switzerland, United Kingdom, United States;

• *Industrial*—Argentina, Belarus, Bosnia and Herzegovina, Brazil, Bulgaria, Chile, Colombia, Croatia, Czech Republic, Estonia, Georgia, Greece, Hungary, Republic of Korea, Latvia, Lithuania, Macedonia, Malta, Mexico, Philippines, Poland, Portugal, Romania, Russian Federation, Slovakia, Slovenia, Taiwan, Turkey, Ukraine, Uruguay, Venezuela, Yugoslavia; and

• *Agrarian*—Albania, Armenia, Azerbaijan, Bangladesh, China, Dominican Republic, Egypt, El Salvador, India, Iran, Jordan, Moldova, Morocco, Nigeria, Pakistan, Peru, South Africa, Tanzania, Uganda, Vietnam, Zimbabwe.

Latin American countries included in the Latino-Barometer surveys, the greatest differences in political interest and participation were those between countries.

In the IEA surveys conducted in Chile and Colombia,[15] 17-year-olds were significantly more likely than 14-year-olds to express an interest in politics. In Chile, 46 percent of 14-year-olds said they were interested in politics, whereas in Colombia, 63 percent of students agreed with that statement (Torney-Purta, Schwille, and Amadeo, 1999). It remains unclear what generates these national differences. However, in both countries younger respondents were more likely to express interest in future participation in such activities as writing letters to newspapers, joining a political party, or running for public office. Amadeo et al. (2002) hypothesized that older students, in particular those closer in age to direct and formal political participation, are more critical of the effectiveness of such activities. When differences in political intent were found, male students were more likely than female students to expect to participate in conventional political activities (Amadeo et al., 2002).

Very little empirical research has been conducted on students' level of civic knowledge in developing countries. The 14-year-old students in Chile and Colombia had the lowest mean scale scores of all 28 countries for "total civic knowledge." Chile scored 88 and Colombia scored 86 compared with an international mean of 100. There were no significant gender differences. In these two countries, 75 percent of students scored below the international average for content knowledge and interpretive skills. Despite this, they had higher than average scores for conventional citizenship, expected participation in political activities, and more positive attitudes toward immigrants (Amadeo et al., 2002; Torney-Purta, Schwille, and Amadeo, 1999).

Feminist critiques of studies of political participation often note that politics is traditionally defined as a masculine activity, whereas the issues that supposedly sway women, such as the environment and health issues, are not seen as political in nature, underestimating women's actual interest and engagement with politics (Bourque and Grossholtz, 1998). Furthermore, the gender differences shown in Table 6-3 and discussed by Inglehart and Norris (2003) may also reflect the relative political agency of women in some of these countries. If young women do not feel that they have a voice in formal political spheres, or if they are denied full representation in gov-

---

[15]The International Association for the Evaluation of Educational Achievement conducted surveys among students in 28 countries. Most of the countries were in North America and Europe; Chile, and Colombia were the only developing countries sampled, and subsequent discussion of the IEA surveys is restricted to these two countries.

erning bodies, they may not perceive their opinions to matter. Likewise, while some survey results may indicate that young people are less engaged with political issues and activities than older members of society, this may also reflect their different sphere of concerns. Groups that feel disengaged from broader political dialogues may invest their interest and attention in issues that seem to reflect self-interest or that are "close to home" (Eliasoph, 1997).

### Voting Behaviors

One of the most direct activities by which a citizen living in a democracy can participate in formal politics is by voting. In literature on the United States and Europe, young people tend to be less likely to register and vote than older adults. While one hypothesis is that young people are less interested in voting, others attribute the difference to the phase of the life cycle (Lagos and Rose, 1999) or to the alternate ways of engaging with politics practiced by young people (Buckingham, 2000). Furthermore, young people are more transient than older adults—they may be living far from their home address if they have gone away to study or to work, and they may be moving more frequently. Depending on a country's rules about voter registration, this mobility may make it difficult for them to register and vote in the appropriate district.

Because the timing of elections varies from country to country, it is difficult for comparative surveys to adequately capture recent voting behavior. For instance, the Barometer surveys gauge voting behavior by focusing on the ability of the respondent to name the party for which they would vote if an election were to be held on the next day. While examining the responses from Latin America, Lagos and Rose (1999) found that, although there are differences in the political involvement of young and older people, age alone does not predict the voting behavior.

Inglehart and Norris (2003) compared voting behaviors in each of the three development categories previously mentioned (see footnote 14) by age and sex. Although they found no evidence that the gender gap was smaller in the younger cohorts than in the older cohorts, younger respondents in the least developed countries were more likely to report voting than older respondents. They hypothesized that improvements in human capital, such as literacy, education, and exposure to the mass media, had benefited both men and women, so that even as younger women had better voting behavior than older women, the gender gap continued. Furthermore, many of the countries included in the least developed category are among the most recently emerging democracies, indicating that in areas in which the prospect of voting is new, young people may not have the same biases against participation that are found in developed countries.

## Willingness to Serve in Armed Forces

Young people in most countries surveyed by the WVS reported a high willingness to fight for their country should a war arise, as shown in Table 6-4. In almost all countries, more than two-thirds of young people said that they would be willing to fight for their country, with the value higher among young men than young women. One exception to this general pattern was Uruguay, where 41 percent of young men felt willing to fight for their country. Low willingness to fight is also notable in the high-income countries, particularly Japan, where fewer than 30 percent of young people reported willingness to fight in the event of war.[16] Compared with other responses, there was also a high proportion of respondents who said they didn't know what they would do in such a situation. Many of the countries in which young men are the most willing to fight should the need arise, such as Azerbaijan, China, the Philippines, and Turkey, are countries that have compulsory recruitment. Furthermore, these numbers may be slightly higher than if calculations were restricted to 18-24-year-olds, since older members of the 18-34 age group may have already served in their country's armed forces.

## Political Party Membership

In established and transitional democracies, political party membership is an important mechanism for political participation. Members of political parties are often directly engaged in activities that link the state to the general population, such as involvement in campaigns, signing petitions, registering new voters, and attending political rallies. Inglehart and Norris (2003) found that men were more likely than women to belong to a political party. Table 6-5 looks at membership rates for each country surveyed by the WVS. Not only are men more likely than women to belong to a political party, but also in almost every country surveyed, younger people are slightly less likely to participate than older people. However, party membership rates are strikingly low, less than 50 percent in most countries. One exception is Armenia, where party membership is compulsory.

While active party membership remains relatively low, actual party affiliation is a very salient identity issue in modern states with contested ethnic politics. In his analysis of Zambia, one researcher found that affiliation with a political party was a strong predictor of political participation, particularly in the immediate posttransition period (Bratton, 1999:570).

---

[16]Japan is exceptionally low, presumably because they have no standing army.

TABLE 6-4 Percentage Willing to Fight for Country in a War, Should the Need Arise

| Region and Country | Male (Ages) | | Female (Ages) | |
|---|---|---|---|---|
| | 18-34 | 35+ | 18-34 | 35+ |
| Caribbean/Central America | | | | |
| Mexico | 61.7 | 70.3 | 52.2 | 50.8 |
| Dominican Republic | 76.0 | 77.8 | 64.4 | 70.4 |
| Eastern/Southern Africa | | | | |
| Nigeria[a] | 70.1 | 64.0 | 50.8 | 46.7 |
| South America | | | | |
| Argentina | 53.4 | 66.7 | 53.2 | 56.0 |
| Brazil | 70.9 | 80.0 | 62.8 | 65.3 |
| Chile | 80.3 | 71.7 | 64.4 | 63.1 |
| Peru | 86.8 | 90.9 | 81.0 | 82.3 |
| Uruguay | 40.6 | 54.3 | 42.9 | 47.6 |
| Venezuela | 83.8 | 81.0 | 76.8 | 70.5 |
| SE/SW Asia | | | | |
| Bangladesh | 93.0 | 85.1 | 69.6 | 61.2 |
| China | 93.3 | 90.7 | 87.0 | 85.9 |
| India[b] | 88.5 | 85.1 | 78.4 | 71.7 |
| Pakistan[c] | n.a. | n.a. | n.a. | n.a. |
| Philippines | 85.2 | 83.0 | 85.4 | 83.2 |
| Middle East | | | | |
| Turkey | 94.4 | 96.8 | 94.3 | 93.6 |
| Former Soviet Asia | | | | |
| Armenia | 79.5 | 77.6 | 58.0 | 61.5 |
| Azerbaijan | 95.2 | 94.1 | 90.9 | 86.0 |
| Georgia | 83.9 | 79.0 | 52.4 | 54.2 |
| Developed Countries | | | | |
| Germany | 52.5 | 53.2 | 25.5 | 38.4 |
| Japan | 20.1 | 26.2 | 2.1 | 11.6 |
| South Korea | 90.5 | 90.2 | 69.5 | 77.0 |
| Spain | 53.2 | 56.7 | 40.7 | 48.0 |
| USA | 79.8 | 82.0 | 51.6 | 58.0 |
| TOTAL | 78.4 | 78.0 | 52.4 | 57.7 |

[a]The sample in Nigeria is restricted to urban areas.
[b]The sample in India is restricted to those who are literate.
[c]This question was not asked in Pakistan.
NOTE: n.a. = not available.
SOURCES: 1995-1998 World Values Surveys.

Many transitional democracies, including Zambia, have recently emerged from situations of single-party rule. In many of these countries, new forms of party membership have found strong connections to ethnic identity. These links between political participation and identity politics become increasingly relevant to the transition to adulthood in countries in which few economic opportunities exist outside the civil service; when a single dominant political party controls access to education or employment, as for example in Cameroon (see Box 6-1), party affiliation mediates one's inclusion or exclusion from these opportunities (Fokwang, 2003).

## Youth and Elected Office

Most citizenship rights are granted at the national level, but some local governments recognize young people as civic and social participants in the community by including youth representatives in community councils and through rites of passage ceremonies that confer an adult status on young people. Initiatives that encourage local municipalities to recognize and promote children's rights have increased with such international programs as the Child Friendly Cities program (Riggio, 2002; Riggio and Kilbane, 2000). Formally established in 2000, the program has conducted research, advocacy, and networking to promote children's participation in governmental processes.

Local governments have effectively included young people in decision-making and planning in recent years. One example of youth participation in local governance is in Barra Mansa, Brazil, where over 6,000 young people ages 9-15 have participated in discussions and neighborhood assemblies aimed at improving city services (Guerra, 2002). In all, 18 boys and 18 girls are elected by other children to serve on the children's council. The council meets regularly, sets priorities for needs, manages an annual budget of US$125,000, and oversees the implementation of projects—all based on the input and priorities of the children.

## Young People and Activism

It is conventional wisdom that young people and students are among the most active in the general population, in organizing as well as participating in public protests and outcries against repressive governments and harsh economic policies. Although students have rarely been the primary leaders of nationalist or revolutionary movements, they have often played an influential role and have been recognized as legitimate political actors (Altbach, 1989; Braungart and Braungart, 1993; Moller, 1968). For example, Iranian young people have become extremely active in the postrevolutionary period, particularly since early 1997, taking part in presi-

TABLE 6-5 Percentage with Political Party Membership

| | Membership Active | | | | Membership | | | |
|---|---|---|---|---|---|---|---|---|
| | Male | | Female | | Male | | Female | |
| Region and Country | 18-34 | 35+ | 18-34 | 35+ | 18-34 | 35+ | 18-34 | 35+ |
| Caribbean/Central America | | | | | | | | |
| Mexico | 27 | 29 | 18 | 21 | 11 | 11 | 5 | 9 |
| Dominican Republic | 35 | 42 | 29 | 39 | 12 | 22 | 7 | 13 |
| Eastern/Southern Africa | | | | | | | | |
| Nigeria[a] | 52 | 40 | 42 | 34 | 9 | 11 | 3 | 4 |
| South America | | | | | | | | |
| Argentina | 12 | 15 | 6 | 8 | 3 | 4 | 3 | 2 |
| Brazil | 14 | 20 | 10 | 13 | 6 | 10 | 5 | 8 |
| Chile | 16 | 20 | 14 | 15 | 3 | 5 | 1 | 2 |
| Colombia | 13 | 14 | 10 | 8 | 6 | 9 | 4 | 4 |
| Peru | 16 | 23 | 11 | 14 | 2 | 6 | 1 | 2 |
| Uruguay | 16 | 20 | 12 | 13 | 8 | 7 | 3 | 5 |
| Venezuela | 14 | 15 | 12 | 14 | 4 | 5 | 3 | 4 |
| SE/SW Asia | | | | | | | | |
| Bangladesh | 33 | 24 | 10 | 4 | 24 | 12 | 4 | 2 |
| China | 12 | 24 | 7 | 10 | 4 | 11 | 4 | 4 |
| India[b] | 23 | 27 | 9 | 13 | 12 | 14 | 4 | 5 |
| Pakistan[c] | n.a. | n.a. | n.a. | n.a. | n.a. | n.a. | n.a. | n.a. |
| Philippines | 8 | 5 | 11 | 5 | 3 | 2 | 6 | 3 |

| | | | | | | | | |
|---|---|---|---|---|---|---|---|---|
| Middle East | | | | | | | | |
| Turkey | 12 | 20 | 3 | 3 | 7 | 13 | 0 | 2 |
| Former Soviet Asia | | | | | | | | |
| Armenia | 99 | 100 | 100 | 100 | 1 | 2 | 0 | 1 |
| Azerbaijan | 7 | 11 | 4 | 3 | 3 | 2 | 2 | 1 |
| Georgia | 6 | 4 | 2 | 5 | 3 | 3 | 1 | 2 |
| Developed Countries | | | | | | | | |
| Germany | 8 | 14 | 5 | 7 | 3 | 6 | 2 | 3 |
| Japan | 5 | 10 | 2 | 4 | 3 | 3 | 0 | 1 |
| South Korea | 12 | 15 | 9 | 11 | 3 | 5 | 1 | 2 |
| Spain | 13 | 7 | 10 | 6 | 3 | 2 | 1 | 1 |
| USA | 42 | 53 | 41 | 54 | 20 | 21 | 19 | 21 |
| TOTAL | 39 | 49 | 38 | 46 | 18 | 21 | 17 | 20 |

[a]The sample in Nigeria is restricted to urban areas.
[b]The sample in India is restricted to those who are literate.
[c]This question was not asked in Pakistan.
NOTE: n.a. = not available.
SOURCES: 1995-1998 World Values Surveys.

**BOX 6-1**
**The Struggle for Citizenship in Contemporary Cameroon**

Anthropologist Jude Fokwang (2003) examined the ways in which young adults in Cameroon negotiated scarce resources and opportunities to achieve full social and political citizenship. Although Cameroon has made efforts toward democratic reform, its government continues to be characterized as an ethnic oligarchy, dominated by a single political party and consistently named one of the most corrupt governments in the world.

Extensive interviews with young people in the cities of Yaounde and Buea led Fokwang to classify their strategies into three categories: (1) individuals or members of groups who saw themselves as an elite-in-the-making and characterized their transition to adult citizenship as an easy process facilitated by their connections to the ruling political party and other state institutions; (2) individuals or members of groups who chose to remain independent from party politics but were willing to use both government and private resources to achieve their goals; and (3) individuals whose transition to adult citizenship had an antistate perspective or who yearned for an alternative way to achieve adult citizenship, such as via migration.

As a case study, Fokwang offered the experience of Carlson, a graduate of the École Normale Superieur, a professional school of the University of Yaounde that prepared secondary school teachers. Although he took the public entry examinations, he was not chosen as one of 80 government candidates who would be employed by the government following graduation. Instead, he enrolled as a private candidate in the program. Despite graduating at the top of his class, Carlson was unable to secure a permanent teaching job. Unable to pay the bribes necessary to obtain a place in another training program, he remained dependent on his father for financial support and worried about his prospects for achieving full adulthood.

Even if Carlson had been a member of one of the youth associations associated with the ruling political party, there would still be no easy guarantee of the "right" connections. Although some members of youth political organizations felt that their loyalty to the government entitled them to jobs or elite education, others expressed disillusionment with the system of patronage. In this context of restricted options, the motivations and ambitions of young people were influenced by national conditions. Without sufficient social and material capital, full citizenship—conceptualized by youth as the achievement of adult responsibilities—remains elusive.

dential elections and national political movements as a unified voting bloc, as political activists, and as a newly respected political reference group (Mashayekhi, 2001). Elsewhere, Mische (1996) described the role of youth political organizations in organizing the 1992 rallies against presidential corruption in Brazil, and many credit the young people in South Africa for providing the momentum that overturned the system of apartheid (Marks, 2001). These are examples of situations in which large and diverse groups of young people have successfully mobilized to create a political space in which their opinions can be heard.

Further qualitative research should be conducted in different national and cultural contexts to understand how political voice and action may be manifested in different forms. For example, in the late 1980s, urban young people in Senegal protested the political system that denied them an active role in government and failed to create economic opportunities for educated young people. Groups of young people created civil society-based police forces and social services in areas in which the government was perceived as a weak actor (Diouf, 1996). This creativity was a statement against the existing distribution of power as well as an attempt to put forward an alternative. These types of locally specific actions are difficult to capture in large, cross-country surveys. Nonetheless, the surveys that are available provide valuable information about the willingness of young people to become involved in their communities and to participate in various forms of political protest.

Using 1990 WVS data, Tilley (2002) tested whether young people are beginning to share more values and attitudes across countries than they do with older generations in their own cultures, an ostensible result of globalization and the spread of postmaterialist values. He grouped countries that shared similar backgrounds and histories, creating categories he called Anglo-Saxon, Nordic, Hispanic,[17] Western European, Central European, and Eastern European. Tilley found that gender and national grouping factors had a much more sizable and significant impact than age group on attitudes concerning religious beliefs, women's roles, and life satisfaction. However, one category in which a person's age was a better predictor than his or her nationality was willingness to participate in political activities. This included signing petitions, engaging in boycotts, attending demonstrations, taking part in strikes, or occupying buildings. Young people were found to be more likely to engage in these activities. Tilley found that the regions with the least willingness to do so were young people from South America and the formerly Communist Eastern Europe—countries with formerly repressive political regimes and perhaps weak civil societies (Tilley, 2002).

The 1995-1998 World Values Surveys show that the majority of young people expressed the intent to participate in a petition, a boycott, or a lawful demonstration (Table 6-6).[18] In the majority of countries surveyed,

---

[17]"Hispanic" is the only category that includes developing countries; it includes Argentina, Brazil, Chile, Mexico, Portugal, and Spain. Information on other developing countries was not collected until the 1995 round of the World Values Survey.

[18]Since past participation in political activity is partially dependent on the availability of opportunities to act, the table measures the intention of respondents to participate in these activities. This includes those respondents who either "have done" or "might do" each activity.

TABLE 6-6 Percentage with Intent to Participate in Various Protest Activities ("have done" or "would do"), Respondents Ages 18-34

| Region and Country | Petition | | Boycott | | Demonstration | | More Than One | |
|---|---|---|---|---|---|---|---|---|
| | Male | Female | Male | Female | Male | Female | Male | Female |
| Caribbean/Central America | | | | | | | | |
| Mexico | 76 | 70 | 42 | 36 | 54 | 48 | 61 | 54 |
| Dominican Republic | 74 | 61 | 30 | 22 | 75 | 69 | 69 | 57 |
| Eastern/Southern Africa | | | | | | | | |
| Nigeria[a] | 43 | 32 | 45 | 29 | 58 | 42 | 48 | 33 |
| South America | | | | | | | | |
| Argentina | 69 | 66 | 16 | 14 | 52 | 49 | 50 | 46 |
| Brazil | 85 | 87 | 38 | 29 | 71 | 74 | 70 | 73 |
| Chile | 63 | 55 | 22 | 13 | 53 | 43 | 48 | 40 |
| Peru | 66 | 59 | 19 | 13 | 46 | 41 | 46 | 38 |
| Uruguay | 67 | 73 | 26 | 23 | 21 | 26 | 30 | 33 |
| Venezuela | 55 | 57 | 19 | 16 | 42 | 35 | 39 | 33 |
| SE/SW Asia | | | | | | | | |
| Bangladesh | 66 | 47 | 58 | 32 | 68 | 48 | 64 | 40 |
| China[c] | n.a. | n.a. | n.a. | n.a. | n.a. | n.a. | n.a. | n.a. |
| India[b] | 56 | 38 | 51 | 34 | 48 | 30 | 54 | 37 |
| Pakistan[c] | n.a. | n.a. | n.a. | n.a. | n.a. | n.a. | n.a. | n.a. |
| Philippines | 29 | 32 | 18 | 17 | 24 | 22 | 21 | 23 |

383

| | | | | | | | |
|---|---|---|---|---|---|---|---|
| **Middle East** | | | | | | | |
| Turkey | 64 | 50 | 35 | 19 | 51 | 28 | 48 | 26 |
| **Former Soviet Asia** | | | | | | | |
| Armenia | 56 | 50 | 44 | 28 | 62 | 48 | 56 | 41 |
| Azerbaijan | 30 | 18 | 19 | 10 | 48 | 31 | 28 | 15 |
| Georgia | 32 | 35 | 25 | 21 | 43 | 43 | 32 | 33 |
| **Developed Countries** | | | | | | | |
| Germany | 98 | 99 | 83 | 78 | 85 | 83 | 93 | 92 |
| Japan | 65 | 68 | 40 | 49 | 29 | 26 | 41 | 43 |
| South Korea | 88 | 89 | 86 | 78 | 70 | 57 | 88 | 81 |
| Spain | 72 | 65 | 36 | 27 | 74 | 67 | 67 | 61 |
| USA | 89 | 93 | 66 | 67 | 62 | 66 | 72 | 75 |
| TOTAL | 82 | 76 | 52 | 42 | 56 | 47 | 62 | 53 |

[a]The sample in Nigeria is restricted to urban areas.
[b]The sample in India is restricted to those who are literate.
[c]This question was not asked in China and Pakistan.
NOTE: n.a. = not available.
SOURCE: 1995-1998 World Values Surveys.

young people are most willing to sign a petition and least willing to engage in a boycott. This is particularly true in the South American and Central American countries and for Turkey as well, where twice as many young people are willing to sign a petition as are willing to engage in a boycott. In contrast, young people in the Asian countries are considerably less likely to report the intention to participate in any of these activities. Furthermore, young men are more willing than young women to engage in these forms of protest.

Nonetheless, even these expressions of political intent are limited. In less than half of these countries do more than 50 percent of surveyed young men intend to engage in more than one of these three political activities, and only in Brazil, the Dominican Republic, and Mexico do more than 50 percent of surveyed young women (Table 6-6). However, this should not be interpreted directly as a sign of youth apathy for political engagement. Boycotting goods and services may be a political activity, but it is closely connected to the availability of alternatives and the financial and social means to exercise choice. Likewise, participation in lawful demonstrations may be restricted by the perceived space for action in civil society and the nature of the political environment.

Inglehart and Norris (2003) broke down participation rates in political protest by national development level (see footnote 14) and birth cohort. They found that not only are respondents from developing countries less likely to have participated in protest activism, but also that there is a larger gender gap in participation than in more developed countries. Furthermore, respondents younger than 30 are less likely to have participated in protest activism than adults ages 30-59, although both of these cohorts are more likely to have engaged in protest activities than respondents ages 60 and older. To some extent, the difference between the two younger adult cohorts may be attributed to the fact that older adults have had more years to engage in protest activities. More interestingly, once such characteristics as education, class, age, union membership, and religiosity are included in the analysis, gender does not have a significant impact on the rate of participation in protest activism. Therefore, Inglehart and Norris conclude that as women have greater opportunities to continue their education and enter the labor force, they may become more likely to participate in protest activities.

The IEA studies also asked students if they would participate in various protest activities. Students from Chile and Colombia were much more likely to expect to participate in such political activities as collecting money for a social cause, collecting signatures for a petition, and participating in a protest march than their counterparts from Western and Eastern Europe. For example, while 83 percent of upper secondary students surveyed in Chile expected to collect money for a social cause, the international mean for the entire sample was only 55 percent.[19] Similarly, 77 percent of 14-year-olds and 78 percent of 17-year-olds in Chile said they would probably or definitely collect signatures for a petition, whereas these percentages were 43 and 42 percent, respectively, for the international sample. While older respondents were willing to engage in traditional political activities, they expressed greater interest in engaging in activities that had a direct impact on the community (Amadeo et al., 2002).

In the IEA study of 14-year-olds, students in all countries were much more likely to report expecting to engage in activities like collecting money (59 percent) or signing petitions (45 percent) than they were to participate in more confrontational activities like blocking traffic (15 percent) or occupying buildings (14 percent). Significant gender differences emerged—girls were more likely to expect to collect money for a social cause, whereas boys were more likely to expect to participate in a march, spray-paint protest slogans, block traffic, or occupy buildings. There were no significant gender differences for collecting signatures for a petition (Amadeo et al., 2002).

Nonetheless, these surveys provide little information about the issues that drive young people's participation in formal politics, community organizing, and forms of protest. There has been some investigation of new types of organizing that are occurring in the context of globalization. These include growing international networks that form around issues ranging from labor rights, trade policies, environmental protection, and reproductive health to shared tastes in music. This new form of organization takes place in a context in which advances in information technology and travel, as well as the rise in a global human rights platform, have facilitated participation in transnational social movements (Keck and Sikkink, 1998). Young people are also more likely than older adults to use the Internet and recent communication technologies (Suoranta, 2003); research is needed to understand how the methods and goals of youth activists differ from the protest activities of older adults and from the practices of young people in the past.

## Young People and Civic Participation

Research on social capital and organizational membership suggests that participating in voluntary groups is associated with access to information, economic and political resources, and social support (Putnam, 2000; Putnam, Leonardi, and Nanetti, 1993; van Deth et al., 1999). Involvement in civic organizations provides young people with the opportunity to ex-

---

[19]The international mean of the IEA study of 17-year-olds is based on results from Chile, Colombia, Cyprus, Czech Republic, Denmark, Estonia, Israel, Latvia, Norway, Poland, Portugal, Russia, Slovenia, Sweden, and Switzerland.

pand their social connections outside the home and develop new skills. Longitudinal research in the United States has started to identify linkages between participation in civic activities as a youth and leadership and involvement as an adult; these trajectories are especially strong for young women (Damico, Damico, and Conway, 1998; Hart, Atkins, and Ford, 1998; Verba, Schlozman, and Brady, 1995; Youniss, McLellan, and Yates, 1997).

The World Values Surveys asked participants whether they were active members of religious organizations, sports organizations, arts organizations, unions, political parties, environmental groups, professional organizations, charity organizations, or other organizations. According to the WVS, the greatest participation rates for young adults were consistently found in religious, sports, and arts or educational organizations (Table 6-7). Participation rates in unions, political parties, environmental organizations, professional organizations, charities, and other organizations were between 5 and 10 percent, whereas participation rates in church, sports, and art organizations were nearly double that. Young men were more likely than young women to participate in most organizations, with the exception of church organizations and charities. Young people (both boys and girls) are also more likely than older adults to participate in sports, arts, and environmental organizations and less likely to participate in church organizations and charities. Participation in unions, political parties, and professional organizations appears to be more closely related to gender than age. However, it is worth noting that the World Values Surveys do not collect information on participation in organizations more specific to certain regional contexts, such as self-help associations (e.g., savings associations, burial associations, neighborhood watch) or groups concerned with local matters (e.g., school or housing associations). While the inclusion of these categories may complicate cross-national comparisons, it might more closely capture the extent of community involvement.

The UNICEF Young Voices Surveys asked young people whether they belonged to at least one organized group, club, or association. In the overall findings for Europe and Central Asia, while there were no large gender or socioeconomic differences, younger adolescents ages 9-13 (48 percent) were more likely to be involved than older adolescents ages 14-17 (38 percent), probably because they are more likely to be enrolled in school, where some of these activities take place. Of the children in Central Asian countries who were polled, 37 percent reported belonging to a group or club (UNICEF, 2001a:77).[20] In Latin America and the Caribbean, a total of 52 percent

---

[20]The countries polled included Kazakhstan, Kyrgyzstan, Tajikistan, Turkmenistan, and Uzbekistan. Data on individual countries in Central Asia were not available.

reported belonging to some organized peer group, with those in the Caribbean reporting the highest participation (70 percent). And 31 percent reported participating in a sports group, 16 percent reported belonging to a religious group, and 8 percent reported belonging to an artistic association (UNICEF, 2000:109). The breakdown by country for Latin America and the Caribbean is shown in Table 6-8. More informal types of participation, including playing sports informally with friends and other neighborhood children, are unlikely to be included in these data, but it is likely to be the more formal activities that cultivate social and leadership skills and the inclination to become active in other aspects of the community.

The levels of participation in various community organizations and activities provide some insight into the level of connectedness that young people may feel to their community, as well as the likelihood of some positive socialization experience through interaction with peers, adults outside the nuclear or extended family, and exposure to new ideas and opportunities. These extrafamilial social networks may mediate access to the resources, opportunities, and aspirations that young people utilize as they assume more adult roles and responsibilities. Therefore, associational membership serves as one indicator of a young person's social capital.

However, not all associations foster a young person's prosocial development. Negative social capital may be carried in associations that exclude outsiders, place excessive claims on group members, restrict individual freedoms, and exercise downward leveling norms (Portes, 1998), such as youth involvement in gang activity. In Nicaragua, young men formed street gangs in reaction to the anarchic conditions during the transition from war to peace during the late 1980s and early 1990s. These gangs, or *pandillas*, were loyal to their neighborhoods and helped maintain peaceful conditions in their home territory, while practicing low-level violence and petty crime elsewhere. However, as Nicaragua was drawn into the drug trade, the gang members became both consumers and dealers of such drugs as crack cocaine. As the revenue from gang activities has increased, security in communities formerly protected by the *pandillas* has decreased (Rodgers, 2002).

The existence of the gangs was a manifestation of the tension between an effort to build a social structure and the struggle to take advantage of economic opportunities, especially those that exist outside the formal market. While the activities and structure of youth gangs vary widely, they are inherently a distinct social group recognized by the community, bound together by shared values, and collectively associated with illegal activities (Moser and van Bronkhorst, 1999; Pattillo, 1998). While violence and gang activity are associated with high levels of income inequality (Lederman and Loayza, 1999), relative poverty is not a sufficient factor; involvement is also predicated on the availability of free unstructured time.

Participation in social organizations that build positive social capital

TABLE 6-7 Percentage with Membership in Selected Organizations

| | Church/Religious | | | |
|---|---|---|---|---|
| | Male | | Female | |
| Region and Country | 18-34 | 35+ | 18-34 | 35+ |
| Caribbean/Central America | | | | |
| Mexico | 67 | 71 | 73 | 70 |
| Dominican Republic | 65 | 72 | 79 | 81 |
| Eastern/Southern Africa | | | | |
| Nigeria[a] | 55 | 74 | 60 | 72 |
| South America | | | | |
| Argentina | 28 | 30 | 31 | 42 |
| Brazil | 50 | 61 | 61 | 75 |
| Chile | 46 | 55 | 60 | 69 |
| Peru | 52 | 59 | 54 | 61 |
| Uruguay | 22 | 26 | 28 | 48 |
| Venezuela | 42 | 40 | 46 | 50 |
| SE/SW Asia | | | | |
| Bangladesh | 41 | 58 | 12 | 13 |
| China[c] | n.a. | n.a. | n.a. | n.a. |
| India[b] | 28 | 34 | 20 | 29 |
| Pakistan[c] | n.a. | n.a. | n.a. | n.a. |
| Philippines | 25 | 25 | 22 | 21 |
| Middle East | | | | |
| Turkey | 3 | 7 | 2 | 2 |
| Former Soviet Asia | | | | |
| Armenia | 96 | 93 | 97 | 97 |
| Azerbaijan | 5 | 6 | 3 | 3 |
| Georgia | 10 | 7 | 10 | 8 |
| Developed Countries | | | | |
| Germany | 46 | 44 | 57 | 57 |
| Japan | 7 | 11 | 14 | 14 |
| South Korea | 38 | 39 | 47 | 63 |
| Spain | 39 | 37 | 44 | 50 |
| USA | 68 | 74 | 77 | 84 |

[a]The sample in Nigeria is restricted to urban areas.
[b]The sample in India is restricted to those who are literate.
[c]This question was not asked in China and Pakistan.
NOTE: n.a. = not available.
SOURCE: 1995-1998 World Values Surveys.

| Sports/Recreation | | | | Arts/Education | | | |
| Male | | Female | | Male | | Female | |
| 18-34 | 35+ | 18-34 | 35+ | 18-34 | 35+ | 18-34 | 35+ |
| --- | --- | --- | --- | --- | --- | --- | --- |
| 54 | 51 | 43 | 35 | 42 | 40 | 43 | 31 |
| 52 | 42 | 36 | 32 | 39 | 30 | 42 | 40 |
| | | | | | | | |
| 75 | 52 | 54 | 36 | 66 | 41 | 54 | 38 |
| | | | | | | | |
| 27 | 18 | 16 | 7 | 19 | 11 | 20 | 12 |
| 45 | 26 | 20 | 12 | 21 | 19 | 15 | 18 |
| 56 | 43 | 29 | 19 | 32 | 26 | 29 | 29 |
| 46 | 34 | 28 | 20 | 29 | 23 | 24 | 20 |
| 32 | 21 | 20 | 9 | 22 | 14 | 28 | 14 |
| 43 | 30 | 26 | 18 | 29 | 20 | 23 | 15 |
| | | | | | | | |
| 47 | 26 | 14 | 9 | 27 | 22 | 21 | 18 |
| 22 | 13 | 22 | 9 | 15 | 10 | 16 | 8 |
| 36 | 20 | 14 | 10 | 30 | 17 | 20 | 18 |
| n.a. | n.a. | n.a. | n.a. | 0 | 0 | 0 | 0 |
| 16 | 18 | 15 | 16 | 11 | 12 | 11 | 8 |
| | | | | | | | |
| 14 | 7 | 2 | 1 | 3 | 4 | 3 | 2 |
| | | | | | | | |
| 99 | 99 | 100 | 100 | 99 | 100 | 100 | 100 |
| 15 | 5 | 7 | 3 | 7 | 5 | 14 | 6 |
| 18 | 5 | 6 | 2 | 11 | 7 | 17 | 8 |
| | | | | | | | |
| 55 | 44 | 52 | 42 | 12 | 19 | 19 | 22 |
| 20 | 25 | 16 | 19 | 5 | 12 | 9 | 19 |
| 66 | 48 | 48 | 36 | 45 | 28 | 45 | 28 |
| 41 | 17 | 22 | 11 | 22 | 12 | 22 | 8 |
| 57 | 42 | 50 | 34 | 42 | 34 | 49 | 37 |

TABLE 6-8 Percentage of Young People Who Participate in Various Activities

| Region and Country | Sports | Religious | Artistic | None |
|---|---|---|---|---|
| South America | | | | |
| Argentina | 35 | 12 | 7 | 50 |
| Bolivia | 35 | 13 | 14 | 44 |
| Brazil | 27 | 20 | 6 | 51 |
| Chile | 28 | 18 | 10 | 43 |
| Colombia | 34 | 12 | 14 | 46 |
| Ecuador | 26 | 12 | 5 | 57 |
| Guyana | 26 | 34 | 9 | 36 |
| Peru | 34 | 12 | 9 | 46 |
| Uruguay | 32 | 9 | 8 | 47 |
| Venezuela | 33 | 8 | 9 | 50 |
| Caribbean/Central America | | | | |
| Barbados | 46 | 33 | 18 | 16 |
| Dominican Republic | 27 | 17 | 4 | 42 |
| El Salvador | 47 | 13 | 4 | 33 |
| Haiti | 48 | 27 | 4 | 21 |
| Honduras | 32 | 28 | 3 | 34 |
| Guatemala | 34 | 23 | 5 | 48 |
| Jamaica | 42 | 14 | 15 | 32 |
| Mexico | 33 | 15 | 7 | 48 |
| Nicaragua | 24 | 8 | 6 | 59 |
| Panama | 26 | 21 | 14 | 45 |

SOURCE: UNICEF (2000:110).

and enhance capabilities and self-esteem, as well as involvement in more negative activities, are highly mediated by the amount of leisure time that a young person has available to spend on activities in the community. Recent cross-national studies of time use among young people have found that boys have more leisure time than girls; as discussed in Chapter 5, when noneconomic household work (or domestic chores) are included in the equation, young women spend more hours each day working than young men, leaving less time to cultivate social networks or to participate in community organizations (Larson and Verma, 1999; Ritchie, Lloyd, and Grant, 2004). When young people are still enrolled in school, they spend more hours per day in structured activities. After-school programs that lengthen the school day—such as the Program for the Eradication of Child Labor in Brazil, discussed in Chapter 5—not only reduce child labor, but also increase the amount of supervised time that can be used to build prosocial values.

## Young People and Social Inclusion

The concept of citizenship encompasses much more than just a narrowly defined relationship between individuals and the state. As discussed in the previous section, social capital and the strength of the civic environment mediate the transition to adult citizenship. The opportunities for participation that young people experience in their community are instrumental to their development and the types of transitions they make to adulthood. Correspondingly, young people who do not have such opportunities may be more likely to feel alienated, to have a sense of hopelessness, and to engage in high-risk or antisocial behavior (Resnick, 2000). In this section we review research on the ways in which young people engage with their environments, as well as some of the antisocial responses that can occur when formal social, economic, and political structures fail to provide sufficient opportunities and support.

Citizenship implies access to and inclusion in community resources and social networks—these in turn can be protective against involvement in high-risk economic and social activities. Supportive environments for youth development are enhanced by access to functional social systems (such as education and labor markets), compensatory social policies to combat economic polarization, shared values and norms, stable social memberships, and wide participation in social life (Tienda and Wilson, 2002). Young people living in urban slums or poor rural areas may not be in surroundings conducive to creating a sense of community, well-being, or safety. While socioeconomic status informs the existence and quality of citizenship opportunities, social inclusion in one's physical environment often mediates the impact of those limitations. The level of safety that young people feel in their community may facilitate or inhibit their ability to participate in activities like sports, after-school clubs, or other civic activities, and the care and upkeep of neighborhood homes and businesses may create an environment that discourages illicit activity (Cohen et al., 2000). This may be particularly the case for young women who fear sexual harassment or for young people who live in areas of armed conflict. Young people who live in areas of high gang activity may be coerced into active or passive participation in gang politics.

An emerging literature in the United States has pointed out the linkages between the connectedness of young people in their communities and risk-taking behaviors (Brooks-Gunn, 1993; Jessor, Turbin, and Costa, 1998a, 1998b; Kirby, 1999; Resnick et al., 1997). Community connectedness has been found to be inversely associated with behaviors like smoking, drug use, and high-risk sex. Studies attempt to capture the level of connectedness by using such measures as perceptions of cohesion and cooperation in communities as well as the presence of community groups and activities for young people. They also ask who the respondent feels close to and who they trust the most. They may also ask about an individual's feelings of safety in the neighborhood and the presence of gangs.

In a study on young people ages 14-22 living in the context of HIV/AIDS in South Africa, investigators looked at the community factors that may affect sexual behavior and choices (Hallman and Diers, 2004; Rutenberg et al., 2001). Interviewers assessed community characteristics, including physical infrastructure and perceptions of safety. The preliminary results found significant gender differences in the levels of comfort that men and young women felt. Young men had higher degrees of social inclusion, as they often had more friends and felt safe in their neighborhood. They seem to have a greater connection to their community than young women; they were more likely to report help and trust among community members and to have many friends, and less likely to say that they would feel happier if they lived in another community. Results from the same study found that social isolation was associated with higher risk of early sexual debut among boys and girls, and with greater risk of coercive or economically motivated sexual encounters and lower negotiating power in sexual relationships for girls only.

Trust in institutions is an indicator often used in public opinion surveys for assessing individuals' sense of security and faith in their society. The World Values Survey included this topic in its investigations. Results demonstrate that religious institutions consistently topped the list as the most trusted institutions among young adults ages 18-34, with more than 70 percent of respondents in most countries expressing "a great deal" or "quite a lot" of confidence. However, trust in all other institutions varies widely from country to country, with trust in the police and national government consistently low (Table 6-9). The incidence of political repression and corruption in a country's history undoubtedly has a strong affect on these variations. These findings were corroborated in a study of 17-year-olds in 16 countries conducted by the IEA. This survey found that, for all countries, young people trusted government institutions less than they trusted the media. In particular, 17-year-olds had less trust for the government than did 14-year-olds (Amadeo et al., 2002:7).

These patterns of higher trust in community and religious institutions compared with low trust in governmental bodies and officials were also evident in the younger group of adolescents (ages 9-17) interviewed in the UNICEF Young Voices Surveys. Questions about trust were asked in the surveys conducted in Central Asia and Latin America and the Caribbean. In all of the Central and Eastern Europe/Commonwealth of Independent States and Baltic States polled, 56 percent trusted the army, 55 percent trusted the church and religious authorities, 47 percent trusted the police, 40 percent trusted the president or other head of state, and 30 percent trusted the government. These levels did not vary by gender but did decrease with age. For example 62 percent of 9-13-year-olds expressed trust in the police compared with 45 percent of 14-17-year-olds (UNICEF, 2001b:65).[21] Older respondents may have had greater interaction with these institutions than younger respondents, and these experiences may shape the level of trust that they express.

The Young Voices Surveys in Latin America and the Caribbean also asked adolescents about their trust in adults and social institutions, including parents, teachers, the church, the mayor, the government, and the president. Young people trust their mothers (94 percent) and their fathers (90 percent) the most; 85 percent of respondents reported trusting the church. Teachers were trustworthy for 79 percent, but this confidence waned among older adolescents (64 percent) and children from poorer households (68 percent). As with the results from other surveys, adolescents had the least trust in government institutions and their representatives: 38 percent reported trust in the mayor, 36 percent in the president, and 32 percent in the government (UNICEF, 2000:115).[22]

Some researchers hypothesize that confidence in political institutions is declining. Comparisons between the 1981 and 1991 World Values Surveys shows a decrease in confidence in public institutions (but not private ones) in many countries[23] (Newton and Norris, 2000). However, this may be due to the poor performance of governments in these countries (Putnam, Pharr, and Dalton, 2000; Torney-Purta, Schwille, and Amadeo, 1999). Trust in institutions is important to examine further, especially to understand how it affects whether young people feel that they can make an impact on their environment or government and whether they decide to get involved as active citizens, as well as to measure the performance of these institutions.

As described above, the social environment of the community may be associated with the risk behaviors that young people engage in. However, opportunities for connection to social institutions trusted by young people may provide positive alternatives to risk behavior. Beckerleg (1995) documents how young people in a coastal Kenyan town turned to a new Islamic movement as a positive alternative to the disintegration of the Swahili

---

[21]These data were not disaggregated by country in the final report, so this total figure reflects not only the countries of Central Asia and the Caucasus, but also Eastern Europe and the Baltic States.

[22]Results that are presented as regional averages have been weighted to accurately represent the proportion of each nation's youth population in the region.

[23]The early rounds of the World Values Surveys conducted in 1981 and 1991 were restricted mainly to developed countries; Argentina, Mexico, and South Africa were the only developing countries surveyed in both rounds.

TABLE 6-9 Percentage of Respondents with Trust in Various Institutions ("a great deal" or "quite a lot"), Ages 18-34

| Region and Country | Church | | Legal System | |
|---|---|---|---|---|
| | Male | Female | Male | Female |
| Caribbean/Central America | | | | |
| Mexico | 68 | 79 | 41 | 39 |
| Dominican Republic | 70 | 71 | 23 | 12 |
| Eastern/Southern Africa | | | | |
| Nigeria[a] | 81 | 87 | 55 | 54 |
| South America | | | | |
| Argentina | 38 | 44 | 21 | 24 |
| Brazil | 71 | 75 | 51 | 51 |
| Chile | 72 | 80 | 38 | 41 |
| Peru | 61 | 72 | 20 | 16 |
| Uruguay | 49 | 48 | 50 | 47 |
| Venezuela | 72 | 75 | 37 | 36 |
| SE/SW Asia | | | | |
| Bangladesh | 97 | 98 | 73 | 71 |
| China[b] | n.a. | n.a. | n.a. | n.a. |
| India[c] | 60 | 63 | 75 | 68 |
| Pakistan | 80 | 82 | 40 | 64 |
| Philippines | 94 | 95 | 66 | 68 |
| Middle East | | | | |
| Turkey | 69 | 69 | 64 | 77 |
| Former Soviet Asia | | | | |
| Armenia | 60 | 71 | 26 | 32 |
| Azerbaijan | 63 | 65 | 53 | 42 |
| Georgia | 70 | 80 | 41 | 38 |
| Developed Countries | | | | |
| Germany | 21 | 29 | 56 | 55 |
| Japan | 10 | 10 | 73 | 63 |
| South Korea | 39 | 45 | 51 | 53 |
| Spain | 32 | 38 | 41 | 34 |
| USA | 60 | 78 | 38 | 38 |

[a]The sample in Nigeria is restricted to urban areas.
[b]This question was not asked in China.
[c]The sample in India is restricted to those who are literate.
NOTE: n.a. = not available.
SOURCE: 1995-1998 World Values Surveys.

| Press | | National Government | | Civil Service | | Police | |
|---|---|---|---|---|---|---|---|
| Male | Female | Male | Female | Male | Female | Male | Female |
| 51 | 50 | 41 | 41 | 44 | 40 | 32 | 35 |
| 35 | 32 | 18 | 8 | 11 | 8 | 14 | 10 |
| 64 | 57 | 16 | 18 | 66 | 61 | 36 | 39 |
| 28 | 39 | 25 | 18 | 8 | 6 | 21 | 15 |
| 64 | 59 | 42 | 42 | 62 | 59 | 43 | 41 |
| 50 | 51 | 50 | 45 | 41 | 41 | 44 | 48 |
| 26 | 29 | 40 | 35 | 11 | 8 | 22 | 24 |
| 56 | 58 | 29 | 33 | 31 | 42 | 37 | 49 |
| 58 | 63 | 28 | 24 | 29 | 32 | 30 | 25 |
| 67 | 66 | 78 | 77 | 75 | 69 | 36 | 32 |
| n.a. | n.a. | n.a. | n.a. | n.a. | n.a. | n.a. | n.a. |
| 58 | 50 | 54 | 51 | 61 | 53 | 41 | 37 |
| 54 | 61 | 0 | 0 | 47 | 54 | 9 | 27 |
| 73 | 72 | 55 | 61 | 68 | 68 | 58 | 58 |
| 44 | 50 | 45 | 54 | 61 | 71 | 65 | 76 |
| 33 | 38 | 42 | 42 | 32 | 38 | 30 | 31 |
| 40 | 27 | 87 | 86 | 39 | 39 | 44 | 39 |
| 60 | 54 | 45 | 39 | 44 | 43 | 31 | 33 |
| 26 | 21 | 24 | 15 | 34 | 41 | 62 | 62 |
| 73 | 72 | 17 | 18 | 24 | 24 | 70 | 80 |
| 58 | 65 | 34 | 38 | 83 | 83 | 38 | 43 |
| 47 | 40 | 22 | 21 | 34 | 38 | 60 | 52 |
| 26 | 25 | 30 | 34 | 50 | 48 | 67 | 70 |

**BOX 6-2**
**Young Men and Pentecostalism in Tanzania**

As one of the fastest growing cities in Africa, Dar es Salaam, Tanzania, has a large youth population, including rural migrants and refugees from neighboring war-torn countries, including Burundi. Most of these young people operate in the informal economy, outside official state sanctions and within the bounds of an urban youth culture defined by heightened alertness, secret codes, and a celebration of their outcast status. However, anthropologist Marc Sommers (2003) found hidden in this environment a community of young, male Burundi refugees who used their connections to Pentecostalism to leave the refugee settlement camps and find a livelihood in the city.

Strong connections between Pentecostal congregations in the refugee settlement camps and in Dar es Salaam provided a social network that young people can use to migrate to the city. Pentecostal traders recruited young men from the settlements to work for them in exchange for providing protection and guidance in the city. Sommers (2003) found that once in the city, most Burundi refugees chose to keep circumspect lives. Not only were they living illegally outside the official refugee settlements, but also many were ethnic Hutus driven by the fear of the genocide carried out by Burundian Tutsis in the early 1970s. Although few of the young people had ever seen a Tutsi, they restricted their friendships to one or two refugees who could be trusted.

Since young refugee migrants maintained narrow social networks, their connections to Pentecostalism took on increased importance. Nearly all members of the Burundi refugee community in Dar es Salaam attended Pentecostal churches, and each church community provided an atmosphere in which refugees could relax. New migrants were taught how to avoid trouble, and young people were provided with an alternative to violence. Sommers (2003) found that Pentecostalism targeted and accommodated the needs of young refugees, providing a stable point attractive to young people alienated from the state and with few viable life choices available. Although his ethnography identified the survival strategies used by young male Burundi refugees, Sommers recognized young urban migrants as a particularly understudied group, in particular their changing sociocultural roles in the current war and postwar context of many African countries.

community and the increase in local drug use driven by the local tourist economy. The high trust that young people have in religious institutions may indicate their potential use by young people to negotiate social disorder. Box 6-2 describes how young urban migrants used their connections to Pentecostalism to forge positive social networks following their arrival in the city.

Elsewhere, others have concluded that low trust in the effectiveness of the police and the justice system lead to alternative, and often violent, forms of justice and conflict resolution among young people (Noronha et al., 1999; Aitchinson, 1998, as cited in World Health Organization, 2002). In settings in which the police have little control over everyday violence and may be perpetrators of violence themselves, marginalized young people may have few disincentives to the use of violence or petty crime to overcome their lack of social and economic opportunity. During the political and economic unrest in Senegal in the late 1980s, groups of young people formed patrols to replace the weakly functioning police force; although these groups walked the fine line of peacekeeping and vigilante justice, they represented a local response to the existing disorder (Diouf, 1996).

Results described in this section point to the large-scale disillusionment and lack of confidence on the part of young people toward formal government institutions and political participation. However, there is also evidence of higher levels of trust in community organizations and religious institutions. Together, the data in the previous sections suggest that the civic participation and engagement of young people are more active at the local level, although some young people express interest and participate in national-level political and social activities. Citizenship is thus also about a young person's socialization in a community and multiple social environments. Those who have the opportunities to participate in activities outside the home and the freedom to have a voice, interact with others, and develop leadership skills may be able to have a healthier transition to adulthood.

## THE FORMATION OF CITIZENSHIP

What types of institutions and processes contribute in a positive way to the formation of citizenship during adolescence? A broad range of institutional forces shape the formation of citizenship in addition to the formal legal structures previously discussed. These include the formal schooling system, the military or national service, the workplace, civil society and NGOs, and the media. Each of these institutions is also responding to as well as contributing to the global changes discussed in Chapter 2. Each of these is briefly discussed below.

### Role of Formal Schooling

Literacy is one of the most powerful skills that school imparts to young people. The ability to read and write in a commonly written and spoken language, as well as the development of critical analytic skills, an expanded vocabulary, and the mastery of abstract concepts that come with sustained schooling, provides young people with important tools for participating in a changing society.

Those without a basic quality education face multiple barriers in terms of employment, access to health care, and the confidence and ability to fully participate in other activities. Furthermore, education is implicitly a political process (Freire, 2002 [1970]), guided both by national education policies that may change frequently, as government power shifts between political parties, and by the agenda that designs and interprets the content of the curriculum.

The Convention on the Rights of the Child enshrines the right to education in Articles 28 and 29. The language of these articles acknowledges that the opportunity to go to school offers children and adolescents not only academic knowledge, but also core skills that will help them be effective and active community participants. This includes (United Nations, 1989) the "development of respect for the child's parents, his or her own cultural identity, language and values, for the national values of the country in which the child is living, the country from which he or she may originate, and for civilizations different from his or her own. . . . The preparation of the child for responsible life in a free society, in the spirit of understanding, peace, tolerance, equality of sexes, and friendship among all peoples, ethnic, national and religious groups and persons of indigenous origin."

As reflected in the Convention on the Rights of the Child, public schooling typically has multiple goals. In addition to instilling literacy and mathematical skills in young people, public education's goals include fostering a national identity, inculcating a shared history, and promoting cohesion between the diverse constituencies within one geographic boundary. The skills, knowledge, and experiences provided contribute to enabling young people to actively participate in society (Fagerlind and Saha, 1989; Wolpe, 1994). Furthermore, formal schooling also provides a setting in which young people can interact with each other and get involved in new activities. Programs beyond the academic core curriculum, such as school-based sports and drama programs can also increase the social skills and networks of young people. Attending school may be particularly empowering for girls and poor adolescents who have few other opportunities to develop leadership skills and social and economic mobility.

There is a movement in the development field to acknowledge and promote the positive socialization and citizenship-building aspects of formal education. Proponents of this aspect of schooling have been extremely critical of the exclusive focus of recent school reform efforts on the acquisition of human capital to the exclusion of other aspects of education that promote social capital, nationalistic belief systems, and citizenship (Carnoy, 2000; Morrow and Torres, 2000). These critics argue that education has become merely an ingredient in development and a means for integration into a Western-dominated global market. As a result, there have been very little curriculum development and teacher training in school reform efforts to promote civic knowledge and activity.

Nonetheless, all government schools, whether pre- or postreform, teach students about their country, its culture, its history, and its government. Furthermore, many schools offer special programs and curricula designed to address civic knowledge, life skills, and human rights. Some schools may also provide opportunities for students for leadership training through systems of student governance, require community service from students, or host special programs on current social and political topics.

The International Association for the Evaluation of Educational Achievement has conducted tests of students' civic knowledge, attitudes, and practices with respect to citizenship in 28 countries; although most of these surveys were conducted in developed nations, Chile and Colombia were included. In general, students express the view that schools that model democratic practices are the most effective in promoting civic knowledge and engagement. The majority of students in Chile and Colombia "agreed" or "strongly agreed" that school helped them to learn to cooperate with other students, understand people who have different ideas, and protect the environment (89-96 percent). Schools also taught them to care about what happens in different countries, to contribute to community problem solving, to be a patriotic and loyal citizen, and to consider that voting is important (Amadeo et al., 2002; Torney-Purta, Schwille, and Amadeo, 1999).

Schools are, however, a site for both learning and conflict, for socialization and exclusion. The language of instruction, the messages and values conveyed in the text books, and the attitudes and behavior of school principals and teachers in the school toward their students all have an impact on young people's sense of belonging, their integration with peers, and the type of civic identity they assume. A school with an authoritarian teaching style may foster civic attitudes and behavior different from those of a school that involves students in decision making, such as through student councils and teacher-student associations. Even when a national curriculum for civic education is defined, the context of the school environment filters the lessons in particular ways. For instance, in Thailand all secondary schools are mandated to develop students' good citizenship and to teach young people to live in society with peace and harmony. However, Pitiyanuwat and Sujiva's in-depth case study of three schools (2001) shows that these themes were open to interpretation. While all schools stressed the importance of morality, the public school emphasized order, discipline, and social development, the private religious school focused on religious conduct, and the university model school stressed critical thinking and intellectual activity.

Experiences in school can contribute to the development of a sense of agency and leadership skills, or alternatively can reinforce a sense of marginalization. Conflicts with school culture are perhaps stronger among young people coming from social classes that are economically and culturally subordinated (Tenti, 2000). Students from minority or otherwise marginalized groups begin school at a disadvantage to other privileged groups and must work harder to gain the skills and social knowledge to operate effectively in the school environment. Furthermore, poor students may be less likely to attend schools with good quality of instruction or with the resources for extracurricular activities or sports facilities.

### Nonformal Programs for the Formation of Citizenship

The public education system is not the only institution providing civic education. Increasingly, foreign donors and local community organizations create their own programs to promote understanding of democracy, encourage community participation, and create social capital in communities. However, programs targeted at young people have traditionally been school-based, such as those discussed previously. Nonschool-based programs either have focused implicitly on adults or have attempted to draw the most vulnerable young people, such as street children and child prostitutes, back into mainstream social activities (Finkel, 2002; Rizzini, Barker, and Cassaniga, 2002). Even when these programs do exist, there are few published evaluations that provide the controls and statistical rigor necessary to measure the impact of the intervention and remove potential biases.

Analysis of nonschool-based programs is further complicated by the fact that few analyses of adult civic education projects provide information about the ages of adult respondents. Given that the age of majority is 18 in most countries, it is likely that these programs included both younger and older adults. Although the needs of adolescents are very different from those of young adults past the age of majority, adult civic education programs provide important information regarding methods for drawing younger adults into formal political participation.

Bratton and colleagues (1999) looked at the effects on political culture of civics programs conducted by NGOs in Zambia, including street shows conducted by the Foundation for Democratic Process and voter registration and turnout programs administered by the Civic Action Fund. In addition to these specific civic education campaigns, the government supported radio broadcasts that encouraged citizens to register and vote, to refrain from violence, and to serve as democratic role models for the country's school-children (Bratton et al., 1999). Using a national sample of registered voters as a control group, they were able to partially account for possible biases related to self-selection into the civic education programs.

Among their findings was that civic education programs had more influence on civic knowledge than on behavior, and that the impact was mediated by the educational attainment of the respondent. For respondents with no education and no access to the mass media, exposure to the civic education programs had no impact on civic knowledge or behavior. However, among respondents who had more than eight years of education and regular radio access, the civic education programs increased the likelihood that the respondent could identify their political representatives, express tolerant values, and participate in key democratic actions, such as voting in elections (Bratton et al., 1999). These results indicate that those who were more educated or better informed may have been more receptive to the program messages.

In a separate study, Finkel (2002) examined several civic education programs supported by the U.S. Agency for International Development in the Dominican Republic and South Africa. The key outcomes of political participation included taking part in an organized community problem-solving activity, attending a local government meeting, working on an election campaign, and contacting a local elected official. Given that participation in the civic education programs may be associated with an individual's predisposition toward democracy, the motivation to succeed in a democratic society, or the need for sociability, Finkel took account of these self-selection biases using Heckman regression models that controlled for group memberships, political interest, media use, and past voting behavior.

Participation in democracy training had significant effects on local-level participation in four of the seven programs evaluated. However, the strength of the effect varied depending on the length and intensity of the exposure, the extent of the focus on fostering participation, the extent to which the training was participatory, and the level of each individual's prior participatory resources. In no situation was age significant, implying that these programs were just as effective in delivering the message to young adults and newly eligible voters as it was to older adults (Finkel, 2002).

The evaluation of these programs (U.S. Agency for International Development, 2002) observed that program participants had decreased trust in public and government institutions relative to nonparticipants. These differences were associated with an increased knowledge about local government. Whereas decreases in institutional trust have elsewhere been hypothesized as detrimental to civic participation (e.g., Putnam, 2000), in these contexts it appeared that decreased trust was relative to an increased awareness of local corruption and a better understanding of how government should function. Furthermore, there was less trust in the nondemocratic arms of the state, such as the police and the military, than there was for elected officials (Finkel and Sabatini, 2000; U.S. Agency for International Development, 2002). Further research is required to examine under what conditions low levels of institutional trust encourage active citizenship and protest, and under what conditions apathy and a sense of ineffectiveness are fostered. Also, this type of analysis should compare the different outcomes of civic education programs in countries with effective governments and those with corrupt bureaucracies.

While these programs have focused on building knowledge of government and encouraging participation in elections and political processes, their target has often been restricted to citizens of voting age. For younger

citizens, especially adolescents who have not yet reached the age of majority, a focus on civic knowledge may be less important than fostering an
ethic of civic responsibility and participation. In developed countries, many
programs, both school-based and nonschool-based, have encouraged youth
volunteerism as a path to future political engagement (Flanagan et al.,
1998; Pancer and Pratt, 1999; Roker, Player, and Coleman, 1999; Yates,
1999).

Although volunteerism is often grounded in Western attitudes toward
the individual and the responsibilities of the state, some youth programs
have attempted to encourage community participation by directly engaging
young people in service projects. One example is the set of programs known
as Public Achievement, which were first developed in the United States and
then adapted to several developing country contexts. While this program is
very well grounded and tested at its sites in the United States, most of the
projects in developing countries are still in the pilot stage. The first generation of programs in Palestine created 14 groups of young men and women
ages 14-17. In each group, an older mentor used games and discussion to
help the participants identify problems in their community and brainstorm
practical solutions for these problems. Although not all projects were successfully implemented, almost all participants reported an improvement in
their ability to analyze local problems and their confidence to pursue their
goals (Davis, 2004). The evaluation of this pilot phase found that the
success of the program was augmented by the participation of parents and
community members in the program development.

Elsewhere, Rhodes, Mihyar, and El-Rous (2002) spent four years following the young male participants in a separate pilot project in Jordan.
This intervention worked with community leaders and parents in periurban
areas of Amman to create more youth-friendly neighborhoods, working
directly with young men ages 6-14 to develop prosocial values and capabilities and to create safe spaces. By working closely with both young people
and communities, the program reshaped the social terrain in which young
men developed. Whereas young people had previously formed networks
and gangs on the street, turning to violence to resolve issues, the program
created community centers with computers in which boys could safely
meet, conducted summer camps in which the boys received counseling on
peaceful conflict resolution, and forged connections to a national youth
organization to provide vocational training for young community residents
(Rhodes, Mihyar, and El-Rous, 2002).

Beyond the content of these interventions, these two programs brought
young people together in an environment in which they could gain confidence and self-esteem, create peer groups and connections with other young
people from inside and outside their immediate community, and have access to mentors who provided counseling and guidance separate from fam-

ily expectations and obligations. These aspects are shared by a broader set of interventions in the development community that focus on building the livelihoods of adolescents and young adults (Kobayashi, 2004; Population Council and UNICEF, 2003; Population Council and International Center for Research on Women, 2000). The livelihoods approach attempts to expand the capabilities of young people and to create resources and opportunities that make it easier for young people to act on their skills.

While the content of livelihoods programs vary, the greatest emphasis is placed on building economic skills, developing and maintaining positive social relationships, and fostering the ability of young people to exercise critical thinking and have a stake in the negotiation and decision-making that directly affect their lives. Policies and programs are developed in a context sensitive to the status and vulnerabilities of young people during their transition into adulthood. Particular attention is paid to developing social networks of peers, which young people can turn to for social support at future points in their life. This is particularly relevant to young women, because emphasis is placed on increasing community acceptance of female mobility and creating acceptable social connections outside the family (Population Council and International Center for Research on Women, 2000). Altogether, this approach to developing the capacities of young people has great promise for creating spaces in which young people can participate more fully in their communities.

Participation in sports is another excellent way for young people to form peer networks, learn teamwork skills, and exercise leadership. These qualities help prepare them to participate actively in other civic, employment, and social activities. Participation in sports can be especially beneficial for girls, who may not have other opportunities for organized recreation. It also gives them an opportunity to cultivate self-esteem that is based on traits that fall outside traditional gender roles that emphasize beauty, passivity, and domesticity (Brady, 1998). Box 6-3 describes the impact that a sports program had on the self-efficacy of adolescent girls in Kenya.

There has been relatively little research into the impact of sports on the social development of young people in either developed or developing countries. Research from the United States suggests that participation in organized sports may have more positive effects on girls than on boys. Young female athletes who participated in sports were less likely than their nonathlete peers to become pregnant, more likely to delay sex, and more likely to use contraception if sexually active (Miller et al., 1998). However, there has been little research on the causal pathways through which sports participation influences these health and social outcomes, and even less attention to the potential self-selection issue of which young women choose to become athletes, particularly in communities defined by strong gender role bias and restricted female mobility.

---

**BOX 6-3**
**The Mathare Youth Sports Association in Kenya**

The Mathare Youth Sports Association in Kenya is a program that provides sports facilities and social support for young boys and girls. Although begun as a sports league for boys, the association began plans to integrate girls after program managers and members of the boys' team saw women athletes during a trip to Norway in 1992. Initially parents were reluctant to allow their daughters to participate; many expressed concern that involvement would take away time for completing chores or that the increased mobility of young girls would expose them to unsafe spaces. However, as the female participants demonstrated their resourcefulness with time management, many mothers actively encouraged their daughters.

Participation in the program has expanded the gender roles available to young girls in Kenya. Not only have female participants had the chance to build friendships and gain confidence, but participation has created an avenue for escaping the confines of daily routines. Furthermore, there was a conscious effort to work against gender stereotypes in the organization, so that, for example, doing the laundry is a job now shared by boys and girls, and young women are now allowed to drive the garbage clean-up trucks around the site. Today, more than 10 years since the beginning of the women's program, several girls have risen through the ranks to be project managers, coaches, and referees, and a woman now coordinates the girls' soccer program (Brady and Khan, 2002).

---

## Work and Citizenship

Just as schools provide an environment in which young people learn about their rights and responsibilities as citizens, expand their social networks beyond the family, and gain the confidence to act in society, work can also serve as an important way to gain citizenship skills. Paid employment may develop an individual's skills, ability and social standing (Bay and Blekesaune, 2002), and work may serve as a means of identity negotiation, learning to balance responsibilities, and gaining responsibility and sufficiency outside the home sphere (Levison, 2000). The professional and social relationships formed with colleagues facilitate the growth of social capital as well as the cultivation of an environment for the discussion of political ideas. Furthermore, community participation is mediated by the amount of time spent working, the status and stigma associated with one's employment, the intensity and nature of the work, the work environment, and whether any union or other organizing effort is active.

In some developing countries, social legislation connects welfare, pension, and medical benefits provided by the state to the recipients' labor contribution (Joseph, 1996; Lister, 1997). Because the formal labor market participation of young women is much lower than that of young men, their opportunities for citizenship through employment are more limited. However, the gap between young men's and women's employment is narrowing. Young women are further excluded from social and political engagement in public spaces through the burden of their domestic labor, which is heavy during the adolescent years even when they are attending school (Ritchie et al., 2004). These responsibilities leave young women with little leisure time to spend engaged in community organizations or political activism.

However, when paid work is available for women, it can expand the public roles available to them. For instance, Salem, Ibrahim, and Brady (2003) discuss how young women in four rural Egyptian communities used their positions as promoters for a local NGO to participate more fully in their communities and acquire valuable social and political experience—opportunities that are rarely available to adolescent girls in rural Egypt. Although their participation was constrained by patriarchal and age norms, the young women were able to negotiate new public spaces and roles for themselves. Likewise, young women who enter the labor force through factory employment report increased mobility and expanded social relationships beyond the immediate family (Amin et al., 1998; Lynch, 1999).

Nonetheless, some adolescents who work may face the same isolation and lack of opportunities for citizenship and community participation as out-of-school youth confront. The most vulnerable adolescents are those who work while attending school, who work at too young an age, who work without the protection of a caring adult, or who work under hazardous conditions. The structure and intensity of work may prevent working adolescents from accessing or developing protective social and cultural networks. Domestic workers are a good example, because they work away from their family in unfamiliar surroundings and without protection. The time demands of labor constrain the amount of leisure time that is available for civic participation and political engagement. Furthermore, if young people are forced to assume adult labor and income-generating responsibilities but are not given a role in personal and household decision-making, they may become rebellious and alienated (Rhodes, Mihyar, and El-Rous, 2002; Tienda and Wilson, 2002).

Young people at particular risk are those who are neither enrolled in school nor employed outside the household. Rarely are these young people actually doing nothing, but rather are involved in domestic labor and unpaid work in family enterprises. These roles—unregulated and unseen—are a direct reflection of children's lack of agency (Levison, 2000). Using micro-level data from 18 Latin American countries, Menezes-Filho (2003) found that more 16-17-year-olds than 12-13-year-olds were neither in school nor working. This increase in invisibility by age was also found among young women in a nationally representative sample of young people in Pakistan (Sathar et al., 2003a). Young women are of particular risk, since they are more likely than young men to be outside these formal structures. Since the social mobility of young women is often more restricted than that of young men, they are even more vulnerable to exclusion from participation in community activities.

In addition to young people who are engaged in unpaid household labor and unpaid work, there is also concern for those who are looking for work but who are unable to find it. Psychological studies have found that educated unemployed young people express a greater sense of alienation than educated employed ones (Singh, Singh, and Rani, 1996), while others have found that unemployed young people express less confidence in existing political systems, talk less about politics, and more frequently support revolutionary political ideas than their employed peers (Bay and Blekesaune, 2002). For instance, unemployed young people played a vital role in the political movements that shaped Senegal in the late 1980s and early 1990s. Young people in general were largely excluded from the rites of political participation, and the social frustration of the elite and educated turned to political violence to "express [their] disillusionment with the outcome of the restoration of democratic rule" (Diouf, 1996:229). In contrast, poor adolescent girls in rural Ecuador found that their aspirations to participate in a modernized society—built through education and exposure to the media—were thwarted by their lack of access to social capital and the formal economy (Miles, 2000).

## Opportunities for Military or National Service

Military service serves as an important means for expressing patriotic sentiments and developing a sense of civic responsibility. In countries with a modern military, service in the armed forces may be an opportunity to gain valuable technical skills that will lead to future employment. Some countries, such as Bolivia, provide literacy classes to supplement basic training exercises, and enlistment in various specialties may include training in areas in which skills are transferable, such as engineering and medicine (Marshall, 2000).[24] Even when specialization is not available, such experience as driving military vehicles may also transfer into future civilian employment. However, in most countries, only men are subject to compulsory recruitment policies, whereas the enlistment of women is usually voluntary. Furthermore, women in most countries are excluded from combat duty and are often restricted to clerical or medical duties. These limitations often

---

[24]Ellen Marshall, formerly with the U.S. State Department, shared cables from U.S. embassies around the world providing, in response to a series of questions, unclassified information and data, as of 2000, on national military and service programs.

exclude women from eligibility to be an officer, thereby restricting the extent to which they can fully participate or aspire to achieve in these contexts.

Military service may represent an alternative pathway to training and citizenship for young people who have not been successful at school or are unable to afford to continue in school. In countries without compulsory enlistment, it is often young people from the poorest, least educated, and most marginalized segments of society who are encouraged to join the armed forces as an economic and employment alternative. Although this may be the only opportunity for some young people to gain transferable skills, there is concern for the mental and physical well-being of young people who enlist in the military prior to age 18 (Coalition to Stop the Use of Child Soldiers, 2001).

Child soldiers drawn directly from conflict zones are of particular concern. There are an estimated 300,000 child soldiers in the world, defined as young people younger than age 18 who are participating in armed conflict (Coalition to Stop the Use of Child Soldiers, 2001). Although this estimate also includes young people who voluntarily enlisted in formal national service, the most publicized cases are of young people who have been forced into guerrilla groups, such as in the Democratic Republic of the Congo, Sierra Leone, and Sudan. Many of these young men may have been coerced into participation, or else may have been left with few alternatives when family members were killed, wounded, displaced, or otherwise split apart (Richards, 1996). With both the physical environment devastated, as well as all normalcy in social relations at a standstill, these young people do not grow up in an environment that offers much security. Their transition to adult citizenship may be characterized by fear, violence, and insecurity. They may also feel that it is difficult or even impossible to have an impact on their environments.

For young people in some settings, the opportunity to join an independence struggle or civil conflict may be the only way to take up an adult role and contribute to their community (Richards, 1996). Participation in organized resistance can be a forum for political education, learning organizing skills, and leadership. For example, this may have happened among South Africa's young people in their struggle against apartheid (Marks, 2001). Elsewhere, participation in military service has been shown to enhance responsibility, self-esteem, independence, and the ability to control impulses and withstand pressures (Mayseless, 1993).

In addition to military service, national service programs can also serve as institutions that bridge the transition from adolescence to adulthood and foster civic development. Most government-sponsored nonmilitary service programs focus on enhancing development and building the human capital infrastructure. For example, national service programs in Burkina Faso and Ghana assign recent university and polytechnic graduates to rural areas to work in education, health, and agriculture (Marshall, 2000). Not only do these programs benefit rural communities by distributing skilled workers throughout the country, but also national service participants are exposed to the issues and needs of rural civil society.

## Media and Citizenship

As information and communication technologies have become more available throughout the world, the media has assumed an important role in the political socialization of young people. By creating a public space in which information can be distributed and debated, the media can contribute to the construction of adult citizenship values and practices (Buckingham, 2000; Habermas, 1989). Television, radio, newspapers, and the Internet are important sites for the dissemination of political and public health information campaigns, as well as sources of civic information and popular culture.

Aware of the influence of the mass media on young people, the Convention on the Rights of the Child (United Nations, 1989) gives it considerable attention in Article 17, which encourages mass media enterprises to "disseminate information and materials of social and cultural benefits to the child" and to be sensitive to the "linguistic needs of the child who belongs to a minority group or who is indigenous." Although the majority of global media outlets are now dominated by a handful of multinational corporations, there is some indication with respect to television that domestic programming tops the ratings when it is available (Hoskins and Mirus, 1988; Thussu, 2000).

However, the proliferation of information and communication technologies is causing rapid transformations in all areas of life, from the speed with which information can be shared to the support of Internet-based communities that transcend national borders. Young people are among those most engaged with these new forms of communication, filtering and integrating new information to forge their identities and gain new skills (Martin-Barbero, Fox, and White, 1993; Suoranta, 2003). Despite the importance of the media as a globalizing force for cultural change, many parts of the developing world have poor access to most forms of information and communication technologies. Although a recent survey of students in eight cities in India found that 48 percent of school-going youth accessed the Internet at cyber cafes, this disguises the lack of access to the Internet in rural areas and among the poor (NetSense, 2002). While this level of connectivity is promising, it highlights the geographic and socioeconomic distribution of access. Not only is access mediated by the availability of electricity and telephone lines, but the cost of most forms of technology makes household access prohibitively expensive in many parts of the developing world (United Nations Development Programme, 1999).

The Demographic and Health Surveys (DHS) include questions on whether respondents watch television at least once a week, read the newspaper at least once a week, or listen to the radio every day. Furthermore, the DHS household surveys recorded household ownership of televisions, radios, and telephones, providing an indicator of household access to these forms of media. One of the most striking results of the surveys is the large number of young people, primarily in sub-Saharan Africa, who do not have access to any of these three media (Table 6-10).[25] Household ownership of televisions and radios was lowest in these regions, leaving young people largely dependent on accessing these forms of technology at a neighbor's house or other local common viewing areas. In contrast, household ownership of radios was higher then ownership of televisions in all regions except the former Soviet Asia, pointing to its lower cost and reliance on batteries instead of electricity. Across sub-Saharan Africa the radio was the most commonly accessed medium, with more young people listening to radio daily than had regular access to television.

Television and radio have long been employed to disseminate political information and organize political involvement, from broadcasting campaign messages and encouraging voter turnout on election days to providing forums for political debate. For example, radio programs have been used in countries as diverse as Zambia and the Dominican Republic to educate the public about the government, political parties, and the election cycle (Bratton et al., 1999; Finkel, 2002).

Although household ownership of radios roughly corresponds to the number of young people reporting that they listened to the radio regularly, the number who watched television was much higher than household ownership. This means that many may go to a neighbor's house or some type of community center in order to watch television. This is a particularly interesting arena for future research; audience research in developed countries has shown that the social interaction of group viewing and the subsequent discussion of television programs have an important relationship to the interpretation of the message (Lull, 1988). The way in which young people talk about television often bears a strong relationship to attitudes toward civic engagement (Buckingham, 2000). Not only is this likely to be the context in which many political and civic identities are forged, but it is also an opportunity to promote social connectedness.

---

[25]Data for Asia and the Middle East include only the married, a very selective sample at ages 15-19.

TABLE 6-10 Media Access, 15-19-Year-Olds (Weighted Averages)

| Region | Television | | Radio | | | Newspaper | |
| | Watch at Least Once a Week | Household Ownership | Listen Daily | | Household Ownership | Read at Least Once a Week | |
| | Female | Male | | Female | Male | | Female | Male |
|---|---|---|---|---|---|---|---|---|
| Former Soviet Asia | 92 | 90 | 90 | 46 | 26 | 52 | 59 | 39 |
| Western and Middle Africa | 45 | 56 | 20 | 43 | 61 | 58 | 20 | 28 |
| Southern and Eastern Africa | 22 | 21 | 15 | 38 | 41 | 47 | 21 | 21 |
| Caribbean/Central America | 71 | 64 | 51 | 69 | 65 | 68 | 47 | 44 |
| South America | 86 | 90 | 70 | 80 | 76 | 86 | 59 | 60 |

SOURCE: Demographic and Health Surveys.

However, other research has shown that heavy television viewing is associated with a "mainstreaming" of political views. In a study of Argentinean adolescents in Buenos Aires and its surrounding 41 towns, Morgan and Shanahan (1991) found that young people who were heavy television viewers (more than 30 hours a week) were more likely than light viewers (less than 20 hours a week) to agree that people should obey authority and to approve of limits on the freedom of speech. Heavy television viewing was significantly associated with less diversity in outlooks and a decrease in the impact of other demographic influences. Although the data did not allow the researchers to address the nature of this relationship, they hypothesized that, among heavy viewers, time spent watching television may preclude participation in civic activities that might promote more "democratic" political thinking (Morgan and Shanahan, 1991).

Beyond the political spectrum, the images, actions, and words broadcast through the media become part of the common cultural language shared by all members of the audience. Although there are few data available, it is also important to consider how the Internet contributes to the construction of civic knowledge and behavior. Both a source of information and social connections, the Internet is the most rapidly growing form of media today. However, access to the Internet is even more sharply divided globally than any other form of information and communication technology. From 1999 to 2002, global access to the Internet tripled; by the year 2005, it is anticipated that over 1 billion people may be on line (Nua, 2003; United Nations Development Programme, 1999; World Bank, 2003). However, the majority of access is restricted to Europe, Canada, and the United States. As of 2002, the Middle East and Africa combined accounted for only 6 percent of all global Internet use (Nua, 2002). Furthermore, over 80 percent of material on the Internet is posted in English, thereby limiting its potential for anyone who is not fluent (Nua, 2002; United Nations Development Programme, 1999). This digital divide has profound consequences, particularly for a media whose usage is dominated by young people around the globe.

The digital divide is not limited to differentials between countries; in any given nation access is also regulated by education, socioeconomic status, and residence in an urban or rural area (Suoranta, 2003). Not only is access mediated by literacy and fluency in English, but use of the Internet also requires basic computer literacy. Furthermore, there is concern that this difference in access will also expand the knowledge gap, whereby young people with access to the Internet will benefit not only from the content of the knowledge and connections formed, but also from the abstract skills gained from conducting searches for information, processing and filtering what is retrieved, and using the subsequent information (Castells, 2000; Suoranta, 2003).

## CONCLUSIONS AND POLICY RECOMMENDATIONS

### Key Findings

*The political and civic interests and behaviors of young people are important topics for future research.* In recent years, the definition of citizenship has been broadened beyond the individual's relationship with the nation-state to encompass various dimensions of political and civic participation. At the same time, elements of rapid global change, including democratization and the rise of civil society, the growing reach of the media, and the formation of transnational identities, have all contributed to a growing appreciation of the importance of citizenship in the development process. As a result, such issues as the formation of citizenship and the role of young people as citizens have taken on increased prominence and attention in the development literature.

*Youth participation in civil society and political life has recently emerged as an important development objective.* Many international organizations and NGOs now recognize the importance of involving young people in development planning and addressing their needs. Young people are expressing greater voice at the local, national, and international levels and pushing agendas that address their concerns.

*Most developing country governments now recognize 18 as the legal age of majority.* Typically, this is the age at which citizens are given the right to vote and young men are subject to compulsory recruitment to the military. However, significant age gaps still remain between the time at which young people are held responsible for adult actions, such as the age of criminal responsibility and the minimum age for employment, and the age at which they are legally able to express a political voice.

*Current cross-national surveys are inadequate for investigating young people's transition to citizenship.* The results of many surveys that have made the effort to include young adults from developing countries are rarely presented by both age and gender, in part because many have not sampled a sufficient number of young adults to allow more discrete descriptive analysis. Although these characteristics are often included as explanatory variables in regressions, the distinct patterns of involvement by young adults have not been given sufficient attention.

*The set of indicators currently available for measuring the participation, agency, and empowerment of young people are inadequate.* Many of the data sets that measure the political and civic involvement of young people have been adapted from public opinion surveys of adults and are grounded in the traditional indicators of citizenship as derived from Western theory. Few adequately capture regionally specific forms of participation or the collective forms of agency used by young people.

*Men are more likely to participate in traditional political activities than women.* Young men are more likely than young women to express interest in politics, vote, join political parties, although there is some evidence that the gender gap in political interest closes as the gender gap in the educational attainment and labor force participation of women decreases.

*Young people are more likely than older adults to participate in community organizations.* Young men and women are more likely to be involved with arts, sports, and religious activities in almost all of the regions for which there are data; although there are few data available to explain this trend, differences may be due to differences in the discretionary time of young people in comparison to older adults. Among young people, participation in these organizations is highly gendered, with young men more likely to be involved in sports organizations and young women more likely to be engaged with religious or arts activities.

*Young people have greater trust in religious institutions and the press than in public institutions.* They are more likely to express trust in the religious institutions than they are in the national government, the police, or the civil service. Furthermore, there is evidence that older adolescents are less trusting of all institutions than younger adolescents.

## Policy Recommendations

*Governments should work toward greater consistency in operational definitions of adulthood, particularly as they relate to various aspects of the practice of citizenship, including voting, military service, and criminal responsibility.* The panel's review of laws relating to the legal age of majority reveals many inconsistencies across and within countries in ages of majority.

*Civic education should include the acceptance of diversity, the teaching of prosocial values, opportunities for participation in school governance, and media literacy.* The majority of current civic education programs focus on teaching the function and purpose of government and the law. School-based and nonschool-based programs should extend instruction beyond basic civics in order to foster critical thinking and service learning.

*Programs designed to enhance the capabilities of young people should actively address issues of participation in the public domain.* Self-confidence and participation in decision-making influence a young person's self-recognition as a political actor. These skills are closely connected to the economic and social outcomes most frequently addressed.

*Compensatory programs for girls and other disadvantaged groups that combine nonformal education and livelihoods training with opportunities for group participation should be developed in order to help them overcome their social isolation.* When young women and other disadvantaged individuals are able to develop a public sphere of their own, they can be empowered to acquire a sense of self and of personal competence and can gain a network of peers, which can serve as a source of social capital during the transition to adulthood. As young women develop a sense of political competence, they will be able to exercise greater voice in the family, community, and nation-state.

*Priority should be placed on building the infrastructure systems that will provide greater equality of access to information and communication technologies.* Social, economic, and political development is increasingly dependent on access to forms of information and communication technologies. The current digital divide is influenced by the availability of electricity, the cost of services, and the literacy and language requirements of the media. The skills deficit of young people without access to the Internet and other forms of media will only deepen economic inequities.

### Research Recommendations

The social, political, and economic environment in which young people are maturing is changing rapidly. In-depth qualitative research holds the most promise for capturing the diversity of structures, networks, and opportunities that young people use to engage with their communities and to participate in the political sphere. Only after the range of these practices has been identified can quantitative surveys adequately measure the levels and implications of youth participation. Furthermore, it is important that empirical research investigate the roles that ethnicity, religion, and other forms of identity play in shaping the formation and practice of citizenship by young people.

*   How is citizenship actually developed and practiced in developing country contexts? What are the relevant indicators? In what ways do

community-based nonformal organizations provide opportunities for the formation and practice of citizenship?

• How do civic participation and attitudes toward politics differ between young citizens in new democracies and young citizens in established democracies? What does it mean to be a citizen in an authoritarian state?

• What are the appropriate indicators for measuring the agency and community engagement of young people?

• What are the levels and types of political processes that young people participate in? What motivates them to engage or disengage with political processes?

• How does the acquisition of the rights and responsibilities of citizenship relate to the success of other transitions to adulthood?

• How are emerging forms of media (e.g., the Internet, mobile phones, independent radio) affecting the ways in which citizenship formation and practice are evolving?

• How are rising levels of school enrollment influencing the relationship between citizens and the state?

• What are the strategies used by young people to maintain social connections in the developing world's rapidly growing urban centers?

• How have the transnational flows of people, capital, and communication technologies influenced the formation and practice of citizenship and community engagement of young people?

• What forms of transnational activism do young people pursue? How are they changing in response to new information and communication technologies? What issues motivate these movements?

• What role does religion play in expressing political views and identities among young people?

• To what extent is it important to understand how the determinants of citizenship and the impact of citizenship differ by groups defined by such characteristics as gender, class, ethnicity, race, caste, tribe, and religion? To what extent can causal effects be identified for all these aspects of the determinants or the impact of citizenship?

# 7

# The Transition to Marriage

## INTRODUCTION

In all regions of the world, most people over age 30 are either currently in a long-term coresidential sexual union, or they have been at one time in their lives. Even in populations of European origin, who have generally exhibited the smallest percentages of adults ever in unions, the fraction of the population who never married is on the order of 10 or 15 percent (with some exceptions, for example, 19th century Ireland—Watkins, 1986). Given that the vast majority of adults marry, examining the transition to marriage in a particular cultural and historical milieu is crucial to understanding the transition to adulthood in that setting.

It is important to stress, however, that although the transition into marriage is a key component of the transition to adulthood in most contexts, marriage, in and of itself, is not necessarily a marker of adulthood, particularly for the numerous young women who wed during their teenage years. As we discuss in Chapter 1, one of the preconditions for a successful transition to adulthood is the taking on of adult roles in an appropriate time and sequence, giving young people: (1) the opportunity to acquire an appropriate amount of human and social capital, (2) the knowledge and means to sustain health during adulthood, and (3) the capability to make choices through the acquisition of a sense of self and a sense of personal competence. Early marriage is unlikely to satisfy those preconditions. Moreover, marriage during the teenage years is associated with an increased probability of divorce (Goldman, 1981; Singh and Samara, 1996; Tilson and Larsen, 2000), although studies have yet to establish whether it is early marriage per se or the characteristics of those who marry early that increases the risk of dissolution.

Despite the fact that marriage or union formation is nearly universal, many aspects of this transition vary from place to place. This variation makes the meaning of marriage—both in and of itself and in relation to the transition to adulthood more broadly—quite different in different contexts.

In this chapter, we examine various aspects of the transition to marriage with a focus on changes in the last several decades. First, we describe the prevalence of marriage among young people under age 30, focusing especially on the timing of marriage. Second, we consider differentials in age at marriage. Third, we explore some of the global changes described in Chapter 2 and their possible implications for changes in the timing of marriage. Fourth, we look at the terms and conditions of marriage, including the age difference between spouses, polygyny, the decision making process surrounding marriage, consanguinity, the nexus between marital behavior and household formation and structure, and financial transfers between families. Finally, we provide data on changes in the legal age at marriage across countries and review the limited literature on interventions that have been designed to encourage young women and their families to delay marriage. Note that, although constrained by the available data, we give attention to young men as well as women. Given that the literature focuses on the timing and conditions of women's marriage, this concern with the marriage of men is a distinctive feature of our treatment.

## TRENDS IN MARRIAGE PREVALENCE AND TIMING

### Trends in Marriage Prevalence

The data on marriage prevalence and timing among young people come from two sources: the United Nations (UN) Population Division database and the Demographic and Health Surveys (DHS). The advantage of the UN data base is that the data are available for a large number of developing countries; the advantage of the DHS data is that there is information on age at first marriage rather than information simply on current marital status by age. A more extensive discussion of the data, including a discussion of the regional weights we employ and the degree of coverage of each data source, appears in Appendix A at the end of the volume.

Before turning to the findings on marriage trends, a cautionary note is in order. We are assuming here that the reporting of age and marital status in the censuses and surveys on which our analysis is based is accurate. In certain populations, however, this assumption may be questionable. In Africa, where formation of a marital union has been described as a process that takes place in stages, marriage is not a well-defined event and therefore age at marriage is difficult to establish (van de Walle and Meekers, 1994). To the extent that particular rites and ceremonies have lost significance or been eliminated as the population becomes more urbanized and better educated, comparisons over time are problematic. In countries in which, at least officially, early marriage violates newly passed legislation, observed declines in the proportion married at or by a particular age may simply reflect increases in deliberate misreporting. For example, Amin and Al-Bassusi (2003) speculate that, in Bangladesh, the implementation of a new law requiring girls to be at least 18 when they marry resulted in a precipitous and, they believe, improbable decline in the proportion of 15-19-year-olds reporting being married. Feng and Quanhe (1996) report that in China, a gap between the marriage ceremony, when couples are permitted by custom to live together, and marriage registration means that the reporting of age at marriage is problematic, at least in the recent past, when the legal age of marriage was higher than the desired age for many young people. While age misreporting may lead to an exaggeration of change in certain populations, in others it may lead to an underestimation of the decline in early marriage over time. In countries in which age is not reported with a great deal of accuracy, the timing of an event that occurred in the remote past is often estimated to take place closer to the survey than it actually did. Older women are thus more likely to report that a marriage took place at a later age (Blanc and Rutenberg, 1990).

Note also that the definition of marriage used in censuses and standardized surveys varies. For the DHS, marriage is a self-defined state. Respondents are coded as married if they say so in response to questions on whether they are currently or ever married or are living with a man. Age at first marriage is thus typically age at first cohabitation with a partner or husband (Kishor, 2003). As for censuses, countries typically define marriage to reflect the forms of marriage and union that are generally recognized and accepted and obtain information accordingly; as a result, for the most part, data on marriage or union status is largely comparable between censuses and surveys. For example, in Latin America, census questions on marital or union status include the category "consensual union" because this is a widely occurring and acknowledged form of union. However, in countries in which cohabitation or living together is much less common, "consensual union" may not be explicitly included as a category, with the result that this type of arrangement may be underreported. Note that we do not separately assess trends in consensual unions because of variability in how data were collected and fluid definitions of marriage. For DHS data, we could present the percentage of respondents currently in a consensual union, but we are not able to compare cohorts because we do not have information on marriages that began as consensual unions. For the UN database we could compare the percentage of those in a consensual union by age group for two censuses or surveys but only for those countries with a separate consensual union category, which is a subset of countries in which consensual unions are common.

Tables 7-1 and 7-2, based on the UN database, show the percentage of women and men ever in a union[1] by age group from data collected at two different points in time. For women the age groups are 15-19, 20-24, and 25-29, and for men—for whom marriage during the teenage years is rare— they are 20-24 and 25-29. An annualized rate of change is calculated, since the interval between the two times varies by country. Note that for these tables as well as all subsequent tables that present regional data, the individual country data are provided in appendix tables at the end of the chapter.

For all regions except former Soviet Asia and South America, where early marriage was not that common even 10-20 years ago, teenage marriage has declined among women; whereas 27 percent of 15-19-year-old women in the developing world were married in 1970-1989, 21 percent were married in 1990-2000.[2] The reduction in the percentage of married 15-19-year-olds is particularly striking in Africa.[3] The percentage married among 20-24-year-olds has also fallen markedly in most regions, with the exception, again, of South America. While the majority of women in developing countries were married by ages 25-29, there are regions in which 15-25 percent of women were still not married by their late 20s, including South America, the Caribbean and Central America, the Middle East, the former Soviet Asia, and Eastern and Southern Africa, as well as certain countries in Asia (e.g., Myanmar, the Philippines, and Thailand).

For the most part, regions with a relatively high percentage married at younger ages also had a relatively high percentage married at older ages (e.g., Africa) and vice versa (e.g., the former Soviet Asia). The exception is

---

[1]For countries in which consensual union is uncommon, the percentage shown is simply those who ever married.

[2]Given that the rate of growth in cohort size is currently declining in most parts of the developing world including in China, where the rate of decline is accelerating, even if the percentage married at each age were unchanged, it would appear that the percentage of 15-19-year-olds married had increased because the ratio of 15-17-year-olds to 18-19-year-olds would be smaller and, relative to 18-19-year-olds, 15-17-year-olds are less likely to be married. The fact that we observe a reduction in the percentage of 15-19-year-olds married indicates that the true decline in marriage is likely to be slightly larger.

[3]Not all demographers would agree with this observation. Van de Walle and Baker (2004:17) assert that for Africa "there are good reasons to argue that the age at union has changed little." They base this claim on the belief that visiting unions, in which an individual has "stable noncohabiting" partners, have increased. Because most women in a visiting union would not describe themselves as married, they are not categorized as such in the DHS.

China,[4] which ranks very low in the level of young marriage and relatively high in the level of marriage at older ages.

Not only is marriage during the teenage years uncommon among men, but also marriage in the early 20s is much less frequent among men than among women and, in some regions, has declined substantially in recent years. For example, in Eastern and Southern Africa, Eastern Asia, the former Soviet Asia, and the Middle East, there has been a sizeable reduction in the percentage of men married at ages 20-24 in the last decade or so.

By ages 25-29, considerable numbers of men in developing countries have wed. However, in certain regions, marriage is postponed until the 30s for a large fraction of men. In South America and the few countries of Western/Middle Africa for which there are data, this pattern is observed in the earlier period and seems to have stabilized. In the Middle East, where nearly half of men were not married in this age group, and in the former Soviet Asia, there is recent evidence of increasing delay.

In summary, Tables 7-1 and 7-2 reveal declines in the proportion ever married for both sexes in most regions; the exceptions are South America for both men and women and, for men only, Western/Middle Africa and South-central/South-eastern Asia. For six of the eight regional groupings, the patterns for men more or less parallel those for women. The exceptions are Western/Middle Africa, where there are substantial declines in the proportions married for women at ages 15-19 and 20-24 but virtually no change for men at ages 20-24 and 25-29, and South-central/South-eastern Asia, where there is no change for men but declines for women at ages 15-19 and 20-24. While five of the eight regions have had declines in the proportions married among young people of both sexes, in China and the Middle East the change has been most consistent across the three age groups for women and the two age groups for men.

Tables 7-3 and 7-4, which are also based on the UN database, are similar to Tables 7-1 and 7-2 in that they show levels of union formation by age, gender, and time, but they also break countries down by income group as designated by the World Bank, rather than region (World Bank, 2002b).[5] For both men and women there is very little difference in the percentage in a union in the lower middle- and upper middle-income categories. There is

---

[4]For Eastern Asia, data are available only for China, which contains 98 percent of the region's population.

[5]China is excluded from the lower-middle category because it is so numerically dominant that the weighted average for the category simply reflects its percentages. Given that China is the only country in the Eastern Asia regional grouping, the percentages for the country can be found in Tables 7-1 and 7-2.

a large contrast, however, between the low-income category and these other two. That is, men and women in low-income countries married earlier than their counterparts in wealthier countries. Among women, proportions ever married at ages 15-19 and 20-24 have declined in countries in all income categories; however, at ages 25-29, declines have occurred only among those in the more affluent countries, that is, those in the lower middle- and the upper middle-income categories. Among men, while there is evidence of a decline in proportions ever married for those in lower middle- and upper middle-income countries, there is no change over time among men in low-income countries.

### Trends in Marriage Timing

To reflect the earlier timing of marriage among women, we examined the proportions in a union before ages 18, 20, and 25 for women and before ages 20, 25, and 30 for men. We compared these proportions across age groups (20-24, 30-34, and 40-44) in order to get a sense of time trends. Tables 7-5 and 7-6, which are based on the DHS, provide data on the percentage of women ever in a union by ages 18 and 20 for three cohorts and by age 25 for two cohorts by region and income level.

The trends revealed by Table 7-5 are more or less consistent with those shown in Table 7-1. First, the regional rankings essentially follow the same sequence; moreover, the ranking changes little by age group. Western/Middle Africa is generally the region with the greatest percentage of women marrying at young ages, followed by South-central/South-eastern Asia, Eastern/Southern Africa, and the Caribbean and Central America. The Middle East, South America, and the former Soviet Asia have smaller proportions of women who married early. Second, a comparison of the percentage married by ages 18 and 20 across age cohorts indicates that there has been little change in South America, the Caribbean and Central America, and the former Soviet Asia. Indeed, in the former Soviet Asia, a greater percentage of 20-24-year-olds have married early than 30-34-year-olds. Other regions reveal a considerable decline in the percentage married by these ages, with a slightly greater percentage decline by age 18 than by age 20. The fall-off in early marriage is particularly sizeable in the Middle East, where there has been a 49 percent decline between 20-24-year-olds and 40-44-year-olds in the percentage married by age 18, and a 38 percent decline in the percentage married by age 20.

As for marriage by age 25, in all regions except South America, over 80 percent of women have married or are living with a partner by that age, with little change across the 30-34 and 40-44 age cohorts, except for the Middle East and sub-Saharan Africa. Comparing the 30-34-year-old cohort with the 40-44-year-old cohort for all three ages at marriage, it is clear that

TABLE 7-1 Percentage of Women Ever Married by Age, Time Period, and Region[a] (Weighted[b] Averages)

| | | Ages 15-19 | | |
| Region | Region Population Represented | Time 1[c] 1970- 1989 | Time 2 1990- 2000 | Annual Change |
|---|---|---|---|---|
| Africa | | | | |
|   Eastern/Southern Africa | 89.8 | 37.5 | 24.5 | −.75 |
|   Western/Middle Africa | 30.8 | 53.0 | 38.4 | −.89 |
| Asia | | | | |
|   Eastern Asia[d] | 98.1 | 4.2 | 1.3 | −.24 |
|   South-central/South-eastern Asia | 93.3 | 39.6 | 32.3 | −.64 |
|   Former Soviet[e] Asia | 37.8 | 9.4 | 9.6 | .02 |
| Latin America and Caribbean | | | | |
|   Caribbean/Central America | 87.5 | 20.6 | 18.1 | −.27 |
|   South America[f] | 99.9 | 14.4 | 16.3 | .12 |
| Middle East[g] | | | | |
|   Western Asia/Northern Africa | 62.8 | 21.0 | 14.9 | −.59 |
| TOTAL | 86.5 | 26.6 | 20.8 | −.48 |

[a]Regional groupings based on United Nations *World Population Prospects: The 2002 Revision* (2003b).

[b]Weighting is based on United Nations population estimates for year 2000 (*World Population Prospects: The 2000 Revision*, POP/DB/WPP/Rev. 2000/3/F1. February 2001).

[c]For several countries, the first survey/census was before 1970: Chad, Gabon, Cambodia, Palestine, Namibia.

[d]There are 3 countries in this region, China, North Korea, and Mongolia; data are available only for China, which contains 98% of the region's population ages 10-24.

the percentage decline in marriage prevalence is greater during the teenage years, that is, by ages 18 and 20, than it is by age 25. In short, in most regions there has been a greater reduction in early marriage than in marriage during the 20s, suggesting an increase in age at marriage among women in the developing world rather than a retreat from the institution of marriage.

Table 7-6 presents these same data by World Bank income group; however because lower middle- and upper middle-income countries are not as well represented by the DHS, these data are not as useful as the comparable UN data. As with Table 7-3, little difference is observed in the percentage married in the lower middle- and upper middle-income categories, whereas a large contrast between the low-income category and these other two is apparent.

In summarizing the data on trends among women, we must emphasize that while marriage during the teenage years is declining in many regions of

| Ages 20-24 | | | Ages 25-29 | | |
|---|---|---|---|---|---|
| Time 1[c] 1970- 1989 | Time 2 1990- 2000 | Annual Change | Time 1[c] 1970- 1989 | Time 2 1990- 2000 | Annual Change |
| 77.2 | 65.6 | −.71 | 89.2 | 83.4 | −.38 |
| 85.1 | 78.6 | −.40 | 93.5 | 92.3 | −.05 |
| 60.1 | 45.9 | −1.19 | 95.9 | 91.6 | −.36 |
| 80.6 | 77.4 | −.30 | 93.7 | 93.4 | −.02 |
| 61.2 | 54.0 | −.70 | 85.0 | 80.7 | −.42 |
| 59.4 | 56.1 | −.35 | 81.0 | 79.3 | −.20 |
| 51.1 | 51.3 | .03 | 75.9 | 76.0 | .00 |
| 64.5 | 54.6 | −.95 | 87.7 | 81.4 | −.58 |
| 70.8 | 63.9 | −.56 | 91.6 | 89.4 | −.18 |

[e]Former Soviet Asia includes former Soviet Republics in South-central and Western Asia.
[f]15-19-year-old married data not available for Argentina, Survey 1.
[g]Data for Bahrain limited to 15-19 age group, other data in nonstandard age groups.
SOURCES: United Nations Population Division Database on Marriage Patterns (Pop/1/DB/2000/3), 73 countries, 1960-2001. See Appendix Table 7-1a for list of countries.

the world, substantial proportions are still marrying extremely early. Indeed, as Table 7-5 indicates, in six of seven regions, at least one-fifth of women currently ages 20-24 married prior to age 18. The UN Convention on the Rights of the Child defines childhood as extending to the age of 18. Thus, according to these data, outside China, 38 percent of women in developing countries marry as minors.

Recently, Demographic and Health Surveys have been conducted among men in a number of countries in sub-Saharan Africa, Central America and the Caribbean, and the former Soviet Asia. However, only in sub-Saharan Africa and Latin America are there a sufficient number of countries with male surveys to aggregate the data and generate regional averages.[6] Table 7-7 provides regional data on the percentage of men

---

[6]In three other countries, male marriage data are available: Armenia, Kazakhstan, and Turkey.

TABLE 7-2 Percentage of Men Ever Married, by Age, Time Period, and Region (Weighted Averages)

| Region | Region Population Represented | Ages 20-24 | | | Ages 25-29 | | |
|---|---|---|---|---|---|---|---|
| | | Time 1[a] 1970-1989 | Time 2 1990-2000 | Annual Change | Time 1[a] 1970-1989 | Time 2 1990-2000 | Annual Change |
| Africa | | | | | | | |
| Eastern/Southern Africa | 89.8 | 36.0 | 27.8 | -.56 | 71.8 | 66.5 | -.42 |
| Western/Middle Africa | 30.8 | 28.4 | 26.5 | -.10 | 61.6 | 60.5 | -.04 |
| Asia | | | | | | | |
| Eastern Asia | 98.1 | 39.0 | 24.9 | -1.17 | 82.7 | 77.2 | -.46 |
| South-central/South-eastern Asia | 93.3 | 41.6 | 41.4 | -.03 | 77.5 | 77.2 | -.01 |
| Former Soviet Asia | 37.8 | 31.9 | 23.9 | -.81 | 78.0 | 66.0 | -1.20 |
| Latin America and Caribbean | | | | | | | |
| Caribbean/Central America | 87.5 | 38.4 | 37.5 | -.14 | 72.0 | 68.8 | -.36 |
| South America | 99.9 | 28.3 | 29.3 | .06 | 65.3 | 62.8 | -.18 |
| Middle East[b] | | | | | | | |
| Western Asia/Northern Africa | 62.6 | 24.9 | 16.8 | -.78 | 63.0 | 53.4 | -.91 |
| TOTAL | 86.5 | 37.9 | 33.0 | -.41 | 76.0 | 73.1 | -.24 |

[a]For several countries, the first survey/census was before 1970: Chad, Gabon, Cambodia, Palestine, Namibia.

[b]Bahrain excluded; data in nonstandard age groups.

NOTES: For source of regional groupings and population data for weighted averages, see Table 7-1. Further detail can be found in Appendix A.

SOURCES: United Nations Population Division Database on Marriage Patterns (Pop/1/DB/2000/3), 72 countries, 1960-2001. See Appendix Table 7-1b for list of countries.

married by ages 20, 25, and 30 by age group for 29 countries with surveys between 1994 and 2001: 9 in Eastern and Southern Africa, 14 in Western and Central Africa, and 6 in Latin America. As with the data on women, the weighted averages shown are the country's percentage of the region's population ages 10-24 in 2000.

This table indicates slight declines in the proportion of men married across cohorts at ages 20 and 25 in both regions of Africa, declines that are considerably smaller than those seen for women in sub-Saharan Africa. Note that, in comparison to Table 7-2, a smaller decline is observed for Eastern and Southern Africa and a slightly larger decline for Western and Middle Africa. These discrepancies arise because of differences in the countries included in the analyses. Data from Nigeria, which has nearly half of the population of Western Africa and where there has been a considerable decline in early marriage for young men (11 percent married by age 20 among 20-24-year-olds, compared with 19 percent among 40-44-year-olds) are not provided in the UN database. And the DHS was not conducted among men in South Africa, where there has been a large decline in early marriage. In 1985, according to the UN database, 17 percent of South African men ages 20-24 were married, compared with 9 percent in 1996. Among men ages 25-29 the decline is also substantial; half were married in 1985 compared with one-third in 1996.[7] As for South America and the Caribbean and Central America, the DHS data, which are less representative than the UN data, show little change and are broadly consistent with the UN data.

## DIFFERENTIALS IN AGE AT MARRIAGE

Tables 7-8, 7-9, and 7-10 are limited to women ages 20-24 and indicate the percentage ever married by age 18 by years of schooling attained, by an asset index score, and by rural-urban residence, respectively. Table 7-11 is limited to men ages 20-24 from sub-Saharan Africa and Latin America and the Caribbean and indicates the percentage ever married by age 20 by the same three factors: years of schooling attained, an asset index score, and

---

[7]In his recent analysis of DHS data on marriage, Westoff observed that "the trend toward later ages at marriage for women is not evident for men surveyed in sub-Saharan Africa" (Westoff, 2003:1). This assertion is based on changes in the median age at marriage, a measure that is not particularly illuminating when analyzing changes in early marriage if what is happening is that those who marry very young now marry slightly later but still before the median age. Moreover, as noted above, South Africa is missing from the DHS analysis, which distorts the regional estimate for Eastern and Southern Africa.

TABLE 7-3 Percentage of Women Ever Married, by Age, Time Period, Income[a] Group (Weighted Averages)

| Income Level | Income Group Population Represented | Ages 15-19 | | |
| --- | --- | --- | --- | --- |
| | | Time 1[b] 1970-1989 | Time 2 1990-2000 | Annual Change |
| Low | 81.0 | 42.5 | 34.1 | −.66 |
| Lower Middle[c] | 29.4 | 19.6 | 14.5 | −.50 |
| Upper Middle[d] | 92.7 | 15.7 | 14.4 | −.15 |
| TOTAL | 63.9 | 34.6 | 27.8 | −.55 |

[a]World Bank income classifications. SOURCE: World Bank (2002b).

[b]For several countries, the first survey/census was before 1970: Chad, Gabon, Cambodia, Palestine, Namibia.

[c]China excluded; see Table 7-1 for data on China.

[d]15-19-year-old married data not available for Argentina, Survey 1. Data for Bahrain limited to 15-19 age group, other data in nonstandard age groups.

rural-urban residence. Note that the asset index score is based on a methodology used by Filmer and Pritchett (1999) and is generated from answers to questions on ownership of assets and housing characteristics.[8] Weights for each item are derived from principal components analysis. The index is computed separately for each country, and households are then assigned a score based on whether they fall into the top 20 percent, the middle 40 percent, or the bottom 40 percent.

As expected, very large differentials by education, household wealth, and residence are observed for both sexes. Women and men with 8 or more years of schooling are much less likely to marry early than are those with 0-3 years of schooling.[9] Women and men in the top wealth category are much less likely to marry at young ages than are those in the bottom category, and those in urban areas are much less likely to marry early than young people living in the countryside. While these differentials are considerable for women, greater variability exists in the timing of marriage by education than by household economic status or residence. For example, in

---

[8]The asset index reflects the characteristics of the household in which the respondent currently resides; these assets may not belong to the respondent or his or her spouse.

[9]Some of those, ages 20-24 in the 8+ "years of education" category, could still be in school.

| Ages 20-24 | | | Ages 25-29 | | |
|---|---|---|---|---|---|
| Time 1[b]<br>1970-1989 | Time 2<br>1990-2000 | Annual<br>Change | Time 1[b]<br>1970-1989 | Time 2<br>1990-2000 | Annual<br>Change |
| 83.4 | 79.8 | –.25 | 95.0 | 94.6 | –.02 |
| 59.2 | 52.1 | –.63 | 81.6 | 77.4 | –.35 |
| 54.1 | 49.7 | –.42 | 78.3 | 75.4 | –.27 |
| 74.6 | 70.3 | –.49 | 90.1 | 88.6 | –.11 |

NOTES: For source of regional groupings and population data for weighted averages, see Table 7-1. Further detail can be found in Appendix A.
SOURCES: United Nations Population Division Database on Marriage Patterns (Pop/1/DB/ 2000/3), 72 countries, 1960-2001. See Appendix Table 7-1a for list of countries.

Eastern and Southern Africa, over four times as many women with 0-3 years of schooling marry before age 18 as do women with 8+ years of schooling, whereas 1.9 times as many women in low-status households marry before 18 as do women in high-status households, and 1.6 times as many women in rural areas marry before age 18 than do women in urban areas. In contrast, in the regions in which data are available for men, the differentials by socioeconomic status are nearly as large, or larger than, the differentials by schooling, suggesting that household economic status is a potentially more important factor than schooling in determining timing of marriage for men than for women.

## FACTORS AFFECTING THE RISE IN AGE AT MARRIAGE

In all regions of the developing world except for South America, fewer young women are married than in the recent past, and in a number of regions, fewer young men are married as well. The fact that this pattern is quite widespread is support for our assumption that global changes are affecting the transition to adulthood. In trying to assess the mechanism for this transformation, it is important to note that the reduction in marriage is occurring in a diversity of settings. More importantly, for women, the change is occurring not only in the teenage years but also in the 20s, suggesting that policy shifts, such as increases in the legal age at marriage,

TABLE 7-4 Percentage of Men Ever Married, by Age, Time Period, Income[a] Group (Weighted Averages)

| Income Level | Income Group Population Represented | Ages 20-24 | | | Ages 25-29 | | |
|---|---|---|---|---|---|---|---|
| | | Time 1[b] 1970-1989 | Time 2 1990-2000 | Annual Change | Time 1[b] 1970-1989 | Time 2 1990-2000 | Annual Change |
| Low | 81.0 | 40.9 | 40.6 | -.01 | 76.4 | 76.6 | .03 |
| Lower Middle[c] | 29.5 | 30.7 | 24.6 | -.57 | 67.5 | 60.0 | -.67 |
| Upper Middle[d] | 92.7 | 30.8 | 27.9 | -.28 | 68.2 | 62.7 | -.48 |
| TOTAL | 63.9 | 37.6 | 35.9 | -.14 | 73.6 | 71.6 | -.17 |

[a]World Bank income classifications. SOURCE: World Bank Development Indicators, 2002.
[b]For several countries, the first survey/census was before 1970: Chad, Gabon, Cambodia, Palestine, Namibia.
[c]China excluded; see Table 7-2 for data on China.
[d]Bahrain excluded; data in nonstandard age groups.
NOTES: For source of regional groupings and population data for weighted averages, see Table 7-1. Further detail can be found in Appendix A.
SOURCES: United Nations Population Division Database on Marriage Patterns (Pop/1/DB/2000/3), 71 countries, 1960-2001. See Appendix Table 7-1b for list of countries.

TABLE 7-5 Percentage of Women Ever Married by Ages 18, 20, and 25, by Age at Time of Survey and Region (Weighted Averages)

| Region | Population Represented | Age 18 | | | Age 20 | | | Age 25 | |
|---|---|---|---|---|---|---|---|---|---|
| | | 20-24 | 30-34 | 40-44 | 20-24 | 30-34 | 40-44 | 30-34 | 40-44 |
| Africa | | | | | | | | | |
| Eastern/Southern Africa | 91.7 | 36.5 | 45.7 | 52.8 | 54.6 | 62.9 | 69.2 | 83.6 | 88.2 |
| Western/Middle Africa[a] | 75.2 | 44.8 | 55.0 | 57.9 | 60.1 | 69.5 | 73.6 | 88.7 | 92.6 |
| Asia | | | | | | | | | |
| South-central/South-eastern Asia | 86.0 | 41.5 | 54.2 | 57.6 | 59.5 | 71.0 | 74.3 | 90.4 | 92.4 |
| Former Soviet Asia | 68.4 | 15.9 | 10.9 | 14.2 | 49.9 | 39.7 | 45.9 | 87.8 | 87.2 |
| Latin America and Caribbean | | | | | | | | | |
| Caribbean/Central America | 21.0 | 34.9 | 35.7 | 38.4 | 53.3 | 53.7 | 58.1 | 82.3 | 82.5 |
| South America | 74.1 | 22.7 | 22.5 | 21.9 | 38.0 | 39.7 | 39.6 | 73.1 | 75.2 |
| Middle East | | | | | | | | | |
| Western Asia/Northern Africa | 54.8 | 23.2 | 35.1 | 45.5 | 39.8 | 52.2 | 64.2 | 81.7 | 87.2 |
| TOTAL—All DHS | 59.8 | 37.7 | 48.2 | 52.0 | 55.5 | 65.0 | 69.1 | 87.2 | 89.8 |

[a]Gabon excluded; data on women unavailable at time of this analysis.
NOTES: For source of regional groupings and population data for weighted averages, see Table 7-1. Further detail can be found in Appendix. A
SOURCES: Demographic and Health Surveys tabulations from 51 countries, 1990-2001. See Appendix Table 7-2 for list of countries.

TABLE 7-6 Percentage of Women Ever Married by Ages 18, 20, and 25, by Age at Time of Survey and Income[a] Level of Country (Weighted Averages)

| Income Level | Population Represented | Age 18 | | | Age 20 | | | Age 25 | | |
|---|---|---|---|---|---|---|---|---|---|---|
| | | 20-24 | 30-34 | 40-44 | 20-24 | 30-34 | 40-44 | 30-34 | 40-44 | |
| Low | 88.9 | 42.5 | 54.7 | 58.3 | 60.9 | 71.5 | 75.4 | 90.8 | 93.2 | |
| Lower Middle | 18.8 | 16.1 | 21.3 | 25.4 | 34.6 | 41.9 | 47.2 | 74.0 | 77.6 | |
| Upper Middle[b] | 53.1 | 20.9 | 22.8 | 25.1 | 35.7 | 40.1 | 44.0 | 73.0 | 76.9 | |
| TOTAL—All DHS | 59.8 | 37.7 | 48.2 | 52.0 | 55.5 | 65.0 | 69.1 | 87.2 | 89.8 | |

[a]World Bank income classifications.
[b]Gabon excluded; data on women unavailable at time of this analysis.
NOTES: For source of regional groupings and population data for weighted averages, see Table 7-1. Further detail can be found in Appendix A.
SOURCES: Demographic and Health Surveys from 51 countries, 1990-2001. See Appendix Table 7-2 for list of countries.

TABLE 7-7 Percentage of Men Ever Married by Ages 20, 25, and 30, by Age at Time of Survey (Weighted Averages)

| Region | Population Represented | Age 20 | | | Age 25 | | Age 30 | |
|---|---|---|---|---|---|---|---|---|
| | | 20-24 | 30-34 | 40-44 | 30-34 | 40-44 | 30-34 | 40-44 |
| Africa | | | | | | | | |
| Eastern/Southern Africa | 69.5 | 13.8 | 20.0 | 21.3 | 59.3 | 61.0 | 86.7 | 87.7 |
| Western/Middle Africa | 75.5 | 12.0 | 16.2 | 17.5 | 47.7 | 50.9 | 77.0 | 76.5 |
| Latin America and Caribbean | | | | | | | | |
| Caribbean/Central America | 13.7 | 22.2 | 20.4 | 21.9 | 55.3 | 58.0 | 76.0 | 80.1 |
| South America | 60.3 | 14.0 | 18.2 | 10.8 | 58.7 | 57.4 | 80.7 | 85.6 |
| TOTAL—All DHS | 60.5 | 13.5 | 18.1 | 16.9 | 54.8 | 56.2 | 81.1 | 82.7 |

NOTES: For source of regional groupings and population data for weighted averages, see Table 7-1. Further detail can be found in Appendix A.
SOURCES: Demographic and Health Surveys tabulations from 29 countries, 1994-2001. See Appendix Table 7-3 for list of countries.

TABLE 7-8 Percentage of Women Ages 20-24 Ever Married by Age 18, by Years of Schooling and Region[a] (Weighted Averages)

| Region | Population Represented | Years of Schooling | | |
|---|---|---|---|---|
| | | 0-3 | 4-7 | 8+ |
| Africa | | | | |
|    Eastern/Southern Africa | 91.7 | 51.2 | 38.6 | 12.6 |
|    Western/Middle Africa[b] | 75.2 | 70.5 | 36.8 | 14.1 |
| Asia | | | | |
|    South-central/South-eastern Asia[c] | 28.0 | 55.7 | 44.0 | 17.3 |
| Latin America and Caribbean | | | | |
|    Caribbean/Central America | 21.0 | 55.5 | 43.9 | 14.7 |
|    South America | 74.1 | 41.7 | 30.3 | 10.8 |
| Middle East | | | | |
|    Western Asia/Northern Africa[d] | 49.6 | 38.9 | 25.6 | 6.4 |
| TOTAL—All DHS | 34.4 | 53.2 | 37.6 | 13.5 |

[a]Former Soviet Asia excluded because too few women with less than 8+ years of schooling.

[b]Gabon excluded; data on women unavailable at time of this analysis.

[c]India and Pakistan excluded; lack the all women weight.

[d]Yemen excluded; lacks the all women weight.

NOTES: For source of regional groupings and population data for weighted averages, see Table 7-1. Further detail can be found in Appendix A.

SOURCES: Demographic and Health Surveys tabulations from 44 countries, 1990-2001. See Appendix Table 7-4 for list of countries.

or social shifts, such as the expansion of education, or ideological shifts, such as a change in norms regarding very early marriage, cannot fully explain the changes observed.

There is a substantial literature on the forces behind postponement of marriage among young women, although much of it is speculative, rather than based on rigorous analysis of data. For example, in her discussion of the increase in the age at first marriage among women in Africa, Hertrich argues that, in contrast to earlier generations, there is now a "recognition of a social status for women other than that of wife and mother" (Hertrich, 2002:12). In the two sections that follow we focus on factors, which may be associated with changes in age of marriage, that we are able to address more systematically—namely, education and labor force participation.[10]

---

[10]For a discussion of potential determinants of female age at marriage besides education and labor force participation, see Mensch, Singh, and Casterline (2005).

TABLE 7-9 Percentage of Women Ages 20-24 Ever Married by Age 18, by Household Economic Status and Region[a] (Weighted Averages)

| Region | Population Represented | Low (bottom 40%) | Middle (mid 40%) | High (top 20%) |
|---|---|---|---|---|
| Africa | | | | |
| Eastern/Southern Africa | 91.7 | 44.6 | 37.1 | 23.6 |
| Western/Middle Africa[b] | 75.2 | 61.4 | 42.5 | 24.0 |
| Asia | | | | |
| Former Soviet Asia | 68.4 | 19.0 | 13.8 | 13.3 |
| Latin America and Caribbean | | | | |
| Caribbean/Central America | 21.0 | 49.6 | 32.3 | 15.5 |
| South America[c] | 72.4 | 31.6 | 19.6 | 14.1 |
| TOTAL—All DHS | 70.9 | 44.7 | 32.4 | 20.2 |

[a] These tabulations do not include countries with ever-married samples, since there is no all women weight for socioeconomic status. Thus the Middle East and South-central and South-eastern Asia are excluded.
[b] Gabon is excluded; data on women unavailable at time of this analysis.
[c] Paraguay excluded; no asset data available.
NOTES: For source of regional groupings and population data for weighted averages, see Table 7-1. Further detail can be found in Appendix A.
SOURCES: Demographic and Health Surveys tabulations from 38 countries, 1990-2001. See Appendix Table 7-4 for list of countries.

TABLE 7-10 Percentage of Women Ages 20-24 Ever Married by Age 18, by Rural-Urban Residence and Region (Weighted Averages)

| Region | Population Represented | Rural | Urban |
|---|---|---|---|
| Africa | | | |
|    Eastern/Southern Africa | 91.7 | 41.0 | 25.3 |
|    Western/Middle Africa[a] | 75.2 | 52.2 | 30.1 |
| Asia | | | |
|    South-central/South-eastern Asia | 86.0 | 48.4 | 24.3 |
|    Former Soviet Asia | 68.4 | 17.9 | 13.9 |
| Latin America/Caribbean | | | |
|    Caribbean/Central America | 21.0 | 44.5 | 27.6 |
|    South America | 74.1 | 31.4 | 20.3 |
| Middle East | | | |
|    Western Asia/Northern Africa | 54.8 | 28.3 | 16.7 |
| TOTAL—All DHS | 59.8 | 44.4 | 23.9 |

[a]Gabon excluded; data on women unavailable at time of this analysis.
NOTES: For source of regional groupings and population data for weighted averages, see Table 7-1. Further detail can be found in Appendix A.
SOURCES: Demographic and Health Surveys tabulations from 51 countries, 1990-2001. See Appendix Table 7-4 for list of countries.

## Role of Education for Women

The increase in girls' educational attainment during the last several decades is widely viewed as the primary cause for the delay in marriage of women (Mathur, Greene, and Malhotra, 2003; United Nations Commission on Population and Development, 2002). In discussions of the positive association between education and age at marriage of women, the autonomy-enhancing effect of school is generally emphasized (Lloyd and Mensch, 1999). While empirical validation of the particular mechanisms is lacking, education is said to give young women greater influence over the timing of marriage and the choice of partner.

Education is also thought to broaden a girl's perspective on the world, increasing her aspirations and providing her with a more Western outlook on life (Lloyd and Mensch, 1999). Finally, there is a suggestion that education lengthens the marriage search process because of a general tendency for women to marry higher status men (Lloyd and Mensch, 1999).

A purely mechanistic reason exists for the association between education and marriage; school in most countries is incompatible with marriage and childbearing as a matter of policy. However, only in early-marrying societies can such policies influence age at marriage (Lindstrom and Brambila Paz, 2001). While it is frequently asserted that early marriage

TABLE 7-11 Percentage of Men Ages 20-24 Ever Married by Age 20, by Years of Schooling, Rural-Urban Residence, Household Economic Status, and Region (Weighted Averages)

| Category | South America | Caribbean/ Central America | Eastern/ Southern Africa | Western/ Middle Africa[a] |
|---|---|---|---|---|
| Years of Schooling | | | | |
| 0-3 | 20.7 | 24.6 | 20.9 | 21.0 |
| 4-7 | 18.0 | 30.9 | 16.7 | 14.5 |
| 8+ | 10.0 | 13.9 | 6.5 | 6.0 |
| Residence | | | | |
| Rural | 13.4 | 26.5 | 15.5 | 16.0 |
| Urban | 14.0 | 18.2 | 8.2 | 5.1 |
| Socioeconomic Status | | | | |
| High | 8.7 | 15.0 | 5.3 | 4.7 |
| Middle | 12.2 | 22.6 | 13.6 | 11.6 |
| Low | 19.8 | 25.4 | 21.1 | 18.5 |
| Population Represented | 60.3 | 13.7 | 69.5 | 75.5 |

[a]Gabon included only for residence; missing schooling and household data on men. Niger excluded from schooling; no respondents ages 20-24 with 8 or more years of schooling.

NOTES: For source of regional groupings and population data for weighted averages, see Table 7-1. Further detail can be found in Appendix A.
SOURCES: Demographic and Health Surveys tabulations from 29 countries, 1994-2001. Insufficient data to aggregate by region for Asia and Middle East, which are excluded. See Appendix Table 7-5 for list of countries.

deprives girls of educational opportunities, widespread evidence that they are withdrawn from school to marry is lacking, except perhaps in such early-marrying countries as Bangladesh, where girls leave school if an appropriate marriage partner is found (Amin, Mahmud, and Huq, 2002). For the most part, countries in which considerable proportions of young women marry at young ages are the same ones in which educational attainment is low. Hence for most women there is likely to be a distinct gap between school leaving and the earliest ages at which marriage might occur. Figure 7-1 shows, for seven countries for which data are available, that a sizeable lag exists between school leaving and marriage not only among young men but also among young women.[11] These graphs, based on questions on current status, compare transitions out of school and into marriage from ages 10 to 29 using census data from the end of the 1990s, providing a rough indicator of the number of years between school leaving and marriage. For example, in Kenya for girls, there is approximately a three-year gap between the age at which 50 percent are out of school and 50 percent are married. In Iran there is a five-year gap, and in China over a six-year gap.

Not only is the link between the transition out of school and into marriage not particularly close for most countries, but also an examination of DHS data indicates that there is not as tight an association between trends in education and age of marriage as one might expect given the emphasis in the literature on the dominant role of educational change as a cause of nuptiality change. Indeed, the region with the largest increase in educational attainment among young people—South-central and Southeastern Asia—is not the region with the largest decline in early marriage. Moreover, while years of schooling have increased in Latin America in the last few decades, almost no change has occurred in age at marriage.

An analysis of the change in the percentage of women ages 20-24 and 40-44 married by age 18 as a function of the change in grades of school attained in 49 DHS countries indicates a weaker association (R = −.46) than

---

[11]Large public use samples from the two most recent censuses for Mexico (1990 and 2000), Kenya (1989 and 1999), and Vietnam (1989 and 1999) are available from the Integrated Public Use Microdata Series (IPUMS) International web site at the University of Minnesota (http://www.ipums.umn.edu). We also use the 1990 and 2001 surveys of Brazil's Pesquisa Nacional por Amostra de Domicilios (PNAD); the 1993 South Africa Integrated Household Survey, SALDRU/World Bank, and September 2000 South Africa Labour Force Survey, Statistics South Africa, courtesy of David Lam (University of Michigan); the Child Health and Nutrition Survey in China from 1989 and 1997, courtesy of Emily Hannum (University of Pennsylvania); the 1987 Social and Economic Survey of Households, Statistical Center of Iran, and 1998 Household Expenditure and Income Survey, Statistical Center of Iran, courtesy of Djavad Salehi-Isfahani (Virginia Polytechnic University).

one might expect, given the determining power often attributed to educational change (Mensch, Singh, and Casterline, 2005). Furthermore, a regression analysis of the amount of intercohort change in early marriage that might be expected to follow from the intercohort change in educational attainment in 39 DHS countries reveals that, in 15 countries, the expected change exceeds the observed change. That is, the magnitude of the decline in early marriage between cohorts is less than would be expected given the increase in schooling (see Mensch, Singh, and Casterline, 2005, for a detailed description of the methodology and findings).[12] Indeed, in about half of these 15 countries, the probability of early marriage actually increases between cohorts despite the increase in schooling.

The pattern in the majority of countries, however, is that the percentage marrying at early ages declined from the older to the younger cohort, and this observed decline exceeds the expected decline. The regional differences are considerable. In Latin America and the Caribbean, the expected decline in early marriage following from increased schooling far exceeds the actual decline. In many of these countries, of course, the probability of early marriage has not changed. Perhaps there is a threshold beyond which increased schooling is not associated with a change in age of marriage. By contrast to Latin America, for about two-thirds of sub-Saharan African countries, half or more of the decline in early marriage can be linked to increased schooling. In sum, the rise in schooling hardly appears to be the entire story, although in sub-Saharan Africa a substantial fraction of the reduction in early marriage is associated with the expansion in education.

### Links with Women's Labor Force Participation

Not only is increased schooling widely believed to contribute to the delay in marriage among young women, but also access to wage employment is frequently cited in discussions of rising age at marriage (Mathur, Greene, and Malhotra, 2003). It seems logical that there are greater opportunity costs associated with marriage for young women who are in the paid labor force. Indeed, a daughter's enhanced income-earning potential is ar-

---

[12]Logit regressions were estimated for each cohort. Then the coefficients from one cohort were applied to the other cohort to calculate a predicted logit of early marriage for each woman, which was then transformed into a predicted probability. The mean of these probabilities is the expected proportion marrying early, and the expected proportion minus the observed is the expected change in early marriage due to schooling change. This analysis was conducted only in the 39 countries in which the DHS interviewed all women, not just ever-married women. This exclusion effectively eliminates South-central and South-eastern Asia and the Middle East from this analysis.

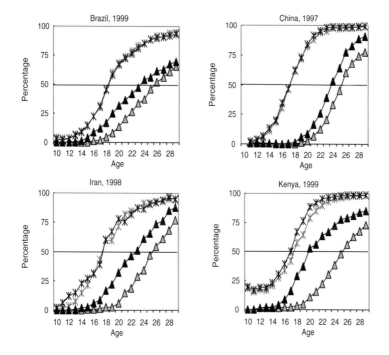

FIGURE 7-1 School and marriage status by single years of age, most recent year. SOURCE: Large public use samples from most recent censuses for Mexico (2000), Kenya (1999), Vietnam (1999), available from IPUMS-International web site at the University of Minnesota (http://www.ipums.umn.edu). Also included are the 1999 survey of Brazil's Pesquisa Nacional por Amostra de Domicilios (PNAD); the

gued to be a strong rationale for a parent's willingness to postpone marriage (Jejeebhoy, 1995). In Bangladesh, for example, where purdah holds sway and cash employment outside the home has been extremely limited for women, adolescent girls who migrate from rural areas to work in the garment industry marry significantly later than their peers from the sending communities who have not had such opportunities (Box 7-1). While those who migrate are likely to be selective for certain characteristics predisposing them to later marriage, the differences in marriage rates are so great— 31 percent of 20-24-year-old garment workers who were not married before beginning work married by age 18 compared with 71 percent of the same age group in the sending villages—that it suggests that the experience of work has been transformative for some (Amin et al., 1998).

Analyses of data from the World Fertility Surveys, in which, unlike in

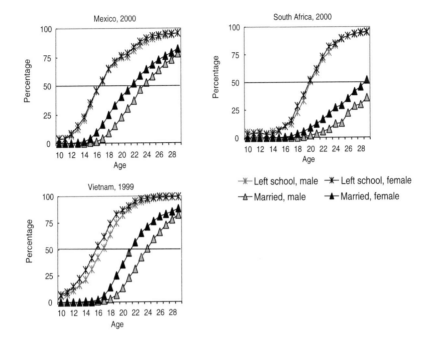

September 2000 South Africa Labour Force Survey, Statistics South Africa, courtesy of David Lam (University of Michigan); the Child Health and Nutrition Survey in China from 1997, courtesy of Emily Hannum (University of Pennsylvania); the 1998 Household Expenditure and Income Survey, Statistical Center of Iran, courtesy of Djavad Salehi-Isfahani (Virginia Polytechnic University).

the DHS,[13] women were asked about the timing of work relative to marriage, indicate that, controlling for grades attained, women who worked prior to marriage wed later than those who did not work. While those who had jobs in the modern sector had the latest age at marriage, even those who worked in traditional occupations married later than those who did no work at all, evidence that it is not only longer exposure to the possibility of work that produces the association between labor force participation and age at marriage but also that women who work postpone marriage (United Nations, 1987).[14]

---

[13]In the DHS, women were only asked about current work.

[14]The argument is that if the positive association between work and age at marriage were simply an artifact of the lengthier exposure to the possibility of employment among those who delayed marriage, then one would not expect a gradient in age of marriage by type of occupation (United Nations, 1987).

**BOX 7-1**
**Does Factory Work Discourage Early Marriage for Women?**
**Evidence from Bangladesh**

Since the first garment factory was established in Bangladesh in the late 1970s, the export of manufactured goods (especially garments) has expanded to become a principal component of the nation's development strategy. By 1995, the number of factories operating in Bangladesh had grown from 700 in 1985 to 2,400 factories, employing approximately 1.2 million people, 90 percent of whom are women (Amin et al., 1998:186). The majority migrate from rural areas to work in the factories and are young and unmarried. Traditional Bangladeshi society is characterized by very early marriage and childbearing (Amin et al., 1998). However, a study conducted by Amin and colleagues (1998) examines how increased opportunities for young women's labor force participation in Bangladesh may be delaying their age at marriage.

In their interviews with young female factory workers, Amin et al. (1998) found that, for some, the decision to pursue factory work is part of a household strategy to improve the household's economic situation. For others, it is a personal decision, made with parental permission, to avoid domestic work, to save for one's dowry, or to delay early marriage. As one young factory worker explained: "I knew my father wanted to marry me off, so I went to my cousin who was a garment worker in Dhaka and had come home for a holiday and I told her I wanted to go with her to Dhaka" (Amin et al., 1998:191).

Data from the study indicate that factory work appears to reduce the incidence of marriage for the young women surveyed. Of those women who were unmarried when they started factory work, only 31 percent of those ages 20-24, and 29 percent of those age 25-29, were married by the age of 18. The rates of early marriage for factory workers are much lower compared to their nonworking counterparts: the percentage of nonworkers from sending villages married by age 18 was 71 percent among 20-24-year-olds and 82 percent among 25-29-year-olds. For nonworkers from comparable nonsending villages, these percentages were 84 and 91, respectively.

Factory work imparts adult skills, such as how to manage income, save money, and budget for expenses, even if young women may not have complete control over their earnings. It exposes adolescent girls to new information, social networks, and lifestyles and raises the opportunity costs of their time. According to Amin et al. (1998:197), "Garment work has direct implications for girls' reproductive health by enabling them to delay marriage, and by motivating workers to delay childbearing even when they are married."

In the United States there is evidence from analysis of recent census data that better labor market conditions for young women reduce marriage rates (Blau, Kahn, and Waldfogel, 2000). Although it seems plausible that the increasing labor force participation of women may be a factor in later age at marriage among women in the developing world, such a causal link has not been established empirically. First, the necessary analysis has not been undertaken. Such analyses require time-series data of good quality and sophisticated econometric models to address the potential endogeneity biases. Not only is there an issue of reverse causality, noted above, whereby delayed marriage may increase the likelihood of entry into the labor force, but the same elements that predispose women to work may encourage later marriage. Second, there are several country examples that challenge an association between the expansion of paid work for women and delayed marriage. In Latin America, the labor force participation of women has risen (see Chapter 5) at the same time that age of marriage has remained fairly stable. In Egypt, the age of marriage has increased considerably while employment opportunities for women have declined substantially (Amin and Al-Bassusi, 2003). In Sri Lanka, employment has no bearing on a young women's expected age of marriage; late age of marriage is desirable regardless of current work status (Malhotra and Tsui, 1996).

### Explanations for Changes in Male Age at Marriage

If the increase in educational attainment dominates discussions of the rise in the age of marriage of women, what explanation is given for changes in young men's age at marriage? In comparison to women, there is little research that examines the reasons for changes in marriage age for men. Some researchers offer similar explanations for men as for women arguing that the extended educational path taken by men in recent years in many countries may contribute to the rise in their age of marriage (Hertrich, 2002). Yet it is economic reasons that are commonly invoked as the primary reason for the delay in marriage of men (see, for example, Williams and Guest, 2002). For example, in Sri Lanka, with increasing industrialization, a man's job status, which was not considered important in the past—particular where subsistence agriculture was the dominant form of economic life—is now said to be critical in determining when he marries (De Silva, 1997).

To the best of our knowledge, there are few studies that investigate the association between economic status—whether employment or income—and marriage patterns of men in the developing world. One notable exception is the work of Antoine and his colleagues (Antoine, Djire, and Laplante, 1995). Using hazard models, they compared age at marriage among three birth cohorts in Dakar, Senegal, and found that the employment status of men had a significant impact on the likelihood of marriage. Moreover, while men of the earlier generation (born between 1930 and 1944) who were unemployed were equally likely to marry as their working counterparts, men in the younger cohorts (born between 1955 and 1964) who were unemployed were significantly and substantially less likely to marry. Apparently economic uncertainty was more a factor in the decision to marry for the younger generation than for the older generation.

There is some discussion in the literature, although for the most part not systematic analysis, that marriage has become more burdensome financially in the last several decades. In the case of African societies, the changing nature of bridewealth, with cash payments replacing payments in kind, is believed to be a contributing factor in delaying marriage of men because more time is needed to acquire the necessary sums and because the responsibility for payments is said to be shifting from the future husband's extended family to the bridegroom himself (Enel, Pison, and Lefebvre, 1994; Isiugo-Abanihe, 1994; National Research Council, 1993: Chapter 3). (See the section below for a discussion of bridewealth.) More fundamentally, a transformation is said to have emerged in many societies in the nature of the household economy and concomitantly in the necessities essential for the establishment of a household. As has been argued for Indonesia, "the assumption in the past that marriage formed a basic productive economic unit for farming or trading, has been modified by the current requirement that basic consumption needs such as capital for a house, or consumer goods, and basic educational attainments must be achieved before a marriage can 'wisely' take place" (Hull, 2002:5).

In countries as diverse as Nigeria and Egypt, researchers have observed that the cost of marriage apparently factors much more into the decision about the timing of a man's marriage than it did earlier. In Nigeria, the oil boom in the 1970s fueled a change in brides' expectations of what purchases grooms needed in order to marry (National Research Council, 1993: Chapter 3). In Egypt, where housing, furniture, and appliances are required for marriage and "the bulk of financial obligations . . . are still borne . . . by the groom and his family," the cost of marriage is estimated to have increased dramatically in the last 30 years (Singerman and Ibrahim, 2003:97). While there has not been a rigorous analysis linking the cost of setting up a household with the timing of marriage in Egypt, the fact that the proportion of individuals in the census marriage registration category, *katb al-kitaab*, in which the marriage is registered but the couple has yet to establish a marital residence, increased fourfold between 1986 and 1996, while the annual rate of marriage barely changed, is an indirect indication that rising costs have lead to a delay in the ceremony (Singerman and Ibrahim, 2003). While this piece of evidence does not firmly establish a link between the rise in the age of marriage and the costs of marriage, there is enough anecdotal data from Egypt and responses from surveys about the financial burdens of marriage to warrant further investigation.

Perhaps increasing exposure to Western media has altered consumer norms and raised the expectations of young people worldwide, so that men feel obligated to postpone marriage until they have acquired the resources needed to establish a household. Given the current numbers of young people in the developing world and the difficulty of ensuring adequate employment opportunities, one can imagine a scenario in which postponement of marriage among men until their 30s or beyond could become more commonplace. The question is whether the rising cost of establishing a household affects the timing of marriage for most young men, or whether, perhaps, those who are worse off are paradoxically less constrained financially and marry at younger ages.

It is also worthwhile considering whether late marriage is viewed as desirable by young men who may be frustrated by their inability to establish a household, even if that inability stems from rising expectations and not from declining economic circumstances. Furthermore, although marriage in no way imposes sexual exclusivity on men, it is very likely that a postponement in the age at marriage leads to increases in the number of sexual partners before marriage and therefore greater exposure to HIV and other sexually transmitted infections.[15]

Not only might delayed marriage among men be considered by some to be problematic but also, given the increasingly distorted sex ratios at birth in some Asian countries as a result of a strong preference for male offspring and sex-selective abortion, there is speculation that substantial numbers of men will never marry. Referred to by the Chinese as "bare branches," that is, "male branches of a family tree that would never bear fruit because no marriage partner might be found for them," these men are said to be a destabilizing force in society (Hudson and den Boer, 2002:11). Hudson and den Boer, two political scientists who have examined this phenomenon, are alarmed about the destructive consequences for India and China, as well as "the nations of the world," of large numbers of unmarried men (Hudson and den Boer, 2002:12):

> Theory suggests that compared with other males in society, bare branches will be prone to seek satisfaction through vice and violence, and will seek to capture resources that will allow them to compete on a more equal

---

[15]Qualitative evidence from Zimbabwe, where approximately 25 percent of the population is infected with HIV suggests that early childbearing, presumably combined with early marriage, is one strategy adopted by young people to prevent transmission of HIV to spouses and children (Grieser et al., 2001).

footing with others. These theoretical predictions are substantiated by empirical evidence so vast and so compelling as to approach the status of social science verity.

While there is no historical precedent on a national scale for as distorted a sex ratio as China currently has, it is not clear that the situation is as dire as Hudson and den Boer make out. First, according to the UN Population Division, the sex ratio at birth in China is currently estimated to be 1.09 rather than the more normal 1.05, hardly that calamitous.[16] Second, Chinese men may respond by delaying rather than forgoing marriage; they also may be more likely to choose spouses outside the standard age range. Finally, as women become scarce, the hope is that their value will rise and the sex ratio will adjust.

## THE TERMS AND CONDITIONS OF MARRIAGE

While there is a considerable body of literature on the timing of marriage, much less research exists on the terms and conditions of marriage and how they vary by age of the woman at marriage and over time. In particular, little is known about changes in the entry into marriage—the process of acquiring a spouse and the financial exchanges between families—and the nature of marital relations among those newly wed. Yet the marriage experience is at the very core of gender dynamics in most societies. In this next section we review the existing literature on this subject and summarize what little is known about the marital process and marital life for young people in the developing world and how they have changed in recent years.

### Age Differences Between Spouses

The magnitude of the age gap between spouses is often regarded as a measure of equity in marriage (Amin and Cain, 1997; Cain, 1984). An analysis of World Fertility Survey data from 28 countries found that the age gap is more likely to be small in countries in which women have relatively high status, there is a bilateral kinship structure (i.e., descent is traced through both parents), and there is neolocal residence following marriage (i.e., the newly married couple lives independently rather than with the relatives of either the wife or the husband). Interestingly, demographic determinants of the age gap, such as the age structure of the pool of potential matches, would appear to matter less than fundamental features of the marriage and family system, suggesting there are clear preferences with

---

[16]See http://esa.un.org/unpp/p2k0data.asp.

regard to age differences (Casterline, Williams, and McDonald, 1986:13). Although there is very little documentation of the effects of a large age gap on a young bride and it is difficult to disentangle social-structural factors that are a consequence of a large age difference from those that are determinants (Casterline, Williams, and McDonald, 1986), it is reasonable to assume that adolescent girls with much older partners are hindered in their capacity to negotiate with their spouses about sex and reproduction as well as other aspects of domestic life.

Previous analyses of survey data in developing countries indicate that the age difference between spouses is inversely related to the wife's age at marriage, even after controlling for education (Mensch, 1986; Mensch, Bruce, and Greene, 1998). Figure 7-2a summarizes recent DHS data on age differences between spouses by age of marriage of the wife. Note that this analysis is restricted to currently married women ages 25-34 because the question on the age of one's spouse or partner is asked only of women who are married at the time of the survey. Note also that the analysis is restricted to those in first marriages, because higher order marriages tend to take place at older ages well after the transition to adulthood has taken place. The graph confirms that women who marry prior to age 18 are more likely to have spouses who are older. It also shows that there is as much, if not more variation among regions as within regions by age. Age differences are largest in Western and Middle Africa, where polygyny is still common and teenagers often become junior wives of older men. Age differences are smallest in the former Soviet Asia.

Figure 7-2b presents parallel data from the DHS but instead plots age differences as a function of male age at marriage for the same sample of women. As Casterline, Williams, and McDonald (1986) observed nearly 20 years ago in their analysis of World Fertility Survey data, age differences vary much more as a function of male age at marriage than of female age at marriage because of the greater variance in male age at marriage. Note, however, that no new information is actually provided by this graph, since male age at marriage is equal to female age at marriage plus the age difference. Nevertheless, these findings are broadly consistent with a model in which men accept or choose from a limited age range of marriageable women irrespective of their own age. In some regions, older grooms actually marry younger brides than do younger grooms, possibly a consequence of arranged marriage.

Given that there has been an increase in age of marriage for both men and women in most regions of the world, it is not obvious what the trends are with regard to age differences. In her analysis of data from 55 of 56 African countries[17] over the last 50 years, Hertrich (2002) notes a decline in

---

[17]The only country without data is Western Sahara.

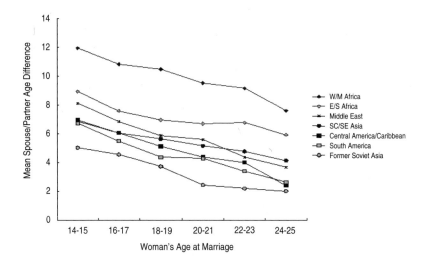

FIGURE 7-2a Mean spouse/partner age difference by woman's age at marriage, women 25-34.
SOURCE: Demographic and Health Surveys.

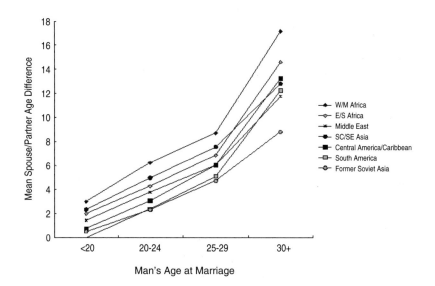

FIGURE 7-2b Mean spouse/partner age difference by man's age at marriage, men married to women 25-34.
SOURCE: Demographic and Health Surveys.

the difference between male and female median age of marriage.[18] She observed that the age difference, while inversely correlated with woman's age at marriage for the last 40 years and positively correlated with male age at marriage from the mid-1950s through the end of the 1970s, is now not associated with male age at marriage. Quisumbing and Hallman (2005), in their examination of International Food Policy Research Institute (IFPRI) survey data, observed a decrease in the age difference between spouses in Bangladesh,[19] Ethiopia, Mexico, and Guatemala, and no change in the Philippines and South Africa, countries in which the age gap between husbands and wives was not large to begin with.[20]

Table 7-12 compares the distribution of spouse or partner age differences from 42 DHS countries by two age groups, 25-29 and 45-49, among women currently in first marriages. There are two potential problems with this analysis. First, although the vast majority of those ages 25-29 who will eventually marry have already done so, in certain regions first marriage does extend into the 30s or later. Given that the age gap between spouses is inversely related to age at marriage, the distribution of spousal age differences observed here for the younger group may be slightly biased upward in countries in which substantial numbers of women marry late.

Second and more significantly, the sample of 45-49-year-olds is unlikely to be representative of all ever-married 45-49-year-olds in regions in which marital dissolution is considerable. The last column of the table indicates the percentage of ever-married women who are currently in a first marriage by age group. There is a considerable range. While 90 percent of ever-married women ages 45-49 in the Middle East are currently married, only 52 percent of their counterparts in Eastern and Southern Africa are. Not only are there a number of regions with a substantial percentage of ever-married women not in a first marriage, but also the sample of those who are in first marriages is likely to be selective. Women ages 45-49 who are still in first marriages at the time of the survey are likely to have spouses closer in age to themselves than women who are widowed. Moreover, if

---

[18]"Although the decline in the differences between the medians is strongly suggestive of a decline in the median or mean age difference, it is not conclusive. The difference between the medians only equals the median difference when a distribution is symmetrical, in which case the median equals the mean" (Mensch, 1986:231).

[19] In contrast to the IFPRI data from Bangladesh, which were collected in 1996 and 1997 in rural areas, the DHS data, which are national, indicate, if anything, a slight increase in the age difference between spouses.

[20]The data are retrospective and capture marriages that were initiated during different periods: Bangladesh, 1945-1994, the Philippines, 1945-1984, Ethiopia, 1955-1989, South Africa, 1955-1999, Mexico, 1930-1999, and Guatemala, 1970-1999.

TABLE 7-12 Percentage Distribution of Spouse/Partner Age Differences, Among Women Currently in First Marriage, by Age (Weighted Averages)

| Region | Population Represented | 0-5 Years | |
|---|---|---|---|
| | | 45-49 | 25-29 |
| Africa | | | |
| Eastern/Southern Africa | 79.2 | 47.4 | 51.9 |
| Western/Middle Africa | 66.9 | 29.2 | 31.7 |
| Asia | | | |
| South-central/South-eastern Asia | 67.6 | 52.2 | 53.9 |
| Former Soviet Asia | 68.4 | 74.4 | 84.5 |
| Latin America and Caribbean | | | |
| Caribbean/Central America | 21.0 | 63.3 | 61.3 |
| South America | 72.4 | 68.6 | 66.2 |
| Middle East | | | |
| Western Asia/Northern Africa | 40.7 | 54.2 | 53.9 |
| TOTAL | 64.2 | 51.9 | 53.5 |

NOTES: All cases where the woman is reported as older than her husband are included in the 0-5 category. For source of regional groupings and population data for weighted averages, see Table 7-1. Further detail can be found in Appendix A.

there is an inverse relationship between the stability of marriage and the spousal age gap, then the mean age difference observed for women ages 45-49 who are currently in a first marriage will be lower than that for all ever-married women ages 45-49.

Comparing age differences among 45-49-year-olds with 25-29-year-olds indicates a narrowing of the gap over time, especially in Eastern and Southern Africa, Western and Middle Africa, the Middle East, and South-central and South-eastern Asia, where there has been a decline in the proportion of women marrying men more than 10 years older, and an increase, in Eastern and Southern Africa, in the proportion of women with an age gap of 5 years or less. Age differences, which were already small in former Soviet Asia, are also narrowing. As discussed above, it is likely that the table underestimates the decline in age differences, because the percentage of women ages 45-49 with an 11+ age difference is undoubtedly larger than observed.

That age differences are shrinking is a function of the fact that the pace of decline in marriage prevalence by age is greater among women than men. For example, in Jordan there has been a sizeable reduction in the age difference between spouses; only 11 percent of women ages 25-29 are

| 6-10 Years | | 11+ Years | | % Ever Married Who Are Currently in a First Marriage | |
|---|---|---|---|---|---|
| 45-49 | 25-29 | 45-49 | 25-29 | 45-49 | 25-29 |
| 28.3 | 30.9 | 24.3 | 17.3 | 52 | 71 |
| 25.8 | 34.6 | 45.0 | 33.7 | 64 | 80 |
| 28.9 | 34.2 | 18.9 | 11.9 | 88 | 95 |
| 19.6 | 13.3 | 6.0 | 2.2 | 73 | 86 |
| 23.3 | 24.6 | 13.5 | 14.1 | 68 | 76 |
| 20.2 | 23.4 | 11.2 | 10.3 | 66 | 84 |
| 28.2 | 33.4 | 17.6 | 12.7 | 90 | 96 |
| 27.3 | 32.0 | 20.9 | 14.4 | | |

SOURCES: Demographic and Health Surveys tabulations from 42 countries, 1994-2001. Côte d'Ivoire, Indonesia, Morocco, Namibia, Pakistan, Paraguay, Senegal, Tanzania, and Yemen excluded; surveys had no question regarding current age of spouse. Gabon data unavailable at time of this analysis. See Appendix Table 7-6 for list of countries.

married to men more than 10 years their senior, whereas 21 percent of women ages 35-39 have husbands who are that much older. The proportion of women ages 20-24 who are married dropped from 64 to 48 percent between 1979 and 1994, whereas the proportion of men ages 25-29 who are married declined only from 66 to 58 percent during that period.

More research is needed on the association between the spousal age gap and how marriage is experienced by the couple, especially in situations in which a young wife is married to a much older man. When gender roles are highly segregated and the vast majority of wives lack power relative to their husbands, it is not clear whether most women would choose a younger husband with whom they might have a slightly better bargaining position over an older man who was better off financially. In addition, when the age gap between a husband and a wife is large, there has been little attempt to analyze whether it is the early age at marriage that limits a woman's ability to influence or share decision making with her spouse, whether it is the large age difference between the woman and her husband, or whether it is some other factor altogether. Indeed, one would think that when the age gap between spouses has remained constant or declined only minimally and the age of marriage of women has risen, the significance of the gap is likely to have diminished. A 15-year-old woman marrying a 25-year-old man probably has a lesser role in household decision making than a 25-year-old woman marrying a 35-year-old man.

## Polygyny

Polygyny is one of the distinctive features of marital regimes in sub-Saharan Africa, especially in Western Africa. Polygynous unions are typically characterized by a large age gap between spouses, with women marrying young and men delaying marriage until at least their 20s, when they are able to acquire bridewealth. More common in societies with patrilineal descent systems and in which traditional religion holds sway, the prevalence of polygyny is expected to decline with increasing urbanization, schooling, and exposure to the West (Timaeus and Reynar, 1998).

An analysis of trends in polygyny in sub-Saharan Africa from the mid-1970s through 1996 revealed little change in the proportion of married women in polygynous unions; among 11 countries with multiple surveys, only Ghana and Kenya exhibited large declines, although there is some indication that the practice was also waning in Côte d'Ivoire, Rwanda, and Uganda (Timaeus and Reynar, 1998).

In Table 7-13 we have updated this analysis. We have added 19 surveys conducted since 1997 to the original 39 (in 25 countries). Multiple surveys are now available for 20 countries. Declines are observed in Cameroon, Côte D'Ivoire, Ghana, Kenya, Malawi, Nigeria, Rwanda, and Togo. Aggregate analyses of all married women ages 15-49 may obscure changes that could be occurring among younger women.

Table 7-14 provides information on the prevalence of polygyny for married women ages 20-29. Note that because women are more likely to be part of a polygynous union as they age, to detect change over time, one should compare across surveys but not age groups. Of the 20 countries with multiple surveys, the incidence of polygyny has declined in about half: Benin, Cameroon, Ghana, Kenya, Madagascar (where it was already very low), Malawi, Mali (possibly), Nigeria, and Togo.

The DHS data indicate that, even with these declines, polygyny is still a prominent element of marriage in sub-Saharan Africa. The social linkages that marriage creates and the economic gain and prestige that polygynous alliances imply for extended families apparently far outweigh the costs to individual women (Blanc and Gage, 2000). However, the practice has evolved over time. Noncoresidential arrangements for wives have emerged, particularly among the wealthy in urban areas (Antoine and Nanitelamia, 1996; Locoh, 1994; Wittrup, 1990).

In addition, while polygyny was traditionally practiced by the relatively affluent, there is the emergence of what has been termed "the polygyny of

TABLE 7-13 Percentage of Currently Married Women in Polygynous Unions in Sub-Saharan Africa

| Country | WFS 1977-1982 | DHS-I 1986-1990 | DHS-II 1990-1993 | DHS-III 1993-1996 | DHS-III 1997-1999 | DHS-IV 1998-2001 |
|---|---|---|---|---|---|---|
| Benin | 34.6 | | | 49.6 | | 46.3 |
| Burkina Faso | | | 51.1 | | 54.7 | |
| Burundi | | 11.6 | | | | |
| Cameroon | 39.7 | | 38.6 | | 33.1 | |
| Central African Republic | | | | 28.5 | | |
| Côte d'Ivoire | 41.4 | | | 36.6 | 35.0 | |
| Ghana | 34.4 | 32.6 | | 27.7 | | 22.7 |
| Guinea | | | | 49.6 | | 53.7 |
| Kenya | 29.5 | 23.4 | | 19.5 | 16.3 | |
| Lesotho | 8.5 | | | | | |
| Liberia | | 38.0 | | | | |
| Madagascar | | | 3.5 | | 4.0 | |
| Malawi | | | 32.2 | | | 17.2 |
| Mali | | 45.1 | | 44.3 | | |
| Namibia | | | 12.6 | | | |
| Niger | | | 36.2 | | 37.6 | |
| Nigeria | 43.1 | | 40.9 | | 35.7 | |
| Rwanda | 18.4[a] | | 14.4 | | | 12.3 |
| Senegal | 48.5 | 46.5 | 47.3 | | 46.0 | |
| Sudan (Northern) | 16.8 | 20.2 | | | | |
| Tanzania | | | 27.5 | 28.8 | | |
| Togo | | 52.3 | | | 43.5 | |
| Uganda | | 34.2 | | 29.9 | | 32.7 |
| Zambia | | | 17.7 | 17.1 | | |
| Zimbabwe | | 16.6 | | 18.6 | | 15.5 |

[a]Not a WFS survey although it had a similar design and questionnaire.
SOURCES: Timaeus and Reynar (1998) and Demographic and Health Surveys tabulations from 1986-2001.

TABLE 7-14 Percentage of Currently Married Women Ages 20-29 in Polygynous Unions in Sub-Saharan Africa

| County and Year of Survey | Ages | |
| --- | --- | --- |
| | 20-24 | 25-29 |
| Benin 1996 | 39.0 | 46.2 |
| Benin 2001 | 32.8 | 41.7 |
| Burkina Faso 1992-1993 | 40.5 | 50.4 |
| Burkina Faso 1998-1999 | 43.4 | 48.6 |
| Cameroon 1991 | 31.6 | 36.1 |
| Cameroon 1998 | 25.4 | 29.5 |
| Côte d'Ivoire 1994 | 27.3 | 34.2 |
| Côte d'Ivoire 1998-1999 | 27.0 | 27.5 |
| Ghana 1988 | 25.5 | 28.5 |
| Ghana 1993 | 18.9 | 21.7 |
| Ghana 1998 | 13.2 | 15.8 |
| Kenya 1989 | 17.8 | 17.7 |
| Kenya 1993 | 12.6 | 15.2 |
| Kenya 1998 | 9.2 | 15.0 |
| Madagascar 1992 | 6.8 | 7.0 |
| Madagascar 1997 | 4.2 | 4.2 |
| Malawi 1992 | 13.0 | 22.1 |
| Malawi 2000 | 11.3 | 18.1 |
| Mali 1987 | 36.0 | 39.7 |
| Mali 1995-1996 | 30.0 | 40.6 |
| Niger 1992 | 26.1 | 36.0 |
| Niger 1998 | 29.2 | 36.7 |
| Nigeria 1990 | 33.7 | 35.8 |
| Nigeria 1999 | 26.5 | 30.6 |
| Rwanda 1992 | 8.4 | 9.8 |
| Rwanda 2000 | 8.0 | 9.1 |
| Senegal 1986 | 33.2 | 41.0 |
| Senegal 1992-1993 | 33.1 | 42.6 |
| Senegal 1997 | 35.0 | 42.5 |
| Tanzania 1992 | 18.6 | 27.4 |
| Tanzania 1996 | 20.1 | 27.3 |
| Togo 1988 | 39.9 | 51.1 |
| Togo 1998 | 28.6 | 37.8 |
| Uganda 1988 | 31.8 | 32.4 |
| Uganda 1995 | 23.2 | 32.0 |
| Uganda 2000-2001 | 25.5 | 31.9 |
| Zambia 1992 | 10.8 | 17.3 |
| Zambia 1996 | 10.0 | 16.6 |
| Zimbabwe 1988 | 11.7 | 14.0 |
| Zimbabwe 1994 | 12.4 | 18.2 |
| Zimbabwe 1999 | 14.8 | 15.2 |

SOURCE: Demographic and Health Surveys tabulations from 1987-2001.

poverty" (Antoine and Nanitelamia, 1996), which refers to the situation in which a man who does not have the means to take on another wife marries a woman involved in a remunerative activity. In so doing, a relatively poor man can acquire the social prestige that comes with additional wives without having to assume the responsibility for her economic well-being.

Finally, new arrangements, referred to as having "outside wives" (Karanja, 1994; Mann, 1994), "away matches," or "le deuxième bureau" (Clignet, 1987), serve as functional substitutes without the same degree of commitment that polygyny entails. These have been attributed in part to economic constraints that make it difficult for men to afford the bridewealth for more than one wife. Indeed, in Lesotho, men ascribe the emergence of the institution of *bonyatsi* (that is, extramarital relations of a more or less long-term nature) to the escalating costs of bridewealth payments (Speigel, 1991). Because polygyny appears to be thriving in these alternative forms, data on changes in its prevalence may not be reliable.

The changing nature of polygyny among some groups is not only a reflection of difficult economic circumstances that make it hard for men to support more than one wife (Solway, 1990), but also a manifestation of cultural persistence. There is even some evidence of a return to polygyny among intellectuals who practiced monogamy earlier in life but now reject it at later stages as "an external imposition not adapted to African realities" (Antoine and Nanitelamio, 1996; see also van der Vliet, 1991). In justifying a polygynous lifestyle, men tend to emphasize the sexual aspects of the practice with less consideration for the traditional economic obligations involved in maintaining several wives and numerous children (Ferraro, 1991; van der Vliet, 1991; Wittrup, 1990).

While there is a large literature on the distinctive features of polygyny and the characteristics of those who are in a polygynous union (see, for example, Bledsoe and Pison, 1994: Section IV), less is known about the experiences of young married women in polygynous unions. What is married life like for a young woman who becomes a junior wife to an older husband? How does she relate to the senior wife? Does the adolescent girl have any say in the decision to enter or remain in a polygynous union?

## Spousal Choice

As discussed in Chapter 1, our conception of a successful transition to adulthood recognizes the value of increased agency as adolescence progresses. In the domain of marriage, this agency takes the form of participation in the choice of partner and the timing of the union. An emphasis on the involvement of the young person in the marriage process is consistent with an emerging international consensus. Article 16 of the UN Convention on the Elimination of All Forms of Discrimination Against Women includes the right to choose a spouse and to enter marriage with "free and full consent." In December 2003, Pakistan's highest court legalized so called free-will marriages[21]; the ruling enables women 18 and older to marry without obtaining the consent of a parent or guardian.

One potential factor contributing to the reduction in early marriage among women is a movement away from arranged marriages (Hull, 2002; Malhotra and Tsui, 1996). Hull (2002:8) asserts for Indonesia that the increase in the age of marriage "has come about due to the shift of the locus of marriage decision making from parents to children," which he attributes, in turn, to the expansion in educational attainment among young women. It is generally believed that the process of parental selection is simply less time-consuming than that of individual searching. Furthermore, when parents are involved in spouse selection, it is argued that daughters are married off early because of a concern with preserving their sexual purity. Indeed, one frequently cited reason for parental involvement in spouse selection is that, in allowing a daughter to explore potential partners for herself, she is more likely to initiate sex before marriage. Another motivation for a parent involved in mate selection to marry a daughter off early is that girls are thought to be compliant in the choice of spouse when they are young (UNICEF, 2001b).

While it stands to reason that there is an association between age of marriage and the spouse selection process, little research exists linking the two. Moreover, even if there is a link, a rise in the age of marriage does not necessarily imply that the practice of arranged marriage is being eliminated (Malhotra and Tsui, 1996). Correspondingly, the absence of a shift in age of marriage does not necessarily signify that there has been no change in the process of spouse selection. Malhotra (1991:566), one of the few researchers who has investigated spouse choice found that, in Java, "younger cohorts are having considerable input into marriage decisions without also marrying considerably later." And in Sri Lanka, those who choose their own spouses marry earlier than those who have arranged marriages, a finding that the researchers note is "relatively unusual among Asian societies" (Malhotra and Tsui, 1996:488).

While there is an extensive literature on the age of marriage of women, fewer studies have investigated parental control over spouse choice and how it may be changing. In fact it is the rare demographic survey that even includes questions that would permit an investigation of the process of spouse selection and how it differs by gender. The lack of current data has led some researchers to assume that arranged marriages are still the norm in

---

[21]See http://www.irinnews.org/print.asp?ReportID= 38641.

some parts of the world. An article on marriage in Kenya written in 2003 cites William Goode's seminal volume on the family, which was published over 30 years ago, to buttress the claim that "[m]arriages were, and continue to be, arranged by relatives and friends in almost every African society" (Luke and Munshi, 2003:6).

Several surveys from 20-30 years ago included questions on the respondent's role in spouse selection. The 1979-1980 Asian Marriage Survey—conducted in Indonesia, Pakistan, the Philippines, and Thailand among married women ages 15-45 and a sample of their husbands—included a question about who chose the spouse, although only in Indonesia, Pakistan, and the Philippines were these data analyzed and only in the former two were there substantial proportions in some form of arranged marriages. There were four response categories: totally initiated and arranged by a parent, by a parent with the respondent's approval, by the respondent with a parent's approval, and totally initiated and arranged by the respondent (Domingo and King, 1992; Malhotra, 1991). In a longitudinal survey in the Kautara district of Sri Lanka in 1989 and 1992-1993, in addition to a question on who was the main decision-maker in spouse selection, there were more probing questions on parental involvement in the process, parental objection to the spouse (if the respondent did the choosing), and whether the respondent was consulted (if the parent did the selection) (Malhotra and Tsui, 1996).[22]

Why has there been relatively little interest in the spouse selection process among demographers in recent years? Perhaps because so much focus has been on the rise in age of marriage and its implications for the decline in fertility, a matter of critical importance to population researchers, other aspects of the nuptiality transition have been relatively neglected. Yet the part played by the potential bride and groom in choosing a spouse undoubtedly has consequences for conjugal relations, including gender roles in marriage and decision making between partners, especially decisions about the number, spacing, and upbringing of children. As Malhotra (1991:550) notes: "in cultures where marriages traditionally have been

---

[22]In the IFPRI research program, Strengthening Development Policy Through Gender Analysis, which includes an investigation of the marriage process, surveys have been conducted in eight developing countries. While the focus of these surveys is on material exchanges around marriage and the underlying determinants of spouse characteristics (see Quisumbing and Hallman, 2005), a direct question was included on spouse choice in Bangladesh (1997) and Ethiopia (1997). The Mexico (1999) survey had the following question: "Did your in-laws talk with your parents to ask for your hand, or make any agreements before the union or when you left (to be) with your husband?" Up to now, there has been no analysis by IFPRI of the data generated by these questions (personal communication, Kelly Hallman).

arranged, the extent to which young people become independent of parents in choosing their life partners has implications for their obligations to the family, the financial and social support they can expect from parents, their postmarital residence, sexual activity and fertility behavior."

The data that exist on the relative involvement of parents and young people in the selection of marriage partners suggest that in a number of societies in which arranged marriage was a common feature of the marriage process, there has been a movement in recent years toward self-choice. This decline in kin control or increase in a young woman's involvement in mate selection has been documented with survey data in China (Feng and Quanhe, 1996; Whyte, 1990; Xiaohe and Whyte, 1990), Togo (Gage and Meekers, 1995), Indonesia (Malhotra, 1991), and India (Jejeebhoy and Halli, 2005), and asserted to be occurring throughout sub-Saharan Africa (Lesthaeghe, Kaufman, and Meekers, 1989; National Research Council, 1993:116-151) and parts of Asia (Choe, Westley, and Retherford, 2002). In Togo, the proportion of first marriages that were arranged declined from 37 percent in 1970 to 24 percent in the period 1980-1988, a trend that Gage and Meekers (1995) associate with increased education and urbanization. A survey in 1987 of nearly 600 women in Chengdu, China, the capital of Sichuan Province, revealed that arranged marriages, in which the couple often did not meet until the wedding day, declined from 69 percent of marriages between 1933 and 1948 to 1 percent in 1958-1965 to 0 percent in the 1980s. While the adoption of a new marriage law in 1950 outlawed arranged marriage, a "family revolution" was apparently beginning in urban areas in the several decades before the Communist takeover in 1949, due to greater exposure to the West (Whyte, 1990).

Bledsoe and Cohen (National Research Council, 1993:Chapter 3) argue that increasing wage labor in sub-Saharan Africa provides young men with a degree of independence from their family, giving them greater control over whom they marry. Banerjee (1999:8), in his discussion of contemporary marriage patterns, makes the same argument about India: "New opportunities for market employment altered the balance of power in the family and kinship system" and this "economic independence allowed adult children to acquire more power over spouse selection." An ethnographic account of changing social norms with regard to marriage among the Orma of northeastern Kenya observed a shift in bargaining power in favor of young men and women; moreover, young women are now gaining support in both the civil and the Muslim courts against "forced" marriages (Ensminger and Knight, 1997).

Comparison of spouse selection patterns across cohorts in Indonesia, as noted above, reveals that both men and women—but particularly women, whose parents were traditionally more involved in spouse selection—are increasingly likely to choose their spouse. While family background and education are significant determinants of spouse choice for women in Indonesia, only living away from the parental home before marriage is significant for men, evidence that status concerns are more important for daughters' than sons' marriages (Malhotra, 1991). Although cohort comparisons of the Asian Marriage Survey data in Pakistan have not been published, differentials among socioeconomic and residential groups suggest that, with increasing education and labor force participation of women prior to marriage, participation of daughters in the choice of husbands will rise (Domingo and King, 1992). The question is whether self-choice may increase even in the absence of changes in the economic role of women. As Malhotra (1991:559) observed for Indonesia, the increase in self-choice across cohorts is not simply a result of a transformation in the composition of the population; rather there are more "fundamental secular" changes at work. While she doesn't specify what these changes are, increasing access to Western media, especially movies and magazines, undoubtedly plays a role in the movement toward self-choice.

The cross-cultural study of romantic love, described as a newly flourishing field in anthropology, is indirect evidence of the pervasive influence of Western ideas about romantic love that has emerged in recent years (Ahearn, 2001). Ahearn's ethnographic study of a Nepalese village west of Kathmandu[23] describes a shift away from arranged and capture marriages[24] in the 1980s and 1990s and a movement toward love marriages (Box 7-2). Among men, approximately 20 percent of marriages between 1960 and 1982 in the village involved the son making his own choice, compared with over 60 percent of marriages between 1983 and 1998. Correspondingly, among women, about 10 percent of marriages in the earlier period involved the daughter selecting her spouse, compared with over 50 percent in the later period.[25] Ahearn attributes this transformation to a dramatic increase in literacy during the last 20 years: 95 percent of married women born between 1937 and 1951 were illiterate, compared with 67 percent of those born between 1952 and 1962 and only 9 percent born after 1962. With this growth in formal schooling and literacy classes, the writing of love letters

---

[23]A 10-hour drive followed by a half-day walk from Kathmandu.

[24]Capture marriages are marriages where the bride is abducted, sometimes with the complicity of her family. Ahearn (2001:106) mentions two reasons for capture marriage: (1) the groom or bride's family cannot afford the costs associated with a wedding; and (2) the groom becomes "so infatuated" with the woman.

[25]While "coercion" is much less common, gender equity in the spouse selection process is far from being realized; it is the woman who consents to the man's proposal.

**BOX 7-2**
**Literacy and Love: Education, Globalization, and**
**Changing Marriage Patterns in Rural Nepal**

"Life is an infinite circle . . . in the whole 'world' there must be few individuals who do not bow down to love. Sarita, I'm helpless, and I have to make friends of a notebook and pen in order to place this helplessness before you. Love is the sort of thing that anyone can feel. . . . Napoleon, who with bravery conquered the 'world,' united it, and took it forward, was astounded when he saw one particular widow. Certainly, history's pages are colored with accounts of such individuals who love each other. . . . Love is the union of two souls. The 'main' meaning of loving is 'life success.' I'm offering you an invitation to love" (excerpt from a love letter written to Sarita from her eventual husband, Bir Bahadur, in spring 1992).

As globalization proceeds, it brings many changes in terms of communication and culture. The spread of education and the availability of mass media and literature in remote places often create unanticipated cultural and social changes. In rural Nepal, literacy rates and formal education have increased, and magazines, books, and films from India and "the West" have become more accessible. Traditional courtship and marriage practices also appear to be changing. The interplay of these changes is evident in some areas of Nepal with the emergence of the courtship practice of writing love letters.

In her ethnographic study of a rural village in Nepal, "Junigau," Laura Ahearn's (2001) findings indicate that the percentage of arranged marriages and capture marriages decreased significantly between 1960 and 1998, while the number of elopements rose sharply after 1983. Paralleling this trend, female literacy rates in Junigau increased sharply, from about 5 percent for women born before 1951, to 91 percent for those born after 1963 (2001). Ahearn argues that rising literacy rates coupled with increased access to magazines, radio, film, school texts, and other books have familiarized villagers with "new structures of feeling" about such concepts as nationalism, Hinduism, democracy, modernization, economic and educational success, romantic love, personal agency, and individual choice. According to Ahearn, not only did the increase in female literacy in Junigau in the 1990s make possible the emergence of new courtship practices and facilitated self-initiated marriages, but it also reinforced certain gender ideologies and undercut some avenues to social power, especially for women (2001).

Ahearn's research depicts how Junigau couples' aspirations have shifted toward desires for companionate marriages and attitudes that women must consent to marriage. However, she maintains that coercion in marriage and existing gender hierarchies have not been eliminated, and that increased female literacy does not necessarily lead to more choices and better lives for men and women. A central message of Ahearn's ethnography is that the social transformations taking place in Junigau involve changes in marriage practices facilitated by love letters and increased literacy, as well as changes in villagers' conceptions of individual agency and personhood.

and the practice of elopement increased markedly. The textbooks used in government schools and literacy classes as well as the film magazines that are now widely read appear to have exposed villagers to notions of romantic love and resulted in an increased sense of agency on the part of the younger generation.

Although mutual attraction clearly plays a more prominent role in spousal choice in many of the countries discussed above, for the most part data are lacking about whether a "dating culture"[26] has replaced a system of arranged marriage. Whyte's survey in Chengdu, China, is an exception; he did explore dating behavior, finding that the majority of women who married between 1977 and 1987 had only one romance, and that romance was with a future spouse prior to marriage (Whyte, 1990).

It would appear that the Western model of dating and total freedom of mate choice has yet to take hold in many developing countries. Indeed, to the extent that the young person is involved in the spouse selection process in countries in which arranged marriage was normative in the past, parents still play a role.[27] In Indonesia, the marriage choice type showing the greatest increase is self-selection with parental approval (Malhotra, 1991). In Chengdu, China, while arranged marriages were no longer reported to exist in the late 1980s, parents were involved in spouse selection in over 40 percent of marriages (Whyte, 1990). In India, Banerjee (1999) does not believe that love marriages have replaced arranged marriages; rather, arranged marriage has been transformed from "an unconsented to a consented model." A similar observation is made more recently for Indonesia by Hull (2002), for Taiwan by Thornton, Chang, and Lin (1994), and for Africa by Isiugo-Abanihe (1994) and Meekers (1993). This more nuanced categorization challenges simplistic notions of marriage systems as being either traditional—serving only the needs of the larger family—or modern, in which the conjugal bond leaves no room for parental involvement (Malhotra and Tsui, 1996).

In what way does a reduced role by the family in the spouse selection process affect the relationship between the bride and the groom? In countries in which arranged marriage used to be the norm, a move toward more individual choice is said to have had important implications for sexual behavior. Data from China, Korea, Malaysia, and Taiwan indicate that the

---

[26]Whyte (1990) defines a dating culture as one where young adults have opportunities to meet removed from adult supervision and where romantic relationships don't necessarily lead to marriage.

[27]Note that this observation is based on surveys that were conducted over 15 years ago. It is possible that increasing exposure to Western culture during the 1990s has given rise to more dating and less parental involvement in spouse selection more recently.

changing nature of partner selection beginning in the 1960s has been associated with an increase in premarital sex, a rise in coital frequency in the
first years of marriage, and a corresponding decline in the first birth interval
(Feng and Quanhe, 1996; Rindfuss and Morgan, 1983; Thornton et al.,
1994). Indeed, Rindfuss and Morgan (1983:259-260) asserted some 20
years ago that "a very quiet sexual revolution has been occurring in Asia
that may be more far reaching and profound than the very vocal sexual
revolution that has been occurring in the West." However, studies from
Vietnam and Indonesia suggest that, when premarital sex is reported by
women, it is more often sex with a future spouse rather than with a more
casual partner (Hull, 2002; Mensch, Clark, and Anh, 2003).

### Consanguineous Marriage

A marriage is generally designated as consanguineous if the couple
shares one recent ancestor; generally the label is attached to marriages
between second cousins or closer relatives (Bittles, 1994). Given that arranged marriages are said to be on the decline, one might expect a reduction
in the proportion of young people who are in consanguineous unions,
although the countries for which there is information on trends in consanguinity are not the same as those for which there is information on trends in
arranged marriage. Surprisingly, according to the data available, the prevalence of consanguineous marriage appears to have changed little in recent
years. A comprehensive analysis of survey data in the Middle East, Northern Africa, and Western Asia found that the proportion of first cousin
marriages declined in only 3 of 18 countries, and then only slightly
(Casterline and El-Zeini, 2003).[28] One-fifth to one-half of all marriages in
these populations is estimated to be consanguineous (Hussain and Bittles,
1999:449).

Sholkamy (2001) and Casterline and El-Zeini (2002) give several arguments as to why cousin marriage is still common in the Arab region. For the
groom and his family, the financial burden is thought to be reduced when
he marries a relative, since the bride and her family are presumed to make
fewer demands for furniture and housing. For the bride, her treatment by
the groom and his mother is thought to be better (Hussain and Bittles,
1999). Moreover, assets are consolidated when the wife marries in the
family. In Southern Asia, where the burden of dowries is high (see discussion of dowry below), marriage to a relative is considered "a more eco-

---

[28]Data on consanguinity analyzed by Casterline and El Zeini (2003) come from the Gulf
Family Health Surveys (GFHS), the Pan-Arab Project for Child Development Surveys
(PAPCHILD), and the DHS.

nomically feasible choice" (Bittles, 1994:576). Perhaps the rationale provided by Casterline and El-Zeini that is most revealing of the day-to-day life of adolescents may also hold true in Southern Asia. They argue that a young person is more likely to form a romantic association with a cousin because opportunities to interact with nonrelatives of the opposite sex are rare.

Casterline and El-Zeini (2002:7) argue that, given the "compelling factors" favoring cousin marriage, "it is not surprising" that rates of consanguinity remain quite high. Alan Bittles, who has written more on this subject than any other researcher, agrees, observing that in the absence of legislation prohibiting the practice, the prevalence of marriages between relatives in those parts of the world in which it is common is unlikely to fall in the near future. He claims, however, that over the long term, a decline in family size should lead to a reduction in the pool of available relatives, as should the reduction in arranged marriages and the increase in age at marriage. Casterline and El-Zeini (2002) dispute this. They argue that, when fertility is high, competition for cousins is also high. With microsimulation, they show, in the demographic regimes they are considering—Egypt, Morocco, and Yemen—the availability of first cousins for marriage is affected more by declines in mortality than fertility.[29]

Because there is so little information about the nature of spouse relations, it is not known how marriages between relatives differ from marriages between those who are unrelated. There is an assertion that consanguineous unions are exploitative of women, because the family link is ostensibly much tighter than the conjugal bond when women marry kin (Hussain, 1999). However, it is not clear that the conjugal bond is any stronger in arranged marriages between nonrelatives. Furthermore, the claim that consanguineous relationships are particularly exploitative is entirely speculative and may be based on the fact that it is generally lower status women and those with less education who are more likely to marry relatives (Hussain and Bittles, 1998). One can as easily make an argument that consanguineous marriages are protective of women, since the wife is living among her own kin who presumably are more likely to be on the watch for abusive behavior from a spouse. Indeed, Dyson and Moore (1983), seeking to explain regional variations in demographic behavior in India in the 1970s, argued that, in consanguineous marriages, women have higher value to both their natal and their conjugal families, with a resulting increase in autonomy and quality of life and lower fertility and child mortality.

---

[29]They also show that the availability of first cousins varies considerably depending on the assumption made about spousal age differences.

## Financial Transfers: Bride-Price, Dowry, and Assets Brought to Marriage

In many developing countries, especially in Africa and Southern Asia, marriage has traditionally involved not only the selection of a mate by one's family but also the transfer of gifts, cash, valuables, and consumer goods from the groom's family to the bride's or vice versa. When this transfer is from the bride's family to the groom's family, it is known as dowry or more precisely groom-price; when the transfer is from the groom's family to the bride's family, it is known as bridewealth or bride-price. The direction and amount of the transfer may affect the timing of marriage as well as the relationship between husband and wife, particularly in the early years of marriage, as well as, just as importantly given the nature of living arrangements, the relationship between the groom or bride and his or her spouse's family.

The conventional explanation given for bride-price is that, in societies in which women do much of the agricultural work, this transfer, whether in cash or in kind, reimburses the bride's family for the loss of her future labor (Amin and Cain, 1997; Boye et al., 1991). The explanation given for dowry is that it compensates men in societies in which women's labor has little market value (Amin and Cain, 1997). Dowry has taken a somewhat different form in developing countries than it did in Western Europe historically, where it was considered a premortem inheritance for the bride (Billig, 1992). Whereas in Europe, the intended recipient of the dowry was the bride, in Southern Asia, the dowry is not given to the bride; rather, property and payments are transferred to the groom and his family. Billig (1992) and others thus argue that the correct expression for this transfer is not dowry, in the traditionally European sense, but groom-price.

By far, the more common form of exchange is from the groom's family to the bride's. Murdock's *Ethnographic Atlas* indicates that, as of the early 1980s in approximately two-thirds of the 1,267 societies catalogued, bridewealth is normative, whereas dowry is prevalent in just 6 percent (cited in Bhat and Halli, 1999). However, the countries in which dowry is common have much larger populations. Moreover, the literature on dowry is more extensive, perhaps because the value of the transfer is much greater in dowry and therefore the impact on the parties involved that much more significant.

### Bridewealth

In sub-Saharan Africa, where bride-price dominates, it traditionally took the form of gifts of food and drink (van de Walle and Meekers, 1994). For example, among the Kassem and Nankam of northern Ghana, kola nuts and guinea fowl were given by the boy to the girl's family as part of the courtship process to signal his intention to marry their daughter (Mensch et al., 1999). However, according to van de Walle and Meekers (1994:62), while ritual gifts of drinks and kola nuts are known to be common in Western Africa, "we know of no systematic ethnography of the custom."

It would appear, from the little research that has been conducted, that this giving of gifts by the man to the family of the woman is becoming less customary in sub-Saharan Africa. "Education, urban living, and the importance of mutual consent in unions have all played roles," as has the rise of "imported forms of civil or religious marriage (which clearly involve a ceremony)" (van de Walle and Meekers, 1994:57). Indeed, a recent study of the changing nature of adolescence among the Kassem and Nankam revealed that older adults felt that the traditional marriage process is now being bypassed, and they are much less involved in choosing a spouse for their offspring. Complained a 70-year-old man who was interviewed: "[In] our time, when you saw a girl and were interested in her, you sent kola nuts and tobacco to her father to declare your intention. But nowadays, you people do not do that; you've taken the white man's ways" (cited in Mensch et al., 1999:105).

While this ritual giving of kola nuts and other foodstuffs by the groom to the bride's family is becoming less common, there is some suggestion that it is being replaced by the transfer of cash and more expensive gifts (Cooper, 1995). According to researchers who have analyzed marriage laws in the countries of the Sahel, postindependence marriage codes in Burkina Faso, Mali, and Senegal do not abolish bride-price but regulate it, in part out of a concern that it has become so inflated as to make marriage prohibitive for the man (Boye et al., 1991). In Eastern and Southern Africa there was an escalation in the real value of bridewealth payments during the colonial and early independence years (1950s and 1960s), which is attributed to the rise in the value of women's agricultural work with cash cropping (Mulder, 1995). An analysis of the pattern of bridewealth payments in Kenya, which is said to conform to other Eastern and Southern African populations, indicates a slight decline in payments in the 1970s and 1980s. It is ascribed to a reduction in women's labor and reproductive value with increasing shortages of land and alternative investment opportunities, as well as a rise in premarital pregnancies. An analysis of bridewealth payments among the Ibo in Nigeria from 1970-1987 also indicates a decline in the value in real terms (Isiugo-Abanihe, 1994). However, the financial burden on the groom is said to have increased because of declines in income, a situation that is probably not unique to Nigeria. Not only has the nature of financial payments apparently shifted with the changing economy, but also young men are increasingly believed to shoulder the burden of bridewealth themselves (National Research Council, 1993:Chapter 3). Among the Orma, who reside in northeastern Kenya, the increase in bargaining power of young people relative to their parents as a result of greater financial independence has led both to a decline in bridewealth and a reduction in the age difference between spouses. "Young women are more inclined to choose young men as marriage partners [rather than rich older men] and young men have less need of bridewealth to ensure a supply of marriage partners" (Ensminger and Knight, 1997:11-12).

In communities in which the cost of bridewealth has increased, various forms of nonmarital cohabitation, often without parental consent, have emerged (Meekers, 1994). Among the Iteseo of Uganda and Kenya, for example, Nagashima (1987) notes that there is a reversal in the order in which cohabitation and negotiation of the bridewealth occur. Formerly marriages were arranged and cohabitation occurred after the bridewealth was negotiated and the main part of it handed over to the bride's family. Now the opposite situation generally prevails. Moreover, payments are often made in piecemeal over many years.

Much of the discussion of changes in the nature and amount of bridewealth is based on only a few studies. Nonetheless, it is important to emphasize that there is likely to be enormous variability in these practices both within ethnic groups and across the different parts of the subcontinent. Given the lack of more comprehensive data, it is not possible to assess whether the practice of bridewealth is becoming less prevalent throughout sub-Saharan Africa, nor whether it has become more of a burden with increasing monetization, nor whether there is any relationship between the cost of bride-price and the timing of marriage.

Increasingly, bride-price is drawing criticism as a practice that essentially commodifies women and gives the husband proprietary rights over his wife. In Africa there is an incipient movement to reform the practice. The Mifumi Domestic Violence and Bride-price Project, based in Uganda, successfully campaigned for the reform of bride-price in the Tororo district. In December 2001, the community voted to make bride-price a nonrefundable gift, so that if a woman wants to divorce her husband, she may do so without her family having to refund the bride-price. These efforts have continued with the first International Conference on Bride-price and Development in February 2004 at Makerere University in Kampala. The goal of the conference was to develop an action plan to reduce or remove the significance of bride-price as a hindrance to gender equality and development (see http://www.Mifumi.org).

## Dowry

In contrast to sub-Saharan Africa, for which the literature on marriage transfers is somewhat dated and to a large extent limited to ethnographies, there is a considerable body of recent studies of dowry in South Asia. A common theme underlies this research, namely, that dowry (or groom-price) has replaced bride-price in India and Bangladesh to the detriment of women.

Among demographers, a view has emerged that the increase in the prevalence and monetary value of dowry in India beginning in the second half of the twentieth century is due to the relative availability of men and women at the appropriate ages of marriage. Because of declining infant and child mortality, and because women marry men who are considerably older, a "marriage squeeze" has emerged; in other words, there is now an excess supply of women of marriageable ages. In addition, as maternal mortality began to fall, there were fewer widowers available for women to marry. When there are too few men of marriageable age, families compete for the eligible men by paying higher dowries (Bhat and Halli, 1999; Billig, 1992; Caldwell, Reddy, and Caldwell, 1983; Deolalikar and Rao, 1998). Some have argued that the increase in dowry should not be attributed entirely to a marriage squeeze. According to Botticini and Siow (2003), growing consumerism and affluence have also contributed to dowry inflation. They suggest that the upper caste practice of hypergamous marriages, that is, women marrying more economically successful spouses, has influenced the larger society.

While India is the focus of research on dowry, the experience of other Southern Asian countries should also be considered. In rural Nepal, where declines in mortality have also created a deficit of eligible men of marriageable age, dowry has yet to emerge as a common practice, although it is increasingly prevalent in Kathmandu (Ahearn, 2001:89).[30] Amin and Cain (1997:300) observe that Bangladesh is more patriarchal than South India and, in their analysis of data from two villages in the northern part of the country, note that one response to a marriage squeeze and a rise in dowry is

---

[30]Interestingly, it has been suggested that the excess supply of marriageable women may have some perversely positive effects on women's status. Bhat and Halli (1999) argue that the rise in the mean age at first marriage in India is due to the marriage squeeze and that, given the low levels of schooling, it is not the increase in education that has led to a rise in the age of marriage. Indeed, they assert that the deficit of eligible men may induce women to stay in school. Caldwell et al. (1983), in their analysis of marriage change in South India in the early 1980s, also argued that the delay in marriage and the decline in age differences between spouses were a function of the marriage squeeze. They asserted that the delay in marriage, while paralleling an increase in contraceptive use, could not be attributed to a desire for reduced family size. And, as do Bhat and Halli (1999), they predicted an increase in the education of girls as society became more accustomed to unmarried girls beyond the age of menarche (Caldwell et al., 1983:361).

an increase in the level of village endogamy, since marriages within the village obviate the necessity of payments to the groom's family.[31]

There is considerable discussion in the literature that the emergence of dowry or excessive dowry payments has undermined the status of women even in the face of increasing education. In India, even researchers refer to dowry as being "evil" and mention is frequently made of daughter-only families becoming destitute and young wives committing suicide and being beaten or burned because of dowry demands (Bhat and Halli, 1999; Suguna, 1998; Sureender, Kahn, and Radhakrishman, 1997).

Although marriages involving dowry are still pervasive in much of Southern Asia, some economists contend that the practice will disappear with increasing urbanization and modernization. Botticini and Siow (2003) assert that, when labor markets become more developed and sons no longer work in family businesses, residential arrangements will move from a virilocal (i.e., residence with the husband's kin) to a neolocal pattern. When married sons move away, there is no reason, so the argument goes, for daughters to be given their share of the family estate at marriage. Instead parents can transfer wealth in the form of human capital investments and bequests to both their daughters and sons. Anderson (2003) argues that the reason dowry has persisted in India is because of caste. She claims that when status is determined by wealth rather than caste, dowry eventually disappears, as it did as Europe. Using a theoretical model of dowry payments, she maintains that in caste-based societies, such as India, increased heterogeneity in income within a caste "necessarily leads to increases in dowry payments," because brides are willing to pay more to marry up (Anderson 2003:273). However, her argument does not take account of the situation in Bangladesh in which dowry is also rising but a formal caste structure does not exist.[32]

## Other Financial Transfers

Not only is it important to explore the changing nature of formal transfers that take place prior to and during the early years of marriage and the impact they have on the nature of marriage, but it is also critical to understand whether contemporary marriage arrangements have changed elsewhere in the developing world. Quisumbing and Hallman (2005) note

---

[31]Incidentally, Amin and Cain (1997:300) argue that in contrast to India, the increase in age of marriage in their study sites is not a function of the marriage squeeze but instead is attributable to exogenous shifts in the education of boys and girls and the imposition of a legal minimum age at marriage.

[32]We thank Sajeda Amin for bringing this point to our attention.

that even in countries in which dowry and bride-price are common, they constitute only a small fraction of the physical assets and human capital that men and women bring to marriage. An examination of survey data from six developing countries—Bangladesh, Ethiopia, Mexico, Guatemala, the Philippines, and South Africa—reveals that: (1) in three of the six countries, there has been an equalization of human capital at marriage, measured as gaps in schooling attainment; in two of the six countries, there has been no change; and in one, Ethiopia, the gap has widened because increases in schooling, while occurring for both sexes, have favored men more than women; (2) there are no clear trends with regard to changes in landownership at marriage; and (3) in five of the six countries, the gap in husband-wife assets brought to marriage has either increased (Latin America) or remained unchanged (Bangladesh, the Philippines, and South Africa), and in Ethiopia it has decreased due to new land collectivization policies. They conclude that while a reduction in the gap in school attainment bodes well for improvement in the balance of power between spouses, the fact that control of assets remains in the hands of men may have implications for household welfare, given the critical role played by women in the well-being of offspring.

## Living Arrangements After Marriage

One potential explanation for later age at marriage in the developing world is a change in the living arrangements of young adults from matrilocal and patrilocal residence to neolocal residence. Rather than establishing residence with the wife's or husband's natal family, newly married couples may set up independent households. The literature on household structure and poverty suggests that the establishment of independent households is a function of income; rising incomes are associated with increased demand for privacy and autonomy and smaller and less complex households (Lloyd, 1998). The desire for a separate residence might therefore lead the couple, especially the young man, to delay marriage. Of course one must also consider that the direction of causation could be reversed, that changing norms about age at marriage may bring about a change in household structure: postponement of marriage may result in greater accumulation of resources and increased demand for a household separate from parents.

Is there any evidence for changing living arrangements and increased economic independence among young people in developing countries? The literature on this subject is very thin. In her 1995 volume on household composition in Latin America, De Vos considered the living arrangements of young people. However, her analysis is based on World Fertility Survey data that are over 30 years old. Although she didn't separate the married from the single nor did she explore trends, De Vos does provide data on the percentage who no longer live with parents. She found that the majority of young adults ages 20-34 of both sexes had left parental households and set up separate residences (De Vos, 1995). In Chengdu, China, postmarital residence with the groom's family declined from 45 percent for women married between 1933 and 1948 to 28 percent for women married from 1977 to 1987, according to the survey conducted in 1987. Correspondingly, the fraction of women living on their own with spouses increased from 39 to 51 percent during the same time period (Whyte, 1990). Presumably this pattern of increasing neolocal residence has continued as exposure to Western culture has grown (Whyte, 2003).

For several DHS countries information exists on living arrangements at two points in time. However, the data are restricted to surveys from DHS II and DHS III and thus can reveal only change that has taken place in the 1990s.[33] There are 10 countries with two surveys at least six years apart in which individual data can be linked to household data. Table 7-15 indicates the percentage of married women ages 20-29 in these 10 countries living in nuclear households in the early 1990s and then 6-10 years later. To measure independence more precisely, we also computed the percentage who live in nuclear households and are household heads or spouses of heads. For this analysis we define a nuclear household to include a head, the spouse of the head, and children and nonrelatives, if any. The expectation is that most married women who live in nuclear households would be heads or spouses of heads. We assume that if a married woman lives in a nuclear household, she and her husband are more likely to be financially independent of parents and other family members than if they lived with them.

Of the 10 countries, only 4—Burkina Faso, Egypt, Nigeria, and Peru—indicate a substantial increase in the proportion of married women living in

---

[33]DHS I Surveys could not be used for this analysis. For some surveys, there is no variable in the household roster to describe each individual's relationship to the household head; it is therefore impossible to determine whether an individual lives in a nuclear household (e.g., Bolivia, Brazil, Dominican Republic, Indonesia, Mali, Nepal, Senegal, and Zimbabwe). Other surveys, for example, Colombia, Guatemala, and Egypt, contain a variable to describe the relationship of household members to the household head, but they do not distinguish between relatives and relatives-in-law within a generation (e.g., children and children-in-law have the same numerical code). There are also instances (e.g., for Ghana and Uganda) in which the household roster contains a question regarding whether or not a household member's parents also reside in the same household. While this variable may enable a proxy for nuclear households, it is not comparable to the standards used in the table. Finally, several surveys (Kenya, Peru, and Togo) do contain the variable for a household member's relationship to the household head, but the data sets contain incomplete identification variables that prohibit the merging of information from the household roster into the individual survey.

nuclear households. Given the small number of countries and the short interval between surveys, it is not possible to come to any conclusions about the living arrangements of young married women in most developing countries or about the association between an increase in age at marriage and a change in household structure. Clearly, data are needed from more countries over a longer period before one can measure changes in household structure and observe whether a link exists between household composition and the timing of marriage.

## POLICIES AND INTERVENTIONS TO DELAY MARRIAGE

Both women's rights and reproductive health advocates assume that there are harmful consequences of early marriage for young women. Yet research has not established the causal links between early marriage and poor outcomes, e.g., reduced schooling, greater social isolation, uninformed sexual relations, increased poverty, etc. In the absence of study designs that control for confounding factors that are both a cause and consequence of early marriage, it is not possible to assess what the short and long term effects of child marriage are. Is it early marriage in and of itself that is problematic or is it the socioeconomic characteristics of women who marry early? Are the consequences of early marriage context dependent? That is, are women's lives altered more by early marriage in countries where the status of women is higher or lower? As educational attainment and labor force participation of women rise within a country, do the consequences of early marriage increase as well as the selectivity of those who marry young? Note that, to the extent that early marriage has consequences for women, these consequences are likely to be a function of the fact that those who marry at a young age also bear children early. (An extensive discussion of the consequences of early childbearing is found in Chapter 8.)

Despite the absence of rigorous studies establishing the deleterious effects of early marriage, this issue has been of great concern to many who view marriage prior to age 18 as a human rights violation. Indeed, there is a growing attention to policies and programs designed to reduce early marriage.

### Laws Regulating Marriage

While laws on age at marriage are increasingly being examined, no study has investigated the connection between changing laws and trends in age at marriage across countries. That laws are often inconsistent within countries may contribute to the complicated legal situation. A review of policies affecting marriage in seven English-speaking African countries indicates that in some countries, for example, Nigeria and Kenya, local and

TABLE 7-15 Percentage of Currently Married Women Ages 20-29 Living in Nuclear Households[a] and Percentage Who Live in Nuclear Households Who Are Either the Household Head or the Spouse of the Head[b]

| Country | Year of Survey | Region[c] | % Nuclear Household | |
| | | | 20-24 | 25-29 |
| --- | --- | --- | --- | --- |
| Colombia | 1990 | SA | 61.0 | 69.2 |
| Colombia | 2000 | SA | 59.6 | 65.0 |
| Peru | 1991 | SA | 52.7 | 61.7 |
| Peru | 2000 | SA | 60.6 | 68.7 |
| Tanzania | 1992 | E/S Africa | 42.5 | 53.2 |
| Tanzania | 2000 | E/S Africa | 43.8 | 51.4 |
| Burkina Faso | 1992-1993 | W/M Africa | 51.4 | 50.9 |
| Burkina Faso | 1999 | W/M Africa | 58.0 | 58.9 |
| Cameroon | 1991 | W/M Africa | 49.9 | 48.4 |
| Cameroon | 1997 | W/M Africa | 49.4 | 47.2 |
| Nigeria | 1990 | W/M Africa | 61.6 | 62.2 |
| Nigeria | 1999 | W/M Africa | 70.7 | 71.4 |
| Egypt | 1992 | ME | 38.0 | 48.5 |
| Egypt | 2000 | ME | 46.3 | 54.6 |
| Bangladesh | 1993-1994 | SC/SE Asia | 47.8 | 59.0 |
| Bangladesh | 1999-2000 | SC/SE Asia | 41.4 | 52.1 |
| India | 1992 | SC/SE Asia | 20.7 | 32.5 |
| India | 1998-2000 | SC/SE Asia | 21.8 | 34.0 |
| Indonesia | 1991 | SC/SE Asia | 56.0 | 66.9 |
| Indonesia | 1997 | SC/SE Asia | 55.2 | 68.3 |

[a]Nuclear household includes household head, spouse of head, children, adopted and foster children, and nonrelatives.

[b]For all countries except Burkina Faso, Egypt, and India, information from the household data was merged with the individual data; in Burkina Faso, Egypt, and India all necessary information was available in the household roster.

| % Live in a Nuclear Household and Are Head/Spouse of Head | | | | | |
| --- | --- | --- | --- | --- | --- |
| 20-24 | 25-29 | Urban | Rural | Total | N |
| 58.4 | 68.7 | 65.8 | 60.0 | 64.9 | 892 |
| 59.8 | 64.6 | 60.4 | 67.3 | 62.9 | 653 |
| 52.6 | 60.9 | 50.2 | 73.8 | 57.9 | 1,633 |
| 59.7 | 68.2 | 56.6 | 73.4 | 65.3 | 1,923 |
| 41.6 | 53.0 | 42.6 | 48.2 | 47.3 | 2,397 |
| 42.9 | 50.8 | 44.7 | 48.4 | 47.2 | 1,023 |
| 49.2 | 50.2 | 37.2 | 57.2 | 49.8 | 3,169 |
| 56.9 | 58.4 | 46.0 | 60.8 | 57.8 | 2,900 |
| 49.6 | 47.7 | 41.4 | 57.1 | 48.7 | 853 |
| 48.9 | 46.3 | 41.1 | 51.5 | 47.5 | 1,103 |
| 60.8 | 61.5 | 61.7 | 60.9 | 61.2 | 2,449 |
| 68.2 | 69.8 | 71.2 | 68.2 | 69.1 | 1,403 |
| 36.8 | 48.2 | 59.0 | 34.1 | 44.1 | 4,832 |
| 44.5 | 53.9 | 65.8 | 40.4 | 50.3 | 7,000 |
| 46.2 | 58.4 | 49.8 | 52.6 | 52.2 | 3,863 |
| 39.9 | 51.8 | 40.4 | 48.4 | 46.0 | 3,727 |
| 18.9 | 31.8 | 28.3 | 25.3 | 26.2 | 61,792 |
| 20.3 | 33.3 | 28.1 | 27.8 | 27.9 | 58,950 |
| 54.9 | 66.5 | 55.3 | 64.6 | 61.8 | 7,843 |
| 54.3 | 67.8 | 57.5 | 64.0 | 62.2 | 9,287 |

cKey: SA = South America; E/S Africa = Eastern and Southern Africa; W/M Africa = Western and Middle Africa; ME = Middle East; SC/SE Asia = South-central/South-eastern Asia.

SOURCE: Demographic and Health Surveys.

religious laws contradict national laws. In other countries, for example, Tanzania, penal codes contradict national laws (Center for Reproductive Law and Policy, 1997a). Reproductive rights advocates believe that laws specifying a minimum age at marriage are rarely enforced; rather, customary practice takes precedence over civil law (Boye et al., 1991). While most countries have laws specifying a minimum age at marriage, these are thought to be rarely enforced. Indeed, in some countries, the actual age at marriage is close to or even lower than the legal age (UNICEF, 2001b).

Table 7-16 gives the minimum age at marriage without parental consent for men and women in civil marriages (International Planned Parenthood Foundation and International Women's Rights Action Watch, 2000). For 50 of the 81 countries, the minimum age is at least 18 for both sexes. In 32 countries the age specified is lower for women than for men, which according to the International Planned Parenthood Federation is based on ideas of women's inferiority and implies that women need fewer years to prepare for marriage because their duties are confined to childbearing or domestic roles.

Have laws on age at marriage changed in recent years? For 55 countries data are available on the legal minimum age at marriage in 1990 and 2000 (Table 7-17). The legal age is now higher for women in 23 countries and for men in 20, which indicates a significant change in social norms regarding early marriage. Moreover, in 17 countries the legal age changed more for women than for men, signifying an attempt to equalize gender differences in age at marriage. Finally, in two countries, Malawi and Trinidad, where no law existed in 1990, there are now laws. Only in three countries has the legal age been lowered since 1990: in Yemen and Uruguay the age is now lower for both men and women, and in Ethiopia the age is lower for men.

Even if laws on age at marriage are not obeyed and little association exists between the legal minimum age at marriage and the percentage of the population that marries early, it is possible that the level of attention now given to early marriage by human rights advocates and a broad range of nongovernmental organizations (NGOs)—internationally and within countries—may have contributed to the increase in the age at marriage among women. Advocacy in opposition to child marriage and discussion at United Nations conferences has undoubtedly contributed to changes in legislation. (See Mensch, Singh, and Casterline, 2005, for a discussion of the association between the legal age at marriage and the prevalence of early marriage.)

## Interventions to Raise the Age at Marriage

To the best of our knowledge, outside Asia, there are no known interventions designed explicitly to reduce early marriage in societies in which substantial numbers of girls wed during their teenage years. In Bangladesh, India, and Nepal, where the legal age at marriage for women is 18, but large proportions of girls marry before then, there are now governmental and NGO efforts directed at lowering the incidence of teen marriage.

In China, the Marriage Laws of 1950 and 1980 specified minimum legal ages of marriage, 20 for males and 18 for females in 1950 and 22 for males and 20 for females in 1980 (Hannum and Liu, 2005). The "later-longer-fewer" family planning policy of 1970 and the one child policy of 1979, designed to reduce the pace of childbearing, also encouraged later age at marriage. However, scholars disagree as to whether these governmental edicts have led to the secular rise in age at marriage. Data from the first half of the twentieth century indicate that age of marriage rose prior to these decrees, leading Whyte and Parish (1984) to argue that urbanization and industrialization and not governmental intervention were behind the transformation. Wolf (1986:101) disagrees, arguing that the level of modernization in China was insufficient to bring about such a "sharp rise in age at marriage." Trends in age at marriage since 1980 suggest that both the policies and the socioeconomic environment figured into couples' decisions about when to wed during the last two decades of the century. The 1980 Marriage Law somewhat paradoxically "relaxed" the age restrictions on marriage. Marriage registration was no longer under the control of the family planning program, but instead was supervised by departments of civil affairs. As a result, age of marriage for women fell during the 1980s. However, since 1987 age at marriage began to rise again with "rapid economic development . . . and stronger implementation of the policy promoting late marriage" (Zeng, 2000:96).

In the Indian states of Andra Pradesh, Haryana, Karnataka, Madhya Pradesh, Punjab, Rajasthan, and Tamil Nadu, programs have been developed that provide a financial incentive to girls to postpone marriage until the age of 18 or later. In addition, scholarships and credit for schooling and income-generating activities are available for participating families. In three of the states, program eligibility is based on the fertility and contraceptive status of the girls' parents. The Haryana program, known as Apni Beti Apna Dhan (Our Daughters Our Wealth), provides 3,000 rupees (approximately $70) to the family of the girl: a gift of 500 rupees within 15 days of the birth and a further investment of 2,500 rupees in a small savings scheme. If the girl remains unmarried at age 18, the gift is expected to be worth about 25,000 rupees. Families are eligible if they fall below the poverty line, if they are members of certain low castes, and if they have three or fewer children. While documentation of some of these programs exists, they have not yet been evaluated either in terms of short-term outcomes, for example, changing the sex ratio at birth, or in terms of longer term objectives, for

TABLE 7-16 Legal Minimum Age at Marriage Without Parental Consent: 2000 (81 countries)

| Country | Region | Male | Female |
|---|---|---|---|
| Nicaragua | Caribbean/Central America | 15 | 14 |
| Panama | Caribbean/Central America | 16 | 15 |
| Barbados | Caribbean/Central America | 18 | 18 |
| Costa Rica | Caribbean/Central America | 18 | 18 |
| Cuba | Caribbean/Central America | 18 | 18 |
| Dominican Republic | Caribbean/Central America | 18 | 18 |
| Guatemala | Caribbean/Central America | 18 | 18 |
| Haiti | Caribbean/Central America | 18 | 18 |
| Jamaica | Caribbean/Central America | 18 | 18 |
| Trinidad & Tobago | Caribbean/Central America | 18 | 18 |
| El Salvador | Caribbean/Central America | 21 | 21 |
| Honduras | Caribbean/Central America | 21 | 21 |
| | | | |
| Ethiopia | Eastern/Southern Africa | 18 | 15 |
| Kenya | Eastern/Southern Africa | 18 | 18 |
| Madagascar | Eastern/Southern Africa | 18 | 18 |
| Malawi | Eastern/Southern Africa | 18 | 18 |
| Mauritius | Eastern/Southern Africa | 18 | 18 |
| Namibia | Eastern/Southern Africa | 18 | 18 |
| South Africa | Eastern/Southern Africa | 18 | 18 |
| United Republic of Tanzania | Eastern/Southern Africa | 18 | 15 |
| Zimbabwe | Eastern/Southern Africa | 18 | 18 |
| Burundi | Eastern/Southern Africa | 21 | 18 |
| Rwanda | Eastern/Southern Africa | 21 | 21 |
| Uganda | Eastern/Southern Africa | 21 | 21 |
| Zambia | Eastern/Southern Africa | 21 | 21 |
| | | | |
| Mongolia | Eastern Asia | 18 | 18 |
| | | | |
| Yemen | Middle East | 15 | 15 |
| Turkey | Middle East | 17 | 15 |
| Egypt | Middle East | 18 | 16 |
| Iraq | Middle East | 18 | 18 |
| Jordan | Middle East | 18 | 17 |
| Morocco | Middle East | 18 | 15 |
| Libyan Arab Jamahiriya | Middle East | 20 | 20 |
| Tunisia | Middle East | 20 | 20 |
| Algeria | Middle East | 21 | 18 |
| | | | |
| Bolivia | South America | 16 | 14 |
| Peru | South America | 16 | 14 |
| Venezuela | South America | 16 | 16 |
| Argentina | South America | 18 | 16 |
| Brazil | South America | 18 | 16 |
| Chile | South America | 18 | 18 |

## TABLE 7-16 Continued

| Country | Region | Male | Female |
|---|---|---|---|
| Colombia | South America | 18 | 18 |
| Ecuador | South America | 18 | 18 |
| Guyana | South America | 18 | 18 |
| Uruguay | South America | 18 | 18 |
| Paraguay | South America | 20 | 20 |
| Lao People's Democratic Republic | South-central/South-eastern Asia | 18 | 18 |
| Pakistan | South-central/South-eastern Asia | 18 | 18 |
| Philippines | South-central/South-eastern Asia | 18 | 18 |
| Sri Lanka | South-central/South-eastern Asia | 18 | 18 |
| Indonesia | South-central/South-eastern Asia | 19 | 16 |
| Bhutan | South-central/South-eastern Asia | 20 | 16 |
| Cambodia | South-central/South-eastern Asia | 20 | 18 |
| Thailand | South-central/South-eastern Asia | 20 | 20 |
| Viet Nam | South-central/South-eastern Asia | 20 | 18 |
| Bangladesh | South-central/South-eastern Asia | 21 | 18 |
| India | South-central/South-eastern Asia | 21 | 18 |
| Nepal | South-central/South-eastern Asia | 21 | 18 |
| Myanmar | South-central/South-eastern Asia | none | 20 |
| Georgia | Former Soviet Asia | 16 | 16 |
| Armenia | Former Soviet Asia | 17 | 17 |
| Azerbaijan | Former Soviet Asia | 18 | 18 |
| Kazakhstan | Former Soviet Asia | 18 | 17 |
| Kyrgyzstan (Kyrgyz Republic) | Former Soviet Asia | 18 | 18 |
| Tajikistan | Former Soviet Asia | 18 | 18 |
| Liberia | Western/Middle Africa | 16 | 16 |
| Cameroon | Western/Middle Africa | 18 | 15 |
| Central Africa Republic | Western/Middle Africa | 18 | 18 |
| Democratic Republic of the Congo | Western/Middle Africa | 18 | 15 |
| Gabon | Western/Middle Africa | 18 | 15 |
| Guinea | Western/Middle Africa | 18 | 17 |
| Guinea-Bissau | Western/Middle Africa | 18 | 15 |
| Nigeria | Western/Middle Africa | 18 | 18 |
| Burkina Faso | Western/Middle Africa | 20 | 17 |
| Senegal | Western/Middle Africa | 20 | 16 |
| Togo | Western/Middle Africa | 20 | 17 |
| Ghana | Western/Middle Africa | 21 | 21 |
| Mali | Western/Middle Africa | 21 | 18 |
| Sierra Leone | Western/Middle Africa | 21 | 18 |
| Chad | Western/Middle Africa | none | 14 |
| Gambia | Western/Middle Africa | none | none |

SOURCE: IPPF and IWRAW (2000).

TABLE 7-17 Legal Minimum Age at Marriage Without Parental Consent: 1990 and 2000 (55 countries)

| Country | Region | 2000 Male | 2000 Female | 1990 Male | 1990 Female |
|---|---|---|---|---|---|
| Panama | Caribbean/Central America | 16 | 15 | 14 | 12 |
| Costa Rica | Caribbean/Central America | 18 | 18 | 15 | 15 |
| Nicaragua | Caribbean/Central America | 15 | 14 | 15 | 14 |
| Barbados | Caribbean/Central America | 18 | 18 | 16 | 16 |
| Dominican Republic | Caribbean/Central America | 18 | 18 | 16 | 15 |
| El Salvador | Caribbean/Central America | 21 | 21 | 16 | 14 |
| Guatemala | Caribbean/Central America | 18 | 18 | 16 | 14 |
| Jamaica | Caribbean/Central America | 18 | 18 | 16 | 16 |
| Cuba | Caribbean/Central America | 18 | 18 | 18 | 18 |
| Honduras | Caribbean/Central America | 21 | 21 | 18 | 16 |
| Mexico | Caribbean/Central America | 18 | 18 | 18 | 18 |
| Trinidad and Tobago | Caribbean/Central America | 18 | 18 | none | none |
| Zambia | Eastern/Southern Africa | 21 | 21 | 16 | 16 |
| Madagascar | Eastern/Southern Africa | 18 | 18 | 17 | 14 |
| Kenya | Eastern/Southern Africa | 18 | 18 | 18 | 18 |
| Mauritius | Eastern/Southern Africa | 18 | 18 | 18 | 15 |
| Rwanda | Eastern/Southern Africa | 21 | 21 | 18 | 15 |
| Uganda | Eastern/Southern Africa | 21 | 21 | 18 | 16 |
| United Republic of Tanzania | Eastern/Southern Africa | 18 | 15 | 18 | 15 |
| Ethiopia | Eastern/Southern Africa | 18 | 15 | 20 | 15 |
| Malawi | Eastern/Southern Africa | 18 | 18 | none | none |
| Mongolia | Eastern Asia | 18 | 18 | 18 | 18 |
| China | Eastern Asia | | | 22 | 20 |
| Turkey | Middle East | 17 | 15 | 17 | 15 |
| Egypt | Middle East | 18 | 16 | 18 | 16 |
| Iraq | Middle East | 18 | 18 | 18 | 18 |

| Country | Region | | | | |
|---|---|---|---|---|---|
| Yemen | Middle East | 15 | 15 | 19 | 16 |
| Libyan Arab Jamahiriya | Middle East | 20 | 20 | 20 | 16 |
| Tunisia | Middle East | 20 | 20 | 20 | 17 |
| Chile | South America | 18 | 18 | 14 | 12 |
| Ecuador | South America | 18 | 18 | 14 | 12 |
| Paraguay | South America | 20 | 20 | 14 | 12 |
| Venezuela | South America | 16 | 16 | 14 | 12 |
| Bolivia | South America | 16 | 14 | 16 | 14 |
| Peru | South America | 16 | 14 | 16 | 14 |
| Argentina | South America | 18 | 16 | 18 | 16 |
| Brazil | South America | 18 | 16 | 18 | 16 |
| Colombia | South America | 18 | 18 | 18 | 18 |
| Guyana | South America | 18 | 18 | 18 | 18 |
| Uruguay | South America | 18 | 18 | 21 | 21 |
| Sri Lanka | South-central/South-eastern Asia | 18 | 18 | 16 | 12 |
| Thailand | South-central/South-eastern Asia | 20 | 20 | 17 | 17 |
| Philippines | South-central/South-eastern Asia | 18 | 18 | 18 | 18 |
| Indonesia | South-central/South-eastern Asia | 19 | 16 | 19 | 16 |
| Viet Nam | South-central/South-eastern Asia | 20 | 18 | 20 | 18 |
| Liberia | Western/Middle Africa | 16 | 16 | 16 | 16 |
| Nigeria | Western/Middle Africa | 18 | 18 | 16 | 16 |
| Burkina Faso | Western/Middle Africa | 20 | 17 | 18 | 15 |
| Gabon | Western/Middle Africa | 18 | 15 | 18 | 15 |
| Guinea | Western/Middle Africa | 18 | 17 | 18 | 17 |
| Senegal | Western/Middle Africa | 20 | 16 | 20 | 16 |
| Togo | Western/Middle Africa | 20 | 17 | 20 | 17 |
| Ghana | Western/Middle Africa | 21 | 21 | 21 | 21 |
| Mali | Western/Middle Africa | 21 | 18 | 21 | 18 |
| Sierra Leone | Western/Middle Africa | 21 | 18 | 21 | 18 |

SOURCE: IPPF and IWRAW (1990, 2000).

example, delaying marriage (Greene, 1997; Mensch, Bruce, and Greene, 1998; Population Council, 1999).

In Aurangabad district in the Indian state of Maharashtra, an intensive life-skills program has been developed by the Institute for Health Management-Pachod to: (1) improve the social and health status of adolescent girls, (2) promote self-esteem, and (3) delay age at marriage. Unmarried adolescent girls ages 12-18 are enrolled in an intensive life-skills course taught by trained village women; the course meets for an hour each weekday evening for one year. To evaluate the intervention, annual data on age of marriage have been collected from 17 study and 18 control villages since 1997 (International Center for Research on Women and Institute of Health Management-Pachod, 2003). Although there is an indication that the percentage of girls marrying before age 18 has declined in the study villages, as with the other interventions, a rigorous evaluation has yet to be conducted.

In the Terai area of Nepal near the Indian border, a participatory approach to improving adolescent reproductive health has been developed by two U.S. NGOs, Engender-Health and International Center for Research on Women, in conjunction with Nepali partners (Mathur, Mehta, and Malhotra, 2004). The intervention, carried out over a 12-24 month period in one rural and one urban community, consisted of eight components: adolescent-friendly services, peer education and counseling, an information and education campaign, adult peer education, youth clubs, street theater on social norms, efforts to improve livelihood opportunities, and teacher training. The project used a quasi-experimental[34] design, with the baseline survey conducted among 14-21-year-olds in 1999 and the end-line survey conducted among a different cross-section of 14-25-year-olds in 2003. One of the outcomes the intervention was designed to affect is age of marriage. Simple descriptive data indicate that in the urban site marriage among 14-21-year-olds declined by 53 percent at the study site and by 47 percent at the control site. In the rural area, there was virtually no change in the percentage married at the study site and an increase at the control site. Although the intervention was unusually comprehensive, it is difficult to draw conclusions about project impact from the statistical analysis that the researchers have conducted thus far as part of the evaluation (see Mathur, Mehta, and Malhotra, 2004, Appendix A). Given that a quasi-experimental design was used, appropriate multivariate models are needed to draw conclusions about the efficacy of the intervention in raising age at marriage.

---

[34]The design is a quasi-experiment rather than a true experiment because individuals were not randomly assigned to be in the experimental or control group; assignment was based on geographic area (Campbell and Stanley, 1963).

In 1994 the government of Bangladesh initiated a scholarship scheme throughout the country for girls enrolled in grades 6 and 9, which was later extended to girls in grades 7 and 8. Provided the girl attends school 65 percent of the time and maintains a certain grade point average, her school is given a certain allotment and she is given a monthly stipend ranging from the equivalent of 1 to 2 U.S. dollars. Parents of the girls are required to sign an agreement guaranteeing that their daughters will not marry before the age of 18. While an assessment of the effect of this program on secondary school enrollment reveals that girls' school attendance increased (Khandker, Pitts, and Fuwa, 2003), there has not been a rigorous analysis of the effect on age at marriage. However, data collected in villages prior to the program's implementation and then again in 1995, 1996, and 2000 indicate, somewhat unexpectedly, little change in the percentage of adolescent girls who marry (Amin and Arends-Kuenning, 2001; Arends-Kuenning and Amin, 2000).

As noted above, we are unaware of any interventions in sub-Saharan Africa, where marriage during the teenage years is also widespread, to directly influence the timing of marriage. However, there are experimental programs designed to improve the status of adolescent girls that, if successful, are likely to delay marriage. The Milles Jeunes Filles project in Burkina Faso, a governmental effort begun in 1994 to educate adolescent girls in cultivation techniques, is a two-year residential program that enrolls 1,000 girls ages 14-18 per year. In addition to learning how to grow crops, girls are given training in literacy, reproductive health, dressmaking, and financial management. At the end of the two-year program, each participant is given a small sum of money to return to her home community and purchase supplies. While the program does not have an explicit goal to raise the age of marriage of girls, one of the desired outcomes is a delay in marriage and an increase in the ability of girls to select their own husbands (Saloucou, Brady, and Chong, forthcoming).

## CONCLUSIONS AND RECOMMENDATIONS

### Key Findings

*Compared with previous generations, a smaller proportion of young women and men are married in most regions of the developing world.* The regions that are clear exceptions to this trend are South America for men and women, and South-central and South-eastern Asia for men. Men still marry at older ages than women. While only one-third of men in the developing world are married by ages 20-24, nearly two-thirds of women are married at this age. Moreover, in certain regions, most notably the Middle East, marriage is postponed until the 30s for a large fraction of men.

*The decline in early marriage is quite widespread, lending support to the notion that global changes are affecting the transition to adulthood.* Not only is the reduction in marriage occurring in a diversity of settings, but it is also occurring, in some regions, over a relatively wide age span, suggesting that policy shifts, such as increases in the legal age at marriage, social shifts, such as the expansion of education, or ideological shifts, such as a change in norms regarding very early marriage, may all contribute to but cannot fully explain the changes observed.

*While women are less likely to be married during the teenage years than in the past, child marriage, defined as marriage prior to age 18, is still widespread and represents a major human rights violation.* According to DHS data, nearly 40 percent of women in countries representing 60 percent of the population of the developing world marry before the age of 18; the proportion ranges from around 40-45 percent in South-central and Southeastern Asia, to approximately 35 percent in the Caribbean and Central America, to about 20-25 percent in South America and the Middle East, to about 15 percent in former Soviet Asia.

*Large differentials by education, household wealth, and residence exist in the percentage of young women married by age 18 and young men married by age 20.* Women and men with eight or more years of schooling, who live in urban areas and are in the top wealth category, are much less likely to marry early than their less well educated, rural, and poorer counterparts. While differentials by schooling level for women are large, the link between the transition out of school and into marriage is not that close in most countries. That is, there is a sizeable gap between the time when most young people exit school and when they marry. While the increase in educational attainment is associated with a substantial proportion of the decline in early marriage, there is still a considerable fraction of the decline that is not associated with the expansion in schooling.

*The age gap between spouses appears to be narrowing, especially in subSaharan Africa and South-central and South-eastern Asia, the regions where it has been largest.* That age differences are shrinking reflects the fact that the pace of increase in age of marriage is greater among women than men. While research is lacking on the effects of a large age gap on marital roles, there is reason to believe that marriages of young women and older men are less equitable.

*There is some evidence of growing agency on the part of young women with regard to marriage.* While there are few data sets to assess changes in the spouse selection process, in countries in which information is available and arranged marriage was a standard feature of the marriage process, there appears to be a movement in recent years toward greater involvement by young people in choosing a partner. There is a suggestion that this shift toward individual choice may have important implications for sexual behavior both before marriage and in the first years of marriage.

*The economics of marriage appears to be changing.* While there are insufficient data to assess whether the practices of bridewealth and dowry are becoming less prevalent in the societies in which they have been widespread, there is evidence of a rise in the value of dowry in Southern Asia and, if not an escalation in the value of bride-price in the last 10 or 20 years in sub-Saharan Africa, a possible increase in the burden on the groom, who is more likely to shoulder the responsibility of bridewealth himself rather than rely on his family.

*The legal age of marriage for both men and women has risen in many countries in the last decade.* Data on the minimum age at marriage without parental consent for men and women for civil marriages indicate that in 50 of 81 countries the minimum is at least 18 for both sexes; in 32 countries the age specified for women is lower than that for men. In 23 of 55 countries for which there are data both in 1990 and 2000, there has been an increase in the legal age of marriage for women in 23 countries and for men in 20.

*Evaluations of interventions to raise the age of marriage of women are rare.* While governmental and NGO efforts have emerged to encourage later age at marriage in a number of countries, these interventions need to be better documented and evaluated.

## Policy Recommendations

*The panel recommends that governments that have not already done so pass legislation prohibiting marriage before age 18.* Article 16, No. 2 of the UN Convention on the Elimination of All Forms of Discrimination Against Women states that "The betrothal and the marriage of a child shall have no legal effect, and all necessary action, including legislation, shall be taken to specify a minimum age for marriage and to make the registration of marriages in an official registry compulsory." In a number of countries, the legal age of marriage for women is still under 18. Although the UN Convention on the Rights of the Child does not mention child marriage, it does define childhood as extending up to age 18. There-fore, a number of countries are in violation of UN conventions by permit-ting marriage before that age.

*The panel recommends that where a substantial proportion of women marry before the legal age at marriage, governments should make an effort to educate parents and their daughters about the existing law.* Information could be disseminated through billboards, radio, and television, as well as through the school curriculum.

*The panel recommends that legislative bodies should establish, and courts should enforce, laws that grant men and women "the same right freely to choose a spouse and to enter marriage only with their free and full con-sent," as specified in the UN Convention on the Elimination of All Forms of Discrimination Against Women.* For women especially, this right is often not available.

*The panel recommends that governments address the issue of excessive dowry and bridewealth payments, which have the effect of promoting too early marriage for women and of possibly delaying marriage for men be-yond an age that is considered desirable.* Public relations campaigns to reduce financial transactions at marriage may help both to dissuade fami-lies from marrying their daughters off too early and to enable men not to wait too long to marry; these efforts would have the added benefit of reducing very large age differences between spouses.

*Finally, in countries in which substantial proportions of girls still marry before the age of 18, the panel encourages policies and programs promoting later age at marriage and evaluations to determine if these interventions are effective.* A number of creative programs have been developed in India and Bangladesh to encourage families to delay the marriage of their daughters. However, to the best of our knowledge, few of these initiatives have been adequately assessed, and few such interventions have been implemented in sub-Saharan Africa, where early marriage is common. One model for re-ducing early marriage in Africa is that employed by Tostan, a Senegalese NGO working to eradicate female genital mutilation.[35] Tostan's approach is to conduct education programs, followed by public declarations whereby the community makes a collective promise not to perform female genital

---

[35]See http://www.popcouncil.org/rhfp/tostan/tostan.html for a summary of the Tostan pro-gram.

mutilation on their daughters. Such a model could also be employed to reduce early marriage.

## Research Recommendations

Although demographers have documented shifts in age at marriage, many questions remain about the process of marriage and the factors underlying changes in the timing and conduct of marriage. The following questions, if answered, would go a long way in explaining the timing, process, and content of marriage in the developing world.

- What factors encourage a delay in age of marriage of women? Changing norms, changing gender roles, changing economic circumstances, changing living arrangements, specifically increases in the prevalence of nuclear households?
- What factors affect the age of marriage of men? How do men's decisions about marital timing influence those of women and vice-versa?
- Are rising expectations of young people with greater exposure to Western media leading to delays in age at marriage of both men and women?
- What are the implications of a rise in the labor force participation of young women for the timing of marriage and for the terms and conditions of marriage?
- What is it about schooling that affects the age of marriage for women? With regard to traditional gender roles, do textbooks and teachers reinforce or challenge the status quo?
- What is the effect of changing laws on age at marriage and on the timing of marriage for women?
- In regions in which a large fraction of women still marry early, for example, Southern Asia and Western Africa, are there any interventions that have had an impact on the prevalence of early marriage, even if that was not their original intent?
- What is the effect of changing marriage markets on trends in age at marriage?
- How have the nature and cost of financial transfers at marriage changed, and what implications do these changes have for relations between marital partners?
- What fraction of young people have no say in the decision about the timing of marriage and the choice of spouse?
- In societies in which arranged marriage is common, how does the practice vary by age at marriage?
- What are the consequences of early marriage on spousal choice, decision making in marriage, and marital satisfaction and stability?

- What is the association between marital status and HIV risk for both men and women?
- What are the implications of changing age at marriage and greater autonomy of spousal choice on sexual behavior, both before and after marriage?
- Does the age gap between spouses affect the conduct of marriage or the nature of spousal relations?
- What are the consequences of late marriage for men? Are there any negative psychosocial or reproductive health effects of delaying marriage, particularly in societies in which interaction between unmarried men and women is limited?
- What is the effect of high rates of HIV on the terms and conditions of marriage in sub-Saharan Africa?
- How are living arrangements after marriage changing? Is there an increased nucleation of households? If so, how does that affect the experience of marriage for the newly married couple?
- What is the effect of changing marriage patterns on intergenerational relations?
- What are the differences between consensual marriage and formal marriage in terms of marital experience and the stability of marriage?

**APPENDIX TABLES 7-1 TO 7-6 FOLLOW**

APPENDIX TABLE 7-1a Percentage of Women Ever Married, by Age and
Time Period

| Country | Survey Year 1 | Note | Survey Year 2 | Note | Survey Interval |
|---|---|---|---|---|---|
| Argentina | 1980 | | 1991 | * | 11 |
| Azerbaijan | 1989 | [a]**1 | 1999 | | 10 |
| Bahrain | 1981 | | 1991 | | 10 |
| Bangladesh | 1981 | | 1991 | | 10 |
| Belize | 1980 | ** | 1991 | | 11 |
| Benin | 1979 | [a] | 1996 | [b] | 17 |
| Bolivia | 1988 | * | 1998 | [c] | 10 |
| Botswana | 1981 | | 1991 | * | 10 |
| Brazil | 1980 | ** | 1996 | [b] | 16 |
| Burkina Faso | 1985 | [f]* | 1999 | [c] | 14 |
| Burundi | 1979 | | 1990 | *** | 11 |
| Cambodia | 1962 | * | 1998 | | 36 |
| Cameroon | 1987 | [a]* | 1998 | [c,f] | 11 |
| Cape Verde | 1980 | * | 1990 | * | 10 |
| Central African Republic | 1975 | | 1994–1995 | [c] | 19.5 |
| Chad | 1964 | [a] | 1996 | [c] | 32 |
| Chile | 1982 | | 1992 | | 10 |
| China | 1987 | [a] | 1999 | | 12 |
| Colombia | 1973 | ** | 1993 | * | 20 |
| Comoros | 1980 | *** | 1996 | [c] | 16 |
| Côte d'Ivoire | 1978 | | 1994 | [c] | 16 |
| Dominican Republic | 1981 | | 1996 | [c] | 15 |
| Ecuador | 1974 | ** | 1990 | ** | 16 |
| Egypt | 1986 | | 1996 | * | 10 |
| El Salvador | 1971 | * | 1992 | | 21 |
| Ethiopia | 1984 | | 2000 | [f] | 16 |
| Gabon | 1961 | [a] | 2000 | [c] | 39 |
| Gambia | 1983 | * | 1993 | * | 10 |
| Guatemala | 1973 | * | 1990 | [a] | 17 |
| Guyana | 1980 | * | 1991 | [a]* | 11 |
| Haiti | 1989 | [f] | 2000 | [f] | 11 |
| India | 1981 | * | 1992–1993 | [a] | 11.5 |
| Indonesia | 1980 | | 1990 | | 10 |
| Iran | 1986 | ** | 1996 | * | 10 |
| Jordan | 1979 | | 1994 | * | 15 |
| Kazakhstan | 1989 | *1 | 1999 | * | 10 |
| Kenya | 1969 | * | 1998 | [c] | 29 |
| Kyrgyzstan | 1989 | *1 | 1999 | | 10 |
| Malawi | 1987 | *** | 2000 | [f] | 13 |
| Malaysia | 1980 | | 1991 | | 11 |

| Ages | | | | | | | | |
|---|---|---|---|---|---|---|---|---|
| 15 to 19 | | | 20 to 24 | | | 25 to 29 | | |
| Survey 1 | Survey 2 | Annual Change | Survey 1 | Survey 2 | Annual Change | Survey 1 | Survey 2 | Annual Change |
| n.a. | 12.4 | | 48.1 | 45.2 | −0.3 | 75.4 | 73.8 | −0.1 |
| 9.4 | 12.8 | 0.3 | 51.3 | 49.0 | −0.2 | 77.5 | 76.1 | −0.1 |
| 14.9 | 6.7 | −0.8 | n.a. | 40.9 | | n.a. | 68.8 | |
| 68.7 | 51.3 | −1.7 | 94.9 | 89.5 | −0.5 | 98.7 | 97.6 | −0.1 |
| 9.1 | 7.9 | −0.1 | 34.3 | 30.9 | −0.3 | 54.2 | 48.2 | −0.5 |
| 52.2 | 29.1 | −1.4 | 90.1 | 79.5 | −0.6 | 97.1 | 94.3 | −0.2 |
| 11.1 | 12.2 | 0.1 | 52.6 | 53.4 | 0.1 | 79.5 | 80.5 | 0.1 |
| 7.3 | 5.4 | −0.2 | 31.2 | 27.2 | −0.4 | 53.1 | 48.0 | −0.5 |
| 15.0 | 16.8 | 0.1 | 52.6 | 52.6 | 0.0 | 76.0 | 78.5 | 0.2 |
| 44.9 | 34.8 | −0.7 | 90.1 | 90.3 | 0.0 | 96.4 | 97.9 | 0.1 |
| 19.2 | 7.0 | −1.1 | 72.6 | 60.2 | −1.1 | 89.9 | 86.5 | −0.3 |
| 14.9 | 12.4 | −0.1 | 68.4 | 60.6 | −0.2 | 90.6 | 83.2 | −0.2 |
| 38.5 | 35.8 | −0.2 | 72.2 | 73.6 | 0.1 | 86.0 | 89.1 | 0.3 |
| 4.6 | 6.7 | 0.2 | 31.7 | 32.3 | 0.1 | 59.3 | 53.4 | −0.6 |
| 46.8 | 42.3 | −0.2 | 81.7 | 81.2 | 0.0 | 90.4 | 90.8 | 0.0 |
| 72.6 | 48.6 | −0.8 | 97.6 | 92.2 | −0.2 | 99.2 | 98.4 | 0.0 |
| 9.2 | 11.7 | 0.2 | 43.0 | 43.8 | 0.1 | 69.9 | 69.8 | 0.0 |
| 4.2 | 1.3 | −0.2 | 60.1 | 45.9 | −1.2 | 95.9 | 91.6 | −0.4 |
| 13.5 | 18.2 | 0.2 | 48.8 | 51.8 | 0.1 | 70.9 | 71.3 | 0.0 |
| 31.0 | 11.5 | −1.2 | 77.8 | 48.4 | −1.8 | 94.5 | 76.9 | −1.1 |
| 53.8 | 27.7 | −1.6 | 82.9 | 69.6 | −0.8 | 91.8 | 90.8 | −0.1 |
| 20.7 | 28.9 | 0.5 | 56.7 | 66.1 | 0.6 | 77.7 | 86.1 | 0.6 |
| 19.5 | 18.0 | −0.1 | 59.3 | 55.1 | −0.3 | 78.7 | 76.3 | −0.2 |
| 20.7 | 14.5 | −0.6 | 60.6 | 56.1 | −0.4 | 86.3 | 87.1 | 0.1 |
| 20.4 | 15.9 | −0.2 | 56.3 | 49.9 | −0.3 | 74.6 | 71.9 | − 0.1 |
| 60.9 | 30.0 | −1.9 | 94.4 | 73.1 | −1.3 | 98.6 | 90.4 | −0.5 |
| 62.7 | 22.4 | −1.0 | 87.0 | 61.3 | −0.7 | 95.1 | 82.0 | −0.3 |
| 55.2 | 38.8 | −1.6 | 85.1 | 74.8 | −1.0 | 94.9 | 90.9 | −0.4 |
| 28.4 | 24.2 | −0.2 | 67.2 | 66.8 | 0.0 | 82.9 | 85.2 | 0.1 |
| 11.8 | 6.9 | −0.4 | 44.1 | 26.6 | −1.6 | 66.1 | 45.4 | −1.9 |
| 14.5 | 19.4 | 0.4 | 52.3 | 57.3 | 0.5 | 84.7 | 79.9 | −0.4 |
| 44.1 | 39.9 | −0.4 | 86.0 | 89.0 | 0.3 | 96.7 | 98.9 | 0.2 |
| 30.1 | 18.2 | −1.2 | 77.7 | 64.3 | −1.3 | 92.6 | 88.8 | −0.4 |
| 34.2 | 17.9 | −1.6 | 74.2 | 60.5 | −1.4 | 90.6 | 85.2 | −0.5 |
| 20.5 | 12.9 | −0.5 | 64.4 | 48.2 | −1.1 | 86.7 | 73.3 | −0.9 |
| 8.9 | 7.4 | −0.2 | 63.1 | 52.7 | −1.0 | 86.8 | 80.5 | −0.6 |
| 35.9 | 16.7 | −0.7 | 81.4 | 65.1 | −0.6 | 93.5 | 87.3 | −0.2 |
| 10.9 | 11.5 | 0.1 | 70.7 | 65.9 | −0.5 | 91.0 | 88.4 | −0.3 |
| 43.6 | 36.8 | −0.5 | 88.3 | 87.7 | 0.0 | 96.4 | 98.2 | 0.1 |
| 10.3 | 7.6 | −0.2 | 48.7 | 39.8 | −0.8 | 79.1 | 74.1 | −0.4 |

*Continued*

## APPENDIX TABLE 7-1a Continued

| Country | Survey Year 1 | Note | Survey Year 2 | Note | Survey Interval |
|---|---|---|---|---|---|
| Maldives | 1985 | * | 1995 | ****2 | 10 |
| Mali | 1976 | *** | 1995–1996 | [c] | 19.5 |
| Mauritania | 1988 | [a]* | 2000–2001 | [f] | 12.5 |
| Mauritius | 1972 | * | 1990 | [f]* | 18 |
| Mexico | 1980 | * | 1990 | * | 10 |
| Morocco | 1982 | | 1994 | | 12 |
| Mozambique | 1980 | ** | 1997 | [c] | 17 |
| Myanmar | 1973 | [a] | 1991 | | 18 |
| Namibia | 1960 | * | 1991 | * | 31 |
| Nepal | 1981 | | 1991 | * | 10 |
| Nicaragua | 1971 | * | 1998 | | 27 |
| Niger | 1988 | * | 1998 | [c] | 10 |
| Occ. Palestinian Territory | 1967 | [e]* | 1997 | [e] | 30 |
| Pakistan | 1981 | | 1998 | [d] | 17 |
| Panama | 1980 | | 1990 | | 10 |
| Paraguay | 1982 | * | 1992 | * | 10 |
| Peru | 1981 | * | 1996 | [c] | 15 |
| Philippines | 1980 | * | 1995 | * | 15 |
| Puerto Rico | 1980 | *** | 1990 | ** | 10 |
| Rwanda | 1978 | * | 1996 | [c]** | 18 |
| Senegal | 1978 | [c] | 1997 | [c] | 19 |
| South Africa | 1985 | | 1996 | *** | 11 |
| Sudan | 1983 | [a]*** | 1993 | [a]* | 10 |
| Tanzania | 1978 | * | 1996 | [c] | 18 |
| Thailand | 1980 | * | 1990 | * | 10 |
| Trinidad & Tobago | 1980 | * | 1990 | ** | 10 |
| Tunisia | 1984 | * | 1994 | * | 10 |
| Turkey | 1980 | | 1990 | * | 10 |
| Uganda | 1969 | * | 1995 | [c] | 26 |
| Uruguay | 1985 | | 1996 | | 11 |
| Venezuela | 1974 | | 1990 | ** | 16 |
| Zambia | 1980 | * | 1999 | *** | 19 |
| Zimbabwe | 1982 | * | 1999 | [c] | 17 |

Unless otherwise noted, source of survey data is UN Statistics Division.
[a] SOURCE: U.S. Bureau of the Census, International Database.
[b] SOURCE: U.S. Bureau of the Census, International Database, National Demographic and Health Survey.
[c] SOURCE: National Demographic and Health Survey.
[d] UN Statistics Division—preliminary.
[e] UN Statistics Division and U.S. Bureau of the Census, International Database.
[f] SOURCE: Other or Unidentified.

| Ages | | | | | | | | |
|---|---|---|---|---|---|---|---|---|
| 15 to 19 | | | 20 to 24 | | | 25 to 29 | | |
| Survey 1 | Survey 2 | Annual Change | Survey 1 | Survey 2 | Annual Change | Survey 1 | Survey 2 | Annual Change |
| 51.2 | 46.9 | −0.4 | 92.0 | 82.4 | −1.0 | 97.7 | 94.7 | −0.3 |
| 51.1 | 49.7 | −0.1 | 88.0 | 87.6 | 0.0 | 95.9 | 95.8 | 0.0 |
| 36.0 | 27.8 | −0.7 | 68.0 | 60.4 | −0.6 | 85.0 | 79.6 | −0.4 |
| 13.2 | 11.3 | −0.1 | 53.9 | 51.3 | −0.1 | 82.7 | 76.1 | −0.4 |
| 20.5 | 15.9 | −0.5 | 59.9 | 54.2 | −0.6 | 81.6 | 78.7 | −0.3 |
| 18.5 | 12.8 | −0.5 | 59.6 | 44.1 | −1.3 | 83.0 | 64.9 | −1.5 |
| 52.4 | 47.1 | −0.3 | 90.3 | 88.8 | −0.1 | 95.4 | 94.1 | −0.1 |
| 22.0 | 10.7 | −0.6 | 64.5 | 44.0 | −1.1 | 83.4 | 67.6 | −0.9 |
| 11.2 | 6.7 | −0.1 | 53.5 | 28.7 | −0.8 | 79.6 | 51.2 | −0.9 |
| 50.8 | 46.6 | −0.4 | 86.9 | 87.1 | 0.0 | 94.7 | 96.3 | 0.2 |
| 22.1 | 31.9 | 0.4 | 62.0 | 69.0 | 0.3 | 80.8 | 85.9 | 0.2 |
| 75.3 | 61.9 | −1.3 | 94.2 | 88.9 | −0.5 | 98.0 | 97.4 | −0.1 |
| 17.2 | 24.2 | 0.2 | 60.7 | 64.0 | 0.1 | 86.2 | 80.1 | −0.2 |
| 29.4 | 20.6 | −0.5 | 71.8 | 61.4 | −0.6 | 91.3 | 93.9 | 0.2 |
| 20.2 | 21.4 | 0.1 | 60.1 | 55.9 | −0.4 | 80.2 | 77.3 | −0.3 |
| 14.3 | 16.6 | 0.2 | 49.8 | 53.5 | 0.4 | 71.7 | 74.4 | 0.3 |
| 14.5 | 12.5 | −0.1 | 51.1 | 52.3 | 0.1 | 75.0 | 77.1 | 0.1 |
| 14.1 | 9.6 | −0.3 | 54.5 | 42.3 | −0.8 | 78.9 | 71.8 | −0.5 |
| 14.7 | 13.2 | −0.1 | 53.8 | 45.6 | −0.8 | 80.6 | 73.2 | −0.7 |
| 15.4 | 9.3 | −0.3 | 70.5 | 55.7 | −0.8 | 94.5 | 81.7 | −0.7 |
| 55.0 | 29.0 | −1.4 | 84.3 | 62.8 | −1.1 | 95.1 | 83.6 | −0.6 |
| 5.2 | 3.4 | −0.2 | 34.0 | 22.3 | −1.1 | 59.9 | 47.5 | −1.1 |
| 28.8 | 20.6 | −0.8 | 69.5 | 55.4 | −1.4 | 90.5 | 80.3 | −1.0 |
| 37.6 | 25.3 | −0.7 | 83.9 | 75.5 | −0.5 | 94.6 | 92.6 | −0.1 |
| 16.7 | 14.7 | −0.2 | 56.5 | 51.6 | −0.5 | 79.1 | 74.5 | −0.5 |
| 11.5 | 9.0 | −0.3 | 32.1 | 27.5 | −0.5 | 55.1 | 49.6 | −0.6 |
| 6.7 | 3.0 | −0.4 | 41.0 | 27.7 | −1.3 | 75.4 | 62.3 | −1.3 |
| 21.0 | 15.2 | −0.6 | 72.7 | 61.8 | −1.1 | 92.5 | 87.2 | −0.5 |
| 49.7 | 49.9 | 0.0 | 86.8 | 87.7 | 0.0 | 93.2 | 94.2 | 0.0 |
| 11.3 | 12.8 | 0.1 | 48.8 | 44.8 | −0.4 | 76.1 | 73.0 | −0.3 |
| 13.5 | 17.7 | 0.3 | 48.4 | 50.6 | 0.1 | 86.5 | 71.2 | −1.0 |
| 31.6 | 23.9 | −0.4 | 80.3 | 67.9 | −0.7 | 92.0 | 86.3 | −0.3 |
| 26.1 | 22.7 | −0.2 | 76.5 | 71.9 | −0.3 | 90.7 | 90.2 | 0.0 |

NOTE: n.a. = not available.
* Status "unknown" for ≤ 1% of total of those 15+ deducted.
** Status "unknown" for > 1% but ≤ 2% of total of those 15+ deducted.
*** Status "unknown" for > 2% but ≤ 5% of total of those 15+ deducted.
**** Status "unknown" for > 5% of total of those 15+ deducted.
[1] Survey 1 uses 16-19-year-old data.
[2] Over 50 percent 15-19-year-olds "unknown" status.

APPENDIX TABLE 7-1b Percentage Men Ever Married, by Age and
Time Period

| Country | Survey Year 1 | Note | Survey Year 2 | Note | Survey Interval |
|---|---|---|---|---|---|
| Argentina | 1980 | | 1991 | * | 11 |
| Azerbaijan | 1989 | [a]**1 | 1999 | | 10 |
| Bahrain | 1981 | | 1991 | | 10 |
| Bangladesh | 1981 | | 1991 | | 10 |
| Belize | 1980 | ** | 1991 | | 11 |
| Benin | 1979 | [a] | 1996 | [b] | 17 |
| Bolivia | 1988 | * | 1998 | [c] | 10 |
| Botswana | 1981 | | 1991 | * | 10 |
| Brazil | 1980 | ** | 1996 | [b] | 16 |
| Burkina Faso | 1985 | [f]* | 1999 | [c] | 14 |
| Burundi | 1979 | | 1990 | *** | 11 |
| Cambodia | 1962 | * | 1998 | | 36 |
| Cameroon | 1987 | [a]* | 1998 | [c,f] | 11 |
| Cape Verde | 1980 | * | 1990 | * | 10 |
| Central African Republic | 1975 | | 1994–1995 | [c] | 19.5 |
| Chad | 1964 | [a] | 1996 | [c] | 32 |
| Chile | 1982 | | 1992 | | 10 |
| China | 1987 | [a] | 1999 | | 12 |
| Colombia | 1973 | ** | 1993 | * | 20 |
| Comoros | 1980 | *** | 1996 | [c] | 16 |
| Côte d'Ivoire | 1978 | | 1994 | [c] | 16 |
| Dominican Republic | 1981 | | 1996 | [c] | 15 |
| Ecuador | 1974 | ** | 1990 | ** | 16 |
| Egypt | 1986 | | 1996 | * | 10 |
| El Salvador | 1971 | * | 1992 | | 21 |
| Ethiopia | 1984 | | 2000 | [f] | 16 |
| Gabon | 1961 | [a] | 2000 | [c] | 39 |
| Gambia | 1983 | ** | 1993 | * | 10 |
| Guatemala | 1973 | * | 1990 | [a] | 17 |
| Guyana | 1980 | * | 1991 | [a]* | 11 |
| Haiti | 1989 | [f] | 2000 | [f] | 11 |
| India | 1981 | * | 1992–1993 | [a] | 11.5 |
| Indonesia | 1980 | | 1990 | | 10 |
| Iran | 1986 | ** | 1996 | * | 10 |
| Jordan | 1979 | | 1994 | * | 15 |
| Kazakhstan | 1989 | *1 | 1999 | * | 10 |
| Kenya | 1969 | * | 1998 | [c] | 29 |
| Kyrgyzstan | 1989 | *1 | 1999 | | 10 |
| Malawi | 1987 | *** | 2000 | [f] | 13 |
| Malaysia | 1980 | | 1991 | | 11 |

| Ages | | | | | | | | |
| 15 to 19 | | | 20 to 24 | | | 25 to 29 | | |
| Survey 1 | Survey 2 | Annual Change | Survey 1 | Survey 2 | Annual Change | Survey 1 | Survey 2 | Annual Change |
|---|---|---|---|---|---|---|---|---|
| n.a. | 2.7 | | 25.8 | 25.6 | 0.0 | 64.1 | 61.1 | −0.3 |
| 1.3 | 2.5 | 0.1 | 21.8 | 16.8 | −0.5 | 70.0 | 57.0 | −1.3 |
| 1.9 | 0.5 | −0.1 | n.a. | 12.8 | | n.a. | 45.3 | |
| 6.7 | 5.0 | −0.2 | 40.3 | 31.6 | −0.9 | 78.8 | 73.6 | −0.5 |
| 1.7 | 1.4 | 0.0 | 20.2 | 18.1 | −0.2 | 47.3 | 39.8 | −0.7 |
| 5.3 | n.a. | | 33.8 | 27.3 | −0.4 | 70.7 | 64.9 | −0.3 |
| 2.9 | 5.2 | 0.2 | 34.2 | 33.6 | −0.1 | 70.2 | 67.5 | −0.3 |
| 0.9 | 2.3 | 0.1 | 6.5 | 9.0 | 0.2 | 30.6 | 29.1 | −0.2 |
| 2.3 | 4.3 | 0.1 | 29.9 | 29.0 | −0.1 | 67.3 | 65.0 | −0.1 |
| 2.5 | 1.4 | −0.1 | 23.6 | 22.1 | −0.1 | 58.6 | 61.0 | 0.2 |
| 5.0 | 0.8 | −0.4 | 45.1 | 26.7 | −1.7 | 76.7 | 70.5 | −0.6 |
| 2.0 | 3.0 | 0.0 | 34.2 | 41.5 | 0.2 | 79.5 | 78.5 | 0.0 |
| 3.4 | 4.2 | 0.1 | 22.6 | 28.0 | 0.5 | 56.7 | 58.2 | 0.1 |
| 0.8 | 1.1 | 0.0 | 15.9 | 14.7 | −0.1 | 56.4 | 47.5 | −0.9 |
| 13.4 | 8.1 | −0.3 | 49.8 | 45.6 | −0.2 | 74.5 | 76.6 | 0.1 |
| 10.1 | 5.9 | −0.1 | 53.9 | 43.7 | −0.3 | 83.0 | 75.2 | −0.2 |
| 2.2 | 5.3 | 0.3 | 24.5 | 25.4 | 0.1 | 63.5 | 59.8 | −0.4 |
| 1.4 | 1.2 | 0.0 | 39.0 | 24.9 | −1.2 | 82.7 | 77.2 | −0.5 |
| 3.0 | 5.4 | 0.1 | 24.7 | 30.6 | 0.3 | 58.0 | 58.9 | 0.0 |
| 1.6 | 3.1 | 0.1 | 19.9 | 15.0 | −0.3 | 60.1 | 41.9 | −1.1 |
| 3.1 | 2.0 | −0.1 | 25.5 | 19.2 | −0.4 | 55.8 | 49.4 | −0.4 |
| 4.0 | 4.4 | 0.0 | 24.9 | 32.3 | 0.5 | 56.8 | 70.3 | 0.9 |
| 3.9 | 4.5 | 0.0 | 34.0 | 33.5 | 0.0 | 66.9 | 65.2 | −0.1 |
| 10.4 | 2.1 | −0.8 | 19.3 | 11.8 | −0.7 | 56.0 | 49.2 | −0.7 |
| 3.4 | 4.5 | 0.1 | 32.7 | 34.5 | 0.1 | 64.2 | 63.4 | 0.0 |
| 6.1 | 3.4 | −0.2 | 47.4 | 23.7 | −1.5 | 84.6 | 70.8 | −0.9 |
| 7.2 | 4.0 | −0.1 | 38.6 | 29.2 | −0.2 | 65.3 | 60.9 | −0.1 |
| 2.9 | 1.7 | −0.1 | 15.9 | 12.4 | −0.4 | 47.6 | 42.7 | −0.5 |
| 8.0 | 7.8 | 0.1 | 45.3 | 45.9 | 0.0 | 75.1 | 78.4 | 0.2 |
| 1.5 | 0.9 | −0.1 | 23.8 | 12.1 | −1.1 | 59.0 | 33.9 | −2.3 |
| 5.8 | 2.6 | −0.3 | 28.4 | 29.8 | 0.1 | 68.7 | 48.1 | −1.9 |
| 12.5 | 8.9 | −0.3 | 43.9 | 51.1 | 0.6 | 78.5 | 84.8 | 0.5 |
| 3.6 | 2.4 | −0.1 | 40.6 | 28.3 | −1.2 | 80.5 | 71.0 | −1.0 |
| 6.8 | 2.6 | −0.4 | 41.4 | 27.4 | −1.4 | 81.5 | 72.8 | −0.9 |
| 1.4 | 1.5 | 0.0 | 25.7 | 16.2 | −0.6 | 66.0 | 57.6 | −0.6 |
| 1.5 | 1.4 | 0.0 | 35.2 | 25.9 | −0.9 | 79.4 | 67.0 | −1.2 |
| 3.7 | 0.7 | −0.1 | 27.5 | 22.6 | −0.2 | 67.6 | 64.9 | −0.1 |
| 1.2 | 1.2 | 0.0 | 37.5 | 28.4 | −0.9 | 86.2 | 76.7 | −1.0 |
| 5.7 | 4.0 | −0.1 | 46.5 | 41.8 | −0.4 | 82.2 | 86.4 | 0.3 |
| 1.3 | 1.4 | 0.0 | 19.6 | 14.3 | −0.5 | 60.1 | 51.0 | −0.8 |

*Continued*

APPENDIX TABLE 7-1b Continued

| Country | Survey Year 1 | Note | Survey Year 2 | Note | Survey Interval |
|---|---|---|---|---|---|
| Maldives | 1985 | * | 1995 | ****2 | 10 |
| Mali | 1976 | ** | 1995–1996 | [c] | 19.5 |
| Mauritania | 1988 | [a]* | 2000–2001 | [f] | 12.5 |
| Mauritius | 1972 | * | 1990 | [f]* | 18 |
| Mexico | 1980 | * | 1990 | * | 10 |
| Morocco | 1982 | | 1994 | | 12 |
| Mozambique | 1980 | ** | 1997 | [c] | 17 |
| Myanmar | 1973 | [a] | 1991 | | 18 |
| Namibia | 1960 | * | 1991 | * | 31 |
| Nepal | 1981 | | 1991 | * | 10 |
| Nicaragua | 1971 | * | 1998 | | 27 |
| Niger | 1988 | * | 1998 | [c] | 10 |
| Occ. Palestinian Territory | 1967 | [e]* | 1997 | [e] | 30 |
| Pakistan | 1981 | | 1998 | [d] | 17 |
| Panama | 1980 | | 1990 | | 10 |
| Paraguay | 1982 | * | 1992 | * | 10 |
| Peru | 1981 | ** | 1996 | [c] | 15 |
| Philippines | 1980 | * | 1995 | * | 15 |
| Puerto Rico | 1980 | *** | 1990 | ** | 10 |
| Rwanda | 1978 | * | 1996 | [c]** | 18 |
| Senegal | 1978 | [c] | 1997 | [c] | 19 |
| South Africa | 1985 | | 1996 | *** | 11 |
| Sudan | 1983 | [a]*** | 1993 | [a]* | 10 |
| Tanzania | 1978 | * | 1996 | [c] | 18 |
| Thailand | 1980 | * | 1990 | ** | 10 |
| Trinidad & Tobago | 1980 | ** | 1990 | ** | 10 |
| Tunisia | 1984 | * | 1994 | * | 10 |
| Turkey | 1980 | | 1990 | * | 10 |
| Uganda | 1969 | * | 1995 | [c] | 26 |
| Uruguay | 1985 | | 1996 | | 11 |
| Venezuela | 1974 | | 1990 | ** | 16 |
| Zambia | 1980 | * | 1999 | *** | 19 |
| Zimbabwe | 1982 | * | 1999 | [c] | 17 |

Unless otherwise noted, source of survey data is UN Statistics Division.
[a] SOURCE: U.S. Bureau of the Census, International Database.
[b] SOURCE: U.S. Bureau of the Census, International Database, National Demographic and Health Survey.
[c] SOURCE: National Demographic and Health Survey.
[d] UN Statistics Division—preliminary.
[e] UN Statistics Division and U.S. Bureau of the Census, International Database.
[f] SOURCE: Other or Unidentified.

| Ages | | | | | | | | |
|------|------|--------|------|------|--------|------|------|--------|
| 15 to 19 | | | 20 to 24 | | | 25 to 29 | | |
| Survey 1 | Survey 2 | Annual Change | Survey 1 | Survey 2 | Annual Change | Survey 1 | Survey 2 | Annual Change |
| 10.2 | 6.3 | −0.4 | 61.2 | 41.1 | −2.0 | 86.8 | 78.5 | −0.8 |
| 1.8 | 4.6 | 0.1 | 16.8 | 28.9 | 0.6 | 52.4 | 67.9 | 0.8 |
| 3.5 | 0.5 | −0.2 | 16.2 | 8.1 | −0.6 | 46.9 | 39.7 | −0.6 |
| 0.7 | 0.6 | 0.0 | 16.0 | 12.6 | −0.2 | 56.1 | 45.0 | −0.6 |
| 7.0 | 5.4 | −0.2 | 40.7 | 38.1 | −0.3 | 74.6 | 70.5 | −0.4 |
| 2.1 | 1.1 | −0.1 | 19.5 | 11.0 | −0.7 | 55.2 | 36.5 | −1.6 |
| 8.4 | 3.8 | −0.3 | 56.3 | 57.6 | 0.1 | 85.6 | 87.6 | 0.1 |
| 7.8 | 3.3 | −0.3 | 44.8 | 30.1 | −0.8 | 76.3 | 62.4 | −0.8 |
| 0.9 | 1.1 | 0.0 | 15.5 | 10.4 | −0.2 | 42.2 | 32.6 | −0.3 |
| 25.9 | 20.0 | −0.6 | 59.2 | 61.7 | 0.3 | 80.5 | 87.3 | 0.7 |
| 4.0 | 8.6 | 0.2 | 36.1 | 46.4 | 0.4 | 68.2 | 74.2 | 0.2 |
| 11.2 | 4.2 | −0.7 | 46.4 | 41.8 | −0.5 | 81.2 | 83.6 | 0.2 |
| 2.3 | 2.1 | 0.0 | 29.1 | 27.9 | 0.0 | 69.9 | 71.1 | 0.0 |
| 7.6 | 6.1 | −0.1 | 35.6 | 30.0 | −0.3 | 68.8 | 62.9 | −0.4 |
| 3.4 | 4.7 | 0.1 | 31.1 | 30.9 | 0.0 | 64.9 | 59.9 | −0.5 |
| 1.3 | 2.1 | 0.1 | 23.5 | 27.4 | 0.4 | 60.4 | 61.5 | 0.1 |
| 3.2 | 2.7 | 0.0 | 28.0 | 31.4 | 0.2 | 61.5 | 60.6 | −0.1 |
| 3.7 | 3.3 | 0.0 | 36.7 | 25.4 | −0.8 | 72.7 | 59.9 | −0.9 |
| 3.5 | 4.7 | 0.1 | 37.2 | 30.9 | −0.6 | 73.6 | 62.9 | −1.1 |
| 3.1 | 2.1 | −0.1 | 38.3 | 28.4 | −0.5 | 78.3 | 65.6 | −0.7 |
| 1.6 | n.a. | | 14.2 | 8.1 | −0.3 | 49.3 | 36.2 | −0.7 |
| 0.9 | 0.8 | 0.0 | 16.5 | 8.6 | −0.7 | 50.4 | 33.3 | −1.5 |
| 3.2 | 1.8 | −0.1 | 21.0 | 14.1 | −0.7 | 54.6 | 43.2 | −1.1 |
| 3.5 | 2.9 | 0.0 | 34.6 | 29.2 | −0.3 | 71.4 | 73.1 | 0.1 |
| 4.2 | 4.0 | 0.0 | 33.6 | 29.6 | −0.4 | 73.0 | 64.6 | −0.8 |
| 1.3 | 1.2 | 0.0 | 14.6 | 10.6 | −0.4 | 43.5 | 34.8 | −0.9 |
| 0.0 | 0.0 | 0.0 | 8.5 | 3.7 | −0.5 | 48.1 | 29.0 | −1.9 |
| 7.9 | 4.3 | −0.4 | 38.1 | 28.2 | −1.0 | 80.7 | 74.2 | −0.7 |
| 7.3 | 11.4 | 0.2 | 42.6 | 55.1 | 0.5 | 69.3 | 82.6 | 0.5 |
| 2.0 | 3.5 | 0.1 | 26.7 | 26.9 | 0.0 | 64.2 | 59.7 | −0.4 |
| 1.9 | 5.5 | 0.2 | 25.3 | 31.3 | 0.4 | 69.6 | 59.1 | −0.7 |
| 2.0 | 2.0 | 0.0 | 30.8 | 26.5 | −0.2 | 72.9 | 66.3 | −0.3 |
| 2.0 | 0.8 | −0.1 | 29.9 | 23.6 | −0.4 | 72.6 | 73.0 | 0.0 |

NOTE: n.a. = not available.

\* Status "unknown" for ≤ 1% of total of those 15+ deducted.

\*\* Status "unknown" for > 1% but ≤ 2% of total of those 15+ deducted.

\*\*\* Status "unknown" for > 2% but ≤ 5% of total of those 15+ deducted.

\*\*\*\* Status "unknown" for > 5% of total of those 15+ deducted.

[1] Survey 1 uses 16-19-year-old data.

[2] Over 50 percent 15-19-year-olds "unknown" status.

APPENDIX TABLE 7-2 Percentage of Women Ever Married by Ages 18, 20, 25 by Age at Time of Survey in 51 DHS Countries

| Country and Year of Survey | Married by Age 18 | | | Married by Age 20 | | | Married by Age 25 | |
|---|---|---|---|---|---|---|---|---|
| | 20-24 Year-Olds | 30-34 Year-Olds | 40-44 Year-Olds | 20-24 Year-Olds | 30-34 Year-Olds | 40-44 Year-Olds | 30-34 Year-Olds | 40-44 Year-Olds |
| Armenia, 2000 | 19.1 | 16.8 | 11.9 | 37.2 | 48.8 | 38.9 | 87.7 | 78.2 |
| Bangladesh, 1999-2000 | 65.3 | 80.8 | 89.4 | 75.4 | 90.2 | 95.1 | 98.1 | 98.4 |
| Benin, 1996 | 38.8 | 46.9 | 46.1 | 65.4 | 67.8 | 69.7 | 91.1 | 95.3 |
| Bolivia, 1998 | 21.2 | 24.0 | 22.1 | 38.5 | 41.8 | 42.9 | 76.2 | 78.4 |
| Brazil, 1996 | 23.7 | 23.3 | 21.0 | 38.8 | 40.8 | 39.3 | 75.1 | 76.8 |
| Burkina Faso, 1998-1999 | 62.3 | 64.8 | 64.0 | 84.1 | 84.4 | 87.5 | 96.5 | 97.7 |
| Cameroon, 1998 | 43.4 | 56.8 | 60.8 | 61.2 | 71.9 | 76.7 | 88.2 | 92.7 |
| Central African Republic, 1994-1995 | 57.0 | 57.0 | 64.6 | 73.5 | 75.4 | 80.6 | 89.8 | 91.0 |
| Chad, 1996-1997 | 71.4 | 71.1 | 77.9 | 86.3 | 84.9 | 86.9 | 97.8 | 97.0 |
| Colombia, 2000 | 21.4 | 18.7 | 24.4 | 37.1 | 35.5 | 39.7 | 65.9 | 71.2 |
| Comoros, 1996 | 29.7 | 47.4 | 54.5 | 39.8 | 61.8 | 69.0 | 80.2 | 90.1 |
| Côte d'Ivoire, 1998-1999 | 33.2 | 46.1 | 49.7 | 49.5 | 64.4 | 66.1 | 82.8 | 88.9 |
| Dominican Republic, 1996 | 37.6 | 36.6 | 42.4 | 53.4 | 53.0 | 58.0 | 81.8 | 81.5 |
| Egypt, 2000 | 19.5 | 34.6 | 43.0 | 35.9 | 50.8 | 59.5 | 81.7 | 83.8 |
| Ethiopia, 1999 | 49.1 | 74.0 | 79.4 | 64.7 | 85.2 | 91.4 | 94.9 | 98.6 |
| Ghana, 1998-1999 | 35.5 | 41.8 | 40.7 | 56.4 | 62.3 | 65.0 | 88.5 | 88.0 |
| Guatemala, 1998-1999 | 34.3 | 38.4 | 40.1 | 55.5 | 56.7 | 60.1 | 86.1 | 83.2 |
| Guinea, 1999 | 64.5 | 69.7 | 68.5 | 78.8 | 81.1 | 82.3 | 94.5 | 96.6 |
| Haiti, 2000 | 24.1 | 25.0 | 26.0 | 43.0 | 43.2 | 49.8 | 74.7 | 77.8 |
| India, 1998-2000 | 46.2 | 59.8 | 63.1 | 65.6 | 77.4 | 80.8 | 93.7 | 95.8 |
| Indonesia, 1997 | 29.6 | 42.2 | 49.1 | 47.0 | 60.1 | 67.2 | 84.6 | 89.2 |
| Jordan, 1997 | 13.5 | 20.1 | 35.0 | 26.5 | 35.0 | 53.0 | 67.3 | 83.3 |
| Kazakhstan, 1999 | 14.4 | 6.6 | 7.7 | 39.9 | 31.9 | 29.3 | 83.4 | 80.8 |

| | | | | | | | | |
|---|---|---|---|---|---|---|---|---|
| Kenya, 1998 | 24.6 | 37.2 | 48.0 | 46.1 | 55.7 | 66.1 | 82.5 | 90.4 |
| Kyrgyz Republic, 1997 | 21.2 | 10.4 | 15.7 | 58.4 | 40.2 | 46.7 | 88.5 | 91.6 |
| Madagascar, 1997 | 40.4 | 40.4 | 49.5 | 61.5 | 57.9 | 63.6 | 84.4 | 86.0 |
| Malawi, 2000 | 46.9 | 53.9 | 55.7 | 72.9 | 75.8 | 77.0 | 94.7 | 93.7 |
| Mali, 2001 | 65.4 | 68.4 | 66.0 | 80.9 | 80.2 | 80.4 | 93.8 | 95.0 |
| Morocco, 1992 | 18.4 | 31.6 | 42.9 | 31.4 | 50.4 | 64.1 | 75.1 | 88.7 |
| Mozambique, 1997 | 56.6 | 55.6 | 59.9 | 77.8 | 72.5 | 76.3 | 90.6 | 93.2 |
| Namibia, 1992 | 11.5 | 14.7 | 14.1 | 20.1 | 24.7 | 28.2 | 50.4 | 53.3 |
| Nepal, 2000-2001 | 56.1 | 65.5 | 69.6 | 74.5 | 82.3 | 84.2 | 94.9 | 96.3 |
| Nicaragua, 1997-1998 | 50.3 | 46.6 | 49.4 | 65.6 | 65.6 | 67.4 | 87.4 | 90.3 |
| Niger, 1998 | 76.6 | 86.4 | 89.1 | 85.1 | 91.4 | 95.5 | 97.9 | 99.6 |
| Nigeria, 1999 | 39.6 | 52.0 | 56.1 | 52.7 | 64.9 | 70.3 | 86.3 | 91.9 |
| Pakistan, 1990-1991 | 31.6 | 47.8 | 44.8 | 48.9 | 63.1 | 60.9 | 87.7 | 87.7 |
| Paraguay, 1990 | 24.2 | 23.5 | 23.4 | 40.5 | 43.1 | 44.4 | 74.9 | 74.3 |
| Peru, 2000 | 18.7 | 22.7 | 23.3 | 33.6 | 38.0 | 39.2 | 69.5 | 70.1 |
| Philippines, 1998 | 14.6 | 18.0 | 20.2 | 27.5 | 34.2 | 36.8 | 68.3 | 71.7 |
| Rwanda, 2000 | 19.5 | 19.7 | 21.5 | 41.6 | 40.0 | 45.0 | 82.0 | 87.0 |
| Senegal, 1997 | 36.1 | 55.7 | 61.9 | 50.6 | 70.0 | 76.6 | 87.5 | 94.5 |
| South Africa, 1997 | 7.9 | 14.2 | 15.1 | 14.2 | 26.9 | 30.3 | 51.5 | 59.9 |
| Tanzania, 1999 | 39.3 | 44.9 | 61.2 | 61.8 | 68.2 | 78.9 | 88.8 | 92.7 |
| Togo, 1998 | 30.5 | 40.6 | 40.4 | 48.4 | 62.8 | 61.0 | 89.0 | 89.2 |
| Turkey, 1998 | 23.0 | 27.9 | 43.0 | 42.8 | 47.5 | 66.2 | 82.4 | 89.3 |
| Uganda, 2000-2001 | 53.9 | 52.6 | 59.5 | 74.7 | 74.4 | 76.7 | 92.4 | 94.8 |
| Uzbekistan, 1996 | 15.3 | 12.7 | 18.0 | 55.7 | 42.7 | 56.2 | 90.1 | 91.3 |
| Vietnam, 1997 | 12.4 | 14.7 | 13.2 | 35.9 | 34.8 | 34.6 | 76.9 | 77.6 |
| Yemen, 1991-1992 | 49.2 | 72.5 | 71.3 | 62.6 | 82.4 | 79.8 | 94.4 | 92.4 |
| Zambia, 1996-1997 | 44.2 | 51.7 | 57.8 | 64.3 | 69.8 | 76.4 | 90.7 | 94.4 |
| Zimbabwe, 1999 | 28.7 | 28.0 | 39.4 | 52.9 | 54.1 | 62.3 | 85.3 | 90.0 |

APPENDIX TABLE 7-3 Percentage of Men Ever Married by Ages 20, 25, and 30 by Age at Time of Survey in 32 DHS Countries

| Country and Year of Survey | Married by Age 20 | | | Married by Age 25 | | Married by Age 30 | |
|---|---|---|---|---|---|---|---|
| | 20-24 Year-Olds | 30-34 Year-Olds | 40-44 Year-Olds | 30-34 Year-Olds | 40-44 Year-Olds | 30-34 Year-Olds | 40-44 Year-Olds |
| Armenia, 2000 | 5.0 | 5.2 | 3.5 | 52.3 | 62.3 | 85.7 | 86.6 |
| Benin, 1996 | 14.3 | 20.6 | 21.5 | 59.5 | 58.4 | 85.2 | 84.8 |
| Bolivia, 1998 | 18.1 | 20.4 | 19.2 | 61.1 | 61.8 | 82.5 | 79.1 |
| Brazil, 1996 | 13.7 | 18.3 | 9.7 | 59.0 | 58.3 | 81.5 | 86.9 |
| Burkina Faso, 1998-1999 | 9.3 | 9.6 | 11.5 | 48.1 | 46.8 | 82.9 | 76.6 |
| Cameroon, 1998 | 15.2 | 13.1 | 11.4 | 49.2 | 52.4 | 73.3 | 80.5 |
| Central African Republic, 1994-1995 | 28.5 | 28.9 | 28.4 | 62.7 | 57.5 | 84.9 | 74.7 |
| Chad, 1996-1997 | 26.1 | 26.1 | 26.1 | 69.9 | 65.2 | 92.5 | 90.9 |
| Comoros, 1996 | 8.7 | 14.3 | 13.0 | 44.2 | 48.1 | 74.0 | 72.2 |
| Côte d'Ivoire, 1998-1999 | 9.9 | 11.0 | 18.2 | 39.5 | 54.1 | 72.3 | 74.8 |
| Dominican Republic, 1996 | 18.6 | 18.9 | 12.1 | 56.3 | 54.9 | 80.0 | 77.1 |
| Ethiopia, 1999 | 12.1 | 20.1 | 24.7 | 53.9 | 56.4 | 81.5 | 85.2 |

| | | | | | | |
|---|---|---|---|---|---|---|
| Gabon, 2000 | 21.5 | 22.9 | 24.4 | 57.6 | 68.3 | 79.4 | 85.1 |
| Ghana, 1998-1999 | 12.1 | 18.4 | 13.3 | 51.3 | 48.7 | 80.0 | 77.4 |
| Guinea, 1999 | 10.5 | 16.1 | 8.7 | 45.1 | 36.9 | 69.7 | 69.2 |
| Haiti, 2000 | 15.8 | 14.9 | 26.5 | 44.8 | 52.4 | 64.2 | 78.1 |
| Kazakhstan, 1999 | 9.5 | 7.9 | 6.1 | 61.8 | 67.9 | 80.6 | 92.1 |
| Kenya, 1998 | 7.6 | 11.6 | 11.6 | 50.1 | 59.1 | 84.9 | 87.4 |
| Malawi, 2000 | 14.8 | 23.3 | 26.7 | 69.1 | 72.6 | 94.1 | 93.5 |
| Mali, 2001 | 9.7 | 11.0 | 4.4 | 47.1 | 33.3 | 78.1 | 68.8 |
| Mozambique, 1997 | 30.8 | 29.7 | 27.8 | 72.7 | 78.5 | 90.6 | 90.7 |
| Nicaragua, 1997-1998 | 38.7 | 32.1 | 29.1 | 71.6 | 71.9 | 89.6 | 88.1 |
| Niger, 1998 | 21.0 | 26.0 | 33.7 | 64.8 | 73.8 | 89.6 | 90.6 |
| Nigeria, 1999 | 10.8 | 16.7 | 19.5 | 45.8 | 50.9 | 76.7 | 74.8 |
| Peru, 1996 | 14.7 | 17.3 | 14.8 | 56.3 | 50.2 | 74.8 | 79.1 |
| Senegal, 1997 | 2.5 | 4.2 | 7.8 | 23.6 | 37.4 | 50.1 | 70.0 |
| Tanzania, 1999 | 12.2 | 21.9 | 19.2 | 60.1 | 53.1 | 88.8 | 86.9 |
| Togo, 1998 | 9.5 | 18.4 | 16.9 | 51.8 | 53.5 | 77.5 | 82.0 |
| Turkey, 1998 | 27.5 | 12.8 | 25.8 | 63.1 | 72.2 | 92.6 | 94.5 |
| Uganda, 2000-2001 | 21.5 | 25.2 | 26.9 | 70.4 | 72.3 | 92.5 | 91.9 |
| Zambia, 1996-1997 | 11.3 | 15.7 | 20.3 | 61.8 | 57.1 | 86.4 | 86.7 |
| Zimbabwe, 1999 | 7.6 | 14.0 | 14.1 | 58.2 | 59.7 | 88.1 | 87.8 |

APPENDIX TABLE 7-4 Percentage of Women Ages 20-24 Ever Married by Age 18, by Years of Schooling, Household Economic Status, and Rural-Urban Residence in DHS Countries

| | Years of Schooling | | |
|---|---|---|---|
| Country and Year of Survey | 0-3 | 4-7 | 8+ |
| Armenia, 2000 | n.a. | n.a. | n.a. |
| Bangladesh, 1999-2000 | 84.7 | 67.1 | 33.2 |
| Benin, 1996 | 43.9 | 28.6 | 1.9 |
| Bolivia, 1998 | 39.8 | 34.3 | 12.2 |
| Brazil, 1996 | 41.3 | 30.5 | 12.9 |
| Burkina Faso, 1998-1999 | 69.2 | 40.8 | 9.5 |
| Cameroon, 1998 | 76.6 | 42.3 | 21.8 |
| Central African Republic, 1994-1995 | 59.6 | 58.1 | 39.2 |
| Chad, 1996-1997 | 74.6 | 56.8 | 30.8 |
| Colombia, 2000 | 39.0 | 22.6 | 2.2 |
| Comoros, 1996 | 37.6 | 29.1 | 15.1 |
| Côte d'Ivoire, 1998-1999 | 42.0 | 33.3 | 6.5 |
| Dominican Republic, 1996 | 74.7 | 61.1 | 22.3 |
| Egypt, 2000 | 41.2 | 27.9 | 7.6 |
| Ethiopia, 1999 | 53.7 | 42.9 | 15.5 |
| Ghana, 1998-1999 | 45.3 | 37.3 | 29.2 |
| Guatemala, 1998-1999 | 48.5 | 38.8 | 7.3 |
| Guinea, 1999 | 71.2 | 50.8 | 20.6 |
| Haiti, 2000 | 37.7 | 23.0 | 10.6 |
| India, 1998-2000 | n.a. | n.a. | n.a. |
| Indonesia, 1997 | 50.2 | 43.0 | 12.5 |
| Jordan, 1997 | 19.7 | 28.6 | 11.0 |
| Kazakhstan, 1999 | n.a. | n.a. | n.a. |
| Kenya, 1998 | 52.0 | 39.2 | 14.4 |
| Kyrgyz Republic, 1997 | n.a. | n.a. | n.a. |

| Household Economic Status | | | Residence | |
| Low (bottom 40%) | Middle (mid 40%) | High (top 20%) | Rural | Urban |
|---|---|---|---|---|
| 28.7 | 15.5 | 10.7 | 30.8 | 12.1 |
| n.a. | n.a. | n.a. | 69.9 | 48.2 |
| 51.0 | 37.5 | 17.3 | 46.1 | 27.8 |
| 35.7 | 18.3 | 10.4 | 35.1 | 16.8 |
| 29.9 | 21.9 | 15.9 | 30.1 | 22.2 |
| 72.0 | 68.6 | 38.6 | 69.9 | 32.0 |
| 59.8 | 39.8 | 27.8 | 51.3 | 30.2 |
| 59.4 | 59.2 | 48.5 | 59.2 | 54.2 |
| 73.2 | 72.6 | 64.8 | 73.6 | 64.7 |
| 34.8 | 14.5 | 13.4 | 33.7 | 18.4 |
| 39.8 | 32.1 | 10.8 | 33.0 | 22.5 |
| 47.3 | 35.2 | 14.7 | 43.0 | 23.5 |
| 58.5 | 31.2 | 18.4 | 50.3 | 31.6 |
| n.a. | n.a. | n.a. | 26.1 | 11.4 |
| 59.8 | 50.3 | 31.8 | 53.2 | 31.8 |
| 41.0 | 39.7 | 20.3 | 41.6 | 25.3 |
| 49.6 | 33.5 | 11.6 | 43.9 | 24.7 |
| 81.2 | 65.0 | 40.3 | 75.3 | 46.2 |
| 32.5 | 27.0 | 10.3 | 30.7 | 17.8 |
| n.a. | n.a. | n.a. | 54.0 | 25.9 |
| n.a. | n.a. | n.a. | 38.4 | 13.2 |
| n.a. | n.a. | n.a. | 15.3 | 13.1 |
| 15.3 | 13.8 | 13.0 | 16.7 | 12.4 |
| 30.3 | 26.4 | 14.7 | 26.2 | 20.7 |
| 23.7 | 20.2 | 17.7 | 22.3 | 18.6 |

*Continued*

## APPENDIX TABLE 7-4 Continued

| Country and Year of Survey | Years of Schooling | | |
|---|---|---|---|
| | 0-3 | 4-7 | 8+ |
| Madagascar, 1997 | 49.7 | 38.2 | 19.3 |
| Malawi, 2000 | 60.7 | 52.2 | 18.4 |
| Mali, 2001 | 71.9 | 44.5 | 18.2 |
| Morocco, 1992 | 25.4 | 14.2 | 2.9 |
| Mozambique, 1997 | 64.5 | 44.6 | 8.6 |
| Namibia, 1992 | 25.8 | 17.0 | 2.6 |
| Nepal, 2000-01 | 68.8 | 50.3 | 22.2 |
| Nicaragua, 1997-1998 | 71.4 | 64.6 | 26.3 |
| Niger, 1998 | 84.7 | 56.1 | 15.1 |
| Nigeria, 1999 | 81.4 | 33.1 | 11.2 |
| Pakistan, 1990-1991 | n.a. | n.a. | n.a. |
| Paraguay, 1990 | 46.9 | 29.3 | 11.5 |
| Peru, 2000 | 48.0 | 39.5 | 10.2 |
| Philippines, 1998 | 42.0 | 34.3 | 8.6 |
| Rwanda, 2000 | 26.2 | 17.7 | 10.4 |
| Senegal, 1997 | 48.5 | 18.9 | 3.2 |
| South Africa, 1997 | 17.1 | 16.1 | 6.3 |
| Tanzania, 1999 | 58.7 | 35.8 | 4.1 |
| Togo, 1998 | 40.5 | 21.1 | 4.2 |
| Turkey, 1998 | 44.5 | 28.4 | 6.4 |
| Uganda, 2000-2001 | 69.8 | 58.4 | 18.0 |
| Uzbekistan, 1996 | n.a. | n.a. | n.a. |
| Vietnam, 1997 | 27.4 | 12.9 | 8.0 |
| Yemen, 1991-1992 | n.a. | n.a. | n.a. |
| Zambia, 1996-1997 | 58.7 | 52.9 | 18.7 |
| Zimbabwe, 1999 | 79.7 | 46.5 | 17.4 |
| Number of countries included: | 44 | 44 | 44 |

NOTE: n.a = not available.

| Household Economic Status | | | Residence | |
| Low (bottom 40%) | Middle (mid 40%) | High (top 20%) | Rural | Urban |
|---|---|---|---|---|
| 51.4 | 41.2 | 17.7 | 43.9 | 31.6 |
| 50.5 | 52.8 | 30.2 | 50.4 | 32.3 |
| 72.6 | 69.2 | 42.0 | 74.3 | 45.7 |
| n.a. | n.a. | n.a. | 24.2 | 12.9 |
| 67.6 | 52.4 | 42.6 | 59.7 | 47.0 |
| 14.3 | 13.2 | 4.6 | 13.7 | 8.1 |
| n.a. | n.a. | n.a. | 58.7 | 38.4 |
| 64.9 | 40.3 | 28.2 | 60.5 | 44.6 |
| 86.7 | 83.9 | 48.3 | 85.7 | 45.7 |
| 62.5 | 31.6 | 16.7 | 45.9 | 26.4 |
| n.a. | n.a. | n.a. | 36.9 | 21.3 |
| n.a. | n.a. | n.a. | 31.7 | 18.4 |
| 36.3 | 13.8 | 5.0 | 34.9 | 12.3 |
| n.a. | n.a. | n.a. | 20.4 | 10.7 |
| 22.8 | 18.0 | 17.5 | 19.2 | 20.5 |
| 56.0 | 46.7 | 14.5 | 53.1 | 15.4 |
| 12.5 | 5.2 | 4.3 | 12.3 | 4.7 |
| 48.9 | 41.0 | 25.4 | 47.6 | 22.5 |
| 41.9 | 30.8 | 17.4 | 40.8 | 16.9 |
| n.a. | n.a. | n.a. | 26.6 | 19.4 |
| 62.6 | 54.6 | 39.2 | 58.9 | 33.7 |
| 18.9 | 12.3 | 13.0 | 16.0 | 14.1 |
| n.a. | n.a. | n.a. | 14.4 | 5.1 |
| n.a. | n.a. | n.a. | 53.9 | 35.7 |
| 55.2 | 46.4 | 28.4 | 52.3 | 34.1 |
| 35.0 | 31.5 | 16.2 | 35.9 | 20.6 |
| 38 | 38 | 38 | 51 | 51 |

APPENDIX TABLE 7-5 Percentage of Men Ages 20-24 Ever Married by Age 20, by Years of Schooling, Household Eeconomic Status, and Rural-Urban Residence in DHS Countries

| Country and Year of Survey | Years of Schooling | | |
|---|---|---|---|
| | 0-3 | 4-7 | 8+ |
| Armenia, 2000 | n.a. | n.a. | n.a. |
| Benin, 1996 | 19.0 | 13.5 | 3.1 |
| Bolivia, 1998 | 36.5 | 34.2 | 14.5 |
| Brazil, 1996 | 18.0 | 16.1 | 9.6 |
| Burkina Faso, 1998-1999 | 11.5 | 9.4 | 0.9 |
| Cameroon, 1998 | 24.2 | 15.6 | 12.5 |
| Central African Republic, 1994-1995 | 29.6 | 33.9 | 20.5 |
| Chad, 1996-1997 | 29.6 | 24.0 | 17.5 |
| Comoros, 1996 | 6.7 | 5.6 | 14.0 |
| Côte d'Ivoire, 1998-1999 | 14.5 | 8.4 | 5.4 |
| Dominican Republic, 1996 | 19.2 | 23.9 | 12.2 |
| Ethiopia, 1999 | 13.1 | 15.8 | 0.8 |
| Gabon, 2000 | n.a. | n.a. | n.a. |
| Ghana, 1998-1999 | 5.4 | 25.6 | 10.5 |
| Guinea, 1999 | 15.3 | 0.0 | 8.4 |
| Haiti, 2000 | 17.2 | 26.1 | 9.2 |
| Kazakhstan, 1999 | 0.0 | 14.3 | 5.1 |
| Kenya, 1998 | 16.0 | 13.4 | 5.1 |
| Malawi, 2000 | 23.8 | 22.1 | 5.5 |
| Mali, 2001 | 11.7 | 6.4 | 5.4 |
| Mozambique, 1997 | 48.0 | 22.7 | 12.4 |
| Nicaragua, 1997-1998 | 45.3 | 49.6 | 24.2 |
| Niger, 1998 | n.a. | n.a. | n.a. |
| Nigeria, 1999 | 27.2 | 15.9 | 4.4 |
| Peru, 1996 | 32.8 | 24.7 | 11.0 |
| Senegal, 1997 | 5.8 | 0.1 | 0.0 |
| Tanzania, 1999 | 24.2 | 9.6 | 14.7 |
| Togo, 1998 | 19.0 | 9.1 | 2.5 |
| Turkey, 1998 | 0.0 | 34.7 | 17.0 |
| Uganda, 2000-2001 | 27.0 | 29.0 | 5.8 |
| Zambia, 1996-1997 | 13.1 | 13.1 | 5.2 |
| Zimbabwe, 1999 | 17.6 | 17.9 | 8.7 |
| Number of countries included: | 29 | 29 | 29 |

NOTE: n.a = not available.

| Household Economic Status | | | Residence | |
| Low (bottom 40%) | Middle (mid 40%) | High (top 20%) | Rural | Urban |
|---|---|---|---|---|
| 5.2 | 4.2 | 6.1 | 5.2 | 4.9 |
| 21.6 | 14.9 | 4.6 | 22.2 | 5.3 |
| 27.7 | 20.6 | 6.4 | 26.5 | 15.8 |
| 18.5 | 11.3 | 9.7 | 11.2 | 14.3 |
| 12.7 | 8.8 | 6.7 | 11.2 | 4.7 |
| 24.3 | 13.0 | 8.5 | 20.1 | 7.7 |
| 37.3 | 24.5 | 19.3 | 39.5 | 19.0 |
| 33.7 | 25.7 | 18.0 | 30.2 | 18.1 |
| 9.4 | 8.3 | 8.5 | 3.9 | 15.7 |
| 16.5 | 9.6 | 2.6 | 14.3 | 5.0 |
| 22.4 | 17.0 | 11.1 | 19.4 | 18.0 |
| 20.7 | 10.2 | 2.0 | 13.9 | 2.3 |
| n.a. | n.a. | n.a. | 31.0 | 19.4 |
| 12.8 | 15.0 | 2.9 | 16.8 | 4.9 |
| 15.4 | 13.7 | 1.1 | 15.3 | 4.7 |
| 15.1 | 20.8 | 8.1 | 22.8 | 8.2 |
| 4.1 | 15.2 | 7.0 | 7.5 | 11.0 |
| 10.5 | 8.3 | 3.8 | 7.7 | 7.5 |
| 19.0 | 16.4 | 6.2 | 17.2 | 5.0 |
| 15.3 | 8.0 | 7.0 | 11.2 | 7.7 |
| 58.4 | 26.5 | 6.1 | 34.1 | 22.3 |
| 47.2 | 34.1 | 32.6 | 43.5 | 35.3 |
| 18.6 | 32.0 | 9.9 | 26.9 | 7.4 |
| 19.9 | 8.8 | 3.4 | 14.4 | 3.3 |
| 25.4 | 15.3 | 3.5 | 23.2 | 11.7 |
| 4.1 | 3.0 | 0.4 | 4.7 | 0.8 |
| 16.4 | 12.4 | 7.6 | 14.0 | 7.8 |
| 11.8 | 12.8 | 1.6 | 14.0 | 3.9 |
| 36.9 | 21.3 | 10.0 | 31.1 | 25.3 |
| 23.9 | 22.9 | 14.4 | 22.4 | 18.1 |
| 14.0 | 15.6 | 2.3 | 13.6 | 8.6 |
| 9.7 | 9.2 | 2.3 | 10.7 | 3.8 |
| 31 | 31 | 31 | 32 | 32 |

APPENDIX TABLE 7-6 Percentage Distribution of Spouse/Partner Age Differences, Among Women Currently in First Marriage, by Age in 42 DHS Countries

| | Spouse/Partner Age Difference | | | | | |
|---|---|---|---|---|---|---|
| | 0-5 Years | | 6-10 Years | | 11+ Years | |
| Country and Year of Survey | 25-29-Year-Olds | 45-49-Year-Olds | 25-29-Year-Olds | 45-49-Year-Olds | 25-29-Year-Olds | 45-49-Year-Olds |
| Armenia, 2000 | 55.0 | 70.7 | 36.4 | 20.5 | 8.6 | 8.7 |
| Bangladesh, 1999-2000 | 25.4 | 20.5 | 47.5 | 36.0 | 27.1 | 43.5 |
| Benin, 2001 | 44.8 | 33.1 | 27.5 | 23.4 | 27.7 | 43.5 |
| Bolivia, 1998 | 73.6 | 75.2 | 19.4 | 17.0 | 7.0 | 7.8 |
| Brazil, 1996 | 65.7 | 70.8 | 24.1 | 18.9 | 10.2 | 10.3 |
| Burkina Faso, 1998-1999 | 39.9 | 40.3 | 23.6 | 15.8 | 36.5 | 44.0 |
| Cameroon, 1998 | 35.5 | 34.1 | 29.2 | 19.7 | 35.3 | 46.3 |
| Central African Republic, 1994-1995 | 52.9 | 52.4 | 28.1 | 20.1 | 19.1 | 27.4 |
| Chad, 1996-1997 | 33.7 | 25.3 | 33.7 | 22.4 | 32.6 | 52.2 |
| Colombia, 2000 | 66.2 | 59.6 | 21.5 | 24.8 | 12.2 | 15.6 |
| Comoros, 1996 | 33.3 | 22.5 | 30.6 | 29.2 | 36.0 | 48.3 |
| Dominican Republic, 1996 | 54.6 | 54.4 | 28.0 | 30.3 | 17.4 | 15.3 |
| Egypt, 2000 | 43.5 | 44.4 | 38.3 | 30.6 | 18.3 | 24.9 |
| Ethiopia, 1999 | 41.8 | 25.0 | 35.6 | 39.2 | 22.6 | 35.9 |
| Ghana, 1998-1999 | 50.7 | 36.9 | 28.5 | 29.6 | 20.8 | 33.6 |
| Guatemala, 1998-1999 | 71.7 | 70.3 | 20.3 | 17.7 | 8.0 | 11.9 |

| | | | | | |
|---|---|---|---|---|---|
| Guinea, 1999 | 13.4 | 15.6 | 30.0 | 26.1 | 56.6 | 58.3 |
| Haiti, 2000 | 50.2 | 62.1 | 30.1 | 24.8 | 19.7 | 13.1 |
| India, 1998-2000 | 53.8 | 52.6 | 35.2 | 30.2 | 10.9 | 17.2 |
| Jordan, 1997 | 57.0 | 41.1 | 32.6 | 38.2 | 10.4 | 20.7 |
| Kazakhstan, 1999 | 83.0 | 85.3 | 14.9 | 9.1 | 2.0 | 5.6 |
| Kenya, 1998 | 47.4 | 47.9 | 35.0 | 28.8 | 17.6 | 23.3 |
| Kyrgyz Republic, 1997 | 85.7 | 64.9 | 11.8 | 27.3 | 2.5 | 7.8 |
| Madagascar, 1997 | 59.9 | 66.2 | 27.3 | 18.3 | 12.8 | 15.5 |
| Malawi, 2000 | 61.6 | 61.3 | 28.5 | 27.0 | 9.9 | 11.7 |
| Mali, 2001 | 20.5 | 21.7 | 37.1 | 30.2 | 42.3 | 48.0 |
| Mozambique, 1997 | 53.4 | 50.4 | 26.2 | 21.3 | 20.3 | 28.2 |
| Nepal, 2000-2001 | 71.9 | 58.3 | 21.8 | 25.9 | 6.3 | 15.8 |
| Nicaragua, 1997-1998 | 66.8 | 62.8 | 19.9 | 22.3 | 13.4 | 14.9 |
| Niger, 1998 | 30.4 | 30.3 | 37.3 | 32.4 | 32.3 | 37.3 |
| Nigeria, 1999 | 27.3 | 26.7 | 38.2 | 26.6 | 34.5 | 46.7 |
| Peru, 2000 | 67.5 | 66.5 | 23.0 | 22.4 | 9.5 | 11.1 |
| Philippines, 1998 | 74.4 | 80.7 | 18.3 | 13.9 | 7.3 | 5.4 |
| Rwanda, 2000 | 57.2 | 78.1 | 27.0 | 12.3 | 15.9 | 9.5 |
| South Africa, 1998 | 59.5 | 69.4 | 25.8 | 18.6 | 14.7 | 12.0 |
| Togo, 1998 | 46.4 | 35.4 | 29.3 | 23.3 | 24.2 | 41.3 |
| Turkey, 1998 | 65.5 | 66.4 | 27.9 | 24.7 | 6.6 | 8.9 |
| Uganda, 2000-2001 | 56.8 | 42.3 | 30.2 | 30.1 | 13.0 | 27.6 |
| Uzbekistan, 1996 | 89.0 | 70.6 | 9.6 | 23.9 | 1.4 | 5.6 |
| Vietnam, 1997 | 80.1 | 74.9 | 16.9 | 16.1 | 3.0 | 9.0 |
| Zambia, 2001-2002 | 52.6 | 33.9 | 35.2 | 37.1 | 12.2 | 29.1 |
| Zimbabwe, 1999 | 54.8 | 44.3 | 26.7 | 28.8 | 18.5 | 26.9 |

# 8

# The Transition to Parenthood

## INTRODUCTION

Becoming a parent for the first time is a major transition at any age, and it is especially so for an adolescent or young adult. While age is one important indicator of readiness for parenthood, other factors, such as family circumstances and social support systems, are also important and can influence young parents' chances of success. Furthermore, in the context of rapid and persistent global changes discussed throughout this book—including rising rates of return to postprimary schooling, the pervasiveness of market-led economic change, advances in medical knowledge and practice, democratization and the rise of civil society, expansion of knowledge sharing networks, and the emergence and spread of new communicable diseases—the prerequisites for preparedness to be a parent are changing and the significance and consequences of early childbearing are assuming new meanings.

Our discussion suggests that success as a first-time parent in many of the contexts in which young people are growing up today is more likely to be ensured if other adult transitions occur *prior* to parenthood. This is because each of these other transitions to adult roles—to work, to citizenship, and to marriage—prepares the way for parenthood and contributes resources for success. While this sequencing does not ensure success and success can occur through a variety of transition pathways, many of the social and institutional supports for effective parenthood are built around this sequencing and therefore are particularly supportive of it. For example, in most settings, schooling is often not an option for parents, particularly mothers, although in this area change is beginning to be seen.

The moment that young people become first-time parents, they become major actors in shaping the health and well-being of the next generation. There is a vast and growing literature on the determinants of success in early childhood. Not surprisingly, parental income, schooling, health knowledge, and the availability of community services have all been documented to be important to child survival and early childhood health and development in a diverse range of developing country settings (Bicego and Boerma, 1993; Cleland and van Ginneken, 1988; Hales et al., 1999; Mahy 2003; United Nations 1991; World Health Organization, 2000). The literature on rates of returns to schooling documents empirically the myriad social benefits that come from investing in schooling, particularly for girls, including smaller family size, better child health, and greater investments in schooling for the next generation. Because of the many global changes we have discussed, there is also increasing recognition that motherhood involves not only a caretaking role but also a role as an economic provider, as has always been the case for fatherhood (Bruce, Lloyd, and Leonard, 1995).

Social concerns about the implications of premature parenthood arise for several reasons. One is the potential health consequences for very young women of pregnancy and birth if their physiological development is incomplete. Other consequences may include premature exit from school, reduced earnings prospects, reduced chances of community participation and the acquisition of social capital, a heightened possibility of divorce or single parenthood, and a greater risk of living in poverty. These other consequences of early parenthood are likely to be greater for young women than young men; in most societies, women have the primary responsibility of child care and childrearing, and parenthood for them often coincides with a shrinking of opportunities and reduced scope for independent action.

We begin with an empirical overview of trends in the timing of first parenthood in developing countries, relying primarily on data from the Demographic and Health Surveys (DHS), which are unique in their careful and comparable measurement of women's birth histories (see Appendix A for further discussion). While the data on young men are more limited, we explore age patterns of parenthood for both. We then go into more depth on early motherhood, presenting data on trends as well as a review of the literature on consequences. Next, we present data on the sequencing of parenthood with marriage, including trends in premarital childbearing as well as trends in the length of the first birth interval. After reviewing the limited evidence on the consequences of premarital childbearing, we explore some of the factors affecting the changing context of first-time parenthood, including the rise of formal schooling, the rise in paid employment among women, changes in health and health behaviors, in particular HIV, and finally changes in access to and use of prenatal and delivery services, with particular implications for the service context surrounding first births. We draw on both qualitative and quantitative research material to describe the changing context of first parenthood. In our brief discussion of policies and programs affecting the transition to parenthood, we focus primarily on those that position young people for success as first-time parents.

## THE TIMING OF THE TRANSITION TO PARENTHOOD

### Gender Differences in Age Patterns of First Parenthood

As noted above, information on the timing of fatherhood is scarce, and it is difficult to obtain comparable indicators for men and women. Data on the age patterns of first parenthood are one of the few measures available

TABLE 8-1 Parenthood by Age and Sex (percentage)—Weighted[a] Regional Averages, DHS Countries

| Region and Country | Regional Population (male) | Who Ever Fathered a Child, Among Men Ages: | | | |
|---|---|---|---|---|---|
| | | 15-19 | 20-24 | 25-29 | 30-34 |
| Africa | | | | | |
| Eastern/Southern Africa | 49.3 | 1.7 | 24.0 | 65.4 | 86.6 |
| Western/Middle Africa | 71.4 | 1.5 | 13.4 | 49.7 | 79.6 |
| Asia[b] | | | | | |
| South-central/ | | | | | |
| South-eastern Asia | n.a. | n.a. | n.a. | n.a. | n.a. |
| Former Soviet Asia[c] | n.a. | n.a. | n.a. | n.a. | n.a. |
| Latin America and Caribbean | | | | | |
| Caribbean/ | | | | | |
| Central America | 13.7 | 1.7 | 26.8 | 56.8 | 79.0 |
| South America | 60.3 | 3.0 | 23.1 | 53.7 | 77.9 |
| Middle East | | | | | |
| Western Asia/ | | | | | |
| Northern Africa | n.a. | n.a. | n.a. | n.a. | n.a. |
| TOTAL—All DHS | 56.2 | 2.1 | 20.8 | 55.7 | 81.0 |

[a]Weighting is based on United Nations population estimates for year 2000 (*World Population Prospects: The 2000 Revision*, POP/DB/WPP/Rev. 2000/3/F1. February 2001).

[b]Eastern Asia not included; no DHS available.

[c]Former Soviet Asia includes former Soviet Republics in South-central and Western Asia.

for both. Table 8-1 shows that the proportion of men ages 15-19 who report that they have had a child is extremely low: 2-3 percent in the regions for which information is available. This is much lower than the proportion of adolescent women ages 15-19 who have done so (6-21 percent). Even at ages 20-24, young men are much less likely to have made the transition to fatherhood than young women: about 25 percent have done so in Latin America, compared with twice as many young women (50-60 percent). The differential is even larger in sub-Saharan Africa, where young women are three to five times as likely to have become a parent in their early 20s as young men. By their late 20s, however, 50-65 percent of men in Latin America and sub-Saharan Africa have become fathers, although this proportion is still lower than that among women of this age (74-89 percent). Gender differences in age patterns of parenthood reflect spousal age differences, discussed in Chapter 7.

| Regional Population (female) | Who Ever Had a Child, Among Women Ages: | | | |
|---|---|---|---|---|
| | 15-19 | 20-24 | 25-29 | 30-34 |
| 91.7 | 18.4 | 69.9 | 89.1 | 95.1 |
| 75.2 | 21.1 | 64.4 | 85.8 | 93.6 |
| | | | | |
| 86.0 | 15.2 | 59.8 | 84.7 | 92.7 |
| 68.4 | 5.6 | 55.1 | 86.1 | 93.9 |
| | | | | |
| 21.0 | 17.3 | 60.5 | 82.4 | 91.2 |
| 74.1 | 13.9 | 49.8 | 74.7 | 87.5 |
| | | | | |
| 54.9 | 6.8 | 43.5 | 74.1 | 88.4 |
| 77.8 | 15.2 | 59.2 | 83.6 | 92.3 |

NOTES: n.a. = not available. Regional groupings based on United Nations *World Population Prospects: The 2002 Revision* (United Nations, 2003b).
SOURCES: Demographic and Health Surveys tabulations from 51 countries (females) and 26 countries (males). See Appendix Table 8-1 for data from each country.

## Trends in the Distribution of Ages at First Motherhood

We compare the distribution of ages at first birth among women from three cohorts: those who were ages 40-44 at the time of the most recent DHS survey (born roughly in the 1950s), those who were ages 30-34 (born roughly in the 1960s), and those who were ages 20-24 (born roughly in the 1970s). In Table 8-2 we present the ages when 25 percent, 50 percent, and 75 percent of women had made the transition to motherhood, by region, using life table analysis.

The first thing to observe about the table is that, for the youngest cohort, a quarter of women remain childless until after age 24 in all regions. This substantial and worldwide pattern is apparent from the footnotes in

TABLE 8-2 Age of Transition to First Motherhood by Quartile— Weighted Region and Income Averages, DHS Countries

| Region or Income Level | 25th Quartile | | |
|---|---|---|---|
| | 20-24 | 30-34 | 40-44 |
| Region | | | |
| Africa | | | |
| Eastern/Southern Africa | 17.9 | 17.2 | 17.0 |
| Western/Middle Africa | 17.4 | 16.8 | 16.4 |
| Asia | | | |
| South-central/South-eastern Asia[a] | 18.2 | 17.6 | 17.7 |
| Former Soviet Asia | 19.9 | 20.2 | 20.0 |
| Latin America and Caribbean | | | |
| Caribbean/Central America | 18.4 | 18.1 | 18.2 |
| South America | 19.0 | 19.2 | 19.4 |
| Middle East | | | |
| Western Asia/Northern Africa[a] | 20.1 | 18.8 | 18.5 |
| Income Level[d] | | | |
| Low | 18.0 | 17.4 | 17.4 |
| Lower Middle | 19.9 | 19.3 | 19.0 |
| Upper Middle | 19.1 | 19.0 | 19.2 |
| TOTAL—All DHS | 18.3 | 17.8 | 17.7 |

[a]Quartiles for SC/SE Asia and Middle East are computed from countries where the DHS only interviews ever married women.

[b]20-24-year-olds from the following countries have not reached the 75th quartile for first births: Armenia, Kazakhstan, Ghana, Nigeria, Senegal, Comoros, South Africa, Bolivia, Brazil, Colombia, Paraguay, Peru, Dominican Republic, Haiti, Nicaragua, Indonesia, Pakistan, Philippines, Vietnam, Jordan, Morocco, Turkey, and Yemen.

[c]In Western Asia/Northern Africa, 20-24-year-old females in Jordan and Morocco have not reached the 50th quartile for first births.

the eighth column of Table 8-2. These footnotes indicate that for no region in the world has a 75th percentile in the age distribution of first birth been reached by the age of 24 for women born in the 1970s. Of course, in both subregions of Latin America and the Caribbean this was true of women born in the 1950s and 1960s as well. This can be seen in the last (tenth) column of the table, which shows that, in South America, at least a quarter of women ages 40-44 were childless until past age 26. This later pattern of childbearing is also apparent in the Middle East for older cohorts. In Africa and Asia, however, 75 percent of the oldest and the middle cohorts were mothers by age 23. If this pattern had remained unchanged, we would have been able to include data in the fifth column of the table for the youngest

| 50th Quartile | | | | 75th Quartile | | |
|---|---|---|---|---|---|---|
| 20-24 | 30-34 | 40-44 | | 20-24 | 30-34 | 40-44 |
| 20.0 | 19.3 | 19.0 | | $b$ | 22.1 | 21.8 |
| 20.3 | 19.5 | 19.2 | | $b$ | 22.8 | 22.5 |
| 20.8 | 19.9 | 20.0 | | $b$ | 23.2 | 23.1 |
| 21.6 | 21.9 | 21.7 | | $b$ | 24.2 | 24.2 |
| 21.0 | 20.9 | 20.3 | | $b$ | 24.5 | 24.1 |
| 22.3 | 22.1 | 22.1 | | $b$ | 26.9 | 26.3 |
| $c$ | 21.7 | 21.0 | | $b$ | 26.0 | 24.5 |
| 20.5 | 19.7 | 19.7 | | $b$ | 22.8 | 22.7 |
| $c$ | 22.2 | 21.7 | | $b$ | 26.8 | 25.9 |
| 22.3 | 21.7 | 21.7 | | $b$ | 26.0 | 25.3 |
| $c$ | 20.2 | 20.1 | | $b$ | 23.6 | 23.3 |

$d$World Bank income classifications.

NOTES: In order to estimate an accurate exposure time, unmarried females in the household roster were identified and censored at their age at the time of the interview plus 0.5 years.

For source of regional groupings and population data for weighted averages, see Table 8-1. Further detail can be found in Appendix A.

SOURCES: Demographic and Health Surveys tabulations, see Appendix Table 8-2 for data from each country.

cohort where footnotes are indicated; recent delays in the timing of parenthood in these two regions make such an estimate for the youngest cohort impossible.

In former Soviet Asia, South America, Central America, and the Caribbean, there is very little change in the age patterns of first-time parenthood, as the table shows. For all three cohorts, a quarter of women in former Soviet Asia are mothers by age 20 and half by age 21.5; in South America, a quarter of women are mothers by age 19 and half by age 22. In the case of Central America and the Caribbean, the age pattern of first parenthood has stayed roughly the same for the past 10 years, with a quarter becoming mothers by age 18 and half by age 21; in the previous 10 years there was a one-year rise in the median age at first-time parenthood. Figure 8-1 depicts these regional trends with data from an illustrative country from each region. Uzbekistan and Colombia are the countries that best exemplify the regions in which there has been little change in the distribution of ages of first-time motherhood, particularly in recent years.

Table 8-2 shows that in South Asia and the Middle East, there has been an overall shift in the distribution of age at first birth toward an older pattern. The changes are particularly notable between the younger two cohorts in South Asia, where this increase has occurred in most countries. Exceptions are Nepal, where there has been a slight decline in the age of motherhood overall, and Vietnam, where things have been constant. In most countries in Southern Asia, the change has been moderate. In the youngest cohort, a quarter of women ages 20-24 became mothers by 18.2, up from 17.7 among women ages 40-44. Among the younger women in Southern Asia we examined, half were mothers by age 20.8, which is up from age 20 among those ages 40-44. We illustrate this modal pattern in Figure 8-1 with information on Indonesia.

In the Middle East, the increase in the age at first-time motherhood has been more substantial. In the oldest cohort, a quarter of women were mothers by age 18.5, and this milestone was reached by the youngest women at age 20.1. The most notable change in this region is that, for the youngest cohort, half of the women living in the countries of the Middle East for which there are data were childless at age 24. In Figure 8-1 we illustrate this dramatic shift with detailed data for Jordan.

In Eastern and Southern Africa, there has been an intercohort increase in the age by which a quarter of women have become mothers of about a year, from 17 to 17.9. There has also been an increase of about a year in the median age at first birth from 19 to 20. We illustrate the overall trend for this region in Figure 8-1 with data on Ethiopia. This is an accurate depiction of the experience of most of the people in this region, including those in the very populous country of Kenya (the data in Table 8-2 are weighted). Nevertheless, it is important to note that in most of the countries in this

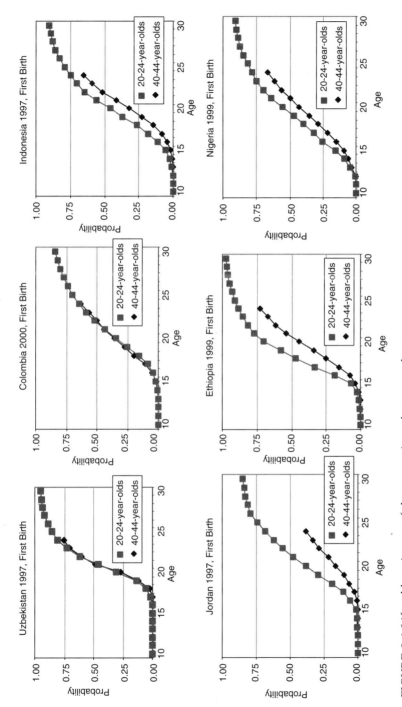

FIGURE 8-1 Life table estimates of the proportion who are mothers.
SOURCE: Demographic and Health Surveys.

region one observes very little intercohort change in the age at the transition to motherhood, specifically in Madagascar, Malawi, Mozambique, Namibia, Rwanda, South Africa, Uganda, and Zimbabwe.

The aggregate data from Western and Middle Africa in Table 8-2 show similar trends but mask even more diversity in the region than was observed for Eastern and Southern Africa. An increase in the age at first-time motherhood can be observed in several countries: Benin, Côte d'Ivoire, Ghana, Senegal, Togo, and Nigeria, which is depicted in Figure 8-1. We note, however that there are at least three other patterns in this region. In Burkina Faso, Cameroon, Guinea, and Niger, one observes no change in the age distribution of first-time motherhood. In the Central African Republic and Chad, there is a crossover in the age distribution across cohorts. For the youngest cohort, women exhibit a lower probability of motherhood at young ages, compared with their older counterparts. Finally, in Mali there is a decline in the average age at transition to motherhood.

We have adapted Winsborough's (1978) definition of the duration of a transition specifically as the numbers of years separating the age at which a quarter of women become first-time mothers and the age at which three-quarters of women become first-time mothers (i.e., the age difference for the interquartile range). Using this approach, comparing women born in the 1950s with women born in the 1960s, the duration of the transition to parenthood has remained about the same for most regions but has widened slightly in Latin America and substantially in the Middle East (see Figure 8-2).[1] The diversity across regions remains striking, however, with almost 8 years separating the first and the third quartiles in the Middle East and South America and only four years separating these two quartiles in the former Soviet Asia. Thus, in the Middle East and South America, there is much greater diversity among women in the timing of first motherhood than in other regions. These comparisons are not possible for the youngest cohort because, by this definition, the transition to motherhood for this cohort is still incomplete.

The duration of the earlier portion of the transition to motherhood as measured by the difference in ages between the first and second quartiles has remained remarkably stable over the past 20 years in sub-Saharan Africa, but there has been a small increase in Latin America and the Caribbean and Southern Asia (see Table 8-2). It is likely that the duration of the early part of the transition is also becoming longer in the Middle East as

---

[1]This is a measure first used by Winsborough (1978) to describe trends in the duration of various transitions for young men in the United States, including exit from school, entrance into the labor market, entrance into the military, and first marriage.

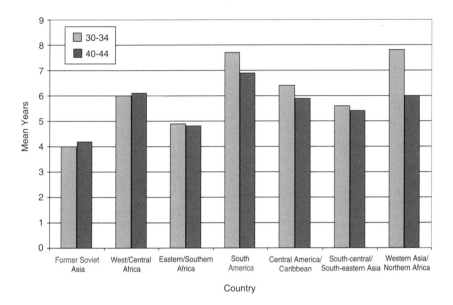

FIGURE 8-2 Changes in duration of transition to first motherhood: Difference in years between age at first quartile and third quartile of age distribution.
SOURCE: Demographic and Health Surveys.

well, but a full comparison is not possible because less than 50 percent of the youngest cohort has had their first child.

## EARLY CHILDBEARING

Parenthood's demanding and enduring obligations, its potential to limit human capital accumulation, and its far-reaching consequences have led scholars and policy makers to be concerned about "premature" transitions to parenthood (Luker, 1996; Nathanson, 1991). The term "adolescent parenthood" is often used to connote parenthood that takes place: (1) before young women are physiologically mature enough for safe motherhood; and (2) before an age when young people have typically acquired the full complement of skills, experience, and social network connections that will enable them to perform the role of parent well and to fulfill the other obligations of adulthood to the best of their ability.

Before commencing our discussion of early childbearing, we remind the reader that our conceptual framework defines adolescent parenthood in historically and geographically specific ways. The ideal approach would be to reflect in each specific context on how the distal and proximate settings

(Boxes B and C of Figure 2-1) shape the opportunities for young people to acquire the stocks of human and social capital that they need for successful adulthood (Box D of Figure 2-1). This conceptualization leads to a context-specific definition of premature parenthood as parenthood that occurs at an age prior to the age at which most young people in that setting typically complete the minimal level of human capital accumulation.

The need for comparative analyses, however, has led the panel to choose two cutoffs to define adolescent parenthood: parenthood before age 18—the age of adulthood as defined by the UN Convention on the Rights of the Child—and parenthood before age 16. The latter of these, for young women, may be a legitimate absolute indicator of premature parenthood, since it is possible that pregnancy and birth before this age are dangerous to the mother and to the child for reasons that are biological and do not vary by setting or culture.

### Trends in Early Childbearing

Table 8-3 presents data by region on the percentage of young women who become mothers by age 16 and by age 18. We focus the comparison on the differences between women born in the 1950s (women ages 40-44 in the table), women born in the 1960s (women ages 30-34 in the table), and women born in the 1970s (women ages 20-24 in the table).

The first thing to observe from the table is that over 10 percent of young women still have their first child before the age of 16 in Western and Middle Africa. In other regions, levels of childbearing at this early age range from less than 1 percent in the former Soviet Asia to almost 9 percent in Eastern and Southern Africa and in South Asia. Furthermore, in Western and Middle Africa, the percentage among the youngest cohort still having their first child below age 18 is over 30 percent. Substantial percentages persist for women having a first birth before age 18 in most regions, with over 20 percent in Southern Asia, Central America and the Caribbean, and Eastern and Southern Africa and 16 percent in South America.

The next thing to notice is that the pace of decline in rates of first parenthood by age varies dramatically across regions but is more similar within regions regardless of whether age 16 or age 18 is chosen as the critical measure of early parenthood. Among regions in which the percentage having very early first births (whether by 16 or 18) was substantial among the oldest cohort—Western and Middle Africa, Eastern and Southern Africa, and Southern Asia—declines have been largest in absolute terms and among the largest in percentage terms. In the Middle East, the declines have been largest in percentage terms, having started from a much lower base. In South America, where rates of early motherhood for the older cohort were much lower in comparative terms, there has been an actual

TABLE 8-3 Percentage of Women Giving Birth by Age 16 and by Age 18—Weighted Regional and Income Averages, DHS Countries

| Region or Income Level | Birth by Age 16 | | | Birth by Age 18 | | |
|---|---|---|---|---|---|---|
| | 20-24 | 30-34 | 40-44 | 20-24 | 30-34 | 40-44 |
| Region | | | | | | |
| Africa | | | | | | |
| Eastern/Southern Africa | 8.5 | 13.3 | 16.0 | 26.9 | 34.3 | 38.4 |
| Western/Middle Africa | 13.4 | 18.6 | 20.6 | 30.9 | 36.3 | 38.6 |
| Asia | | | | | | |
| South-central/South-eastern Asia | 9.3 | 12.0 | 13.8 | 24.2 | 31.1 | 32.1 |
| Former Soviet Asia | 0.2 | 0.2 | 0.2 | 4.1 | 2.9 | 3.5 |
| Latin America and Caribbean | | | | | | |
| Caribbean/Central America | 6.8 | 8.2 | 8.7 | 21.7 | 23.2 | 24.0 |
| South America | 4.3 | 3.7 | 3.4 | 16.3 | 14.4 | 12.3 |
| Middle East | | | | | | |
| Western Asia/Northern Africa | 3.1 | 5.5 | 6.5 | 11.2 | 18.1 | 20.8 |
| Income Level[a] | | | | | | |
| Low | 9.9 | 13.2 | 15.2 | 25.8 | 32.6 | 34.2 |
| Lower Middle | 2.9 | 4.0 | 5.1 | 11.3 | 14.3 | 16.1 |
| Upper Middle | 3.9 | 4.4 | 3.4 | 15.5 | 16.1 | 14.2 |
| TOTAL—All DHS | 8.5 | 11.3 | 12.9 | 23.1 | 28.9 | 30.2 |

[a]World Bank income classifications.

NOTE: For source of regional groupings and population data for weighted averages, see Table 8-1. Further detail can be found in Appendix A.

SOURCE: Demographic and Health Surveys tabulations, see Appendix Table 8-6 for data from each country.

increase in the percentage having a birth by age 18 from 12 to 16 percent. And in the former Soviet Asia, the percentage experiencing early parenthood remains extremely low (whether measured by age 16 or 18) with little further decline possible.

When the country data are aggregated by income level rather than region (bottom panel of Table 8-3), one sees that the percentage of women who became mothers by age 16 is nearly 3 times higher in low-income than in middle-income countries, but it has declined in the lower two income groups and increased in the high-middle-income group of countries (composed mostly of countries in Latin America), although remaining at a very low level. Similar patterns are apparent for the percentage of young women who become mothers by age 18. There has thus been some narrowing of the range of first parenthood experience across regions.

Table 8-4 provides information on educational and residential differentials in the percentage who become mothers by age 18 (the patterns are similar for the percentage becoming mothers by age 16 and therefore are not shown separately).[2] We chose broad educational groupings so as to assure sufficient sample sizes in each category.[3] Here we note that, in every region of the world, premature motherhood occurs much more often among young women who have low levels of schooling rather than higher levels of schooling and more often among rural women than urban women. For young women with less than four years of schooling, the percentage becoming a mother before age 18 currently ranges from 21 percent in the Middle East to 48 percent in Western and Central Africa.

In addition, Panel A of Table 8-4 gives some insight into how the changes we described in Table 8-3 have occurred differentially by educational background and residential status. With respect to differential trends by educational attainment, marked declines in the percentage who make the transition to motherhood by 18 are apparent in Western and Middle Africa, Eastern and Southern Africa and South Asia for all but the least educated group. In the Middle East, the overall decline occurred among the two less educated groups. In South America, the increase in the percentage who become mothers before age 18 occurred across all educational groups, while in Central America and the Caribbean the overall decline in the percentage who are mothers by age 18 masks an increase in

---

[2]A small percentage of young women ages 20-24 are still attending school (see Table 3-1) and therefore their education is not yet complete. Because motherhood typically interrupts schooling, those having a birth prior to age 18 are able to accumulate fewer years of schooling.

[3]Nonetheless, we recognize that in some regions, certain educational groupings can become highly selective, with the degree of selectivity varying across cohorts. Thus these comparisons, while interesting, have to be interpreted with caution.

this percentage among the lower two educational groups. The very different trends in early childbearing by school levels across regions underscores how the social context—even when measured as crudely as world region—modifies the effects of individual-level characteristics (such as schooling) on the transition to adulthood. In particular, not only is it likely that these crude schooling categories represent different things in different places but also that factors other than schooling are differentially important in different settings.

In Panel B of Table 8-4 we can see that for all regions of the developing world, whatever the direction of the overall change in the prevalence of early childbearing, the trends for women from both rural and urban areas were in a consistent direction. However, in regions experiencing declines, the absolute size of the declines were greater in urban than rural areas in sub-Saharan Africa and Southern Asia, leading to a widening gap between urban and rural areas in the prevalence of early parenthood in these regions. Early parenthood, however, remains a much more common phenomenon in rural areas. Urban-rural differentials in the percentage having a child before age 18 are particularly dramatic in Western and Middle Africa and in South-central and South-eastern Asia, where there are 14 percentage point differentials between rates of early childbearing in urban and rural areas. Unfortunately, we are not able to present differentials by household wealth, because household wealth is measured at the time of the survey and the births have occurred at various points in the past.

## Consequences of Early Childbearing

### Health Consequences of Early Childbearing

As previously discussed in Chapter 4, the evidence on the age pattern of maternal mortality is conflicting. While some evidence suggests that first parenthood below age 18 or 20 may carry more health risks than first parenthood at slightly older ages, other data suggest that the risks, if they exist at all, are more likely to be concentrated at younger ages (e.g., ages 15-16). Despite these uncertainties in the evidence, popular concern about childbearing below age 18 tends to focus on maternal health concerns (e.g., Save the Children, 2004; United Nations, 2004).

While more evidence is needed on whether adolescent mothers experience poorer outcomes than do older mothers, it is critical to note, particularly for health policy and programs, that maternal morbidity and mortality in the developing world for women at any age, including adolescents, are greatly influenced by poverty, poor nutrition, and limited access to medical services for problems of pregnancy and delivery. The data presented in Table 8-4 indicate that a higher percentage of rural and less well educated

TABLE 8-4 Percentage of Women Giving Birth by Age 18, by Years of Schooling, and Residence, DHS Countries

| | Ages 20-24 | | | Ages 40-44 | | |
|---|---|---|---|---|---|---|
| | Years of Schooling | | | Years of Schooling | | |
| Panel A | 0-3 | 4-7 | 8+ | 0-3 | 4-7 | 8+ |
| Region | | | | | | |
| Africa | | | | | | |
| Eastern/Southern Africa | 39.5 | 32.0 | 11.3 | 42.5 | 37.8 | 17.3 |
| Western/Middle Africa | 47.6 | 28.4 | 10.0 | 42.1 | 37.1 | 17.6 |
| Asia[a] | | | | | | |
| South-central/South-eastern Asia | 34.2 | 24.4 | 7.1 | 34.3 | 31.0 | 13.8 |
| Latin America and Caribbean | | | | | | |
| Caribbean/Central America | 38.4 | 27.7 | 7.5 | 31.5 | 19.4 | 7.7 |
| South America | 34.6 | 21.3 | 6.6 | 19.4 | 13.5 | 3.5 |
| Middle East[b] | | | | | | |
| Western Asia/Northern Africa | 20.9 | 11.3 | 2.1 | 28.9 | 19.6 | 2.6 |
| Income Level[c] | | | | | | |
| Low | 39.9 | 27.7 | 8.9 | 40.2 | 36.0 | 16.5 |
| Lower Middle | 26.6 | 17.5 | 3.8 | 24.9 | 18.7 | 4.7 |
| Upper Middle | 32.9 | 21.4 | 7.8 | 22.3 | 14.7 | 4.1 |

| Panel B | Ages 20-24 | | Ages 40-44 | |
|---|---|---|---|---|
| | Rural | Urban | Rural | Urban |
| Region | | | | |
| Africa | | | | |
| Eastern/Southern Africa | 29.7 | 20.9 | 39.0 | 33.7 |
| Western/Middle Africa | 35.8 | 21.4 | 40.5 | 34.2 |
| Asia | | | | |
| South-central/South-eastern Asia | 28.6 | 13.2 | 34.9 | 25.5 |
| Former Soviet Asia | 4.7 | 3.6 | 4.1 | 2.6 |
| Latin America and Caribbean | | | | |
| Caribbean/Central America | 28.7 | 16.4 | 29.2 | 19.5 |
| South America | 23.8 | 14.2 | 15.8 | 11.2 |
| Middle East | | | | |
| Western Asia/Northern Africa | 14.5 | 8.1 | 25.3 | 17.8 |
| | | | | |
| Income Level[c] | | | | |
| Low | 30.1 | 15.3 | 36.5 | 27.6 |
| Lower Middle | 16.5 | 8.4 | 20.5 | 13.0 |
| Upper Middle | 20.7 | 13.7 | 16.5 | 13.4 |

[a]Countries from former Soviet Asia are excluded from this table because the majority of respondents have completed eight or more years of education. Also excluded are India and Pakistan because they lack the all women weight.

[b]Yemen excluded; it lacks the all women weight.

[c]World Bank income classifications.

NOTES: For source of regional groupings and population data for weighted averages, see Table 8-1. Further detail can be found in Appendix A.

SOURCE: Demographic and Health Surveys tabulations, see Appendix Tables 8-4a and 8-4b for data from each country.

women give birth as children, and these are the women who are most likely to be poor. Young women in impoverished settings are likely to be less well nourished and to be still completing physical growth in the late teens; for adolescent mothers in these settings, these factors are linked to increased risk of obstructed labor and of such complications as obstetric fistula during delivery (Senderowitz, 1995).[4]

The research on adverse reproductive outcomes affecting the infant is more definitive. For example, analyses of longitudinal data for more than 20,000 live births in the early 1980s in urban areas of Mali and Burkina Faso reveal that pregnancies to women under age 18 were associated with lower birthweight and greater mortality, particularly during the second year of life (LeGrand and Mbacké, 1993). Retrospective analysis of clinical records from 15,207 women who gave birth in 1989 in an urban hospital in Mozambique also found significant differences in the birthweights of infants born to teenage mothers compared with older mothers and greater likelihood of obstetric complications (Bacci, et al., 1993). Analysis of over 8,000 life births between 1990 and 1992 in Matlab, Bangladesh, found a significantly higher rate of neonatal mortality among teenage mothers (Alam, 2000). The average infant mortality rate for infants born to mothers under 20 was 100 (per 1,000 live births) compared with rates of 72 and 74 among mothers ages 20-29 and 30-39, and 94 among mothers ages 40-49, based on 49 countries with DHS surveys (Alan Guttmacher Institute, 2002).

Yet even in the presence of such findings, some social scientists remain skeptical. Geronimus (1987) argues that the background factors controlled for in most analyses fail to account for unobserved heterogeneity. In particular, she argues that women who give birth at a young age are selected for certain social characteristics that predispose them to having poorer outcomes. While there may indeed be some intrinsic risk associated with young maternal age, the consensus seems to be that, holding other factors (such as poverty and nutritional status) constant, except for teens younger than age 15 or 16, "if young pregnant women have access to . . . programs and use them, their health and their chances of delivering a healthy baby improve to levels almost on a par with those of older women" (Senderowitz, 1995:19). A study of over 5,000 teenage mothers who delivered in 1994 in a Hong Kong hospital found that, even in the presence of preterm labor, which is more common among teenagers, neonatal outcomes are favorable if adequate antenatal care is available (Lao and Ho, 1997).

---

[4]Indeed, in developed countries, cephalopelvic disproportion is extremely uncommon even among very young mothers, because nutrition is adequate, physical development is achieved during the early teen years, and there is access to adequate medical care during delivery, especially cesarean section (Zabin and Kiragu, 1998).

## Social and Economic Consequences of Early Childbearing

McCauley and Salter (1995:16), in a population report entitled "Meeting the Needs of Young Adults" that focuses primarily on developing country adolescents, state: "For young women just beginning their adult lives, the risks of childbearing do not end with delivery. Compared with a woman who delays childbearing until her 20s, the woman who has her first child before age 20 is more likely to: obtain less education, have fewer job possibilities and lower income, be divorced or separated from her partner, and live in poverty."

Implicit here is the suggestion that early childbearing *causes* negative outcomes. While this is certainly a plausible hypothesis, there is insufficient evidence to make this assertion. Not only is the research from the developing world on the social and economic impact of adolescent childbearing extremely thin, but, more importantly, the few studies that exist lack statistical rigor. In order to adequately assess the consequences of adolescent fertility, it is critical to address selection bias, namely that those who give birth as teens differ fundamentally from those who delay. Yet, to the best of our knowledge, no developing country study has effectively done this.

Mayra Buvinic, one of the few researchers to investigate the consequences of adolescent childbearing in the developing world, acknowledges that her studies in Barbados, Chile, Guatemala, and Mexico "were not able to separate clearly the differences due to individual factors and the event of childbearing itself" (Buvinic, 1998:202). For the most part, Buvinic and others (Alatorre and Atkin, 1998; Engle and Smidt, 1996; Russell-Brown, Engle, and Townsend, 1992) used retrospective data to compare adolescent mothers regardless of marital status to women who had their first birth at age 20 or older. While they did not investigate the effects of early childbearing on educational attainment, they did investigate economic consequences and consequences for marriage.

These researchers found that, on a variety of measures, those who gave birth during adolescence were in worse shape economically than those who delayed childbearing. In Mexico, where a sample of women who initiated childbearing between 1987 and 1989 in a major hospital in Mexico City were followed up four years after their first birth, mothers who gave birth before age 18 were six times more likely to live in poverty compared with women who gave birth for the first time at age 21 or later.

In Chile, using retrospective data from Santiago, a sample of women first interviewed in 1990 who had a child ages 5 to 9, were reinterviewed in 1991. For analysis purposes the sample was divided into poor and nonpoor women. Among the poor women, controlling for schooling but not for years in the labor force, those who gave birth at 19 or younger had significantly lower wages than those who gave birth after age 20. The issue of the potential endogeneity of adolescent childbearing and wages was not addressed, however; in addition, the analysis failed to control for the fact that women who work in this setting are a selective group. Buvinic also noted that adolescent childbearing in Mexico and Guatemala (for which she analyzed retrospective data on 850 women collected in 1967, 1974, and 1988) was significantly associated with poverty status measured by an index of housing quality in the two countries and socioeconomic status in Mexico. Although economic status as a child was controlled, it is not clear whether economic status immediately prior to childbirth was accounted for.

It is interesting that in none of the four countries Buvinic studied did adolescent childbearing affect marital status. Those who gave birth early were as likely to marry in subsequent years, although in Chile (where this issue was explored) those who gave birth in their 20s were significantly more likely to be living with the father of the child five years after the birth.

Another study in Nigeria compares the life course of adult Yoruba women who had a birth in adolescence regardless of marital status with those who delayed childbearing into their 20s (Omololu, 1994). Compared with women who had their first child in their 20s, women who had their first birth during their adolescent years were more likely to have more children by the time of the survey, more likely to be second wives, and more likely to receive assistance from parents. The author argues that in many cases, partners and families of orientation were unsupportive, contributing to the higher levels of poverty among adolescent mothers compared with others. Social adjustment during pregnancy and in the first year of birth in southwest Nigeria was characterized by an end to schooling, difficult parental relations, and peer difficulties for the adolescent mother.

A prospective study in Forteleza, Brazil of young women experiencing early pregnancy compares those who sought prenatal care from a clinic with those who sought postabortion care. Preliminary findings suggest that while sociodemographic characteristics of the two groups were relatively similar, adolescents who continued the pregnancy were more likely than those who opted for abortion to have dropped out of school as a result of the pregnancy. Yet those who underwent induced abortion reported significantly lower levels of self-esteem, a difference attributed in part to the circumstances surrounding the unwanted pregnancy and abortion seeking in this setting, in which abortion is legally restricted. While these differences continued to be manifested at one and five years following the pregnancy, they had narrowed considerably by year five; about three-fifths of young women in both groups reported high self-esteem, and about one-third were still students (Bailey and Bruno, 2001).

While the findings from these studies are suggestive, they are, as noted above, far from definitive. In the absence of study designs that control for confounding factors that are both a cause and consequence of early child-bearing, it is not possible to assess the short-term and long-term effects of adolescent childbearing.

## THE SEQUENCING OF PARENTHOOD WITH MARRIAGE

Although parenthood continues to occur largely within a socially recognized union (typically marriage) regardless of age, most literature about first parenthood focuses on premarital childbearing, with a particular focus on adolescents (a topic we will return to). However, given that marital childbearing remains the most typical pattern (Mensch, Bruce, and Greene, 1998), we start this discussion of sequencing of parenthood within marriage by considering the timing of first birth within marriage.

First to set the context, however, we explore trends in the proportion of births that occur after union formation or marriage (Table 8-5).[5] For this analysis, we do not distinguish between premarital and postmarital conceptions, because we are interested in the social context in which the birth occurs, not the social context in which the conception occurs. Overall, among 20-24-year-olds, 91 percent of young women have their first birth after marriage. The decline has been very slight in the last 20 years. Patterns vary substantially by region, however, as do trends. For those countries in the Middle East and Asia, where data were collected only on married women, we have to assume that unmarried women have not given birth; thus any premarital births that are captured in the data are those reported by women who are currently married. The proportion of births that occur within marriage varies from a low of 70 percent in Eastern and Southern Africa and 74 percent in South America to highs of 97 percent in Southern Asia and close to 100 percent in the Middle East. There is also an inverse correlation between a country's level of income and the proportion of births that occur within marriage.

Premarital births represent a rising proportion of births in Eastern and Southern Africa, South America, and in upper middle-income countries (Table 8-5). There was much greater homogeneity across regions 20 years ago than there is today in the proportion of births that occur within marriage. A discussion of trends in the percentage of young women having a birth premartially and the implications of out-of-wedlock motherhood fol-

---

[5]As previously explained in Chapter 7, in data from the DHS, marriage is a self-defined state. Respondents are coded as married if they say so in response to questions on whether they are currently or ever married or are living with a man. Thus age at first marriage is typically age at first cohabitation with a partner or husband (Kishor, 2003).

TABLE 8-5 Percentage of Births That Occur Within Marriage, of All Births, DHS Countries

| Region or Income Level | After Marriage | | | Marital Births That Occur Within First 7 Months of Marriage | | |
|---|---|---|---|---|---|---|
| | 20-24 | 30-34 | 40-44 | 20-24 | 30-34 | 40-44 |
| Region | | | | | | |
| Africa | | | | | | |
| Eastern/Southern Africa | 69.9 | 73.9 | 79.2 | 14.9 | 15.3 | 15.5 |
| Western/Middle Africa | 81.9 | 83.9 | 84.0 | 15.8 | 15.3 | 16.9 |
| Asia | | | | | | |
| South-central/South-eastern Asia | 97.1 | 96.8 | 97.1 | 14.9 | 13.2 | 11.5 |
| Former Soviet Asia | 97.1 | 96.4 | 96.6 | 5.0 | 5.8 | 5.6 |
| Latin America and Caribbean | | | | | | |
| Caribbean/Central America | 88.6 | 90.8 | 89.8 | 11.1 | 13.0 | 12.2 |
| South America | 74.4 | 84.1 | 86.0 | 23.7 | 17.6 | 13.4 |
| Middle East | | | | | | |
| Western Asia/Northern Africa | 99.5 | 98.5 | 97.9 | 3.4 | 6.3 | 6.9 |
| Income Level[a] | | | | | | |
| Low | 93.3 | 93.5 | 94.2 | 14.5 | 13.4 | 12.5 |
| Lower Middle | 88.8 | 90.9 | 91.8 | 12.1 | 12.3 | 10.5 |
| Upper Middle | 72.4 | 81.3 | 83.7 | 19.8 | 15.1 | 11.6 |
| TOTAL—All DHS | 90.7 | 92.0 | 92.9 | 14.8 | 13.4 | 12.2 |

[a]World Bank income classifications.

NOTES: For source of regional groupings and population data for weighted averages, see Table 8-1. Further detail can be found in Appendix A.
SOURCES: Demographic and Health Surveys tabulations, see Appendix Table 8-5 for data from each country.

lows our discussion of trends in the first birth interval and the significance of the first marital birth.

## Trends in the First Birth Interval

The first birth interval is demographic jargon for the duration of the period between union formation and the first birth. Among women who give birth after marriage, the shorter the first birth interval, the tighter the association between marriage and first birth. Among women for whom the timing of marriage coincides with the timing of sexual debut, the first birth interval cannot be shorter than the normal gestational period of a pregnancy—typically nine months. Among women who are sexually experienced at the time of marriage, the act of getting married may be associated with readiness for childbirth or may even be triggered by pregnancy. Either way, short first birth intervals also connote a strong association between marriage and parenthood.

Table 8-6 presents data on the median number of months from marriage to first birth for those who married before their first birth by cohort, by region, and by country income level. The table reveals that the length of time between marriage and motherhood is declining all over the world. This is true in every region except former Soviet Asia and it is true for countries of all income levels. As a result of these changes, the variation across regions in the median length of the first birth interval is narrowing. Among women ages 40-44, the median length of the first birth interval ranged across regions from 13 to 26 months. Among the youngest cohort, the range had narrowed from a low of 14 months in former Soviet Asia to a high of 21 months in Western and Middle Africa. It is notable that first birth intervals as short as 14 to 16 months are now apparent in Latin America and the Caribbean, the Middle East, and former Soviet Asia. Twenty years ago, such short intervals were prevalent only in the countries of former Soviet Asia. While DHS data are not available on China, a steady and even more rapid decline in the length of the first birth interval had been documented by Feng and Quanhe (1996) using China's two per thousand Fertility and Birth Control Survey of 1988. They estimate that the first birth interval fell from an average of 22 months for the cohort marrying in 1970 to 16 months on average for the cohort marrying in 1986.

Young married women, then, are becoming mothers for the first time sooner after marriage or union formation than did women who are 20 years their senior. This shortening of the time between marriage and first birth is likely to be due to a combination of factors. First, the preference to begin family building soon after marriage clearly continues to be very strong, and this preference may have increased in strength in places in which women have begun to marry later. Indeed, marriages may be more likely now than

TABLE 8-6 Trends in Median Length of First Birth Interval Among Women Having Their First Birth After Marriage,[a] DHS Countries

| Region or Income Level | Median Birth Interval | | |
|---|---|---|---|
| | 20-24 | 30-34 | 40-44 |
| Region | | | |
| Africa | | | |
|   Eastern/Southern Africa | 18.2 | 24.1 | 25.6 |
|   Western/Middle Africa | 21.2 | 22.4 | 24.6 |
| Asia | | | |
|   South-central/South-eastern Asia | 19.3 | 20.2 | 22.9 |
|   Former Soviet Asia | 13.9 | 12.8 | 12.8 |
| Latin America and Caribbean | | | |
|   Caribbean/Central America | 15.3 | 16.3 | 16.7 |
|   South America | 15.4 | 18.2 | 17.0 |
| Middle East | | | |
|   Western Asia/Northern Africa | 15.8 | 17.5 | 21.8 |
| Income Level[b] | | | |
|   Low | 19.6 | 20.7 | 23.2 |
|   Lower Middle | 13.6 | 15.3 | 16.2 |
|   Upper Middle | 16.7 | 22.7 | 23.8 |
| TOTAL—All DHS | 18.6 | 20.3 | 22.5 |

[a]The birth interval is constructed from a life table and is restricted to all first births that occurred after marriage. Women who are married but have not yet given birth are censored at the date of their interview.

[b]Based on World Bank income classifications.

NOTES: For source of regional groupings and population data for weighted averages, see Table 8-1. Further detail can be found in Appendix A.

SOURCES: Demographic and Health Surveys tabulations, see Appendix Table 8-6 for data from each country.

in the past to be timed to coincide with readiness for parenthood and to be with partners who have established a romantic relationship.[6] Second, improvements in general health may have resulted in improved fecundity, especially in regions in which substantial proportions of women marry before age 16. Third, the proportion of women who are pregnant at the time of marriage may be on the rise in some settings. Finally, it is possible that, among women who were pregnant before they married, there is a

---

[6]Feng and Quanhe (1996) point out that in traditional China, when marriages were arranged, the initiation of sex was often delayed after marriage because of restrictions on the conduct of young married couples. The narrowing of the birth interval in China is partially attributed to increased sexual relations among newly married couples.

greater reluctance on the part of older women relative to younger women to report their marriage age accurately, thus differentially biasing estimates of the length of the first birth interval.

The extent to which first births that occur within marriage are the result of premarital conceptions can be approximated by looking at the proportion of first birth intervals that are less than 8 months in duration. The second panel of Table 8-5 shows an enormous range across regions in the prevalence of short birth intervals among the youngest women, from 24 percent in South America to 3 percent in the Middle East. The data also indicate a slight rise overall in the percentage of all first marital birth intervals that are shorter than 8 months, from 12 to 15 percent over the last 20 years. This rise is explained by the increase in the prevalence of short birth intervals in South America, from 13 to 24 percent over 20 years as well as the more modest but demographically significant rise in Southern Asia from 12 to 15 percent. The rise in Southern Asia is largely driven by the rise in India—which represents 59 percent of the population surveyed by the DHS in this region—from 16 to 20 percent. Data from China show an increase in the percent of marital births conceived premaritally from 1 to 5 percent from 1970 to 1988 (Feng and Quanhe, 1996).

An important implication of these findings is that many of the global changes that are affecting the timing of first marriage are also affecting the timing of first parenthood because of the very tight link between these two transitions. Despite evidence of premarital sexual activity and pregnancy, it is marriage or union formation that continues to define, for the most part, the timing of parenthood in the developing world. National survey data underscore a strong direct relationship between marriage and child-bearing: as age of marriage rises, age at first parenthood also rises. Thus, much of the discussion in Chapter 7 of factors affecting the timing of first marriage become equally salient to a discussion of trends in the age at first birth. In particular, it was shown that there is not as tight an association between trends in age of marriage and trends in education as one might expect, given the extensive literature documenting the strong cross-sectional association between years of schooling and marriage age. For example, while enrollment rates and labor force participation rates have risen substantially in Latin America for young people in their late teens and early 20s, there has been little change in the age of marriage or first parenthood. Similar trends in other regions have been associated with delayed marriage and childbearing.

## Significance of the First Marital Birth

In many settings, particularly in Asia and sub-Saharan Africa, women are expected to bear a child as soon as possible after marriage in order to

secure themselves in the marital home; infertility is deeply feared and results, for many women, in abandonment and mistreatment (Adepoju and
Mbugua, 1997; Jejeebhoy, 2000). A study in rural Maharashtra, India,
highlights the extent to which newly married young women face pressure to
begin childbearing as soon as possible after marriage (Barua and Kurz,
2001). In this study, fertility within a year of marriage was a prime concern
to young women and their husbands and mothers-in-law; any gynecological condition perceived to limit fertility prospects tended to receive prompt
treatment. Mothers-in-law strongly objected to any delay, and young
women themselves were motivated to have a child in the first year of
marriage to satisfy social obligations and strengthen their own position in
the marital family. This study was limited to brides between ages 15 and
19; we do not know whether older brides would face similar pressures.

In some contexts, a marriage does not receive full social recognition
until the arrival of the first birth or until the first pregnancy is celebrated.
Van Hollen (2003) describes the Seemantham ritual in Tamil Nadu, which
is performed in preparation for a woman's first delivery. This ceremony,
which was traditionally a way to celebrate and legitimize the marital union,
has been reinvented in a more modern guise, with the elaborate exchange of
gifts and display of conspicuous consumption, representing a final phase of
the economic exchanges associated with the marriage itself (Box 8-1).

### Trends in Premarital Childbearing

Chapter 4 documents the worldwide decline in age at menarche and
Chapter 7 describes the increase in the age at marriage or union formation.
These two facts together mean that, on average, there has been a worldwide
increase in the length of the period during which young people are exposed
to the risk of having premarital sex. And Chapter 4 provides evidence that
premarital sex prior to age 18 is increasing. But it is by no means a given
that increasing levels of sex before marriage are leading to increases in
premarital childbearing of the same magnitude. There are examples of
populations in which a strong taboo against becoming a parent outside
marriage persists even after norms forbidding sex outside marriage have
weakened; the most notable examples are Japan (Retherford, Ogawa, and
Matsukura, 2001) and several Central and Southern European countries
(Kiernan, 1999).

Table 8-7 shows trends in the percentage of young women having their
first birth before marriage across three cohorts for three ages marking
phases of the transition to adulthood: age 18, age 20, and age 25. The
overall level of premarital childbearing across all developing countries
remains very low, with no more than 5 percent of women having a pre-

**BOX 8-1**
**Celebrating a Woman's First Pregnancy in Tamil Nadu**

In Tamil Nadu, the Seemantham ceremony marks a woman's passage into motherhood and celebrates her fertility. Seemantham is a ritual performed widely throughout Tamil Nadu by Hindus, Muslims, and Christians in preparation for a woman's first delivery, and its primary functions are to satisfy the pregnant woman's *ācai* ("desire, craving, passion"), bless her, and ensure a safe delivery and a healthy baby. In her ethnography of childbearing in Tamil Nadu, Cecilia Van Hollen (2003) examines how processes of modernization have impacted the use of different birthing technologies and transformed reproductive rituals. Contrary to assumptions that as childbirth becomes increasingly modernized women will rely less on traditional birth practices and rituals, Van Hollen found that in Tamil Nadu, the modernization of childbirth and the intensification of birth-related rituals like Seemantham are occurring simultaneously. The nature and form of this ritual are being transformed, however, as market-led growth, rising consumerism, and other appendages of globalization take hold.

Seemantham has become much more elaborate and expensive, according to the women, scholars, and religious figures interviewed by Van Hollen. Food has always been a central feature of the ceremony, but the amount of food has multiplied and sweets have taken on a more important role. Expectant first-time mothers are now more likely to receive cash, gold, and consumer items, like household appliances, and in greater amounts. The husbands' families often request certain gifts, unlike in the past when guests brought gifts they had chosen. There is an increasing emphasis on displaying food and gifts at the Seemantham, which was not true in the past.

The reinvention of the Seemantham tradition is associated with the rising trend of conspicuous consumption that has occurred along with growing privatization and economic liberalization in Tamil Nadu and throughout Southern Asia. According to Van Hollen (2003:78), Seemantham has come to represent a "convergence of the desires for new consumer technologies and for the display of wealth through ritual," a trend that parallels the intensification of dowry practices throughout India. She discusses how these changes create a double burden for the families of first-time mothers: "The growing economic burden of Seemantham (and other ritual gifts associated with the reproductive continuum) was compounded by the fact that the pregnant woman's family in Tamil Nadu was also largely responsible for the medical expenses associated with childbirth. This was particularly true of the first delivery, since the pregnant woman almost always returned home for that delivery but not necessarily for consecutive deliveries" (p. 111).

In spite of the increasing financial burden of Seemantham, young women and their families continue to perform the Seemantham because it is tradition, and not doing so could hurt a family's prestige. Seemantham is also seen as a symbol of legitimacy of the marital union, a means to legitimize love marriages and resolve any familial conflict they incite. Van Hollen contends that as Seemantham is reinvented, it simultaneously increases social and economic burdens on families and reinforces the reverence for first-time mothers and their auspicious fertility.

TABLE 8-7 Trends in Percentage of Women Having First Birth Before Marriage (by Ages 18, 20, 25)—Weighted Regional and Income Averages, DHS Countries

| Region or Income level | Premarital Birth by Age 18 | | | Premarital Birth by Age 20 | | | Premarital Birth by Age 25 | |
|---|---|---|---|---|---|---|---|---|
| | 20-24 | 30-34 | 40-44 | 20-24 | 30-34 | 40-44 | 30-34 | 40-44 |
| Region | | | | | | | | |
| Africa | | | | | | | | |
| Eastern/Southern Africa | 8.0 | 8.9 | 7.3 | 14.5 | 14.8 | 11.5 | 21.0 | 16.4 |
| Western/Middle Africa | 5.7 | 7.0 | 8.1 | 8.0 | 9.1 | 10.6 | 11.6 | 12.5 |
| Asia | | | | | | | | |
| South-central/South-eastern Asia | 0.4 | 0.8 | 0.8 | 0.5 | 1.0 | 1.1 | 1.3 | 1.3 |
| Former Soviet Asia | 0.3 | 0.3 | 0.1 | 0.8 | 0.9 | 0.9 | 2.5 | 2.8 |
| Latin America and Caribbean | | | | | | | | |
| Caribbean/Central America | 2.8 | 2.3 | 4.0 | 4.2 | 4.2 | 5.7 | 6.8 | 8.3 |
| South America | 4.1 | 3.3 | 3.0 | 8.1 | 6.3 | 5.8 | 11.1 | 9.9 |
| Middle East | | | | | | | | |
| Western Asia/Northern Africa | 0.0 | 0.4 | 0.7 | 0.1 | 0.6 | 0.9 | 0.8 | 1.2 |
| Income Level[a] | | | | | | | | |
| Low | 1.7 | 2.3 | 2.3 | 2.6 | 3.2 | 3.1 | 4.1 | 3.8 |
| Lower Middle | 1.9 | 1.4 | 1.6 | 3.5 | 3.1 | 3.3 | 5.7 | 5.6 |
| Upper Middle | 5.0 | 5.1 | 4.1 | 9.7 | 9.2 | 7.4 | 14.7 | 12.5 |
| TOTAL—All DHS | 2.0 | 2.5 | 2.4 | 3.4 | 3.8 | 3.6 | 5.4 | 44.9 |

[a]World Bank income classifications.

NOTES: For source of regional groupings and population data for weighted averages, see Table 8-1. Further detail can be found in Appendix A.

SOURCES: Demographic and Health Surveys tabulations, see Appendix Table 8-7 for data from each country.

marital birth by the age of 25. However, these rates vary substantially across regions.

The proportion of all women ages 20-24 who had their first birth before marriage and before age 20 (including those who did so and who are still never-married) is a useful summary indicator of the prevalence of premarital childbearing. Comparison of younger and older women (women ages 20-24, 30-34, and 40-44) provides a measure of change in childbearing among unmarried adolescent women over the period of 20 years before the survey. Indeed, change in this indicator may have a great influence on perceptions of whether unmarried adolescent childbearing is prevalent or not.

Among all young women ages 20-24, a significant minority in most countries of sub-Saharan Africa and Latin America and the Caribbean become parents during their adolescent years, before entry into a union or marriage. This proportion is about 8-14 percent in sub-Saharan Africa and South America but lower in Central America and the Caribbean. The percentage giving birth prior to marriage has increased slightly in South America (from 6 percent among women ages 40-44 to 8 percent among women ages 20-24). The percentage giving birth prior to marriage and before age 20 has also increased in Eastern and Southern Africa (from 12 to 15 percent). At the same time, slight declines have occurred in the Caribbean (from 6 to 4 percent) and Western and Middle Africa (from 11 to 8 percent). However, none of these changes is large in absolute size.

Compared with low-income and lower middle-income countries, premarital childbearing in the upper middle-income group of countries is somewhat higher, and the level has increased slightly over the past two decades. In the late 1990s, about 10 percent of women had a child before marriage and before age 20 in the upper middle-income group of countries, compared with 3-4 percent in the other two income categories.

Figure 8-3 shows the range of prevalence of premarital childbearing among women born in the 1960s and 1970s and the extent to which there has been an increase among the young women in the sample. Most rates cluster well below 10 percent. Another group of countries, mainly countries in Eastern and Southern Africa, have rates in the 10 to 20 percent range. A few from the same region have rates of 30 percent or above. In most but not all countries, there have been increases in the last 10 years, but these increases have been very small.

## Implications of Premarital Childbearing

Concerns about the consequences of premarital childbearing arise because the birth occurs outside the social support structure provided by marriage and therefore often without the support of the baby's father and

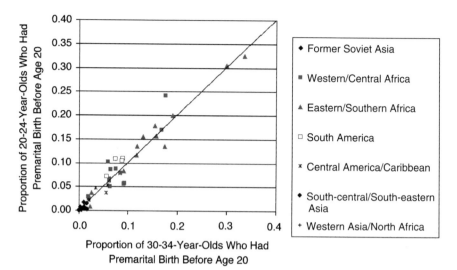

FIGURE 8-3 Change in percentage of young women having premarital birth by age 20.
SOURCE: Demographic and Health Surveys.


his family and sometimes without the support of the girl's family as well. Never-married adolescent mothers are much more likely than married adolescent mothers to report that their recent birth was unplanned (i.e., unwanted or mistimed). In most countries, this difference is very large—often the proportion is twice as high among unmarried mothers, half or more of whom report that the birth was unplanned in 22 of the 27 countries in Singh's (1998) review. Many are concerned about the situation of women who make the transition to motherhood both at a young age and before marriage. If being young and unmarried places mothers at risk, the reasoning goes, then young women with both characteristics are particularly likely to have an unsuccessful transition to adulthood. For developing countries, in societies in which the levels of premarital sexual activity are moderate and on the increase, but where taboos against nonmarital motherhood remain strong, becoming a mother as an unmarried woman constitutes a barrier to successful adulthood. Whether or not becoming a mother outside marriage is a barrier to adult success in these populations is therefore a question that merits investigation by researchers and, if it is found to be so, the attention of policy makers.

In some settings, however, particularly in sub-Saharan Africa, childbirth confers on teenagers the valued status of motherhood. Indeed, parenthood can be seen as an acceptable pathway to adult status in cases in which marriage is either unlikely or delayed by lack of money or other resources (Nsamenang, 2002). Among the Turkana, a group that remains traditional and relatively untouched by the forces of modernization in Kenya, premarital childbearing is socially acceptable (Shell-Duncan and Wimmer, 1999). When a premarital birth occurs, the father typically pays a set fee to the mother's family and custody of the child remains permanently with the mother's family. If the young parents later decide to wed, the father must purchase custody of the child for an additional fee.

Van Driel (1996) notes with reference to Botswana that the stigma of premarital childbearing appears to be disappearing with the rise in its prevalence, compared with the old days, when "the child of an unmarried girl who was not betrothed would often be killed at birth or live a life full of humiliation and insults" (p. 58).

In other contexts, unmarried adolescent motherhood is viewed as very undesirable by parents and the community. In a study in Nigeria (Aina and Odebiyi, 2000) focus group discussions with community members revealed a lack of empathy with unmarried young mothers and a tendency to associate their status as unmarried mothers with such factors as unstable or broken homes, family poverty, uneducated parents, and rape or harassment. In Cameroon, while having a premarital birth may make marriages more likely in the short run, it significantly jeopardizes a single woman's marriage chances in the long run (Calvès, 1999). In some communities, such as the Gusii of Kenya, single mothers continue to be socially and economically marginalized with respect to their kin groups. Despite the increasing prevalence of consensual unions and out-of-wedlock births among the Gusii, unwed mothers are still considered an embarrassment to the clan (Hakansson, 1994).

Stern (1995) shows that, in Mexico, early, unmarried parenthood takes on different meanings for young people from different sociocultural backgrounds. Among traditional rural settings, adolescents tend to have few life choices, and existing norms support adolescent motherhood as an accepted starting point for the formation of a family. The marginal urban sector is also characterized by relatively high levels of early, unmarried childbearing, but in this group, family support for adolescent motherhood is much more variable, and young women perceive pregnancy and motherhood as one means of escaping parental controls or family instability. Among lower class and lower middle-class urban families, in contrast, most parents and their adolescent children have high aspirations for increased education and livelihood options, and these are perceived as incompatible with early, unmarried parenthood; as a result, when they do occur, pregnancy and parenthood among adolescents are seen as an unexpected event limiting aspirations of upward social mobility, and efforts are made to postpone these transitions. Finally, young people from middle- and upper middle-class families who have high educational aspirations and remain economically and socially dependent on their parents into their 20s tend to have greater skills in negotiation, are better able to exercise contraceptive and reproductive choices, and if pregnancy occurs, are more likely than other groups to have planned it.

A creative way to avoid the social consequences of early childbearing among young women who are motivated to continue their education is described by Johnson-Hanks (2002) in her ethnography of motherhood among young educated Beti women in Cameroon (see Box 8-2). By delaying the assumption of the socially recognized role of mother, transferring major child care responsibilities to grandparents and other kin and remaining in school, young women are able to continue their preparation for adulthood before taking on the social status of mother. Kaufman, de Wet, and Stadler (2000) report that in South Africa, where premarital childbearing is also common, parents are willing to support their daughter's schooling even after childbirth, because young women who are educated tend to bring more bridewealth. As a result the second birth, and official parenthood, tends to be delayed until after marriage which does not take place until schooling is completed.

The establishment and social recognition of paternity are often problematic when birth occurs outside marriage. One reason is that paternal recognition can jeopardize further education and training for young men because it requires the payment of damages and the provision of financial support (Kaufman, de Wet and Stadler, 2000). In Osun state, Nigeria, the phenomenon of a supportive partner was found to be so rare in the case of a premarital birth that the original study design, to compare adolescent mothers with unsupportive partners with those having supportive ones, had to be abandoned, since only two such adolescents could be found (Aina and Odebiyi, 2000). In Cameroon, about a third of children born out of wedlock in the study area were not recognized by the biological father, with the consequence that financial support was not provided (Calvès, 2000).

## FACTORS AFFECTING THE CHANGING CONTEXT OF FIRST PARENTHOOD

Many of the changes noted in earlier chapters are changing the context in which decisions about first-time parenthood are being made as well as the experience of it. In this section, we discuss the implications of some of these changes for transitions to parenthood. In particular, we focus on some of the possible implications for first parenthood of a rise in school enrollment rates during the teens and early 20s, a rise in young women's participation in the labor force, changes in health and health behaviors, and changes in access to and use of prenatal and delivery services.

**BOX 8-2**
**Postponing Motherhood Until the Second Child Among Educated Young Beti Women in Southern Cameroon**

Jennifer Johnson-Hanks' (2002) ethnography of motherhood among young, educated Beti women in Southern Cameroon explores the complex relationship between student and motherhood roles. Beti schoolgirls who become pregnant often face disrespect by others and feelings of shame. The stigma of schoolgirl pregnancy is not tied to negative perceptions of premarital sex, but to the characterization of pregnant schoolgirls as unprepared for motherhood, uneducated, and undisciplined. Many Beti women believe that a first birth should take place in the context of marriage, and marriage and first birth should follow getting an education and establishing one's career. The shame associated with schoolgirl pregnancy comes in part from the expectation that these girls will drop out of school once their baby is born, cutting short their trajectory toward a successful life that includes a stable livelihood and household.

However, Johnson-Hanks found that the majority of girls in secondary school who became pregnant stayed in school for at least a year after giving birth. In fact, she found no discernible correlation among the 184 Beti women she interviewed between early childbearing and age at marriage, first employment, or school leaving. Using the example of a young Beti woman named Marie, Johnson-Hanks illustrates the point that Beti women can effectively postpone socially recognized motherhood and continue their schooling after the first birth.

Marie left school to give birth to her first child. At her father's insistence and in order to avoid a "shameful entry into motherhood," Marie went to live with the family of her child's father and deliver her baby. After some time, Marie found living in her in-laws' home intolerable and longed to go back to her own family and continue her studies. She returned to her father's home, leaving her son with his father's family, and subsequently relinquished her rights to claim him as her child. Marie returned to school and rarely saw or spoke of her child. Johnson-Hanks (2002:876) observes, "Her childbearing career will begin when she bears another child, with a man she intends to marry, at some later point in her educational and professional trajectory. She has been effectively relieved of any stigma from, or even connection to, her premarital birth, regularly referring to herself as an adolescent girl (*ngon*)."

Since it is the status of being a mother that potentially disrupts a woman's schooling among the Beti, a woman's first birth doesn't necessarily end her schooling career. "The locally perceived conflict between schooling and childbearing applies not to all births but only in situations in which the biological mother is socially recognized as a mother. . . . Schooling and childbearing are neither mutually exclusive nor strictly ordered; the one-time mother again becomes a girl when she dons the school uniform" (p. 874).

First births are often distinct from subsequent births for Beti women. As Johnson-Hanks observed, "Beti women who have borne children are not necessarily mothers" in their eyes or the eyes of local society, nor have they made the transition to adulthood by giving birth—they can still be considered girls.

## Rise in School Enrollment Among Adolescents

Many empirical studies show a negative relationship between education and fertility and in particular between educational attainment and the timing of the first birth in developing countries (e.g., Choe, Thapa, and Achmad, 2001; Gupta and da Costa Leite, 1999; Gupta and Khan, 1995; Welti, 2002). Both outcomes stem from a common set of causes: declines in family size, a rise in parental schooling, and rising rates of return to higher levels of schooling and rapid urbanization. While some young mothers find ways to continue in school, childbearing or marriage often mark the end of schooling. Figure 8-4 shows the relationship between enrollment and fertility among young women ages 15-19 in developing regions. While on average fertility among young women is much lower in countries in which enrollment rates remain high, countries with similar enrollment rates show substantial variation in the percentage of 15-19-year-old women who have had a birth. This largely reflects a substantial variation across countries in levels of early fertility among the nonenrolled because, with a few exceptions, women still find it difficult to combine schooling and motherhood, even when allowed to return (see further discussion under the section on policies and programs).

With a rising percentage of young women attending school after the age of puberty, however, a growing percentage of them are exposed to pregnancy while attending school. Evidence presented in Chapter 4 established that adolescent girls who attend school are half as likely as their unmarried peers who are out of school to have ever had sex. Nonetheless, with more of them attending school during ages when they are risk of . pregnancy, it is likely that an increasing percentage of births among young women will occur to those who became pregnant while attending school.

In Figure 8-5, we show a scatter plot of country-level data on the proportion of 15-19-year-olds currently enrolled in school and the proportion of those who had had a birth by age 18 who gave pregnancy as the reason for dropping out of school. The figure is based on data from the 28 DHS surveys conducted since 1995 that included questions on reasons for dropout.[7] The figure shows that the greater the level of enrollment in a country, the more likely it is that young mothers in that country give pregnancy as a reason for school dropout. Obviously, if enrollment rates are very low at this age, relatively few young women will have attended school at a time when pregnancy was even a potential cause of dropout. This is clearly the case for countries with enrollment rates below 20 percent

---

[7]These include 19 countries in sub-Saharan Africa as well as Bolivia, Brazil, Colombia, Dominican Republic, Guatemala, Kazakhstan, Nicaragua, Peru, and the Philippines.

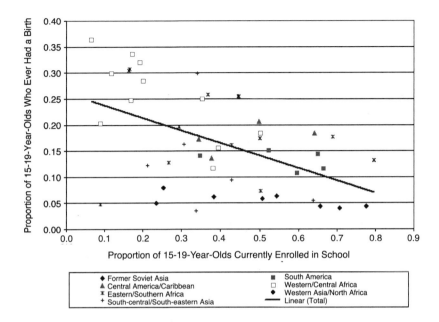

FIGURE 8-4 Current school enrollment and childbearing, 15-19-year-olds.
SOURCE: Demographic and Health Surveys.

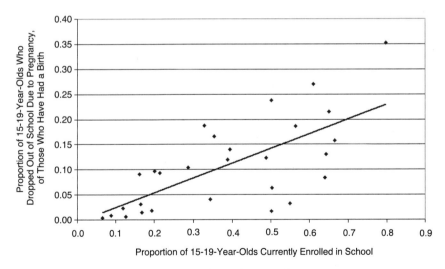

FIGURE 8-5 School enrollment and school dropout due to pregnancy, 15-19-year-olds.
SOURCE: Demographic and Health Surveys.

at this age. As enrollment rates rise, the chance that the timing of pregnancy and school dropout will coincide becomes much greater. Nonetheless, among countries with an enrollment rate of 50 percent or more for this age group, the relative importance of schoolgirl pregnancy varies widely across countries, suggesting that variations in the school context across countries may play a role in mediating reproductive behavior among adolescents.

Most literature on pregnancy in developing countries makes the implicit assumption that young women who report that they drop out of school because they are pregnant would have continued in school otherwise (e.g., Ferguson, 1988; Meekers and Ahmed, 1999; Meekers, Gage, and Zhan, 1995). Pregnancy may be an ex post explanation but not a cause. Indeed, rather than pregnancy causing dropout, the lack of social and economic opportunities for girls and young women and the noneconomic household work burdens they carry, coupled with the gender inequities of the school system, may result in unsatisfactory school experiences, poor academic performance, and acquiescence in or endorsement of early motherhood (Lloyd and Mensch, 1999). Moreover, for young women who become pregnant unintentionally, a nonsupportive school environment may contribute to their decision to proceed with the pregnancy rather than having an abortion in order to continue in school.[8]

Using life table analysis to assess the importance of pregnancy as a factor in school dropout in rural Kenya, Mensch et al. (2001) found that only 3 percent of dropouts by the age of 19 could be attributed to pregnancy, given the sequencing of events in the reporting of the young women's retrospective schooling and fertility history. Of those young women who had ever attended school and become pregnant, however, the association between pregnancy and dropout was strong—all of those who had become pregnant had dropped out of school. Thus a rise in school enrollment increases the percentage of adolescents who are exposed to the risk of a pregnancy while attending school.

Furthermore, in countries in which enrollments are high and premarital childbearing is common, one would expect that school systems will increasingly find ways to accommodate girls who want to remain in school. For example, in South Africa, where enrollment and premarital fertility are high, young mothers are allowed to return to school. Although this policy was formalized in 1996, it was upheld by many school principals prior to that date. According to Kaufman, Maharaj, and Richter (1998), approximately 34 percent of girls younger than age 24 who had had a child during their teenage years were attending secondary school as far back as 1993.

---

[8]Typically it is only those pregnancies that result in births that are ultimately reported and linked to school dropout.

As noted earlier, young mothers in Cameroon are also allowed to return to school (see Box 8-2). Indeed, in some settings, marriage may be a greater barrier to school attendance than parenthood, because of the increased time married women typically spend on noneconomic household work. Among young women who are able to continue in school as young mothers, however, it is often difficult to balance child care and school work and as a result school performance may suffer. In a case study of schoolgirl mothers in Burkina Faso, Gorgen, Laier, and Diesfeld (1993) describe the challenges faced by the very small minority of young women who were able to return to school after childbirth in terms of time demands and child care responsibilities.

### Rise in Formal Sector Work Among Young Women

In Chapter 7, we review the literature on the implications of the rise in formal sector work among young women for marriage timing. While appropriate data are limited and causal interpretations are difficult, there is some evidence suggesting that opportunities for labor market work, in particular work in the formal sector, contribute to marriage delays. By extension, given the tight link between the timing of marriage or union formation and parenthood, we can conclude that the rise in modern sector work may also contribute to delays in the timing of first birth.

We know very little about the extent to which new mothers are able to combine labor market work with new motherhood and, if so, how they manage both. It is clearly much easier to accommodate motherhood and work at home or in rural settings in which mothers can work in the fields and tend their children at the same time. The physical separation of the home and the workplace that often arises with work in the formal sector, most relevant in urban areas, makes the roles of worker and mother less compatible and presents new challenges to young mothers. Box 8-3 outlines the implications of this for urban wives who work in the modern sector in Malaysia and who have to give up their jobs and depend on their husbands after childbirth because of the lack of available child care. While traditional mothers were able to combine work and new motherhood, this is no longer possible for modern mothers in urban Malaysia. Wolf (1992) tells a similar story about factory workers in Indonesia who are forced to leave the factory, not at the time of marriage but at the time of first birth, due to the lack of child care options.

Among women who do continue factory work after marriage, there is some evidence that this is made possible largely through the support of other female family members. Cameron et al. (1998) undertook an investigation of child care arrangements among young women who returned to factory work after the birth of a child despite the 7 day per week, 12 hour

## BOX 8-3
## From Rural Daughters, to Urban Wage Workers, to Modern Mothers: Bidayuh Women Migrants in Kuching, Malaysia

In the Malaysian state of Sarawak, unprecedented rates of urbanization and the increasing penetration of the market economy into rural areas have increased the need and demand for cash in most villages. Since there are limited cash-earning opportunities in rural villages, most households rely on remittances from members who have migrated to cities to work. The expansion of Sarawak's urban middle class after the economic boom of the 1980s and 1990s led to greater employment opportunities in the personal service sector, which increased the demand for rural female migrants' labor. The majority of female migrants in Sarawak reside in the capital city of Kuching, arriving as single women between the ages of 15 and 34.

Sim's (2001) ethnographic study of rural Bidayuh women who migrated to Kuching examines how these women experience motherhood in their new urban environment, how household gender relations change, and how their experiences differ from those of their kin back in the village. The Bidayuh, a minority ethnic group, represent the second largest group of rural migrants in Sarawak. The majority of Bidayuh women Sim interviewed migrated to Kuching with the motivation to become modern and independent, earn money, and undergo a "transformation from rural daughters into urban wage workers" (Sim, 2001:156). Upon marrying and having their first child in Kuching, however, most of these women withdrew from the labor force, staying at home to raise their children.

"People say that women without a permanent job should marry and look after her own children. . . . Even if she has a decent job, she should stop if her husband earns a big salary because it is better to look after her own children. My sister in the village carries her child to the fields when she works. How can a child grow this way?" (Alison, a Bidayuh housewife; Sim, 2001:151-152). This quote illustrates urban women's attitudes about modern motherhood and the disparity between rural and urban Bidayuh women's approach to combining work and motherhood. There are significant structural factors that contribute to this disparity: affordable child care is almost nonexistent for low-paid working women in Kuching, whereas rural women can rely on kin to help with child care and incorporate child care into their daily work routine. Therefore, becoming a modern mother for an urban Bidayuh woman means leaving her job to become a housewife, an outcome that Sim (2001) argues derives from economic pragmatism rather than the adoption of Western ideals about motherhood.

In addition, rural-to-urban migration is changing the family form for Bidayuh women and men. In the village, the well-being of a family is considered a collective effort, since individual contributions are generally nonmonetary and hard to distinguish. This contrasts with family life in the city, in which men take on the new identity of breadwinner as they become the primary wage earners and the non-wage-earning members (including their wives) become their dependents. Since becoming a mother effectively marks the end, at least for a number of years, of urban Bidayuh women's wage-earning opportunities in the city (although many women report wanting to return to work after their children are grown), these women become dependent on their husbands after having a child, more so than their sisters and mothers still living in the village.

per day work schedule in Bangladeshi garment factories. The most common arrangement was for the child to be cared for by the maternal grandmother or by another female relative.

## Changes in Health and Health Behaviors

Various changes in health and health behaviors have implications for the transition to first-time parenthood, sometimes improving health prospects for mothers and their children and sometimes worsening them. On one hand, prospects are improved by increased prenatal care and hospital births and by mothers being better nourished. On the other hand, they are worsened by increased prevalence of HIV/AIDS (particularly in sub-Saharan Africa), increased smoking by mothers (U.S. Surgeon General, 2001) and by the inverse association between breastfeeding and increased schooling (Grummer-Strawn, 1996).

The implications of these trends for new mothers remain relatively unexplored but in many cases are likely to become increasingly important. For example, there has been no particular attention to the question of how living in a context in which HIV/AIDS is prevalent or where there is access to antiretroviral therapy affects reproductive decision-making related to the timing of first-time parenthood. Nonetheless, there is evidence from focus group discussions with both single and married men and women in Zimbabwe that some are opting to have children earlier than otherwise in order to have them before they contract the disease or while they are still healthy enough to take care of them (Grieser et al., 2001). A qualitative study in urban Zambia found that women would be concerned if they found out that they were HIV positive while pregnant because pregnancy could "bring out" the disease and accelerate the deterioration of their health. Most men and women interviewed felt that women should not continue childbearing if they test positive for HIV and should instead use contraception to prevent pregnancy (Rutenberg, Biddlecom, and Kaona, 2000).

A recent review of the literature on HIV/AIDS and fertility by the United Nations (2002b) found that seropositive status discourages continuing reproduction because of concerns about the detrimental effects of pregnancy on HIV-positive women's health, mother-to-child transmission of HIV, and the welfare of children born to a HIV-positive parent. This is more problematic for those who have never had children, given the high social and cultural premium on childbearing. One of the many reasons why the development of an efficacious microbicide as an HIV/AIDS prevention measure is so critical is because a microbicide that is not spermicidal would allow women who wanted to get pregnant to do so without risking infection (Harrison, Rosenburg, and Bowcut, 2003; Population Council and Family Health International, 2001).

### Changes in Access to and Use of Prenatal and Delivery Services

Young women who are giving birth to their first child face special risks because the probability of poor outcomes is higher for first births. Furthermore younger mothers face special risks at delivery, because they are likely to be less well educated, come from a rural area, live in a poorer household, and be less well nourished. Very young parenthood also carries heightened risks for physiological reasons. Adequate monitoring and care during pregnancy and at delivery can compensate to some extent for these factors, reducing the probability of poor outcomes (World Health Organization, 1992). Over the past decades, due in large part to concerted efforts by international agencies and country governments, awareness of the benefits of antenatal care, medical attendance at delivery (and in particular emergency obstetric care), and postpartum care have greatly increased and programmatic action has to some extent also improved (Family Care International, 1997).

Survey data show that the proportion of women who make at least one prenatal care visit is moderately high: the World Health Organization (WHO) estimates (circa 1996) that 65 percent of pregnant women obtain some prenatal care in the developing world on average (World Health Organization, 1997). Although these estimates are for women of all ages, they probably reflect the situation of adolescent mothers, given that DHS data show little variation by age in the use of antenatal care or attendance at delivery. There is some regional variation in access to antenatal care: the proportion obtaining some care is much higher, for example, in Eastern Asia (80 percent, including China) and Latin America and the Caribbean (73 percent), but is lower (50-60 percent) in South-central Asia and in Western, Middle, and Northern Africa. Nevertheless, in some of the poorest countries, this proportion is even lower (e.g., 29 percent in Ethiopia and 37 percent in Chad for adolescent women, based on DHS surveys). A limitation of this statistic is that, although it is an indicator of pregnant women obtaining some basic care during pregnancy, it does not suggest whether the care started early in pregnancy or whether the frequency of visits was sufficient to match women's level of risk (World Health Organization, 1997).

The proportion who are attended at delivery by a trained medical professional (nurse, midwife, or doctor) is somewhat lower: 40 percent deliver in a health facility, but 53 percent are attended by a skilled professional (the difference is those who deliver at home but have a medical professional present). In some regions, the gap between antenatal care and attendance at delivery is much greater: for example, in Eastern, Middle, and Western Africa and in South-central Asia, an estimated 34-42 percent are attended by a medical professional at delivery. Estimates of the trend in the proportion who are attended by a professional at delivery show some small gains from 1985 to 1996: from 48 to 53 percent in the developing world as a whole; 49 to 53 percent in Asia; 34 to 42 percent in Africa; and 64 to 75 percent in Latin America and the Caribbean (World Health Organization, 1997).

## POLICIES AND PROGRAMS

Given the changing context of parenthood, policies and programs of particular interest for promoting successful transitions to first-time parenthood include those that (1) help young people have the option of delaying the first birth until they have completed their education and training, (2) allow new mothers whose schooling, training, or work were disrupted by pregnancy to return to school if they wish, and (3) support first-time parents in the adoption of family planning to allow proper spacing of a second birth. Evaluations of the impact of various programs in sexual and reproductive health designed for young people are fully reviewed in Chapter 4. We are not aware of evaluations in other policy domains with implications for first-time parents. Indeed, to our knowledge very few such programs specifically targeted to newly married couples or first-time parents are currently in operation. Even in a country like China, where marriage and family planning policy has impacted on the lives of all young people in the country for several generations, there has been no deliberate attempt by the government to influence the spacing of the first birth (Feng and Quanhe, 1996).

About 10 years ago, school policies as they related to pregnant students were reviewed for sub-Saharan Africa (National Research Council, 1993b). At that time, most policies required expulsion from school at the time of pregnancy, with some countries allowing for reentry under certain conditions after birth. We were able to update that review and add some data from South America (see Box 8-4). It would appear that the diversity of policies has increased with a growing number of countries allowing for more liberal reentry policies and some even allowing pregnant girls to remain in school during their pregnancy (e.g., Burkina Faso, Cameroon, Chile, Peru). An increasing number of countries allows for a return to school after some period of maternity leave. The extent to which these policies are actually implemented has not been documented, and the effects of such policies have not been evaluated. However, policies are more likely to follow changes in behavior than to lead those changes.

A recent review of programs addressed to married adolescents in developing countries found that most of the relatively few available were addressed to engaged or newly married women or couples but not to first-time parents (Graft, Haberland, and Goldberg, 2003). The Population Council's

## BOX 8-4
## School Policies Related to Pregnancy Policy

| Country | Policy |
|---------|--------|
| | ***Expulsion*** |
| Mozambique (Chilisa, 2002) | Young women are expelled from school once it is discovered that they are pregnant. |
| Togo (Chilisa, 2002) | Young women are required to drop out of school once it is discovered that they are pregnant. |
| Zanzibar (Chilisa, 2002) | Young women are required to drop out of school once it is discovered that they are pregnant. |
| Mali (FAWE, 2000) | Pregnant young women are expelled and not allowed to reenter school after delivery. |
| | ***Continuation*** |
| Cameroon (Chilisa, 2002) | Maternity leave is not required and is negotiable for pregnant young women, who may return to school immediately after the delivery. They can arrange for extra classes so as not to fall behind in their studies because of pregnancy. |
| Peru (Annual Review of Population Law Database, 2004) | The New Code of Children and Adolescents asserts that mothers who are children or adolescents shall not be hindered from beginning or continuing their education. |
| Madagascar (Chilisa, 2002) | Young women may return to school immediately after the delivery, and maternity leave is not compulsory. |
| Namibia (Chilisa, 2002; FAWE, 2000) | After delivery, a young woman may return immediately to school upon the approval of a social worker who has confirmed that the baby has adequate child care. The policy takes into account the academic, physical, and psychological needs of mother and baby and provides for action against men (particularly teachers) responsible for the pregnancy. |
| Chile (Gonzalez, 2004; Murray et al., 2000; UNICEF, 2003) | A law was approved in 2000 that guarantees the rights of young women to continue and complete their education despite pregnancy and to demand necessary facilities from their schools. As of 2004, pregnant young women or young mothers cannot be prevented from registering for classes or be expelled from school, even if their attendance rate is below 85 percent. |

| Country | Policy |
|---------|--------|
| Burkina Faso (Gorgen et al., 1993) | Pregnant young women may remain in school during their pregnancy and may return directly after delivery. |
| | ***Reentry*** |
| Guinea-Conkary (FAWE, 2000) | Young women are temporarily suspended from school during pregnancy and allowed to reenter after a specified amount of time after delivery. |
| Kenya (Chilisa, 2002; FAWE, 2000) | As of 1994, young women may return to school after a specified period of compulsory maternity leave. School administers decide whether they may reenter the same school or be transferred to another school. |
| Botswana (FAWE, 2000) | Pregnant young women are barred from taking exams. It is encouraged that young men responsible for pregnancies discontinue their studies for a period of time and young women take a year-long maternity leave after delivery. Before a young woman is readmitted to school, she must produce the birth certificate for her baby, produce her own identity certificate, meet the age admission requirement, and produce a testimonial and school report from her previous school. |
| Malawi (Chilisa, 2002; O'Gara, Benoliel, and Sutton, 1999; Rugh, 2000) | The policy was recently changed so that both young women and young men must drop out of school until the baby is born and may return to school once child care arrangements have been made. |
| South Africa (Chilisa, 2002) | Young women are expelled immediately once their pregnancy is discovered, and they are readmitted 12 months after delivery. |
| Zambia (Chilisa, 2002; UNICEF, 2003) | As of 1997, young women are required to take a 12-month leave from school after delivery. Very few young women return to school because of stigma and fears of abuse at school. |

first-time parents' project in Gujurat and West Bengal is fairly unusual in its focus on young married women at the time of first birth. The intervention is currently under way and will be evaluated using a quasi-experimental design. It provides information and services to young married women, their husbands, and their families in two communities using both home visits and group membership activities that take place during pregnancy and during the postpartum period.

## CONCLUSIONS AND RECOMMENDATIONS

### Key Findings

Our review of the literature and our data analysis lead to the following conclusions:

*While parenthood remains nearly universal in all societies, the timing and context in which young women experience this transition remain highly variable across the developing world.* In every society, young men become parents at later ages than young women, allowing them more time to invest and prepare for their responsibilities as parents.

*In many parts of the developing world, rates of early childbearing remain substantial.* The percentage of young people giving birth before age 18—the internationally recognized age of adulthood as defined by the UN Convention on the Rights of the Child—remains in excess of 30 percent in Western and Middle Africa and in excess of 20 percent in South-central and South-eastern Asia, Eastern and Southern Africa, and Central America and the Carribean. In some countries of these regions, over 10 percent have had a birth before the age of 16.

*While the percentage of young women having a birth before the age of 16 or 18 is declining almost everywhere, rates of decline vary substantially.* The highest rates of decline have occurred in the Middle East, starting from a very low base, and declines have also been substantial in sub-Saharan Africa and Southern Asia. In South America, where rates have been comparatively low, there has been some increase in early childbearing in recent years. The prevalence of early childbearing is highest among poor countries and, within countries, among rural residents and the least educated.

*In some regions, most young women make the transition to motherhood quite quickly after a certain age, while in other regions, ages of first motherhood are spread out over a much longer period.* In the Middle East and South America, the range of ages across which women have their first birth, which was already almost the widest, is getting wider, while in other regions it is remaining about the same.

*In all regions, at least a quarter of women remain childless until age 24, and in some regions until several years beyond age 24.* In Africa and Asia, this occurred for the first time among the youngest cohort, born in the 1970s. In the Middle East, 50 percent of women are still childless at age 24.

*The overwhelming majority of births occur within marriage.* Among those who give birth after marriage, the length of time between marriage and motherhood is declining everywhere.

*Patterns of premarital childbearing vary substantially across regions.* In most regions, less than 5 percent of all women have had a child before marriage and before age 20. However, reported rates in sub-Saharan Africa exceed 10 percent in 11 countries and in many South American countries range from 5 to 10 percent. The implications of premarital childbearing for the parents vary substantially across societies.

*Some countries have seen recent small increases in rates of premarital childbearing.* As a result the percentage of births occurring to young women that are premarital has been rising, and these increases have been most notable in Eastern and Southern Africa and South America.

*Gaps in research on first-time parenthood include all aspects of fatherhood, the determinants of and impacts of early parenthood, the implications of recent global changes on transitions to first-time parenthood, and the consequences of early parenthood.* Basic research is needed on the timing of fatherhood and on the attitudes of young men regarding pregnancy and fatherhood. Although there is plentiful evidence that early childbearing is correlated with negative outcomes, rigorous research confirming a causal role for age at birth in producing these outcomes does not exist. Major global changes, such as rises in enrollment rates during late adolescence, rising rates of labor force participation among young women, and rising HIV/AIDS prevalence among young women in Africa are likely to have important implications for the transition to parenthood, but little is currently known about their implications.

## Policy Recommendations

Systematic evaluations of policies and programs directed at the transition to first parenthood are almost nonexistent. The research findings summarized in this chapter, however, have some implications for policy and programs.

*Prenatal and delivery services should reach out to and give attention to the special needs of first-time parents.* First-time parents require information and education about pregnancy, delivery, breastfeeding, nutrition, and healthy baby care as well as contraception and fatherhood. Other family members who are involved in supporting first-time parents, particularly new mothers, may also benefit from participating in programs designed to support, prepare, and train new parents. In areas with high HIV prevalence, new parents also need to know about the risks of mother-to-child transmission of HIV, means of reducing this risk, and the importance of voluntary counseling and testing for HIV and other sexually transmitted infections.

*Family planning programs should reach out to newly married individuals and couples and assist them in planning their first births so that they are well timed.* Family planning programs are often not well designed to meet the needs of the newly married, particularly newly married young women. Young people who are recently married or had their first birth immediately after marriage need assistance in thinking about family-building strategies and taking control of the timing of their pregnancies.

*Schools should remove any barriers preventing young parents from returning to school.* Complementary programs that can assist young mothers with child care are needed to help adolescent women who have had a child and been forced to interrupt their education to return to school and complete it.

*In settings in which girls still become parents as children, there is a need to evaluate the effectiveness of interventions designed to increase awareness in the general community (and among young women and men themselves) of the advantages for later success as an adult of delaying the age of first parenthood.* Interventions could take the form of public education campaigns through the media, for example.

*There is a need to evaluate the effectiveness of family life education programs and life-skills programs in schools that include discussions of the responsibilities of parenthood, the knowledge and skills required for successful parenthood, and the importance of planning and good timing in the curriculum.* It is important to assess whether the addition of these topics could contribute to greater success in transitions to first parenthood.

## Research Recommendations

Many of the questions listed below cannot be answered without new data collection or in-depth studies. The panel's recommendations on new research strategies are discussed in Chapter 9. Our focus on transitions, their interrelationships, and their determinants and consequences lead us to see the following research questions as particularly compelling.

- How is the context of premarital childbearing changing, and what implications do these changes have for the likelihood of a successful transition?
- What are the determinants of early parenthood, including individual, family, and community characteristics and policies?
- What are the fertility desires of newly married couples, and how are they formed? Of young unmarried women?
- What are the distinguishing features of first-time parenthood as an adolescent, and as a young adolescent?
- What are the short-term and long-term consequences of starting parenthood at an early age and of starting parenthood with an unwanted child—for individuals, families, and communities?
- How are changes in the timing of first-time parenthood affecting transitions into and out of school and work and, in turn, how are changes in schooling and work transitions affecting the timing of marriage and parenthood?
- What are the differences between young men and women in their experiences with the transition to parenthood, and how are they changing? What are young men's attitudes and expectations with respect to parenthood, and how are they shared?
- What are the implications of HIV/AIDS for the timing and context of first-time parenthood?

## APPENDIX TABLES 8-1 TO 8-7 FOLLOW

## APPENDIX TABLE 8-1 Parenthood by Age and Sex, DHS Countries (Percentage)

| Country and Year of Survey | Ever Had a Child | | | | | | | |
| --- | --- | --- | --- | --- | --- | --- | --- | --- |
| | Males | | | | Females | | | |
| | 15-19 | 20-24 | 25-29 | 30-34 | 15-19 | 20-24 | 25-29 | 30-34 |
| Armenia, 2000 | 1.4 | 18.3 | 60.6 | 87.1 | 4.4 | 44.3 | 81.7 | 91.1 |
| Bangladesh, 1999-2000 | | | | | 29.8 | 72.7 | 91.4 | 96.7 |
| Benin, 2001 | 2.9 | 29.4 | 62.0 | 83.8 | 15.4 | 66.4 | 90.3 | 96.2 |
| Bolivia, 1998 | 3.1 | 22.6 | 52.6 | 77.7 | 11.5 | 54.6 | 82.3 | 92.1 |
| Brazil, 1996 | 0.7 | 14.9 | 53.2 | 87.7 | 14.3 | 49.2 | 73.8 | 87.8 |
| Burkina Faso, 1998-1999 | 2.6 | 21.6 | 50.4 | 77.8 | 20.2 | 84.0 | 95.7 | 98.2 |
| Cameroon, 1998 | 4.7 | 38.4 | 71.2 | 89.9 | 25.0 | 68.0 | 90.5 | 95.1 |
| Central African Republic, 1994-1995 | 2.9 | 26.8 | 66.0 | 89.5 | 28.4 | 77.2 | 88.6 | 93.3 |
| Chad, 1996-1997 | | | | | 29.8 | 84.6 | 95.6 | 97.3 |
| Colombia, 2000 | | | | | 15.1 | 51.5 | 76.9 | 85.3 |
| Comoros, 1996 | 0.5 | 9.4 | 32.3 | 67.5 | 7.3 | 40.8 | 70.1 | 85.2 |
| Côte d'Ivoire, 1998-1999 | 3.3 | 26.6 | 44.0 | 81.9 | 24.7 | 71.2 | 88.3 | 94.1 |
| Dominican Republic, 1996 | 1.3 | 21.0 | 54.4 | 79.7 | 18.3 | 58.4 | 80.6 | 90.9 |
| Egypt, 2000 | | | | | 5.8 | 43.3 | 77.2 | 90.2 |
| Ethiopia, 1999 | 0.3 | 14.5 | 59.2 | 79.7 | 12.8 | 61.9 | 85.4 | 95.5 |
| Ghana, 1998-1999 | 0.6 | 13.5 | 45.2 | 79.7 | 11.7 | 60.8 | 82.4 | 93.9 |
| Guatemala, 1998-1999 | 17.3 | 67.3 | 88.3 | 93.5 | | | | |
| Guinea, 1999 | 1.8 | 16.2 | 52.1 | 73.0 | 32.0 | 77.2 | 92.6 | 96.3 |
| Haiti, 2000 | 0.8 | 20.5 | 47.3 | 74.2 | 13.6 | 49.5 | 74.7 | 87.3 |
| India, 1998-2000 | | | | | 16.4 | 64.2 | 87.8 | 93.9 |
| Indonesia, 1997 | | | | | 9.4 | 53.3 | 79.6 | 90.7 |
| Jordan, 1997 | | | | | 4.0 | 30.8 | 61.4 | 76.5 |
| Kazakhstan, 1999 | | | | | 4.4 | 46.3 | 81.2 | 91.0 |

| | | | | | | | | |
|---|---|---|---|---|---|---|---|---|
| Kenya, 1998 | 1.1 | 18.0 | 56.5 | 86.8 | 17.3 | 69.2 | 92.6 | 97.3 |
| Kyrgyz Republic, 1997 | | | | | 6.3 | 65.5 | 90.0 | 94.5 |
| Madagascar, 1997 | | | | | 30.7 | 76.6 | 87.9 | 91.9 |
| Malawi, 2000 | 3.0 | 32.9 | 82.0 | 95.2 | 25.4 | 83.3 | 96.0 | 97.0 |
| Mali, 1995-1996 | 0.2 | 18.9 | 61.5 | 80.2 | 33.6 | 84.9 | 93.6 | 96.6 |
| Morocco, 1992 | | | | | 4.9 | 33.9 | 57.0 | 79.7 |
| Mozambique, 1997 | 3.1 | 42.3 | 71.7 | 89.2 | 30.4 | 78.9 | 93.2 | 96.1 |
| Namibia, 1992 | | | | | 17.7 | 63.3 | 81.4 | 92.8 |
| Nepal, 2000-2001 | | | | | 16.2 | 70.5 | 91.7 | 95.5 |
| Nicaragua, 1997-1998 | 3.9 | 46.0 | 76.3 | 85.8 | 22.1 | 66.8 | 84.8 | 92.9 |
| Niger, 1998 | 0.8 | 23.0 | 70.6 | 88.1 | 36.3 | 82.4 | 94.6 | 97.0 |
| Nigeria, 1999 | 1.8 | 11.9 | 45.5 | 77.0 | 18.4 | 55.7 | 81.6 | 91.3 |
| Pakistan, 1990-1991 | | | | | 12.2 | 45.7 | 77.0 | 90.8 |
| Paraguay, 1990 | | | | | 14.1 | 56.4 | 80.3 | 91.8 |
| Peru, 2000 | 2.0 | 24.0 | 57.9 | 77.5 | 10.7 | 48.0 | 72.9 | 87.0 |
| Philippines, 1998 | | | | | 5.5 | 38.5 | 70.2 | 84.5 |
| Rwanda, 2000 | | | | | 4.8 | 54.9 | 86.2 | 94.6 |
| Senegal, 1997 | | | | | 18.2 | 58.2 | 81.7 | 94.9 |
| South Africa, 1998 | | | | | 13.2 | 58.3 | 81.6 | 93.2 |
| Tanzania, 1999 | | | | | 19.7 | 78.4 | 92.0 | 94.4 |
| Togo, 1998 | 1.5 | 15.1 | 53.9 | 76.6 | 15.5 | 59.1 | 88.2 | 96.1 |
| Turkey, 1998 | | | | | 7.9 | 46.1 | 77.2 | 89.8 |
| Uganda, 2000-2001 | 5.2 | 40.2 | 82.0 | 95.5 | 25.6 | 84.4 | 95.6 | 96.5 |
| Uzbekistan, 1996 | 6.2 | 59.6 | 88.7 | 95.8 | | | | |
| Vietnam, 1997 | | | | | 3.5 | 43.9 | 74.9 | 86.6 |
| Yemen, 1991-1992 | 1.3 | 31.9 | 72.9 | 88.0 | 10.9 | 56.0 | 83.9 | 94.4 |
| Zambia, 1996-1997 | | | | | 23.9 | 78.8 | 91.9 | 96.2 |
| Zimbabwe, 1999 | 0.3 | 16.8 | 61.2 | 90.4 | 16.2 | 69.3 | 92.3 | 94.8 |
| Number of Countries: | 26 | 26 | 26 | 26 | 51 | 51 | 51 | 51 |

APPENDIX TABLE 8-2 Age of Transition to First Motherhood by
Quartile, DHS Countries

| Country and Year of Survey | 25th Quartile | | |
| --- | --- | --- | --- |
| | 20-24 | 30-34 | 40-44 |
| Armenia, 2000 | 19.9 | 19.6 | 20.2 |
| Bangladesh, 1999-2000 | 16.4 | 16.1 | 15.5 |
| Benin, 2001 | 18.1 | 17.2 | 17.3 |
| Bolivia, 1998 | 18.8 | 18.8 | 19.3 |
| Brazil, 1996 | 19.0 | 19.3 | 19.6 |
| Burkina Faso, 1998-1999 | 17.5 | 17.5 | 17.3 |
| Cameroon, 1998 | 17.3 | 16.8 | 16.9 |
| Central African Republic, 1994-1995 | 17.0 | 16.8 | 16.4 |
| Chad, 1996-1997 | 16.4 | 16.2 | 15.8 |
| Colombia, 2000 | 18.8 | 19.4 | 19.0 |
| Comoros, 1996 | 19.4 | 17.4 | 17.5 |
| Côte d'Ivoire, 1998-1999 | 17.0 | 16.3 | 16.5 |
| Dominican Republic, 1996 | 18.3 | 18.3 | 18.1 |
| Egypt, 2000 | 20.2 | 18.7 | 18.5 |
| Ethiopia, 1999 | 18.1 | 16.5 | 16.5 |
| Ghana, 1998-1999 | 18.3 | 17.8 | 17.7 |
| Guatemala, 1998-1999 | 18.0 | 17.7 | 17.9 |
| Guinea, 1999 | 16.1 | 16.1 | 16.0 |
| Haiti, 2000 | 19.3 | 19.1 | 19.1 |
| India, 1998-2000 | 17.7 | 17.3 | 17.3 |
| Indonesia, 1997 | 19.3 | 18.1 | 17.9 |
| Jordan, 1997 | 21.5 | 20.2 | 18.6 |
| Kazakhstan, 1999 | 20.2 | 20.4 | 20.5 |
| Kenya, 1998 | 18.2 | 17.4 | 16.7 |
| Kyrgyz Republic, 1997 | 19.3 | 20.3 | 20.0 |
| Madagascar, 1997 | 17.3 | 17.3 | 16.7 |

| 50th Quartile | | | 75th Quartile | | |
| --- | --- | --- | --- | --- | --- |
| 20-24 | 30-34 | 40-44 | 20-24 | 30-34 | 40-44 |
| 22.8 | 21.3 | 22.3 |      | 24.0 | 26.0 |
| 18.8 | 18.0 | 17.2 | 22.7 | 20.6 | 19.8 |
| 20.3 | 19.6 | 19.8 | 23.3 | 22.7 | 22.6 |
| 21.6 | 21.4 | 21.6 |      | 24.8 | 25.0 |
| 22.4 | 22.1 | 22.3 |      | 26.8 | 26.4 |
| 19.1 | 19.2 | 19.2 | 20.9 | 21.1 | 21.3 |
| 19.4 | 18.8 | 18.9 | 23.9 | 21.1 | 22.2 |
| 18.9 | 19.3 | 18.8 | 21.8 | 22.3 | 22.9 |
| 18.3 | 18.3 | 18.1 | 20.4 | 21.3 | 22.0 |
| 22.1 | 22.4 | 21.8 |      | 27.7 | 26.3 |
| 23.8 | 20.9 | 20.0 |      | 26.3 | 24.4 |
| 19.4 | 19.1 | 18.6 | 22.8 | 22.4 | 21.8 |
| 21.2 | 21.3 | 20.8 |      | 25.2 | 25.3 |
| 23.2 | 21.6 | 21.3 | 24.9 | 25.6 | 25.3 |
| 20.7 | 18.5 | 18.3 | 24.6 | 21.3 | 20.7 |
| 21.0 | 20.0 | 19.9 |      | 23.2 | 22.7 |
| 20.4 | 20.3 | 19.8 | 23.1 | 22.9 | 23.2 |
| 18.2 | 18.3 | 18.5 | 21.3 | 21.0 | 21.8 |
| 22.1 | 22.3 | 21.2 |      | 27.0 | 25.4 |
| 20.2 | 19.4 | 19.6 | 23.6 | 22.4 | 22.4 |
| 21.8 | 20.7 | 20.5 |      | 24.6 | 24.0 |
|      | 24.0 | 21.3 |      | 31.9 | 25.2 |
| 22.3 | 22.1 | 22.5 |      | 24.9 | 25.3 |
| 20.3 | 19.4 | 18.8 | 22.8 | 22.2 | 21.3 |
| 20.8 | 21.8 | 21.6 | 23.0 | 24.2 | 23.8 |
| 19.3 | 19.9 | 18.8 | 22.0 | 23.8 | 23.3 |

*Continued*

## APPENDIX TABLE 8-2 Continued

| Country and Year of Survey | 25th Quartile | | |
| --- | --- | --- | --- |
| | 20-24 | 30-34 | 40-44 |
| Malawi, 2000 | 17.6 | 16.9 | 16.9 |
| Mali, 2001 | 16.5 | 16.3 | 16.8 |
| Morocco, 1992 | 20.9 | 19.4 | 18.4 |
| Mozambique, 1997 | 16.6 | 16.7 | 16.0 |
| Namibia, 1992 | 18.6 | 18.3 | 18.7 |
| Nepal, 2000-2001 | 17.7 | 18.0 | 18.1 |
| Nicaragua, 2001 | 17.7 | 17.3 | 17.3 |
| Niger, 1998 | 16.4 | 15.9 | 15.9 |
| Nigeria, 1999 | 17.5 | 16.8 | 16.0 |
| Pakistan, 1990-1991 | 19.3 | 18.0 | 18.3 |
| Paraguay, 1990 | 18.9 | 19.1 | 19.2 |
| Peru, 2000 | 19.3 | 19.0 | 18.8 |
| Philippines, 1998 | 20.7 | 20.1 | 19.8 |
| Rwanda, 2000 | 19.5 | 19.8 | 19.9 |
| Senegal, 1997 | 17.8 | 17.1 | 17.0 |
| South Africa, 1998 | 18.4 | 18.0 | 18.7 |
| Tanzania, 1999 | 17.8 | 17.3 | 16.3 |
| Togo, 1998 | 18.5 | 17.8 | 17.6 |
| Turkey, 1998 | 19.8 | 19.1 | 18.4 |
| Uganda, 2000-2001 | 16.8 | 16.5 | 16.5 |
| Uzbekistan, 1996 | 19.9 | 20.1 | 19.8 |
| Vietnam, 1997 | 20.5 | 20.6 | 21.7 |
| Yemen, 1991-1992 | 19.0 | 17.2 | 18.4 |
| Zambia, 2001-2002 | 17.3 | 17.2 | 16.8 |
| Zimbabwe, 1999 | 18.3 | 18.2 | 17.7 |

| 50th Quartile | | | | 75th Quartile | | |
|---|---|---|---|---|---|---|
| 20-24 | 30-34 | 40-44 | | 20-24 | 30-34 | 40-44 |
| 19.3 | 18.8 | 18.9 | | 21.0 | 20.9 | 21.3 |
| 18.4 | 18.4 | 19.2 | | 20.8 | 21.2 | 22.0 |
|  | 22.2 | 20.9 | |  | 28.5 | 24.2 |
| 18.7 | 19.1 | 18.5 | | 21.3 | 21.8 | 23.2 |
| 20.8 | 20.4 | 21.0 | | 23.9 | 24.2 | 24.3 |
| 19.2 | 19.7 | 19.9 | | 21.0 | 21.8 | 22.4 |
| 20.2 | 19.5 | 19.4 | |  | 22.8 | 22.4 |
| 18.2 | 17.3 | 17.8 | | 20.7 | 19.8 | 20.6 |
| 21.2 | 20.1 | 19.4 | |  | 24.0 | 23.0 |
| 22.9 | 20.8 | 21.7 | |  | 24.5 | 25.3 |
| 21.7 | 21.7 | 21.6 | |  | 25.8 | 25.8 |
| 22.6 | 21.8 | 21.7 | |  | 26.7 | 26.2 |
| 24.1 | 23.3 | 22.8 | |  | 28.1 | 27.8 |
| 21.7 | 22.2 | 22.0 | | 24.6 | 24.8 | 24.5 |
| 20.9 | 19.4 | 19.7 | |  | 22.8 | 22.4 |
| 21.0 | 20.2 | 20.9 | |  | 23.8 | 24.3 |
| 19.4 | 19.1 | 17.8 | | 21.5 | 21.1 | 20.3 |
| 21.0 | 19.8 | 20.1 | | 24.8 | 22.8 | 22.8 |
| 22.9 | 21.8 | 20.4 | |  | 25.5 | 23.3 |
| 18.3 | 18.5 | 18.7 | | 20.4 | 20.5 | 21.2 |
| 21.2 | 21.8 | 21.3 | | 23.9 | 23.8 | 23.3 |
| 22.9 | 22.8 | 23.1 | |  | 26.3 | 26.8 |
| 23.8 | 19.8 | 22.2 | |  | 23.3 | 26.6 |
| 19.0 | 18.8 | 18.3 | | 21.5 | 21.1 | 20.3 |
| 20.2 | 20.2 | 19.8 | | 23.0 | 23.1 | 21.9 |

558

APPENDIX TABLE 8-3 Percentage of Women Giving Birth by Age 16 and by Age 18, DHS Countries

| Country and Year of Survey | Birth by 16 | | | Birth by 18 | | |
|---|---|---|---|---|---|---|
| | 20-24 | 30-34 | 40-44 | 20-24 | 30-34 | 40-44 |
| Armenia, 2000 | 0.4 | 0.1 | 0.2 | 8.0 | 3.7 | 3.3 |
| Bangladesh, 1999-2000 | 19.5 | 23.6 | 33.6 | 43.7 | 50.4 | 58.5 |
| Benin, 2001 | 7.7 | 14.0 | 13.2 | 23.8 | 33.3 | 32.8 |
| Bolivia, 1998 | 3.7 | 4.3 | 4.5 | 16.0 | 16.8 | 14.2 |
| Brazil, 1996 | 4.3 | 3.5 | 2.8 | 16.0 | 14.4 | 10.8 |
| Burkina Faso, 1998-1999 | 9.7 | 11.3 | 12.5 | 33.1 | 32.4 | 34.6 |
| Cameroon, 1998 | 12.7 | 14.4 | 16.4 | 33.2 | 41.2 | 39.5 |
| Central African Republic, 1994-1995 | 13.1 | 14.9 | 20.4 | 37.7 | 35.9 | 40.6 |
| Chad, 1996-1997 | 19.7 | 21.8 | 27.4 | 45.4 | 45.5 | 48.0 |
| Colombia, 2000 | 4.8 | 3.6 | 4.2 | 18.9 | 12.7 | 14.9 |
| Comoros, 1996 | 5.4 | 15.0 | 16.9 | 17.0 | 29.5 | 31.5 |
| Côte d'Ivoire, 1998-1999 | 13.3 | 20.2 | 21.3 | 35.0 | 40.6 | 42.6 |
| Dominican Republic, 1996 | 6.5 | 8.0 | 9.0 | 21.6 | 21.9 | 24.0 |
| Egypt, 2000 | 2.7 | 5.4 | 7.2 | 9.5 | 19.3 | 21.4 |
| Ethiopia, 1999 | 7.3 | 17.6 | 17.4 | 24.2 | 43.1 | 46.0 |
| Ghana, 1998-1999 | 4.7 | 9.7 | 9.5 | 19.9 | 26.5 | 28.3 |
| Guatemala, 1998-1999 | 8.1 | 9.1 | 8.1 | 23.8 | 27.3 | 25.6 |
| Guinea, 1999 | 22.9 | 22.5 | 24.4 | 47.3 | 45.5 | 44.8 |
| Haiti, 2000 | 3.9 | 5.2 | 6.2 | 15.2 | 14.3 | 16.3 |
| India, 1998-2000 | 10.7 | 13.4 | 14.0 | 27.6 | 35.1 | 35.3 |
| Indonesia, 1997 | 3.9 | 8.8 | 10.7 | 14.0 | 23.1 | 25.7 |

| | | | | | | |
|---|---|---|---|---|---|---|
| Jordan, 1997 | 0.4 | 1.1 | 5.2 | 6.0 | 9.2 | 18.9 |
| Kazakhstan, 1999 | 0.6 | 0.4 | 0.1 | 5.9 | 3.4 | 1.6 |
| Kenya, 1998 | 8.8 | 12.4 | 18.6 | 23.2 | 32.5 | 38.5 |
| Kyrgyz Republic, 1997 | 0.0 | 0.0 | 0.0 | 4.2 | 2.3 | 2.5 |
| Madagascar, 1997 | 13.5 | 14.2 | 16.0 | 32.2 | 31.6 | 40.1 |
| Malawi, 2000 | 8.7 | 14.7 | 17.0 | 30.3 | 38.5 | 39.6 |
| Mali, 2001 | 19.0 | 21.3 | 17.1 | 45.0 | 45.5 | 36.8 |
| Morocco, 1992 | 1.5 | 4.3 | 8.3 | 7.3 | 13.8 | 20.4 |
| Mozambique, 1997 | 17.0 | 20.1 | 23.0 | 43.2 | 36.6 | 44.8 |
| Namibia, 1992 | 4.6 | 9.0 | 7.1 | 17.8 | 22.3 | 20.0 |
| Nepal, 2000-2001 | 4.3 | 3.5 | 5.0 | 26.0 | 23.8 | 23.7 |
| Nicaragua, 2001 | 9.6 | 11.5 | 14.0 | 28.1 | 30.8 | 33.2 |
| Niger, 1998 | 19.1 | 26.0 | 25.5 | 46.5 | 58.8 | 51.9 |
| Nigeria, 1999 | 14.1 | 20.8 | 24.4 | 27.7 | 33.6 | 39.0 |
| Pakistan, 1990-1991 | 7.7 | 9.4 | 11.7 | 17.1 | 24.4 | 21.9 |
| Paraguay, 1990 | 3.7 | 4.1 | 3.5 | 16.0 | 16.2 | 14.2 |
| Peru, 2000 | 3.6 | 4.6 | 5.6 | 14.2 | 16.0 | 16.4 |
| Philippines, 1998 | 1.5 | 2.1 | 2.5 | 7.1 | 9.1 | 10.6 |
| Rwanda, 2000 | 2.2 | 1.8 | 2.9 | 9.2 | 9.7 | 10.4 |
| Senegal, 1997 | 9.7 | 13.1 | 13.8 | 25.8 | 34.7 | 33.4 |
| South Africa, 1998 | 4.7 | 7.8 | 5.7 | 20.3 | 24.6 | 18.3 |
| Tanzania, 1999 | 6.7 | 11.9 | 21.5 | 26.5 | 34.8 | 51.1 |
| Togo, 1998 | 7.6 | 12.1 | 10.3 | 18.9 | 28.0 | 28.1 |
| Turkey, 1998 | 2.2 | 4.2 | 3.6 | 11.0 | 14.8 | 20.0 |
| Uganda, 2000-2001 | 14.1 | 18.2 | 20.0 | 41.9 | 43.0 | 42.2 |
| Uzbekistan, 1996 | 0.0 | 0.1 | 0.3 | 2.6 | 2.6 | 4.7 |
| Vietnam, 1997 | 0.3 | 0.7 | 0.7 | 4.1 | 4.4 | 3.8 |
| Yemen, 1991-1992 | 11.3 | 13.2 | 10.8 | 27.0 | 35.3 | 22.7 |
| Zambia, 2001-2002 | 8.9 | 10.4 | 16.5 | 34.6 | 37.4 | 44.9 |
| Zimbabwe, 1999 | 6.0 | 7.4 | 12.0 | 19.1 | 23.3 | 28.3 |

APPENDIX TABLE 8-4a Percentage of Women Giving Birth by Age 18, by Years of Schooling, DHS Countries

| Country and Year of Survey | 20-24 | | | 40-44 | | |
|---|---|---|---|---|---|---|
| | 0-3 | 0-4 | 8+ | 0-3 | 0-4 | 8+ |
| Bangladesh, 1999-2000 | 61.7 | 44.4 | 14.6 | 62.7 | 56.9 | 33.6 |
| Benin, 2001 | 29.5 | 11.2 | 2.4 | 35.1 | 23.3 | 18.2 |
| Bolivia, 1998 | 31.4 | 26.2 | 8.7 | 17.9 | 20.7 | 6.5 |
| Brazil, 1996 | 34.4 | 19.8 | 7.4 | 17.5 | 11.8 | 2.7 |
| Burkina Faso, 1998-1999 | 36.1 | 24.5 | 10.0 | 35.1 | 31.0 | 7.7 |
| Cameroon, 1998 | 53.0 | 36.8 | 17.2 | 41.8 | 41.0 | 28.8 |
| Central African Republic, 1994-1995 | 39.4 | 38.5 | 26.7 | 40.0 | 50.2 | 27.9 |
| Chad, 1996-1997 | 48.2 | 30.0 | 16.6 | 47.6 | 56.3 | 51.6 |
| Colombia, 2000 | 36.3 | 19.1 | 2.5 | 21.7 | 12.4 | 3.9 |
| Comoros, 1996 | 24.0 | 16.4 | 4.3 | 33.2 | 22.2 | 0.0 |
| Côte d'Ivoire, 1998-1999 | 38.8 | 41.6 | 13.3 | 40.3 | 55.7 | 30.9 |
| Dominican Republic, 1996 | 50.3 | 38.4 | 10.3 | 36.0 | 29.1 | 9.9 |
| Egypt, 2000 | 24.4 | 12.2 | 2.1 | 29.5 | 20.6 | 2.6 |
| Ethiopia, 1999 | 26.1 | 24.2 | 8.4 | 46.8 | 43.8 | 8.8 |
| Ghana, 1998-1999 | 29.9 | 19.0 | 14.5 | 30.0 | 37.3 | 23.0 |
| Guatemala, 1998-1999 | 35.8 | 22.4 | 6.1 | 31.0 | 13.3 | 9.2 |
| Guinea, 1999 | 51.6 | 43.1 | 14.2 | 46.3 | 41.1 | 28.9 |
| Haiti, 2000 | 22.4 | 18.3 | 5.4 | 20.4 | 7.9 | 1.4 |
| Indonesia, 1997 | 30.2 | 20.4 | 4.6 | 30.5 | 29.7 | 9.3 |

| | | | | | | |
|---|---|---|---|---|---|---|
| Jordan, 1997 | 9.2 | 14.5 | 4.7 | 25.1 | 28.5 | 9.7 |
| Kenya, 1998 | 46.8 | 37.2 | 13.8 | 46.8 | 43.1 | 15.2 |
| Madagascar, 1997 | 42.9 | 27.8 | 11.3 | 48.0 | 34.5 | 11.9 |
| Malawi, 2000 | 40.2 | 31.8 | 12.8 | 44.0 | 36.6 | 18.8 |
| Mali, 2001 | 50.0 | 27.6 | 10.9 | 38.0 | 36.6 | 15.0 |
| Morocco, 1992 | 10.6 | 4.4 | 0.8 | 21.6 | 23.4 | 2.0 |
| Mozambique, 1997 | 46.5 | 39.6 | 13.5 | 46.9 | 28.6 | 25.0 |
| Namibia, 1992 | 35.6 | 20.7 | 9.8 | 24.9 | 18.6 | 10.3 |
| Nepal, 2000-2001 | 31.4 | 26.3 | 9.1 | 24.3 | 22.2 | 3.5 |
| Nicaragua, 2001 | 52.9 | 38.8 | 10.1 | 44.4 | 37.5 | 11.5 |
| Niger, 1998 | 51.1 | 35.3 | 11.1 | 52.8 | 40.3 | 10.1 |
| Nigeria, 1999 | 54.9 | 28.0 | 7.5 | 45.4 | 33.9 | 12.8 |
| Paraguay, 1990 | 34.8 | 16.5 | 10.0 | 22.8 | 13.5 | 0.9 |
| Peru, 2000 | 34.3 | 33.3 | 6.9 | 27.4 | 23.7 | 7.8 |
| Philippines, 1998 | 23.1 | 17.5 | 3.8 | 21.7 | 15.9 | 5.4 |
| Rwanda, 2000 | 12.1 | 8.0 | 6.8 | 12.9 | 6.1 | 2.3 |
| Senegal, 1997 | 33.5 | 15.8 | 4.4 | 35.3 | 34.4 | 9.0 |
| South Africa, 1998 | 41.0 | 38.3 | 16.8 | 26.2 | 23.8 | 11.9 |
| Tanzania, 1999 | 40.4 | 23.7 | 2.8 | 52.8 | 51.1 | 26.7 |
| Togo, 1998 | 25.7 | 12.5 | 0.6 | 31.3 | 21.6 | 10.9 |
| Turkey, 1998 | 23.1 | 13.5 | 2.4 | 32.1 | 16.0 | 2.2 |
| Uganda, 2000-2001 | 52.9 | 46.8 | 14.0 | 42.6 | 44.1 | 34.9 |
| Vietnam, 1997 | 7.1 | 5.1 | 2.5 | 8.6 | 5.2 | 0.9 |
| Zambia, 2001-2002 | 46.2 | 40.4 | 19.0 | 48.7 | 48.1 | 31.2 |
| Zimbabwe, 1999 | 50.0 | 35.7 | 11.0 | 38.5 | 24.9 | 15.9 |

APPENDIX TABLE 8-4b Percentage of Women Giving Birth by Age 18, by Residence, DHS Countries

| Country and Year of Survey | 20-24 | | 40-44 | |
|---|---|---|---|---|
| | Rural | Urban | Rural | Urban |
| Armenia, 2000 | 14.2 | 4.4 | 4.5 | 2.6 |
| Bangladesh, 1999-2000 | 47.4 | 29.9 | 59.1 | 56.2 |
| Benin, 2001 | 30.1 | 15.0 | 32.9 | 32.6 |
| Bolivia, 1998 | 30.2 | 11.5 | 17.9 | 12.4 |
| Brazil, 1996 | 21.8 | 14.7 | 12.9 | 10.4 |
| Burkina Faso, 1998-1999 | 36.6 | 19.0 | 35.0 | 32.5 |
| Cameroon, 1998 | 41.3 | 19.9 | 38.7 | 41.2 |
| Central African Republic, 1994-1995 | 38.6 | 36.7 | 35.6 | 48.1 |
| Chad, 1996-1997 | 46.4 | 42.2 | 48.6 | 46.3 |
| Colombia, 2000 | 30.0 | 16.3 | 22.9 | 12.5 |
| Comoros, 1996 | 18.8 | 13.2 | 28.3 | 40.7 |
| Côte d'Ivoire, 1998-1999 | 43.7 | 26.4 | 42.9 | 42.1 |
| Dominican Republic, 1996 | 30.0 | 17.7 | 30.6 | 20.9 |
| Egypt, 2000 | 12.7 | 5.6 | 28.6 | 14.1 |
| Ethiopia, 1999 | 25.9 | 17.2 | 46.8 | 41.1 |
| Ghana, 1998-1999 | 22.9 | 14.9 | 29.6 | 25.4 |
| Guatemala, 1998-1999 | 31.6 | 16.0 | 30.8 | 19.3 |
| Guinea, 1999 | 55.7 | 33.0 | 46.4 | 40.4 |
| Haiti, 2000 | 18.1 | 12.4 | 19.2 | 12.6 |
| India, 1998-2000 | 32.8 | 14.2 | 39.2 | 26.1 |
| Indonesia, 1997 | 18.9 | 4.8 | 29.0 | 18.7 |
| Jordan, 1997 | 6.8 | 5.9 | 22.9 | 18.3 |
| Kazakhstan, 1999 | 5.7 | 6.2 | 1.0 | 2.1 |
| Kenya, 1998 | 25.1 | 18.7 | 41.0 | 23.4 |
| Kyrgyz Republic, 1997 | 3.7 | 5.4 | 2.9 | 1.7 |
| Madagascar, 1997 | 36.0 | 22.3 | 45.2 | 29.4 |
| Malawi, 2000 | 32.3 | 21.8 | 40.4 | 33.8 |
| Mali, 2001 | 51.4 | 31.1 | 36.8 | 37.1 |
| Morocco, 1992 | 10.0 | 4.7 | 20.2 | 20.7 |
| Mozambique, 1997 | 44.2 | 40.1 | 47.4 | 31.7 |
| Namibia, 1992 | 17.5 | 18.2 | 18.0 | 24.1 |
| Nepal, 2000-2001 | 26.8 | 20.7 | 23.4 | 26.3 |
| Nicaragua, 2001 | 38.4 | 22.2 | 40.5 | 29.5 |
| Niger, 1998 | 52.1 | 27.4 | 53.7 | 44.2 |

## APPENDIX TABLE 8-4b Continued

| Country and Year of Survey | 20-24 | | 40-44 | |
| --- | --- | --- | --- | --- |
| | Rural | Urban | Rural | Urban |
| Nigeria, 1999 | 31.7 | 19.4 | 42.3 | 31.9 |
| Pakistan, 1990-1991 | 20.2 | 11.2 | 21.8 | 22.1 |
| Paraguay, 1990 | 20.6 | 12.5 | 18.2 | 10.8 |
| Peru, 2000 | 26.2 | 9.4 | 22.3 | 14.0 |
| Philippines, 1998 | 9.4 | 5.5 | 12.7 | 8.9 |
| Rwanda, 2000 | 7.9 | 13.8 | 11.1 | 5.1 |
| Senegal, 1997 | 34.5 | 15.3 | 36.0 | 30.0 |
| South Africa, 1998 | 24.8 | 17.0 | 16.8 | 19.1 |
| Tanzania, 1999 | 29.4 | 20.4 | 49.2 | 56.7 |
| Togo, 1998 | 25.9 | 9.6 | 30.5 | 23.5 |
| Turkey, 1998 | 15.1 | 9.0 | 25.6 | 17.2 |
| Uganda, 2000-2001 | 45.0 | 29.5 | 43.2 | 34.5 |
| Uzbekistan, 1996 | 3.1 | 1.8 | 6.0 | 3.1 |
| Vietnam, 1997 | 4.6 | 2.2 | 4.4 | 1.9 |
| Yemen, 1991-1992 | 29.1 | 21.1 | 21.0 | 29.6 |
| Zambia, 2001-2002 | 39.9 | 27.3 | 44.9 | 44.8 |
| Zimbabwe, 1999 | 26.2 | 12.8 | 29.2 | 26.1 |

APPENDIX TABLE 8-5 Percentage of Births That Occur Within Marriage, of All Births, DHS Countries

| Country and Year of Survey | Within Marriage | | | Within 7 Months of Marriage | | |
|---|---|---|---|---|---|---|
| | 20-24 | 30-34 | 40-44 | 20-24 | 30-34 | 40-44 |
| Armenia, 2000 | 99.4 | 98.2 | 98.7 | 0.8 | 2.4 | 1.4 |
| Bangladesh, 1999-2000 | 98.7 | 96.7 | 97.5 | 5.7 | 7.7 | 5.8 |
| Benin, 2001 | 86.0 | 85.5 | 85.6 | 24.0 | 28.2 | 22.4 |
| Bolivia, 1998 | 70.7 | 79.7 | 79.7 | 21.4 | 19.3 | 16.7 |
| Brazil, 1996 | 76.5 | 87.1 | 88.6 | 25.1 | 18.0 | 12.7 |
| Burkina Faso, 1998-1999 | 85.6 | 85.4 | 85.7 | 21.6 | 21.6 | 24.9 |
| Cameroon, 1998 | 68.9 | 74.5 | 79.5 | 14.0 | 9.6 | 14.8 |
| Central African Republic, 1994-1995 | 82.3 | 88.2 | 92.5 | 8.4 | 10.0 | 10.1 |
| Chad, 1996-1997 | 95.7 | 96.4 | 98.1 | 6.9 | 7.2 | 8.5 |
| Colombia, 2000 | 68.2 | 77.5 | 82.1 | 21.4 | 14.8 | 11.6 |
| Comoros, 1996 | 95.7 | 96.1 | 93.1 | 12.4 | 12.9 | 13.8 |
| Côte d'Ivoire, 1998-1999 | 59.1 | 66.2 | 72.3 | 19.5 | 17.0 | 16.4 |
| Dominican Republic, 1996 | 94.2 | 95.6 | 95.2 | 6.9 | 9.0 | 7.1 |
| Egypt, 2000 | 99.9 | 99.3 | 99.1 | 2.4 | 8.1 | 10.1 |
| Ethiopia, 1999 | 96.2 | 95.1 | 95.8 | 5.8 | 9.4 | 9.6 |
| Ghana, 1998-1999 | 84.1 | 88.0 | 90.3 | 11.7 | 22.5 | 21.3 |
| Guatemala, 1998-1999 | 86.3 | 86.7 | 85.3 | 14.8 | 18.8 | 16.0 |
| Guinea, 1999 | 87.6 | 89.2 | 90.4 | 19.1 | 17.2 | 19.8 |
| Haiti, 2000 | 85.1 | 91.6 | 89.2 | 11.2 | 11.7 | 13.5 |
| India, 1998-2000 | 96.1 | 96.3 | 96.6 | 20.3 | 17.9 | 15.5 |
| Indonesia, 1997 | 99.0 | 97.3 | 96.9 | 8.5 | 7.7 | 7.4 |
| Jordan, 1997 | 100.0 | 99.6 | 99.3 | 0.1 | 1.0 | 1.3 |

| | | | | | | |
|---|---|---|---|---|---|---|
| Kazakhstan, 1999 | 93.9 | 94.1 | 94.3 | 12.8 | 14.2 | 10.6 |
| Kenya, 1998 | 58.5 | 66.8 | 74.2 | 18.7 | 19.6 | 19.5 |
| Kyrgyz Republic, 1997 | 98.2 | 97.2 | 98.7 | 3.5 | 2.8 | 3.1 |
| Madagascar, 1997 | 71.5 | 77.6 | 77.7 | 22.9 | 20.5 | 18.7 |
| Malawi, 2000 | 85.7 | 86.5 | 93.2 | 14.2 | 13.1 | 14.1 |
| Mali, 2001 | 84.4 | 88.2 | 90.8 | 13.2 | 13.9 | 14.7 |
| Morocco, 1992 | 99.7 | 98.2 | 98.0 | 0.9 | 3.1 | 4.0 |
| Mozambique, 1997 | 77.1 | 79.2 | 78.8 | 20.2 | 21.1 | 30.2 |
| Namibia, 1992 | 26.2 | 42.0 | 49.8 | 16.7 | 18.2 | 11.4 |
| Nepal, 2000-2001 | 99.0 | 98.9 | 98.9 | 3.1 | 2.9 | 3.9 |
| Nicaragua, 2001 | 91.2 | 91.4 | 92.7 | 9.1 | 8.5 | 9.5 |
| Niger, 1998 | 94.2 | 96.6 | 95.3 | 9.3 | 11.6 | 9.2 |
| Nigeria, 1999 | 83.6 | 83.7 | 81.0 | 16.6 | 14.2 | 17.0 |
| Pakistan, 1990-1991 | 100.0 | 100.0 | 100.0 | 3.0 | 1.6 | 3.0 |
| Paraguay, 1990 | 73.8 | 80.8 | 81.5 | 15.0 | 11.5 | 10.3 |
| Peru, 2000 | 71.9 | 77.7 | 78.6 | 21.0 | 19.9 | 20.0 |
| Philippines, 1998 | 93.2 | 93.6 | 94.9 | 17.1 | 14.7 | 9.0 |
| Rwanda, 2000 | 89.2 | 92.0 | 95.7 | 4.9 | 6.1 | 6.9 |
| Senegal, 1997 | 77.8 | 86.4 | 91.6 | 14.8 | 13.2 | 13.2 |
| South Africa, 1998 | 19.6 | 37.3 | 47.8 | 22.4 | 17.6 | 17.2 |
| Tanzania, 1999 | 73.4 | 73.3 | 85.0 | 12.8 | 16.5 | 15.1 |
| Togo, 1998 | 81.7 | 82.0 | 82.9 | 20.3 | 20.3 | 18.5 |
| Turkey, 1998 | 99.2 | 97.5 | 96.2 | 4.1 | 5.8 | 4.8 |
| Uganda, 2000-2001 | 79.3 | 74.5 | 80.5 | 13.3 | 14.0 | 13.6 |
| Uzbekistan, 1996 | 98.5 | 97.3 | 97.3 | 1.4 | 2.0 | 3.7 |
| Vietnam, 1997 | 99.4 | 98.2 | 98.3 | 5.6 | 3.8 | 3.6 |
| Yemen, 1991-1992 | 98.4 | 98.6 | 99.0 | 10.7 | 7.8 | 8.5 |
| Zambia, 2001-2002 | 71.0 | 76.2 | 81.9 | 16.9 | 13.4 | 11.4 |
| Zimbabwe, 1999 | 76.5 | 79.1 | 78.3 | 20.2 | 19.2 | 17.5 |

APPENDIX TABLE 8-6 Trends in Median Length of First Birth Interval Among Women Having Their Birth After Marriage, DHS Countries

| Country and Year of Survey | Median Birth Interval | | |
|---|---|---|---|
| | 20-24 | 30-34 | 40-44 |
| Armenia, 2000 | 12 | 12 | 12 |
| Bangladesh, 1999-2000 | 24 | 30 | 32 |
| Benin, 2001 | 15 | 13 | 14 |
| Bolivia, 1998 | 14 | 16 | 19 |
| Brazil, 1996 | 16 | 19 | 17 |
| Burkina Faso, 1998-1999 | 20 | 20 | 22 |
| Cameroon, 1998 | 23 | 30 | 36 |
| Central African Republic, 1994-1995 | 20 | 20 | 20 |
| Chad, 1996-1997 | 20 | 22 | 21 |
| Colombia, 2000 | 14 | 17 | 16 |
| Comoros, 1996 | 17 | 21 | 22 |
| Côte d'Ivoire, 1998-1999 | 20 | 25 | 25 |
| Dominican Republic, 1996 | 17 | 17 | 18 |
| Egypt, 2000 | 13 | 15 | 17 |
| Ethiopia, 1999 | 24 | 25 | 26 |
| Ghana, 1998-1999 | 21 | 18 | 17 |
| Guatemala, 1998-1999 | 12 | 15 | 17 |
| Guinea, 1999 | 17 | 21 | 21 |
| Haiti, 2000 | 17 | 17 | 16 |
| India, 1998-2000 | 20 | 20 | 23 |
| Indonesia, 1997 | 16 | 17 | 20 |
| Jordan, 1997 | 14 | 13 | 14 |
| Kazakhstan, 1999 | 13 | 11 | 11 |
| Kenya, 1998 | 15 | 20 | 19 |
| Kyrgyz Republic, 1997 | 12 | 12 | 12 |
| Madagascar, 1997 | 17 | 20 | 19 |
| Malawi, 2000 | 14 | 15 | 15 |
| Mali, 2001 | 21 | 21 | 23 |
| Morocco, 1992 | 17 | 20 | 22 |
| Mozambique, 1997 | 20 | 24 | 22 |
| Namibia, 1992 | 21 | 30 | 30 |
| Nepal, 2000-2001 | 23 | 27 | 34 |
| Nicaragua, 2001 | 17 | 17 | 15 |
| Niger, 1998 | 25 | 24 | 29 |

## APPENDIX TABLE 8-6 Continued

| Country and Year of Survey | Median Birth Interval | | |
|---|---|---|---|
| | 20-24 | 30-34 | 40-44 |
| Nigeria, 1999 | 22 | 23 | 26 |
| Pakistan, 1990-1991 | 21 | 22 | 24 |
| Paraguay, 1990 | 15 | 18 | 21 |
| Peru, 2000 | 14 | 16 | 17 |
| Philippines, 1998 | 12 | 13 | 13 |
| Rwanda, 2000 | 13 | 14 | 15 |
| Senegal, 1997 | 19 | 22 | 23 |
| South Africa, 1998 | 20 | 47 | 57 |
| Tanzania, 1999 | 16 | 16 | 14 |
| Togo, 1998 | 17 | 18 | 17 |
| Turkey, 1998 | 16 | 15 | 18 |
| Uganda, 2000-2001 | 16 | 20 | 21 |
| Uzbekistan, 1996 | 15 | 14 | 14 |
| Vietnam, 1997 | 14 | 15 | 18 |
| Yemen, 1991-1992 | 25 | 33 | 56 |
| Zambia, 2001-2002 | 15 | 16 | 17 |
| Zimbabwe, 1999 | 12 | 14 | 17 |

APPENDIX TABLE 8-7 Trends in Percentage of Women Having First Birth Before Marriage (by ages 18, 20, 25), DHS Countries

| Country and Year of Survey | Premarital Birth by Age 18 | | |
| --- | --- | --- | --- |
| | 20-24 | 30-34 | 40-44 |
| Armenia, 2000 | 0.2 | 0.1 | 0.1 |
| Bangladesh, 1999-2000 | 0.3 | 1.5 | 1.4 |
| Benin, 2001 | 2.9 | 4.8 | 3.5 |
| Bolivia, 1998 | 5.8 | 4.5 | 3.9 |
| Brazil, 1996 | 3.5 | 3.0 | 2.8 |
| Burkina Faso, 1998-1999 | 6.4 | 6.8 | 8.2 |
| Cameroon, 1998 | 10.5 | 10.0 | 10.5 |
| Central African Republic, 1994-1995 | 5.7 | 4.2 | 2.3 |
| Chad, 1996-1997 | 1.4 | 1.8 | 1.2 |
| Colombia, 2000 | 6.3 | 3.1 | 2.9 |
| Comoros, 1996 | 0.5 | 1.1 | 2.3 |
| Côte d'Ivoire, 1998-1999 | 16.9 | 14.1 | 12.1 |
| Dominican Republic, 1996 | 1.3 | 1.3 | 1.1 |
| Egypt, 2000 | 0.0 | 0.0 | 0.2 |
| Ethiopia, 1999 | 0.5 | 2.0 | 2.1 |
| Ghana, 1998-1999 | 4.0 | 4.2 | 3.3 |
| Guatemala, 1998-1999 | 3.9 | 2.9 | 6.9 |
| Guinea, 1999 | 5.4 | 5.3 | 5.8 |
| Haiti, 2000 | 2.7 | 1.6 | 3.5 |
| India, 1998-2000 | 0.5 | 0.9 | 0.8 |
| Indonesia, 1997 | 0.2 | 1.0 | 1.6 |
| Jordan, 1997 | 0.0 | 0.1 | 0.2 |
| Kazakhstan, 1999 | 0.8 | 0.2 | 0.3 |
| Kenya, 1998 | 11.0 | 11.0 | 8.7 |
| Kyrgyz Republic, 1997 | 0.4 | 0.3 | 0.1 |
| Madagascar, 1997 | 9.7 | 8.6 | 9.5 |
| Malawi, 2000 | 4.7 | 7.1 | 3.5 |
| Mali, 2001 | 7.1 | 5.8 | 2.9 |
| Morocco, 1992 | 0.1 | 0.4 | 0.7 |

| Premarital Birth by Age 20 | | | Premarital Birth by Age 25 | | |
|---|---|---|---|---|---|
| 20-24 | 30-34 | 40-44 | 30-34 | 40-44 | |
| 0.2 | 0.3 | 0.2 | 1.3 | 0.9 | |
| 0.3 | 1.6 | 1.6 | 1.6 | 1.6 | |
| 5.0 | 6.3 | 6.5 | 9.1 | 9.7 | |
| 10.8 | 8.9 | 8.3 | 15.6 | 15.2 | |
| 7.2 | 5.5 | 4.9 | 9.0 | 8.0 | |
| 7.9 | 8.5 | 9.5 | 10.0 | 10.8 | |
| 17.0 | 16.8 | 15.6 | 21.3 | 18.6 | |
| 10.3 | 5.9 | 3.0 | 8.8 | 5.0 | |
| 2.4 | 2.1 | 1.2 | 2.6 | 1.7 | |
| 10.8 | 7.2 | 6.8 | 14.2 | 12.6 | |
| 1.0 | 1.1 | 3.3 | 1.7 | 3.3 | |
| 24.2 | 17.6 | 19.4 | 27.0 | 22.9 | |
| 2.2 | 2.0 | 2.2 | 2.8 | 3.6 | |
| 0.0 | 0.0 | 0.3 | 0.0 | 0.3 | |
| 0.9 | 2.4 | 2.2 | 2.6 | 2.3 | |
| 6.2 | 6.2 | 4.6 | 8.5 | 6.9 | |
| 5.3 | 5.8 | 9.4 | 10.6 | 13.0 | |
| 6.7 | 6.2 | 7.1 | 8.4 | 8.4 | |
| 4.8 | 3.4 | 5.2 | 5.3 | 8.2 | |
| 0.6 | 1.0 | 0.9 | 1.2 | 1.1 | |
| 0.2 | 1.5 | 2.0 | 2.0 | 2.2 | |
| 0.0 | 0.2 | 0.5 | 0.3 | 0.5 | |
| 1.7 | 1.0 | 2.1 | 3.5 | 4.4 | |
| 20.0 | 19.1 | 14.9 | 28.3 | 20.8 | |
| 0.8 | 0.3 | 0.1 | 1.6 | 0.8 | |
| 15.5 | 13.0 | 13.5 | 17.3 | 16.7 | |
| 8.4 | 9.1 | 4.6 | 11.7 | 5.5 | |
| 8.8 | 7.5 | 4.3 | 9.3 | 5.7 | |
| 0.1 | 0.5 | 1.2 | 0.8 | 1.3 | |

*Continued*

## APPENDIX TABLE 8-7 Continued

| Country and Year of Survey | Premarital Birth by Age 18 | | |
|---|---|---|---|
| | 20-24 | 30-34 | 40-44 |
| Mozambique, 1997 | 9.0 | 6.2 | 9.1 |
| Namibia, 1992 | 12.6 | 14.3 | 12.1 |
| Nepal, 2000-2001 | 0.2 | 0.3 | 0.1 |
| Nicaragua, 2001 | 2.8 | 3.9 | 2.5 |
| Niger, 1998 | 1.8 | 1.6 | 2.0 |
| Nigeria, 1999 | 4.5 | 7.7 | 10.7 |
| Pakistan, 1990-1991 | 0.0 | 0.0 | 0.0 |
| Paraguay, 1990 | 4.8 | 5.6 | 4.3 |
| Peru, 2000 | 3.7 | 4.4 | 3.9 |
| Philippines, 1998 | 0.6 | 0.5 | 0.7 |
| Rwanda, 2000 | 1.6 | 1.5 | 0.6 |
| Senegal, 1997 | 5.1 | 3.5 | 2.0 |
| South Africa, 1998 | 17.3 | 18.4 | 12.7 |
| Tanzania, 1999 | 7.0 | 9.0 | 7.2 |
| Togo, 1998 | 3.2 | 6.1 | 5.8 |
| Turkey, 1998 | 0.1 | 1.0 | 1.4 |
| Uganda, 2000-2001 | 9.4 | 12.2 | 9.6 |
| Uzbekistan, 1996 | 0.1 | 0.4 | 0.0 |
| Vietnam, 1997 | 0.2 | 0.4 | 0.2 |
| Yemen, 1991-1992 | 0.0 | 0.0 | 0.0 |
| Zambia, 2001-2002 | 10.7 | 10.8 | 9.8 |
| Zimbabwe, 1999 | 5.8 | 8.1 | 7.1 |

| Premarital Birth by Age 20 | | | Premarital Birth by Age 25 | |
|---|---|---|---|---|
| 20-24 | 30-34 | 40-44 | 30-34 | 40-44 |
| 13.5 | 11.9 | 12.2 | 15.7 | 13.9 |
| 30.4 | 30.0 | 22.7 | 46.4 | 41.1 |
| 0.2 | 0.4 | 0.2 | 0.6 | 0.4 |
| 3.7 | 5.5 | 3.5 | 6.8 | 5.2 |
| 2.9 | 1.9 | 2.1 | 2.2 | 2.2 |
| 5.8 | 9.3 | 13.2 | 10.9 | 15.0 |
| 0.0 | 0.0 | 0.0 | 0.0 | 0.0 |
| 10.5 | 8.8 | 7.8 | 14.4 | 13.5 |
| 7.8 | 8.4 | 8.7 | 14.4 | 14.7 |
| 1.5 | 1.6 | 1.5 | 3.4 | 2.9 |
| 3.8 | 2.5 | 1.0 | 6.3 | 2.6 |
| 8.6 | 6.5 | 3.6 | 9.9 | 5.4 |
| 32.5 | 33.7 | 24.6 | 51.7 | 43.1 |
| 15.7 | 15.7 | 9.5 | 20.0 | 11.3 |
| 5.7 | 9.1 | 8.7 | 12.8 | 12.5 |
| 0.1 | 1.6 | 1.7 | 2.0 | 2.6 |
| 13.6 | 17.5 | 13.5 | 22.3 | 15.8 |
| 0.4 | 1.0 | 0.5 | 2.3 | 2.6 |
| 0.2 | 0.5 | 0.6 | 1.3 | 1.4 |
| 0.0 | 0.0 | 0.0 | 0.0 | 0.0 |
| 17.8 | 15.4 | 13.7 | 20.5 | 16.6 |
| 11.7 | 11.7 | 12.8 | 17.0 | 18.0 |

# PART IV

# Conclusions

# 9

# The Way Forward

## INTRODUCTION

The juxtaposition of rapid global change, emergent opportunities, glaring inequities, and resource constraints has focused the attention of policy makers on a shared concern for the elimination of global poverty, with all its attendant negative consequences. The UN Millennium Development Goals, adopted by the United Nations in 2000, recognize the urgent need to accelerate the pace of development in the poorest countries and among the most disadvantaged populations in order to bring greater convergence of experience and opportunity across nations and among individuals. The future will soon be in the hands of the largest generation of young people ever born. Almost universally, these young people will aspire to have healthy lives, progress beyond their parents in school, have a say in their futures, secure productive livelihoods, participate in their communities, find happiness in marriage or other partnership, and raise a family.

The UN Millennium Development Goals are targeted to the elimination of extreme poverty but were not originally developed with a particular focus on young people. However, in the panel's view, the successful achievement by 2015 or beyond of many of these goals will require that policy makers center their attention on young people. There is an urgent need to identify and implement, with a renewed commitment of resources, promising and cost-effective investments that will allow the rapidly growing population of young people to expand their capacities during their adolescent years while staying safe and healthy. Investments not made during this phase of the life cycle often are opportunities missed for a lifetime. Young people growing up in disadvantaged circumstances cannot achieve their full potential if they have only their families to support them. Facilitating young peoples' success in this stage of life cannot be the responsibility of parents alone but must also be a responsibility shared with the international community, national and local governments, schools, health service providers, communities, employers, nongovernmental organizations (NGOs), and last but not least, the research community.

The panel's charge was to review research findings on the transition to adulthood in developing countries in order to identify research gaps and promising program and policy options for young people. The fulfillment of this challenging assignment has involved the review and integration of multiple literatures on many topics and from many disciplines as well as the careful analysis of comparative data sets. The result is a very long book. In this short concluding chapter, we summarize key cross-cutting findings, make policy and program recommendations based on these findings, identify knowledge gaps, and highlight fruitful directions for future research. Because each individual chapter includes a summary of key findings and a discussion of research needs specific to its topic area, we limit ourselves here to some of the overarching research issues. These include both age-old questions that remain unanswered as well as new themes that are reflective of emergent interests and trends. The panel acknowledges the research challenges that are particular to the study of this phase of the life cycle and suggests directions for future research that could go a long way toward meeting some of these challenges and making more effective links between research and policy.

## CONTEXT AND CHANGE

Context and change are two central themes that have guided the panel's conceptual approach to the study of transitions to adulthood in developing countries. The report begins by identifying key contextual domains at the international, national, and local levels that have the potential to affect transitions to adulthood. The panel put a special emphasis on the compilation and comparative analysis of the very best recent empirical data on each domain of the transition to adulthood in order to document what is known about it, in particular recent changes in these transitions. For each domain of the transition, the results of existing literature, including behavioral research and policy evaluation, are interpreted as much as possible in terms of the panel's conceptual framework. Differences in transitions by gender and by socioeconomic status are given special attention throughout. Differences by other categorizations, such as race, ethnicity, caste, tribe, religion, and language group, may also be very important in particular contexts, but these categorizations differ substantially across developing countries, so we have not been able to incorporate these myriad differences as much as those for gender and socioeconomic status, which are more common across societies.

Young people born recently have, for the most part, seen dramatic improvements in their health, education, and employment opportunities compared with those born earlier. These changes have been supported by significant parental and social investments and have also been accelerated by rapid globalization. The challenge for the future is to see that young people in the poorest countries, in which demographic transitions have begun more recently, as well as poor young people residing in countries in which demographic transitions are much further along, will experience at least the same level of progress; otherwise existing global inequalities will widen further.

## CHANGING TRANSITIONS TO ADULTHOOD

For most young people growing up in developing countries (except in sub-Saharan Africa), health conditions for young people are continuing to improve steadily, as they have over the past 20 years. However, behavioral choices that adolescents make at this age have critical implications for their health and mortality in early and later phases of their adulthood, particularly in the context of HIV/AIDS.

HIV/AIDS is now the leading cause of death among 15-29-year-old young women in sub-Saharan Africa. And, because of the heavy weight of deaths in Africa in the global total of deaths at this age, HIV/AIDS is also the leading cause of death among this age group globally. For this reason, unprotected sex during these years is one of the most dangerous behaviors for young people, given its potential consequences for later health and mortality.

Promising new program models are beginning to emerge to address the reproductive health needs of adolescents. These include multicomponent community-based programs as well as youth development and livelihood programs.

School participation and attainment have important and mostly positive associations with young people's health. Across almost 50 countries with varying levels of enrollment and very different school environments, the panel found that girls who are currently enrolled in school are substantially less likely to have had sex than their unmarried peers who are not currently enrolled. While many adolescent reproductive health programs have yet to prove their effectiveness, policies enabling more young people to remain in school and progress to secondary school emerge as particularly promising for the achievement of better health during the teenage years as well as over the life cycle.

Adolescent health and mortality rates would be better for young women, however, if it were not for the high rates of pregnancy and childbearing that still occur during this phase of the life cycle. Deaths from maternal causes remain a major factor in the health profile of young women in many developing countries. In Western and Middle Africa, the percentage of young people giving birth before age 18—the internationally recognized age of adulthood as defined by the UN Convention on the Rights of the Child—remains in excess of 30 percent, while in Southern Asia, Eastern and Southern Africa, and Central American and the Caribbean, rates of early childbearing remain over 20 percent. On average, rates of early childbearing have declined by over 20 percent in the past 20 years; the percentage of young women marrying before the age of 18 has declined even more rapidly but still remains unacceptably high at 38 percent.

Young people spend a growing share of their adolescent years attending school. With a decline in the age of puberty and a rise in the age of marriage and childbearing, reproductive and work transitions to adulthood are now occurring simultaneously. In order for young people to stay in school, have a healthy transition to adulthood, have productive experiences in the labor market before marriage and childbearing, and develop a readiness for parenthood, they face the challenge of managing their sexuality while continuing to develop their capabilities in school and work. With a growing percentage of young people making their sexual debut before marriage as the age of marriage rises, there is a growing need for accessible family planning and reproductive health services so that young people can protect their health, avoid pregnancy, and delay childbearing until they are ready.

Global trends in fertility, mortality, health, urbanization, and education have all contributed positively to the rapid rise in school enrollment rates that has occurred during the teenage years, particularly among girls, in most developing countries in recent years. This increase in enrollment rates has occurred in conjunction with very rapid growth in the sheer numbers of young people coming of school age. While data on trends in learning outcomes do not exist, however, the results of recent internationally comparable standardized tests raise serious concerns about how much students are actually learning in school and, therefore by extension, about school quality. Furthermore, evidence suggests that the pedagogical practice of rote learning remains widespread, a practice that does not reward critical thinking—an increasingly important skill in the context of rapid global economic change.

The economic returns to schooling at the secondary and tertiary levels are consistently high (and differentially high for young women). In addition, the gap between the returns at higher versus lower levels of schooling is widening, thus putting an increasing premium on secondary schooling for later success in adulthood. It is not known whether this shift in rates of return is largely due to globalization or whether other factors, such as declines in school quality, could also have played a role. Young people with secondary or more schooling are increasingly advantaged relative to their less educated peers in the labor market, in terms of earnings, job stability, and upward mobility. Indeed, in relative terms, their less educated peers are worse off than their parents were in terms of skills and marketability.

Despite the very rapid growth in the size of youth cohorts, it would appear that, in much of Latin America and Asia where data exist, the formal and informal labor markets have effectively absorbed increasing numbers of young people over the past 20 years, including a growing number of young women, without large increases in unemployment rates. Some countries, particularly in Asia, have succeeded in reaping a demographic dividend as a result in terms of economic growth. However, the challenge of youth employment remains substantial in some of the poorer countries of Asia, sub-Saharan Africa, and the Middle East, which are currently experiencing unprecedented growth in the size of their youth populations. Rates of growth in the size of the potential youth labor force (ages 15-24) have now peaked in most countries, even though the absolute numbers continue to grow.

Young people who grow up in poor households are likely to achieve significantly less success in their transitions to adulthood. Because of rapid population growth, poor young people are about as numerous today as they were in the past, despite declining poverty rates; the number of young people ages 10-24 in developing countries living on less than $1 a day at the turn of the twenty-first century is estimated at roughly 325 million. They are more likely to work as children, more likely to drop out of primary school (and in some cases never have a chance to go to school at all), more likely to engage in risky sexual behavior (not always voluntary), more likely to marry and bear children early and less likely to find stable and remunerative employment as adults. A substantial majority of the poor by most measures still live in Asia. However, sub-Saharan Africa is a region of special concern because the prevalence of poverty has been increasing there, while declining elsewhere, at the same time that the population of young people is growing more rapidly than in other parts of the developing world.

Some trends suggest a convergence of experiences of young people around the world; other trends suggest just the opposite. Converging trends include increases in school attendance among young people, declining rates of child labor, rising rates of labor market participation among young women, and closing gender gaps in schooling. The economies in which young people are growing up are also tending to converge in terms of their structure of production, urbanization, and increasing intranational and international communication and transportation (Behrman and Sengupta, 2005).

In contrast, there is a divergence of experiences across regions. Young people making the transition to adulthood in Asia, where the majority of young people live, have been doing so in rapidly expanding economies. Most young people in Africa, the Middle East, and Latin America and the Caribbean have been making these transitions in stagnant or even declining economies. Furthermore, health among young people is improving in most places but deteriorating in sub-Saharan Africa. While marriages take place at older ages in most parts of the world, there has been no recent delay in marriage in Latin America and the Caribbean, despite continuing increases in school enrollment rates among young people. While rates of early child-bearing have decreased substantially in most parts of the world, they have increased slightly in South America. While the percentage of young people having sex before age 18 is rising in some places, it is declining in others. While some young people are engaged in wars and civil strife, others are voting for the first time. While some young people are accessing the Internet, others have never been to school. Thus, despite global changes that have led to a convergence of experiences among young people in certain domains of life, the experiences of many young people remain sharply divergent.

Young women have been making very rapid progress in school, and gender gaps in school enrollment and attainment are closing. Indeed, they have been eliminated in Latin America and the Caribbean and a few other countries. Young women are also much more likely to enter the paid labor force than in the past. As marriage is delayed in most parts of the world, age gaps between spouses are narrowing. This is typically interpreted as a sign that the traditional disadvantage that women experience in marriage, in terms of access to resources and a role in decision-making, is declining slightly. Furthermore, there is some evidence that, relative to the past, marriages are more likely to involve some choice of partner on the part of the bride and groom. Nonetheless, young women's overall work burden, as measured in weekly hours, still exceeds that of young men, even when they are students, and these differences in work burdens continue to shape adult gender roles. Furthermore, in many parts of the world, the content of textbooks and the attitudes and behavior of teachers continue to socialize boys and girls into traditional gender role expectations, even as overall levels of grade attainment rise.

Globalization and trends toward greater democratization have changed the opportunities for youth civic and political engagement. At the same time that young people express greater voice at the local, national, and international levels, there is greater awareness among young people of global diversity and inequality as a result of globalization, democratization, rising rates of schooling, and growing access to the media. Recent survey data show that a majority of young men in many Latin American and Asian countries express an interest in politics and a willingness to engage in political activism, whereas young women appear somewhat less inclined to express these views.

Concepts of citizenship go beyond political participation to embrace various forms of participation in the life of the community. A variety of institutions are potentially important actors in encouraging young people to become more active in the community. However, comparative data are lacking on the extent and nature of community participation among young people or on the roles that various institutions play in encouraging or discouraging participation.

## Lessons from Policy and Program Experience

Although evaluations of interventions in the fields of education and sexual and reproductive health are abundant, only in the field of education did we find many that met the panel's rules of evidence. The quality of evaluation research is improving rapidly, however, as the standards of evidence applied become more rigorous.

Recent evaluations of interventions in schooling have shown that conditional grants or targeted subsidies can be effective strategies for increasing school attendance and grade attainment among disadvantaged groups, as well as for reducing child labor. The long-term implications of these policies are unknown, however. Success in the long run requires that improvements in education lead to a decline in poverty in the next generation, so that the conditions that fostered child labor are also improved.

Most other evaluation studies in the education field have measured the impact of one or several discrete policy or program changes among a much wider array of factors affecting either the demand or the supply of schooling. Both positive and negative results have been documented, but effects are usually small in size and context-specific. Systemic reforms are rarely evaluated, although they are increasingly being implemented. After a decade of active research and experimentation with a range of school innovations, many development experts are now calling for systemic school reform, but specific roadmaps are lacking.

Recently published and ongoing evaluations of sexual and reproductive health progress are using more rigorous evaluation designs and more appropriate statistical methods. To date, insufficient data exist to evaluate the relative effectiveness of different approaches. Furthermore, the cost-effectiveness of various approaches has not been assessed. Sexual and reproductive health interventions have generally been more successful at influencing knowledge and attitudes than at changing behavior. Furthermore, there is no evidence that these interventions contribute to greater sexual experimentation among young people. Among those programs that were able to demonstrate behavioral impact, the magnitude of the effect has generally been modest. Given past experience, many now see multiple-component community-based programs as well as comprehensive youth development or livelihoods strategies as more promising approaches than single-component strategies.

Evaluations of interventions to provide job training, promote livelihoods, delay marriage and childbearing among young women, or promote citizenship and provide citizenship education are rare. While governmental and NGO efforts have emerged in each of these domains, these interventions need to be better documented and evaluated.

## POLICY AND PROGRAM RECOMMENDATIONS

Some of the panel's recommendations are derived from careful empirical studies of policy and program effects that met our rules of evidence. Others emerge from the identification of problem areas through literature reviews and data analyses. They address areas that are potentially encompassed within the scope of the UN Millennium Development Goals and others that are not within their current scope but are nonetheless of vital importance for young people. In the panel's view, policies and programs, if they are to be effective, will need to be evidence-based, appropriate to the local context, and developed in cooperation with developing country governments and local communities.

### Poverty

The UN Millennium Development Goals, the international community's unprecedented agreement initiated in 2000, are targeted on the elimination of extreme poverty but were not originally developed with a particular focus on young people. In the panel's view, the successful achievement by 2015 or beyond of many of these goals will require that policy makers center their attention on young people. Young people currently growing up in poverty face much greater health risks in both the short and longer term and are much less likely to attend schools of adequate quality, to complete primary school, to find secure and productive employment, to have opportunities for community participation, to marry well, or to be able to provide good care and support to their children. Young women who are poor are particularly disadvantaged.

Policies and programs designed to enhance successful transitions for young people, whether they are reproductive health programs, programs to enhance school quality or reduce dropout rates, job training programs, livelihood or civic education programs, or programs for first-time parents, should be targeted to the poor, particularly poor young women, who are often doubly disadvantaged. Evaluation research shows that important actors in the system—parents, students, teachers, employers, and administrators—can be very responsive to well-designed incentive programs.

## Schooling

At their best, schools have the capacity to enhance success in all transitions to adulthood through the acquisition of literacy in a commonly spoken language and the transmission of knowledge and means to sustain health, prosocial values and citizenship knowledge and skills, and decision-making, negotiating, and leadership skills and skills for lifelong learning. While the panel supports the UN Millennium Development Goals for education, it does not see the achievement of these goals—universal primary school completion rates and the elimination of gender disparities at all levels of schooling—as sufficient for the next generation of young people to acquire the skills necessary for successful transitions to adulthood. The rapidity of global change and changing patterns of employment require that policy makers give equal attention to investments in school quality in order to ensure adequate learning outcomes at the primary level as well as to create a stronger base for further expansions in enrollment at the secondary level. The panel also identified carefully targeted subsidies as a particularly promising way to increase enrollment and reduce the prevalence of child labor among the poor.

Declines in fertility and improvements in child health have been shown to have contributed to past increases in the demand for schooling. Policies and programs supporting further progress in these areas are likely to continue to contribute to future growth in school enrollment and attainment.

## Gender Equality and the Empowerment of Women

The panel's recommendations on gender equality emphasize the promotion of gender-equitable treatment in the classroom, the development of compensatory educational and training programs for disadvantaged and out-of-school youth, particularly girls, and the adoption of policies and programs that support delays in marriage in places where girls still marry before the age of 18. Addressing gender problems in society will call for interventions that affect all social classes.

## Health, Including Sexual and Reproductive Health

The panel has identified maternal mortality as one of the major causes of death and morbidity for young women and HIV/AIDS as the major cause of death and morbidity for young people in sub-Saharan Africa. In the view of the panel, programs designed to reduce risky and unprotected sex among young people are critical to successful transitions and are likely to require multipronged and multisectoral approaches that are culturally appropriate and community based, including active collaboration between the health and education sectors. Indeed, some of the most important reproductive health interventions for young people may lie outside the health sector. For example, school participation and attainment appear to have important and mostly positive associations with young people's health; unmarried girls who remain enrolled during their teens are substantially less likely to have had sex than their unmarried nonenrolled peers. Thus resources spent on expanding opportunities for secondary schooling for girls may have a direct impact on their reproductive health.

No single strategy is likely to be effective in changing sexual behavior on its own and no single program is likely to be able to serve the needs of all young people. In particular, most family planning and reproductive health programs designed to serve young people have neglected the special needs of married adolescents, a particularly disadvantaged group.

## Youth Employment

Policies and programs with implications for young people's successful transition to work in developing countries exist at all levels of action. However, labor market regulations that are commonly enacted in developing countries for the purpose of improving the terms and conditions of employment put young people at a disadvantage in competing for jobs in the formal labor market and encourage the growth of an informal, unregulated sector: young people are likely to fare better in a labor market in which employers do not face excessive regulation or where government incentives encourage firms to invest in training.

The panel has also noted that too often policies affecting aid and trade are not coordinated. For example, trade sanctions against products produced with child labor or against countries known to violate international labor standards relating to child labor are likely to do more harm than good in contexts in which poverty is persistent and the family economy still relies on child labor. In general, trade and agricultural subsidies in developed countries compromise the competitiveness of products and services produced in developing countries and are more likely to hurt than to help poor children and their families, even when the intention of trade policies is humanitarian rather than protectionist. Thus, while the focus of this report has been on policies and programs directly targeted to young people, the panel notes that agricultural and trade policies aimed at reducing nonmarket imperfections in the terms of trade between developed and developing countries could potentially be a far more effective means of helping the poorest people in the world, particularly young people, seeking decent and productive employment opportunities appropriate to their skills.

Evaluation should be adopted as an integral part of policy and program innovation for all interventions designed to enhance successful transitions to adulthood. If rigorous evaluation becomes a routine part of a phased implementation, lessons can be learned and adjustments made before implementation goes to scale, increasing the chances of success.

## KEY KNOWLEDGE GAPS

Much more is known about basic patterns and trends than about the determinants of these trends or the consequences of these trends for later phases of the life course. Much more is known about the timing of some transitions—in particular, school leaving, marriage, and first birth—and much less about the context and content of those transitions (e.g., skills acquired in school, migration for school or marriage or economic arrangements surrounding marriage). The understanding of the timing of other transitions, such as the transition to work, the transition to citizenship or the transition to household manager, remain murky due to the greater difficulty of defining a beginning or an end to the transition. Furthermore, the individuality of the research subjects rarely emerges because the primary focus of research on transitions in developing countries is on the interrelationships between the variables that surround individuals rather than on the individuals themselves. Even so, these interrelationships can be explored only descriptively, given the cross-sectional nature of much of the available survey data. Moreover, there is very little systematic cross-cultural information on some possibly critical aspects of young people and their transitions to adulthood, such as their mental health. Finally, the rapidity of global change itself limits the transferability of lessons learned in one context to other contexts, unless these contexts are well specified. As a result, lessons for policies and programs are currently relatively limited and are confined to single-sector interventions in the areas of education and reproductive health.

Gaps in knowledge that emerge from the juxtaposition of our conceptual framework and our compilation of solid evidence form the basis of research questions that are provided at the end of each chapter. From these, the following cross-cutting research questions emerge.

*What are the implications of rising rates of school attendance among young people for health and reproductive health?* Students appear to be less likely to engage in sex, more likely to use contraception, and possibly more likely to resort to abortion when they remain in school. Given the possible significance of school enrollment for reproductive health during the teenage years, it is important to learn more about what it is about schools, and the potential opportunities that schools can open up, that can make a difference for health and reproductive health.

*What are the links between poverty, economic opportunity, and risk behaviors?* There is much anecdotal evidence that poverty is associated with various kinds of risk-taking by parents or young people that compromises the health of young people either during the transition or later in life. Examples include children not completing their schooling level, children taking up work at young ages in unsafe environments, students exchanging sex for money to pay school fees, parents marrying off their young daughters to older men, young girls participating in trafficking to meet the demand of older men for safe sex with virgins, pregnant teenagers resorting to unsafe abortions, and jobless teenagers getting in trouble with drugs and alcohol. Solid empirical evidence is surprisingly slim.

*What are the implications of the HIV/AIDS epidemic for the transition to first-time parenthood?* Parenthood continues to be highly valued even in contexts in which getting pregnant can be risky to the health of mother and child. Little is known about how young men and women negotiate the transition to parenthood under these difficult circumstances or how best to support them in the process.

*What are the implications of rapid demographic change for intrafamilial resource allocation, with particular implications for investments in young people?* While there has been much research on intrafamilial resource allocation, that research has not been situated in the dynamic context of demographic change or focused in particular on the implications for young people. The marriage market might be an interesting example. Changing cohort size has led to a marriage squeeze, and rising dowry has led to delays in marriage and more women working before marriage to raise money for the dowry. While cohort sizes are beginning to decline in some parts of the developing world, they will continue to rise in other parts of the developing world for many years to come. There may be lessons learned in some settings that can be applied to others.

*What is the explanation for the rapid rise in girls' schooling? Why are enrollment and grade attainment rising more rapidly for young women than young men?* Possible explanations include declining family size affecting quality-quantity trade-offs in the family, changing rates of return in the job market or the marriage market that could be affected by global demographic or economic shifts, changes in the relative costs of schooling due to policy interventions encouraging girls' schooling relative to boys', or changing norms about the value of schooling and women's place in society.

*What are the determinants and the implications of differences among groups categorized by ethnicity, race, caste, tribe, language, and religion for successful transitions to adulthood?* From casual observations of individual societies, it appears that these differences are important. The options appear different for Sunni and Sufi young people in many countries in the Middle East; for young people of indigenous, African, and European descent in Latin American and the Caribbean; for young people from various tribal groups in sub-Saharan Africa, the Middle East, and isolated areas of Asia; for young people of different castes in South Asia; for overseas Chinese and other young people in various countries in Asia; and for religious and language minorities and those belonging to majority groups throughout the developing world. However, because of the global sweep of this report, we have not been able to consider the myriad of such differences. But in the consideration of any particular context, such differences may be very important.

*How is globalization affecting job opportunities for children, young women, and young men?* While data on labor force participation are generally available by age, data on occupational distributions are not. It is thus very difficult to tease out how the changing distribution of job opportunities is affecting young people in particular. For example, we do not know whether young women fare better or worse than older women in terms of occupational discrimination. We do not know whether rapid urbanization has created new demands in the labor market for child workers.

*How are patterns of migration (both national and international) changing among young people in response to globalization, rapid urbanization and changing employment prospects?* Young people migrate in search of better schools, better jobs, and better marriage opportunities; sometimes they are forced to move due to conflict or environmental disasters. We would expect that the rapid changes documented in the report would have important implications for migration patterns. However little is known about how these migration flows are changing or about the implications of these changes for transitions to adulthood.

*What are the explanations for delays in the age of family formation for both men and women? What are the implications of very late marriage ages for men?* The traditional explanation—increases in educational participation and attainment—does not explain the trends fully. Possible explanations include demographic shifts affecting the marriage market; changing views and expectations surrounding marriage, childbearing, and childrearing; and shifts in early work patterns.

*What elements of school quality are critical for successful transitions to work, marriage, citizenship, and parenthood? Do students from disadvantaged backgrounds have special needs in each of these domains? How can these aspects of school quality be improved?* Most research on school quality has concentrated on aspects of schooling that are expected to affect cognitive competencies. There has been little attention to other valued outcomes of schooling, including the socialization of the young to attitudes that are prosocial and gender equitable, the teaching of languages of global commerce, the teaching of job-related skills including computer literacy, and the transmission of knowledge supporting healthful behaviors.

*What are the near-term and long-term consequences of very early or very late marriage and childbearing for reproductive health, education, work, and citizenship roles in the context of rapid global change?* While global standards and norms increasingly see marriage below age 18 as inappropriate, there has been no rigorous research exploring the subsequent consequences for young people, in terms of other role transitions, of marrying while still a child. These consequences are likely to vary by context. Furthermore, age at marriage for men in some parts of the world is rising to unprecedented levels. Are there implications of these trends for reproductive health and overall satisfaction and well-being?

*How are the social norms, values, perceptions of opportunity, and goal aspirations changing among young men and women in the context of rapid global change? What consequences do these changes have for behaviors and successful transitions?* While most surveys of young people ask questions designed to solicit their views on various topics, there are rarely longitudinal data designed to explore whether these views have changed. These changes may have important implications for all aspects of the transition to adulthood, including the formation of citizenship, one of the adult roles about which the least is known.

*Do such experiences as secondary school attendance, work for cash during the middle or later phases of adolescence, participation in sports, livelihood programs, or other group or community activities, particularly for young women, increase young people's sense of agency, self-esteem, identity, and decision-making skills? Do these types of experiences enhance success in other transitions?* Very little is known about agency among children and young people and how it is changing. There is some information that young people have greater choice of marriage partners than in the past, but little else. Economic models of decision-making typically include parents as major players in the lives of young people. Changes in the pace and timing of transitions may require that models be adapted to encompass the transition in decision-making roles that occurs during the transition to adulthood.

In addition to the many cross-cutting questions laid out above, new research areas are emerging as a result of global change that need attention as well:

- The role of the media in forming and changing social norms, values, perceptions of opportunity, cultural identity, and goal aspirations.
- The relationship between citizenship education and gender role socialization.

- The cost-effectiveness of policy interventions designed to enhance schooling and health outcomes, including both direct and indirect effects.
- The role of culture and context in adolescent development, emotionally, physically, and cognitively.
- The consequences of health behaviors developed during adolescence for health and well-being in later life.
- The role of the military or national service in the transition to work and citizenship.
- The particular needs of out-of-school young people and the effectiveness of alternative pathways to the acquisition of capabilities, resources, and opportunities to enhance success.
- The implications for transitions to adulthood of the rapid expansion of noncommunicable diseases, mental health conditions, and injuries in developing countries.
- How do civic participation and attitudes toward politics differ between young citizens in new democracies and young citizens in established democracies? What does it mean to be a citizen in an authoritarian state?
- What factors affect the age of marriage of men? How do men's decisions about marital timing influence those of women and vice-versa?

## DIRECTIONS FOR FUTURE RESEARCH

Many gaps remain in the knowledge about transitions to adulthood in developing countries, their determinants and consequences, and how they are changing. While we have focused on specific research questions in each of the chapters and have summarized the main cross-cutting themes and emergent questions above, we have not yet discussed what types of data and what styles of research would be most fruitful in order to deepen knowledge of the transitions to adulthood and at the same time to keep up with the very rapid and accelerating changes that are occurring in young people's lives. We have postponed this discussion to the end of the book, because our recommendations cut across research topics and it would therefore be repetitive to treat these recommendations in each individual chapter. Furthermore, we hope that the next generation can explore the ways in which various transitions interconnect and interact and to see changes in transitions unfolding as they are occurring rather than retrospectively through the filtered memories of adults.

In order for research to yield insights about the transitions to adulthood and lessons for programs and policies that go beyond the specific research context, the research must be situated in a behavioral model and must identify and measure critical elements of the context in a way that allows for comparison across time and space. The juxtaposition of global change, adolescent development, and cultural diversity in the panel's conceptual framework presents a simultaneous challenge to research along three very different dimensions. Without good behavioral theory and contextual specification, it is hard to generalize and draw lessons for the future from even the very best designed research studies.

From the very rich experience of researchers in the West on transitions to adulthood, there is much to be gained from building multidisciplinary research teams; following cohorts over prolonged periods of time; and measuring a full range of social, psychological, health, and economic outcomes while deploying a mix of research methods. Jessor (1996), commenting some years back on the state of research on adolescent development in the United States, stated that "there is a growing commitment to methodological pluralism and more frequent reliance on the convergence of findings from multiple and diverse research procedures (p.4)." The same cannot yet be said for the state of research on adolescent development in developing countries.

Researchers exploring transitions to adulthood in developing countries currently depend primarily on the cross-sectional household survey. It measures and describes trends in key demographic markers of the transition, such as the timing of first sex, marriage, and childbearing as well as school enrollment and employment status but rarely looks beyond these markers to capture the quality of the developmental experience or its implications for later life success. Drawing causal inferences from cross-sectional surveys is also challenging, given the likelihood that some key behavioral determinants were not or cannot be measured, leaving webs of causation difficult to untangle even when sophisticated statistical techniques are employed. Furthermore, poor contextual specification has made it difficult to apply lessons learned in one setting to other cultural settings in which the configuration of risks and opportunities for young people are also very different.

In order to deepen the research on transitions to adulthood in developing countries, increased sensitivity is needed to some of the challenges of collecting data from a population group that straddles the divide between childhood and adulthood. These young people are gaining knowledge, cognitive capacities, common sense, opinions, and agency as they mature. Their parents may be their guardians at the youngest ages but often not at the end of the transition. Cultural sensitivities about privacy and consent vary in different contexts. Young people are highly mobile, and the households they live in at the end of the transition may suggest very little about their natal experiences, particularly in places where marriages are exogamous or urbanization is occurring rapidly. All of these features of growing up have implications for research approaches. Researchers working on this age group must be thoughtful about these issues in their research designs and provide research protocols that make their approach transparent to users.

In the sections that follow we (1) recommend ways that existing data collection operations can be enhanced; (2) identify promising research approaches, not always new but underutilized, that would significantly deepen the understanding of transitions; and (3) suggest how program and policy evaluation can be more effectively integrated into policy innovation.

## Enhancement of Existing Data Collection and Compilation Operations

The cross-national comparability of the Demographic and Health Surveys (DHS) data has been a great asset to the work of the panel. In the recommendations below, we have placed an emphasis on the encouragement of cross-national comparability in other large multinational survey efforts.

*The publication of comparable data by age*: To substantially increase the comparability and usability of data published by various UN agencies (e.g., United Nations Educational, Scientific and Cultural Organization [UNESCO], International Labour Organization [ILO]; World Health Organization [WHO]; United Nations Children's Fund [UNICEF]; and the Joint United Nations Programme on HIV/AIDS [UNAIDS]) on topics related to transitions to adulthood, such as education, work, marriage, childbearing, health, and mortality, among others, the panel strongly recommends that data always be collected by age and published, at a minimum, in 5-year age groups (10-14, 15-19, 20-24) rather than in broader or open age ranges. As changes occur rapidly during these ages, it is important that age groups be narrowly constructed and consistent and that data be collected at regular intervals for the monitoring of trends.

*The development and publication of rating systems for data quality:* Data quality can vary for many reasons, not only those that relate to data collection techniques, but also for reasons that relate to the built-in penalties or rewards that are incurred by respondents, collectors, or reporters of data if data are reported accurately. Such incentive and disincentive structures exist at all levels. The panel recommends that international agencies responsible for publishing cross-national data develop a transparent rating system of data quality, drawing on statistical expertise outside their own institutions, so that users will have a better understanding of variations in data quality when undertaking data analysis. The introduction of such a rating system would also encourage national data collection systems to be more answerable to concerns about data quality. Greater investments in the training of government statisticians would also support the improvement of data quality.

*The expansion of access to national censuses and surveys:* The panel benefited in its data analysis from the limited international census data currently available from the University of Minnesota's Integrated Public Use Microdata Series (IPUMS), which is housed in the Minnesota Population Center. In order to analyze recent trends in various transitions simultaneously, the panel relied on our own members and other colleagues on an ad hoc basis to access other data sets and ultimately found relatively few that were sufficiently well documented to be used. Thus, given our own experience, we recommend very strongly that international and bilateral agencies as well as other donors require public access and support the costs of necessary documentation and archival capacity when providing financial support for data gathering. We also recommend that such efforts as the IPUMS data base be well funded so that country statistical offices and other data gathering operations have a central repository through which their data can be shared.

*The adaptation of DHS questionnaires to address adolescent issues:* In most of Asia and the Middle East, DHS surveys continue to be restricted to ever-married women. With delays in the age of marriage and an increasing likelihood that the prevalence of premarital sex will rise further it is important to standardize approaches to data collection so that the comparability of data is enhanced and emergent trends in the transition to adulthood can be documented. Furthermore, at a minimum, the addition of just a few questions on the ages of entry and exit from school and the age of entry into the labor force would allow for a clearer sequencing of reproductive and work behaviors so that interrelationships between school attendance, labor force participation, and reproductive behaviors could be more fully explored.

*The expansion of World Values Surveys, Barometer surveys, and other value and opinion surveys to be more representative of young people through the transition to adulthood and to allow for better indicators of community participation:* Currently, neither the World Values Surveys nor the Barometer surveys have been designed to give special attention to young people. Sample sizes are too small to single out for analysis those under age 25 or subgroups of particular interest, in particular differentials by ethnicity, caste, religion, race, tribe, or language group. Furthermore, samples tend to be biased toward the more educated and the more urban. While sample weights allow the analyst to make corrections for these biases, the underlying samples are too small to derive confident estimates. Those who are poor, rural, and less educated, are the most likely to be disenfranchised; more needs to be known about the practice of citizenship and community participation of these groups.

## Promising Research Strategies

*The greater use of multidisciplinary, multimethod panel research designs:* During the transition years, most young people graduate or leave school, have sex, enter the military or national service, get their first job, leave home, become a parent, get married, and have many other experiences as well, all for the first time. This is a very busy phase of life when change happens rapidly and can have long-lasting effects. The timing and sequencing of transitions have important implications for success in adult life. Nonetheless, we are not aware of data collection efforts of this kind in developing countries that have followed cohorts starting at the age of school entry and continuing through labor force entry, leaving home, marriage, and parenthood or linked these transitions to the context of young peoples' lives through data on schools, communities, parents, and employers. The panel recommends the launching of three to four sustained longitudinal studies of contemporary cohorts of young people in a few developing countries currently experiencing very rapid change (possibly one in each major region). These should focus on multiple outcomes simultaneously and be sustained for 10 to 20 years. They should be designed to allow for comparative analysis, be informed by theory, and be sensitive to critical dimensions of context. In some cases, it is likely to be desirable to build on previous nationally representative household longitudinal surveys and to follow young people as they age, whether or not they separate from their parental household, because this would enable building on extensive existing data sets. Examples of such possibilities include the Indonesian Family Life Survey, the Mexican Family Life Survey, and the Vietnamese Living Standards Measurement Survey.

*The development of research protocols that allow for a more in-depth exploration of adolescent development in different contexts:* A full understanding of adolescent development during the transition to adulthood has eluded the grasp of the conventional research design: its characteristic reliance on survey methods; its typical focus on one or two problems, such as sex, or drugs, or labor market participation; its concern with context being almost exclusively the family, rarely the larger ecology of school and friends and neighborhood; its conceptual interest confined largely to risk factors; its explanatory unit being variables rather than persons; and its source of data limited to the respondent alone. What has been missed in most such research is a sense of the full complexity of an adolescent's life, an understanding of the choices and decisions that shape the course of its development and an appreciation of the meanings and interpretations the young person attributes to daily life experience. Yet such knowledge is essential in foretelling the future and in predicting the role the adolescent will play in determining it. The desired understanding we advocate is likely to be obtained through qualitative or mixed-method approaches.

There have been salutary changes in adolescent developmental studies that promise to overcome at least some of the limitations of traditional inquiry. Theory-derived surveys mapping more comprehensively both individual-level and contextual attributes, engaging a wider range of behavior, prosocial as well as problematic, concerned with protective factors as well as risk factors, and eliciting characterizations of the multiple settings of daily life—family, school, neighborhood, community, or friends—are not only feasible but increasingly available. Furthermore, theory-derived qualitative inquiries with selected subsamples of the survey population can be used simultaneously to enlarge understanding of the survey findings. Finally, systematic engagement of other observers in the life of young people—parents, teachers, friends, neighbors—as part of the same research enterprise not only can illuminate the daily context a young person traverses, but also can provide independent, external information against which to appraise a young person's reports. Ambitious as this may sound, it is a way of designing research that would strengthen our understanding of the lives of young people in transition to adulthood in developing societies. Implementing such an approach is strongly recommended by the panel where feasible; where constraints prevent full implementation, it is an approach to be approximated as closely as possible.

### Integration of Well-Designed Evaluation Studies into Policy Innovation

Very few policies and programs have been properly evaluated, whether they are designed to address the needs of young people or other population groups. Proper evaluation requires not only a scientifically sound research design and an independence between researcher and program implementer but also a thorough documentation of the content and context of the intervention. Without the latter, empirically validated success or failure is difficult to interpret, making scaling up or replication problematic. Proper evaluation also requires a full accounting for costs as well as both direct and indirect program effects. The suitability of a particular policy is determined not only by its effectiveness but also by its cost-benefit ratio in relationship to alternative policies or programs that might achieve the same objectives.

Reliable estimates of the effects of various interventions for young people can be found mainly in the area of formal schooling. Few studies, however, include adequate data on costs, making the comparison of programs according to cost-effectiveness next to impossible (Knowles and Behrman, 2005).

The panel recommends that evaluation be adopted as an integral part of policy and program innovation for all interventions designed to enhance successful transitions to adulthood. If rigorous evaluation becomes a routine part of a phased implementation, lessons can be learned and adjustments made before implementation goes to scale, increasing the chances of success.

Proper evaluation requires preprogram baseline data, knowledge about what population the sample is representing (ensured, for example, by stratified random sampling of the population), means of comparing an individual affected by the program with what that same individual would have been likely to do without the program (through random assignment to treatment and control samples or through statistical methods such as matching), longitudinal data to follow the impact over time, and community-level data to investigate the impact of context on individual behaviors and to permit use of statistical methods to control for behavioral choices (e.g., instrumental variables).

The development of evaluation designs should explore direct and indirect effects. The transition to adulthood is multifaceted. A program designed to increase school enrollment is likely to have impacts on other aspects of the transition to adulthood. Evaluations of schooling interventions often look at implications for labor force participation but rarely explore reproductive outcomes. It is likely that increased school attendance will have consequences for reproductive health and behavior but it is currently difficult to assess and compare the effectiveness of schooling interventions to reproductive health interventions for young people in terms of their reproductive health benefits. The same could be said for the impact of reproductive health programs on school retention.

Evaluations should be set up for a sufficient amount of time to assess longer term outcomes. This would allow program and policy objectives that are usually expressed in terms of outcomes, such as higher test scores, delayed age of marriage, reductions in the prevalence of risky sexual behaviors, condom use, or reduced rates of HIV infection to be properly assessed against their objectives rather than against various correlates of these outcomes such as attitudes and behaviors that can be measured more quickly but may or may not ultimately lead to the desired objectives.

## CONCLUSIONS

At the end of such a long and complex report, it is important to leave the reader with a few key themes. First, on average, the chances for young people living in developing countries to complete successful transitions to adulthood have increased thanks to the many increased opportunities and improved conditions created by recent global changes, although prospects for success for young women still lag behind young men. However, because 70 percent of young people in developing countries live in Asia, this statement is most strongly reflective of the experience of Asian young people. Second, because of continuing population growth, poor young people are almost as numerous today as they were in the past. In the panel's judgment, poverty is the greatest enemy of successful transitions. Third, young people in sub-Saharan Africa appear to be experiencing diminished chances for successful transitions to adulthood given the poor economic conditions and the HIV/AIDS pandemic, at the same time that their numbers are increasing relative to the population of young people in other regions. In the context of continuing global change and differential prospects for success, the panel sees policies that support universal basic schooling of adequate quality so as to create a stronger base for the continuing expansion of secondary enrollment and promote health during this phase of the life cycle as essential in their own right but also important because of their roles in promoting success in other domains.

Ultimately, this report is not just a story about transitions but also the product of a field in transition. Not only does globalization bring changes in the lives of young people, but it also changes the nature of the research enterprise, with expanding opportunities for data and knowledge sharing across countries and disciplines as well as new research techniques for more rigorous analysis and policy evaluation. The story we leave with the reader is rich, dynamic, and complex but incomplete, because change continues and because our angles of vision on the past have been limited by the information at hand.

# References

Abah, O.S., and Okwori, J.Z. (2002). Agendas in encountering citizens in the Nigerian context. *IDS Bulletin, 33*(2), 24-29.

Abou-Zahr, C., and Wardlaw, T. (2003). *Antenatal care in developing countries: Promises, achievements, and missed opportunities.* Geneva, Switzerland: World Health Organization.

Acharya, A. (1999). Southeast Asia's democratic moment. *Asian Survey, 39*(3), 418-432.

Adato, M. (2000). *The impact of PROGRESA on community social relationships.* Washington, DC: International Food Policy Research Institute.

Adebanwi, W.T. (2002). *The carpenter's revolt: Oodua people's congress, youth, citizenship and democracy in Nigeria.* (Research Report, SSRC African Youth Fellowship Program.) New York: Social Science Research Council.

Adepoju, A., and Mbugua, W. (1997). The African family: An overview of changing forms. In A. Adepoju (Ed.), *Family, population, and development in Africa* (pp. 41-59). London, England: Zed Books.

Admassie, A., and Singh Bedi, A. (2003). *Attending school, two r's and child work in rural Ethiopia.* University of Addis Ababa, Ethiopia and Institute of Social Studies, The Netherlands. Available: http://ctool.gdnet.org/conf_docs/Admassie_paper.pdf [January 20, 2004].

Adorno, S. (2002). Youth crime in Sao Paulo: Myths, images, and facts. In S. Rotker (Ed.), *Citizens of fear: Urban violence in Latin America* (pp. 102-116). New Brunswick, NJ: Rutgers University Press.

Aedo, C., and Nuñez, S. (2001). *The impact of training policies in Latin America and the Caribbean: The case of Programa Joven.* Adelaide, Australia: National Centre for Vocational Education Research. Available: http://www.cinterfor.org.uy/public/english/region/ampro/cinterfor/temas/youth/doc/aedo/aedo.pdf [February 2005].

Agarwal, B. (1994). *A field of one's own: Gender and land rights in South Asia.* New York: Cambridge University Press.

Agha, S. (2000). *An evaluation of adolescent sexual health programs in Cameroon, Botswana, South Africa, and Guinea.* (Population Services International Research Division, Working Paper No. 29.) Silver Spring, MD: Population Association of America.

Agha, S. (2002). An evaluation of the effectiveness of a peer sexual health intervention among secondary school students in Zambia. *AIDS Education and Prevention Review, 14*(4), 269-281.

Agyei, W., and Epema, E. (1992). Sexual behavior and contraceptive use among 15-24 year-olds in Uganda. *International Family Planning Perspectives, 18*(1), 13-17.

Ahearn, L.M. (2001). *Invitations to love: Literacy, love letters, and social change in Nepal.* Ann Arbor, MI: University of Michigan Press.

Ahlburg, D.A., and Amer, M. (2004). *Labour market mobility among Egyptian youth.* Paper presented at the Workshop on Gender, Work, and Family in the Middle East and North Africa, June 9, Tunisia, Mahdia.

Ahmed, A., and del Ninno, C. (2002). *Food for education program in Bangladesh: An evaluation of its impact on educational attainment and food security.* (FCND Brief No. 138.) Washington, DC: International Food Policy Research Institute, Food Consumption and Nutrition Division.

Ahmed, M., Chabbott, C.J.A., and Pande, R. (1994). *Primary education for all: Learning from the BRAC experience.* Washington, DC: BRAC Printers.

Ahmed, N., and Andersson, R. (2002). Differences in cause-specific patterns of unintentional injury mortality among 15-44 year-olds in income-based country groups. *Accident, Analyis, and Prevention, 34*(4), 541-551.

Aina, O.A., and Odebiyi, A.I. (2000). *Transmission of poverty: Experiences of unmarried adolescent mothers in Osun State, Nigeria.* Unpublished manuscript, Department of Sociology and Anthropology, Obafemi Awolowo University, Ile-Ife, Nigeria.

Aitchinson, J. (1998). Violence and youth in South Africa: Causes, lessons, and solutions for a violent society. In *São Paulo without fear: A diagnosis of urban violence* (pp. 121-132). Rio de Janiero, Brazil: Garamond Press.

Ajayi, A., Clark, W., Erulkar, A., Hyde, K., Lloyd, C.B., Mensch, B.S., Ndeti, C., Ravitch, B., Masiga, E., and Gichaga, S. (1997). *Schooling and the experience of adolescents in Kenya.* New York and Nairobi, Kenya: Population Council and Government of Kenya Ministry of Education.

Ajuwon, A.J., Akin-Jimoh, I., Olley, B.O., and Akintola, O. (2001). Perceptions of sexual coercion: Learning from young people in Ibadan, Nigeria. *Reproductive Health Matters, 9*(17), 128-136.

Akabayashi, H., and Psacharopoulos, G. (1999). The trade-off between child labor and human capital formation: A Tanzanian case study. *Journal of Development Studies, 35*(5), 120-140.

Alam, N. (2000). Teenage motherhood and infant mortality in Bangladesh: Material age-dependent effect of parity one. *Journal of Biosocial Science, 32*(2), 229-236.

Alatorre, R.J., and Atkin, L.C. (1998). De abuela a madre, de madre a hijas: Repeticion intergeneracional del embarazo adolescente y la pobreza (From grandmother to mother, from mother to children: Intergenerational repetition of adolescent pregnancy and poverty). In B. Schmukler (Ed.), *Transformaciones de la Familia en America Latina y el Caribe: Una Perspectiva de Genero (Transformation in Families: Changes in Gender Relations and the Situation of Children in Latin America)* (pp. 419-450). Mexico City: Population Council/Editores Asociados Mexicanos.

Alderman, H., Behrman, J.R., Lavy, V., and Menon, R. (2001). Child health and school enrollment: A longitudinal analysis. *Journal of Human Resources, 36*(1), 185-205.

Alderman, H., Hoddinott, J., and Kinsey, B. (2003). *Long-term consequences of early childhood malnutrition.* (FCND Brief No. 168.) Washington, DC: International Food Policy Research Institute, Food Consumption and Nutrition Division.

Ali, M.M., Cleland, J., and Shah, I.H. (2003). Trends in reproductive behavior among young single women in Colombia and Peru: 1985-1999. *Demography, 40*(4), 659-673.

Almond, G., and Verba, S. (1963). *The civic culture.* Princeton, NJ: Princeton University Press.

Altbach, P.G. (1989). *Student political activism: An international reference handbook.* New York: Greenwood Press.

Amadeo, J.-A., Torney-Purta, J., Lehmann, R., Husfeldt, V., and Nikolova, R. (2002). *Executive summary: Civic knowledge and engagement: An IEA study of upper secondary students in sixteen countries.* Amsterdam: International Association for the Evaluation of Educational Achievement.

Amin, S., and Al-Bassusi, N.H. (2003). *Wage work and marriage: Perspectives of Egyptian working women.* (Policy Research Division Working Paper No. 171.) New York: Population Council.

Amin, S., and Arends-Kuenning, M. (2001). *What does it mean to be a vulnerable child in rural Bangladesh?* Paper presented at Session S48 Demography of Vulnerable Populations, International Union for the Scientific Study of Population General Conference, August 20-25, Salvador, Brazil.

Amin, S., and Cain, M. (1997). The rise of dowry in Bangladesh. In G.W. Jones, R.M. Douglas, J.C. Caldwell, and R.M. D'Souza (Eds.), *The continuing demographic transition* (pp. 290-306). Oxford, England: Clarendon Press.

Amin, S., Diamond, I., Naved, R.T., and Newby, M. (1998). Transition to adulthood of female garment-factory workers in Bangladesh. *Studies in Family Planning, 29*(2), 185-200.

Amin, S., and Lloyd, C.B. (2002). Women's lives and rapid fertility decline: Some lessons from Bangladesh and Egypt. *Population Research and Policy Review, 21,* 275-317.

Amin, S., Mahmud, S., and Huq, L. (2002). *Kishori Abhijan: Baseline survey report on rural adolescents in Bangladesh.* Dhaka: Government of Bangladesh, UNICEF and Ministry of Women and Children Affairs.

Amnesty International. (2000). *Hidden scandal, secret shame: Torture and ill treatment of children.* London, England: Author.

Amnesty International. (2002). *Burundi. Poverty, isolation, and ill treatment: Juvenile justice in Burundi.* London, England: Author.

Amnesty International. (2003). *Philippines. A different childhood: The apprehension and detention of child suspects and offenders.* London, England: Author.

Anderson, B. (1983). *Imagined communities: Reflections on the origin and spread of nationalism.* New York: Verso Press.

Anderson, J., and Herencia, C. (1983). *L'image de la femme et de l'homme dans les livres scolaires peruviens.* Paris, France: UNESCO.

Anderson, S. (2003). Why dowry payments declined with modernization in Europe but are rising in India. *Journal of Political Economy, 111*(2), 269-310.

Anderson-Levitt, K.M., Bloch, M., and Soumare, A.M. (1998). Inside classrooms in Guinea: Girls' experiences. In M. Bloch, J. Beoku-Betts, and R. Tabachnick (Eds.), *Women and education in sub-Saharan Africa* (pp. 99-130). Boulder, CO: Lynne Rienner.

Angrist, J.D., Bettinger, E., Bloom, E., King, E., and Kremer, M. (2002). Vouchers for private schooling in Colombia: Evidence from a randomized natural experiment. *American Economic Review, 92*(5), 1535-1558.

Angrist, J.D., and Krueger, A.B. (1991). Does compulsory school attendance affect schooling and earnings? *Quarterly Journal of Economics, 106*(4), 979-1014.

Angrist, J.D., and Lavy, V. (1997). The effect of a change in language of instruction on the returns to schooling in Morocco. *Journal of Labor Economics, 15*(1), S48-S76.

Angrist, J.D., and Lavy, V. (1999). Using Maimonides' rule to estimate the effect of class size on scholastic achievement. *Quarterly Journal of Economics, 114*(2), 533-575.

Anh, T.S., Knodel, J., Lam, D., and Friedman, J. (1998). Family size and children's education in Vietnam. *Demography, 35*(1), 57-70.

Anker, R. (1998). *Gender and jobs: Sex segregation of occupations in the world.* Geneva, Switzerland: International Labour Office.

Anker, R. (2000). The economics of child labour: A framework for measurement. *International Labour Review, 139*(3), 257-280.

Annual Review of Population Law Database. (2004). Available: http://www.law.harvard.edu/programs/annual_review [May 21, 2004].

Antoine, P., Djire, M., and LaPlante, B. (1995). Les déterminants socioéconomiques de la sortie du célibat à Dakar. *Population, 50*(1), 95-117.

Antoine, P., and Nanitelamio, J. (1996). Can polygyny be avoided in Dakar? In K. Sheldon (Ed.), *Courtyards, markets, city streets: Urban women in Africa* (pp. 129-152). Boulder, CO: Westview Press.

Antunes, M.C., Stall, R.D., Paiva, V., Peres, C.A., Paul, J., Hudes, M., and Hearst, N. (1997). Evaluating an AIDS risk reduction program for young adults in public night schools in Sao Paulo, Brazil. *AIDS, 11*(Supplement 1), S121-S127.

Appadurai, A. (1996). *Modernity at large: Cultural dimension of globalization.* Minneapolis: University of Minnesota.

Appleton, S. (1995). *Exam determinants in Kenyan primary school: Determinants and gender differences.* Washington, DC: Economic Development Institute of the World Bank.

Aras, R.Y., Pai, N.P., and Jain, S.G. (1987). Termination of pregnancy in adolescents. *Journal of Postgraduate Medicine, 33*(3), 120-124.

Arends-Kuenning, M., and Ahmed, A.U. (2004a). *Do crowded classrooms crowd out learning? Evidence from the food for education program in Bangladesh.* (FCND Brief No. 149.) Washington, DC: International Food Policy Research Institute, Food Consumption and Nutrition Division.

Arends-Kuenning, M., and Ahmed, A.U. (2004b). *Does the impact of the food for education program in Bangladesh differ by gender? An analysis of children's academic achievement.* Paper prepared for the Committee on the Status of Women in the Economics Profession session, Education and Gender at the 2004 ASSA Meetings, January 6.

Arends-Kuenning, M., and Amin, S. (2000). *The effects of schooling incentive programs on household resource allocation in Bangladesh.* (Policy Research Division Working Paper Report No. 133.) New York: Population Council.

Arnett, J.J. (2002). The psychology of globalization. *American Psychologist, 57*(10), 774-783.

Arnett, J.J. (2003). Conceptions of the transition to adulthood among emerging adults in American ethnic Groups. *New Directions for Child and Adolescent Development, 100*(June), 63-75.

Arnett, J.J. (2004). *Emerging adulthood: The winding road from the late teens through the twenties.* New York: Oxford University Press.

Assaad, R. (1997a). The effects of public sector hiring and compensation policies on the Egyptian labor market. *The World Bank Economic Review, 11*(1), 85-118.

Assaad, R. (1997b). The employment crisis in Egypt: Current trends and future prospects. In *Research in Middle East economics* (pp. 39-66, Volume 2). Greenwich, CT: JAI Press.

Assaad, R. (2002). The transformation of the Egyptian labor market: 1988-98. In R. Assaad (Ed.), *The Egyptian labor market in an era of reform* (pp. 3-64). Cairo, Egypt: The American University in Cairo Press.

Bacci, A., Manhica, G.M., Machungo, F., Bugalho, A., and Cuttini, M. (1993). Outcome of teenage pregnancy in Maputo, Mozambique. *International Journal of Gynecological Obstetrics, 40*(1), 19-23.

Bachrach, C., and McNicoll, G. (2003). Notes and commentary. Causal analysis in the population sciences: A symposium. *Population and Development Review, 29*(3), 443-447.

Bailey, P., and Bruno, Z. (2001). *Consecuencias del embarazo y aborto entre las adolescentes del nordeste de Brasil: 1 año y 5 años después.* Presented at the International Conference on Unwanted Pregnancy and Induced Abortion and Public Health Implications for Latin America and the Caribbean, Cuernavaca, Mexico, November 12-14.

Baker, R., and Hinton, R. (2001). Approaches to children's work and rights in Nepal. *Annals of the American Academy of Political and Social Sciences, 575*(May), 176-193.

Balmer, D.H., Gikundi, E., Billingsley, M.C., Kihuho, F.G., Kimani, M., Wang'ondu, J., and Njoroge, H. (1997). Adolescent knowledge, values, and coping strategies: Implications for health in sub-Saharan Africa. *Journal of Adolescent Health, 21*(1), 33-38.

Banerjee, A.V., Cole, S., Duflo, E., and Linden, L. (2003). *Remedying education: Evidence from two randomized experiments in India.* (Poverty Action Lab Paper No. 4.) Cambridge, MA: Poverty Action Lab.

Banerjee, A.V., Jacob, S., Kremer, M., Lanjouw, J., and Lanjouw, P. (2000). *Promoting school participation in rural Rajasthan: Results from some prospective trials.* Unpublished manuscript, Harvard University, Cambridge, MA.

Banerjee, A.V., Kremer, M., Lanjouw, J., and Lanjouw, P. (2002). *Teacher-student ratios and school performance in Udaipur, India: A prospective evaluation.* Unpublished manuscript, Harvard University, Cambridge, MA.

Banerjee, K. (1999). Gender stratification and the contemporary marriage market in India. *Journal of Family Issues, 20*(5), 648-676.

Bankole, A., Darroch, J.E., and Singh, S. (1999). Determinants of trends in condom use in the United States, 1988-1995. *Family Planning Perspectives, 31*(6), 264-272.

Bankole, A., Singh, S., and Haas, T. (1999). Characteristics of women who obtain induced abortion: A worldwide review. *International Family Planning Perspectives, 25*(2), 68-77.

Baris, E., Brigden, L.W., Prindiville, J., da Costa e Silva, V.L., Chitanondh, H., and Chandiwana, S. (2000). Research priorities for tobacco control in developing countries: A regional approach to a global consultative process. *Tobacco Control, 9*(Summer), 217-233.

Barker, D.J.P. (1998). *Mothers, babies, and health in later life* (2nd ed.). Edinburgh, Scotland: Churchill Livingstone.

Barker, D.J.P. (2003). *The developmental origins of adult disease.* Paper presented at the World Health Organization Expert Consultation Towards the Development of a Strategy for Promoting Optimal Fetal Growth, Geneva, Switzerland, November 25-27.

Barker, G. (2002). *Adolescents, social support, and selp-seeking behavior: An international literature review and program consultation with recommendations for action.* Prepared for the World Health Organization, Department of Child and Adolescent Health and Development.

Barnett, B. (2000). Programs for adolescents: Reproductive health merit badge for scouts. *Network, 20*(3), 24-32.

Barnett, T., and Whiteside, A. (2002). *AIDS in the twenty-first century: Disease and globalization.* New York: Palgrave Macmillan.

Barreto, T., Campbell, O.M.R., Davies, J.L., Fauveau, V., Filippi, V.G.A., Graham, W.J., Mamdani, M., Rooney, C.I.F., and Toubia, N.F. (1992). Investigating induced abortion in developing countries: Methods and problems. *Studies in Family Planning, 23*(3), 159-170.

Barros, R.P., and Lam, D. (1996). Income inequality, inequality in education, and children's schooling attainment in Brazil. In N. Birdsall and R.H. Sabot (Eds.), *Opportunity foregone: Education in Brazil* (pp. 337-366). Baltimore, MD: Johns Hopkins University Press for the Inter-American Development Bank.

Barua, A., and Kurz, K. (2001). Reproductive health seeking by married adolescent girls in Maharashtra, India. *Reproductive Health Matters, 9*(17), 53-62.

Basu, A. (1995). Women's roles and the gender gap in health and survival. In M. Das Gupta, L.C. Chen, and T.N. Krishman (Eds.), *Women's health in India: Risk and vulnerability.* Bombay, India: Oxford University Press.

Basu, K. (1999). Child labor: Cause, consequence, and cure, with remarks on international labor standards. *Journal of Economic Literature, 37*(3), 1083-1119.

Basu, K. (2003a). The economics of child labor. *Scientific American, 289*(4), 84-91.

Basu, K. (2003b). *Globalization and marginalization: A reexamination of development policy.* (Working Paper No. 026.) London, England: Bureau for Research in Economic Analysis of Development.

Basu, K., and Tzannatos, Z. (2003). The global child labor problem: What do we know and what can we do? *The World Bank Economic Review, 17*(2), 147-174.

Basu, K., and Van, P.H. (1998). The economics of child labor. *The American Economic Review, 88*(3), 412-427.

Baumer, E.P., and South, S.J. (2001). Community effects on youth sexual activity. *Journal of Marriage and the Family, 63,* 540-554.

Bay, A.-H., and Blekesaune, M. (2002). Youth, unemployment, and political marginalization. *International Journal of Social Welfare, 11*(2), 132-139.

Beckerleg, S. (1995). Brown sugar or Friday prayers: Youth choices and community building in coastal Kenya. *African Affairs, 94*(374), 23-38.

Beegle, K., Dehejia, R., and Gatti, R. (2003). *Child labor, crop shocks, and credit constraints.* (NBER Working Paper No. 10088.) Cambridge, MA: National Bureau of Economic Research.

Beegle, K., Dehejia, R., and Gatti, R. (2004). *Why should we care about child labor?* (Policy Research Division Working Paper No. 3479.) Washington, DC: World Bank.

Behrman, J.R. (1996). The impact of health and nutrition on education. *The World Bank Research Observer, 11*(1), 23-37.

Behrman, J.R. (1997). *Women's schooling and child education: A survey.* Philadelphia: University of Pennsylvania.

Behrman, J.R., and Birdsall, N. (1983). The quality of schooling: Quantity alone is misleading. *The American Economic Review, 73*(5), 928-946.

Behrman, J.R., Birdsall, N., and Szekely, M. (2003). *Economic policy and wage differentials in Latin America.* (Working Paper No. 29.) Washington, DC: Center for Global Development.

Behrman, J.R., Deolalikar, A.B., Tinakorn, P., and Chandoevwit, W. (2000). *The effects of the Thai economic crisis and of Thai labor market policies on labor market outcomes.* Bangkok: Thailand Development Research Institute.

Behrman, J.R., Duryea, S., and Szekely, M. (1999). *Schooling investments and aggregate conditions: A household-survey-based approach for Latin America and the Caribbean.* Washington, DC: Inter-American Development Bank.

Behrman, J.R., Duryea, S., and Szekely, M. (2004). *Schooling investments and aggregate conditions: A household-survey-based investigation for Latin America and the Caribbean.* (Working Paper No. 407.) Philadelphia: University of Pennsylvania.

Behrman, J.R., Foster, A.D., Rosenzweig, M.R., and Vashishtha, P. (1999). Women's schooling, home teaching, and economic growth. *Journal of Political Economy, 107*(4), 682-714.

Behrman, J.R., Hoddinott, J., Maluccio, J.A., Quisumbing, A., Martorell, R., and Stein, A.D. (2003). *The impact of experimental nutritional interventions on education into adulthood in rural Guatemala: Preliminary longitudinal analysis.* Paper presented at the Second Meeting of the Social Policy Monitoring Network Health and Nutrition, Rio de Janeiro, Brazil, November 6-7.

Behrman, J.R., and Knowles, J.C. (1998). Population and reproductive health: An economic framework for policy evaluation. *Population and Development Review, 24*(4), 697-738.

Behrman, J.R., and Knowles, J.C. (1999). Household income and child schooling in Vietnam. *The World Bank Economic Review, 13*(2), 211-256.

Behrman, J.R., and Knowles, J.C. (2002). *Assessing the economic benefits of investing in youth in developing countries.* (Departmental Working Paper No. 28888.) Washington, DC: World Bank.

Behrman, J.R., and Rosenzweig, M.R. (1994). Caveat emptor: Cross-country data on education and the labor force. *Journal of Development Economics, 44*(1), 147-171.

Behrman, J.R., and Rosenzweig, M.R. (1999). Ability biases in schooling returns and twins: A test and new estimates. *Economics of Education Review, 18*(2), 159-167.

Behrman, J.R., and Rosenzweig, M.R. (2002). Does increasing women's schooling raise the schooling of the next generation? *American Economic Review, 92*(1), 323-334.

Behrman, J.R., and Sengupta, P. (2002). *The returns to female schooling in developing countries revisited.* Unpublished manuscript, Department of Economics, University of Pennsylvania.

Behrman, J.R., and Sengupta, P. (2005). The changing contexts in which youth are transitioning to adulthood in developing countries: Have developing economies been converging toward developed economies? In National Research Council and Institute of Medicine, *The changing transitions to adulthood in developing countries: Selected studies.* C.B. Lloyd, J.R. Behrman, N.P. Stromquist, and B. Cohen (Eds.). Committee on Population and Board on Children, Youth, and Families. Division of Behavioral and Social Sciences and Education. Washington, DC: The National Academies Press.

Behrman, J.R., Sengupta, P., and Todd, P. (2000). *The impact of PROGRESA on achievement test scores in the first year.* Washington, DC: International Food Policy Research Institute.

Behrman, J.R., Sengupta, P., and Todd, P. (2002*). Progressing through PROGRESA: An impact assessment of Mexico's school subsidy experiment.* Washington, DC: International Food Policy Research Institute.

Behrman, J.R., and Zhang Z. (1995). Gender issues and employment in Asia. *Asian Development Review, 13*(2), 1-49.

Bell, C., Devarajan, S., and Gersbach, H. (2003). *The long-run economic costs of AIDS: Theory and an application to South Africa.* Washington, DC: World Bank.

Benavot, A., and Kamens, D. (1989). *The curricular content of primary education in developing countries.* (Report No. WPS-237.) Washington, DC: World Bank, Education and Employment Division.

Bennell, P., Hyde, K., and Swainson, N. (2002). *The impact of the HIV/AIDS epidemic on the education sector in sub-Saharan Africa: A synthesis of the findings and recommendation of three country studies.* Brighton, England: Center for International Education, University of Sussex.

Bennett, L.R. (2001). Single women's experiences of premarital pregnancy and induced abortion in Lombok, Eastern Indonesia. *Reproductive Health Matters, 9*(17), 37-43.

Berman, S., and Hein, K. (1999). Adolescents and STDs. In K. Holmes, P. Sparling, P. Mardh, S. Lemon, W. Stamm, P. Piot, and J. Wasserheit (Eds.), *Sexually transmitted diseases* (pp. 129-142, 3rd ed.). New York: McGraw Hill.

Berry, B.J.L., Conkling, E.C., and Ray, D.M. (1997). *The global economy in transition* (2nd ed.). Upper Saddle River, NJ: Prentice Hall.

Bertrand, J., Magnani, R., and Rutenberg, N. (1996). *Evaluating family planning programs with adaptations for reproductive health.* (The Evaluation Project. USAID, Contract Number, DPE-3060-C-00-1054-00.) Washington, DC: U.S. Agency for International Development.

Bhat, P.N.M., and Halli, S.S. (1999). Demography of brideprice and dowry: Causes and consequences of the Indian marriage squeeze. *Population Studies: A Journal of Demography, 53*(2), 129-148.

Bhave, G., Lindan, C.P., Hudes, E.S., Desai, S., Wagle, U., Tripathi, S.P., and Mandel, J.S. (1995). Impact of an intervention on HIV, sexually transmitted diseases, and condom use among sex workers in Bombay, India. *AIDS, 9*(Supplement 1), S21-S30.

Bicego, G.T., and Boerma, J.T. (1993). Maternal education and child survival. *Social Science and Medicine, 36*(9), 1207-1227.

Bicego, G.T., Rutstein, S., and Johnson, K. (2003). Dimensions of the emerging orphan crisis in sub-Saharan Africa. *Social Science and Medicine, 56*(6), 1235-1247.

Billig, M.S. (1992). The marriage squeeze and the rise of groomprice in India's Kerala State. *Journal of Comparative Family Studies, 23*(2), 197-216.

Binder, M., and Scrogin, D. (1999). Labor force participation and household work of urban schoolchildren in Mexico: Characteristics and consequences. *Economic Development and Cultural Change, 48*(1), 123-154.

Biraimah, K.C. (1980). The impact of western schools on girls expectations: A Togolese case. *Comparative Education Review, 24*(Supplement), S197-S209.

Birdsall, N., and Chester, L.A. (1987). Contraception and the status of women: What is the link? *Family Planning Perspectives, 19*(1), 14-18.

Bittles, A.H. (1994). The role and significance of consanguinity as a demographic variable. *Population and Development Review, 20*(3), 561-584.

Blanc, A.K. (2001). The effect of power in sexual relationships on sexual and reproductive health. *Studies in Family Planning, 32*(3), 189-213.

Blanc, A.K., and Gage, A.J. (2000). Men, polygyny, and fertility over the life course in sub-Saharan Africa. In C. Bledsoe, S. Lerner, and J.I. Guyer (Eds.), *Fertility and the male life-cycle in the era of fertility decline* (pp. 163-187). New York: Oxford University Press.

Blanc, A.K., and Rutenberg, N. (1990). Assessment of the quality of data on age at first sexual intercourse, age at first marriage, and age at first birth in the demographic and health surveys. In Institute of Resource Development/Macro Systems Inc., *An assessment of DHS-I data quality* (volume 1, pp. 41-79). Columbia, MD: DHS Methodological Reports.

Blanc, A.K., and Way, A.A. (1998). Sexual behavior and contraceptive knowledge and use among adolescents in developing countries. *Studies in Family Planning, 29*(2), 106-116.

Blanc, A.K., Wolff, B., Gage, A.J., Ezeh, A.C., Neema, S., and Ssekamaatte-Ssebuliba, J. (1996). *Negotiating reproductive outcomes in Uganda.* Calverton, MD: ORC Macro International and Institute of Statistics and Applied Economics.

Blau, F.D. (1997). *Trends in the well-being of American women: 1970-1995.* (NBER Working Paper No. 6206.) Cambridge, MA: National Bureau of Economic Research.

Blau, F.D., Kahn, L.M., and Waldfogel, J. (2000). *Understanding young women's marriage decisions: The role of labor and marriage market conditions.* (NBER Working Paper No. 7510.) Cambridge, MA: National Bureau of Economic Research.

Bledsoe, C.H. (1992). The cultural transformation of western education in Sierra Leone. *Africa, 62*(2), 182-202.

Bledsoe, C.H., and Pison, G. (1994). *Nuptiality in sub-Saharan Africa: Contemporary anthropological and demographic perspectives.* Oxford, England: Clarendon Press and Oxford University Press.

Bloom, D.E., Canning, D., and Sevilla, J. (2002). *The demographic dividend: A new perspective on the economic consequences of population change (population matters). A RAND program of policy-relevant research communication.* Santa Monica, CA: RAND.

Bloom, D.E., Mahal, A., Christiansen, L., de Silva, A., de Sylva, S., Dias, S.M., Jayasinghe, S., Jayaweera, S., Mahawewa, S., Sammugam, T., and Tantrigama, G. (1997). Socioeconomic dimensions of the HIV/AIDS epidemic in Sri Lanka. In D. Bloom, (Ed.), *The economics of HIV and AIDS: The case of South Africa and South East Asia* (Chapter 3). New York: Oxford University Press.

Bloom, D.E., and Williamson, J.G. (1998). Demographic transitions and economic miracles in emerging Asia. *The World Bank Economic Review, 12*(3), 419-455.

Blum, R.W., McNeely, C., and Nonnemaker, J. (2002). Vulnerability, risk, and protection. *Journal of Adolescent Health, 31*(Supplement 1), 28-39.

Bohmer, L., and Kirumira, E. (1997). *Access to reproductive health services: Participatory research with Ugandan adolescents.* Unpublished Final Report and Working Paper, Pacific Institute for Women's Health and Child Health and Development Centre, Makerere University, Kampala, Uganda.

Bolu, O., Lindsey, C., Peterman, T., Kamb, M., Bolan, G., Zenilman, J., Douglas, J., Malotte, K., and Rogers, J. (2002). *Once is not enough: Re-screening sexually transmitted disease (STD): Clinic patients in six months to detect new, unrecognized STD.* Paper presented (for the Project RESPECT Study Group) at the 2002 CDC National STD Prevention Conference, San Diego, CA, March 4-7.

Bommier, A., and Lambert, S. (2000). Education demand and age at school enrollment in Tanzania. *Journal of Human Resources, 35*(1), 177-203.

Bongaarts, J. (2000). Dependency burdens in the developing world. In N. Birdsall, A.C. Kelley, and S. Sinding (Eds.), *Population matters: Demographic change, economic growth, and poverty in the developing world* (pp. 55-64). New York: Oxford University Press.

Bongaarts, J., and Watkins, S.C. (1996). Social interactions and contemporary fertility transitions. *Population and Development Review, 22*(4), 639-682.

Booth, M. (2002). Arab adolescents facing the future: Enduring ideals and pressures to change. In B.B. Brown, R.W. Larson, and T.S. Saraswathi (Eds.), *The world's youth: Adolescence in eight regions of the globe* (pp. 207-242). Cambridge, England: Cambridge University Press.

Borooah, V.K., and Iyer, S. (2002). *Vidya, veda, and varna: The influence of religion and caste on education in rural India.* (ICER Working Paper No. 32-2002.) Torino, Italy: International Centre for Economic Research.

Botero, J., Djankov, S., La Porta, R., Lopez-de-Silanes, F., and Shliefer, A. (2003). *The regulation of labor.* (NBER Working Paper No. 9756.) Cambridge, MA: National Bureau of Economic Research.

Botticini, M., and Siow, A. (2003). Why dowries? *American Economic Review, 93*(4), 1385-1398.

Bound, J., and Johnson, G. (1992). Changes in the structure of wages in the 1980s: An evaluation of alternative explanations. *American Economic Review, 82*, 371-392.

Bourdieu, P. (1985). The forms of capital. In J.G. Richardson (Ed.), *Handbook of theory and research for the sociology of education* (pp. 241-258). New York: Greenwood.

Bourguignon, F., Ferreira, F.H.G., and Leite, P.G. (2003) Conditional cash transfers, schooling, and child labor: Micro-simulating Brazil's Bolsa Escola program. *The World Bank Economic Review, 17*(2), 229-254.

Bourque, S., and Grossholtz, J.P. (1998). Politics as an unnatural practice: Political science looks at female participation. In A. Phillips (Ed.), *Feminism and politics* (pp. 23-43). Oxford, England: Oxford University Press.

Boyden, J. (1997). Childhood and the policy makers: A comparative perspective on the globalization of childhood. In A. James and A. Prout (Eds.), *Constructing and reconstructing childhood: Contemporary issues in the sociological study of childhood* (2nd ed., pp. 190-215). London, England: Falmer Press.

Boyden, J., Ling, B., and Myers, W. (1998). *What works for working children.* Florence, Italy: UNICEF.

Boye, A.K., Hill, K., Isaacs, S., and Gordis, D. (1991). Marriage law and practice in the Sahel. *Studies in Family Planning, 22*(6), 343-349.

Boyer, D., and Fine, D. (1992). Sexual abuse as a factor in adolescent pregnancy. *Family Planning Perspectives, 24*(4), 11.

Brady, M. (1998). Laying the foundation for girls' healthy futures: Can sports play a role? *Studies in Family Planning, 29*(1), 79-82.

Brady, M., and Khan, A.B. (2002). *Letting girls play: The Mathare youth sports association's football program for girls.* New York: Population Council.

Bratton, M. (1999). Political participation in a new democracy: Institutional considerations from Zambia. *Comparative Political Studies, 32*(5), 549-588.

Bratton, M., Alderfer, P., Bowser, G., and Temba, J. (1999). The effects of civic education on political culture: Evidence from Zambia. *World Development 27*(5), 807-824.

Braungart, R., and Braungart, M. (1993). Historical generations and citizenship. *Research in Political Sociology, 6,* 139-174.

Bray, M. (2003). *Adverse effects of private supplementary tutoring: Dimensions, implications, and government responses.* Paris, France: UNESCO, International Institute for Educational Planning.

Brieger, W.R., Delano, G.E., Lane, C.G., Oladep, O., and Oyediran, K.A. (2001). West African youth initiative: Outcome of a reproductive health education program. *Journal of Adolescent Health, 29*(6), 436-446.

Brockerhoff, M.P. (2000). An urbanizing world. *Population Bulletin, 55*(3), 3-45.

Bronfenbrenner, U., and Morris, P.A. (1998). The ecology of developmental processes. In W. Damon and R.M. Lerner (Eds.), *Handbook of child psychology* (pp. 993-1028). New York: John Wiley and Sons.

Brooks-Gunn, J. (1993). Why do adolescents have difficulty adhering to health regimes? In N.A. Krasnegor, L. Epstein, S.B. Johnson, and S.J. Yaffe (Eds.), *Developmental aspects of health compliance behavior* (pp. 125-152). Hillsdale, NJ: Lawrence Erlbaum.

Brown, A.D., Jejeebhoy, S.J., Shah, I., and Yount, K. (2001). *Sexual relations among young people in developing countries: Evidence from WHO case studies.* (Occasional Paper No. 4.) Geneva, Switzerland: World Health Organization, Department of Reproductive Health and Research.

Brown, D.K., Deardorff, A.V., and Stern, R.M. (2003). Child labor: Theory, evidence, and policy. In K. Basu, H. Horn, L. Román, and J. Shapiro (Eds.), *International labor standards: History, theory, and policy options* (pp. 195-247). Malden, MA: Blackwell.

Brown, P.H. (2001). Choosing to die: A growing epidemic among the young. *Bulletin of the World Health Organization, 79*(12), 1175-1177.

Brown, P.H., and Park, A. (2002). Education and poverty in rural China. *Economics of Education Review, 21*(6), 523-541.

Browning, M., Bourguignon, F., Chiappori, P.A., and Lechene, V., (1994). Income and outcomes: A structural model of intrahousehold allocation. *Journal of Political Economy, 102*(6), 1067-1097.

Bruce, J., Lloyd, C.B., and Leonard, A. (1995). *Families in focus: New perspectives on mothers, fathers, and children.* New York: Population Council.

Bruns, B., Mingat, A., and Rakotomalala, R. (2003). *Achieving universal primary education by 2015: A chance for every child.* Washington, DC: World Bank.

Buchmann, C. (2002). Getting ahead in Kenya: Social capital, shadow education, and achievement. In B. Fuller and E. Hannum (Eds.), *Schooling and social capital in diverse cultures* (pp. 133-159). Greenwich, CT: JAI Press.

Buckingham, D. (2000). *The making of citizens: Young people, news, and politics.* London, England: Routledge.

Busse, M. (2002). Do labor standards affect comparative advantage in developing countries? *World Development, 30*(11), 1921-1932.

Bustillo, I. (1993). Latin America and the Caribbean. In E.M. King and A.M. Hill (Eds.), *Women's education in developing countries: Barriers, benefits and policies* (pp. 175-210). Baltimore, MD: Johns Hopkins University Press.

Butchart, A., and Engstrom, K. (2002). Sex and age-specific relations between economic development, economic inequality, and homicide rates in people aged 0-24 years: A cross-sectional analysis. *Bulletin of the World Health Organization, 80*(10), 797-805.

Buvé, A., Lagarde, E., Caraël, M., Hayes, R.J, Auvert, B., Ferry, B., Robinson, N.J., Anagonou, S., Kanhonou, L., and Laourou, M. (2001). Interpreting sexual behaviour data: Validity issues in the multicentre study of actors determining the differential spread of HIV in four African cities. *AIDS, 15*(Supplement 4), S117-S126.

Buvinic, M. (1998). The costs of adolescent childbearing: Evidence from Chile, Barbados, Guatemala, and Mexico. *Studies in Family Planning, 29*(2), 201-209.

Cain, M. (1984). *Women's status and fertility in developing countries: Son preference and economic security.* (Working Paper No. 682.) Washington, DC: World Bank.

Caldwell, J.C. (1969). *African rural-urban migration: The movement to Ghana's towns.* Canberra: Australian National University Press.

Caldwell, J.C., Caldwell, P., Caldwell, B.K., and Pieris, I. (1998). The construction of adolescence in a changing world: Implications for sexuality, reproduction, and marriage. *Studies in Family Planning, 29*(2), 137-153.

Caldwell, J.C., Reddy, P.H., and Caldwell, P. (1983). The causes of marriage change in South India. *Population Studies, 37*(3), 343-361.

Call, K.T., Riedel, A.A., Hein, K., McLoyd, V., Petersen, A., and Kipke, M. (2002). Adolescent health and well-being in the twenty-first century: A global perspective. *Journal of Research on Adolescence, 12*(1), 69-98.

Calvès, A.E. (1999). Marginalization of African single mothers in the marriage market: Evidence from Cameroon. *Population Studies: A Journal of Demography, 53*(3), 291-301.

Calvès, A.E. (2000). Premarital childbearing in urban Cameroon: Paternal recognition, child care, and financial support. *Journal of Comparative Family Studies, 31*(4), 443-461.

Calvès, A.E. (2002). Abortion risk and decisionmaking among young people in urban Cameroon. *Studies in Family Planning, 33*(3), 249-260.

Cameron, J. (2003). Hormonal mediation of physiological and behavioral processes that influence fertility. In National Research Council, *Offspring: Human fertility behavior in biodemographic perspective* (pp. 104-139). Panel for the Workshop on the Biodemography of Fertility and Family Behavior. K.W. Wachter and R.A. Bulatao (Eds.). Committee on Population. Division of Behavioral and Social Sciences and Education. Washington, DC: The National Academies Press.

Cameron, S., Kandule, N., Leng, J., and Arnold, C. (1998). *Urban child care in Bangladesh.* Westport, CT: Save the Children (USA).

Campbell, D., and Stanley, J.C. (1963). *Experimental and quasi-experimental designs for research.* Chicago, IL: Rand McNally.

Canals-Cerda, J., and Ridao-Cano, C. (2003). *The dynamics of school and work in rural Bangladesh.* (Royal Economic Society Annual Conference Series Paper No. 36.) Available: http://www.res.org.uk/society/annualconf.asp [accessed February 2005].

Cantor, C., and Neulinger, K. (2000). The epidemiology of suicide and attempted suicide among young Australians. *Australian and New Zealand Journal of Psychiatry, 34*(3), 370-387.

Card, D. (2000). *Estimating the return to schooling: Progress on some persistent econometric problems.* (NBER Working Paper No. 7769.) Cambridge, MA: National Bureau of Economic Research.

Carnoy, M. (2000). Globalization and educational reform. In N.P. Stromquist and K. Monkman (Eds.), *Globalization and education: Integration and contestation across cultures* (pp. 43-62). Lanham, MD: Rowman and Littlefield.

Carnoy, M., and Rhoten, D. (2002). What does globalization mean for educational change? A comparative approach. *Comparative Education Review, 46*(1), 1-9.

Carnoy, M., and Torres, C.A. (1994). Educational change and structural adjustment: A case study of Costa Rica. In J. Samoff (Ed.), *Coping with crisis: Austerity, adjustment, and human resources* (pp. 64-99). London and New York: UNESCO and Cassell.

Carr, D. (1997). *Female genital cutting: Findings from the demographic and health surveys program.* Calverton, MD: ORC Macro International.

Casassus, J., Froemel, J.E., Palafox, J.C., and Cusato, S. (1998). *Primer estudio internacional comparativo sobre lenguaje, matematica y factores asociados en tercero y cuarto grado.* Santiago, Chile: UNESCO.

Case, A., and Deaton, A. (1999). School inputs and educational outcomes in South Africa. *Quarterly Journal of Economics, 114*(3), 1047-1084.

Case, A., Paxson, C., and Ableidiner, J. (2004). Orphans in Africa: Parental death, poverty, and school enrollment. *Demography, 41*(3), 483-508.

Caselli, G., Meslé, F., and Vallin, J. (2002). Epidemiologic transition theory exceptions. *Genus, 58*(2), 54-67.

Cash, K., Anasuchatkul, B., and Busayawong, W. (1995). *Experimental educational interventions for AIDS prevention among Northern Thai single migratory factory workers.* (ICRW Women and AIDS Research Program Report Series No. 9.) Washington, DC: International Center for Research on Women.

Castells, M. (2000). *The rise of the network society.* Malden, MA: Blackwell.

Casterline, J.B., and El-Zeini, L.O. (2002). *The changing demography of kinship in the Arab region: A microsimulation analysis.* Paper presented at annual meeting of Population Association of America. Atlanta, GA.

Casterline, J.B., Williams, L., and McDonald, P. (1986). The age difference between spouses: Variations among developing countries. *Population Studies, 40*(3), 353-374.

Cattell, M.G. (1994). Nowadays it isn't easy to advise the young: Grandmothers and granddaughters among Abaluyia of Kenya. *Journal of Cross-Cultural Gerontology, 9*(2), 157-178.

Celantano, D.D., Bond, K., Lyles, C.M., Eiumtrakul, S., Go, V.F.L., Beyrer, C., Nelson, K., Khamboonruang, C., and Vaddhannaphutttii, C. (2000). Preventive intervention to reduce sexually transmitted infections: A field trial I, the Royal Thai Army. *Archives of Internal Medicine 160*(4), 535-540.

Celentano, D.D., Nelson, K.E., Lyles, C.M., Beyrer, C., Eiumtrakul, S., Go, V.F.L., Kuntolbutra, S., and Khamboonruang, C. (1998). Decreasing incidence of HIV and sexually transmitted diseases in young Thai men: Evidence for success of the HIV/AIDS control and prevention program. *AIDS, 12*, F29-F36.

Celli, J.B., and Obuchi, R. (2003). Entry, participation, income, and consolidation: Young adult labor market experience in Latin America. In S. Duryea, A. Cox Edwards, and M. Ureta (Eds.), *Critical decisions at a critical age: Adolescents and young adults in Latin America* (pp. 145-178). Washington, DC: Inter-American Development Bank.

Chen, S., and Ravallion, M. (2001). How well did the world's poorest fare in the 1990s? *Review of Income and Wealth, 47*(3), 283-300.

Chen, S., and Wang, Y. (2001). *China's growth and poverty reduction: Recent trends between 1990 and 1999.* (Policy Research Division Working Paper No. 2651.) Washington, DC: World Bank.

Chilisa, B. (2002). National policies on pregnancy in education systems in sub-Saharan Africa: The case of Botswana. *Gender and Education, 14*(1), 21-35.

Choe, M.K., Kiting, A.S., Lin, H.–S., Podhisita, C., Raymundo, C., and Thapa, S. (2002b). *The youth tobacco epidemic in Asia.* (East-West Center Working Papers Population Series No. 108-117.) Honolulu, HI: East-West Center.

Choe, M.K., and Lin, H.-S. (2001). Effect of education on premarital sex and marriage in Taiwan. (East-West Center Working Papers Population Series No. 108-16.) Honolulu, HI: East-West Center.

Choe, M.K., and Raymundo, C.M. (2001). *Initiation of smoking, drinking, and drug-use among Filipino youths.* (East-West Center Working Papers Population Series No. 108-7.) Honolulu, HI: East-West Center.

Choe, M.K., Thapa, S., and Achmad, S.I. (2001). Surveys show persistence of teenage marriage and childbearing in Indonesia and Nepal. *Asia-Pacific Population and Policy, 58,* 1-4.

Choe, M.K., Westley, S.B., and Retherford, R.D. (2002). *Tradition and change in marriage and family life: The future of population in Asia.* Honolulu, HI: East-West Center.

Chumlea, C.W., Schubert, C.M., Roche, A.F., Kulin, H.E., Lee, P.A., Himes, J.H., and Sun, S.S. (2003). Age at menarche and racial comparisons in U.S. girls. *Pediatrics, 111*(1), 110-113.

Cincotta, R.P., Engelman, R., and Anastasion, D. (2003). *The security demographic: Population and civil conflict after the cold war.* Washington, DC: Population Action International.

Clark, S. (2004). Early marriage and HIV risks in sub-Saharan Africa. *Studies in Family Planning, 35*(3), 149-160.

Cleland, J.G., and van Ginneken, J.K. (1988). Maternal education and child survival in developing countries: The search for pathways of influence. *Social Science and Medicine, 27*(12), 1357-1368.

Clemens, M. (2004). *The long walk to school: International education goals in historical perspective.* Washington, DC: Center for Global Development.

Clignet, R. (1987). On dit que la polygamie est morte, vive la polygamie! In D. Parkin and D. Nyamwaya (Eds.), *Transformations of African marriage* (pp. 199-209). Manchester, England: Manchester University Press.

Coalition to Stop the Use of Child Soldiers. (2001). *Child soldiers global report.* London, England: Author.

Cohen, D., Spear, S., Scribner, R., Kissinger, P., Mason, K., and Wildgen, J. (2000). Broken windows and the risk of gonorrhea. *American Journal of Public Health, 90*(2), 230-236.

Cohen, M. (1998). Sexually transmitted diseases enhance HIV transmission: No longer a hypothesis. *Lancet, 351*(Supplement 3), 5-7.

Colclough, C., and Al-Samarrai, S. (2000). Achieving schooling for all: Budgetary expenditures on education in sub-Saharan Africa and South Asia. *World Development, 28*(11), 1927-1944.

Colclough, C., and Lewin, K. (1993). *Educating all the children: Strategies for primary schooling in the south.* Oxford, England: Clarendon Press.

Condon, R. (1988). *Inuit youth: Growth and change in the Canadian Arctic.* New Brunswick, NJ: Rutgers University Press.

Contreras, D. (2003). *Vouchers, school choice, and the access to higher education.* New Haven, CT: Yale University.

Cooper, B.M. (1995). Women's worth and wedding gift exchange in Maradi, Niger, 1907-89. *Journal of African History, 36*(1), 121-140.

Coplan, P., Okonofua, F.E., Temin, M., Ogonor, J.T., Omorodion, F.I., Kaufman, J.A., and Hegenhougen, H.K. (1999). Sexual behavior and health care-seeking behavior for sexually transmitted diseases among Nigerian youth. *International Family Planning Perspectives, 25*(4), 186-190, 195.

Cornia, G.A., Patel, M., and Zagonari, F. (2002). The impact of HIV/AIDS on the health system and child health. In G.A. Cornia (Ed.), *AIDS, public policy and child well-being* (Chapter 13). Florence, Italy: UNICEF.

Corten, A. (2001). Transnationalised religious needs and political delegitimisation. In A. Corten and R. Marshall-Fratani (Eds.), *Between babel and Pentecost: Transnational Pentecostalism in Africa and Latin America* (pp. 106-123). Bloomington: Indiana University Press.

Corten, A., and Marshall-Fratani, R. (Eds.) (2001). Introduction. In *Between Babel and Pentecost: Transnational Pentecostalism in Africa and Latin America* (pp. 1-21). Bloomington: Indiana University Press.

Costa, F.M., Jessor, R., Donovan, J.E., and Fortenberry, J.D. (1995). Early initiation of sexual intercourse: The influence of psychosocial unconventionality. *Journal of Research on Adolescence, 5,* 93-121.

Cox, C., and Lemaitre, M.J. (1999). Market and state principles of reform in Chilean education: Policies and results. In G. Perry and D.M. Leipziger (Eds.), *Chile: Recent policy lessons and emerging challenges* (pp. 149-188). Washington, DC: World Bank.

Creel, L. (2001). *Abandoning female genital cutting: Prevalence, attitudes, and efforts to end the practice.* Washington, DC: Population Reference Bureau.

Cunningham, W.V., and Maloney, W.F. (2000). *Child labor and schooling decisions.* Washington, DC: World Bank.

Cutler, D.M. (2004). *Behavioral health interventions: What works and why?* In National Research Council, *Critical perspectives on racial and ethnic differences in health in late life* (pp. 643-674). N.B. Anderson, R.A. Bulatao, and B. Cohen (Eds.). Panel on Race, Ethnicity, and Health in Later Life. Committee on Population. Division of Behavioral and Social Sciences and Education. Washington, DC: The National Academies Press.

Dalton, R.J. (1996). *Citizen politics.* Chatham, NJ: Chatham House.

Damico, A.J., Damico, S.B., and Conway, M.M. (1998). The democratic education of women: High school and beyond. *Women and Politics, 19*(2), 2-11.

Dare, O.O., and Cleland, J.G. (1994). Reliability and validity of survey data on sexual behavior. *Health Transition Review, 4*(Supplement), 93-110.

Davidson, J., and Kanyuka, M. (1992). Girls' participation in basic education in southern Malawi. *Comparative Education Review, 36*(4), 446-466.

Davis, S. (2004). *Quaker Palestine youth program evaluation.* Amman, Jordan: American Friends Service Committee.

de Onis, M., Frongillo, E.A., and Blossner, M. (2000). Is malnutrition declining? An analysis of changes in levels of child malnutrition since 1980. *Bulletin of the World Health Organization, 78*(10), 1222-1233.

De Silva, W.I. (1997). The Ireland of Asia: Trends in marriage timing in Sri Lanka. *Asia-Pacific Population Journal, 12*(2), 3-24.

De Vos, S.M. (1995). *Household composition in Latin America.* New York: Plenum Press.

de Walque, D. (2002). *How does the impact of an HIV/AIDS information campaign vary with educational attainment? Evidence from rural Uganda.* (Discussion Paper Series No. 2002-16.) Chicago: University of Chicago, Population Research Center.

Deaton, A. (2001). Counting the world's poor: Problems and possible solutions. *The World Bank Research Observer, 16*(2), 125-147.

Deaton, A. (2002). Is world poverty falling? *Finance and Development, 39*(2).

Deaton, A. (2003). Measuring poverty in a growing world? (NBER Working Paper No. 9822.) Cambridge, MA: National Bureau of Economic Research.

Deaton, A., and Dreze, J. (2002). Poverty and inequality in India: A reexamination. *Economic and Political Weekly*, September 7, 3729-3748.

DeGraff, D.S., Bilsborrow, R.E., and Herrin, A.N. (1993). The implications of high fertility for children's time use in the Philippines. In C.B. Lloyd (Ed.), *Fertility, family size, and structure: Consequences for families and children.* New York: Population Council.

Dehejia, R.H., and Gatti, R. (2002). *Child labor: The role of income variability and access to credit across countries.* (NBER Working Paper No. 9018.) Cambridge, MA: National Bureau of Economic Research.

Deininger, K. (2003). Does cost of schooling affect enrollment by the poor? Universal primary education in Uganda. *Economics of Education Review, 22*(3), 291-305.

Deolalikar, A.B., and Rao, V. (1998). The demand for dowries and bride characteristics in marriage: Empirical estimates for rural South-Central India. In M. Krishnaraj, R. Sudarshan, and A. Shariff (Eds.), *Gender, population, and development* (pp. 122-140). Oxford, England: Oxford University Press.

Desai, S., and Jain, D. (1994). Maternal employment and changes in family dynamics: The social context of women's work in rural South India. *Population and Development Review, 20*(1), 115-136.

Deutsch, R., Morrison, A., Piras, C., and Nopo, H. (2002). *Working within confines: Occupational segregation by gender in three Latin American countries.* Washington, DC: Inter-American Development Bank, Sustainable Development Department Technical Paper Series.

Diamond, L., and Plattner, M.F. (2001). *The global divergence of democracies.* Baltimore, MD: Johns Hopkins University Press.

DiCenso, A., Guyatt, G., Willan, A., and Griffiith, L. (2002). Interventions to reduce unintended pregnancies among adolescents: Systematic review of randomized controlled trials. *British Medical Journal, 324*(7374), 1426-1435.

Dietz, M.G. (1998). Context is all: Feminism and theories of citizenship. In A. Phillips (Ed.), *Feminism and politics* (pp. 378-400). Oxford, England: Oxford University Press.

DiFranza, J.R., Savageau, J.A., Rigotti, N.A., Fletcher, K., Ockene, J.K., McNeill, A.D., Coleman, M., and Wood, C. (2002). Development of symptoms of tobacco dependence in youths: 30 month follow up data from the DANDY study. *Tobacco Control, 11*(3), 228-235.

Diouf, M. (1996). Urban youth and Senegalese politics: Dakar 1998-1994. *Public Culture, 8*(2), 225-250.

Domingo, L.J., and King, E.M. (1992). The role of the family in the process of entry to marriage in Asia. In E. Berquo and P. Xenos (Eds.), *Family systems and cultural change* (pp. 87-108). New York: Oxford University Press.

Duflo, E. (2001). Schooling and labor market consequences of school construction in Indonesia: Evidence from an unusual policy experiment. *American Economic Review, 91*(4), 795-813.

Dunbar, M. (2004). *SHAZ! Shaping the health of adolescents in Zimbabwe.* Paper presented at the Women's Global Health Initiative/University of California, San Francisco, October.

Duraisamy, P. (2002). Changes in returns to education in India, 1983-94: By gender, age-cohort, and location. *Economics of Education Review, 21*(2), 609-622.

Duraisamy, P., James, E., Lane, J., and Tan, J.P. (1997). *Is there a quantity-quality tradeoff as enrollments increase? Evidence from Tamil Nadu, India.* (Policy Research Working Paper No. 1768.) Washington, DC: World Bank.

Durston, J. (1995). *The changing situations of rural youth: Challenges and opportunities.* Santiago, Chile: UN Economic Commission for Latin America and the Caribbean (ECLAC).

Duryea, S., and Arends-Kuenning, M. (2003). School attendance, child labor, and local labor market fluctuations in urban Brazil. *World Development, 31*(7), 1165-1178.

Duryea, S., Lam, D., and Levison, D. (2003). *Effects of economic shocks on children's employment and schooling in Brazil.* (Population Studies Center Research Report No. 03-541.) Ann Arbor, MI: PSC Publications.

Duryea, S., Jaramillo, O., and Pagés, C. (2003). *Latin American labor markets in the 1990s: Deciphering the decade.* (Research Department Working Paper No. 486.) Washington, DC: Inter-American Development Bank.

Duryea, S., Hoek, J., Lam, D., and Levison, D. (Forthcoming). Dynamics of child labor: Labor force entry and exit in urban Brazil. In P. Orazem, G. Sedlacek, and Z. Tzannatos (Eds.), *Child labor in Latin America.* Washington, DC: World Bank and Inter-American Development Bank.

du Toit, B.M. (1987). Menarche and sexuality among a sample of black South African schoolgirls. *Social Science and Medicine, 24*(7), 561-571.

Dwyer, D., and Bruce, J. (1988). *A home divided: Women and income in the third world.* Stanford, CA: Stanford University Press.

Dyson, T., and Moore, M. (1983). On kinship structure, female autonomy, and demographic behavior in India. *Population and Development Review, 9*(1), 35-60.

Easterly, W. (2001). *The elusive quest for growth: Economists' adventures and misadventures in the tropics.* Cambridge, MA: MIT Press.

Eckersley, R., and Dear, K. (2002). Cultural correlates of youth suicide. *Social Science and Medicine, 55*(6), 1891-1904.

Edmonds, E.V. (2003). *Does child labor decline with improving economic status?* (NBER Working Paper No. 10134.) Cambridge, MA: National Bureau of Economic Research.

Edmonds, E.V., and Pavcnik, N. (2002). *Does globalization increase child labor? Evidence from Vietnam.* (NBER Working Paper No. 8760.) Cambridge, MA: National Bureau of Economic Researh.

Eggleston, E., Jackson, J., Rountree, W., and Pan, Z. (2000). Evaluation of a sexuality education program for young adolescents in Jamaica. *Pan American Journal of Public Health, 7*(2), 102-112.

Egypt Ministry of Health and Population. (2001). *National maternal mortality study: Egypt, 2000.* Cairo, Egypt: Author, Directorate of Maternal and Child Health Care.

Ehrenfeld, N. (1999). Female adolescents at the crossroad: Sexuality, contraception, and abortion in Mexico. In A. Mundigo and C. Indriso (Eds.), *Abortion in the developing world: Findings from WHO case studies* (pp. 368-386). New Delhi, India: Vistaar Publications.

El-Gibaly, O., Ibrahim, B., Mensch, B.S., and Clark, W.H. (2002). The decline of female circumcision in Egypt: Evidence and interpretation. *Social Science and Medicine, 52*(1), 205-220.

El Mahdi, A. (2002). The labor absorption capacity of the informal sector in Egypt. In R. Assaad (Ed.), *The Egyptian labor market in an era of reform* (pp. 99-130). Cairo, Egypt: The American University in Cairo Press.

El-Sanabary, N. (1993). Middle East and North Africa. In E.M. King and A.M. Hill (Eds.), *Women's education in developing countries: Barriers, benefits, and policies* (pp. 136-174). Baltimore, MD: Johns Hopkins University Press.

El-Tawila, S., Wassef, H., Lloyd, C.B., Mensch, B.S., and Gamal, Z. (2000). *The school environment in Egypt: A situation analysis of public preparatory schools.* Cairo, Egypt: Population Council.

El–Tawila, S., Ibrahim, B., El-Gibaly, O., El Sahn, F., and Lee, S. (1999). *Transitions to adulthood: A national survey of Egyptian adolescents.* Cairo, Egypt: Population Council.

Eliasoph, N. (1997). Close to home: The work of avoiding politics. *Theory and Society, 26(5)*, 605-647.

Ellison, N. (1997). Towards a new social politics: Citizenship and reflexivity in late modernity. *Sociology, 31(4)*, 697-711.

Ellison, P.T. (2001*). Reproductive ecology and human evolution.* Chicago, IL: Aldine.

Eloundou-Enyegue, P.M., and Calvès, A.E. (2003). *Till marriage takes her away: Testing an economic argument for gender discrimination in education in Cameroon.* Unpublished manuscript, Cornell University.

Emerson, P.M., and Souza, A.P. (2002). *From childhood to adulthood: The effect of child labor activities on adult earnings in Brazil.* Paper presented at the 2002 Latin American and Caribbean Economic Association meeting, Madrid, Spain, October 11-13.

Emerson, P.M., and Souza, A.P. (2003). Is there a child labor trap? Intergenerational persistence of child labor in Brazil. *Economic Development and Cultural Change, 51(2)*, 375-398.

Enel, C., Pison, G., and Lefebvre, M. (1994). Migration and marriage change: A case study of Mlomp, a Joola village in rural Senegal. In C. Bledsoe and G. Pison (Eds.), *Nuptiality in Sub-Saharan Africa: Contemporary anthropological and demographic perspectives* (pp. 92-116). Oxford, England: Clarendon Press.

Engerman, S.L. (2003). The history and political economy of international labor standards. In K. Basu, H. Horn, L. Román, and J. Shapiro (Eds.), *International labor standards: History, theory, and policy options* (pp. 9-83). Malden, MA: Blackwell.

Engle, P.L., and Smidt, R.K. (1996). *Influences of adolescent childbearing and marital status at first birth on rural Guatemalan women and children.* (Population Report Series J, No. 41.) New York and Washington, DC: Population Council and International Center for Research on Women.

Ensminger, J., and Knight, J. (1997). Changing social norms: Common property, bridewealth, and clan exogamy. *Current Anthropology, 38(1)*, 1-24.

Erikson, E. (1968). *Identity, youth, and crisis.* New York: Norton.

Ersado, L. (2002). *Child labor and school decisions in urban and rural areas: Cross-country evidence.* (FCND Discussion Paper No. 145.) Washington, DC: International Food Policy Research Institute.

Erulkar, A.S., and Mensch, B.S. (1997a). *Gender differences in dating experiences and sexual behavior among adolescents in Kenya.* Paper presented at the 23rd Population Conference of the International Union for the Scientific Study of Population, Beijing, China, October 11-17.

Erulkar, A.S., and Mensch, B.S. (1997b). *Youth centers in Kenya: Evaluation of the Family Planning Association in Kenya Programme.* New York: Population Council.

Erulkar, A.S., Etyang, L.I.A., Onoka, C., Nyagah, F.K., and Muyonga, A. (2004). Behavior change evaluation of a culturally consistent reproductive health program for young Kenyans. *International Family Planning Perspectives, 30*(2), 58-67.

Facio, A., and Micocci, F. (2003). Emerging adulthood in Argentina. *New Directions for Child and Adolescent Development, 100*(June), 21-31.

Fagerlind, I., and Saha, L.J. (1989). *Education and national development: A comparative perspective.* New York: Pergamon.

Family Care International. (1997). *The safe motherhood action agenda: Priorities for the next decade.* (Report on the Safe Motherhood Technical Consultation, October 13-23.) New York: Author and Inter-Agency Group for Safe Motherhood.

Featherstone, M., Lash, S., and Robertson, R. (1995). *Global modernities.* London, England: Sage.

Feng, W., and Quanhe, Y. (1996). Age at marriage and the first birth interval: The emerging change in sexual behavior among young couples in China. *Population and Development Review, 22*(2), 299-320.

Ferguson, A. (1998). *Schoolgirl pregnancy in Kenya: Report of a study of discontinuation rates and associated factors.* Nairobi, Kenya: Ministry of Health, Division of Family Health.

Fernandez Davila, M., Alarcon, W., Ortega, P., and Sanchez, R. (1986). *Imagenes de la mujer y el varon en la vision de las ciencias sociales.* Lima, Peru: Instituto Nacional de Investigaciones y Desarrollo de la Educacion.

Ferraro, G.P. (1991). Marriage and conjugal roles in Swaziland: Persistence and change. *International Journal of Sociology of the Family, 21*(Autumn), 89-128.

Filmer, D. (1998). *The socioeconomic correlates of sexual behavior: Results from an analysis of Demographic and Health Survey data.* Washington, DC: World Bank.

Filmer, D. (2003). *School availability and school participation in 21 developing countries.* Paper presented at the annual meeting of the Population Association of America, Minneapolis, MN, May 1-3.

Filmer, D., and Pritchett, L.H. (1999). The effect of household wealth on educational attainment: Evidence from 35 countries. *Population and Development Review, 25*(1), 85-120.

Filmer, D., and Pritchett, L.H. (2001). Estimating wealth effects without expenditure data, or tears: An application to educational enrollments in states of India. *Demography, 38*(1), 115-132.

Finkel, S.E. (2002). Civic education and the mobilization of political participation in developing democracies. *Journal of Politics, 64*(4), 994-1020.

Finkel, S.E., and Sabatini, C. (2000). Civic education, civil society, and political mistrust in a developing democracy: The case of the Dominican Republic. *World Development, 28*(11), 1851-1874.

Fitzgerald, A.M., Stanton, B.F., Terrieri, N., Shipena, H.L.X., Kahihuata, J., Ricardo, I.B., Galbraith, J.S., and De Jaeger, A.M. (1999). Use of western-based HIV risk-reduction interventions targeting adolescents in an African setting. *Journal of Adolescent Health, 25*(3), 52-61.

Flanagan, C.A., Bowes, J.M., Jonsson, B., Csapo, B., and Sheblanova, E. (1998). Ties that bind: Correlates of adolescents' civic commitments in seven countries. *Journal of Social Issues, 54*(3), 457-475.

Flanagan, C.A., Jonsson, B., Botcheva, L., Csapo, B., Bowes, J., Macek, P., Averina, I., and Sheblanova, E. (1999). Adolescents and the social contract: Developmental roots of citizenship in seven countries. In M. Yates and J. Youniss (Eds.), *Roots of civic identity: International perspectives on community service and activism in youth* (pp. 135-155). Cambridge, England: Cambridge University Press.

Flanagan, D., Williams, C., and Mahler, H. (1996). *Peer education in projects supported by AIDSCAP: A study of 21 projects in Africa, Asia, and Latin America.* Research Triangle Park, NC: Family Health International.

FOCUS on Young Adults. (2001). *Advancing young adult reproductive health: Actions for the next decade.* Washington, DC: Author.

FOCUS on Young Adults, Care International. (2000). *Impact of an adolescent reproductive health education intervention undertaken in garment factories in Phnom Penh, Cambodia.* Washington, DC: Author.

Fogel, R.W. (1994). Economic growth, population theory, and physiology: The bearing of long-term processes on the making of economic policy. *American Economic Review, 84*(3), 369-395.

Fokwang, J. (2003). Ambiguous transitions: Mediating citizenship among youth in Cameroon. *Africa Development, 28*(1), 173-201.

Forum for African Women Educationalists (FAWE) (2000). Adolescent sexuality and pregnancy. *FAWE News, 8*(3), 16-20.

Foster, A.D., and Rosenzweig, M.R. (1996). Technical change and human-capital returns and investments: Evidence from the Green Revolution. *American Economic Review, 86*(4), 931-953.

Freedom House. (2004). *Freedom in the world 2003: The annual survey of political rights and civil liberties.* Lanham, MD: Rowman and Littlefield.

Freire, P. (2002). *Pedagogy of the oppressed.* New York: Continuum.

Fuller, B., and Snyder, C.W. (1991). Vocal teachers, silent pupils? Life in Botswana classrooms. *Comparative Education Review, 35*(2), 274-294.

Furstenberg, F.F., Cook, T.D., Sampson, R., and Slap, G.E. (2002). Early adulthood in cross-national perspective: Preface. *Annals of the American Academy of Political and Social Science, 580*(2), 6-15.

Gage, A.J. (1998). Sexual activity and contraceptive use: The components of the decision-making process. *Studies in Family Planning, 29*(2), 154-166.

Gage, A.J., and Meekers, D. (1995). The changing dynamics of family formation: Women's status and nuptiality in Togo. In P. Makinwa-Adebusoye and A.-M. Jensen (Eds.), *Women and demographic change in sub-Saharan Africa* (pp. 15-38). Liege, Belgium: International Union for the Scientific Study of Population.

Gage, A.J., Sommerfelt, A.E., and Piani, A.L. (1996). *Household structure, socioeconomic level, and child health in sub-Saharan Africa.* (DHS Surveys Analytical Reports No. 1.) Calverton, MD: ORC Macro International.

Gajalakshmi, C.K., Jha, P., Ranson, K., and Nguyen, S. (2000). Global patterns of smoking and smoking-attributable mortality. In P. Jha and F. Chaloupka (Eds.), *Tobacco control in developing countries* (pp. 11-39). Oxford, England: Oxford University Press.

Gallart, M.A. (2001). Poverty, youth, and training: A study on four countries in Latin America. *Compare, 31*(1), 113-128.

Ganatra, B. (2000). *Unsafe abortion in South and South-east Asia: A review of the evidence.* In Proceedings of the WHO Technical Consultation on Unsafe Abortion, Geneva, Switzerland, August 27-28.

Ganatra, B., and Hirve, S. (2002). Induced abortions among adolescent women in rural Maharashtra, India. *Reproductive Health Matters, 10*(19), 76-85.

Gaventa, J. (2002). Introduction: Exploring citizen participation and accountability. *IDS Bulletin, 33*(2), 1-11.

Geronimus, A.T. (1987). On teenage childbearing and neo-natal mortality in the United States. *Population and Development Review, 13*(2), 245-279.

Ghellab, Y. (1998). *Minimum wages and youth unemployment.* (Employment and Training Paper No. 26.) Geneva, Switzerland: International Labour Office.

Gill, I., and Fluitman, F. (1997). *Skills and change: Constraints and innovation in the reform of vocational education and training.* Geneva, Switzerland, and Washington, DC: International Labour Organization and World Bank.

Glewwe, P. (2002). Schools and skills in developing countries: Education policies and socioeconomic outcomes. *Journal of Economic Literature, 40*(2), 436-482.

Glewwe, P., Grosh, M., Jacoby, H., and Lockheed, M. (1995). An eclectic approach to estimating the determinants of achievement in Jamaican primary education. *The World Bank Economic Review, 9*(2), 231-258.

Glewwe, P., Ilias, N., and Kremer, M. (2003). *Teacher incentives.* (NBER Working Paper No. 9671.) Cambridge, MA: National Bureau of Economic Research.

Glewwe, P., and Jacoby, H. (1994). Student achievement and schooling choice in low income countries: Evidence from Ghana. *Journal of Human Resources, 29*(3), 843-864.

Glewwe, P., and Jacoby, H. (2004). Economic growth and the demand for education: Is there a wealth effect? *Journal of Development Economics, 74*(1), 33-51.

Glewwe, P., Jacoby, H., and King, E. (2001). Early childhood nutrition and academic achievement: A longitudinal analysis. *Journal of Public Economics, 81*(September), 345-368.

Glewwe, P., Kremer, M., and Moulin, S. (2001). *Textbooks and test scores: Evidence from a randomized evaluation in Kenya.* Washington, DC: World Bank, Development Research Group.

Glewwe, P., Kremer, M., Moulin, S., and Zitzewitz, E. (2004). Retrospective vs. prospective analyses of school inputs: The case of flip charts in Kenya. *Journal of Development Economics, 74*(1), 251-268.

Global Youth Tobacco Survey Collaborating Group (GYTS) (2002). Tobacco use among youth: A cross country comparison. *Tobacco Control, 11*(3), 252-270.

Global Youth Tobacco Survey Collaborating Group (GYTS) (2003). Differences in worldwide tobacco use by gender: Findings from the Global Youth Tobacco Survey. *Journal of School Health, 73*(6), 207-215.

Glover, E.K., Erulkar, A.S., and Nerquaye-Tetteh, J. (1998). *Youth centers in Ghana: Assessment of the planned parenthood association of Ghana programme.* Nairobi, Kenya: Population Council and Planned Parenthood Association of Ghana.

Glynn, J.R., Caraël, M., Auvert, B., Kahindo, M.J., Musonda, R., Kaona, F., and Buvé, A. (2001). Why do young women have a much higher prevalence of HIV than young men? A study in Kisumu, Kenya and Ndola, Zambia. *AIDS, 15*(Supplement 4), S51-S60.

Glynn, J.R., Caraël, M., Buvé, A., Anagonou, S., Zekeng, L., Kahindo, M., and Musonda, R. (2004). Does increased general schooling protect against HIV infection? A study in four African cities. *Tropical Medicine and International Health, 90*(1), 4-14.

Goldin, C. (1990). *Understanding the gender gap: An economic history of American women.* New York: Oxford University Press.

Goldman, N. (1981). Dissolution of first unions in Colombia, Panama, and Peru. *Demography, 18*(4), 659-679.

Goldstone, J.A. (2002). Population and security: How demographic change can lead to violent conflict. *Journal of International Affairs, 56*(1), 3-24.

Gonzalez, G. (2004). *No more discrimination against pregnant students.* Inter Press Service News Agency, March 10. Available: http://www.ipsnews.net/interna.asp?idnews=22783 [May 21, 2004].

Gorgen, R., Laier, B., and Diesfeld, H.J. (1993). Problems related to schoolgirl pregnancies in Burkina Faso. *Studies in Family Planning, 24*(5), 283-294.

Gorgen, R., Yansane, M.L., Marx, M., and Millimounou, D. (1998). Sexual behavior and attitudes among unmarried urban youth in Guinea. *International Family Planning Perspectives, 24*(2), 65-71.

Graft, A., Haberland, N., and Goldberg, R. (2003). *Addressing married adolescent needs: A review of programs.* Paper presented at WHO/UNFPA/Population Council Technical Consultation on Married Adolescents, Geneva, Switzerland, December 9-12.

Greene, M.E. (1997). *Watering the neighbour's garden: Investing in adolescent girls in India.* (Regional Working Papers.) New Delhi, India: Population Council.

Greenhalgh, S. (1988). Intergenerational contracts: Familial roots of sexual stratification. In T.D. Dwyer, and J. Bruce (Eds.), *A home divided: Women and income in the Third World* (pp. 39-70). Stanford, CA: Stanford University Press.

Griesbach, D., Amos, A., and Currie, C. (2003). Adolescent smoking and family structure in Europe. *Social Science and Medicine, 56*(1), 41-52.

Grieser, M., Gittelsohn, J., Shankar, A.V., Koppenhaver, T., Legrant, Y.K., Marindo, R., Mavhu, W.M., and Hill, K. (2001). Reproductive decision-making and the HIV/AIDS epidemic in Zimbabwe. *Journal of Southern Africa Studies, 27*(2), 255-243.

Griliches, Z. (1977). Estimating the returns to schooling: Some econometric problems. *Econometrica, 45*(1), 1-22.

Grootaert, C., and Kanbur, R. (1995). Child labour: An economic perspective. *International Labour Review, 134*(2), 187-203.

Grosh, M., and Glewwe, P. (2000). *Designing household questionnaires for developing countries: Lessons from fifteen years of the living standards measurement study.* Washington, DC: World Bank.

Gruber, J., and Zinman, J. (2000). *Youth smoking in the U.S.: Evidence and implications.* (NBER Working Paper No. 7780.) Cambridge, MA: National Bureau of Economic Research.

Grummer-Strawn, L. (1996). The effect of changes in population characteristics on breast-feeding trends in fifteen developing countries. *International Journal of Epidemiology, 25*(1), 94-102.

Guerra, E. (2002). Citizenship knows no age: Children's participation in the governance and municipal budget of Barra Mansa, Brazil. *Environment and Urbanization, 14*(2), 71-84.

Gueye, M., Castle, S., and Konate, M.K. (2001). Timing of first intercourse among Malian adolescents: Implications for contraceptive use. *International Family Planning Perspectives, 27*(2), 56-62, 70.

Gunnarsson, V., Orazem, P.F., and Sanchez, M.A. (2003). *Child labor and school achievement in Latin America.* (Department of Economics Working Paper No. 03023.) Ames: Iowa State University.

Gupta, N. (2000). Sexual initiation and contraceptive use among adolescent women in Northeast Brazil. *Studies in Family Planning, 31*(3), 228-238.

Gupta, N., and da Costa Leite, I. (1999). Adolescent fertility behavior: Trends and determinants in Northeastern Brazil. *International Family Planning Perspectives, 25*(3), 125-130.

Gupta, R.B., and Khan, M.E. (1995). *Teenage fertility in U.P.: Some results from baseline survey in Uttar Pradesh.* Paper presented at the Workshop on Strategy Formulation to Reduce Teenage Fertility in Uttar Pradesh, India, organized by U.P. Academy of Administration, Nainital, May 15-16.

Gureje, O. (1991). Gender and schizophrenia: Age at onset and sociodemographic attributes. *Acta Psychiatrica Scandinavia 83*(5), 402-405.

Habermas, J. (1989). *The structural transformation of the public sphere.* Cambridge, MA: MIT Press.

Haddad, L., Brown, L., Ritcher, A., Smith, L. (1995). The gender dimensions of economic adjustment policies: Potential interactions and evidence to date. *World Development, 23*(6), 881-896.

Haddad, L., Hoddinott, J., and Alderman, H. (1997). *Intrahousehold resource allocation in developing countries: Models, methods, and policy.* Baltimore, MD: Johns Hopkins University Press.

Hakansson, N.T. (1994). The detachability of women: Gender and kinship in processes of socioeconomic change among the Gusii of Kenya. *American Anthropologist, 21*(3), 516-538.

Halcón, L., Blum, R.W., Beuhring, T., Pate, E., Campbell, S., and Venema, A. (2003). Adolescent health in the Caribbean: A regional portrait. *American Journal of Public Health, 93*(11), 1851-1857.

Hales, S., Howden-Chapman, P., Salmond, C., Woodward, A., and Mackenbach, J. (1999). National infant mortality rates in relation to gross national product and distribution of income. *Lancet, 354*(9195), 2047.

Hallman, K. (2004). *Socioeconomic disadvantage and unsafe sexual behaviors among young women and men in South Africa.* (Policy Research Division Working Paper No. 190.) New York: Population Council.

Hallman, K., and Diers, J. (2004). *Social inclusion and economic vulnerability: Adolescent HIV and pregnancy risk factors in South Africa.* Paper presented at the annual meeting of the Population Association of America, Boston, MA.

Handwerker, W.P. (1993). Gender power differences between parents and high-risk sexual behaviour by their children: AIDS/STD risk factors extend to a prior generation. *Journal of Women's Health, 2*(3), 301-316.

Hannum, E. (2002). Educational stratification by ethnicity in China: Enrollment and attainment in the early reform years. *Demography, 39*(1), 95-117.

Hannum, E., and Liu, J. (2005). Adolescent transitions to adulthood in reform-era China. In National Research Council and Institute of Medicine, *The changing transitions to adulthood in developing countries: Selected studies.* C.B. Lloyd, J.R. Behrman, N.P. Stromquist, and B. Cohen (Eds.). Committee on Population and Board on Children, Youth, and Families. Division of Behavioral and Social Sciences and Education. Washington, DC: The National Academies Press.

Hanushek, E.A., and Kim, D. (1995). *Schooling, labor force quality, and economic growth.* (NBER Working Paper No. 5399.) Cambridge, MA: National Bureau of Economic Research.

Harbison, R.W., and Hanushek, E.A. (1992). *Educational performance of the poor: Lessons from rural Northeast Brazil.* Washington, DC: Oxford University Press (for World Bank).

Hargreaves, J.R., and Glynn, J.R. (2002). Educational attainment and HIV-1 infection in developing countries: A systematic review. *Tropical Medicine and International Health, 7*(6), 489-498.

Harrison, P.F., Rosenberg, Z., and Bowcut, J. (2003). Topical microbicides for disease prevention: Status and challenges. *Clinical Infectious Diseases, 36*(3), 1290-1294.

Hart, D., Atkins, R., and Ford, D. (1998). Urban America as a context for the development of moral identity in adolescence. *Journal of Social Issues, 54*(3), 513-530.

Harvey, B., Stuart, J., and Swan, T. (2000). Evaluation of a drama-in-education programme to increase AIDS awareness in South African high schools: A randomized community intervention trial. *Internaional Journal of STD and AIDS, 11*(3), 105-111.

Heady, C. (2003). The effect of child labor on learning achievement. *World Development, 31*(2), 385-398.

Heckman, J.J., and Li, X. (2003). *Selection bias, comparative advantage, and heterogeneous returns to education.* (NBER Working Paper No. 9877.) Cambridge, MA: National Bureau of Economic Research.

Heise, L.L., Moore, K., and Toubia, N. (1995). *Sexual coercion and reproductive health: A focus on research.* New York: Population Council.

Heise, L.M., Ellsberg, M., and Gottemoeller, M. (1999). Ending violence against women. *Population Reports, Series L*(11), 1-43.

Heitmeyer, W. (2002). Have cities ceased to function as "integration machines" for young people? In M. Tienda and W.J. Wilson (Eds.), *Youth in cities: A cross-national perspective* (pp. 87-112). New York: Cambridge University Press.

Hertrich, V. (2002). *Nuptiality and gender relationships in Africa: An overview of first marriage trends over the past 50 years.* Paper presented at annual meeting of Population Association of America, Atlanta, GA.

Herz, B., and Sperling, G.B. (2004). *What works in girls' education: Evidence and policies from the developing world.* New York: Council on Foreign Relations.

Hewett, P.C., and Lloyd, C.B. (2005). Progress towards education for all: Trends and current challenges for sub-Saharan Africa. In National Research Council and Institute of Medicine, *The changing transitions to adulthood in developing countries: Selected studies.* C.B. Lloyd, J.R. Behrman, N.P. Stromquist, and B. Cohen (Eds.). Committee on Population and Board on Children, Youth, and Families. Division of Behavioral and Social Sciences and Education. Washington, DC: The National Academies Press.

Hewett, P.C., Mensch, B., and Erulkar, A.S. (2003). *Consistency in the reporting of sexual behavior among adolescent girls in Kenya: A comparison of interview methods.* (Policy Research Division Working Paper No 182.) New York: Population Council.

Hewett, P.C., Mensch, B., and Erulkar, A.S. (2004). The feasibility of computer-assisted survey interviewing in Africa: Experience from two rural districts in Kenya. *Social Science Computer Review, 22*(3), 319-334.

Hill, K. (2003). *Adult mortality in the developing world: What we know and how we know it.* Paper presented at the Training Workshop on HIV/AIDS and Adult Mortality in Developing Countries, United Nations Population Division, New York, September 8-13.

Hoj, L., da Silva, D., Hedegaard, K., Sandström, A., and Aaby, P. (2002). Factors associated with maternal mortality in rural Guinea-Bissau. A longitudinal population-based study. *BJOG: An International Journal of Obstetrics and Gynaecology, 109*(7), 792-799.

Holland, J., Blackburn, J., and Chambers, R. (1998). *Whose voice? Participatory research and policy change.* London, England: Intermediate Technology.

Hornik, R., and McAnany, E. (2001). Mass media and fertility change. In National Research Council, *Diffusion processes and fertility transition: Selected perspectives* (pp. 208-239). J.B. Casterline (Ed.). Committee on Population. Division of Behavioral and Social Sciences and Education. Washington, DC: National Academy Press.

Horowitz, A.W., and Wang, J. (2004). Favorite son? Specialized child laborers and students in poor LDC households. *Journal of Development Economics, 73*(2), 631-642.

Hoskins, G., and Mirus, R. (1988). Reasons for U.S. dominance of the international trade in television programmes. *Media, Culture, and Society, 10*(5), 499-515.

Howell, J. (2000). The political economy of Xiamen special economic zone. In Y.M. Yeung and D.K.Y. Chu (Eds.), *Fujian: A coastal province in transition and transformation* (pp. 119-142). Hong Kong: Chinese University Press.

Hsieh, C.T., and Urquiola, M. (2003). *When schools compete, how do they compete? An assessment of Chile's nationwide school voucher program.* (NBER Working Paper No. 10008.) Cambridge, MA: National Bureau of Economic Research.

Hudson, V.M., and den Boer, A. (2002). A surplus of men, a deficit of peace: Security and sex ratios in Asia's largest states. *International Security, 26*(4), 5-38.

Huebler, F., and Loaiza, E. (2002). *Child labor and school attendance in sub-Saharan Africa: Empirical evidence from UNICEF's multiple indicator cluster surveys (MICS).* New York: UNICEF Strategic Information Section, Division of Policy and Planning.

Hull, T.H. (2002). *The marriage revolution in Indonesia.* Paper presented at Population Association of America annual meeting, Australian National University, May 9-11.

Human Rights Watch. (1994a). *Final justice: Police and death squad homicides of adolescents in Brazil*. New York: Author.

Human Rights Watch. (1994b). *Generation under fire: Children and violence in Colombia*. New York: Author.

Human Rights Watch. (1996). *Police abuse and killings of street children in India*. New York: Author.

Human Rights Watch. (1997a). *Guatemala's forgotten children: Police violence and arbitrary detention*. New York: Author.

Human Rights Watch. (1997b). *Juvenile injustice: Police abuse and detention of street children in Kenya*. New York: Author.

Human Rights Watch. (1999a). *Nobody's children: Jamaican children in police detention and government institutions*. New York: Author.

Human Rights Watch. (1999b). *Prison bound: The denial of juvenile justice in Pakistan*. New York: Author.

Hussain, R. (1999). Community perceptions of reasons for preference for consanguineous marriages in Pakistan. *Journal of Biosocial Science, 31*(4), 449-461.

Hussain, R., and Bittles, A.H. (1998). The prevalence and demographic characteristics of consanguineous marriages in Pakistan. *Journal of Biosocial Science, 30*(2), 261-275.

Hussain, R., and Bittles, A.H. (1999). Consanguineous marriage and differentials in age at marriage, contraceptive use, and fertility in Pakistan. *Journal of Biosocial Science, 31*(1), 121-138.

Hyde, K. (1997). *Sexual education programmes in African schools: A review*. Paper presented at National Academy of Sciences' Workshop on Adolescent Sexuality and Reproductive Health in Developing Countries, Washington, DC, March 24-25.

Ibrahim, B.L., and Wassef, H. (2000). Caught between two worlds: Youth in the Egyptian hinterland. In R. Meijer (Ed.), *Alienation or integration of Arab youth: Between family, state and street* (pp. 161-189). London, England: Curzon.

Ilahi, N., Orazem, P.F., and Sedlacek, G. (Forthcoming). How does working as a child affect wages, income, and poverty as an adult? In P.F. Orazem, G. Sedlacek, and Z. Tzannatos (Eds.), *Child labor in Latin America*. Washington, DC: World Bank and Inter-American Development Bank.

INDEPTH Network. (2002). *Population and health in developing countries*. Ottawa: International Development Research Centre.

Inglehart, R., and Norris, P. (2003). *Rising tide: Gender equality and cultural change around the world*. New York: Cambridge University Press.

Institute of Medicine. (1996). *In her lifetime: Female morbidity and mortality in sub-Saharan Africa*. Committee to Study Female Morbidity and Mortality in Sub-Saharan Africa. C.P. Howson, P.F. Harrison, D. Hotra, and M. Law (Eds.), Board on International Health. Washington, DC: National Academy Press.

Institute for Reproductive Health. (2001). *Reaching adolescents at family planning clinics: Applying the reproductive health awareness model*. (The Awareness Project Research Update.) Washington, DC: Institute for Reproductive Health, Georgetown University Medical Center.

Inter-American Development Bank. (2003a). *Good jobs wanted: Labor markets in Latin America. 2004 report on economic and social progress in Latin America*. Washington, DC: Author.

Inter-American Development Bank. (2003b). *Ideas for development in the Americas*. (Volume 2, September, based on 2004 report on Economic and Social progress in Latin America.) Available: www.iadb.org/res/publications [January 2004].

International Center for Research on Women and Institute of Health Management-Pachod. (2003). *Increasing low age at marriage in rural Maharashtra, India: Update 1.* Washington, DC, and Maharashtra, India: Authors.

International Crisis Group. (2004). *Pakistan: Reforming the education sector.* (ICG Asia Report No. 84.) Islamabad, Pakistan:Author.

International Food Policy Research Institute. (2003). *Annual report: Agriculture, food security, nutrition and the Millennium Development Goals.* Washington, DC: Author.

International Labour Office. (2002a). *Every child counts: New gobal estimates on child labour.* (International programme on the elimination of child labour, statistical information and monitoring programme on child labour.) Geneva, Switzerland: Author.

International Labour Office. (2002b). *A future without child labour: Global report 2002.* (Report of the Director-General.) Geneva, Switzerland: Author.

International Labour Office. (2003). *Working out of poverty: Report of the Director-General.* (International Labour Conference, 91st Session.) Geneva, Switzerland: Author.

International Labour Office, Labor Statistics Division. (2003). *LABORSTA home page.* Available: http://laborsta.ilo.org [November 24, 2003].

International Planned Parenthood Federation and International Women's Rights Action Watch. (1990). *Reproductive rights.* (The Hubert H. Humphrey Institute of Public Affairs at the University of Minnesota.) Suffolk, England: Lavenham Press.

International Planned Parenthood Federation and International Women's Rights Action Watch. (2000). *Reproductive rights.* (The Hubert H. Humphrey Institute of Public Affairs at the University of Minnesota.) London, England: Terracotta Press.

International Road Traffic and Accident Database. (2002). *Brief overview.* Available: http://www.bast.de/htdocs/fachthemen/irtad/english/englisch.html [March 2003].

Isiugo-Abanihe, U.C. (1994). Consequences of bridewealth changes on nuptiality patterns among the Ibo of Nigeria. In C. Bledsoe and G. Pison (Eds.), *Nuptiality in sub-Saharan Africa: Contemporary anthropological and demographic perspectives* (pp. 74-91). Oxford, England: Clarendon Press.

Jackson, J., Leitch, J., Lee, A., Eggleston, E., and Hardee, K. (1998). *The Jamaica adolescent study: Final report.* (Prepared by Fertility Management Unit, University of the West Indies, Kingston, Jamaica, and Women's Studies Project.) Research Triangle Park, NC: Family Health International.

Jacoby, H. (1994). Borrowing constraints and progress through school: Evidence from Peru. *Review of Economics and Statistics, 76*(1), 151-160.

Jacoby, H., and Skoufias, E. (1997). Risk, financial markets, and human capital in a developing country. *Review of Economic Studies, 64*(3), 311-335.

Jafarey, S., and Lahiri, S. (2002). Will trade sanctions reduce child labour? The role of credit markets. *Journal of Development Economics, 68*(1), 137-156.

Jalan, J., and Glinskaya, E. (2003). *Improving primary school education in India: An impact assessment of DPEP I.* New Delhi, India, and Washington, DC: Indian Statistical Institute and World Bank.

Jeffrey, R., and Basu, A.M. (1996). *Girl's schooling, women's autonomy, and fertility change in South Asia.* New Delhi, India: Sage.

Jejeebhoy, S.J. (1993). Family size, outcomes for children, and gender disparities: The case of rural Maharashtra. In C.B. Lloyd (Ed.), *Fertility, family size, and structure: Consequences for families and children* (pp. 445-479). New York: Population Council.

Jejeebhoy, S.J. (1995). *Education and women's age at marriage.* In S.J. Jejeebhoy, *Women's education, autonomy, and reproductive behaviour: Experience from developing countries* (pp. 60-77). Oxford, England: Clarendon Press.

Jejeebhoy, S.J. (1998). Adolescent sexual and reproductive behavior: A review of the evidence from India. *Social Science and Medicine, 46*(10), 1275-1290.

Jejeebhoy, S.J. (2000). Adolescent sexual and reproductive behaviour: A review of the evidence from India. In R. Ramasubban and S.J. Jejeebhoy (Eds.), *Women's reproductive health in India* (pp. 40-101). Jaipur, India: Rawat.

Jejeebhoy, S.J., and Bott, S. (2003). *Non-consensual sexual experiences of young people: A review of evidence from developing countries.* (Regional Working Paper Series No.16.) New Delhi, India: Population Council.

Jejeebhoy, S.J., and Halli, S.S. (2005). Marriage patterns in rural India: Influence of sociocultural context. In National Research Council and Institute of Medicine, *The changing transitions to adulthood in developing countries: Selected studies.* C.B. Lloyd, J.R. Behrman, N.P. Stromquist, and B. Cohen (Eds.). Committee on Population and Board on Children, Youth, and Families. Division of Behavioral and Social Sciences and Education. Washington, DC: The National Academies Press.

Jensen, R. (2003). *Equal treatment, unequal outcomes? Generating gender inequality through fertility behavior.* Cambridge, MA: Harvard University John F. Kennedy School of Government.

Jernigan, D.H. (2001). *Global status report: Alcohol and young people.* Geneva, Switzerland: World Health Organization.

Jessor, R. (1984). Adolescent development and behavioral health. In J.D. Matarazzo, S.M. Weiss, J.A. Herd, N.E. Miller, and S.M. Weiss (Eds.), *Behavioral health: A handbook of health enhancement and disease prevention* (pp. 69-90). New York: Wiley.

Jessor, R. (1991). Risk behavior in adolescence: A psychosocial framework for understanding and action. *Journal of Adolescent Health, 12*(2), 597-605.

Jessor, R. (1996). Ethnographic methods in contemporary perspective. In R. Jessor, A. Colby, and R.A. Shweder (Eds.), *Ethnography and human development: Context and meaning in social inquiry* (Chapter 1). (The John D. and Catherine T. MacArthur Foundation Series on Mental Health and Development.) Chicago, IL: University of Chicago Press.

Jessor, R., Turbin, M.S., and Costa, F.M. (1998a). Protective factors in adolescent health behavior. *Journal of Personality and Social Psychology: Personality Processes and Individual Differences, 75*(3), 788-800.

Jessor, R., Turbin, M.S., and Costa, F.M. (1998b). Risk and protection in successful outcomes among disadvantaged adolescents. *Applied Developmental Science, 2*, 194-208.

Jessor, R., Turbin, M.S., Costa, F.M., Dong, Q., Zhang, H., and Wang, C. (2003). Adolescent problem behavior in China and the United States: A cross-national study of psychosocial protective factors. *Journal of Research on Adolescence, 13*(3), 329-360.

Jewkes, R., Levin, J., Mbananga, N., and Bradshaw, D. (2002). Rape of girls in South Africa. *Lancet, 359*(9303), 319-320.

Jewkes, R., Vundule, C., Maforah, F., and Jordaan, E. (2001). Relationship dynamics and teenage pregnancy in South Africa. *Social Science and Medicine, 52*(5), 733-744.

Jha, P., and Chaloupka, F.J. (1999). *Curbing the epidemic: Governments and the economics of tobacco control.* Washington, DC: World Bank.

Ji, J. (1999). *Committed suicide in the Chinese rural areas: Updates on global mental and social health.* Newsletter of the World Mental Health Project 3(1). Available: http://www.hms.harvard.edu/dsm/wmhp/updates/news0301/suic0301.htm [March 2003].

Ji, J., Kleinman, A., and Becker, A.E. (2001). Suicide in contemporary China: A review of China's distinctive suicide demographics in their sociocultural context. *Harvard Review of Psychiatry, 9*(1), 1-12.

Jimenez, E., and Paqueo, V. (1996). Do local contributions affect the efficiency of public primary schools? *Economics of Education Review, 15*(4), 377-386.

Jimenez, E., and Sawada, Y. (1999). Do community-managed schools work? An evaluation of El Salvador's EDUCO program. *The World Bank Economic Review, 13*(3), 415-441.

Jiraphongsa, C., Danmoensawat, W., Greenland, S., Frerichs, R., Siraprapasiri, T., Glik, D.C., and Detels, R. (2002). Acceptance of HIV testing and counseling among unmarried young adults in Northern Thailand. *AIDS Education and Prevention, 14*(2), 89-101.

Johnson-Hanks, J. (2002). On the limits of life stages in ethnography: Toward a theory of vital conjunctures. *American Anthropologist, 104*(3), 865-880.

Johnston, L.D., O'Malley, P.M., and Bachman, J.G. (2003). *Teen smoking continues to decline in 2003, but declines are slowing.* Ann Arbor, MI: University of Michigan News and Information Services. Available: www.monitoringthefuture.org [April 2004].

Jolly, R. (1991). Adjustment with a human face: A UNICEF record and perspective on the 1980s. *World Development, 19*(12), 1807-1821.

Joseph, S. (1996). Gender and citizenship in Middle Eastern states. *Middle East Report,* January-March, 4-10.

Joseph, S. (1997). The public/private: The imagined boundary in the imagined nation/state/ community: The Lebanese case. *Feminist Review, 57*(1), 73-92.

Kabeer, N. (2000). Resources, agency, achievements: Reflections on the measurement of women's empowerment. In *Discussing women's empowerment: Theory and practice* (Sida Studies No. 3, pp. 17-57). Stockholm: Swedish International Development Cooperation Agency.

Kabeer, N. (2002). Citizenship, affiliation, and exclusion: Perspectives from the South. *IDS Bulletin, 33*(2), 12-23.

Kac, G., Coelho, M.A.D.S.C., and Velasquez-Melendez, G. (2000). Secular trend in age at menarche for women born between 1920 and 1979 in Rio de Janeiro, Brazil. *Annals of Human Biology, 27*(4), 423-428.

Kamb, M.L., Fishbein, M., Douglas, J.M., Jr., and Rhodes, F. (1998). Efficacy of risk-feduction counseling to prevent human immunodeficiency virus and sexually transmitted diseases: A randomized controlled trial. *Journal of American Medical Association, 280*(13), 1161-1167.

Karanja, W.W. (1994). The phenomenon of outside wives: Some reflections on the possible influence on fertility. In C. Bledsoe and G. Pison (Eds.), *Nuptiality in sub-Saharan Africa: Contemporary anthropological and demographic perspectives* (pp. 194-214). New York: Oxford University Press.

Kaufman, C.E., Clark, S., Manzini, N., and May, J. (2002). *How community structures of time and opportunity shape adolescent sexual behavior in South Africa.* (Policy Research Division Working Paper Report No. 159.) New York: Population Council.

Kaufman, C.E., de Wet, T., and Stadler, J. (2000). Adolescent pregnancy and parenthood in South Africa. (Policy Research Division Working Paper No. 136.) New York: Population Council.

Kaufman, C.E., Maharaj, P., and Richter, L. (1998). *Children's schooling in South Africa: Transitions and tensions in households and communities.* Paper presented at the annual meeting of the Population Association of America, Chicago, IL.

Kaufmann, D., Kraay, A., and Zoida-Lobatón, P. (2002). *Governance matters II: Update indicators for 2000-01.* (Policy Research Working Paper No. 2772.) Washington, DC: World Bank.

Keck, M.E., and Sikkink, K. (1998). *Activists beyond borders: Advocacy networks in international politics.* Ithaca, NY: Cornell University Press.

Kelley, A.C. (1996). The consequences of rapid population growth on human resource development: The case of education. In D.A. Ahlburg, A.C. Kelley, and K.O. Mason (Eds.), *The impact of population growth on well-being in developing countries* (pp. 67-137). Berlin/Heidelberg, Germany: Springer-Verlag.

Kestler, E., and Ramírez, L. (2000). Pregnancy-related mortality in Guatemala, 1993-1996. *Pan American Journal of Public Health, 7*(1), 41-45.

Khandker, S.R., Pitt, M.M., and Fuwa, N. (2003). *Subsidy to promote girls' secondary education: The female stipend program in Bangladesh.* Paper presented at the 68th Annual Meeting of the Population Association of America, Minneapolis, MN, May 1-3.

Khilnani, S. (1997). *The idea of India.* London, England: Hamish Hamilton.

Kielland, A., and Sanogo, I. (2002). *Burkina Faso: Child labor migration from rural areas: The magnitude and the determinants.* Washington, DC: World Bank.

Kiernan, K. (2001). European perspectives on nonmarital childbearing. In L. Wu and B. Wolfe (Eds.), *Out of wedlock: Causes and consequences of nonmarital fertility* (pp. 77-108). New York: Russell Sage Foundation.

Kim, J., Alderman, H., and Orazem, P.F. (1998). *Can cultural barriers be overcome in girls' schooling? The community support program in rural Balochistan.* (Working Paper Series on Impact Evaluation of Education Reforms, Development Research Group No. 10.) Washington, DC: World Bank.

Kim, J., Alderman, H., and Orazem, P.F. (1999). Can private school subsidies increase enrollment for the poor? The Quetta Urban Fellowship Program. *The World Bank Economic Review, 13*(3), 443-465.

Kim, Y.M., Marangwanda, C., Nyakaura, R., and Chibatamoto, P. (1998*). Impact of the promotion of youth responsibility project campaign on reproductive health in Zimbabwe 1997-1998.* Baltimore, MD, and Harara: Johns Hopkins University Center for Communication Programs and Zimbabwe National Family Planning Council.

Kim, Y.M., Kols, A., Nyakauya, R., Marangwanda, C., and Chibatamoto, P. (2001). Promoting sexual responsibility among young people in Zimbabwe. *International Family Planning Perspectives, 27*(1), 11-19.

King, E.M., and Mason, A.D. (2001*). Engendering development: Through gender equality in rights, resources, and voice.* (World Bank Policy Research Report.) New York: World Bank and Oxford University Press.

King, E.M., and Ozler, B. (1998). *What's decentralization got to do with learning? The case of Nicaragua's school autonomy reform.* Paper presented at the annual meetings of the American Educational Research Association, San Diego, CA, April 13-17.

King, E.M., Orazem, P.F., and Wohlgemuth, D. (1999). Central mandates and local incentives: The Colombia education voucher program. *The World Bank Economic Review, 13*(3), 467-491.

Kinsman, J., Nakiyingi, J., and Kamali, A.W.J. (2001). Condom awareness and intended use: Gender and religious contrasts among school pupils in rural Masaka, Uganda. *AIDS Care, 13*(2), 215-220.

Kiragu, K. (2001). *Youth and HIV/AIDS: Can we avoid catastrophe?* (Population Reports Series L, Number 12.) Baltimore, MD: Johns Hopkins University, Population Information Program.

Kirby, D. (1997). *No easy answers: Research findings on programs to reduce sexual risk-taking and teen pregnancy.* Washington, DC: National Campaign to Prevent Teen Pregnancy Task Force on Effective Programs and Research.

Kirby, D. (1999). *Asking for reasons why.* Washington, DC: National Campaign to Prevent Teen Pregnancy.

Kirby, D. (2001). *Emerging answers: Research findings on programs to reduce teen pregnancy.* Washington, DC: National Campaign to Prevent Teen Pregnancy.

Kirby, D., and Coyle, K. (1997). Youth development programs. *Children and Youth Services Review, 19*(5/6), 437-454.

Kishor, S. (2003). *Uses and limitations of DHS data on age and characteristics of first marriages.* Paper presented at UNICEF Global Consultation on Indicators: Female Genital Mutilation/Cutting and Early Marriage, New York, November 11-13.

Knight, J.B., and Sabot, R.H. (1990). *Education, productivity, and inequality: The East African natural experiment.* Washington, DC: World Bank.

Knodel, J. (1997). The closing of the gender gap in schooling: The case of Thailand. *Comparative Education, 33*(1), 61-86.

Knowles, J.C., and Behrman, J.R. (2005). Assessing the economic returns to investing in youth in developing countries. In National Research Council and Institute of Medicine, *The changing transitions to adulthood in developing countries: Selected studies.* C.B. Lloyd, J.R. Behrman, N.P. Stromquist, and B. Cohen (Eds.). Committee on Population and Board on Children, Youth, and Families. Division of Behavioral and Social Sciences and Education. Washington, DC: The National Academies Press.

Kobayashi, Y. (2004). *Economic livelihoods for street children: A review.* Bethesda, MD: Development Alternatives.

Korenman, S., and Neumark, D. (1997). *Cohort crowding and youth labor markets: A cross-national analysis.* (NBER Working Paper No. 6031.) Cambridge, MA: National Bureau of Economic Research.

Kouwonou, K., and Mukahirwa, P. (2000). *Enquête evaluation du centre des jeunes de* l'ATBEF Connaissances, attitudes et pratiques sexuelles des jeunes de Lomé, Abidjan, Côte d'Ivoire: Focus on Young Adults: Unité de recherche démographique, Université de Lomé and Santa Familiale et Prévention du SIDA.

Kremer, M., Moulin, S., Myatt, D., and Namunyu, R. (1997). *The quality-quanity tradeoff in education: Evidence from a prospective evaluation in Kenya.* Unpublished manuscript, Massachusetts Institute of Technology.

Krueger, A. (1997). International labor standards and trade. In M. Bruno and B. Pleskovic (Eds.), *Annual world bank conference on development economics.* Washington, DC: World Bank.

Krueger, A.B. (2002). A model for evaluating the use of development dollars, south of the border. *The New York Times* (May 2), Section C: Economic Scene.

Krueger, A.B., and Lindahl, M. (2001). Education for growth: Why and for whom? *Journal of Economic Literature, 39*(December), 1101-1136.

Krug, E.G., Dahlberg, L.L., Mercy, L.A., Zwi, A.B., and Lozano, R. (2002). *World report on violence and health.* Geneva, Switzerland: World Health Organization.

Kuate-Defo, B. (1998). Trends and determinants of adolescent childbearing and contraceptive use. In B. Kuate-Defo (Ed.), *Sexuality and reproductive health during adolescence in Africa with special reference to Cameroon* (pp. 175-201). Ottawa, Canada: University of Ottawa Press.

Kuate-Defo, B. (2005). Multilevel modeling of influences on transitions to adulthood in developing countries with special reference to Cameroon. In National Research Council and Institute of Medicine, *The changing transitions to adulthood in developing countries: Selected studies.* C.B. Lloyd, J.R. Behrman, N.P. Stromquist, and B. Cohen (Eds.). Committee on Population and Board on Children, Youth, and Families. Division of Behavioral and Social Sciences and Education. Washington, DC: The National Academies Press.

Kulpoo, D. (1998). *The quality of education—some policy suggestions based on a survey of schools: Mauritius, SACMEQ policy research: Report No. 1.* Southern Africa Consortium for Monitoring Educational Quality, Ross, K.N. (Series Editor). Paris, France: International Institute for Educational Planning and UNESCO.

Lacey, M. (2003). Primary schools in Kenya, fees abolished, are filled to overflowing. *The New York Times* (January 7, 2003), A8.

Lagarde, E., Carael, M., Glynn, J.R., Kanhonou, L., Abega, S.C., Kahindo, M., Musonda, R., Auvert, B., and Buve, A. (2001). Study group on the heterogeneity of HIV epidemics in African cities 2001: Educational level is associated with condom use within nonspousal partnerships in four cities of sub-Saharan Africa. *AIDS, 15*(4), 1399-1408.

Lagos, M., and Rose, R. (1999). Young people in politics: A multi-continental survey. *Studies in Public Policy, 316*(Supplement), 17-24.

Lam, D., and Duryea, S. (1999). The effects of education on fertility, labor supply, and investments in children, with evidence from Brazil. *Journal of Human Resources, 34*(1), 160-192.

Lam, D., and Leibbrandt, M. (2003). *What has happened to inequality in South Africa since the end of apartheid?* Unpublished manuscript, University of Michigan.

Lam, D., and Marteleto, L. (2002*). Small families and large cohorts: The impact of the demographic transition on schooling in Brazil.* (PSC Research Report No. 02-519.) Ann Arbor: University of Michigan, Population Studies Center.

Lam, D., and Marteleto, L. (2005). Small families and large cohorts: The impact of the demographic transition on schooling in Brazil. In National Research Council and Institute of Medicine, *The changing transitions to adulthood in developing countries: Selected studies.* C.B. Lloyd, J.R. Behrman, N.P. Stromquist, and B. Cohen (Eds.). Committee on Population and Board on Children, Youth, and Families. Division of Behavioral and Social Sciences and Education. Washington, DC: The National Academies Press.

Lam, D., and Schoeni, R. (1993). Effects of family background on earnings and returns to schooling: Evidence from Brazil. *Journal of Political Economy, 101*(4), 213-243.

Lao, T.T., and Ho, L.F. (1997). Outcome of teenage pregnancy in Hong Kong. *Human Reproduction, 12*(10), 2303-2305.

Larson, R., and Verma, S. (1999). How children and adolescents spend time across the world: Work, play, and developmental opportunities. *Psychological Bulletin, 125*(6), 701-736.

Lassibille, G., Tan, J.-P., and Sumra, S. (2000). Expansion of private secondary education: Lessons from recent experience in Tanzania. *Comparative Education Review, 44*(1), 1-28.

Lavy, V. (1996). School supply constraints and children's educational outcomes in rural Ghana. *Journal of Development Economics, 51*(December), 291-314.

Leach, F., Fiscian, V., Kadzamira, E., Lemani, E., and Nacgajabga, P. (2003). *An investigative study of the abuse of girls in African Schools.* London, England: Policy Division, Department of International Development, Government of United Kingdom.

Lechner, F.J., and Boli, J. (Eds.). (2000). *The globalization reader.* Malden, MA: Blackwell Publishers.

Lederman, D., and Loayza, N. (1999). What causes crime and violence? In C. Moser and S. Lister (Eds.), *Violence and social capital* (pp. 7-11). (Proceedings of the LCSES Seminar Series, 1997-1998.) Washington, DC: World Bank.

Lee, B.S., and Schultz, T.P. (1982). Implications of child mortality reduction in fertility and population growth in Korea. *Journal of Economic Development, 7*(1), 21-44.

Lee, J.W., and Barro, R.J. (1997). *Schooling quality in a cross section of countries.* (NBER Working Paper No. 6198.) Cambridge, MA: National Bureau of Economic Research.

LeGrand, T.K., and Mbacké, C.S.M. (1993). Teenage pregnancy and child health in the urban Sahel. *Studies in Family Planning, 24*(3), 137-149.

Leon, D., and Walt, G., (Eds.). (2001). *Poverty, inequality, and health: An international perspective.* Oxford, England: Oxford University Press.

Lesthaeghe, R.J., Kaufman, G., and Meekers, D. (1989). The nuptiality regimes in sub-Saharan Africa. In R.J. Lesthaeghe (Ed.), *Reproduction and social organization in sub-Saharan Africa* (pp. 238-333). Berkeley: University of California Press.

Levison, D. (2000). Children as economic agents. *Feminist Economics, 6*(1), 125-134.

Levison, D., and Moe, K.S. (1998). Household work as a deterrent to schooling: An analysis of adolescent girls in Peru. *Journal of Developing Areas, 32*(3), 339-356.

Levison, D., Moe, K.S., and Knaul, F.M. (2001). Youth education and work in Mexico. *World Development, 29*(1), 167-188.

Levison, D., Anker, R., Ashraf, S., and Barge, S. (1996). *Is child labour really necessary in India's carpet industry?* (Labour Market Paper No. 15.) Geneva, Switzerland: International Labour Office.

Levitt-Dayal, M., and Motihar, R. (2000). *Adolescent girls in India choose a better future: An impact assessment.* Washington, DC: The Centre for Development and Population Activities.

Levy, V. (1985). Cropping pattern, mechanization, child labor, and fertility behavior in a farming economy: Rural Egypt. *Economic Development and Cultural Change, 33*(4), 777-791.

Lewinsohn, P.M., Hops, H., Roberts, R.E., Seeley, J.R., and Andrews, J.A. (1993). Adolescent psychopathology: I. Prevalence and incidence of depression and other DSM-III-R disorders in high school students. *Journal of Abnormal Psychology, 102*(1), 133-144.

Libreros, D. (2002). *Tensiones de las politicas educativas en Colombia: Balance y perspectivas.* Bogota, Colombia: Universidad Pedagogica Nacional.

Lindstrom, D.P., and Brambila Paz, C. (2001). Alternative theories of the relationship of schooling and work to family formation: Evidence from Mexico. *Social Biology, 48*(3-4), 278-297.

Lister, R. (1997). *Citizenship: Feminist perspectives.* New York: New York University Press.

Lloyd, C.B. (1994). Investing in the next generation: The implications of high fertility at the level of the family. In R. Cassen (Ed.), *Population and development: Old debates, new conclusions* (pp. 181-202). Washington, DC: Overseas Development Council.

Lloyd, C.B. (1998). Household structure and poverty: What are the connections? In M. Livi-Bacci and G. De Santis (Eds.), *Population and poverty in the developing world* (pp. 84-102). Oxford, England: Clarendon Press.

Lloyd, C.B., and Blanc, A.K. (1996). Children's schooling in sub-Saharan Africa: The role of fathers, mothers, and others. *Population and Development Review, 22*(2), 265-298.

Lloyd, C.B., El-Tawila, S., Clark, W.H., and Mensch, B.S. (2003). The impact of educational quality on school exit in Egypt. *Comparative Education Review, 47*(4), 444-467.

Lloyd, C.B., and Grant, M.J. (2005. Growing up in Pakistan: The separate experiences of males and females. In National Research Council and Institute of Medicine, *The changing transitions to adulthood in developing countries: Selected studies.* C.B. Lloyd, J.R. Behrman, N.P. Stromquist, and B. Cohen (Eds.). Committee on Population and Board on Children, Youth, and Families. Division of Behavioral and Social Sciences and Education. Washington, DC: The National Academies Press.

Lloyd, C.B., and Hewett, P.C. (2004). *Universal primary schooling in sub-Saharan Africa: Is gender equity enough?* Unpublished manuscript, Population Council, New York.

Lloyd, C.B., and Mensch, B. (1999). Implications of formal schooling for girls' transitions to adulthood in developing countries. In National Research Council, *Critical perspectives on schooling and fertility in the developing world* (pp. 80-104). C.H. Bledsoe, J.B. Casterline, J.A. Johnson-Kuhn, and J.G. Haaga (Eds.). Committee on Population. Commission on Behavioral and Social Sciences and Education. Washington, DC: National Academy Press.

Lloyd, C.B., Mensch, B.S., and Clark, W.H. (2000). The effects of primary school quality on school dropout among Kenyan girls and boys. *Comparative Education Review, 44*(2), 113-147.

Lloyd, C.B., and Montgomery, M.R. (1997). *The consequences of unintended fertility: Potential implications for investments in children.* (International Population Conference.) Liege, Belgium: International Union for the Scientific Study of Population.

Lloyd, C.B., Mete, C., and Sathar, Z.A. (2005). The effect of gender differences in primary school access, type, and quality on the decision to enroll in rural Pakistan. *Economic Development and Cultural Change, 53*(3).

Lo, F.C., and Yeung, Y.M. (1996). *Emerging world cities in Pacific Asia.* Tokyo, Japan: United Nations University Press.

Lockheed, M.E. (1993). The condition of primary education in developing countries. In H.M. Levin and M.E. Lockheed (Eds.), *Effective schools in developing countries* (pp. 20-40). Washington, DC: Falmer Press.

Lockheed, M.E., and Verspoor, A.M. (1991). *Improving primary education in developing countries.* Washington, DC: Oxford University Press for the World Bank.

Locoh, T. (1994). Social change and marriage arrangements: New types of union in Lomé, Togo. In C. Bledsoe and G. Pison (Eds.), *Nuptiality in sub-Saharan Africa: Contemporary anthropological and demographic perspectives* (pp. 215-230). New York: Oxford University Press.

Loeber, R., Farrington, D.P., Stouthamer-Loeber, M., and Van Kammen, W.B. (1998). In R. Jessor (Ed.), *New perspectives on adolescent risk behavior* (pp. 90-149). Cambridge, England: Cambridge University Press.

Lombardo, C., Zakus, D., and Skinner, H. (2002). Youth social action: Building a global latticework through information and communication technologies. *Health Promotion International, 17*(4), 363-371.

Lucas, R.E.B. (1997). Internal migration in developing countries. In M.R. Rosenzweig and O. Stark (Eds.), *Handbook of population and family economics.* Amsterdam: Elsevier.

Lugo, B.M. (1999). School-to-work transition in Mexico: An overview of recent experiences. In D. Stern and D.A. Wagner (Eds.), *International perspectives on the school-to-work transition* (pp. 311-334). Cresskill, NJ: Hampton Press.

Luke, N. (2003). Age and economic asymmetries in the sexual relationships of adolescent girls in sub-Saharan Africa. *Studies in Family Planning, 34*(2), 67-86.

Luke, N., and Munshi, K. (2003). *What role does marriage play in urban Africa? Evidence from a high HIV area in Kenya.* (Department of Economics Working Paper No. 03-20.) Cambridge, MA: Massachusetts Institute of Technology.

Luker, K. (1996). *Dubious conceptions: The politics of teenage pregnancy.* Cambridge, MA: Harvard University Press.

Lull, J. (Ed.). (1988). *World families watch television.* Beverly Hills, CA: Sage.

Lundberg, S., and Pollack, R.A. (1993). Separate-spheres bargaining and the marriage market. *Journal of Political Economy, 101*(6), 988-1010.

Lundberg, S.J., Pollack, R.A., and Wales, T.J. (1997). Do husbands and wives pool their resources? Evidence from the United Kingdom Child Benefit. *Journal of Human Resources, 32*(3), 463-480.

Luo, L., Wu, S.Z., Chen, X.Q., Li, M., and Pullum, T.W. (1995). Induced abortion among unmarried women in Sichuan Province, China. *Contraception, 51*(1), 59-63.

Luster, T., and Small, S. (1997). Sexual abuse and sexual risk-taking among sexually abused girls. *Family Planning Perspectives, 29*(5), 200-203.

Lynch, C. (1999). The good girls of Sri Lankan modernity: Moral orders of nationalism and capitalism. *Identities, 6*(1), 55-89.

Maddaleno, M., and Silber, T.J. (1993). An epidemiological view of adolescent health in Latin America. *Journal of Adolescent Health, 14*(8), 595-604, 655-663.

Magadi, M., Agwanda, A., Obare, F., and Taffa, N. (2004). *Comparing maternal health indicators between teenagers and older women in sub-Saharan Africa: Evidence from DHS.* Paper presented at the Population Association of American Annual Meeting, Boston, MA, April 1-3.

Magnani, R., Macintyre, K., Karim, A.M., Brown, L., and Hutchinson, P. (2003). *The impact of life skills education on adolescent sexual risk behaviors.* (Horizons Research Summary.) Washington, DC: Population Council.

Magnani, R., Robinson, A., Seiber, E., and Avila, G. (2000*). Evaluation of arte y parte: An adolescent reproductive health communications project implemented in Asunción, San Lorenzo and Fernande de la Mora, Paraguay.* Final report prepared for FOCUS on Young Adults, Washington, DC.

Magnani, R.J., Seiber, E.E., Gutierrez, E.Z., and Vereau, D. (2001). Correlates of sexual activity and condom use among secondary-school students in urban Peru. *Studies in Family Planning, 32*(1), 53-66.

Mahy, M. (2003). *Childhood mortality in the developing world: A review of evidence from the Demographic and Health Surveys.* (DHS Comparative Report No. 4.) Calverton, MD: ORC Macro International.

Mahy, M., and Gupta, N. (2002*). Trends and differentials in adolescent reproductive behavior in sub-Saharan Africa.* (DHS Analytical Studies No. 3.) Calverton, MD: ORC Macro International.

Malhotra, A. (1991). Gender and changing generational relations: Spouse choice in Indonesia. *Demography, 28*(4), 549-570.

Malhotra, A., and Degraff, D.S. (1997). Entry versus success in the labor force: Young women's employment in Sri Lanka. *World Development, 25*(3), 379-394.

Malhotra, A., and Tsui, A.O. (1996). Marriage timing in Sri Lanka: The role of modern norms and ideas. *Journal of Marriage and the Family, 58*(2), 476-490.

Malhotra, A., Nyblade, L., Parasuraman, S., MacQuarrie, K., Kashyap, N., and Walia, S. (2003). *Realizing reproductive choice and rights: Abortion and contraception in India.* Washington, DC: International Center for Research on Women.

Maluccio, J.A. (Forthcoming). Education and child labor: Experimental evidence from a Nicaraguan conditional cash transfer program. In P. Orazem, G. Sedlacek, and Z. Tzannatos (Eds.), *Child labor in Latin America.* Washington, DC: World Bank and Inter-American Development Bank.

Maluccio, J.A., and Flores, R. (2004). *Impact evaluation of a conditional cash transfer program: The Nicaraguan Red de Protección Social.* (FCND Discussion Paper.) Washington, DC: International Food Policy Research Institute.

Mamdani, M. (1996). *Citizen and subject: Contemporary Africa and the legacy of late colonialism.* Princeton, NJ: Princeton University Press.

Mann, K. (1994). The impact of Christianity on Yoruba marriage, gender, and Fertility. In C. Bledsoe and G. Pison (Eds.), *Nuptiality in sub-Saharan Africa: Contemporary anthropological and demographic perspectives* (pp. 167-193). Oxford, England: Clarendon Press.

Manser, M., and Brown, M. (1979). Bargaining analysis of household decisions. In C.B. Lloyd, E. Andrews, and C. Gilroy, (Eds.), *Women in the labor market* (pp. 43-50). New York: Columbia University Press.

Manser, M., and Brown, M. (1980). Marriage and household decision-making: A bargaining analysis. *International Economic Review, 21*(1), 31-44.

Mansilla, M.E. (1981). *La socializacion y los estereotipos sexuales: Estudio de los textos escolares de E.B.R.* Lima, Peru: Pontificia Universidad Catolica del Peru.

Marks, M. (2001). *Young warriors: Youth politics, identity and violence in South Africa.* Johannesburg, South Africa: Witwatersrand University Press.

Marr, D., and Rosen, S. (1998). Chinese and Vietnamese youth in the 1990s. *The China Journal, 40*(4), 145-172.

Marshall, T.H. (1950). *Citizenship and social class.* Cambridge, England: Cambridge University Press.

Marston, C., and Cleland, J. (2003). Relationships between contraception and abortion: A review of the evidence. *International Family Planning Perspectives. 29*(1), 6-13.

Marteleto, L. (2001). Children's schooling in Brazil: Do number and siblings composition matter? In *Annals of the XXIV IUSSP meeting*, Salvador, August. Liege, Belgium: International Union for the Scientific Study of Population.

Martin, M.O., Gregory, K.D., and Stemler, S.E. (1999a). *TIMSS 1999 technical report.* Available: wysiwyg://11/http://timss.bc.edu/timss1999i/tech_report.html [March 2003].

Martin-Barbero, J., Fox, E., and White, R.A. (1993). *Communication, culture, and hegemony: From media to mediations.* London, England: Sage.

Marty, M.E., and Appleby, R.S. (Eds.). (1993). *Fundamentalisms and the state: Remaking polities, economies, and militance.* Chicago, IL: University of Chicago Press.

Mashayekhi, M. (2001). The revival of the student movement in post-revolutionary Iran. *International Journal of Politics, Culture, and Society, 15*(2), 283-313.

Mason, A., Merrick, T., and Shaw, P. (Eds.). (1999). *Population economics, demographic transition, and development: Research and policy implications.* Washington, DC: World Bank.

Masterson, J.M., and Swanson, J.H. (2000). *Female genital cutting: Breaking the silence, enabling change.* Washington, DC: International Center for Research on Women.

Mathur, S., Greene, M., and Malhotra, A. (2003). *Too young to wed: The lives, rights, and health of young married girls.* Washington, DC: International Center for Research on Women.

Mathur, S., Mehta, M., and Malhotra, A. (2004). *Youth reproductive health in Nepal: Is participation the answer?* Washington, DC, and New York: International Center for Research on Women and Engender Health.

Mayseless, O. (1993). Attitudes toward military service among Israeli youth. In D. Ashkenazy (Ed.), *The military in the service of society and democracy.* Westport, CT: Greenwood Press.

McCauley, A.P., and Salter, C. (1995). *Meeting the needs of young adults.* (Population Report Series J, No. 41.) Baltimore, MD: Johns Hopkins School of Public Health.

McElroy, M.B., and Horney, M.J. (1981). Nash-bargained household decisions: Toward a generalization of the theory of demand. *International Economic Review, 22*(2), 333-347.

McGinn, N.F. (1997). The impact of globalization on national education systems. *Prospects: Quarterly Review of Comparative Education, 28*(1), 41-54.

Meekers, D. (1993). The noble custom of Roora: The marriage practices of the Shona of Zimbabwe. *Ethnology, 32*(1), 35-54.

Meekers, D. (1994). Combining ethnographic and survey methods: A study of the nuptiality patterns of the Shona of Zimbabwe. *Journal of Comparative Family Studies, 25*(3), 313-328.

Meekers, D. (1998). *The effectiveness of targeted social marketing to promote adolescent reproductive health: The case of Soweto, South Africa.* (Research Division Working Paper No. 16.) Washington, DC: Population Services International.

Meekers, D., and Ahmed, G. (1999). Pregnancy-related school dropout in Botswana. *Population Studies, 53*(2), 195-209.

Meekers, D., Gage, A., and Zhan, L. (1995). Preparing adolescents for adulthood: Family life education and pregnancy-related school expulsion in Kenya. *Population Research and Policy Review, 14*(1), 91-110.

Meekers, D., Stallworthy, G., and Harris, J. (1997). *Changing adolescents' beliefs about protective sexual behavior: The Botswana Tsa banana program.* (Research Division Working Paper No. 3.) Washington, DC: Population Services International.

Mehrotra, S. (1998). Social development in high-achieving countries: Common elements and diversities. In S. Mehrotra and R. Jolly (Eds.), *Development with a human face: Experiences in social achievement and economic growth* (pp. 21-61). Oxford, England: Oxford University Press.

Meinzen-Dick, R., Brown, L.R., Sims Feldstein, H., and Quisumbing, A.R. (1997). *Gender, property, and natural resources.* Washington, DC: International Food Policy Research Institute.

Meinzen-Dick, R., and Pradhan, R. (2001). Implications of legal pluralism for natural resource management. *IDS Bulletin, 32*(4), 10-17.

Melchiorre, A. (2002). *At what age are school children employed, married, and taken to court?* The Raoul Wallenberg Institute of Human Rights and Humanitarian Law. Available: http://right-to-education.org/content/index_9.html [March 2004].

Menezes-Filho, N.A. (2003). Adolescents in Latin America and the Caribbean: How do they decide to allocate their time? In S. Duryea, A. Cox Edwards, and M. Ureta (Eds.), *Critical decisions at a critical age: Adolescents and young adults in Latin America* (pp. 91-144). Washington, DC: Inter-American Development Bank.

Mensch, B.S. (1986). Age differences between spouses in first marriages. *Social Biology, 33*(3-4), 229-240.

Mensch, B.S., and Lloyd, C.B. (1998). Gender differences in the schooling experiences of adolescents in low-income countries: The Case of Kenya. *Studies in Family Planning, 29*(2), 167-184.

Mensch, B.S., Bruce, J., and Greene, M.E. (1998). *The uncharted passage: Girls' adolescence in the developing world.* New York: Population Council.

Mensch, B.S., Clark, W.H., and Anh, D.N. (2003). Adolescents in Vietnam: Looking beyond reproductive health. *Studies in Family Planning, 34*(4), 249-262.

Mensch, B.S., Hewett, P.C., and Erulkar, A.S. (2003). The reporting of sensitive behavior by adolescents: A methodological experiment in Kenya. *Demography, 40*(2), 247-268.

Mensch, B.S., Singh, S., and Casterline, J. (2005). Trends in the timing of first marriage among men and women in the developing world. In National Research Council and Institute of Medicine, *The changing transitions to adulthood in developing countries: Selected studies.* C.B. Lloyd, J.R. Behrman, N.P. Stromquist, and B. Cohen (Eds.). Committee on Population and Board on Children, Youth, and Families. Division of Behavioral and Social Sciences and Education. Washington, DC: The National Academies Press.

Mensch, B.S., Bagah, D., Clark, W.H., and Binka, F. (1999). The changing nature of adolescence in the Kassena-Nankana district of Northern Ghana. *Studies in Family Planning, 30*(2), 95-111.

Mensch, B.S., Clark, W.H., Lloyd, C.B., and Erulkar, A. (2001). Premarital sex, schoolgirl pregnancy, and school quality in rural Kenya. *Studies in Family Planning, 32*(4), 285-301.

Mensch, B.S., Grant, M.J., Blanc, A., and Clarke, S. (2005). *The changing context of sexual initiation in developing countries.* Paper accepted for presentation at annual meeting of International Union for the Scientific Study of Population, Tours, France.

Mensch, B.S., Ibrahim, B.L., Lee, S.M., and El-Gibaly, O. (2003). Gender role attitudes among Egyptian adolescents. *Studies in Family Planning, 34*(1), 8-18.

Mete, C. (2004). The inequality implications of highly selective promotion practices. *Economics of Education Review, 23*(3), 301-314.

Meyer, J.W. (1992). Background: A perspective on the curriculum and curricular research. In J.W. Meyer, D.H. Kamens, A. Benavot, Y.-K. Cha, and S.-Y. Wong (Eds.), *School knowledge for the masses: World models and national primary curricular categories in the twentieth century* (pp. 18-27). Washington, DC: Falmer Press.

Mgalla, Z., Schapink, D., and Boerma, J.T. (1998). Protecting school girls against sexual exploitation: Development of a guardian programme in Tanzania. *Reproductive Health Matters, 7*(12), 19.

Michaelowa, K. (2001). Primary education quality in Francophone sub-Saharan Africa: Determinants of learning achievement and efficiency considerations. *World Development, 29*(10), 1699-1716.

Miguel, E., and Kremer, M. (2004). Worms: Identifying impacts on education and health in the presence of treatment externalities. *Econometrica, 72*(1), 159-217.

Milanovic, B. (2003). The two faces of globalization: Against globalization as we know it. *World Development, 31*(4), 667-683.

Miles, A. (2000). Poor adolescent girls and social transformations in Cuenca, Ecuador. *Ethos, 28*(1), 54-74.

Millennium Project Task Force. (2004). *Task force 3 interim report on primary education.* Washington, DC: Millennium Project Task Force on Education and Gender Equality.

Miller, K.E., Sabo, D., Farrell, M.P., Barnes, G.M., and Melnick, M.J. (1998). Athletic participation and sexual behavior in adolescents: The different worlds of boys and girls. *Journal of Health and Social Behavior, 39*(2), 108-123.

Mincer, J. (1962). Labor force participation of married women: A study of labor supply. In H. Gregg Lewis (Ed.), *Aspects of labor economics* (pp. 63-97). Princeton, NJ: Princeton University Press.

Mische, A. (1996). Projecting democracy: The formation of citizenship across youth networks in Brazil. In C. Tilly (Ed.), *Citizenship, identity, and social history* (pp. 150-159). Cambridge, England: Press Syndicate of the University of Cambridge.

Mizala, A., and Romaguera, P. (2000). School performance and choice. *The Journal of Human Resources, 35*(2), 392-417.

Mmari, K., and Magnani, R. (2003). Does making clinic-based reproductive health services more "youth friendly" increase service utilization by adolescents: Evidence from Lusaka, Zambia. *Journal of Adolescent Health, 33*(4), 259-270.

Moffitt, R. (2003). Causal analysis in population research: An economist's perspective. *Population and Development Review, 29*(3), 448-458.

Moghadam, A. (2003). *A global resurgence of religion.* (Working Paper No. 03-03.) Cambridge, MA: Harvard University, Weatherhead Center for International Affairs.

Mohan, D. (2003). Road traffic injuries: A neglected pandemic. *Bulletin of the World Health Organizaton, 81*(9), 684-685.

Moktar, M., and Wahba, J. (2002). Informalization of labor in Egypt. In R. Assaad (Ed.), *The Egyptian labor market in an era of reform* (pp. 131-158). Cairo, Egypt: The American University in Cairo Press.

Moller, H. (1968). Youth as a force in the modern world. *Comparative Studies in Society and History, 10*(3), 237-260.

Montgomery, M.R., Arends-Kuenning, M., and Mete, C. (2001). The quantity-quality transition in Asia. In C. Chu and R. Lee (Eds.), *Population and economic change in East Asia.* New York: Population Council.

Montgomery, M.R., and Lloyd, C.B. (1999). Excess fertility, unintended births and children's schooling. In National Research Council, *Critical perspectives on schooling and fertility in the developing world* (pp. 216-266). C.H. Bledsoe, J.B. Casterline, J.A. Johnson-Kuhn, and J.G. Haaga (Eds.). Committee on Population. Commission on Behavioral and Social Sciences and Education. Washington, DC: National Academy Press.

Montoya, M. (2003). *La educación sexual desde el Ministerio de Educación Pública*. Paper presented at colloquium on "Gender and Social Equity for All," sponsored by UNESCO and the School of Education, Universidad Catolica del Peru, Lima, August 28.

Morgan, M., and Shanahan, J. (1991). Television and the cultivation of political attitudes in Argentina. *Journal of Communication, 41*(1), 88-103.

Morris, P., and Cogan, J. (2001). A comparative overview: Civic education across six societies. *International Journal of Educational Research, 35*(1), 109-123.

Morrow, M., Ngoc, D.H., Hoang, T.T., and Trinh, T.H. (2002). Smoking and young women in Vietnam: The influence of normative gender roles. *Social Science and Medicine, 55*(10), 681-690.

Morrow, R.A., and Torres, C.A. (2000). The state, globalization, and educational policy. In N.C. Burbules and C.A. Torres (Eds.), *Globalization and education: Critical perspectives* (pp. 27-56). New York: Routledge.

Moser, C., and van Bronkhorst, B. (1999). *Youth violence in Latin America and the Caribbean: Costs, causes, and interventions*. Washington, DC: World Bank.

Moulton, J., Mundy, K., Welmond, M., and Williams, J. (2001). *Paradigm lost? The implementation of basic education reforms in sub-Saharan Africa*. (Sustainable Development Publication Series Technical Paper No. 109.) Washington, DC: U.S. Agency for International Development.

Mpangile, G., Leshabari, M., and Kihwele, D. (1999). Induced abortion in Dar es Salaam, Tanzania: The plight of adolescents. In A. Mundigo and C. Indriso (Eds.), *Abortion in the developing world* (pp. 387-403). London, England: Zed Books.

Mugisha, F., Arinaitwe-Mugisha, J., and Hagembe, B.O.N. (2003). Alcohol, substance and drug use among urban slum adolescents in Nairobi, Kenya. *Cities, 20*(4), 231-240.

Mulder, M.B. (1995). Bridewealth and its correlates: Quantifying changes over time. *Current Anthropology, 36*(4), 573-603.

Mullis, I.V.S., Martin, M.O., Gonzalez, E.J., Gregory, K.D., Garden, R.A., O'Connor, K.M., Chrostowski, S.J., and Smith, T.A. (2000). *TIMSS 1999 international mathematics report: Findings from IEA's repeat of the third international mathematics and science study at the eighth-grade*. Available: http://isc.bc.edu/timss1999i/math_achievement_report.html [March 2003].

Munshi, K., and Rosenzweig, M. (2003). *Traditional institutions meet the modern world: Caste, gender, and schooling choice in a globalizing economy*. (Working Paper No. 038.) Washington, DC: Bureau for Research in Economic Analysis Development.

Murray, C.J., Lopez, A.D., Mathers, C., and Stein, C. (2001). *The global burden of disease 2000 project: Aims, methods, and data sources*. (Global Programme on Evidence for Health Policy Discussion Paper No. 36.) Geneva, Switzerland: World Health Organization.

Murray, N., Toledo, V., Luengo, X., Molina, R., and Zabin, L. (2000). *An evaluation of an integrated adolescent development program for urban teenagers in Santiago, Chile. Focus on Young Adults Program 1995-2000*. Available: http://www.futuresgroup.com/Documents/Chile-IADP.pdf [March 2005].

Myers, W.E. (2001). The right rights? Child labor in a globalizing world. *Annals of the American Academy of Political and Social Science, 575*(May), 38-55.

Nagashima, N. (1987). Aspects of change in bridewealth among the Iteso of Kenya. In D. Parkin and D. Nyamwaya (Eds.), *Transformations of African marriage* (pp. 184-198). Manchester, England: Manchester University Press.

Nantulya, V.M., and Reich, M.R. (2002). The neglected epidemic: Road traffic injuries in developing countries. *British Medical Journal, 321*(11), 1139-1141.

Nathanson, C.A. (1991). *Dangerous passage: The social control of sexuality in women's adolescence*. Philadelphia, PA: Temple University Press.

National Institute of Population Research and Training and ORC Macro International. (2002). *Bangladesh maternal health services and maternal mortality survey 2001: Preliminary report*. Dhaka, Bangladesh, and Calverton, MD: National Institute of Population Research and Training and ORC Macro International.

National Research Council. (1993). *Social dynamics of adolescent fertility in sub-Saharan Africa. Population dynamics of sub-Saharan Africa*. C.H. Bledsoe and B. Cohen (Eds.), Working Group on the Social Dynamics of Adolescent Fertility, Panel on the Population Dynamics of Sub-Saharan Africa. Committee on Population, Commission on Behavioral and Social Sciences and Education. Washington, DC: National Academy Press.

National Research Council. (1997a). *Reproductive health in developing countries: Expanding dimensions, building solutions*. A.O. Tsui, J.N. Wasserheit., and J.G. Haaga (Eds.). Panel on Reproductive Health. Committee on Population. Commission on Behavioral and Social Sciences and Education. Washington, DC: National Academy Press.

National Research Council. (1997b). *The new Americans: Economic, demographic, and fiscal effects of immigration*. J.P. Smith and B. Edmonston (Eds.). Panel on the Demographic and Economic Impacts of Immigration. Committee on Population and Committee on National Statistics. Commission on Behavioral and Social Sciences and Education. Washington, DC: National Academy Press.

National Research Council. (1999). *Critical perspectives on schooling and fertility in the developing world*. C.H. Bledsoe, J.B. Casterline, J.A. Johnson-Kuhn, and J.G. Haaga (Eds.). Committee on Population. Commission on Behavioral and Social Sciences and Education. Washington, DC: National Academy Press.

National Research Council. (2003). *Cities transformed: Demographic change and its implications in the developing world*. Panel on Urban population Dynamics. M. Montgomery, R. Stren, B. Cohen, and H. Reed (Eds.). Committee on Population. Division of Behavioral and Social Sciences and Education. Washington, DC: The National Academies Press.

National Research Council. (2004). *Monitoring international labor standards: Techniques and sources of information*. Committee on Monitoring International Labor Standards. Center for Education. Division of Behavioral and Social Sciences and Education and Policy and Global Affairs Division. Washington, DC: The National Academies Press.

Nelson, L.J., Badger, S., and Wu, B. (2004). The influence of culture in emerging adulthood: Perspectives of Chinese college students. *International Journal of Behavorial Development, 28*(1), 26-36.

Neri, M.C., Gustafsson-Wright, E., Sedlacek, G., and Orazem, P.F. (Forthcoming). The responses of child labor, school enrollment, and grade repetition to the loss of parental earnings in Brazil, 1982-1999. In P.F. Orazem, G. Sedlacek, and Z. Tzannatos (Eds.), *Child labor in Latin America*. Washington, DC: World Bank and Inter-American Development Bank.

NetSense. (2002). *NetKidz: A comprehensive study of internet usage and attitudes of school going children in India*. Pune, India: Author.

Neumark, D. (1998). *Youth labor markets in the U.S.: Shopping around versus staying put*. (NBER Working Paper No. 6581.) Cambridge, MA: National Bureau of Economic Research.

Newton, K., and Norris, P. (2000). Confidence in public institutions: Faith, culture or performance? In S.J. Pharr and R.D. Putnam (Eds.), *Disaffecting democracies: What's troubling the trilateral countries?* (pp. 52-73). Princeton, NJ: Princeton University Press.

Nicholson, H.J., and Postrado, L.T. (1991). *Girls Incorporated preventing adolescent pregnancy: A program development and research project*. New York: Girls Incorporated.

Noorbakhsh, F., and Paloni, A. (2001). Human capital and FDI inflows to developing countries: New empirical evidence. *World Development, 29*(9), 1593-1610.

Nordberg, E. (2000). Injuries as a public health problem in sub-Saharan Africa: Epidemiology and prospects for control. *East African Medical Journal, 77*(Supplement 12), S1-S43.

Noronha, C.V., Machado, E.P., Tapparelli, G., Cordeiro, T.R., Laranjeira, D.H., and Santos, C.A. (1999). Violence, ethnic groups, and skin color: A study on differences in the metropolitan region of Salvador, Bahia, Brazil. *Pan American Journal of Public Health, 5,* 268-277.

Norris, A.E., and Ford, K. (1999). Sexual experiences and condom use of heterosexual, low-income African-American and Hispanic youth practicing relative monogamy, serial monogamy, and nonmonogamy. *Sexually Transmitted Diseases, 26*(2), 17-25.

Nsamenang, A.B. (2002). Adolescence in sub-Saharan Africa: An image constructed from Africa's triple inheritance. In B. Bradford Brown, R. Larson, and T.S. Saraswathi (Eds.), *The world's youth: Adolescence in 8 regions of the globe* (pp. 44-59). Cambridge, England: Cambridge University Press.

Nua Internet Survey. (2002). *How many online?* Available: www.nua.ie/surveys/how_many_online/index.html [April 2004].

Nuñoz, F. (2003). *De que politicas educativas hablamos en el Peru? La incorporación del genero a la educación.* Paper presented at the 51st International Congress of Americanists, Santiago, July 14-18.

Nyanzi, S., Pool, R., and Kinsman, J. (2001). The negotiation of sexual relationships among school pupils in south-western Uganda. *AIDS Care, 13*(1), 83-98.

O'Gara, C., Benoliel, S., and Sutton, M., and Tietjen, K. (1999). *More, but not yet better: An evaluation of USAID's programs and policies to improve girls' education.* (USAID Program and Operations Assessment Report No. 25.) Washington, DC: U.S. Agency for International Development.

O'Higgins, N. (2001). *Youth unemployment and employment policy: A global perspective.* Geneva, Switzerland: International Labour Office.

Obura, A.P. (1991). *Changing images: Portrayal of girls and women in Kenyan textbooks.* Nairobi, Kenya: ACTS Press.

Omololu, F. (1994). *Adolescent childbearing and poverty: Identifying the mechanisms for creation and transmission of poverty in southwestern Nigeria.* Paper presented at the seminar on women, poverty, and demographic change, organized by the International Union for the Scientific Study of Population, Committee on Gender and Population, in collaboration with El Colegio de Mexico, the Mexican Society of Demography, the National Population Council, and the State Population Council of Oaxaca, Mexico, October 25-28.

Onat, T., and Erten, B. (1995). Age at menarche: Relationships to socioeconomic status, growth rate in stature and weight, and skeletal and sexual maturation. *American Journal of Human Biology, 7*(6), 741-750.

ORC Macro International. (2004). *Measure DHS + STAT compiler.* Available: http://www.measuredhs.com [February 2004].

Oreopoulos, P. (2003). *Do dropouts drop out too soon? International evidence from changes in school-leaving laws.* (NBER Working Paper No. 10155.) Cambridge, MA: National Bureau of Economic Research.

Organisation for Economic Co-operation and Development. (2001). *Knowledge and skills for life: First results from OECD programme for international student assessment 2000.* Paris, France: Author.

Organisation for Economic Co-operation and Development and UNESCO Institute for Statistics. (2003). *Literacy skills for the world of tomorrow: Further results from PISA 2000.* Paris, France: Author.

Oro, A.P., and Seman, P. (2001). Brazilian pentecostalism crosses national borders. In A. Corten and R. Marshall-Fratani (Eds.), *Between babel and Pentecost: Transnational Pentecostialism in Africa and Latin America* (pp. 181-195). Bloomington: Indiana University Press.

Over, M., and Piot, P. (1993). HIV infection and sexually transmitted diseases. In D.T. Jamison, W.H. Mosley, A.R. Measham, and J.L. Bobadilla (Eds.), *Disease control priorities in developing countries* (pp. 455-527). New York: Oxford University Press.

Pancer, S.M., and Pratt, M.W.S. (1999). Social and family determinants of community service involvement in Canadian youth. In M. Yates and J. Youniss (Eds.), *Roots of civic identity: International perspectives on community service and activism in youth* (pp. 32-55). New York: Cambridge University Press.

Parent, A.S., Teilmann, G., Juul, A., Skakkebaek, N.E., Toppari, J., and Bourguignon, J.P. (2003). The timing of normal puberty and the age limits of sexual precocity: Variations around the world, secular trends, and changes after migration. *Endocrine Reviews, 24*(5), 668-693.

PASEC. (2002). *PASEC (Presentation du programme d'analyse des systemes educatifs de la Confemen).* Available: www.confemen.org/pasec/program/index.htm [October 28, 2002].

Pasquet, P., Biyong, A.M., and Rikong-Adie, H. (1999). Age at menarche and urbanization in Cameroon: Current status and secular trends. *Annals of Human Biology, 26*(1), 89-97.

Patel, V., and Andrew, G. (2001). Gender, sexual abuse, and risk behaviours in adolescents: A cross-sectional survey in schools in Goa. *National Medical Journal of India, 14*(5), 263-267.

Pateman, C. (1988). *The sexual contract.* Stanford, CA: Stanford University Press.

Patrinos, H.A., and Psacharopoulos, G. (1995). Educational performance and child labor in Paraguay. *International Journal of Educational Development, 15*(1), 47-60.

Patrinos, H.A., and Psacharopoulos, G. (1997). Family size, schooling, and child labor in Peru: An empirical analysis. *Journal of Population Economics, 10*(4), 387-405.

Pattillo, M.E.S. (1998). Sweet mothers and gangbangers: Managing crime in a black middle-class neighborhood. *Social Forces, 76*(3), 747-774.

Pavis, S., Cunningham-Burley, S., and Amos, A. (1998). Health related behavioural change in context: Young people in transition. *Social Science and Medicine, 47*(10), 1407-1418.

Paxson, C., and Schady, N.A. (2000). *Do school facilities matter? The case of the Peruvian Social Fund.* (Policy Research Working Paper No. 2229.) Washington, DC: World Bank.

Peláez Mendoz, J.A., Rodriguez Izquiendo, C., Lammers, R.W., and Blum, R. (1999). Abortion among adolescents in Cuba. *Journal of Adolescent Health, 24*(1), 59-62.

Philliber, S. (1999). *In search of peer power: A review of research on peer-based interventions for teens. Peer potential: Making the most of how teens influence each other.* Washington, DC: National Campaign to Prevent Teen Pregnancy.

Phillips, A. (1998). *Feminism and politics.* Oxford, England: Oxford University Press.

Phiri, A., and Erulkar, A.S. (1997). *A situation analysis of the Zimbabwe national family planning council's youth centres: Baseline Assessment.* Nairobi, Kenya: Zimbabwe National Family Council and Population Council.

Pitiyanuwat, S., and Sujiva, S. (2001). Civics education in Thailand: Three case schools. *International Journal of Educational Research, 35*(1), 93-108.

Pitt, M.M., Rosenzweig, M.P., and Gibbons, D.M. (1993). The determinants and consequences of the placement of government programs in Indonesia. *The World Bank Economic Review, 7*(September 3), 319-348.

Pollitt, E., Gorman, K.S., Engle, P.L., Martorell, R., and Rivers, J. (1993). Early supplemental feeding and cognition: Effects over two decades. *Monographs of the Society for Research in Child Development, Serial No. 235, 58*(7).

Popkin, B.M. (2002). An overview on the nutrition transition and its health implications: The Bellagio meeting. *Public Health Nutrition, 5*(1A), 93-103.

Population Council. (1999). *Our daughters, our wealth: Investing in young girls, Apni Beti Apna Dhan, government of Haryana.* (The Adolescents in Transition Series.) New Delhi, India: Author.

Population Council and Family Health International. (2001). *The case for microbicides: A global priority* (2nd ed.). New York: Author.

Population Council and International Center for Research on Women. (2000). Adolescent girls' livelihoods: Essential questions, essential tools. A report on a workshop. New York: Author.

Population Council and UNICEF. (2003). *The role of social support and economic skill building programs in mitigating adolescents' vulnerabilities: Perspectives and UNICEF's experience to date.* New York: Author.

Porter, K.A. (1996). The agency of children, work, and social change in the South Pare Mountains, Tanzania. *Anthropology of Work Review, 17*(1, 2), 8-19.

Portes, A. (1998). Social capital: Its origins and applications in modern sociology. *Annual Review of Sociology, 24*(August), 1-24.

Post, D. (2001). *Children's work, schooling, and welfare in Latin America.* Boulder, CO: Westview Press.

Post, D., and Pong, S. (2000). Employment during middle school: The effects on academic achievement in the U.S. and abroad. *Educational Evaluation and Policy Analysis, 23,* 273-298.

Pritchett, L. (2004). *Towards a new consensus for addressing the global challenge of the lack of education.* Cambridge, MA: Harvard University, John F. Kennedy School of Government.

Psacharopoulos, G. (1994). Returns to investment in education: A global update. *World Development, 22*(9), 1325-1343.

Psacharopoulos, G., and Patrinos, H.A. (2002). *Returns to investment in education: A further update populatin research.* (Working Paper No. 2881.) Washington, DC: World Bank Latin America and Carribean Region, Education Sector.

Psacharopoulos, G., Rojas, C., and Velez, E. (1993). Achievement evaluation of Colombia's *Escuela Nueva*: Is multigrade the answer? *Comparative Education Review, 37*(3), 263-276.

Pullum, T.W., and Zellner, S. (2000). *The number and sex composition of siblings: International variations, trends, and implications.* Paper presented at annual meeting of Population Association of America, Los Angeles, CA, March 23-25.

Putnam, R. (2000). *Bowling alone: The collapse and revival of American community.* New York: Simon and Schuster.

Putnam, R.D., Leonardi, R., and Nanetti, R.Y. (1993). *Making democracy work: Civic traditions in modern Italy.* Princeton, NJ: Princeton University Press.

Putnam, R.D., Pharr, S.J., and Dalton, R.J. (2000). Introduction: What's troubling the trilateral democracies? In S.J. Pharr and R.D. Putnam (Eds.), *Disaffecting democracies: What's troubling the trilateral countries?* (pp. 3-30). Princeton, NJ: Princeton University Press.

Quisumbing, A.R., and Hallman, K. (2005). Marriage in transition: Evidence on age, education, and assets from six developing countries. In National Research Council and Institute of Medicine, *The changing transitions to adulthood in developing countries: Selected studies.* C.B. Lloyd, J.R. Behrman, N.P. Stromquist, and B. Cohen (Eds.). Committee on Population and Board on Children, Youth, and Families. Division of Behavioral and Social Sciences and Education. Washington, DC: The National Academies Press.

Quisumbing, A.R., and Otsuka, K. (2001). *Land, trees, and women: Evolution of land tenure institutions in Western Ghana and Sumatra.* Washington, DC: International Food Policy Research Institute.

Rama, M. (1996). *The consequences of doubling the minimum wage: The case of Indonesia.* (Policy Research Working Paper No. 1643.) Washington, DC: World Bank.

Ramrakha, S., Caspi, A., Dickson, N., Moffitt, T.E., and Paul, C. (2000). Psychiatric disorders and risky sexual behavior in young adulthood: Cross-sectional study in birth cohort. *British Medical Journal, 321*(7526), 263-266.

Randolph, S.M. (1996). *Evaluation of the Jamaica Red Cross Society' "Together We Can" HIV/AIDS Peer Education Project.* Submitted to the American Red Cross National Headquarters and Jamaica Red Cross Society.

Rani, M., Figueroa, M.E., and Ainsle, R. (2003). The psychosocial context of young adult sexual behavior in Nicaragua: Looking through the gender lens. *International Family Planning Perspectives, 29*(4), 174-181.

Ravallion, M. (2003). *The debate on globalization, poverty, and inequality: Why measurement matters.* (Policy Research Working Paper No. 3038.) Washington, DC: World Bank.

Ravallion, M., and Wodon, Q. (2000). Does child labor displace schooling? Evidence on behavioral responses to an enrollment subsidy. *The Economic Journal, 110*(March), C158-C175.

Ray, R. (2002). Child labor, child schooling, and their interaction with adult labor: Empirical evidence for Peru and Pakistan. *The World Bank Economic Review, 14*(2), 347-367.

Ray, R., and Lancaster, G. (2003). *Does child labour affect school attendance and school performance? Multicountry evidence on SIMPOC data.* (School of Economics, University of Tasmania.) Econometric Society 2004 Australasian Meetings Series No. 68. Available: http://ideas.repec.org/s/ecm/ausm04.html [March 2005].

Resnick, M. (2000). Protective factors, resiliency, and healthy youth development. *Adolescent Medicine, 11*(1), 157-164.

Resnick, M., Bearman, P., Blum, R., and Bauman, K. (1997). Protecting adolescents from harm: Findings from the National Longitudinal Study on Adolescent Health. *Journal of the American Medical Association, 278*(10), 823-832.

Retherford, R.D., Ogawa, N., and Matsukura, R. (2001). Late marriage and less marriage in Japan. *Population and Development Review, 27*(1), 65-102.

Rhodes, C.N., Jr., Mihyar, H.A., and El-Rous, G.A. (2002). Social learning and community participation with children at risk in two marginalized urban neighborhoods in Amman, Jordan. In M. Tienda and W.J. Wilson (Eds.), *Youth in cities: A cross-national perspective* (pp. 191-216). Cambridge, England: Cambridge University Press.

Richards, P. (1996). *Fighting for the rain forest: War, youth, and resources in Sierra Leone.* Oxford, England: James Currey.

Riesebrodt, M. (2000). *Secularization and the global resurgence of religion.* Paper presented at the Comparative Social Analysis Workshop, University of California, Los Angeles, CA, March 9.

Riggio, E. (2002). Child friendly cities: Good governance in the best interests of the child. *Environment and Urbanization, 14*(2), 45-58.

Riggio, E., and Kilbane, T. (2000). The international secretariat for child friendly cities: A global network for urban children. *Environment and Urbanization, 12*(2), 201-205.

Rindfuss, R.R., and Morgan, S.P. (1983). Marriage, sex, and the 1st birth interval: The quiet revolution in Asia. *Population and Development Review, 9*(2), 259-278.

Ritchie, A., Lloyd, C.B., and Grant, M.J. (2004). *Gender differences in time use among adolescents in developing countries: The implications of rising school enrollment rates.* (Policy Research Division Working Paper No. 193.) New York: Population Council.

Ritualo, A.R., Castro, C.L., and Gormly, S. (2003). Measuring child labor: Implications for policy and program design. *Comparative Labor Law & Policy Journal, 24*(2), 401-434.

Rizzini, I., Barker, G., and Cassaniga, N. (2002). From street children to all children: Improving the opportunities of low-income urban children and youth in Brazil. In M. Tienda and W.J. Wilson (Eds.), *Youth in cities: A cross-national perspective* (pp. 113-137). Cambridge, England: Cambridge University Press.

Roberts, B. (1991). The changing nature of informal employment: The Case of Mexico. In G. Standing and V. Tokman (Eds.), *Towards social adjustment: Labor market issues in structural adjustment* (pp. 115-140). Geneva, Switzerland: International Labour Office.

Rodgers, D. (1999). *Youth gangs and violence in Latin America and the Caribbean: A literature survey.* (Latin America and the Caribbean Region Sustainable Development, Working Paper No. 4, Urban Peace Program Series.) Washington, DC: World Bank.

Rodgers, D. (2002). *We live in a state of siege: Violence, crime, and gangs in post-conflict urban Nicaragua.* (Development Studies Institute Work Paper Series No. 02-36.) London, England: London School of Economics.

Rogers, E.M. (1995). *Diffusion of innovations* (4th ed.). New York: Free Press.

Roker, D., Player, K., and Coleman, J. (1999). Exploring adolescent altruism: British young people's involvement in voluntary work and campaigning. In M. Yates and J. Youniss (Eds.), *Roots of civic identity: International perspectives on community service and activism in youth* (pp. 50-61). New York: Cambridge University Press.

Rosaldo, M.Z. (1974). Woman, culture, and society: A theoretical overview. In M. Rosaldo and L. Lamphere (Eds.), *Women, culture, and society* (pp. 17-42). Stanford, CA: Stanford University Press.

Rosati, F.C., and Rossi, M. (2003). Children's working hours and school enrollments: Evidence from Pakistan and Nicaragua. *The World Bank Economic Review, 17*(2), 283-296.

Rosenzweig, M.R. (1995). Why are there returns in schooling? *American Economic Review, 85*(2), 153-158.

Rosenzweig, M.R., and Wolpin, K.J. (1986). Evaluating the effects of optimally distributed public programs. *American Economic Review, 76*(3), 470-487.

Rosenzweig, M.R., and Wolpin, K.J. (2000). Natural "natural experiments" in economics. *Journal of Economic Literature, 38*(December), 827-874.

Ross, J., and Stover, J. (2000). *Effort indices for National Family Planning Programs: 1999 cycle.* Washington, DC: The Future Group.

Rubalcava, L., Teruel, G., and Thomas, D. (2004). *Welfare design, women's empowerment and income pooling.* Paper presented at the Population Association of America Annual Meeting, Minneapolis, MN, May 1-3.

Rucci, G. (2003). *Macro shocks and schooling decisions: The case of Argentina.* Paper presented at the Population Association of America Annual Meeting, Boston, MA, April 1-3.

Rugh, A. (2000). *Starting now: Strategies for helping girls complete primary.* (AGE Technical Report No. 1.) Washington, DC: Academy for Educational Development.

Russell-Brown, P., Engle, P.L., and Townsend, J.W. (1992). *The effects of early childbearing on women's status in Barbados.* (Working Paper Series on family structure, female headship, and maintenance of families and poverty.) New York: Population Council and International Center for Research on Women.

Rutenberg, N., Biddlecom, A.E., and Kaona, F.A.D. (2000). Reproductive decision-making in the context of HIV and AIDS: A qualitative study in Ndola, Zambia. *International Family Planning Perspectives, 26*(3), 124-130.

Rutenberg, N., Kehus-Alons, C., Brown, L., Macintyre, K., Dallimore, A., and Kaufman, C. (2001). *Transitions to adulthood in the context of AIDS in South Africa: Report of wave I.* New York: Population Council.

Saffer, H. (2000). Tobacco advertising and promotion. In P. Jha and F. Chaloupka (Eds.), *Tobacco control in developing countries* (pp. 215-236). Oxford, England: Oxford University Press.

Salaff, J.W. (1981). *Working daughters of Hong Kong: Filial piety or power in the family?* Cambridge, England: Cambridge University Press.

Sala-i-Martin, X. (2002). *The word distribution of income estimated from individual country distributions.* (NBER Working Paper No. 8933.) Cambridge, MA: National Bureau of Economic Research.

Salem, R., Ibrahim, B., and Brady, M. (2003). Negotiating leadership roles: Young women's experience in rural Egypt. *Women's Studies Quarterly, 31*(Fall, 3-4), 174-191.

Saloucou, L., Brady, M., and Chong, E. (Forthcoming). *Adolescent girls in Burkina Faso: A pivot point for social change.* New York: Population Council.

Samoff, J. (1994). *Coping with crisis: Austerity, adjustment, and human resources.* London and New York: UNESCO and Cassell.

Samoff, J., Alfthan, T., Carton, M., Cohen, M., Duvieusart, B., Jallade, L., Lee, E., de Moura Castro, C., Oulai, D., Reiff, H., Tiburcio, L., and Woodhall, M. (1994). Crisis and adjustment: Understanding national responses. In J. Samoff (Ed.), *Coping with crisis: Austerity, adjustment, and human resources* (pp. 5-27). London and New York: UNESCO and Cassell.

Samoff, J., and Sumra, S. (1994). From planning to marketing: Making education and training policy in Tanzania. In J. Samoff (Ed.), *Coping with crisis: Austerity, adjustment and human resources* (pp. 134-172). London and New York: UNESCO and Cassell.

Sathar, Z.A., Lloyd, C.B., and ul Haque, M. (2000). *Investments in children's education and family-building behavior in Pakistan: Findings from rural NWFP and Punjab.* Islamabad, Pakistan: Population Council.

Sathar, Z.A., Lloyd, C.B., Mete, C., and ul Haque, M. (2003a). Schooling opportunities for girls as a stimulus for fertility change in rural Pakistan. *Economic Development and Cultural Change, 51*(3), 677-698.

Sathar, Z.A., Lloyd, C.B., ul Haque, M., Diers, J.A., Faizunnissa, A., Grant, M., and Sultana, M. (2003b). *Adolescents and youth in Pakistan 2001-2002: A nationally representative survey.* Islamabad, Pakistan: Population Council.

Save the Children. (2004). *State of the world's mothers 2004: Children having children.* Westport, CT: Author.

Schaffner, J.A. (2001). Job stability in developing and developed countries: Evidence from Colombia and the United States. *Economic Development and Cultural Change, 49*(3), 511-535.

Schulenberg, J.E., and Zarrett, N.R. (Forthcoming). Mental health in emerging adulthood: Continuities and discontinuities in course, content, and meaning. In J.J. Arnett and J.T. Tanner (Eds.), *Coming of age in the 21st century: The lives and contexts of emerging adults.* Washington, DC: American Psychological Association.

Schultz, T.P. (1971). Rural-urban migration in Colombia. *Reveiw of Economics and Statistics, 53*(2), 157-163.

Schultz, T.P. (2000). *Impact of PROGRESA on school attendance rates in the sampled population.* Washington, DC: International Food Policy Research Institute.

Schultz, T.P. (2002). Why governments should invest more to educate girls. *World Development, 30*(2), 207-225.

Schultz, T.P. (2003). *Evidence of returns to schooling in Africa from household surveys: Monitoring and restructuring the market for education.* New Haven, CT: Yale University.

Schultz, T.P. (2004). School subsidies for the poor: Evaluating the Mexican PROGRESA poverty program. *Journal of Development Economics, 74*(1), 199-250.

Schultz, T.W. (1975). The value of the ability to deal with disequilibria. *Journal of Economic Literature, 13*(3), 827-846.

Schutt-Aine, J., and Maddaleno, M. (2003). *Sexual health and development among youth in the Americas: Program and policy implications.* Washington, DC: Pan American Health Organization.

Sen, A. (1997). Editorial: Human capital and human capability. *World Development, 25*(12), 1959-1961.

Sen, A. (1999). *Development as freedom.* Oxford, England: Oxford University Press.

Senderowitz, J. (1995). *Adolescent health: Reassessing the passage to adulthood.* (Report No. 272.) Washington, DC: World Bank.

Senlet, P., Curtis, S.L., Mathis, J., and Raggers, H. (2001). The role of changes in contraceptive use in the decline of induced abortion in Turkey. *Studies in Family Planning, 32*(1), 41-52.

Shafey, O., Dolwick, S., and Guindon, G.E. (2003). *Tobacco control country profiles* (2nd ed.). Atlanta, GA: American Cancer Society.

Shaheed, F., and Mumtaz, K. (1993). Women's education in Pakistan. In J.K. Conway and S.C. Bourque (Eds.), *The politics of women's education* (pp. 30-42). Ann Arbor: University of Michigan Press.

Shapiro, M. (2000). National times and other times: Re-thinking citizenship. *Cultural Studies, 14*(1), 79-98.

Sharma, V., and Sharma, A. (1995). *Safe sex: A mirage in a desert? The sexual behaviour of adolescent boys in Gujarat, India.* Paper presented at the 6th International Congress on Adolescent Health, Vancouver, Canada.

Shavit, Y., and Kraus, V. (1990). Educational transitions in Israel: A test of the industrialization and credentialism hypotheses. *Sociology of Education, 63*(2), 133-141.

Shelburne, R.C. (2001). An explanation of the international variation in the prevalence of child labour. *The World Economy, 24*(3), 359-378.

Shell-Duncan, B., and Hernlund, Y. (Eds.). (2001). *Female circumcision in Africa: Culture, controversy, and change.* Boulder, CO: Lynne Riener.

Shell-Duncan, B., and Wimmer, M. (1999). Premarital childbearing in northwest Kenya: Challenging the concept of illegitimacy. *Social Biology, 46*(1-2), 47-61.

Sholkamy, H. (2001). Rationales for kin marriages in rural Upper Egypt. In N.S. Hopkins (Ed.), *Cairo papers in social science: The new Arab family* (Vol. 24, Chapter 1-2, pp. 62-79). Cairo, Egypt: The American University in Cairo Press.

Sim, H.C. (2001). Bidayuh housewives in a changing world: Sarawak, Malaysia. *Journal of Anthropological Research, 27*(3), 151-166.

Siña, E.D., Valdivieso, J.B., and Villarroel del Pinto, L. (2003). Birth rates and reproductive risk in adolescents in Chile, 1990-1999. *Pan American Journal of Public Health, 14*(1), 3-8.

Singerman, D., and Ibrahim, B. (2003). The costs of marriage in Egypt: A hidden dimension in the new Arab demography. In N.S. Hopkins (Ed.), *Cairo papers in social science: The new Arab family* (Vol. 24, Chapters 1-2, pp. 80-116).

Singh, L.B., Singh, A.K., and Rani, A. (1996). Alienation: A symptomatic reaction of educated unemployed youth in India. *International Journal of Psychology, 31*(2), 101-110.

Singh, S. (1998). Adolescent childbearing in developing countries: A global review. *Studies in Family Planning, 29*(2), 117-136.

Singh, S., and Bankole A. (2001). *Gender differences in the sexual and contraceptive behavior of young people: Sub-Saharan Africa and Latin America and the Caribbean.* Paper presented at the International Union for the Scientific Study in Population Conference, Salvador, Brazil.

Singh, S., Henshaw, S.K., and Berentsen, K. (2003). Abortion: A worldwide overview. In M.A. Basu (Ed.), *The sociocultural and political aspects of abortion: Global perspectives* (pp. 15-34). Westport, CT: Greenwood.

Singh, S., and Samara, R. (1996). Early marriage among women in developing countries. *International Family Planning Perspectives, 22*(4), 148-157, 175.

Singh, S., and Sedgh, G. (1997). The relationship of abortion to trends in contraception and fertility in Brazil, Colombia, and Mexico. *International Family Planning Perspectives, 23*(1), 4-14.

Sjaastad, L.A. (1962). The costs and returns of human migration. *Journal of Political Economy, 70*(5, Part 2), 80-93.

Skoufias, E. (2001). *PROGRESA and its impacts on the welfare and human capital of adults and children in rural Mexico: A synthesis of the results of an evaluation by the International Food Policy Research Institute.* Washington, DC: International Food Policy Research Institute, Food Consumption and Nutrition Division.

Skoufias, E., and McClafferty, B. (2001). *Is PROGRESA working? Summary of the results of an evaluation by IFPRI.* Washington, DC: International Food Policy Research Institute.

Skoufias, E., and Parker, S.W. (2001). Conditional cash transfers and their impact on child work and schooling: Evidence from the PROGRESA program in Mexico. *Economia, Fall*, 45-96.

Skoufias, E., and Parker, S.W. (2002). *Labor market shocks and their impacts on work and schooling: Evidence from urban Mexico.* (FCND Discussion Paper No. 129.) Washington, DC: International Food Policy Research Institute.

Skoufias, E., and Parker, S.W. (Forthcoming). The impact of PROGRESA on child labor and schooling. In P. Orazem, G. Sedlacek, and Z. Tzannatos (Eds.), *Child labor in Latin America.* Washington, DC: World Bank and Inter-American Development Bank.

Smith, H.L. (2003). Some thoughts on causation as it relates to demography and population studies. *Population and Development Review, 29*(3), 459-469.

Smith, L.C., and Haddad, L. (2000). *Explaining child malnutrition in developing countries: A cross-country analysis.* Washington, DC: International Food Policy Research Institute.

Sobek, M., Ruggles, S., McCaa, R., King, M., and Levison, D. (2002). *Integrated public use microdata series-international: Preliminary version 1.0.* Minneapolis: University of Minnesota, Minnesota Population Center.

Sodhi, G., and Verma, M. (2003). Sexual coercion among unmarried adolescents of an urban slum in India. In S. Bott, S. Jejeebhoy, I. Shaw, and C. Puri (Eds.), *Towards adulthood: Exploring the sexual and reproductive health of adolescents in South Asia* (pp. 91-94). Geneva, Switzerland: World Health Organization.

Solway, J.S. (1990). Affines and spouses, friends, and lovers: The passing of polygyny in Botswana. *Journal of Anthropological Research, 46*(Spring), 41-66.

Sommers, M. (2003). Young, male, and pentecostal: Urban refugees in Dar es Salaam, Tanzania. *Journal of Refugee Studies, 14*(4), 347-370.

Sorenson, S.B., Rutter, C.M., and Aneshensel, C.S. (1991). Depression in the community: An investigation into age of onset. *Journal of Consulting and Clinical Psychology, 59*(4), 541-546.

Speigel, A.D. (1991). Polygyny as a myth: Towards understanding extramarital relations in Lesotho. In A.D. Spiegel and P.A. McAllister (Eds.), *Tradition and transition in southern Africa* (pp. 145-166). Johannesburg, South Africa: Witwatersrand University Press.

Speizer, I.S., Heller, G., and Brieger, W. (2000). *Survey findings from the West African youth initiative project: Final evaluation of peer educator intervention.* Report prepared for Rockefeller Foundation, New York.

Speizer, I.S., Kouwonou, K., Mullen, S., Vignikin, E. (Forthcoming). Evaluation of the ATBEF Youth Center in Lomé, Togo. *African Journal of Reproductive Health.*

Speizer, I.S., Tambashe, B.O., and Tegang, S.-P. (2001). An evaluation of the "Entre Nois Jeunes" peer-educator program for adolescents in Cameroon. *Studies in Family Planning, 32*(4), 339-351.

Standing, G. (1999). Global feminization through flexible labor: A theme revisited. *World Development, 27*(3), 583-602.

Stanton, B., Li, X., Kahihuata, J., Fitzgerald, A.M., Neumbo, S., Kanduuombe, G., Ricardo, I.B., Galbraith, J., Terreri, N., Guevara, I., Shipena, H., Strijdom, J., Clemens, R., and Zimba, R.F. (1998). Increased protected sex and abstinence among Namibian youth following a HIV risk-reduction intervention: A randomized, longitudinal study. *AIDS, 12*(2), 2473-2480.

Stash, S., and Hannum, E. (2001). Who goes to school? Educational stratification by gender, caste, and ethnicity in Napal. *Comparative Education Review, 45*(3), 354-378.

Steinberg, L., and Morris, A.S. (2001). Adolescent development. *Annual Review of Psychology, 52*(1), 83-100.

Stern, C. (1995). Adolescent pregnancy: Meaning and implications for different social sectors. *Demos, Carta Demografica Sobre Mexico, 8*(2), 11-12.

Stewart, L., Sebastini, A., Delgado, G., and Lopez, G. (1996). Consequences of sexual abuse of adolescents. *Reproductive Health Matters, 7*(1), 129-134.

Stock, J.L., Bell, M.A., Boyer, D.K., and Connell, F.A. (1997). Adolescent pregnancy and sexual risk-taking among sexually abused girls. *Family Planning Perspectives, 29*(4), 200-203, 227.

Stromquist, N.P. (1994). Gender and education. In T. Husen and T.N. Postlethwaite (Eds.), *The international encyclopedia of education* (2nd ed., pp. 2407-2412). Tarrytown, NY: Elsevier Science/Pergamon.

Stromquist, N.P., and Monkman, K. (2000a). Defining globalization and assessing its implications on knowledge and education. In N. Stromquist and K. Monkman (Eds.), *Globalization and education: Integration and contestation across cultures* (pp. 21-28). Lanham, MD: Rowman and Littlefield.

Stromquist, N.P., and Monkman, K. (2000b). *Globalization and education: Integration and contestation across cultures.* Lanham, MD: Rowman and Littlefield.

Suguna, B. (1998). Dowry: The position of women in India. In P.R. Reddy and P. Sumangala (Eds.), *Women in development: Perspectives from selected states of India* (pp. 801-824). New Delhi, India: B.R. Publishing.

Summers, L.H. (1994). *Investing in all the people: Educating women in developing countries.* (Report No. 45.) Washington, DC: World Bank.

Summers, T., Kates, J., and Murphy, G. (2002). *The tip of the iceberg: The global impact of HIV/AIDS on youth.* Menlo Park, CA: The Henry J. Kaiser Family Foundation.

Suoranta, J. (2003). *UN world youth report 2003: The global situation of young people.* (Youth and information and communication technologies. UN World Youth Report 2003.) New York: United Nations Department of Economic and Social Development.

Sureender, S., Khan, A.G., and Radhakrishnan, S. (1997). The dowry system and education of female children: Attitudes examined in Bihar, India. *Demography India, 26*(1), 109-122.

Szwarcwald, C.L., Bastos, F.I., Viacava, F., and de Andrade, C.L.T. (1999). Income inequality and homicide rates in Rio de Janeiro, Brazil. *American Journal of Public Health, 89*(6), 845-850.

Tai-Hwan, K., Kwang-Hee, J., and Sung-nam, C. (1999). Sexuality, contraception, and abortion among unmarried adolescents and young adults: The case of Korea. In A. Mundigo and C. Indriso (Eds.), *Abortion in the developing world: Findings from WHO case studies* (pp. 346-367). London, England: Zed Books.

Tan, J.-P., Lane, J., and Lassibille, G. (1999). Student outcomes in Philippine elementary schools: An evaluation of four experiments. *The World Bank Economic Review, 13*(3), 493-508.

Tarr, C.M., and Aggleton P. (1999). Young people and HIV in Cambodia: Meanings, contexts, and sexual cultures. *AIDS Care, 11*(3), 375-384.

Tenti, E. (2000). Culturas juveniles y cultura escolar. *Revista Colombiana De Educación, 8*(40-41), 61-74.

The Alan Guttmacher Institute. (1998). *Into a new world: Young women's sexual and reproductive lives.* New York: Author.

The Alan Guttmacher Institute. (1999). *Sharing responsibility: Woman, society, and abortion worldwide.* New York: Author.

The Alan Guttmacher Institute. (2002). *Family planning can reduce high infant mortality levels: Issues in Brief.* (AGI Series No. 2.) New York: Author.

The Center for Reproductive Rights. (1997a). *Women of the world: Laws and policies affecting their reproductive lives, Anglophone Africa.* New York: The Center for Reproductive Law and Policy.

The Center for Reproductive Rights. (1997b). *Women of the world: Laws and policies affecting their reproductive lives, Latin America and the Caribbean.* New York: The Center for Reproductive Law and Policy.

The Center for Reproductive Rights. (1999). *Adolescent reproductive rights: Laws and policies to improve their health and lives.* New York: The Center for Reproductive Law and Policy.

The Center for Reproductive Rights. (2001). *Adolescent reproductive rights.* New York: The Center for Reproductive Law and Policy.

The Partnership for Child Development. (1999). Short stature and the age of enrollment in primary school: Studies in two African countries. *Social Science and Medicine, 48*, 675-682.

Thomas, D., Schoeni, R.F., and Strauss, J. (1996). *Parental investments in schooling: The roles of gender and resources in urban Brazil.* Los Angeles, CA: RAND.

Thomas, D.S.T. (1938). *Research memorandum on migration differentials.* New York: Social Science Research Council.

Thornton, A., Chang, J.S., and Lin, H.S. (1994). From arranged marriage toward love match. In A. Thornton and H.S. Lin (Eds.), *Social change and the family in Taiwan* (pp. 148-177). Chicago, IL: University of Chicago Press.

Thussu, D.K. (2000). *International communication: Continuity and change.* New York: Oxford University Press.

Tienda, M., and Wilson, W.J. (2002). *Youth in cities: A cross-national perspective.* Cambridge, England: Cambridge University Press.

Tilley, J. (2002). Is youth a better predictor of sociopolitical values than is nationality? *Annals of the American Academy of Political and Social Science, 58*(3), 226-256.

Tilson, D., and Larsen, U. (2000). Divorce in Ethiopia: The impact of early marriage and childlessness. *Journal of Biosocial Science, 32*(3), 355-372.

Timaeus, I.M., and Reynar, A. (1998). Polygynists and their wives in sub-Saharan Africa: An analysis of five Demographic and Health Surveys. *Population Studies, 52*(2), 145-162.

Todd, P., and Wolpin, K. (2003). *Using a social experiment to validate a dynamic behavioral model of child schooling and fertility: Assessing the impact of a school subsidy program in Mexico.* Philadelphia: University of Pennsylvania.

Tomasevski, K. (2001). *Free and compulsory education for all children: The gap between promise and performance.* (Right to Education Primers No. 2.) Lund and Stockholm, Sweden: Raoul Wallenberg Institute and Swedish International Development Cooperation Agency.

Torney-Purta, J., Lehmann, R., Oswald, H., and Schulz, W. (2001). *Executive summary: Citizenship and education in twenty-eight countries. Civic knowledge and engagement at age fourteen.* Amsterdam, Holland: International Association for the Evaluation of Educational Achievement.

Torney-Purta, J., Schwille, J., and Amadeo, J. (1999). *Civic education across countries: Twenty-four national case studies from the IEA civic education project.* Amsterdam, Holland: International Association for the Evaluation of Educational Achievement.

Toubia, N., and Izett, S. (1998). *Female genital mutilation: An overview.* Geneva, Switzerland: World Health Organization.

Treiman, D.J., McKeever, M., and Fodor, E. (1996). Racial differences in occupational status and income in South Africa, 1980 and 1991. *Demography, 33*(1), 111-132.

Turbin, M.S., Jessor, R., and Costa, F.M. (2000). Adolescent cigarette smoking: Health-related behavior or normative transgression? *Prevention Science, 1*(3), 115-124.

Turner, B. (1999). *The sociology of citizenship.* London, England: Sage.

UNAIDS. (1998). *Report on the global HIV/AIDS epidemic, June 1998.* Geneva, Switzerland: Author. Available: http://www.unaids.org/hivaidsinfo/statistics/june98/global_report/index.html [February 2003].

UNAIDS. (2000a). *AIDS and men who have sex with men.* Geneva, Switzerland: Author. Available: http://www.unaids.org/publications/documents/specific/men/mentue2000.pdf [February 2003].

UNAIDS. (2000b). *Report on the global HIV/AIDS epidemic, June 2000.* Geneva, Switzerland: Author. Available: http://www.unaids.org/epidemic_update/report/index.html [February 2003].

UNAIDS. (2002). *Report on the global HIV/AIDS epidemic 2002.* Geneva, Switzerland: Author. Available: http://www.unaids.org/barcelona/presskit/report.html [February 2003].

UNAIDS and WHO. (2003). *AIDS epidemic update: 2003.* Geneva, Switzerland: Author.

UNESCO. (1999). *UNESCO statistical yearbook 1999.* Ogdensburg, NY: Renouf.

UNESCO. (2002a). *Education for all: Is the world on track?* (EFA Global Monitoring Report 2002). Paris, France: Author.

UNESCO. (2002b). *UNESCO home page.* Available: http://portal.unesco.org/uis/ev.php?URL_ID=5045andURL_DO=DO_TOPICandURL_SECTION=201andreload=1036610332 [October 2002].

UNESCO. (2004). *EFA global monitoring report 2003/2004: Gender and education for all, the leap to equality.* Available: http://portal.unesco.org/education/en/ev.php.html [November 2002].

UNICEF. (1998). *Juvenile justice.* (Innocenti Digest 3.) Florence, Italy: Author.

UNICEF. (1999). *Education. The state of the world's children 1999.* New York: Author.

UNICEF. (2000). *Voices of children and adolescents in Latin America and the Caribbean. A regional survey.* Bogotá, Colombia: Author.

UNICEF. (2001a). *Speaking out! Voices of children and adolescents in East Asia and the Pacific. A regional opinion survey.* Bangkok, Thailand: Author.

UNICEF. (2001b). *Young voices opinion survey of children and young people in Europe and Central Asia.* Geneva, Switzerland: Author.

UNICEF. (2002). *Young people and HIV/AIDS: Opportunity in crisis.* New York: UNICEF, UNAIDS, and World Health Organization.

UNICEF. (2003). *The state of the world's children 2004 report: Girls, education, and development.* New York: Author.

UNICEF. (2005). *Psychosocial health projects.* Available: http://www.unicef.org [March 2005].

UNICEF International Child Development Centre. (1998). *What works for working children?* Florence, Italy: Author.

UNICEF and WHO. (1995). *A picture of health? A review and annotated bibliography of the health of young people in developing countries.* Geneva, Switzerland: World Health Organization.

United Nations. (1987). *Ferility behaviour in the context of development: Evidence from the World Fertility Survey.* New York: United Nations Department of International Economic and Social Affairs.

United Nations. (1989). *Convention on the rights of the child.* New York: Author.

United Nations. (1991). *Child mortality in developing countries: Socioeconomic differentials, trends, and implications.* New York: Author.

United Nations. (1994). *Program of action: International conference on population and development.* (Report of the International Conference on Population and Development, Preliminary Version.) New York: Author.

United Nations. (1996). *Platform for action and the Beijing declaration.* New York: Author.

United Nations. (1999a). *Health and mortality issues of global concern. Proceedings of the symposium on health and mortality.* (Brussels, November 1997.) New York: Author.

United Nations. (1999b). *Youth and drugs: A global overview.* Vienna, Austria: United Nations Commission on Narcotic Drugs Economic and Social Council.

United Nations. (2000a). *Optional protocols to the convention on the rights of the child.* New York: Author.

United Nations. (2000b). *World situation with regard to drug abuse, with particular reference to children and youth.* Vienna, Austria: United Nations Commission on Narcotic Drugs Eonomic and Social Council.

United Nations. (2000c). *The world's women 2000: Trends and statistics.* (Social Statistics and Indicators, Series K., No. 16.) New York: Author.

United Nations. (2001). *World population prospects, the 2000 revision, volume 1: Comprehensive tables.* New York: Author.

United Nations. (2002a). *World urbanization prospects: The 2001 revision.* New York: Author.

United Nations. (2002b). *HIV/AIDS and fertility in sub-Saharan Africa: A review of research literature.* New York: United Nations Population Division, Department of Economic and Social Affairs.

United Nations. (2003a). *World population prospects: The 2002 revision CD-Rom.* New York: Author.

United Nations. (2003b). *World population prospects, the 2002 revision, volume 1: Comprehensive tables.* New York: Author.

United Nations. (2003c). *The impact of AIDS.* New York: United Nations Population Division, Department of Economic and Social Affairs.

United Nations. (2003d). *World population prospects, the 2002 revision, volume II: Sex and age distribution of populations.* New York: Author.

United Nations. (2003e). *Global illicit drug trends 2003.* Vienna, Austria: United Nations Office on Drugs and Crime.

United Nations. (2004). *World youth report 2003: The global situation of young people.* New York: Author.

United Nations Commission on Population and Development. (2002). *Reproductive rights and reproductive health: Selected aspects.* New York: Author.

United Nations Development Programme. (1999). *Human development report 1999: Globalization with a human face.* New York: Oxford University Press.

United Nations Development Programme. (2001). *Human development report 2001: Making new technologies work for human development.* New York: Oxford University Press for the UNDP.

United Nations Development Programme. (2002). *Human development report 2002: Deepening democracy in a fragmented world.* New York: Oxford University Press.

United Nations General Assembly. (2003). *Implementation of the United Nations millennium declaration: Report of the secretary-general, A/58/323.* New York: United Nations.

United Nations Population Fund. (2003). *The impact of HIV/AIDS: A population and development perspective.* New York: Author.

United Nations Secretariat. (2003). *World population prospects, the 2002 revision, volume 2: Sex and age distribution of populations.* New York: United Nations.

U.S. Agency for International Development. (2002). *Approaches to civic education: Lessons learned.* (Technical Publication Series.) Washington, DC: Author, Office of Democracy and Governance.

U.S. Surgeon General. (2001). *Women and smoking: A report of the Surgeon General.* Atlanta, GA: National Center for Chronic Disease Prevention and Health Promotion.

Urdall, H. (2004). *The devil in the demographics: The effect of youth bulges on domestic armed conflict, 1950-2000.* (Conflict Prevention and Reconstruction Working Paper No. 14.) Washington, DC: World Bank.

Urquiola, M. (2000). *Identifying class size effects in developing countries: Evidence from rural schools in Bolivia.* (Development Research Group Working Paper No. 2711.) Washington, DC: World Bank.

Vandemoortele, J. (1991). Labor market informalization in sub-Saharan Africa. In G. Standing and V. Tokman (Eds.), *Towards social adjustment: Labor market issues in structural adjustment* (pp. 81-113). Geneva, Switzerland: International Labour Office.

van der Vliet, V. (1991). Traditional husbands, modern wives? Constructing marriages in a South African township. In A.D. Spiegel and P.A. McAllister (Eds.), *Tradition and transition in Southern Africa* (pp. 219-241). Johannesburg, South Africa: Witwatersrand University Press.

van Deth, J.W., Maraffi, M., Newton, K., and Whiteley, P.F. (1999). *Social capital and European democracy.* London, England: Routledge.

van de Walle, E. and Baker, K.R. (2004). *The evolving culture of nuptiality in sub-Saharan Africa.* Paper presented at Perspectives on International Family Change Conference, Population Studies Center, University of Michigan, Ann Arbor, MI, June 3-5.

van de Walle, E., and Meekers, D. (1994). Marriage drinks and Kola nuts. In C. Bledsoe and G. Pison (Eds.), *Nuptiality in sub-Saharan Africa: Contemporary anthropological and demographic perspectives* (pp. 57-73). Oxford, England: Clarendon Press.

van Driel, F. (1996). Marriage: From rule to rarity? Changing gender relations in Botwana. In R. Pairiwala and C. Risseeuw (Eds.), *Shifting circles of support: Contextualising gender and kinship in South Asia and sub-Saharan Africa* (pp. 51-78). London, England: Alta Mira Press.

van Eekelen, W., de Luca, L., and Ismail, N. (2001). *Youth employment in Egypt. InFocus programme on skills, knowledge, and employability skills.* (Working Paper No. 2.) Geneva, Switzerland: International Labour Office.

Van Hollen, C. (2003). *Birth on the threshold: Childbirth and modernity in South India.* Berkley: University of California Press.

VanLandingham, M., Suprasert, S., Grandjean, N., and Sittitrai, W. (1995). Two views of risky sexual practices among northern Thai males: The health belief model and the theory of reasoned action. *Journal of Health and Social Behavior, 36*(2), 195-212.

VanLandingham, M., and Trujillo, L. (2002). Recent changes in heterosexual attitudes, norms, and behaviors among unmarried Thai men: A qualitative analysis. *International Family Planning Perspectives, 28*(1), 6-15.

Van Rossem, R., and Meekers, D. (1999a). *An evaluation of the effectiveness of targeted social marketing to promote adolescent and young adult reproductive health in Cameroon.* (Working Paper No. 19.) Washington, DC: Population Services International Research Division.

Van Rossem, R., and Meekers, D. (1999b). *An evaluation of the effectiveness of targeted social marketing to promote adolescent reproductive health in Guinea.* (Working Paper No. 23.) Washington, DC: Population Services International Research Division.

Varga, C.A. (1997). Sexual decision-making and negotiation in the midst of AIDS: Youth in KwaZulu-Natal, South Africa. *Health Transition Review, 7*(Supplement 3), 45-67.

Varga, C.A. (2001). The forgotten fifty percent: A review of sexual and reproductive health research and programs focused on boys and young men in sub-Saharan Africa. *African Journal of Reproductive Health, 5*(3), 175-195.

Verba, S., Schlozman, K.L., and Brady, H.E. (1995). *Voice and equality: Civic voluntarism in American politics.* Cambridge, MA: Harvard University Press.

Verma, S., and Saraswathi, T.S. (2002). Adolescence in India: Street urchins or Silicon Valley millionaires. In B.B. Brown, R.W. Larson, and T.S. Saraswathi (Eds.), *The world's youth: Adolescence in eight regions of the globe* (pp. 105-140). Cambridge, England: Cambridge University Press.

Visaria, P. (1998). *Unemployment among youth in India: Level, nature, and policy implications.* (Employment and Training Paper No. 36.) Geneva, Switzerland: International Labour Office.

Wade, R.H. (2004). Is globalization reducing poverty and inequality? *World Development, 32*(4), 567-589.

Wang, Y., Keyou, G., and Popkin, B.M. (2000). Tracking of body mass index from childhood to adolescence: A 6-year follow-up study in China. *American Journal of Clinical Nutrition, 72*(2), 1018-1024.

Wang, Y., Monteiro, C., and Popkin, B.M. (2002). Trends of obesity and underweight in older children and adolescents in the United States, Brazil, China, and Russia. *American Journal of Clinical Nutrition, 75*(6), 971-977.

Warren, C.W., Riley, L., Asma, S., Eriksen, M.P., Green, L., Blanton, C., Loo, C., Batchelor, S., and Yach, D. (2000). Tobacco use by youth: A surveillance report from the global youth tobacco survey project. *Bulletin of the World Health Organization, 78*(7), 868-876.

Watkins, S.C. (1986). Regional patterns of nuptiality in Western Europe. In A.J. Coale and S.C. Watkins (Eds.), *The decline of fertility in Europe: The revised proceedings of a conference on the Princeton European Fertility Project* (pp. 314-336). Princeton, NJ: Princeton University Press.

Watstein, S., and Laurich, R. (1991). *AIDS and women: A sourcebook.* Phoenix, AZ: Oryx Press.

Weiss, E., Whelan, D., and Gupta, G.R. (1996). *Vulnerability and opportunity: Adolescents and HIV/AIDS in the developing world.* Washington, DC: International Center for Research on Women.

Welch, F. (1970). Education in production. *Journal of Political Economy, 78*(1), 35-59.

Welti, C. (2002). Adolescents in Latin America: Facing the future with skepticism. In B.B. Brown, R.W. Larson, and T.S. Saraswathi (Eds.), *The world's youth: Adolescence in eight regions of the globe* (pp. 276-306). Cambridge, England: Cambridge University Press.

Westoff, C.F. (2001). *Unmet need at the end of the century.* (DHS Comparative Reports No. 1.) Calverton, MD: ORC Macro International.

Westoff, C.F. (2003). *Trends in marriage and early childbearing in developing countries.* (DHS Comparative Reports No. 5.) Calverton, MD: ORC Macro International.

Westoff, C.F., and Bankole, A. (1995). *Unmet need: 1990-1994.* (DHS Comparative Studies No.16.) Calverton, MD: ORC Macro International.

Westoff, C.F., Sharmanov, A.T., Sullivan, J.M., and Croft, T. (1998). *Replacement of abortion by contraception in three central Asian Republics.* Calverton, MD: The POLICY Project and ORC Macro International.

WHO/UNICEF/UNFPA. (2003). *Maternal mortality in 2000. Estimates prepared by WHO, UNICEF, and UNFPA.* New York: UNICEF.

Whyte, M.K. (1990). Changes in mate choice in Chengdu. In D. Davis and E.F. Vogel (Eds.), *Chinese society on the eve of Tiananmen: The impact of reform* (pp. 181-213). Cambridge, MA: Council on East Asian Studies, Harvard University Press.

Whyte, M.K. (2003). China's revolutions and intergenerational relations. In M.K. Whyte (Ed.), *China's revolutions and intergenerational relations* (pp. 3-30). Ann Arbor: University of Michigan, Center for Chinese Studies.

Whyte, M.K., and Parish, W.L. (1984). *Urban life in contemporary China.* Chicago, IL: University of Chicago Press.

Williams, L., and Guest, M.P. (2002). *Why marry? Attitudes of urban middle-class respondents in Vietnam, Thailand, and the Philippines.* (Population and Development Program Working Paper Series No. 01.01.) Ithaca, NY: Cornell University Department of Rural Sociology.

Williamson, J.G. (2002). *Winners and losers over two centuries of globalization.* Helsinki, Finland: World Institute for Development Economics Research.

Wilson, D., Mparadzi, A., and Lavelle, S. (1991). An experimental comparison of two AIDS prevention interventions among young Zimbabweans. *Journal of Social Psychology, 132*(3), 415-417.

Winsborough, H.H. (1978). Statistical histories of the life cycle of birth cohorts: The transition from schoolboy to adult male. In K.E. Taeuber, L.L. Bumpass, and J.A. Sweet (Eds.), *Social demography* (pp. 231-259). New York: Academic Press.

Wittrup, I. (1990). Me and my husband's wife: An analysis of polygyny among Madinka in the Gambia. *Folk, 2*(1), 117-142.

Wolf, A. (1986). The preeminent role of government intervention in China's family revolution. *Population and Development Review, 12*(1), 101-116.

Wolf, D.L. (1992). *Factory daughters: Gender, household dynamics, and rural industrialization in Java.* Berkeley and Los Angeles: University of California Press.

Wolpe, A. (1994). *Adult education and women's needs: A study of some community organisations in the western Cape.* Cape Town, South Africa: CACE.

Wong, G.W., Leung, S.S., and Law, W.Y. (1996). Secular trend in the sexual maturation of southern Chinese boys. *Acta Paediatrica, 85*(5), 620-621.

Wood, A., and Calandrino, M. (2000). When other giants awaken: Trade and human resources in India. *Economic and Political Weekly,* (December 30), 4677-4694.

Wood, K., Maforah, F., and Jewkes, R. (1998). He forced me to love him: Putting violence on adolescent sexual health agendas. *Social Science and Medicine, 47*(2), 233-242.

World Bank. (1988). *Education in sub-Saharan Africa: Policies for adjustment, revitalization, and expansion.* Washington, DC: Author.

World Bank. (2001). *Engendering development: Through gender equality in rights, resources, and voice.* Washington, DC, and Oxford, England: World Bank and Oxford University Press.

World Bank. (2002a). *Bosnia and Herzegovina: From AID dependency to fiscal self reliance.* (Public Expenditure and Institutional Review Report No. 24297-BIH.) Washington, DC: Author.

World Bank. (2002b). *World development indicators 2002.* Washington, DC: Author.

World Bank. (2003). *World development indicators 2003.* Washington, DC: Author.

World Bank. (2004). *Tobacco control at a glance.* Available: http://www1.worldbank.org/tobacco/pdf/AAG%20Tobacco%206-03.pdf [April 15, 2004].

World Health Organization. (1992). *Antenatal care and maternal health: How effective is it? A review of the evidence.* (Prepared by Cleone Rooney.) Geneva, Switzerland: Author.

World Health Organization. (1995). *A picture of health? A review and annotated bibliography of the health of young people in developing countries.* (WHO/FHE/ADH/95.14.) Geneva, Switzerland and New York: World Health Organization and UNICEF.

World Health Organization. (1997). *Coverage of maternity care: A listing of available information* (4th ed.). Geneva, Switzerland: Author.

World Health Organization. (1999a). *Programming for adolescent health and development.* (WHO Technical Report Series No. 886.) Geneva, Switzerland: Author.

World Health Organization. (1999b). *What in the world works: International consultation on tobacco and youth.* (Singapore, September 28-30, Final Conference Report.) Geneva, Switzerland: Author.

World Health Organization. (2000). *World health report 2002: Reducing risks, promoting healthy life.* (WHO's European Public Health Report 2000.) Geneva, Switzerland: Author.

World Health Organization. (2001a). *The world health report 2001: Mental health, new understanding, new hope.* Geneva, Switzerland: Author.

World Health Organization. (2001b). *Surveys of drinking patterns and problems in seven developing countries.* Geneva, Switzerland: Author.

World Health Organization. (2001c). *Global burden of disease database.* Available: http://www3.who.int/whosis/menu.cfm?path=whosis,mort,mort_info,evidence, burden, burden_estimates,burden_estimates_2001&language=english [July 2004].

World Health Organization. (2002). *The world health report 2002: Reducing risks, promoting healthy life.* Geneva, Switzerland: Author.

World Health Organization. (2003). *Child and adolescent mental health. Fact sheet.* Available: http://www.who.int/child-adolescent-health/New_Publications/ADH/mental_ health _factsheet.pdf [November 2003].

World Health Organization and Centers for Disease Control and Prevention. (2002). *Global youth tobacco survey.* Available: http://www.cdc.gov/tobacco/global/GYTS.htm [November 2003].

World Values Survey. (2003). *SDA means program* (selected study: World Values Surveys 1981-1990-1995.) Available: http://worldvaluessurvey.org/services/index.html [March 2003].

Wright, E.A. (1990). Menarche in plateau state of Nigeria. *West African Journal of Medicine,* 9(3), 204-207.

Xenos, P. (1997). Survey sheds new light on marriage and sexuality in the Philippines. *Asia-Pacific Population and Policy,* 42(July), 2-5.

Xenos, P., Achmad, S., Lin, H., Luis, P.-K., Podhisita, C., Raymundo, C., and Thapa, S. (2001). *The timing of union formation and sexual onset: Asian evidence from young adult reproductive health surveys.* Paper prepared for the 2001 International Conference on Asian Youth at Risk, Taipei, Taiwan, November 26-29.

Xiaohe, X., and Whyte, M.K. (1990). Love matches and arranged marriages: A Chinese replication. *Journal of Marriage and the Family,* 52(3), 709-722.

Xiaoming, S., Yong, W., Choi, K-H, Lurie, P., and Mandel, J. (2000). Integrating HIV prevention education into existing family planning services: Results of a controlled trial of a
community-level intervention for young adults in rural China. *Aids and Behaviors, 4*(1),
103-110.

Yang, G.H., Fan, L.X., Tan, J., Qi, G.M., Zhang, Y., Samet, J.M., Taylor, C.E., Becker, K.,
and Xu, J. (1999). Smoking in China: Findings of the 1996 national prevalence survey.
*Journal of the American Medical Association, 282*(13), 1247-1253.

Yap, Y.-T., Sedlacek, G., and Orazem, P.F. (Forthcoming). Limiting child labor through
behavior-based income transfers: An experimental evaluation of the PETI program in
rural Brazil. In P.F. Orazem, G. Sedlacek, and Z. Tzannatos (Eds.), *Child labor in Latin
America*. Washington, DC: World Bank and Inter-American Development Bank.

Yates, M. (1999). Community service and political-moral discussions among adolescents: A
study of a mandatory school-based program in the United States. In M. Yates and J.
Youniss (Eds.), *Roots of civic identity: International perspectives on community service
and activism in youth* (pp. 16-31). New York: Cambridge University Press.

Yates, M., and Youniss, J. (1999). *Roots of civic identity: International perspectives on
community service and activism in youth*. Cambridge, England: Cambridge University
Press.

Yeung, Y.M. (2000). *Globalization and networked societies: Urban-regional change in Pacific Asia*. Honolulu: University of Hawaii Press.

Yeung, Y.M. (Ed.). (2002). *New challenges for development and modernization: Hong Kong
and the Asia-Pacific region in the new millennium*. Hong Kong: The Chinese University
Press.

Yeung, Y.M., and Chu, D.K.Y. (Eds.). (1998). *Guangdong: Survey of a province undergoing
rapid change* (2nd ed.). Hong Kong: The Chinese University Press.

Yeung, Y.M., and Chu, D.K.Y. (Eds.). 2000. *Fujian: A coastal province in transition and
transformation*. Hong Kong: The Chinese University Press.

Yeung, Y.M., and Hu, X.M. (Eds.) (1992). *China's coastal cities: Catalysts for modernization*. Honolulu: University of Hawaii Press.

Youniss, J., Bales, S., Christmas-Best, V., Diversi, M., McLaughlin, M., and Silbereisen, R.
(2002). Youth civic engagement in the twenty-first century. *Journal of Research on
Adolescence, 12*(1), 121-148.

Youniss, J., McLellan, J.A., and Yates, M. (1997). What we know about engendering civic
identity. *The American Behavioral Scientist, 40*(5), 620-631.

YouthNet and Family Health International. (2003). *New findings from intervention research: Youth reproductive health and HIV prevention*. Arlington, VA: Family Health
International.

Yunes, J., and Rajs, D. (1994). Trends in mortality due to violent causes in the overall
population and among adolescents and young people in the Americas. *Cad Saude Publ
(Rio De Janeiro), 10*(Supplement 1), 88-125.

Zaba, B.J., Boerma, T., Pisani, E., and Baptiste, N. (2002). *Estimation of levels and trends in
age at first sex from African demographic surveys using survival analysis*. (Measure/
Evaluation Working Paper No. WP-02-51.) Chapel Hill: University of North
Carolina.

Zabin, L.S., and Kiragu, K. (1998). The health consequences of adolescent sexual and fertility
behavior in sub-Saharan Africa. *Studies in Family Planning, 29*(2), 210-232.

Zeng, Y. (2000). Marriage patterns in contemporary China. In P. Xizhe and G. Zhigang
(Eds.), *The changing population of China* (pp. 91-114). Oxford, England: Blackwell.

Zheng, Z., Zhou, Y., Zheng, L., and Yang, Y. (2001). Sexual behaviour and contraceptive use among unmarried, young migrant workers in five cities in China. *Reproductive Health Matters, 9*(17), 118-127.

Zlidar, V., Gardner, R., Rutstein, S.O., Morris, L., Goldberg, H., and Johnson, K. (2003). *New survey findings: The reproductive revolution continues.* (Population Reports Series M. No. 17.) Baltimore, MD: Johns Hopkins Bloomberg School of Public Health, The INFO Project.

Zulu, E.M., Dodoo, N.-A., and Chicka-Ezeh, A. (2002). Sexual risk-taking in the slums of Nairobi, Kenya, 1993-98. *Population Studies, 56*(4), 311-323.

# APPENDIX
# A
# Coverage, Definitions, Methods, and Data

This appendix describes operational definitions adopted by the panel, approaches to data analysis, and chapter by chapter discussions of the specific data choices made and the reasons for those choices. The first section of the appendix presents data and methodological issues pertaining to the entire report as well as an introduction to Demographic and Health Survey (DHS) data, which are the only data used extensively in more than one chapter. The second section describes the data and methods used in each of the chapters in Parts II and III of the report.

## ENTIRE REPORT

### Coverage

When data are presented in Chapters 3-8, countries are defined by the panel as developing if they fit the following criteria: (1) location in Africa, Asia, or Latin America and the Caribbean, using United Nations (UN) regional groupings, and (2) classification by the World Bank (2002b) as low, lower-middle, and upper-middle-income countries as of 2000. When the panel judged there to be sufficient coverage in terms of countries within regional groupings for a particular topic, regional averages were presented according to geographic and income categories. For the summary data on the size and distribution of young people in developing countries presented in Table 2-1, we use the United Nations definition of developing countries: "Less developed regions comprise all regions of Africa, Asia (except Japan),

Latin America and the Caribbean plus Melanesia, Micronesia and Polynesia" (United Nations, 2003d:46).

## Regional Groups

**Geographical Categories:** The panel grouped developing countries into eight geographic regions, which were constructed from the geographic subregions used by the United Nations for its population estimates and projections (United Nations, 2003b). For the purposes of the panel report, Latin America and the Caribbean consists of two subregions (the Caribbean and Central America[1] and South America), sub-Saharan Africa consists of two subregions (Western and Middle Africa and Eastern and Southern Africa), Asia includes three subregions (Eastern Asia, South-central, and Southeastern Asia, and former Soviet Asia, which includes eight former Soviet countries from South-central and Western Asia), and the Middle East combines two subregions (Western Asia and Northern Africa). Wherever the data coverage was deemed sufficient to allow population-weighted estimates by geographic region, these are the categories used. This was typically the case for the DHS survey data as well as for the UN data base on marriage prevalence.

**Income Groups:** The World Bank classifies countries ("economies") into four economic groups. In 2000 the range for each of these four groups was as follows: low income (gross national income of $755 or less), lower-middle income ($756 to $2,995), upper-middle income ($2,976 to $9,266), and high income ($9,267 or more) (World Bank 2002b).[2] Whenever the data allowed estimates by country income category, the panel used the first three country income categories described above.

---

[1]Mexico is included in the Central America and Caribbean region even though in some international contexts (e.g., NAFTA) it is considered to be part of North America.

[2]Gross national income is in current U.S. dollars converted using the World Bank Atlas method. The purpose of the Atlas conversion factor is to reduce the impact of exchange rate fluctuations in the cross-country comparison of national incomes. A full explanation can be found on page 380 of World Bank (2002b). Updates of country income groupings on the World Bank Website: http://www.worldbank.org/data/countryclass/classgroups.htm as of September 30, 2002, led the panel to make a few adjustments to these country groupings, including shifting Korea into the high-income group (and therefore out of the developing country group) and adding East Timor in the low-income category, for which no data on income were provided in World Bank (2002b).

## Approaches to Data Analysis

**Trends:** The working group decided to concentrate primarily on data on recent trends, ideally the last two decades of the twentieth century wherever possible. In cases in which recent trend data were not available, we focused primarily on data that were sufficiently recent to characterize contemporary patterns and interrelationships.

Two approaches were used to measure trends: (1) a comparison of comparable data collected for surveys or censuses at two separate points in time, and (2) cross-cohort comparisons within a single recent survey based on the retrospective reporting of specific experiences or events during the transition to adulthood.

**Age Ranges:** The working group decided not to set a rigid range of ages but to explore broad age ranges that would allow a full exploration of transitions. For practical purposes, this usually meant concentrating on ages 10-24, but not always when transitions were found to continue until later ages. In several cases, constraints associated with available data limited our ability to analyze the most conceptually appropriate age group. For example, the DHS surveys restrict their samples of individual women or men, generally to the 15-49-year-old age range. The World Values Surveys do not interview youth younger than age 18. Mortality data by cause as estimated by the World Health Organization (WHO) are presented only for an aggregated age group: 15-29.

**Population Weights:** To provide the basis for statements about broad regional and global trends in cases in which there were sufficient data from each regional grouping to allow some representativeness, data were aggregated by region and income level and weighted according to the size of the population of young people ages 10-24 in 2000 (United Nations, 2001). The aggregated data were produced by calculating a weighted average of a particular statistic using as a weight for each country the percentage of the population of young people from countries with available data that are estimated to reside in that country. When data are available for two periods in time, we weighted both figures with the UN 2000 population estimates. Holding the weight constant allows us to attribute any apparent change between the two years to changes in the indicator rather than changes in the weights (allowing us to look at the average change over the time span).

## Demographic and Health Surveys

The panel used Demographic and Health Surveys extensively for Chapter 3 on schooling, for a few topics in Chapter 4 (sex and contraceptive use), extensively in Chapter 7 on marriage, and exclusively in Chapter 8 on parenthood. Although other data on these topics are available, the DHS data have the special advantage of allowing comparative analysis over time and across countries while controlling for important social and economic factors like urban and rural residence, socioeconomic status, and education level.

For each topic treated, all DHS data from publicly accessible surveys fielded since 1990 that included data for the topic in question were used (see Table A-1). The number of countries included in each analysis varied from 49 to 52 in the education, marriage, and parenthood chapters to as few as 39 in the case of a few topics—sex and contraceptive use—presented in the health chapter. This smaller sample of countries was necessitated because data on these topics for adolescents were not available for countries in which the DHS data were limited to ever-married women samples.

Using the full sample of 52 countries, we can make certain generalizations about the timeliness and representativeness of the DHS. Survey years range from 1990 to 2001 and all but 7 of the 52 surveys were conducted post-1995. The median year of the 52 surveys is 1998. Fewer surveys (32) include data on men, mostly but not exclusively in Latin America and the Caribbean and Africa. The specific number of surveys included in each analysis varies for a variety of reasons, including (1) whether the survey interviewed all women regardless of marital status or only ever-married women of reproductive age, (2) whether a specific question was asked, and (3) whether the data were available at the time the tables were compiled.

Table A-1 provides a listing of all the DHS data sets included in the panel sample along with sample sizes. The sample sizes for the survey of women of reproductive age varied from a little over 3,000 for the small island of Comoros to over 90,000 for the most recent sample in India. Typically, the samples of men are much smaller in size. The DHS data also include a household roster with some basic data on all household members, including the schooling level and current schooling participation of all household members.

Together, the 52 DHS surveys of females provide representative data for 90 percent of the population of low-income countries as defined by the World Bank in 2000, 19 percent of the population in lower middle-income countries, and 53 percent of upper middle-income countries (see Table A-2 for regional and income categories). Thus, overall the DHS data are most representative of the experience in the poorest countries. In addition, DHS surveys of females are representative of the populations in Eastern and Southern Africa (92 percent), South-central and South-eastern Asia (86 percent), Western and Middle Africa (75 percent), South America (74 percent), and the former Soviet Asia (68 percent), but they are less representative of all women in the Middle East (55 percent) and the Caribbean and

Central America (21 percent) (see Table A-2). They include no countries from Eastern Asia, most importantly China, which has over a fifth of the developing world's young people.

## DATA FOR INDIVIDUAL CHAPTERS

The panel's working group on data reviewed data on each topic for quality and coverage before deciding whether or not to treat a topic and, when choices were available, determined which data were best to provide the most accurate and comprehensive information on a particular topic.

### Chapter 3: Schooling

Since 1990, the Demographic and Health Surveys have included comparable questions on school attendance and attainment in all household surveys. In the absence of comparable census data, we have chosen to rely on DHS data for this report, supplemented when available by data on schooling from other household surveys to describe trends and patterns of schooling participation and attainment. These surveys allow us to calculate not only current schooling attendance rates, but also various cohort measures of schooling participation, grade attainment and progression between levels to estimate trends consistently over the past 20 years—a particular goal for the overall panel report. They also allow us to report current attendance figures according to household wealth categories and urban-rural residence. Before making this choice of data source as our primary source for the analysis of schooling patterns and trends, we carefully reviewed the pros and cons of United Nations Education, Scientific and Cultural Organization (UNESCO) data versus DHS data. These considerations are discussed below.

These DHS data are supplemented for Latin America with a collection of household surveys assembled by the Inter-American Bank from the mid-1980s to mid-1990s that covers roughly 93 percent of the population of Latin America and includes more countries than available from DHS in the upper middle-income category (Behrman, Duryea, and Székely, 1999a) and for China with data on eight provinces from the China Health and Nutrition Survey (Hannum and Liu, 2005).[3]

The enrollment ratios published by UNESCO are the most widely used international statistics on education for measuring progress over time and

---

[3]Unfortunately, we were not able to acquire data from the 2000 China census that would allow us to make comparable tabulations.

TABLE A-1 List of Countries with Recent DHS Surveys Used in Analysis, Including Estimates of Youth Population, Dates of Surveys, Sample Sizes, and Chapters in Which Data Were Used

| Country | Survey Date(s) | UN Data Base 2000 (in thousands) | Household Sample Size |
|---|---|---|---|
| | | Youth Population, 10-24 | |
| Armenia | 2000 | 1,068 | 5,980 |
| Bangladesh | 1999-2000 | 44,726 | 9,854 |
| Benin | 1996 (2001) | 2,115 | 5,796 |
| Bolivia | 1998 | 2,601 | 12,109 |
| Brazil | 1996 | 50,868 | 13,283 |
| Burkina Faso | 1998-1999 | 3,976 | 4,812 |
| Cameroon | 1998 | 4,996 | 4,697 |
| Central African Republic | 1994-1995 | 1,199 | 5,551 |
| Chad | 1996-1997 | 2,491 | 6,840 |
| Colombia | 2000 | 12,346 | 10,907 |
| Comoros | 1996 | 240 | 2,252 |
| Côte d'Ivoire | 1998-1999 | 5,595 | 2,122 |
| Dominican Republic | 1996 (1999) | 2,603 | 8,831 |
| Egypt | 2000 | 21,991 | 16,957 |
| Ethiopia | 1999 | 19,988 | 14,072 |
| Gabon | 2000 | 348 | 6,203 |
| Ghana | 1998-1999 | 6,581 | 6,003 |
| Guatemala | 1998-1999 | 3,830 | 5,587 |
| Guinea | 1999 | 2,637 | 5,090 |
| Haiti | 2000 | 2,881 | 9,595 |
| India | 1998-2000 | 298,291 | 92,486 |
| Indonesia | 1997 | 64,059 | 34,255 |
| Jordan | 1997 | 1,610 | 7,335 |
| Kazakhstan | 1999 | 4,631 | 5,844 |
| Kenya | 1998 | 11,306 | 8,380 |
| Kyrgyz Republic | 1997 | 1,533 | 3,672 |

| Female Sample Size 15-49 | Male Sample Size* | Chapters in Which Data Were Used | | | |
|---|---|---|---|---|---|
| | | Education | Health | Marriage | Parenthood |
| 6,430 | 1,719 | Y | Y | Y | Y |
| 10,544** | 2,556 | Y | | Y | Y |
| 6,219 | 2,709 | Y | Y | Y | Y (2001) |
| 11,187 | 3,780 | Y | Y | Y | Y |
| 12,612 | 2,949 | Y | Y | Y | Y |
| 6,445 | 2,641 | Y | Y | Y | Y |
| 5,501 | 2,562 | Y | Y | Y | Y |
| 5,884 | 1,729 | Y | Y | Y | Y |
| 7,454 | 2,320 | Y | Y | Y | Y |
| 11,585 | | Y | Y | Y | Y |
| 3,050 | 795 | Y | Y | Y | Y |
| 3,040 | 886 | Y | Y | Y | Y |
| 8,422 | 2,279 | Y | Y | Y | Y |
| 15,573 | | Y | | Y | Y |
| 15,367 | 2,607 | Y | Y | Y | Y |
| 6,183 | 2,004 | | | Y | |
| 4,843 | 1,546 | Y | Y | Y | Y |
| 6,021 | | Y | Y | Y | Y |
| 6,753 | 1,980 | Y | Y | Y | Y |
| 10,159 | 3,171 | Y | Y | Y | Y |
| 90,303 | | Y | | Y | Y |
| 28,810 | | Y | | Y | Y |
| 5,548 | | Y | | Y | Y |
| 4,800 | 1,440 | Y | Y | Y | Y |
| 7,881 | 3,407 | Y | Y | Y | Y |
| 3,848 | | Y | Y | Y | Y |

*Continued*

## TABLE A-1 Continued

| Country | Survey Date(s) | Youth Population, 10-24 | |
|---|---|---|---|
| | | UN Data Base 2000 (in thousands) | Household Sample Size |
| Madagascar | 1997 | 5,025 | 7,171 |
| Malawi | 2000 | 3,722 | 14,213 |
| Mali | 2001 | 3,652 | 12,285 |
| Morocco | 1992 | 9,501 | 6,577 |
| Mozambique | 1997 | 5,848 | 9,282 |
| Namibia | 1992 | 572 | 4,101 |
| Nepal | 2001 | 7,152 | 8,602 |
| Nicaragua | 1997 (2001) | 1,715 | 11,528 |
| Niger | 1998 | 3,505 | 5,928 |
| Nigeria | 1999 | 37,637 | 7,647 |
| Pakistan | 1990-1991 | 44,432 | 7,193 |
| Paraguay | 1990 | 1,751 | 5,683 |
| Peru | 2000 | 8,058 | 28,900 |
| Philippines | 1998 | 24,319 | 12,407 |
| Rwanda | 2000 | 2,689 | 9,696 |
| Senegal | 1992-1993 (1997) | 3,082 | 3,528 |
| South Africa | 1998-2000 | 13,715 | 12,247 |
| Togo | 1998 | 1,496 | 7,517 |
| Turkey | 1998 | 19,311 | 8,059 |
| Uganda | 2000-2001 | 7,757 | 7,885 |
| United Republic of Tanzania | 1999 | 11,845 | 7,000 |
| Uzbekistan | 1996 | 8,152 | 3,703 |
| Vietnam | 1997 | 25,053 | 7,001 |
| Yemen | 1991-1992 | 5,563 | 12,836 |
| Zambia | 1996-1997 (2001-2002) | 3,521 | 7,286 |
| Zimbabwe | 1999 | 4,489 | 6,369 |

NOTE: Y = Yes.

\* Male sample age ranges vary by country, falling within 12-70 years.

\*\* Female sample age range 10-49 for this country.

| Female Sample Size 15-49 | Male Sample Size* | Chapters in Which Data Were Used | | | |
|---|---|---|---|---|---|
| | | Education | Health | Marriage | Parenthood |
| 7,060 | | Y | Y | Y | Y |
| 13,220 | 3,092 | Y | Y | Y | Y |
| 12,817 | 3,390 | Y | Y | Y | Y |
| 9,256 | 1,336 | Y | | Y | Y |
| 8,779 | 2,335 | Y | Y | Y | Y |
| 5,421 | | Y | Y | Y | Y |
| 8,726 | 2,261 | Y | | Y | Y |
| 13,634 | 2,912 | Y | Y | Y | Y (2001) |
| 7,577 | 3,542 | Y | Y | Y | Y |
| 9,810** | 2,680 | Y | Y | Y | Y |
| 6,611 | 1,354 | Y | | Y | Y |
| 5,827 | | | Y | Y | Y |
| 27,843 | | Y | Y | Y | Y |
| 13,983 | | Y | | Y | Y |
| 10,421 | 2,717 | Y | Y | Y | Y |
| 6,310 | 1,436 | Y | Y (1997) | Y (1997) | Y (1997) |
| 11,735 | | Y | Y | Y | Y |
| 8,569 | 3,819 | Y | Y | Y | Y |
| 8,576 | 1,971 | Y | | Y | Y |
| 7,246 | 1,962 | Y | Y | Y | Y |
| 4,029 | 6,000 | Y | | Y | Y |
| 4,415 | | Y | Y | Y | Y |
| 5,664 | | Y | | Y | Y |
| 5,687 | | | | Y | Y |
| 8,021 | 1,849 | Y | Y | Y | Y |
| 5,907 | 2,609 | Y | Y | Y | Y |

TABLE A-2 Demographic and Health Surveys (DHS)

| Country | Region[a] | Sorted by Region | |
|---|---|---|---|
| | | Most Recent Survey | * = includes Male Survey |
| Dominican Republic | Carib/CA | 1996 | * |
| Guatemala | Carib/CA | 1998-1999 | |
| Haiti | Carib/CA | 2000 | * |
| Nicaragua | Carib/CA | 1997-1998 | * |
| Comoros | E/S Africa | 1996 | * |
| Ethiopia | E/S Africa | 1999 | * |
| Kenya | E/S Africa | 1998 | * |
| Madagascar | E/S Africa | 1997 | |
| Malawi | E/S Africa | 2000 | * |
| Mozambique | E/S Africa | 1997 | * |
| Namibia | E/S Africa | 1992 | |
| Rwanda | E/S Africa | 2000 | |
| South Africa | E/S Africa | 1998 | |
| Tanzania | E/S Africa | 1999 | * |
| Uganda | E/S Africa | 2000-2001 | * |
| Zambia | E/S Africa | 1996-1997 | * |
| Zimbabwe | E/S Africa | 1999 | * |
| Egypt | ME | 2000 | |
| Jordan | ME | 1997 | |
| Morocco | ME | 1992 | |
| Turkey | ME | 1998 | *[b] |
| Yemen | ME | 1991-1992 | |
| Bolivia | SA | 1998 | * |
| Brazil | SA | 1996 | * |
| Colombia | SA | 2000 | |
| Paraguay | SA | 1990 | |
| Peru | SA | 2000 | * |
| Bangladesh | SC/SE Asia | 1999-2000 | |
| India | SC/SE Asia | 1998-2000 | |
| Indonesia | SC/SE Asia | 1997 | |
| Nepal | SC/SE Asia | 2000-2001 | |

| | | Sorted by World Bank Income Categories | |
|---|---|---|---|
| Country | Income | Most Recent Survey | * = includes Male Survey |
| Armenia | Low | 2000 | * b |
| Bangladesh | Low | 1999-2000 | |
| Benin | Low | 1996 | * |
| Burkina Faso | Low | 1998-1999 | * |
| Cameroon | Low | 1998 | * |
| Central African Republic | Low | 1994-1995 | * |
| Chad | Low | 1996-1997 | * |
| Comoros | Low | 1996 | * |
| Côte d'Ivoire | Low | 1998-1999 | * |
| Ethiopia | Low | 1999 | * |
| Ghana | Low | 1998-1999 | * |
| Guinea | Low | 1999 | * |
| Haiti | Low | 2000 | * |
| India | Low | 1998-2000 | |
| Indonesia | Low | 1997 | |
| Kenya | Low | 1998 | * |
| Kyrgyz Republic | Low | 1997 | |
| Madagascar | Low | 1997 | |
| Malawi | Low | 2000 | * |
| Mali | Low | 2001 | * |
| Mozambique | Low | 1997 | * |
| Nepal | Low | 2000-2001 | |
| Nicaragua | Low | 1997-1998 | * |
| Niger | Low | 1998 | * |
| Nigeria | Low | 1999 | * |
| Pakistan | Low | 1990-1991 | |
| Rwanda | Low | 2000 | |
| Senegal | Low | 1997 | * |
| Tanzania | Low | 1999 | * |
| Togo | Low | 1998 | * |
| Uganda | Low | 2000-2001 | * |

*Continued*

## TABLE A-2 Continued

| Country | Region[a] | Sorted by Region Most Recent Survey | * = includes Male Survey |
|---|---|---|---|
| Pakistan | SC/SE Asia | 1990-1991 | |
| Philippines | SC/SE Asia | 1998 | |
| Vietnam | SC/SE Asia | 1997 | |
| Armenia | Soviet | 2000 | *[b] |
| Kazakhstan | Soviet | 1999 | *[b] |
| Kyrgyz Republic | Soviet | 1997 | |
| Uzbekistan | Soviet | 1996 | |
| Benin | W/M Africa | 1996 | * |
| Burkina Faso | W/M Africa | 1998-1999 | * |
| Cameroon | W/M Africa | 1998 | * |
| Central African Republic | W/M Africa | 1994-1995 | * |
| Chad | W/M Africa | 1996-1997 | * |
| Cote d'Ivoire | W/M Africa | 1998-1999 | * |
| Gabon | W/M Africa | 2000 | *[c] |
| Ghana | W/M Africa | 1998-1999 | * |
| Guinea | W/M Africa | 1999 | * |
| Mali | W/M Africa | 2001 | * |
| Niger | W/M Africa | 1998 | * |
| Nigeria | W/M Africa | 1999 | * |
| Senegal | W/M Africa | 1997 | * |
| Togo | W/M Africa | 1998 | * |

[a]Key: Carib/CA (Caribbean and Central America); E/S Africa (Eastern and Southern Africa); ME (Middle East [Northern Africa and Western Asia]); SA (South America); SC/SE Asia (South-central and South-eastern Asia); Soviet (Former Soviet Asia); W/M Africa (Western and Middle Africa).

[b]Male survey data are available for these countries, but not in sufficient number to allow aggregation of data to generate regional averages.

for making cross-national comparisons. Annual enrollment data provided by UNESCO are based on enrollments as reported officially by schools to national ministries of education. These annual enrollment counts are divided by United Nations estimates for the population for the year and ages in question to derive gross or net enrollment ratios for each level of schooling. Gross enrollment ratios, which are available for almost all countries for

| Country | Income | Most Recent Survey | * = includes Male Survey |
|---|---|---|---|
| | | Sorted by World Bank Income Categories | |
| Uzbekistan | Low | 1996 | |
| Vietnam | Low | 1997 | |
| Yemen | Low | 1991-1992 | |
| Zambia | Low | 1996-1997 | * |
| Zimbabwe | Low | 1999 | * |
| Bolivia | Lower middle | 1998 | * |
| Colombia | Lower middle | 2000 | |
| Dominican Republic | Lower middle | 1996 | * |
| Egypt | Lower middle | 2000 | |
| Guatemala | Lower middle | 1998-1999 | |
| Jordan | Lower middle | 1997 | |
| Kazakhstan | Lower middle | 1999 | *b |
| Morocco | Lower middle | 1992 | |
| Namibia | Lower middle | 1992 | |
| Paraguay | Lower middle | 1990 | |
| Peru | Lower middle | 2000 | * |
| Philippines | Lower middle | 1998 | |
| Brazil | Upper middle | 1996 | * |
| Gabon | Upper middle | 2000 | *c |
| South Africa | Upper middle | 1998 | |
| Turkey | Upper middle | 1998 | *b |

cGabon data on women unavailable at time of this analysis; data on men do not include schooling.
NOTE: Middle East, South-central, and South-eastern Asia are excluded from marriage chapter Table 7-9 because the surveys are based on ever-married samples.

multiple decades, relate enrollment in primary or secondary levels regardless of age to the population age group appropriate to each level of schooling. Net enrollment ratios, which are confined to those enrolled in the eligible age range, are conceptually cleaner but less widely available particularly for earlier years, because many countries have not collected data on enrollment by age. Because these data are school based, they have the potential to be broken down into geographic subgroupings but not by household characteristics, such as wealth.

These enrollment data vary in quality according to the quality of the management information systems in each country. The development of good systems is a continuing challenge in many parts of the developing world (Moulton et al., 2001). School reform efforts, which often include improvements in management information systems that make current data more accurate, may compromise comparability over time. Furthermore, in some settings in which financial flows to schools are a function of the level of enrollment, there can be a substantial motivation to inflate reported enrollments.

Some of the shortcomings of UNESCO enrollment data have been discussed in the literature (Behrman and Rosenzweig, 1994; Hewett and Lloyd, 2005; Lloyd, Mensch, and Clark, 2000). While some researchers feel comfortable relying on the enrollment data from UNESCO for trends and cross-country comparisons (e.g., Behrman and Sengupta, 2002), others doubt that the inherent biases in the data are sufficiently consistent across countries or over time to permit firm comparative conclusions about levels, trends, and differentials (Hewett and Lloyd, 2005; Lloyd et al., 2000).

With the establishment of the UNESCO Institute of Statistics (UIS) in 2001, the international community has taken some important steps to improve systems of reporting on literacy and schooling, including launching several special initiatives with the Organisation for Economic Co-operation and Development (OECD) and the World Bank to strengthen the collection and reporting of comparative statistics and indicators. The World Education Indicators program (WEI) launched in 1997 is one example. This program now includes 17 developing countries (Argentina, Brazil, China, Egypt, India, Indonesia, Jamaica, Jordan, Malaysia, Paraguay, Peru, the Philippines, the Russian Federation, Thailand, Tunisia, Uruguay, and Zimbabwe). Eventually this program will permit comparisons between developed and developing country data on a more consistent basis. Recently, Bruns, Mingat, and Rakotomalala (2003) from the World Bank have used UNESCO data to calculate a primary school completion ratio using data from UNESCO on end of year enrollments in the last year of primary school (if available) or beginning-of-year enrollment data for the last year of primary school adjusted for repeaters. These estimates of numbers graduating from primary school are divided by UN estimates of the population of official graduation age to simulate a completion rate and are available now to assess changes in the 1990s.

Relative to data on enrollment from UNESCO, data on school attendance and attainment derived from censuses and national sample surveys have some advantages and some disadvantages. The major advantages include (1) the fact that the data for the numerator and the denominator of any indicator are based on the same underlying population, thus allowing the construction of proper cohort-specific indicators on a consistent basis over time, (2) that data collected from households are more likely to capture current attendance rather than opening-day enrollment, thus providing a much more realistic measure of school participation, and (3) that attendance rates from household data can be compared by household income or wealth groups as well as other household characteristics. The disadvantages of household data include the facts that (1) they often are only collected periodically rather than annually, (2) differential mortality across education groups can bias the estimation of trends,[4] and (3) in the case of household surveys, changing sample frames over time can compromise the comparability of successive surveys. Despite their advantages, household survey data rarely have been used for comparative analysis of educational trends, because of their lack of accessibility on a comparable basis. There has never been an international education survey program similar to the DHS program. Census data are published with a huge lag and, despite much UN technical assistance over the years, often lack comparability when presented in tabular form in printed reports (Lloyd et al., 2000).[5] The fact that DHS data were collected on schooling on a comparable basis has allowed us to take advantages of some of the benefits offered by household data for the study of trends in schooling across countries and regions. See Table A-1 for the list of countries included in the presentation of data on schooling.

The data presented on standardized text scores come primarily from Programme for International Student Assessment (PISA) of the Organisation for Economic Co-operation and Development (OECD) (Organisation for Economic Co-operation and Development, 2001) and from the Third International Mathematics and Science Study (TIMSS) undertaken in 1999 by the International Study Center at Boston College—both international efforts with some participation of developing countries.

---

[4]When using cross-sectional cohort data to estimate trends, there is the danger that growth in schooling attainment will be underestimated if there is differential mortality by schooling in the relevant age groups. Given that we are comparing age groups between 10-14 and 30-34, for which group mortality rates are relatively low, this is unlikely to be a serious source of bias (Lloyd et al., 2000).

[5]There are several current efforts to make census data more accessible: Integrated Public Use Microdata Series (IPUMS, http://www.ipums.umn.edu) based at the University of Michigan and the African Census Analysis Project based at the University of Pennsylvania (http://www. acap.upenn.edu).

## Chapter 4: Health

The panel relied on multiple sources of data for the health chapter, depending on the topic. Data on mortality and morbidity were taken from WHO and the Joint United Nations Programme on HIV/AIDS. DHS surveys were used to analyze data on sexual initiation and on contraceptive use (see Table A-1). While data on sex and contraceptive use among young people have also been collected by the Centers for Disease Control and Prevention as part of their Young Adult Reproductive Health Survey, relatively few developing countries (as defined by the panel) have participated in these surveys and the data are not as easily accessible.[6] The global tobacco surveys were used to describe levels and trends in smoking worldwide. For some topics, regional and global averages were not constructed, either because coverage was limited or because data were available for an insufficient number of countries.

## Chapter 5: Work

The panel relied on data from labor force surveys provided by the International Labour Organization's LABORSTAT (http://laborsta.ilo.org/ from November 24, 2003) trends in labor force participation rates, data on population trends from the UN Population Division, and data collected by the Population Council on time use. To analyze trends in transitions to education and to work for seven case study countries, the panel used large public-use samples from the two most recent censuses for Mexico (1990 and 2000), Kenya (1989 and 1999), and Vietnam (1989 and 1999), which are available from the IPUMS-International web site at the University of Minnesota (www.ipums.umn.edu), as well as the 1992 and 1999 surveys of Brazil's Pesquisa Nacional por Amostra de Domicilios (PNAD); the 1993 South Africa Integrated Household Survey, SALDRU/World Bank and September 2000 South Africa Labour Force Survey, Statistics South Africa, courtesy of David Lam (University of Michigan); the Child Health and Nutrition Survey in China from 1989 and 1997 (http://www.cpc.edu/dataarch/primary), courtesy of Emily Hannum (University of Pennsylvania); and the 1987 Social and Economic Survey of Households, Statistical Center of Iran, and the 1998 Household Expenditure and Income Survey, Statistical Center of Iran, courtesy of Djavad Salehi-Isfahani (Virginia Polytechnic University). These data were also used in Chapter 7.

Other data, typically using countries as examples, were drawn from previously published analyses and used to illustrate various points.

---

[6]See http://www.cdc.gov/reproductivehealth/gp_spanrhs.htm.

## Chapter 6: Citizenship

After an initial exploration of a range of data sets including the World Values Surveys, AfroBarometer surveys, LatinoBarometer surveys, and UNICEF young voices surveys, the panel decided to rely primarily on data from the World Values Surveys collected for the first time in a large sample of developing countries in 1995-1998. This survey project is guided by a steering committee representing all regions of the world. Coordination and distribution of the data are based at the Institute for Social Research at the University of Michigan under the direction of Ronald Inglehart. While this choice meant that we have very little coverage for Africa (except Nigeria, which has about a fifth of the continent's population), we thought that the sampling procedures for the World Values Surveys were better documented than were alternative sources, such as the Afro- and Latino-Barometer surveys. Because of small sample sizes, however, we thought we needed to allow larger age ranges (18-34, 35+) in order to have a sufficient sample size to explore gender differences. These data were supplemented for some topics by published data from the UNICEF young voices surveys.

More recent versions of the World Values Surveys (1999-2000) and AfroBarometer Surveys (1999-2000) are better documented and include more developing countries; however, neither of these newer data sets were publicly available at the time that this chapter was being completed.

## Chapter 7: Marriage

In order to analyze marriage patterns, in particular trends in age at first marriage, it would be desirable to have accurate marriage registration data for at least two points in time. Such data are rarely available for developing countries. The United Nations Population Division collects data on the percentage of the population married in five-year age groups for most developing countries. For the most part, these data are available for men as well as women. For this analysis, we consider all countries in Africa, Asia, and Latin America and the Caribbean, with the exception of those identified by the World Bank as "high income" and those with a population under 140,000[7] in population (World Bank, 2002b). Given the focus on trends, we have identified 73 countries of the 117 that meet our criteria for which recent data,[8] i.e., data collected in 1990 or later, are available and for which there is information from two censuses or surveys at least 10 years apart (see Table A-3). In 2000, the United Nations estimated that

---

[7]If a country had fewer than 140,000 in population, the UN did not provide an exact population figure.

[8]There are a total of 152 countries in the three regions: 13 of these have fewer than 140,000 in population, 17 are listed by the World Bank as high income, and 5 have no World Bank income data, leaving 117 that meet our criteria.

## TABLE A-3 United Nations Database on Marriage

| Sorted by Region | | Sorted by Region Categories | |
| --- | --- | --- | --- |
| Country | Region[a] | Census/Survey Year 1 | Census/Survey Year 2 |
| Belize | Carib/CA | 1980 | 1991 |
| Dominican Republic | Carib/CA | 1981 | 1996 |
| El Salvador | Carib/CA | 1971 | 1992 |
| Guatemala | Carib/CA | 1973 | 1990 |
| Haiti | Carib/CA | 1989 | 2000 |
| Mexico | Carib/CA | 1980 | 1990 |
| Nicaragua | Carib/CA | 1971 | 1998 |
| Panama | Carib/CA | 1980 | 1990 |
| Puerto Rico | Carib/CA | 1980 | 1990 |
| Trinidad and Tobago | Carib/CA | 1980 | 1990 |
| Botswana | E/S Africa | 1981 | 1991 |
| Burundi | E/S Africa | 1979 | 1990 |
| Comoros | E/S Africa | 1980 | 1996 |
| Ethiopia | E/S Africa | 1984 | 2000 |
| Kenya | E/S Africa | 1969 | 1998 |
| Malawi | E/S Africa | 1987 | 2000 |
| Mauritius | E/S Africa | 1972 | 1990 |
| Mozambique | E/S Africa | 1980 | 1997 |
| Namibia | E/S Africa | 1960 | 1991 |
| Rwanda | E/S Africa | 1978 | 1996 |
| South Africa | E/S Africa | 1985 | 1996 |
| Tanzania | E/S Africa | 1978 | 1996 |
| Uganda | E/S Africa | 1969 | 1995 |
| Zambia | E/S Africa | 1980 | 1999 |
| Zimbabwe | E/S Africa | 1982 | 1999 |
| China | EA | 1987 | 1999 |
| Bahrain | ME | 1981 | 1991 |
| Egypt | ME | 1986 | 1996 |
| Jordan | ME | 1979 | 1994 |
| Morocco | ME | 1982 | 1994 |
| Occ. Palestinian Territory | ME | 1967 | 1997 |
| Sudan | ME | 1983 | 1993 |
| Tunisia | ME | 1984 | 1994 |
| Turkey | ME | 1980 | 1990 |
| Argentina | SA | 1980 | 1991 |
| Bolivia | SA | 1988 | 1998 |
| Brazil | SA | 1980 | 1996 |
| Chile | SA | 1982 | 1992 |
| Colombia | SA | 1973 | 1993 |
| Ecuador | SA | 1974 | 1990 |
| Guyana | SA | 1980 | 1991 |
| Paraguay | SA | 1982 | 1992 |
| Peru | SA | 1981 | 1996 |

Sorted by World Bank Income Categories

| U.N. Marriage Data Country | Income | Census/Survey Year 1 | Census/Survey Year 2 |
|---|---|---|---|
| Azerbaijan | Low | 1989 | 1999 |
| Bangladesh | Low | 1981 | 1991 |
| Benin | Low | 1979 | 1996 |
| Burkina Faso | Low | 1985 | 1999 |
| Burundi | Low | 1979 | 1990 |
| Cambodia | Low | 1962 | 1998 |
| Cameroon | Low | 1987 | 1998 |
| Central African Republic | Low | 1975 | 1994-1995 |
| Chad | Low | 1964 | 1996 |
| Comoros | Low | 1980 | 1996 |
| Côte d'Ivoire | Low | 1978 | 1994 |
| Ethiopia | Low | 1984 | 2000 |
| Gambia | Low | 1983 | 1993 |
| Haiti | Low | 1989 | 2000 |
| India | Low | 1981 | 1992-1993 |
| Indonesia | Low | 1980 | 1990 |
| Kenya | Low | 1969 | 1998 |
| Kyrgyz Republic | Low | 1989 | 1999 |
| Malawi | Low | 1987 | 2000 |
| Mali | Low | 1976 | 1995-1996 |
| Mauritania | Low | 1988 | 2000-2001 |
| Mozambique | Low | 1980 | 1997 |
| Myanmar | Low | 1973 | 1991 |
| Nepal | Low | 1981 | 1991 |
| Nicaragua | Low | 1971 | 1998 |
| Niger | Low | 1988 | 1998 |
| Pakistan | Low | 1981 | 1998 |
| Rwanda | Low | 1978 | 1996 |
| Senegal | Low | 1978 | 1997 |
| Sudan | Low | 1983 | 1993 |
| Tanzania | Low | 1978 | 1996 |
| Uganda | Low | 1969 | 1995 |
| Zambia | Low | 1980 | 1999 |
| Zimbabwe | Low | 1982 | 1999 |
| Belize | Lower Middle | 1980 | 1991 |
| Bolivia | Lower Middle | 1988 | 1998 |
| Cape Verde | Lower Middle | 1980 | 1990 |
| China | Lower Middle | 1987 | 1999 |
| Colombia | Lower Middle | 1973 | 1993 |
| Dominican Republic | Lower Middle | 1981 | 1996 |
| Ecuador | Lower Middle | 1974 | 1990 |
| Egypt | Lower Middle | 1986 | 1996 |
| El Salvador | Lower Middle | 1971 | 1992 |

*Continued*

## TABLE A-3 Continued

| Sorted by Region | | Sorted by Region Categories | |
| --- | --- | --- | --- |
| Country | Region[a] | Census/Survey Year 1 | Census/Survey Year 2 |
| Uruguay | SA | 1985 | 1996 |
| Venezuela | SA | 1974 | 1990 |
| Bangladesh | SC/SE Asia | 1981 | 1991 |
| Cambodia | SC/SE Asia | 1962 | 1998 |
| India | SC/SE Asia | 1981 | 1992-1993 |
| Indonesia | SC/SE Asia | 1980 | 1990 |
| Iran | SC/SE Asia | 1986 | 1996 |
| Malaysia | SC/SE Asia | 1980 | 1991 |
| Maldives | SC/SE Asia | 1985 | 1995 |
| Myanmar | SC/SE Asia | 1973 | 1991 |
| Nepal | SC/SE Asia | 1981 | 1991 |
| Pakistan | SC/SE Asia | 1981 | 1998 |
| Philippines | SC/SE Asia | 1980 | 1995 |
| Thailand | SC/SE Asia | 1980 | 1990 |
| Azerbaijan | Soviet | 1989 | 1999 |
| Kazakhstan | Soviet | 1989 | 1999 |
| Kyrgyz Republic | Soviet | 1989 | 1999 |
| Benin | W/M Africa | 1979 | 1996 |
| Burkina Faso | W/M Africa | 1985 | 1999 |
| Cameroon | W/M Africa | 1987 | 1998 |
| Cape Verde | W/M Africa | 1980 | 1990 |
| Central African Republic | W/M Africa | 1975 | 1994-1995 |
| Chad | W/M Africa | 1964 | 1996 |
| Côte d'Ivoire | W/M Africa | 1978 | 1994 |
| Gabon | W/M Africa | 1961 | 2000 |
| Gambia | W/M Africa | 1983 | 1993 |
| Mali | W/M Africa | 1976 | 1995-1996 |
| Mauritania | W/M Africa | 1988 | 2000-2001 |
| Niger | W/M Africa | 1988 | 1998 |
| Senegal | W/M Africa | 1978 | 1997 |

[a]Key: Carib/CA (Caribbean and Central America); E/S Africa (Eastern and Southern Africa); ME (Middle East [Northern Africa and Western Asia]); SA (South America); SC/SE Asia (South-central and South-eastern Asia); Soviet (Former Soviet Asia); W/M Africa (Western and Middle Africa).

there were 1.4 billion young people ages 10-24 in these 117 countries; 87 percent or 1.2 billion were resident in the 73 countries for which marriage trend data are available. Because of the difficulty of interpreting such large volumes of information, we have aggregated these data by UN geographic groupings.

Sorted by World Bank Income Categories

| U.N. Marriage Data Country | Income | Census/Survey Year 1 | Census/Survey Year 2 |
|---|---|---|---|
| Guatemala | Lower Middle | 1973 | 1990 |
| Guyana | Lower Middle | 1980 | 1991 |
| Iran | Lower Middle | 1986 | 1996 |
| Jordan | Lower Middle | 1979 | 1994 |
| Kazakhstan | Lower Middle | 1989 | 1999 |
| Maldives | Lower Middle | 1985 | 1995 |
| Morocco | Lower Middle | 1982 | 1994 |
| Namibia | Lower Middle | 1960 | 1991 |
| Occ. Palestinian Territory | Lower Middle | 1967 | 1997 |
| Paraguay | Lower Middle | 1982 | 1992 |
| Peru | Lower Middle | 1981 | 1996 |
| Philippines | Lower Middle | 1980 | 1995 |
| Thailand | Lower Middle | 1980 | 1990 |
| Tunisia | Lower Middle | 1984 | 1994 |
| Argentina | Upper Middle | 1980 | 1991 |
| Bahrain | Upper Middle | 1981 | 1991 |
| Botswana | Upper Middle | 1981 | 1991 |
| Brazil | Upper Middle | 1980 | 1996 |
| Chile | Upper Middle | 1982 | 1992 |
| Gabon | Upper Middle | 1961 | 2000 |
| Malaysia | Upper Middle | 1980 | 1991 |
| Mauritius | Upper Middle | 1972 | 1990 |
| Mexico | Upper Middle | 1980 | 1990 |
| Panama | Upper Middle | 1980 | 1990 |
| Puerto Rico | Upper Middle | 1980 | 1990 |
| South Africa | Upper Middle | 1985 | 1996 |
| Trinidad and Tobago | Upper Middle | 1980 | 1990 |
| Turkey | Upper Middle | 1980 | 1990 |
| Uruguay | Upper Middle | 1985 | 1996 |
| Venezuela | Upper Middle | 1974 | 1990 |

Coverage varies considerably by region, with approximately 90 percent or more of the population represented by these data in Eastern and Southern Africa, South-central and South-eastern Asia, Eastern Asia, South America, and the Caribbean and Central America, but only 63 percent represented in the Middle East, 31 percent represented in Western and

Middle Africa, and 38 percent represented in the former Soviet Asia. Note that Eastern Asia consists entirely of China, as data are unavailable for the two other countries, Mongolia and North Korea. Populous countries for which data are unavailable include Afghanistan, the Democratic Republic of the Congo, Iraq, Nigeria, Saudi Arabia, Uzbekistan, and Vietnam.

The Demographic and Health Surveys provide additional information to what is available from the United Nations data base (see Tables A-1 and A-2). Respondents' specific age at first marriage is obtained on these surveys, enabling the calculation of the proportion married by a particular age rather than just the percentage of a particular group who are married. In addition, they enable one to examine differentials in the timing of marriage by schooling attainment, place of residence and household economic status and may therefore provide insights into the forces behind the changes we have observed. The one drawback is that the surveys have been conducted in fewer countries than we have UN data for.

Note that regions vary considerably in the number of countries for which DHS surveys have been conducted. Coverage is highest in Eastern and Southern Africa, with approximately 92 percent of the population represented, and lowest in the Caribbean and Central America, where, because no recent survey is available for Mexico—by far the largest country—only about one-fifth of the population is represented. It is also important to keep in mind that no data are available for Eastern Asia, which includes China. Note, however, there are a few countries for which DHS data are available that are not included in the UN database: Armenia, Ghana, Guinea, Madagascar, Nigeria, Togo, Uzbekistan, Vietnam, and Yemen). Indeed, for two regions, Western/Middle Africa and Former Soviet Asia, coverage is considerably higher in the DHS at 75 percent and 68 percent, respectively. As with the UN data, the regional analyses based on the DHS data are weighted averages.

### Chapter 8: Parenthood

All data, for the parenthood chapter, are based on DHS surveys (see earlier discussion of DHS data as well as Tables A-1 and A-2).

APPENDIX
B
Contents
*The Changing Transitions to Adulthood in Developing Countries: Selected Studies*

*Cynthia B. Lloyd, Jere R. Behrman, Nelly P. Stromquist, and Barney Cohen, eds.*

The National Academies Press (2005)

The panel commissioned numerous papers by panel members and other experts that provided much valuable background material that informed the panel's deliberations. Many of these papers constitute useful contributions to the literature in their own right. Selected papers were subsequently modified to incorporate the comments of panel members and reviewers and are available in a companion volume entitled *The Changing Transitions to Adulthood in Developing Countries: Selected Studies.*

# APPENDIX
# C
# Biographical Sketches of
# Panel Members and Staff

**CYNTHIA B. LLOYD** (*Chair*) is director of social science research in the Policy Research Division at the Population Council. She also serves on the National Research Council's Committee on Population. Prior to her work at the Population Council, she was chief of the fertility and family planning studies section at the UN Population Division and an assistant professor of economics, Barnard College, Columbia University. Her fields of expertise include children's schooling, transitions to adulthood, gender and population issues, and household and family demography in developing countries. Lloyd has worked on these issues extensively in Ghana, Egypt, Kenya, Pakistan, and other developing countries as well as comparatively. Her recent research has concentrated on school quality in developing countries and the relationship between school quality, school attendance, and transitions to adulthood. She has M.A. and Ph.D. degrees in economics from Columbia University.

**CARLOS E. ARAMBURÚ** is the executive director of the Consorcio de Invesigacion Economica and Social (CIES) in Lima, Peru, an umbrella organization with 26 affiliates in Peru that supports research, dissemination, and training on economic and social issues related to public policies and programs. He is also the chairperson of the Board at REDESS-Jovenes, an organization focused on adolescents' sexual and reproductive health issues. Aramburú was president of the National Population Council in Peru from 1991-1992 and again in 1996. In addition to working extensively in the policy and program arena, he is the author of numerous articles and books, including a recent coauthored book on adolescent reproductive health and pregnancy in Peru. He has a B.A. in social anthropology from the Catholic University of Peru, a postgraduate diploma in rural development studies from Cambridge University, and M.Sc. in demography from the London School of Economics and Political Sciences.

**NAN MARIE ASTONE** is an associate professor in the Department of Population and Family Health Sciences at Johns Hopkins University, where her work has concentrated on the sociology of adolescence and the demography of life course transitions. She currently serves on the National Research Council and Institute of Medicine's Committee on Adolescent Health and Development. Her research has concentrated on teenage childbearing in the United States, particularly the relationship between teenage childbearing and family and community background factors and the influence of teenage pregnancy and childbearing on education and work of adolescents. In addition to her work on transitions to adulthood, Astone's research addresses child health in the United States and abroad. She has a Ph.D. from the University of Chicago.

**KAUSHIK BASU** is professor of economics and C. Marks professor of international studies at Cornell University. Prior to his work at Cornell, he was professor of economics at the Delhi School of Economics and has served as a visiting professor at a number of universities, including Princeton University, Stockholm University, the London School of Economics, and Harvard University, and was recently a visiting fellow in the office of senior vice president of development economics at the World Bank. His work focuses on development economics and he has written extensively on a number of topics, including inequality, international debt, and various labor issues including child labor. In addition to his academic activities, he publishes a monthly column in *India Today* on economic issues and has had articles and book reviews in several other leading English newspapers and magazines. He has a Ph.D. from the London School of Economics.

**JERE R. BEHRMAN** is the William R. Kenan, Jr. professor of economics at the University of Pennsylvania, where he has been on the faculty since 1965. His research interests include empirical micro economics, economic development, labor economics, human resources, economic demography, and household behaviors. He has worked as a research consultant with numerous national and international organizations, including the World Bank, the Asian Development Bank, and the Inter-American Development Bank. He has been the principal investigator or co-principal investigator on numerous research projects, has lectured widely in the United States and abroad, and has been involved in professional research or lecturing activities in over 40 countries in Asia, Africa, Europe, and Latin America and the

Caribbean. He has received various honors, including being selected as a Fulbright 40th anniversary distinguished fellow, a fellow of the Econometric Society, a Guggenheim Foundation faculty fellow, and a Ford Foundation faculty fellow. He has a Ph.D. from the Massachusetts Institute of Technology.

**ROBERT W. BLUM** is professor and chair of the Department of Population and Family Health Sciences in the Bloomberg School of Public Health at Johns Hopkins University. His research interests include adolescent sexuality, chronic illness, and international adolescent health care issues. He was also co-investigator for the National Longitudinal Study on Adolescent Health, the largest survey of American youth ever undertaken. He is a past president of the Society for Adolescent Medicine; has served on the American Board of Pediatrics; was a charter member of the sub-Board of Adolescent Medicine; and is a past chair of The Alan Guttmacher Institute board of directors. Currently, he chairs the National Research Council and Institute of Medicine's Committee on Adolescent Health and Development. He is a consultant to the World Bank and UNICEF as well as the World Health Organization. He has been awarded the Society for Adolescent Medicine's outstanding achievement award and the American Public Health Association's Herbert Needleman award. He has an M.D. from Howard University College of Medicine, an M.P.H. in maternal and child health and a Ph.D. in hospital and health care administration from the University of Minnesota.

**BARNEY COHEN** (*Study Director*) is director of the National Academies' Committee on Population and assumed the role of study director in September 2003. Since 1992 he has worked at the National Academies on a wide variety of projects, including studies on urbanization, mortality, adolescent fertility and reproductive health, forced migration, aging, the demography of sub-Saharan Africa, HIV/AIDS, the demography of American Indians and Alaska Natives, and racial and ethnic differences in health in later life. Currently, he is working on developing learning partnerships with African Science Academies. He has an M.A. in economics from the University of Delaware and a Ph.D. in demography from the University of California, Berkeley.

**VALERIE DURRANT** (*Study Director*) directed for the panel through August 2003. Her research has examined the status of adolescents in Pakistan and household decision making about the activities of children and youth in developing countries. While at the National Academies, Durrant also worked on projects related to leveraging longitudinal data in developing countries and the economic benefits of investing in youth in developing countries. Prior to joining the Committee on Population, she was a Berelson postdoctoral fellow at the Population Council, where she conducted research on adolescents and on the influence of the status of women on infant and child mortality and children's schooling in Pakistan. Durrant has an M.S. in sociology from Utah State University and a Ph.D. in sociology with an emphasis in demography from the University of Maryland. She is currently a scientific review administrator with the health of the population integrated review group at the Center for Scientific Review at the National Institutes of Health.

**ANASTASIA J. GAGE** is an associate professor in the Department of International Health and Development at Tulane University. Her research spans a number of topics related to maternal, child, and adolescent health in developing countries. Her previous positions include serving as technical officer with the Basic Support for Institutionalizing Child Survival II Project, senior technical advisor at the U.S. Agency for International Development, and assistant professor of sociology at the Pennsylvania State University. She has written articles on adolescent decision making about sexual activity and contraceptive use, premarital childbearing and maternity care in sub-Saharan Africa, and children's schooling and gender in the transition to adulthood. She has a Ph.D. in demography from the University of Pennsylvania.

**SHIREEN J. JEJEEBHOY** is senior program associate, Population Council, New Delhi, India. Prior to joining the Population Council, she was a scientist working on social science research on reproductive health at the World Health Organization where she oversaw a large project on adolescent reproductive health. Previously, she worked as an independent consultant. Her areas of expertise include women's status, education, fertility, and reproductive health in Southern Asia. She was the country coordinator for the India Status of Women and Fertility Survey and has published articles on the reproductive and sexual health of adolescents in India. She has a Ph.D. in demography from the University of Pennsylvania.

**RICHARD JESSOR** is a professor of social and developmental psychology and director of the Research Program on Health Behavior in the Institute of Behavioral Science at the University of Colorado. He has been writing in the area of adolescence in the United States for several decades, notably on adolescent risk behaviors. He is a former member of the Committee on Child Development Research and Public Policy and has served on two panels at the National Research Council and Institute of Medicine, one on high-risk youth and one on adolescent pregnancy and childbearing. Jessor also works on related issues in developing countries. He has a current research project looking at adolescent risk behaviors in Beijing and

Zhengzhou, China. He is a consultant to a number of international organizations, including the World Health Organization and UNICEF, on adolescents and adolescent health. He has an M.A. from Columbia University and a Ph.D. from Ohio State University

**BARTHÉLÉMY KUATE-DEFO** is an associate professor of demography and preventive medicine at the University of Montreal. His research interests include fertility and mortality linkages, sexuality and reproductive health, child nutrition, African demography, and event history and multilevel methods. He is currently the principal investigator on a large Rockefeller Foundation project examining the determinants and consequences of adolescent sexuality and reproductive health in Cameroon. The first phase of the project culminated in the publication of a book on sexuality and reproductive health during adolescence in Africa, with special reference to Cameroon. He has a doctoral degree in demography from the Institut de Demographie de Paris and a Ph.D. in population studies from the University of Wisconsin, Madison. He also has M.S. degrees in epidemiology and demography.

**DAVID A. LAM** is a professor of economics and formerly director of the Population Studies Center at the University of Michigan, Ann Arbor. He was also a member of the National Research Council's Committee on Population. His research focuses on the interaction of economics and demography in developing countries. He has worked extensively in Brazil and South Africa, analyzing the links between education, labor markets, and income inequality. He has served as a Fulbright visiting researcher at the Institute for Applied Economic Research in Rio de Janeiro and as a Fulbright visiting professor at the University of Cape Town. He has recently engaged in research on returns to school quality in Brazil, consequences of economic shocks on children's schooling, and child labor in Brazil. He has an M.A. in Latin American studies from the University of Texas, Austin, and an M.A. in demography and a Ph.D. in economics from the University of California, Berkeley.

**ROBERT J. MAGNANI** is vice president for technical support at the Family Health International (FHI) Institute for HIV/AIDS. Prior to joining FHI, he was professor and chair in the Department of International Health and Development at Tulane University's School of Public Health and Tropical Medicine. Magnani has over 20 years of experience in the international population, health, and nutrition sectors, with extensive program and consulting experience with a number of agencies. He has worked in over 20 developing countries in Africa, Latin America, Asia, and the Pacific. He led the research and evaluation efforts of the FOCUS on Young Adults Program. He has written numerous publications concerning the reproductive health of adolescents and evaluating reproductive health and family planning and health programs aimed at adolescents and others, including both substantive and methodological studies. He has an M.A. in sociology from the State University of New York at Albany and a Ph.D. in demography from Brown University.

**BARBARA S. MENSCH** is a senior associate in the Policy Research Division of the Population Council. Mensch has been involved in research on adolescents and the transition to adulthood in Egypt, Ghana, India, Kenya, and Vietnam, as well as the United States. She coauthored (with Judith Bruce and Margaret Greene) *The Uncharted Passage: Girls' Adolescence in the Developing World,* a seminal report on adolescents in developing countries. Her work on adolescents spans a number of life course events and dimensions of adolescents' lives including education, reproductive health, gender-role socialization, marriage, and livelihoods. She has an M.A. and Ph.D. in sociology and demography from Princeton University and an M.A. in social and political sciences from Cambridge University.

**SUSHEELA SINGH** is vice president for research at The Alan Guttmacher Institute. Singh has been an active researcher in the area of adolescent reproductive health for almost 20 years, conducting research on marriage, sexual activity, contraceptive use, and childbearing in the United States, other developed countries, and developing countries. The majority of her recent work involves comparative studies of adolescents across developing countries and regions. She is the author of journal articles and publications on a variety of topics related to adolescent sexual activity and reproductive health. Her recent publications include articles on gender differences in the timing of first intercourse in 14 countries and sexually transmitted diseases among adolescents in developed countries. She has also been involved in research on age at marriage in developing countries. She has M.A. and Ph.D. degrees in sociology from the University of California, Berkeley.

**NELLY P. STROMQUIST** is a professor at the University of Southern California's Rossier School of Education and an affiliated faculty member of its Center for Feminist Research and Gender Studies. Previously she held research positions at the International Development Research Center in Canada and as a visiting professor at Stanford University; the Federal University of Bahia, Brazil; Florida State University; and the University of California, Los Angeles. She has written extensively on issues of education and gender in developing countries, including books on promoting education for girls and women in Latin America, the politics of educational innovation in developing countries, and gender and grassroots dynamics in Brazil. She has a Ph.D. in education from Stanford University.

# Index

## A

Abortion, 524
    access to, 48
    contraceptive use and, 218
    data sources, 215
    health risks in, 5, 48, 191, 215, 242, 244
    motivation, 218
    policy recommendations, 247
    prevalence, 215-216
    provider characteristics and selection,
        217-218, 244
    research needs, 249
    self-induced, 216
    time during gestation, 216-217, 244
Adult roles, 3, 31
    gender role socialization, 6, 19, 51, 70,
        114-116, 169, 208, 266, 580
    globalization effects, 588
    indicators of successful transition to
        adulthood, 3-4, 26, 416
    role of school in preparation for, 70
    succession of, in transition to adulthood,
        27, 31, 416
Africa
    abortion practices, 218
    access to mass media, 49, 409
    access to perinatal health care, 544, 545
    age differences between spouses, 445-
        447, 448

    age patterns of first parenthood, 509,
        511, 512-514, 516, 518, 519, 548,
        549, 578
    challenges for young people, 596
    child labor trends, 342
    child marriage, 8
    condom use, 183
    contraceptive use, 5, 209-212, 243
    demographic trends, 40-41
    dowry and bridewealth practices, 462-463
    economic growth, 2, 20, 37, 59, 325
    family structure and function, 56, 57
    female genital cutting in, 193
    female-headed households, 324
    HIV/AIDS mortality, 174
    HIV/AIDS patterns and trends, 3, 5, 47,
        174, 179-180, 181, 182, 577, 583-584
    HIV awareness and knowledge, 182
    injury mortality, 187-188
    labor force participation, 579
    marriage patterns and trends, 419, 420,
        421, 423-425, 427, 432, 437, 442,
        450, 456, 460, 479
    maternal mortality, 191
    mortality patterns, 5, 11, 174, 191, 583-
        584
    population growth, 3, 18
    poverty in, 3, 63, 579, 596
    premarital childbearing, 9, 525, 530-
        533, 534-535, 549, 578